Organization Theory and Design

The West Series in Management

Consulting Editors

DON HELLRIEGEL   Texas A & M
JOHN W. SLOCUM, JR.   Southern Methodist University

ALDAG & BRIEF	Managing Organizational Behavior
BURACK	Personnel Management: Cases and Exercises
COSTLEY AND TODD	Human Relations in Organizations, 2d Ed.
DAFT	Organization Theory and Design
DOWNEY, HELLRIEGEL, AND SLOCUM	Organizational Behavior: A Reader
HELLRIEGEL, SLOCUM AND WOODMAN	Organizational Behavior, 3rd Ed.
HITT, MIDDLEMIST, AND MATHIS	Management: Concepts and Effective Practices
HREBINIAK	Complex Organizations
HUSE	Organization Development and Change, 2d Ed.
HUSE	Management, 2d Ed.
KELLEY AND WHATLEY	Personnel Management in Action: Skill Building Experiences, 2d Ed.
MATHIS AND JACKSON	Personnel: Contemporary Perspectives and Applications, 3d Ed.
MORRIS AND SASHKIN	Organization Behavior in Action: Skill Building Experiences
NEWPORT	Supervisory Management: Tools and Techniques
RITCHIE AND THOMPSON	Organization and People: Readings, Cases, and Exercises in Organizational Behavior, 2d Ed.
SCHULER	Effective Personnel Management
SCHULER	Personnel and Human Resource Management
SCHULER, DALTON, AND HUSE	Case Problems in Management, 2d Ed.
SCHULER, McFILLEN, AND DALTON	Applied Readings in Personnel and Human Resource Management
VEIGA AND YANOUZAS	The Dynamics of Organization Theory: Gaining a Macro Perspective

Organization Theory and Design

RICHARD L. DAFT

Texas A & M University

WEST PUBLISHING COMPANY

St. Paul · New York · Los Angeles · San Francisco

Copy editing: Rosalie Koskenmaki
Text design: Steve Lux
Artwork: Scientific Illustrators
Composition: Omegatype Typographers
Cover design: Jack Deskin

Acknowledgments

pages 2-3, Quotation from Jacques Neher. Reprinted with permission from the April 13, 1981 issue of *Advertising Age.* Copyright 1981 by Crain Communications Inc.

pages 24-25, Quotation from Charles Perrow. From *Organizational Analysis: A Sociological View,* by C. Perrow. Copyright © 1970 by Wadsworth Publishing Company, Inc. Reprinted by permission of the publisher, Brooks/Cole Publishing Company, Monterey, California.

pages 26-27, Quotation from Richard M. Cyert. Reprinted by permission of *The Wall Street Journal,* © Dow Jones Company, Inc. 1980. All Rights reserved.

page 35, "In Broken Images" by Robert Graves from *Collected Poems* by Robert Graves. Reprinted by permission of Robert Graves.

pages 88 and **90-91,** Quotations from Charles Perrow. From *Organizational Analysis: A Sociological View,* by C. Perrow. Copyright © 1970 by Wadsworth Publishing Company, Inc. Reprinted by permission of the Publisher, Brooks/Cole Publishing Company, Monterey, California.

pages 122-123, Quotation from Charles Perrow. From *Complex Organizations: A Critical Essay* by Charles Perrow. Copyright © 1979 by Scott, Foresman and Company. Reprinted by permission.

pages 283-284, Quotation from Wendell L. French, Cecil H. Bell, Jr., *Organization Development: Behavioral Interventions for Organization Improvement,* 2nd. ed., © 1978, pp. 3–5. Reprinted by permission of Prentice-Hall, Inc., Englewood Cliffs, N.J.

page 372, Quotation from Robert Townsend. From *Up the Organization,* by Robert Townsend. Copyright © 1970 by Robert Townsend. Reprinted by permission of Alfred A. Knopf, Inc.

page 470, Quotation from Robert Townsend. From *Up the Organization,* by Robert Townsend. Copyright © 1970 by Robert Townsend. Reprinted by permission of Alfred A. Knopf, Inc.

pages 495-496, Quotation from Richard E. Rustin. Reprinted by permission of *The Wall Street Journal,* © Dow Jones & Company, Inc. 1981. All rights reserved.

Library of Congress Cataloging in Publication Data

Daft, Richard L.
    Organization theory and design.

    (West series in management)
    Includes bibliographical references and index.
    1. Organization. I. Title   II. Series.
HD31.D135   1983   658.4   82-19958
ISBN 0-314-69645-8

3rd Reprint—1984

To Kathy

Contents

PART II
THE OPEN SYSTEM   39

PART IV

STRUCTURAL INFLUENCE ON DYNAMIC PROCESSES   259

PART V

MANAGING DYNAMIC PROCESSES 341

PART VI

INTEGRATING THE TOTAL SYSTEM   461

Preface

"Does organization theory have to be so theoretical?" "How will this stuff help me as a manager?" "Organization theory is boring." These comments are typical of what students say about organization theory. Organization theory is widely perceived as complex, abstract, theoretical, and dull. Of course, those of us within the field know differently, but something has been lost in the translation to students and managers. Most O.T. textbooks describe academic theories and abstract concepts drawn from the research literature. The value of these concepts for explaining organizational activities and for solving day-to-day problems has not been conveyed.

This book is written for a single purpose—to describe the usefulness, interest, and applicability of organization theory concepts. Organization theory is intriguing, rich, and helpful. Organization theory frameworks have been developed from contact with real organizations. The concepts can help students and managers explain their organizational world as well as solve pressing problems. This book is written for the student, teacher, or manager who not only wants to understand organization theory, but who wants to understand organizations and to function effectively within them.

Special Features Organizations are abstract entities. Many students do not have organizational experience, especially at the middle and upper organizational levels where O.T. is most applicable. To reach students, a textbook in organization theory has to explain concepts in a simple and clear fashion, and provide real-world illustrations. Several features have been adopted in this book to achieve this outcome.

1. Over 100 case illustrations provide a real-world anchor. Each chapter begins with an introductory case to pull the reader into the material. Several industry and government cases are used within each chapter to

illustrate key concepts and frameworks. Additional examples are sprinkled throughout chapter discussions. Each chapter also ends with one or more cases for analysis that serve as discussion aids for text material. Organization theory is at its best and most powerful when used to explain live organizational situations. This text takes full advantage of organization theory's ability to relate to the real world.

2. The book focuses exclusively on organization theory concepts. At this point in the development of the field, the boundary of organization theory is not defined consistently across textbooks. Most books do include main topics like environment and technology. Other important material, however, such as the sociological view of organization (bureaucracy), or the Carnegie and garbage can models of decision-making, may be omitted. Moreover, topics that are clearly in the domain of organizational behavior, such as leadership and motivation, often appear in organization theory texts. Materials clearly in the domain of organizational behavior are left out of this book.

3. Each chapter is organized into a logical framework. Many O.T. books treat material in sequential fashion, such as, "Here's view A, here's view B, here's view C, and so on." This book shows how the views mesh together. Several chapters conclude with a single contingency framework that organizes the major points into a single scheme.

4. Each chapter sticks to the essential point. The student is not introduced to the confusing theoretical and empirical squabbles that occur among organizational researchers. Most research areas point to a single trend, which is reported here. The essential point then is applied to real organizational situations.

5. Several pedagogical devices are used to enhance student involvement in the material. "A Look Inside . . ." introduces the chapter from an organizational perspective. "In Practice" illustrates theoretical concepts in organizational settings. Frequent figures and tables are used to help students visualize the material. "Summary and Interpretation" tells students which points are important, and what the points mean in the context of organization theory. "Guides to Action" tell students how to use material to analyze cases and manage organizations.

6. The book has been extensively tested on students. First year MBA students and third- and fourth-year undergraduate students have been using the book since the first draft. Feedback from students has been used in the revisions. Complex topics have been rewritten until the explanation is smooth and clear. Abstract concepts have been illustrated with additional case examples. The combination of organization theory concepts and case examples is designed to meet student learning needs, and students have responded very favorably.

Acknowledgements   A most pleasant discovery for me was that textbook writing is a team enterprise. The image I had of a solitary author proved completely inaccurate. The book that has emerged is the integration of ideas and hard work from a number of people to whom I am very grateful.

In one sense, this is a reviewer's book. My reviewers were critical and blunt when things were not going well, and they showered me with suggestions for improvement. Randy Bobbitt, Ohio State University; Tony Butterfield, University of Massachusetts; Don Campbell, Bowling Green State University; Ralph Catalanello, Northern Illinois University; Vince Luchsinger, University of Baltimore; Craig Pinder, University of British Columbia; and David Whetten, University of Illinois, all stayed with me through all or most of the book. Barbara Gricar, Penn State University, and J. B. Ritchie, Brigham Young, reviewed selected chapters. I sincerely thank all of them for their significant contributions to this text.

I owe a special debt to Don Hellriegel and John Slocum, Consulting Editors for the West Series in Management. Their many suggestions were excellent, and the book was literally transformed under their guidance. They both served the dual roles of stern critic and friend. Don championed the original idea of an organization theory textbook, gave me detailed reviews on several chapters, brainstormed solutions when I ran into problems, provided me with liberal use of his personal library, and shared many techniques from his previous writing experience. John did not give up when it looked as if this book might be a lost cause. Through memos, telephone calls, and after-dinner discussions, he helped me acquire a few basic skills for textbook writing. He read each chapter carefully and gave me detailed criticisms and encouragement. John also provided several theoretical ideas and case illustrations when they were applicable. This book still has many shortcomings, but it is much better than it would have been without Don and John's help.

For prompt and accurate typing I would like to thank Necia Mueller, Roberta Perdue, Aurelia Jimenez, Pam Ross, and Chrystal Casanova. They did not completely understand why I just didn't write it correctly the first time, but they pushed ahead anyway with commitment and goodwill through revision after revision after revision.

Several colleagues and students at Texas A & M also contributed to this book. Bob Albanese, Jody Fry, Ricky Griffin, George Rice, David Van Fleet, and Dick Woodman all provided intellectual stimulation and commiseration. Both were needed and appreciated. Several classes of students used the manuscript without complaint and gave me feedback on what they liked and didn't like.

I would like to extend special appreciation to Lee Lyon. Lee co-authored the environment chapter and made extensive contributions to the rest of the book. He also worked hard on a variety of other projects, which gave me time to write.

The editors at West also deserve special mention. Richard Fenton got the book started, and Esther Craig kept it moving. They both were wonderfully helpful and supportive throughout the project. John Lindley, Senior Production Editor, provided several valuable suggestions and helped design the Guides to Action.

Administrators also played a role in this project. As Department Heads, Bill Mobley and Lyle Schoenfeldt maintained an almost perfect scholarly atmosphere here at Texas A&M. They and Dean Bill Muse also provided resources as needed. I also want to thank Richard Hand, who was Dean at Queen's during my formative years. His early guidance enabled me to grow and flourish in organization theory.

There is another kind of support that was crucial to the successful completion of this book. This book was written during evenings, weekends, holidays, and vacations. My wife Kathy and daughters Danielle and Amy learned what it was like to be without a husband and father. Kathy made a special contribution by supporting this book when all of us were sick of it. Kathy's love and encouragement were absolutely essential. We made the best of those Friday and Saturday evenings that were free. Without Kathy's support, the book would not have been written. For that reason the book is dedicated, with love and affection, to her.

R.L.D.

Organization Theory and Design

PART I

Introduction to Organizations

1

Organizations and Organization Theory

JOSEPH SCHLITZ BREWING COMPANY

In the fall of 1976, the cloudy liquid from 10,000,000 bottles and cans of the beer that made Milwaukee famous flowed into the sewer systems of Memphis and Tampa. For months, bulldozers rocked back and forth catatonically in the yards of Joseph Schlitz Brewing Company's facilities in those two cities, destroying the defective product of a brewery gone haywire.

"It was absolutely demoralizing," remembers a Memphis plant worker who observed the secret burial. The bottles and cans crushed by the bulldozers contained hazy or "flaky" beer that had been recalled from taverns and stores across much of the country, lest it poison the loyalty of yet more faithful Schlitz drinkers. "You spend all that time and effort trying to make the best beer you can, and then you have to watch, day in and day out, as it's bulldozed under. We were literally crying in our beer."

During the years since, many thousands of persons associated with Schlitz—stockholders, employees, wholesalers—have shared this worker's sadness as they helplessly watched fortunes, businesses, and careers tumble along with the stature of the once-great company. Consider:

- Since that fateful period in the mid-1970s, volume sales have plummeted about 40%, dropping the brewer from a strong second place in the industry (behind Anheuser-Busch) to a tie for fourth. The flagship Schlitz brand, which for most of the twenty-five years following Prohibition was the country's best-selling beer, now trails far behind six other brands, having lost almost six of every ten customers it had in 1974.

- The value of Schlitz stock nosedived from about $69 a share to a low last year of $5, with investors suffering paper losses in excess of $1.7 billion in the process.
- Independent wholesalers, angry and impatient with the company, have turned their energies to other brands to fill their trucks and stay in business, making long-term prospects for a Schlitz turnaround that much more difficult.[1]

Schlitz's deterioration is a classic story of organizational failure. In the '50s, '60s, and early '70s, Schlitz experienced rapid growth and large profits. Now, suddenly, Schlitz is fighting to stay out of the grave. Schlitz suffers from an image so tarnished that many people are embarrassed to be seen drinking the beer.[2]

How could the number-one brewery collapse so dramatically? How could its management take the largest and richest brewery and ruin its reputation and future prospects? The answer is that Schlitz's situation is the consequence of several organizational mistakes, which began about fifteen years ago.

History　When prohibition was repealed in the 1930s, each brewery had to start from scratch. Under the direction of Erwin C. Uihlein, the Joseph Schlitz Brewing Company pulled into the industry lead in 1947. Schlitz held the lead for ten years, but was not aggressive and did not take advantage of its position. One executive described Schlitz as "a big lion dozing in the sun" during these years.[3] A more aggressive Anheuser-Busch took over the industry lead in 1957.

Loss of the industry lead jolted Schlitz's top management into taking action. A management shake-up followed. Erwin Uihlein became chairman, and his nephew Robert Uihlein became president (both were major stockholders and members of the founding family). They brought in Fred Haviland from Anheuser-Busch to take over marketing. They switched advertising agencies in 1961. These changes led to a series of innovations during the 1960s. The "pop top" can was introduced. So were the company's successful new products—Old Milwaukee and Schlitz Malt Liquor. Schlitz also imprinted American culture with its advertising slogans: "You only go around once in life so you have to grab for all the gusto you can." "Go for it, go for the gusto." "When you're out of Schlitz, you're out of beer."[4]

Their First Mistake　In the late 1960s, Schlitz had abundant cash, and management decided to acquire other companies. Diversification would provide stability and long-run protection against fluctuations in the beer business. Without careful investigation, the vice president in charge of finance pumped $100 million into several ventures, most of which were unprofitable. He was promptly fired. A new financial expert was brought in to sort out the chaotic diversification effort. Several of the early acquisitions were sold, but new big-time acquisitions were never completed. Only a small vinegar and jug-wine producer, along with a grain farm, were acquired. Schlitz had a chance to get Lowenbrau, a German-based beer, but lost out to Miller. Paul Masson was passed up because of the high price.

The diversification effort failed because family interests owned most of the stock. The family had power. After the early diversification mistakes, the family would not risk the loss of short-run dividends for long-run stability. The long-term prospects of Joseph Schlitz Brewing Company would thus rest entirely on its ability to make and sell beer.

Real Trouble Begins Early in 1973, Robert Uihlein was moved up to chairman. For various reasons, the position of president and chief executive officer was not filled for about eighteen months. This is when the real trouble began. Schlitz started to drift because, as Jacques Neher said in his analysis of the company, "no one was minding the store."[5]

Individual departments began working independently of each other. Changes were made in the product without consulting with marketing. Price increases were ordered by the financial department despite warnings from marketing that consumers would not pay them. Schlitz was reorganized into a straight functional structure. The brand management group was disbanded because marketing was no longer receiving priority. The brand management group had been responsible for coordination across departments, which was rapidly being replaced by interdepartmental conflict.

A more insidious and dangerous change was also taking place. Gradually, perhaps without realizing it, Schlitz changed its strategic emphasis from marketing to cost reduction. The dominant group of managers was becoming concerned with production efficiency rather than with advertising, with cost reduction rather than with increased sales and customer allegiance. The bottom line was emphasized at the expense of the company's product and image. Non-marketing people, such as a finance expert and an attorney, were making operating decisions. Schlitz had once become the largest brewer in the country through sound marketing knowledge and principles. Now key decisions were shaped by people who had never sold a case of beer.[6]

The cost-reduction strategy led to two innovations, both in production rather than in new products. The more significant innovation was accelerated batch fermentation, which shortened the fermentation process from twelve days to four. The potential savings were enormous, because beer quality remained high. Anheuser-Busch retaliated with a rumor that Schlitz was brewing "green beer." The less significant innovation was the decision to cheapen the beer. Cheaper ingredients were used because the operating managers believed consumers couldn't tell the difference. Whether the green-beer rumor affected consumers or whether they could actually taste a difference, Schlitz drinkers began to defect from the flagship brand.

The Last Straw Two additional events crippled the company. In 1976, nervous about a pending government requirement to list ingredients on cans of beer, the company dropped an enzyme and added a stabilizer called Chillgarde.[7] Unknown to the company, the stabilizer reacted with another ingredient and caused tiny flakes to appear in the beer after a short time on the shelf. The flakes looked bad and were not discovered until thousands of cases had been sold. The company shifted ingredients to correct the mistake, and this caused the beer to go flat. The result was a complete disaster. "Thousands of Schlitz drinkers who came upon the unappealing (but perfectly safe) beer were making their last purchase of Schlitz."[8] That year Schlitz physically buried 10,000,000 bottles and cans of beer.

The second event was Robert Uihlein's illness. He entered the hospital, learned he had acute leukemia, and was dead two weeks later. The organization was in chaos. Not a single marketing expert was left in the top management group. As one marketing staffer saw it, "It was amateur night at the zoo."[9]

Schlitz was now in a tailspin. Consumers couldn't leave Schlitz beer fast enough. Schlitz's image was severely damaged. In 1977, total corporate sales dropped into third place below Miller Brewing Company. Schlitz replaced managers and reinstalled the brand management group, but nothing helped.[10] By 1980, third place in corporate sales was lost to Pabst, and the Schlitz brand fell into seventh place.

The Present Early in 1982, Stroh Brewing Company purchased a controlling interest of Schlitz stock.[11] The Joseph Schlitz Brewing Company could never rebound from its errors. The company managed to survive, but never regained its competitive edge. The flagship brand still has a poor image, although a recent advertising campaign has halted the downward trend. Frank Sellinger was hired to run the company. His goal is to produce a quality beer and to direct new advertising campaigns.[12] One campaign stresses live taste tests with Miller and Budweiser. A second campaign shows Frank Sellinger describing the beer's good taste and quality.

Schlitz's products are still being sold and may once again prosper in the years to come. But not under an independent Joseph Schlitz Brewing Company. The great brewer is no more.[13]

Welcome to the real world of organization theory. The rise and fall of the Joseph Schlitz Brewing Company illustrates organization theory in action. Schlitz managers were deeply involved in organization theory each day of their working lives. But they never realized it. Schlitz managers didn't understand how the organization related to the environment, or how it should function internally. We can't claim that formal training in organization theory would have prevented Schlitz's troubles. But familiarity with organization theory would have enabled the managers to understand their situation, and to analyze and diagnose what was happening to them. Organization theory enables us to explain what happened to Schlitz. Organization theory also helps us predict what will happen in the future, so we can manage our organizations more effectively. Each of the topics to be covered in this book are illustrated in the Schlitz case. Consider, for example:

Schlitz's lack of effort to ensure consumer satisfaction, and the alienation of instrumental organizations, such as distributors and wholesalers, are issues affecting the organization's environment. To survive and prosper, organizations must both respond to and control elements in the external environment. These issues are discussed in chapter 2.

Profit goals dominated at Schlitz during the early 1970s, to the detriment of such goals as product quality, diversification, and corporate image. Management was unable to balance multiple goals and was not sensitive to multiple indicators of corporate effectiveness over the long term. They were oriented toward short-term profit. These are issues of goals and effectiveness, the topics discussed in chapter 3.

As Schlitz grew and developed, it never took advantage of its size. In the early years, it was a lion dozing in the sun. In later years, Schlitz did not develop into a mature corporation, with impersonal administrative procedures and bureaucratic efficiencies. The family stayed involved too long. These are issues of organizational size and development, which are covered in chapter 4.

The shift to a straight functional structure from a brand-management concept led to coordination problems between departments. Finance and production made decisions to suit their own narrow interests. The organization structure did not reflect task requirements, interdependencies between departments, or a market orientation. These are issues of organization structure and design, which are discussed in chapters 5 and 6.

Companies must change. Schlitz was innovative in the 1960s, and the new products were unusually successful. The production innovations in the 1970s were a disaster. These are issues of innovation and change. Techniques for managing change are described in chapter 7.

Information and control systems at Schlitz were not designed or used properly. Good information about the environment and internal problems was not available. Control was not used to achieve corporate targets. Information and control systems are discussed in chapter 8.

Decision-making at Schlitz was uneven. Several top-level decisions at Schlitz had no rationale. Cheapening the beer and changing ingredients without adequate testing hurt Schlitz badly in the marketplace. Managers were not paying attention to problems, were not following the progress of their solutions, and were not learning from trial and error. These are the types of decision-making issues covered in chapter 9.

The family with dominant ownership used their influence to direct the organization toward their short-run interest rather than toward long-run health and prosperity. Managers were removed when necessary. These are issues of power and politics in organizations, topics of chapter 10.

Within the organization, conflicting points of view emerged. Mechanisms to decrease conflict between departments in order to improve overall corporate performance were not in place. This is an issue of intergroup conflict. Techniques for managing conflict are described in chapter 11.

Schlitz shifted from a market orientation to a concern for production efficiency to achieve profit goals. The misinterpretation of the external environment and internal corporate strengths was the biggest single error Schlitz executives made. These are issues of corporate strategy, which is the concern of top management in corporations. The top management domain is explored in chapter 12.

The Joseph Schlitz Brewing Company illustrates all the topics covered in this book. Of course, organization theory is not limited to Schlitz, nor even to business corporations. Every organization, every manager in every organization, is involved in organization theory. Organization theory applies to elementary schools, universities, welfare agencies, not-for-profit foundations, symphony orchestras, local employment agencies, myriad government departments, and the YMCA. Organization theory draws lessons from these organizations and makes those lessons available to students of organizations. The story of the Joseph Schlitz Brewing Company is important because it demonstrates that large organizations are vulnerable, that lessons are not learned automatically, that organizations are only as strong as their decision-makers. Organization theory provides the tools to make Schlitz, or any other organization, more effective.

Purpose of This Chapter The purpose of this chapter is to explore the nature of organizations and organization theory. Organization theory has developed from the systematic study of organizations by scholars. Systematic research often seems formal and academic, but concepts are obtained from living, ongoing organizations. Organization theory can be very practical, as illustrated in the Schlitz case. It helps people understand, diagnose, and respond to organizational needs and problems. The next section begins with a formal definition of organization, and explores introductory concepts for describing organizations. Then the scope and nature of organization theory is discussed more fully. We consider what organization theory can and cannot do, its usefulness, and how organization-theory models can help people manage complex organizations. The chapter closes with a brief review of the important themes covered in this book.

WHAT IS AN ORGANIZATION?

Organizations are hard to see. We see outcroppings, such as a tall building, or a can of beer, or a friendly employee. But the whole organization is vague and abstract, and may be scattered among several locations. We know organizations are there because they touch us every day. Indeed, they are so common we take them for granted. We hardly notice that we are born in a hospital, have our birth records registered in a government agency, are educated in schools and universities, are raised on food produced on corporate farms, are treated by doctors engaged in a joint practice, buy a house built by a construction company and sold by a real-estate agency, borrow money from a bank, turn to police and fire departments when trouble erupts, use moving companies to change jobs, receive an array of benefits from government agencies, spend forty hours a week working in an organization, and are even laid to rest by a church and undertaker.[14]

Definition   Organizations as diverse as a local hospital and the Joseph Schlitz Brewing Company have characteristics in common. The definition that we use to describe organizations in this book is: **organizations** are social entities that are goal-directed, deliberately structured activity systems with an identifiable boundary.[15] There are four key elements in this definition:

1. *Social Entities.* Organizations are composed of people and groups of people. The building block of a social system is the human being. People interact in patterned ways and perform the essential functions in organizations.
2. *Goal-Directed.* Organizations exist for a purpose. An organization and its members are trying to achieve an end. Participants may have different purposes, and the organization may have several purposes. But organizations exist for one or more purposes without which they would cease to exist.
3. *Deliberately Structured Activity System.* Activity system means that organizations have a technology—they use knowledge to perform work activities. Organizational tasks are deliberately subdivided into separate departments and sets of activities. The subdivision is intended to achieve efficiencies in the work process. The deliberate structure is also characterized by a conscious attempt to coordinate and direct the separate activities.
4. *Identifiable Boundary.* An organization must be able to identify which elements are inside and which are outside its boundary. Membership is distinct. Members normally have some commitment or contract to contribute to the organization in return for money, prestige, or other gain. The organization exchanges resources with the environment, but it must maintain itself as an entity distinct from the environment. A visible boundary is a necessary characteristic of organizing. When random pieces of scrap metal are organized they become a machine distinct from other machines. When sounds are organized they become a song that is distinct from other noise. The boundaries of an organization may change, and may not always be immediately clear, but the organization must have a definable boundary.

ORGANIZATIONS AS SYSTEMS

Open Systems   One of the significant developments in the study of organizations was the distinction between closed and open systems.[16] A **closed system** does not depend on its environment; it is autonomous, enclosed, and sealed off from the outside world. It has all the energy it needs, and can function without the consumption of external resources. Early studies of organizations looked at internal workings to understand and explain organizational design and behavior. Traditional management concepts, including scientific management and industrial engineering, were closed-system approaches. They focused on activities inside the organization. These approaches took the environment for granted and assumed the organization could be made more efficient through internal design. The management of a closed system would be quite easy. The environment would be stable, predictable, and would not cause problems. The primary management issue would be internal efficiency. The closed-system approach to organizations is not really incorrect, but it is not complete.

An **open system** must interact with the environment to survive; it both consumes resources and exports resources to the environment. It cannot seal itself off. It must deal continuously with the environment. Open systems can be enormously complex. Internal efficiency is just one issue, and is sometimes a minor issue. The organization has to find and obtain needed resources, interpret and act on environmental changes, dispose of outputs, and control and coordinate internal activities in the face of environmental disturbances and uncertainty. Even large corporations are vulnerable to the environment. All systems that must interact with the environment to survive are open systems. The human being is an open system. So is planet earth, the city of New York, and the Joseph Schlitz Brewing Company. Indeed, the Schlitz top managers may have forgotten they were part of an open system. They concentrated on internal efficiency rather than on relationships with customers and organizations in the environment.

To understand the whole organization, it should be viewed as a system. The **organization system** is a set of interrelated elements that acquires inputs, transforms them, and discharges outputs to the external environment. Inputs and outputs reflect the dependency on the environment. Interrelated elements mean that people and departments depend upon one another and must work together.

Figure 1.1 illustrates an open system. Inputs include employees, raw materials and other physical resources, information, and financial resources. The transformation process changes these inputs into something of value

Figure 1.1. An Open System.

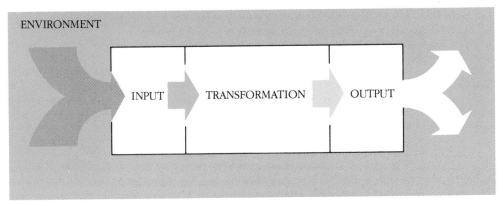

that can be exported back to the environment. Outputs of the system include specific products and services for customers and clients. Outputs may also include employee satisfaction, pollution, and other byproducts of the transformation process.

Organizational
Subsystems

An organization system is composed of several subsystems. The specific functions required for organization survival are performed by subsystems. Each subsystem is a system in its own right, because it has a boundary and absorbs inputs from other subsystems and transforms then into outputs for use by the remainder of the organization. Organizational subsystems perform five essential functions: production, boundary spanning, maintenance, adaptation, and management.[17] These subsystems are illustrated in figure 1.2.

Production   The production subsystem produces the product and service outputs of the organization. This is where the primary transformation takes place. This subsystem is the production department in a manufacturing firm, teachers and classes in a university, and the medical activities in a hospital. In the Joseph Schlitz Brewing Company, the production subsystem is that part of the company that actually manufactures the beer. The remaining subsystems are organized around the production subsystem.

Boundary Spanning   Boundary subsystems handle transactions at organizational boundaries. They control the boundary and are responsible for exchanges with the environment. On the input side, boundary subsystems acquire needed supplies and materials. On the output side, they create demand and deliver outputs. Boundary subsystems work directly with the external environment. At Schlitz, boundary subsystems included marketing on the output side and purchasing on the input side.

Maintenance   The maintenance subsystem is responsible for the smooth operation and upkeep of the organization. Maintenance includes cleaning and painting of buildings and the maintenance of machines. Maintenance activities also include human needs, such as morale, compensation, and physical comfort. Maintenance functions in a corporation like Schlitz include departments such as personnel, the employee cafeteria, and the janitorial staff.

Adaptation   The adaptive subsystem is responsible for organizational change. The adaptive subsystem scans the environment for problems, opportunities and technological developments. It is responsible for providing information and for helping the organization change and adapt. At Schlitz, engineering, research, and the marketing research departments were responsible for the adaptive function.

Management   Management is a distinct subsystem, responsible for directing the other subsystems of the organization. Management provides direction, strategy, goals, and policies for the entire organization. Management also coordinates other subsystems and resolves conflicts between departments.

ENVIRONMENT

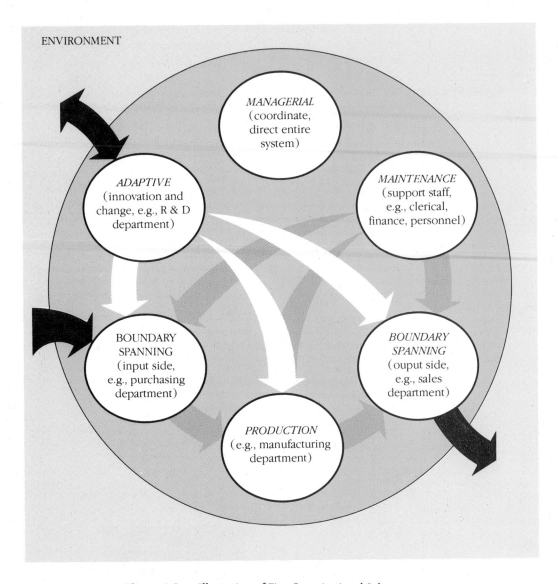

Figure 1.2.   Illustration of Five Organizational Subsystems.

The managerial subsystem is also responsible for developing organization structure and directing tasks within each subsystem. At Schlitz, the management subsystem consisted of the chairman, president, vice presidents, and the managers of functional departments.

The arrows in figure 1.2 show how the five subsystems are interconnected, and indicate the extent to which an organization is an open system. In ongoing organizations, several departments may interact with the environment. Moreover, subsystem functions may overlap. Departments often have multiple roles. Marketing is primarily a boundary spanner, but may also sense problems or opportunities for adaptation. Managers coordinate and direct the entire system, but they are also involved in maintenance, boundary spanning, and adaptation. People and resources in one subsystem overlap and perform other functions in organizations.

Social Systems   We have described human organizations as systems, and some of the characteristics we have identified apply to other systems as well. A thermostat is a system, and so is a houseplant, and a human being. Two things distinguish human organizations from these other systems. First, human beings are the basic building block, so organizations are social systems rather than machine or biological systems. Second, human organizations are incredibly complex, far more complex than other types of systems.

Kenneth Boulding[18] analyzed many systems and concluded that they can be arranged in order from simple to complex, as shown in figure 1.3. The simplest system is a static framework, such as an atom, a map, or a bridge. Dynamic systems, such as the solar system, are at level 2. Control systems, such as a thermostat, are self-regulating within prescribed limits and are at level 3. The simple cell is the beginning of living, self-maintaining systems, and is at level 4. The plant (level 5) and animal (level 6) are more complex living systems. The human being is the most complex living system because it can think, use languages, and is aware of itself. The human is at level 7.

The social organization is the most complex system of all, and is at level 8. The social organization has many characteristics of simpler systems, but it also incorporates new forms of complexity.[19] The sources of this complexity are characteristics formed only in human groups: norms and values are intangible and hard to detect; cultural dimensions such as music and art appear; system elements (humans) display self-awareness; the

Figure 1.3.   Boulding's Scale of System Complexity.
Source: Based on Kenneth E. Boulding, "General Systems Theory: The Skeleton of Science," *Management Science* 2 (1965): 197–207.

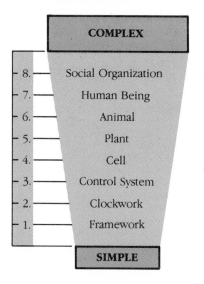

structure of elements and roles continuously changes; and information is processed through abstract forms of language, symbols, and meaning systems.

Organization managers must be sensitive to social-system complexity if they are to understand and cope with organizational systems.[20] In the human organization, a large number of dimensions interact so that it is impossible to completely understand and predict future behavior. These dimensions are interconnected so that changing one element affects the whole system. A single cause does not have a single effect. The human system can be difficult to manage because relevant dimensions are intangible, a large number of variables can influence any situation, variables work in clusters, and external conditions change. When managers oversimplify organizational issues, mistakes will be made, as in the following incident at Alcan.

IN PRACTICE 1.1

Alcan Incorporated

The aluminum company of Canada was extremely proud of its employees. Worker motivation and job satisfaction had high priority. The plant in Kingston, Ontario, had introduced several innovations to improve the quality of life for its workers.

One of the personnel specialists proposed that time clocks be removed from the shop floor. With only limited discussion, the personnel manager agreed that time clocks were demeaning to the workers, and that all workers should be put on straight salary. Approximately 1,000 workers were affected, and for the first few weeks all of them enjoyed the new freedom. But after a few months, several problems emerged. A few workers began to show up late, or leave early, or stay away too long at lunch. Less than 5% of the workers were involved, but the problem had to be managed. People who worked a full shift found it inequitable for other workers to receive full pay.

Supervisors had no previous experience with timekeeping or attendance, and now had great new demands placed upon them. They had to observe and record when the workers came and left. They were also responsible for confronting workers who were late, which required interpersonal skills that many supervisors had not developed. The workers resented the reprimands, which led to a less supportive relationship between themselves and their supervisors. After just a few months, Alcan found it necessary to reduce the supervisors' span of control. Supervisors were unable to manage as many people because of additional responsibilities. Moreover, pay was no longer docked when workers were late because they were on salary. Punishment was a letter written for the worker's file, which required yet more time and additional skills from supervisors. Workers did not want permanent letters in their files, so they filed grievances with the union. As grievances were passed up the hierarchy, both union officials and upper-level managers spent more time handling these disputes, which left less time for other management activities.

As Alcan discovered, the simple time clock was connected to many parts of the organization. The time clock influenced worker tardiness and absenteeism, closeness of supervision, whether supervisors had a coercive or supportive relationship with workers, interpersonal skills, forms of punishment and discipline, span of control, number of grievances, the relationship between union and management, and even the overall work climate in the Kingston plant. About eighteen months after the time clocks were removed, a personnel specialist concluded, after talking with several workers, that "nobody minded punching the time clocks anyway."[21]

The personnel department performed a maintenance function for Alcan. They erred in two ways. First, personnel specialists assumed they understood worker values and attitudes. These are intangible dimensions of organization, and differ from one part of the organization to another. Based perhaps upon their own values, personnel employees assumed that workers found time clocks demeaning, when in fact they did not. Careful investigation is required to assess employee attitudes. Second, the personnel department assumed that one cause had one effect, that removing time clocks would cause greater worker satisfaction. Single cause-effect logic applies to simple systems, but not to human organizations. Time clocks were interconnected with many other dimensions in the organization. Their removal eventually influenced such things as organization structure, worker climate, union-management relations, and supervisor roles. While it is hard to anticipate every outcome of an organizational change, managers should realize that unanticipated outcomes can occur, and plan for them. It can be a mistake to assume that an organization is similar to simpler systems.

DIMENSIONS OF ORGANIZATION

Organizations are open systems, within which the functions of maintenance, production, boundary spanning, adaptation, and management are performed. The next step is to look at dimensions that characterize and describe specific traits of organizations.

Organizational dimensions fall into two types—structure and context. **Structural dimensions** pertain to internal characteristics of organization. **Contextual dimensions** characterize the whole organization, including its environment. Structural dimensions are important because they provide labels to describe organizational differences. These are static dimensions, like personality characteristics in psychology, and they provide a basis for comparison. Contextual dimensions are important because they influence structure. The impact of the three contextual dimensions listed below are analyzed in detail in later chapters. Both structural and contextual dimensions are necessary to evaluate and understand organizations.[22] Key organizational dimensions are listed in table 1.1.

Table 1.1. Structural and Contextual Dimensions of Organizations.

Structural	Contextual
1. Formalization	1. Size
2. Specialization	2. Technology
3. Standardization	3. Environment
4. Hierarchy of Authority	
5. Decentralization	
6. Complexity	
7. Professionalism	
8. Personnel Configuration	

Structural Dimensions

1. Formalization pertains to the amount of written documentation in the organization. Documentation includes procedures, job descriptions, regulations, and policy manuals. These written documents describe behavior and activities. Formalization is often measured by simply counting the amount of documentation within the organization. Figure 1.4 is an example of documentation in a highly formalized university. Even rules for bulletin boards are described in detail.

2. Specialization is the degree to which organizational tasks are subdivided. If specialization is extensive, each employee performs only a narrow range of activities. Specialization is sometimes referred to as the division of labor.

3. Standardization is the extent to which similar work activites are performed in a uniform manner. In a highly standardized organization, work content is described in detail, so similar work is performed the same way across departments or locations.

4. Hierarchy of authority describes who reports to whom and the span of control for each manager. The hierarchy is normally depicted by the vertical lines on an organization chart. Hierarchical authority is related to span of control—the number of employees reporting to a supervisor. When spans of control are narrow, the hierarchy tends to be tall. When spans of control are wide, the hierarchy of authority will be shorter.

5. Centralization refers to the hierarchical level that has authority to make a decision. When decisions are delegated to lower organizational levels, the organization is decentralized. When decision-making authority is kept at the top level, it is centralized. Organizational decisions include the authority to make purchases, set goals, choose suppliers, set prices, and decide marketing territories.[23]

6. Complexity refers to the number of activities or subsystems within the organization. Complexity is measured along two dimensions—vertical and horizontal. Vertical complexity is the number of levels in the hierarchy. Horizontal complexity may be measured as either the number of job titles or departments existing laterally across the organization. The chart in figure 1.5 shows an organization with a vertical complexity score of five. The horizontal complexity for job titles is thirty-four, and the score for departments is seven.

UNIVERSITY BULLETIN BOARD GUIDELINES

Bulletin Board publicity and advertising shall be defined as any method or device for disseminating information or promotional material on the bulletin boards, kiosks, or other public areas of the university.

1. Only recognized campus organizations, university offices, governmental or educational agencies, and students, faculty, and staff advertising personal one-of-a-kind items will be allowed to utilize bulletin boards, kiosks, or other posting areas. Personal one-of-a-kind notices will be limited to those authorized areas marked "Personal Notices."

2. All advertising and publicity located on bulletin boards and kiosks must be no larger than 616 square inches (22 X 28 inches).

3. There will be a maximum of one flyer or poster per bulletin board and no more than four per kiosk of each advertising or publicity notice.

4. Each poster or flyer *must* contain the name of the responsible organization or individual and a clearly visible date of posting.

5. The posting period may not normally exceed three weeks. An expiration date will be considered as one day following the posted event. All personal one-of-a-kind notices will be removed on the first day of each month.

6. Materials presented in a foreign language must have the same information presented in English and must have the name of the organization and posting date printed in English.

7. Materials must be attached to bulletin boards so as not to deface or destroy the surface. Signs, posters, or flyers will be attached to cork boards with tacks and to kiosks with tacks or masking tape. Masking tape will be used on other designated posting areas. No scotch tape is to be used.

8. Materials should not overlap or conceal other advertising.

9. Materials must not be attached to glass surfaces, walls, doors, vending machines, or other unauthorized locations.

10. Particular bulletin boards and specific public areas of the campus may require additional authorizations and/or restrictions by building or area proctors, residence hall councils, or departmental units. Additional restrictions for bulletin boards will be posted.

11. Persons or organizations who post on bulletin boards are responsible for removal of the material when the date for posting has expired.

Figure 1.4.   Example of Organization Formalization.

7. Professionalism is the level of formal education and training of employees. Professionalism is considered high when employees require long periods of training to be job holders in the organization. Professionalism is

generally measured as the average number of years of education of employees, which could be as high as twenty in a medical practice and less than ten in a construction company.

8. Personnel configuration refers to the deployment of people to various functions and departments. Personnel configuration is measured by ratios such as the administrative ratio, the clerical ratio, or the ratio of indirect to direct labor employees. A configuration ratio is measured by dividing the number of employees in a function by the total number of organizational employees.

Contextual Dimensions

1. Size is the number of people in the organization. Since organizations are social systems, size is measured by the count of employees. Other measures such as total sales or amount of assets are related, but do not indicate the size of the human part of the social system.

2. Organizational technology is the nature of the task in the production subsystem, and includes the actions, knowledge, and techniques used to change inputs into outputs. An assembly line is one type of technology. So is a college classroom or an oil refinery, although these technologies differ from one another.

3. The environment includes all elements outside the boundary of the organization. Key elements include the industry, government, customers, suppliers, and the financial community. Most elements that affect the organization are composed of other organizations.

The eleven dimensions above represent variables that can be measured and analyzed for any organization. They provide a basis for measurement and an analysis of characteristics that cannot be seen by the casual observer, yet they reveal significant information about the organization.

IN PRACTICE 1.2

Organization Dimensions

A research team led by Derek Pugh from the Industrial Administration Research Unit of the University of Aston, England, developed profiles of key dimensions for organizations. Their goal was to measure dimensions of organization structure and context, and to compare how these dimensions differed across various types of organizations. The Aston group initially studied the dimensions of fifty-two organizations, of which four organizations are summarized in figure 1.6.

Organization A is a medium-sized firm with a manufacturing technology. The firm has a reasonable degree of specialization, but is relatively low in formalization, standardization, and centralization. The firm is family-owned and has minimum procedures and paperwork, perhaps because employees rely on family expertise and traditional ways of doing things.

Organization B also has a manufacturing technology, but is a large organization. This firm is much more specialized, formalized, and stan-

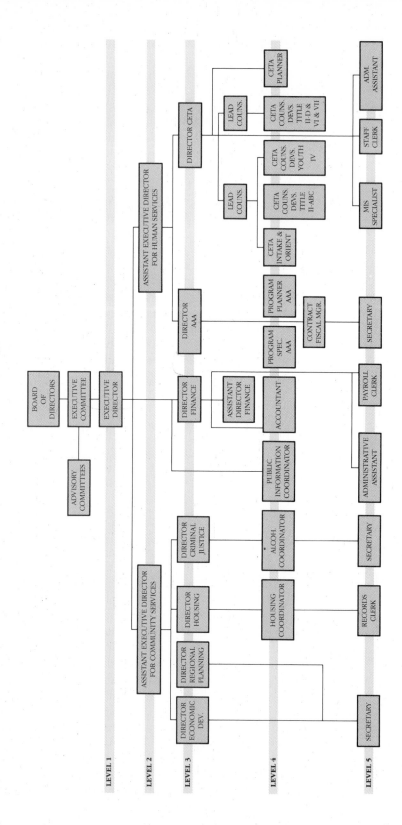

Figure 1.5. Organization Chart Illustrating Vertical and Horizontal Complexity (levels = 5; major departments = 7; job titles = 34).

dardized than organization A. Firm B also has a higher percentage of non-workflow personnel, but is very decentralized.

Organization C also has a manufacturing technology, and its size is similar to organization A. Organization C has a similar division of labor, but formalization and centralization are much higher. This is probably because organization C is owned and run by the government, which uses bureaucratic mechanisms of control. Organization C also has a larger percentage of personnel not engaged in production activities.

Organization D represents another type of organization. It has a retailing technology, and is about the same size as organizations A and C. It operates in a very competitive environment because of other retail chains. Specialization is low, which indicates that employees are involved in a range of activities. Standardization is very low, which means employees can perform tasks in their own way. Organization D is also very informal, although a number of decisions are centralized to upper management.[24]

The four organizations in figure 1.6 represent different structural profiles of technology, specialization, standardization, centralization, and configuration. Organizations can be analyzed along these dimensions, and these dimensions vary widely depending upon contextual factors, such as size, technologies, and environment. Organizational dimensions are examined in more detail in later chapters to determine the appropriate level of each dimension for each organization setting.

Figure 1.6. Structural Characteristics of Four Organizations.
Adapted from D. S. Pugh, D. F. Hickson, C. R. Hinings, and C. Turner, "Dimensions of Organization Structure," *Administrative Science Quarterly* 13 (1968): 80, reprinted by permission.

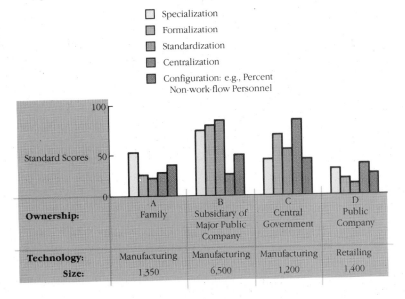

Another aspect of the structural profiles in figure 1.6 is the relationship that occurs among organizational dimensions. For example, organization B, the subsidiary of a public company, is rated highest on the dimensions of specialization, formalization, and standardization. What does this mean? One possible answer is that these dimensions are affected by size, because organization B is three times larger than the other organizations. Thus one relationship we can look for in future chapters is whether size influences structural dimensions. Another possible interpretation is that the three dimensions of specialization, formalization, and standardization may be related to one another. All three dimensions are rated high in company B, low in organizations A and D, and at an intermediate level in organization C. Minor variations exist, but in general the three dimensions seem to exist at comparable levels. These dimensions each may represent some deeper trait, such as bureaucratization, so that they exist in concert.

Centralization, by contrast, seems to be independent of the other structural dimensions. Centralization is lowest in the large subsidiary, and highest in the small government organization. It is also low in the family company. This probably means that centralization is partly a function of size and partly a function of ownership. In a very large organization, decision making has to be decentralized or senior management would be overloaded. Moreover, the interests of the owners are reflected in centralization. A central government may want tight control, while a family may be informal and emphasize delegation to other people.

WHAT IS ORGANIZATION THEORY?

Organization theory is not a body of knowledge. Organization theory is not a collection of facts. Organization theory is a *way of thinking* about organizations. Organization theory is a way to see and analyze organizations more accurately and deeply than one otherwise could. The way to see and think about organizations is based upon patterns and regularities in organizational design and behavior. Organization scholars search for these regularities, define them, measure them, and make them available to the rest of us. The facts from the research are not as important as the general patterns and insights into organizational functioning.

Medical doctors are said to memorize the details of more than a thousand chemicals and drugs by the time they graduate from medical school. Engineers and physicists have precise formulas to calculate with incredible accuracy the stress tolerance of a piece of metal or the amount of force required to lift a satellite into orbit. Accumulation of facts and precise equations are not part of organization theory. The physical and biological sciences have a well-defined body of knowledge, and study often involves learning facts and formulas. Social systems, as we have already discussed, are more ambiguous and complex than physical and biological systems.

Organization theory thus works with less precise relationships. A student of organization theory can acquire a vocabulary to describe organizational characteristics, and learn the patterns and regularities that explain relationships among those characteristics. Those relationships provide the basis for understanding organizational phenomena, diagnosing and analyzing problems, and responding with well-formulated solutions.

Models
One technique for understanding organizational relationships is the use of models. A **model** is a simplified representation of reality. A model is simplified because it never captures reality in its full complexity. A model describes a few important dimensions. Many types of models can be used to represent reality. In a mathematical model, dimensions are represented by abstract numbers, and relationships among dimensions can be computed mathematically. Physical models provide a physical representation of reality. For the movie "Raiders of the Lost Ark," a small-scale physical model was constructed for every set. The models were used to diagnose potential filming problems before the real sets were constructed. Verbal models are a verbal description of reality. An example of a verbal model is the description of eleven dimensions of organizations in the previous section. Schematic models are pictorial representations. A map is a schematic model of a geographical territory, and a wiring diagram is a model of a television set. Figure 1.2 was a schematic model of an organization as a system with five subsystems.

Throughout this book, organizational relationships will be described in terms of models. These models may contain several variables, or as few as two. **Variables** are organizational characteristics that can be measured and that represent key elements of the organization. A model may indicate that organizational size and standardization are positively related. That model would help a person understand and predict that large organizations require greater rules to ensure standard behavior when a large number of people are involved. Even two-variable models can be important if they describe key relationships. When a larger number of variables are involved, as they often are in organizations, the model will be more complicated. Each chapter reports models that can be used to understand important organizational patterns and processes.

Contingency
Organizations are not all alike. A great many problems in organizations stem from the assumption that all organizations can be treated as similar.[25] A consultant may recommend the same management by objectives (MBO) system for a manufacturing firm that was successful in a school system. Or a central government agency may impose the same rules and guidelines on diverse agencies. Or a conglomerate may take over a chain of restaurants and impose the same organizational charts and financial systems that are used in a banking division. These approaches assume that organizations behave according to universal principles, which is not the case.

Contingency means that one thing depends upon another thing, or that one characteristic depends upon another characteristic. What works in one setting may not work in another setting. There are no universal principles that apply to every organization. There is not one best way. Contingency theory means "it depends." The most efficient organization structure may be contingent upon the organization's size and technology. The MBO system may be contingent upon the professional level of employees. Organization charts and financial systems may depend upon the organization's past experience, ownership, environment, and technology. Big mistakes are made when organization contingencies are ignored or not understood, as in the case of the Joseph Schlitz Brewing Company. When the non-marketing executives gained influence, they were able to swing the profit strategy toward internal cost reduction and away from sales and advertising. The financial vice president assumed that cost reduction was a universal principle, and that it would work at Schlitz. Strategy, however, is a contingency variable. Strategy depends upon the nature of the organization. Cost reduction to achieve profits is appropriate in a manufacturing firm that produces a standardized product for industrial consumers. But it is not appropriate for a brand-name product in a consumer market. The organization must build and maintain a favorable image and win customer loyalty to its product line. The failure to appreciate this important contingency was an important reason for Schlitz's downfall.

Most research in organization theory is a search for contingencies. Investigators try to understand the relationships among variables so they can recommend which strategies and structures are appropriate in each situation. Organizations are open systems so one important contingency is the environment. Organization theorists attempt to determine which organization characteristics allow firms to deal effectively with different kinds and rates of environmental change. Other important contingencies are organization size and technology. Since there is no single best way for firms to organize in all situations, the recurring question in organization theory is: What kind of organization does it take to deal with different environments, technologies, or sizes? The answers have great significance for present-day managers.[26]

Levels of Analysis   One of the confusing and sometimes perplexing aspects of organization theory is level of analysis. In systems theory, each system is composed of subsystems. Systems are nested within systems and one level of analysis has to be chosen as the primary focus. Four levels of analysis normally characterize organizations, as illustrated in figure 1.7. The individual human being is the basic building block of organization. The human being is to the organization what a cell is to a biological system. The next higher system level is the group or department. These are collections of individuals who work together and interact to perform subsystem tasks. The next level of analysis is the organization itself. An organization is a collection of groups or departments that combine into the total organization. Organizations themselves can be grouped together into the next higher level of analysis, which is the community. Other organizations make up an important part of an organization's environment.

The concept of systems nested within systems can be extended beyond the four levels in figure 1.7. The individual person is composed of subsystems (e.g., circulatory, respiratory), which are composed of organs (heart,

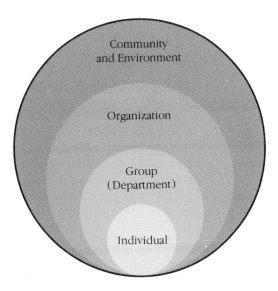

Figure 1.7. Levels of Analysis in Organizations.

lungs), which in turn are composed of cells, and the cells themselves are made up of smaller pieces of matter. The subsystem concept can be narrowed down until one reaches the very smallest unit of matter. Likewise, at higher levels of analysis, communities can be aggregated into a society, societies can be aggregated into the world, the world can be combined with other worlds to form our solar system, solar systems combine to form galaxies, and galaxies combine to form the universe.

Within this range of systems, organization theory focuses on the organizational level of analysis. In the study of social systems, the most powerful sources of causal explanation are the social system itself, and those systems one level above and below. To explain the organization, we should not only look at its characteristics, but also at the characteristics of the environment and of the departments and groups that make up the organization. Additional explanation may be derived by going to levels farther out, such as down to the individual or up to the solar system, but the impact of levels far removed tends to be less powerful. The focus of this book is to understand organizations by examining their characteristics, the nature and relationships among groups that make up the organization, and the collection of organizations that make up the environment.

But what about individuals? Are they included in organization theory? Individuals are the building block of social systems, and their role in organizations is important. Individuals do the behaving, make the decisions, and otherwise provide the energy that makes organizations go.

The answer is that organization theory does consider the behavior of individuals, but in the aggregate. People are important, but are not the focus of analysis in organization theory. Organization theory is a macro examination of organizations because it analyzes the whole organization as a unit.

Organization theory is distinct from organizational behavior. Organizational behavior is the micro approach to organizations because it focuses on the individuals within organizations as the relevant unit of analysis. Organizational behavior examines concepts such as motivation, leadership style, and personality, and is concerned with cognitive and emotional differences among people within organizations. Organization theory is concerned with people aggregated into departments and organizations, and with the differences in structure and behavior of those aggregates. Organization theory is the sociology of organizations, while organizational behavior is the psychology of organizations. Psychology concentrates on the individual person, while sociology concentrates on the social system.

Organization theory can also be characterized as the situation of organization participants. Organizational behavior is concerned with the *person*, organization theory with the person's *situation*. The dilemma between these levels of analysis was described by Perrow, who analyzed both the individual (leadership) and the organization (structure) to explain the success of an automobile manufacturing plant.[27]

IN PRACTICE 1.3

Automobile Assembly Plant

The leadership-structure problem will be illustrated by examining . . . a poor plant leader and a good one who replaced him. A large assembly plant for an automobile company, Plant Y, had 5,000 employees. The poor leader, Mr. Stewart, did not solicit suggestions from his subordinates, bypassed his immediate subordinates, gave orders directly to those two or more levels below him, ruled by edict on the basis of fear rather than incentives, and carried out his threats by firing a number of people. His was a crisis-ridden operation; the only time people came together for meetings was in response to an emergency. Of the six plants in this division of the corporation, Plant Y had the poorest performance record, and it was getting worse.

Mr. Stewart was replaced by Mr. Cooley, who seemed to be a truly effective leader. Cooley mingled with the lower-level managers and foremen to obtain their cooperation and suggestions. At the outset he indicated that, although top management in the corporation thought deadwood should be removed from the staff, he disagreed and would give everyone ample opportunity to show his worth. He encouraged groups to meet regularly to solve common problems and, more important, to engage in long-range planning and consultation to prevent daily crises. He asked for and received money from headquarters to modernize the plant, starting first with the cafeteria and washrooms used by hourly employees. . . . He inspired confidence and loyalty and erased the fear and crisis syndrome that had prevailed. After about six months, the plant started to improve its performance record, and within three years it was the best of the six plants.

The big difference was apparently style of leadership. Cooley was a good leader; Stewart wasn't [but] leadership style was only one of two important factors. The other was that while Stewart received daily orders from division headquarters to correct specific situations, Cooley was left alone. Cooley was allowed to lead; Stewart was told how to lead . . . .

Cooley probably could not have succeeded if the division had not let him alone; leadership was not enough. Therefore, the most important factor was the *situation* in which the two leaders, Cooley and Stewart, operated . . . . Remarkably, many of Cooley's subordinates behaved as ideal leaders should. Yet, they were poor leaders under the old manager. . . .

The same may have held true for Stewart; the stress of a rapid changeover in an old plant, with top management giving him little leeway, may have changed his leadership style. However, it is more likely that Stewart would have been a good leader for a routine situation, but a poor one during such a crisis. So, leadership does play a role, but not necessarily the most important one; it is better to begin, at least, by examining the situation which the leader confronts.[28]

A single contingency, like the amount of decentralization from headquarters to the plant manager, had significant impact on plant productivity and working relationships. The situation, not just leadership style, influenced plant performance.

WHAT ORGANIZATION THEORY CAN DO

Why study organizations? Most people who study organization theory belong to one of two groups—those who are managers or potential managers, and those who will not be managers. For the second group, the reason is to appreciate and understand more about the world around you. Nearly everyone works in an organization. Organization theory will provide an appreciation and understanding of what is happening in the organization. Organizations are a major part of our environment. They affect us enormously. By studying organizations you will know more about that environment, just as you would by studying geology, astronomy, or music.

For people who are or will be managers, organization theory provides significant insight and understanding to help you become better managers. As in the case of the Joseph Schlitz Brewing Company, many managers learn organization theory by trial and error. At Schlitz, the managers did not understand the situation they were in or the contingencies to which they should respond. Organization theory identifies variables and provides models so that managers know how to diagnose and explain what is happening around them, and thus can organize for greater effectiveness.

The study of organization theory is similar to the study of botany. People who do not work with trees find it enjoyable and enlightening to be able to identify and describe trees around them, know their history, their relevant differences, and the role trees play in ecology systems. For a manager at Weyerhauser, however, who is responsible for cutting trees in a forest, the value of botany is much more applied. Botany enables the manager to identify and label trees, and to make decisions about which trees to cut and which to ignore. The manager understands how many and what types of trees to cut down based upon needs for certain kinds of wood, and understands contingency relationships, such as between tree size and wood volume, age and wood quality, or tree type and wood density.

In a very real sense, organization theory can make a manager more competent and more influential. Understanding how and why organizations act lets managers know how to react. The study of organizations enables people to see and understand things that other people cannot see and understand. Occasionally an organization theorist gets involved in the management of an organization. One of the most famous, Richard Cyert, reflects on organization theory and whether it helped him be an effective manager:

IN PRACTICE 1.4

University President

As a professor of organization theory and management I used to wonder about the practical value of these academic fields. For the last eight years, I've had some first-hand experience finding out—as a university president . . . .

Familiarity with management literature has encouraged me to think strategically about the university. Strategic planning is as important to universities as to business firms. At a school like Carnegie-Mellon, for example, where our goals are to be small but excellent, department heads must select a limited number of research areas and concentrate enrollment resources in those areas. A small school can't be all things to all people. So I've tried to enunciate some strategic principles and to develop a strategic planning process within the organization.

For one thing, I've argued, departments must pick strategic areas with an eye to comparative advantage . . . . And I've argued that departments must make decisions that will be compatible with the expected environment for higher education over the next ten years.

Finally, my work in organization theory has helped me understand the behavior of people and departments in a university. It became clear, for example, that our budget procedures were almost guaranteed to lead to deficits, for we started the process by soliciting from each budget unit the amount of money it expected to need in the coming year. Organization theory suggests that expected needs would be inflated, and that it would be difficult politically to reduce the initial estimates significantly. So I decided to reverse the procedure, starting with income estimates and allocating a specific amount of income to each unit based on university priorities.

Knowledge of organization theory has led me to pay considerable attention to reporting relationships. To reduce conflict between academic and nonacademic sides of the university, I hired a scholar to head the institution's business affairs. And to encourage librarians to think of how to use modern technology more effectively, I have them report to the same individual who manages the computer center.

When I was dean at Carnegie-Mellon's Graduate School of Industrial Administration (GSIA), I was constantly fighting the central administration, especially when it required our school to make an overhead payment to the university. Now that I'm president, it's hard for me to understand why the dean doesn't automatically double the inadequate amount the GSIA is asked to pay. Organization theory helps put the problem in perspective; it teaches that the goals of an organization's subgroups will often conflict with the goals of the organization as a whole.[29]

Richard Cyert's experience shows the positive side of what organization theory enabled him to do in the areas of budgeting, goal conflict, and relationships among departments. Organization theory explores many additional areas, which are explained briefly in the next section.

FRAMEWORK FOR THE BOOK

Two Themes   Two themes will appear throughout this book. One theme is the conflict between the ideal of a rational organization and the reality of a social organization. The other theme is management level. Most organization theory topics pertain to upper management levels.

Rational Versus Social Organization   The rational approach to organizations strives for logic and order. This approach assumes the organizational world is stable and predictable. In this view, the manager's job is to arrange efficient work relationships and let the organization run as a clockwork. Cost-benefit analysis and economic logic are the bases upon which decisions should be made. The manager's role is to push the organization as close as possible toward maximum efficiency and rationality. The organization should be characterized by order rather than by disorder, as one early rational theorist wrote:

For social order to prevail in a concern there must, in accordance with the definition, be an appointed place for every employee and every employee must be in his appointed place. Perfect order requires, further, that the place be suitable for the employee and the employee for the place.[30]

The social approach assumes that organizations cannot achieve perfect order. Organizations may not even come close. Complex human organizations can be chaotic, irrational, and disorderly. As an open system, the organization responds to environmental turbulence, uncertainty, internal changes, technological developments, and shifts in consumer demand. Disagreement and conflict emerge. Organizational decisions may be based on power and politics. All these pressures work against order and tend to create disorder.

Management is in the middle of this conflict. Managers must balance the need for both rational and social organization, for order and disorder, and for tight control and looseness, if the organization is to perform effectively. The pressures are illustrated in figure 1.8. If the organization is managed too tightly, it will achieve remarkable efficiencies, but will not be adaptive, will not respond to the environment, and may not meet the needs of its employees. If the organization responds too freely to uncertainty and external changes, anarchy could result. The organization would not achieve sufficient economies and efficiencies to survive.

Throughout this book, issues will be considered from each point of view. The chapters on organization structure emphasize the rational point of view. Those chapters seek to develop models of ideal structure for organizational efficiency. But ideal models are never achieved. The social side of organizations is reflected in the chapters on politics, innovation, conflict, and decision-making. Each organization has to find its own level of rationality. Depending on organizational contingencies, greater rationality or greater social characteristics may be appropriate.

Managerial Level The other theme that appears throughout the book is managerial level. Organizations are usually divided into top, middle, and lower management. These levels are called the institutional level, managerial level, and operational level.[31] These three levels are illustrated in figure 1.9. Institutional managers are responsible for the entire organization. At this level, managers are concerned with goal-setting (e.g., profit, marketshare), strategy, the external environment, and how the organization can cope with the external environment. The institutional level is the domain of top management, and is described in the chapters on size, technology, and organization structure.

The managerial level pertains to major departments within the organization. The marketing department and research departments are examples.

Figure 1.8. Conflicting Pressures for Both Rational and Social System Characteristics.

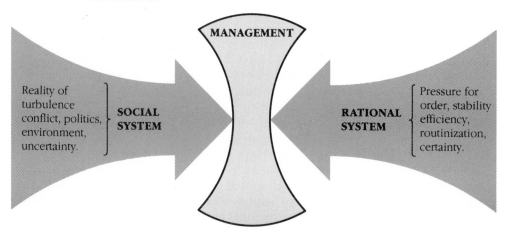

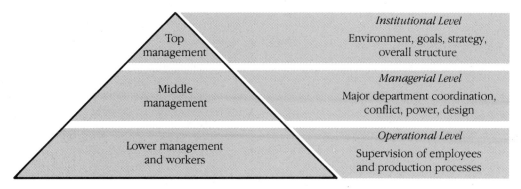

Figure 1.9. Institutional, Managerial, and Operational Levels of Management.

Managers at this level are concerned with the behavior of an entire department, and how the department relates to the rest of the organization. The managerial level is described in the material on work-unit technology, power and politics, intergroup conflict, and information and control systems.

The operational level is at the bottom of the organization. This level pertains to the supervision of employees who operate machines, type letters, teach classes, sell goods, and schedule work. The operational level is concerned with supervisors and individual employees.

This text focuses on the point of view of middle- and top-level managers. They are at the managerial and institutional levels in organizations. They have impact on the total organization. Several chapters treat the organization as a whole and cover techniques and strategies for managing the entire system. The level of major departments is also covered, along with techniques and strategies for management at this level. In many ways, the two levels are similar, but there are also important differences, which are explored in the chapters ahead.

Plan of the Book   The topics within the field of organization theory are interrelated. Chapters are presented so that major ideas unfold in logical sequence. The framework that guides the organization of the book is shown in figure 1.10. Part I introduces the basic idea of organizations as social systems and the nature of organization theory. This discussion provides the basis for Part II, which is about the external environment and goals and effectiveness. Organizations are open systems that exist for a purpose. The nature of the environment and the achievement of that purpose are the topics of Part II.

Part III describes how the organization is structured from the institutional viewpoint. Organization structure is an outgrowth of organizational goals and environment (discussed in Part II). The overall system and how it should be designed based upon size, technology, environment, and goals are explored in this section.

Parts IV and V look inside the organization. Part IV describes how structure can be designed to influence adaptation and change, and information and control. Part V shifts to behavioral processes that exist within and between major organizational departments. The topics of decision-making, power and politics, and intergroup conflict are covered there.

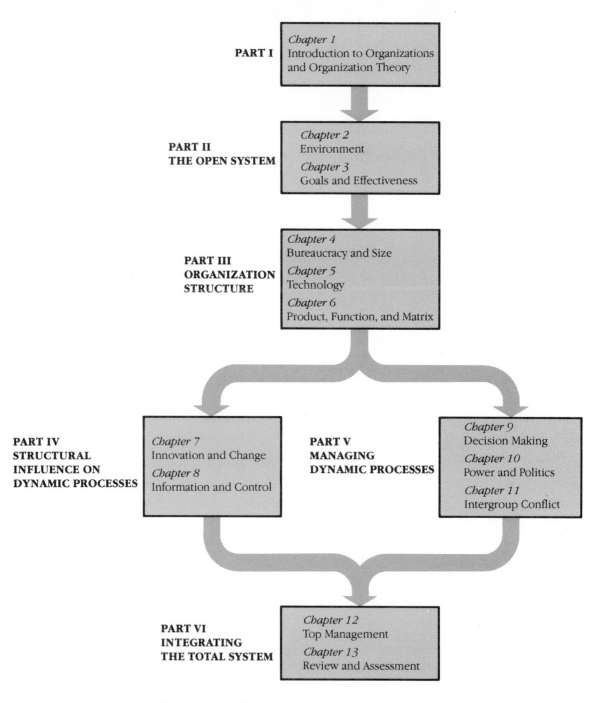

PART I

Chapter 1
Introduction to Organizations
and Organization Theory

**PART II
THE OPEN SYSTEM**

Chapter 2
Environment

Chapter 3
Goals and Effectiveness

**PART III
ORGANIZATION
STRUCTURE**

Chapter 4
Bureaucracy and Size

Chapter 5
Technology

Chapter 6
Product, Function, and Matrix

**PART IV
STRUCTURAL
INFLUENCE ON
DYNAMIC PROCESSES**

Chapter 7
Innovation and Change

Chapter 8
Information and Control

**PART V
MANAGING
DYNAMIC PROCESSES**

Chapter 9
Decision Making

Chapter 10
Power and Politics

Chapter 11
Intergroup Conflict

**PART VI
INTEGRATING
THE TOTAL SYSTEM**

Chapter 12
Top Management

Chapter 13
Review and Assessment

Figure 1.10. Plan for the Book.

Finally, Part VI returns to the institutional level and considers the special role of top managers in organizations. In many ways, top managers are involved in all the issues discussed in Parts I to V. Additional topics are explored so that the overall role of top management and its effect on the organization are understood. The last chapter assesses the topics in the book and relates them to the management of effective organizations. This discussion provides the basis for summarizing and evaluating previous chapters.

Plan of Each Chapter Each chapter begins with an organizational case to illustrate the topic to be covered. Theoretical concepts are introduced and explained in the body of the chapter. Several In Practice sections are included in each chapter to illustrate the concepts and show how they apply to real organization situations. Each chapter closes with a Summary and Interpretation and a Guides to Action section. Guides to Action highlight key points for use in designing and managing organizations. Summary and Interpretation reviews and interprets important theoretical concepts.

SUMMARY AND INTERPRETATION

The single most important idea in this chapter is that organizations are systems. They are open systems, which must adapt to the environment to survive. As social systems, organizations differ from other types of lower-level systems. Organizations are more complex and ambiguous. Thus, the organization is a unique management situation, and concepts developed for simpler mechanical systems do not apply.

The focus of analysis for organization theory is not individual people, but the organization itself. Relevant concepts include the dimensions of organization structure and context. The dimensions of formalization, specialization, standardization, hierarchy of authority, decentralization, complexity, professionalism, configuration, size, technology, and environment provide labels for measuring and analyzing organizations. These dimensions vary widely from organization to organization. Subsequent chapters provide frameworks for analyzing organizations within these concepts.

Another important concept is the difference between organization theory and disciplines in the physical and biological sciences. The usefulness of organization theory is not in the memorization of facts or in the application of precise formulas. Organization theory provides a set of concepts and models that inform the way a person thinks about organizations. Many of these concepts and models are not obvious and will not be learned through trial and error. Organization theory describes the patterns and relationships among organizational dimensions so that if a manager understands one important characteristic, other important dimensions can be predicted. Organization theory enables managers to understand their organizational situation, which is the first step toward effective management and control.

DISCUSSION QUESTIONS

1. What is the definition of organization? Briefly explain each part of the definition.
2. What is the difference between an open and closed system? Can you give an example of a closed system?
3. What are the five subsystems in organizations? If an organization had to go without one system, which one could it give up and survive the longest? Explain.
4. Why are human organizations considered more complex than other types of systems? What is the implication of this complexity for managers?
5. What is the difference between formalization, specialization, and standardization? Do you think an organization high on one of these three dimensions would also be high on the others? Discuss.
6. What is the difference between vertical and horizontal complexity?
7. Figure 1.4 presented a list of rules for bulletin-board use. What might be the reasons for prescribing rules in such detail? Is this helpful or harmful to the organization? To students?
8. Discuss the meaning of the following statement: Organization theory is not a collection of facts. Organization theory is a way of thinking about organizations.
9. What does contingency mean? What are the implications of contingency theories for organization theory?
10. What levels of analysis are typically studied in organization theory? How would this contrast with the level of analysis studied in a course in organizational behavior? A course in sociology?
11. What is the value of organization theory for non-managers? For managers?
12. Early management theorists believed that organizations should strive to be logical and rational, with a place for everything and everything in its place. Do you agree with that approach to the management of organizations? Discuss.
13. How do the institutional, managerial, and operational levels in an organization's hierarchy differ? Which of these hierarchical levels are most relevant to organization theory?

GUIDES TO ACTION

As an organization manager:

1. Do not ignore the external environment or protect the organization from it. Exchange resources with the environment in order to survive and prosper. Because the environment is unpredictable, do not expect to achieve complete order and rationality within the organization. Strive for a balance between order and flexibility.

2. Assign departments to perform the subsystem functions of production, boundary spanning, maintenance, adaptation, and management. Do not endanger the organization's survival and effectiveness by overlooking any of these functions.

3. Think of the organization as an entity distinct from the individuals who work in it. Describe the organization according to its level of size, formalization, decentralization, complexity, specialization, professionalism, personnel configuration, and the like. Use these characteristics to analyze the organization and to compare it to other organizations.

4. Be cautious when applying something that works in one situation to another situation. All organizational systems are not the same. Use organization theory to identify the correct structure, goals, strategy, and the like for each organization.

5. Make yourself a competent, influential manager by using the frameworks and models that organization theory provides to interpret and understand the organization around you. Use organization theory to understand and handle such things as intergroup conflict, power and politics, organization structure, environmental change, and organizational goals. Organization theory can help you see and understand things that other people miss.

Consider these guides when analyzing the following cases and when answering the questions listed after each case.

CASES FOR ANALYSIS

1. ELECTRONIC SYSTEMS COMPANY

The organization chart in figure 1.11 is for a medium-sized company that develops, manufactures, and sells electronic systems for use in automated and self-controlled production machines. The organization chart identifies each of the functions performed within the organization.

Questions
1. Which departments on the organization chart perform each of the five subsystem functions of production, adaptation, maintenance, boundary spanning, and management? Would any of these departments perform more than one of the functions?

2. Estimate the amount of formalization, specialization, standardization, decentralization, complexity, professionalism, and indirect labor ratio for this organization. Sketch a chart similar to figure 1.6. Explain the amount of each dimension you expect to find in the Electronic Systems Company.

2. IN BROKEN IMAGES

Peter Vaill of George Washington University uses poetry to describe how courses in organizations differ from courses in other fields.[32] The poem on page 35 is one he uses to help students think about the correct mental set for approaching material on the behavior of organizations.

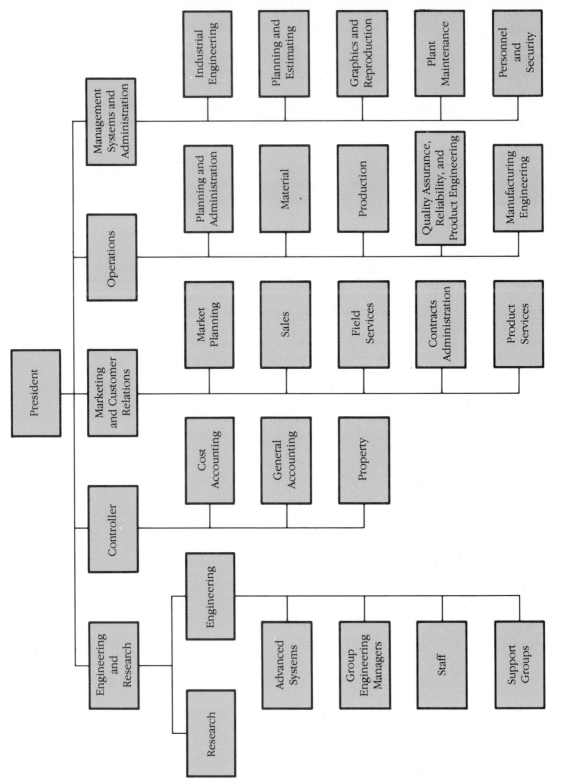

Figure 1.11. Organization Chart for the Electronic Systems Co.

In Broken Images
by
ROBERT GRAVES

He is quick, thinking in clear images;
I am slow, thinking in broken images.

He becomes dull, trusting to his clear images;
I become sharp, mistrusting my broken images.

Trusting his images, he assumes their relevance;
Mistrusting my images, I question their relevance.

Assuming their relevance, he assumes the fact;
Questioning their relevance, I question the fact.

When the fact fails him he questions his senses;
When the fact fails me, I approve my senses.

He continues quick and dull in his clear images;
I continue slow and sharp in my broken images.

He in a new confusion of his understanding;
I in a new understanding of my confusion.[33]

Questions
1. Robert Graves's poem implies that facts are less important than senses. Is that true for organization theory? For statistics? For finance?
2. Do the images in this poem correspond to the rational versus social-systems approach to organizations? Explain.
3. The poem seems to value broken images, confusion, mistrust of facts, and the act of questioning. Is that an appropriate point of view for managers in organizations? For university students? Discuss.

NOTES

1. Jacques Neher, "What Went Wrong," *Advertising Age,* April 13, 1981, p. 61.
2. Mark Schulz, Mike Agar, and Jim Grubert, "The Rise and Fall of Schlitz: A Case Analysis," unpublished manuscript, Texas A & M University, November, 1981, p. 1.
3. Neher, "What Went Wrong," p. 62.
4. Schulz, Agar, and Grubert, "Rise and Fall of Schlitz," p. 1.
5. Neher, "What Went Wrong," p. 64.
6. "Schlitz Puts Top Marketing Men on Leave; Cites Probes," *Advertising Age,* August 30, 1976, p. 2.
7. Jacques Neher, "Lost at Sea," *Advertising Age,* April 20, 1981, p. 49.
8. *Ibid.*
9. *Ibid.,* p. 52.
10. Christy Marshall, "Schlitz Reverts to Brand Management Structure," *Advertising Age,* July 3, 1978, p. 3.

11. "U.S. Conditionally Lets Stroh Buy Schlitz," *The Wall Street Journal,* April 19, 1982, p. 4.

12. Arthur M. Louis, "Schlitz's Crafty Taste Test," *Fortune,* January 26, 1981, pp. 32–34.

13. The analysis of the Joseph Schlitz Brewing Company was inspired by Mark Schulz, Mike Agar, and Jim Grubert, "Rise and Fall of Schlitz."

14. Howard Aldrich, *Organizations and Environments* (Englewood Cliffs, NJ: Prentice-Hall, 1979), p. 3.

15. Arthur G. Bedian, *Organizations: Theory and Analysis* (Hinsdale, IL: Dryden, 1980), p. 4; Aldrich, *Organizations and Environments,* pp. 4–6.

16. James D. Thompson, *Organizations in Action* (New York: McGraw-Hill, 1967), pp. 4–13.

17. Daniel Katz and Robert L. Kahn, *The Social Psychology of Organizations* (New York: John Wiley, 1966), p. 86.

18. Kenneth E. Boulding, "General Systems Theory: The Skeleton of Science," *Management Science* 2 (1956): 197–207.

19. *Ibid.;* Richard L. Daft, "The Evolution of Organization Analysis in *ASQ,* 1959–1979," *Administrative Science Quarterly* 25 (1980): 623–635.

20. Louis R. Pondy and Ian I. Mitroff, "Beyond Open Systems Models of Organization," in Barry M. Staw, ed., *Research in Organizational Behavior* (Greenwood, CT: JAI Press, 1978), 13–40; Richard L. Daft and John C. Wiginton, "Language and Organization," *Academy of Management Review* 4 (1978): 179–192.

21. Personal communication from a personnel manager.

22. The following discussion was heavily influenced by D. S. Pugh, "The Measurement of Organization Structures: Does Context Determine Form?" *Organizational Dynamics* I (Spring, 1973): 19–34; and D. S. Pugh, D. F. Hickson, C. R. Hinings, and C. Turner, "Dimensions of Organization Structure," *Administrative Science Quarterly* 13 (1968): 65–91.

23. D. S. Pugh, "Measurement of Organization Structures," pp. 19–34.

24. *Ibid.*

25. Henry Mintzberg, "Organization Design: Fashion or Fit?" *Harvard Business Review* (January–February, 1981): 103–116.

26. Bertrand Fox, "Forward," in Paul R. Lawrence and Jay W. Lorsch, *Organization and Environment* (Homewood, IL: Irwin, 1969), p. vi.

27. Robert Guest, *Organizational Change* (Homewood, IL: Dorsey Press, 1962).

28. Charles Perrow, *Organizational Analysis: A Sociological View* (Belmont, CA: Wadsworth, 1970), pp. 11–14.

29. Richard M. Cyert, "Does Theory Help?" *The Wall Street Journal,* April 7, 1980, p. 18.

30. Henry Fayol, "General Principles of Management," in H. F. Merrill, ed., *Classics in Management* (New York: American Management Association, 1960), p. 236.

31. Talcott Parsons, *Structure and Process in Modern Societies* (New York: Free Press, 1960).

32. Peter D. Vaill, "Thoughts on Using Poetry in the Teaching of OB," *Exchange: The Organizational Behavior Teaching Journal* 6 (1981): 50–51.

33. Robert Graves, "In Broken Images," *Collected Poems* (Garden City, NY: Anchor Books, 1966), p. 78.

PART **II**
The Open System

2

The External Environment

AMERICAN MOTORS CORPORATION

The product planners of the American Motors Corporation were droning through another meeting, describing the fuel-efficient models on their drawing boards, when Gerald Myers, chairman, interrupted.

What, he asked, were they going to do if the current glut of gasoline continued and prices did not increase in accordance with their projections? What would happen if no market developed for the very fuel-efficient, but expensive cars planned for later in the decade?

Donald E. Peterson, president of the Ford Motor Company, put it this way as he outlined some of the very small cars the company is developing: One big trouble with managing for the future is that the future is unpredictable. For instance, even though everyone agrees that fuel prices will continue to increase, there is always the possibility they won't, and the potential market for urban-type cars will not materialize.

Peterson said the cars were being developed for an era of $4-a-gallon gasoline.

Automakers still bear the scars caused by the rapid changes in consumers' tastes during the 1970s. Small cars were in great demand right after the Middle East war and the oil embargo in 1973, but as prices stabilized, [demand] for large cars increased, and small, efficient imports piled up on the docks.

When gasoline lines returned with the cutoff of Iranian oil to the United States in 1979, fuel economy once again became foremost in the minds of car buyers. The domestic auto makers are still struggling to transform their product lines to satisfy the renewed demand for fuel efficiency.

This chapter was coauthored by Lee Lyon, Texas A&M University.

Harold K. Sperlich, president of North American automotive operations for the Chrysler Corp., said he did not think the current leveling off of gasoline prices at about $1.40 a gallon will bring a renewed demand for big cars powered by V-8 engines.

Our view is that the glut is a short-term plateau and that prices will continue to move up, if only with inflation.

. . . Nevertheless, the auto companies have to decide just how much fuel economy people want and there are some signs that they are putting off commitments to produce [new models]. General Motors is known to have suspended plans to make the smaller-than-subcompact "S" model in the United States and has halted development of some three-cylinder engines that would have given over 70 miles to the gallon in an "S" car.

As Ford executives noted in their presentation, the dollar savings decline with each incremental increase in fuel efficiency, and the payback period from buying a new, more fuel-efficient car is longer than that for an older model.

. . . Although Americans have largely returned to their old driving habits this summer (the American Automobile Association reported that requests for route maps are up about 11% from last year) there is little evidence of a resurgence of the American love affair with big cars.

". . . In the past it was true that people shifted from smaller to larger cars as the economy strengthened," said Sperlich (of Chrysler Corp.). "But I don't think they're going back to their nasty old habits. We see them trading up in luxury, not in size, as good times come back."[1]

Executives at American Motors, Ford, Chrysler, and General Motors have a problem. They are trying to anticipate and predict the future demand for automobiles. Prior to 1974, customers demanded large automobiles. Demand abruptly shifted to smaller cars after 1974. Then demand for large automobiles moved upward until 1979, when small cars again became popular. Consumer demand for automobiles was influenced by the availability and price of gasoline. When gas was in short supply, small cars took priority. Currently, plenty of gas is available, but prices remain high. The price and availability of gasoline in the future is anyone's guess, but will have tremendous impact on the sale of automobiles. Auto executives want to correctly anticipate demand so they can manufacture the right type and number of automobiles.

Discussions like the one above about changes in the environment take place every day in large corporations. In the automobile industry, any number of external changes could have direct impact on the organization. Developments in technology, such as electric cars or the use of methane gas, could disrupt the marketplace. Competing transportation modes—bicycles, motorcycles, buses, and airlines—are trying to take away customers. The government also gets involved with rules about required mileage, consumer safety requirements, and tax benefits for investment in new plants. Labor feels it is not making sufficient wages, but may give back wages to help raise demand for autos and create more jobs. Foreign manufacturers are gaining a reputation for providing higher quality cars at lower prices than American manufacturers can produce. The list could go on and on. If a comprehensive list of the threats and opportunities facing major corporations were developed, the majority of those elements would originate in the external environment.

Purpose of This Chapter

This chapter is concerned with the organization's environment. In a broad sense, the environment is infinite and includes everything outside the organization. Organizations are directly influenced by a subset of external elements that have bearing or impact on the organization. Our analysis will consider only those aspects of technology, economic conditions, government, competitors, and the like to which the organization is sensitive and must respond to survive. Thus, our definition of **organizational environment** is all elements existing outside the boundary of the organization that have the potential to affect all or part of the organization.

Recall from the previous chapter that organizations are open systems. The open-system concept is important because it calls attention to the vulnerability of the organization from the external environment. The open-system concept forces us to look outside the organization to explain the behavior of organizations. Much of the behavior within organizations as well as organizational performance is affected by external factors. Characteristics within the organization, such as structure, goals, technology, strategy, and power, reflect the external environment to some extent. To fully assess management processes, employee behavior, organization design, and performance, the external environment must be analyzed and understood.

The purpose of this chapter is to develop a framework for analyzing organizational environments. We identify external domains that influence organizations. Then we explore how the complexity and rate of change in those domains create uncertainty for the organization. Organizational responses to uncertainty, including structural design and planning systems, are also discussed. Finally, we consider how the organization can manage the external environment. Organizations are not passive entities that simply respond to external changes. Managers can develop strategies for reaching out and controlling those elements that are critical to organization survival and success.

ENVIRONMENTAL DOMAINS

The environment of an organization can be understood by analyzing specific domains. Environmental domains represent those external sectors that influence the behavior and performance of the organization. Nine domains can be analyzed for each organization: industry, raw materials, human resources, financial resources, the market, technology, economic conditions, government, and the larger social culture in which the organization functions. The domains are illustrated in figure 2.1. In any single organization, each domain should be scanned and analyzed for threats and opportunities.

Figure 2.1. Domains in an Organization's Environment.

Industry Industry includes competitors in the same type of business. The recording industry is different from the steel industry or the broadcasting industry. Industry influences the size of the organization, amount of advertising, type of customers, and typical profit margins.

Industry concentration determines the amount of competitive uncertainty for each organization.[2] An industry with a few large companies is considered more uncertain than an industry with many small ones. A competitor may offer higher pay, or better working conditions, or sell its goods at a lower price. Any action by a competitor requires an organizational response or customers and employees may be lost. The decision of a large competitor has great significance for the organization. An example of unusual competitive pressure and a strong response occurred recently in San Antonio.

IN PRACTICE 2.1

Eloy Centeno Food Stores

An independent grocer contends two of the state's largest food store chains are taking losses on items sold in the San Antonio area to drive him out of business.

A full-page advertisement in a local newspaper this week marked the latest round in the food store war.

In the ad, Eloy Centeno accused Kroger Stores, Inc., of Ohio and H.E.B. Stores, Inc., of Corpus Christi of lowering prices in trying to force out the smaller stores so they can have a monopoly and then raise prices—a practice known as predatory pricing and illegal under federal antitrust laws . . . .

Centeno made a plea to consumers, saying if the policies of the large chains were successful in driving out competition, prices would be higher in the long run.

"The consumer is king and if you act individually and collectively, you will be able to bring sanity to a situation which, if left unchecked, will lead to economic disaster for hundreds of allied suppliers, related business and thousands of employees," the advertisement said. "This will also mean higher food prices for you."

Centeno said the stores were taking deliberate losses in San Antonio but compensating by raising prices elsewhere. He said he planned to run his ad in most south Texas newspapers within the next month.

Included in Centeno's ad was a list of prices for H.E.B. stores in San Antonio and other south Texas cities—showing them about 12 percent higher in Corpus Christi, Laredo, San Marcos, Del Rio, and Eagle Pass.[3]

Raw Materials Organizations must acquire raw materials from the external environment. These materials include everything from paper, pencils, and typewriters to patients for a hospital, iron ore for a steel mill, manuscripts for a publisher, or green coffee beans for a coffee distributor. Raw materials are often readily available at a low price. Sometimes raw material supplies are threatened or are available at high prices or not at all.

A few years ago, the price of silver soared from less than $10 per ounce to over $40 per ounce in only a few months. This created a great deal of activity in organizations manufacturing or using photographic film. Faced with rising costs of raw materials, film manufacturers were forced to raise prices. Rising prices tended to reduce the customer's use of film and thus reduced sales.

Major users of photographic film such as X-ray laboratories invested heavily in equipment that would recapture silver washed from film in the developing process. In this way, they could offset part of the higher cost of the film. Then the price of silver plunged to less than $10 per ounce. Investment in expensive silver recovery equipment was no longer attractive, and several film users were stuck with the new equipment.

Human Resources Human resources are employees. Organizations must have a supply of trained, qualified personnel. Without an abundant supply of human raw material, the organization will have a hard time producing output. Managerial talent has been in short supply for many years. Organizations have bid up the price of upper-level managers to keep highly qualified people in their organizations. The demand for MBA degrees has increased at an enormous rate. Business schools, on the other hand, have a difficult time obtaining a supply of qualified professors. Very few graduate students want to go on for their Ph.D. when high salaries are paid for bachelor's and master's degree positions. As a result of short supplies, business schools have to bunch students together in large classes or use less qualified teachers.

Financial Resources Financial resources reflect the availability of money. The stock and bond markets, banks, and insurance companies are included in this environmental domain. Interest rates also influence the availability of money. The availability of cheap money encourages an organization to grow fast. If an organization has to finance growth internally, growth slows down. Extensive borrowing also transfers some control of the company to lending agencies.

Market Customer demand for goods and services represents the market. Hospitals serve patients, schools serve students, supermarkets supply home-makers, airlines move travelers, and government agencies provide benefits to practically everyone. The market influences the organization through demand for the organization's output. If the market is shrinking, the organization must cut back or diversify into other markets. If the market expands, the organization must expand to supply customer needs or lose its standing in the industry.

Customers must be taken care of. Many organizations advertise to increase customer demand for their products. Organizations typically try to understand and anticipate potential market changes. Mistreatment of customers, even by large, influential organizations can have disastrous results. Customers may not only stop doing business with the organization but, as in the following case, they may seek revenge.

IN PRACTICE 2.2

Burroughs Corporation

Attention: Unhappy users of Burroughs B-800 and similar Burroughs computer hardware and software

Our firm is preparing to sue the Burroughs Corporation. We would like to find other firms who, like us, feel that overly zealous computer sales people may have misrepresented the Burroughs B-800 or similar product lines to them. We wish to combine our information in efforts to seek a solution to our problems using all available legal remedies. All responses will be treated confidentially.

Contact Tom Drewes or Tony Leisner, Quality Books, Inc., 400 Anthony Trail, Northbrook, IL 60062.

After Thomas Drewes, president of Quality Books, an Illinois publisher and distributor, placed the advertisement above, more than 500 users of small computer systems came forward with their own horror stories about Burroughs. Not all the unhappy customers were content with griping. Burroughs is being sued by 129 users of its small computer systems.

It seems that many plaintiffs ran into similar problems: the Burroughs salesman promised a system that could run several programs and respond to several terminals at the same time. But if the programs were too big or the terminal traffic too heavy, the central processor slowed down drastically or even stopped. It was especially delicate when running programs for entering orders and controlling inventory.

In its suit, Quality Books is asking damages of $856,000. It claims its Burroughs computer lost track of inventory, billings, shipments, and accounts receivable. After the computer system was installed, Quality says, the processing time for orders lengthened from a few days to as much as six weeks.[4]

Technology Technology is the use of available knowledge and techniques to produce goods and services. The complexity of the technology influences the skill level and organization size required to use the technology. New technological developments also have impact on the organization. If the organization fails to keep up with technological change, it will be forced out of business. The electronics industry has experienced rapid technological changes in recent years. But even in a traditional industry like meat packing, technological change can put companies out of business if they do not adapt:

> *In a business where success or failure hinges on fractions of a cent profit or loss, Idle Wild Foods is just about as good as they come. If there is anyone better, it's Iowa Beef Processors, which revolutionized the way finished beef is produced. The new technology was first perfected in a huge slaughtering and processing plant IBP built at Dakota City, Nebr. in 1967, and overnight most of the competition had to acquire IBP's cost-cutting skills or get out of the business. Most of them got out.[5]*

Economic Conditions Economic conditions reflect the general economic health of the country and region where the organization operates. Unemployment rates, consumer purchasing power, interest rates, inflation, and excess production capacity are all part of external economic health. The availability of supplies, labor, and the demand for output are related to economic conditions. Economic conditions also affect government and not-for-profit organizations. High tax revenues are a direct result of economic prosperity. Contributions to the Salvation Army and the Red Cross go down during periods of economic recession, just when helping agencies experience greater demand for their services. Business-leaders prefer stable economic conditions with moderate growth and prosperity. Violent economic changes restrict business investment and growth, and poor economic conditions have a variety of undesirable side effects.

Government The government includes the regulatory, legal, and political systems that surround the organization. The political system, such as capitalism versus socialism, determines the amount of freedom organizations have to pursue their own ends. In North America, organizations operate in a capitalistic economy, but the government specifies the rules of the game through laws and regulations. The federal government influences organizations through the occupational safety and health administration, fair trade practices, subsidies for certain products and services, punitive damage statutes that encourage or discourage lawsuits against businesses, consumer protection legislation, product safety, requirements for information and labeling, import and export restrictions, and pricing constraints. In some cases, government is the consumer and may purchase most or all of an organization's output. Although some government regulation is necessary, many businesses find it objectionable. Government tries to regulate and protect the larger society, but sometimes regulations have unfortunate consequences for an individual business. The following case illustrates how government regulations affected a small construction company.

IN PRACTICE 2.3

Dante's Construction Company

Sole proprietor of Dante's Construction Co., employer of one carpenter and two laborers, and proud owner of a Ford pickup truck, Dante Di Gaitano, forty-nine, has lately been on the receiving end of the kind of official attention the federal government normally reserves for *Fortune 500* companies.

The first intimation of trouble came in November, 1978, when Di Gaitano received a letter from the Philadelphia field office of OFCCP (Office of Federal Contract Compliance Programs) admonishing him that he had failed to send in his monthly affirmative-action reports. Applicable to any federal construction contract in excess of $10,000, the one-page Form 257 requires contractors to break down the number of hours worked by craft, race, sex, and ethnicity. Figuring that most of the questions didn't really apply to him, Di Gaitano sent back forms for October and November reporting "no activity." He says he felt secure in doing so because one of his two laborers, Robert Sutton, was black: "I'd hired him because we'd worked alongside each other for many years before I went into business on my own—not because anybody in government made me do it."

Unfortunately for Di Gaitano, OFCCP was less interested in the state of his conscience than in his failure to submit any further reports. OFCCP inspector Lee Tolbert went to the Navy Yard construction site to ask Di Gaitano some questions.

Tolbert's first concern was Di Gaitano's record with blacks. Black himself, Tolbert asked to meet alone with laborer Robert Sutton to make sure he had not been harassed. No harassment, Sutton replied; in fact Di Gaitano had been buying him breakfast every morning.

Looking around the site, Tolbert inquired next about separate toilets for women. "What for, when we have no women on the site?" Di Gaitano exploded. No women, Tolbert noted on his checklist.

About five weeks later, Di Gaitano received a "deficiency citation" listing seventeen flaws in his "equal-opportunity posture." Topping the list was Di Gaitano's failure to set himself the goal of filling at least 5 percent of his jobs with women. Among other flaws were failures to conduct and document an outreach program and to publicize Dante's Construction's equal-employment-opportunity policy through the news media, at staff meetings, in the company's "annual report," and in the "company newspaper."

To purge himself of these failings, Di Gaitano was invited to sign an eleven-page, seventeen-section "conciliation agreement" itemizing at least forty-three filing and reporting requirements. Some of them struck Di Gaitano as more than a little odd, like the one "to maintain records that parties and picnics have been posted and available to all employees." If he refused to sign, he could be barred from receiving federal contracts.

Though the government has locked him into a vast paper chase he still does not employ a woman. He briefly had one working for him as a laborer but admits that he was relieved when her mother called him that her daughter could not continue on the job because she had been called up for duty in the National Guard.[6]

Culture Culture includes both the demographic characteristics and the value system within a society. Demographic characteristics include age of the population, income distribution, composition of the work force (age, sex, race), whether people live in rural or urban areas or are migrating from one area to the other, and the incidence of slums, crime, and educational facilities.

Values are also an important component of culture. Protest groups in the 1960s and 1970s tarnished the public image of munitions manufacturers, whose stock was divested from many foundations and university portfolios. A changing value in recent years has been the work ethic. The work force used to be dominated by employees who were concerned with job security and standard of living. In recent years, people want challenging jobs and interesting work and time to enjoy life away from the organization. Other emerging values pertain to consumer safety. Ralph Nader led the movement toward consumers fighting back. Corporations were portrayed by consumer groups as careless and exploitative, which led to many lawsuits against companies.

Value systems are most visible when comparing one country to another. A large automobile plant in Japan will not reduce its work force during slack periods in the same way an American company will. The value system in the Japanese culture encourages companies to treat employees as members of the family. Employees are given lifetime tenure, and are not laid off even when times are bad. Everyone shares the burden equally until conditions improve.

Summary   Each of the nine domains is made up of elements that have the potential to influence the organization. Each domain can be scanned and analyzed by the organization's managers. In most organizations, perhaps three or four domains will be especially important and should be watched closely. Moreover, the domains will affect each other. Economic conditions will affect the market, and government policy affects financial resources. The next section considers how to assess domains and the impact domains have on organizations.

ASSESSING ENVIRONMENTAL UNCERTAINTY

The external environment can be organized into the nine domains described above. The impact of the environment on the organization can be analyzed along two dimensions: the extent to which external domains are simple or complex, and the extent to which they are stable or unstable. The simple-complex and stable-unstable dimensions of the external environment are important because they determine the amount of uncertainty facing the organization.[7] Organizations must cope with and manage uncertainty in order to be effective. **Uncertainty** means that decision-makers do not have information about environmental factors, and they have a difficult time predicting external changes. Uncertainty increases the risk of failure for organizational actions, and makes it difficult to compute costs and probabilities associated with decision alternatives.

Environmental complexity refers to heterogeneity, or the number of external elements that are relevant to an organization's operations.[8] In a complex environment, a large number of diverse external elements will interact with and influence the organization. In a simple environment, as few as three or four external elements influence the organization.

Universities have complex environments. Universities span a large number of technologies, and are a focal point for cultural and value changes. Government regulatory and granting agencies interact with the university, and so do a variety of professional and scientific associations, alumni, parents, foundations, legislators, community residents, international agencies, donors, corporations, and athletic teams. Economic conditions influence the size of student enrollment and the amount of tuition paid. Professors are scarce in certain fields. A large number of external elements thus function simultaneously, which makes the university's environment very complex. On the other hand, a hardware store in a suburban community is in a simple environment. The only external elements of any real importance are the parent company (for supplies) and customers. Government regulation is minimal, and cultural change has little impact. Human resources are not a problem because the store is run by family members or part-time student help.

The **stable-unstable** dimension refers to whether elements in the environment are dynamic.[9] An environmental domain is stable if it remains the same over a period of months or years. Under unstable conditions, environmental elements shift abruptly. Environmental elements change unexpectedly and surprise the organization.

An example of a stable environment would be a public utility.[10] In the rural midwest, demand and supply factors for the public utility are stable. A gradual increase in demand may occur, which is easily predictable over time. Other companies, however, face rapid and unexpected changes in one or more external domains. In the following example of the market domain, demand shifted so rapidly that the plant had to be closed.

IN PRACTICE 2.4

Scullin Steel Co.

Ben Fixman appreciates the story about the man who jumped nude into a cactus and later explained, "It seemed like the thing to do at the time."

So it seemed three years ago when Mr. Fixman decided that Scullin Steel Co. should commit itself to making and selling railroad freight-car castings on long-term contracts with freight-car makers. Such contracts had been unheard of. At the time, the rail-car business was booming, and car manufacturers were jumping at the chance to lock up supplies of the castings they would need.

Or thought they would need. Last year, the rail-car boom had busted. The orders Scullin asserts customers are obliged to place stopped coming in. Scullin had spent more than $10 million on plant improvements to turn out castings. Its plant began losing money, and this month, Mr. Fixman, chairman of Scullin's parent company, Diversified Industries, Inc., closed the plant and laid off about 680 employees.[11]

The simple-complex and stable-unstable dimensions are combined into a framework for environmental assessment in figure 2.2. In the simple, stable environment uncertainty is low. There are only a few external elements to contend with and they tend to remain stable. The complex, stable environment represents somewhat greater uncertainty. A larger number of elements have to be scanned and analyzed in order for the organization to perform well. External elements do not change rapidly in this environment.

Even greater uncertainty is felt in the simple, unstable environment.[12] Rapid change creates uncertainty for managers. Even though the organization

	Simple	Complex
Stable	*LOW UNCERTAINTY* 1. Small number of external elements 2. Elements remain the same or change slowly	*LOW MODERATE UNCERTAINTY* 1. Large number of external elements 2. Elements remain the same or change slowly
Unstable	*HIGH MODERATE UNCERTAINTY* 1. Small number of external elements 2. Elements are in continuous process of change	*HIGH UNCERTAINTY* 1. Large number of external elements 2. Elements are in continuous process of change

Environmental Change (vertical axis: Stable to Unstable)

Environmental Complexity (horizontal axis: Simple to Complex)

Figure 2.2. Framework for Assessing Environmental Uncertainty.
Adapted and reprinted from "Characteristics of Perceived Environments and Perceived Environmental Uncertainty" by Robert B. Duncan published in *Administrative Science Quarterly* 17(3) (1972): 313–327 by permission of *The Administrative Science Quarterly.* Copyright © 1972 by Cornell University.

has few external elements, they are hard to predict and understand. Finally, the greatest uncertainty for an organization occurs in the complex, unstable environment. A large number of elements impinge upon the organization, and they are shifting. Behavior of key elements in the environment is difficult to predict and understand.

A beer distributor functions in a simple, stable environment. Demand for beer changes only gradually. The distributor has an established delivery route, and supplies of beer arrive on schedule. State universities and other large government agencies are in a stable, complex environment. A large number of external elements are present but, although they change, the changes are gradual and predictable. Fashion industries are in simple, unstable environments. Organizations that manufacture and sell women's clothing, or that are involved in the music industry, face shifting supply and demand. Taste and fads change rapidly, and the organization must adapt quickly to keep up. The oil industry and the airline industry face complex, unstable environments. Uncertainty is extremely high. Many external domains are changing simultaneously. In the case of oil companies, environmental groups are filing lawsuits and pressing for new legislation. Oil supplies from the Mideast are unpredictable, public opinion is shifting, often against the oil companies, and the government frequently changes the regulations and tax laws that apply to oil companies. In the case of airlines, over just a few years they have been confronted with deregulation, the entry of regional airlines as a new set of competitors, dramatically increased fuel prices, price wars, shifting customer demand, an air-traffic controller strike and mass firing, and a reduction of scheduled flights.

Environmental domains influence the level of uncertainty within the organization. Taken together, the elements described so far form the overall texture of an organization's environment. Emory and Trist introduced the term "causal texture" to describe how linked environmental elements represent threats or opportunities for the organization.[13] They described four types of causal textures: placid, randomized; placid, clustered; disturbed, reactive; and turbulent field. Each type of environmental texture represents a different type of complexity or change that influences organizational behavior.

Placid, Randomized   This is the simplest organizational environment. It is placid in the sense that elements change slowly. New threats or opportunities are infrequent. This environment is random because when a change does occur it is not predictable and is not coordinated with other environmental elements.

An example is a pharmacy in a small town. Years go by without abrupt changes. Only a few elements are directly connected to the pharmacy. Supplies are purchased on a regular basis from well-established sources. Customers of long standing are drawn from the local community. There is little the pharmacist can do to influence the environment, and occurrences that have a major impact on the pharmacy are unlikely. In this kind of environment, the organization can concentrate on day-to-day business operations. The environment is not a major problem to be considered in a manager's decision-making.

Placid, Clustered   This environment is quite stable, but more complex. Elements in the environment are linked to one another. Elements may act simultaneously to influence the organization. When threats or opportunities appear, they occur in clusters, which is more dangerous for the organization. Since elements may change simultaneously, the organization should try to anticipate and avoid these problems. Some planning and forecasting is important, and day-to-day operations should allow for possible new events in the environment.

A placid, clustered environment was experienced by chemical producers because of disposal procedures for chemical wastes. The simultaneous disruption among several elements, including customers, suppliers, community groups, and state and federal agencies, caused a severe problem for the chemical manufacturers. The external groups were coordinated and formed powerful coalitions demanding greater safety in the disposal of chemical wastes. Organizations in placid, clustered environments should plan and anticipate clustered responses in order to avoid them.

Disturbed, Reactive   In this environment, changes are no longer random. Actions by one organization can disturb the environment and provoke a reaction. The disturbed, reactive environment is made up of large organizations. This is similar to what economists call oligopolistic industries. Large, similar organizations who are visible to one another dominate an industry and market.

A decision by an organization concerning price, advertising, or new products will cause a reaction from competitors, and sometimes from the government or protest groups. Improvement in one organization's position comes at the expense of other organizations. One example was the introduction of a fifty-thousand-mile guarantee by Chrysler Corporation in the early 1960s. It gave Chrysler an advantage, so other automobile companies reacted with similar warranties to offset the advantage. A more recent example of a disturbed, reactive environment was the move by PepsiCo to take away supermarket business from Coca-Cola. The strong advertising and price-cutting campaign of PepsiCo successfully increased market share. Coca-Cola failed to properly assess the strengths and threat of PepsiCo. Coca-Cola has now reacted, and PepsiCo and Coca-Cola are locked into a fierce competitive battle for market share that is reducing profits for both companies. This cola war also caused a serious drop in business for Seven-Up, an innocent bystander in the disturbed, reactive environment.

In disturbed, reactive environments, management's task is to carefully plan decisions and strategic moves to allow for countermoves. Planning no longer considers just the organization's own behavior, but must consider all organizations in the industry. The organization must carefully monitor other organizations and prepare reactions to their moves. The disturbed, reactive environment is more complex and unstable than either the placid, randomized or the placid, clustered environment.

Turbulent Field   The turbulent field is an environment characterized by both complexity and rapid changes. Multiple sectors experience dramatic change, and the changes are connected. The turbulent field usually has overwhelming negative consequences for the organization. The environment changes so dramatically that the organization may perish. This could happen, for example, when simultaneous technological breakthroughs, new government regulations, and changes in consumer preferences occur, such as in the canning industry in England in the 1940s. Within one or two years, most organizations ceased to exist. The distinguishing factor in the turbulent field is the interdependence among environmental elements. By shifting together and influencing one another, the effect on the organization is multiplied. True turbulent fields are rare, but when an environment becomes turbulent, organizational planning is of little value. Changes are so dramatic that they cannot be anticipated. Adaptation represents the best hope for the organization. Table 2.1 summarizes the four environmental textures and the appropriate organizational response.

Table 2-1. Environmental Textures and Management Implications.

Causal Texture	Characteristics	Organizational Response
Placid, randomized	Changes are infrequent, and in single elements.	Concentrate on day-to-day operations. Little planning.
Placid, Clustered	Changes are infrequent, but occur in clusters of linked elements.	Plan and forecast to anticipate and avoid clustered changes.
Disturbed, reactive	External elements react to changes in organization and vice-versa. Organizations are large and visible.	Plan and forecast to anticipate moves and countermoves by other organizations.
Turbulent Field	Environmental domains change frequently and in clusters.	Interpret environment and adapt to survive.

IN PRACTICE 2.5

Procter and Gamble vs. General Foods

Sanka brand had dominated the decaffeinated coffee market in the United States for several years, with about 50% of the market. "Sanka" has almost become a generic term for caffeine-free coffee. Procter & Gamble recently introduced High Point instant decaffeinated coffee to acquire a share of this market. Procter wants to capture at least 10% of the instant coffee business. This move touched off an expensive marketing battle.

Procter & Gamble is spending as much as $30,000,000 on the introduction of High Point. In the third quarter of 1980 alone, Procter spent $10 million in advertising. General Foods responded by tripling its Sanka advertising to over $8,000,000. Then Procter & Gamble mailed dollars-off coupons to housewives all over the country. General Foods responded with an increase in its total promotional spending.

Several manufacturers want a share of the instant coffee market. Taster's Choice and Brim are other contenders. Decaffeinated coffee is a growth market, and appears to be one place where increased profits are possible in the coffee industry.

Not only do these companies have to contend with each other, but new factors loom on the horizon. For one thing, U.S. coffee consumption has been falling steadily over the last twenty years. Consumption has never fully rebounded from the 1975 shortage of coffee beans that sent prices through the roof. Moreover, future price changes are in the offing. Bean prices have fallen 70¢ in the past year, which is an opportunity for all brands. If another shortage sends prices spiraling again, a severe market decline could occur.

Another problem is a government study which indicates that a solvent used in decaffeinated coffee may cause cancer. If tests indicate that cancer is a possibility, all manufacturers may have to stop production and reconstruct their manufacturing process.[14]

The coffee market at this time is disturbed, reactive. A move by any one instant coffee producer to increase market share disturbs the environment and provokes a response from competitors. Managers at Procter & Gamble can plan for those reactions. Other factors, such as the price of coffee beans, the demand for coffee, and government studies and regulations, are potential hazards. If each factor shifted to the worst possible case simultaneously, the environment would be turbulent. Simultaneous cancer scare and high prices could possibly wipe out, at least temporarily, the decaffeinated coffee business.

THE IMPACT OF ENVIRONMENT ON THE ORGANIZATION

Resource Dependence   The discussion so far in this chapter has described how the organization is dependent upon the external environment. All resources come from the environment.[15] Elements in the external environment consume the organization's goods and services, and provide raw materials, employees, financial resources, and technological information. The organization is vulnerable to the external environment when the exchange of resources is endangered. Some external organizations control resources the organization needs. These dependencies give environmental elements power over the organization. If these dependencies are small and isolated, as in the case of the placid, random environment, significant coping is not required. The organization can concentrate on production activites. When external dependencies are large, and are changing, the organization must take steps to cope with these dependencies and reduce them.

Organizations have two coping techniques.[16] The first is internal change. The organization can adapt to the external environment by altering organization structure, internal work patterns, or policies, or planning and forecasting. The second technique is to reach out and change the external environment. The organization can try to reduce environmental change, or to change external conditions in a direction suitable to its own needs. The next section describes internal organization responses to the environment. Organizational structures and processes that are suited to specific environments are discussed. Later sections describe how organizations influence the external environment.

Organization Structure

Structural Complexity   As the complexity in the external environment increases, so does complexity in the organization. The law of requisite variety says that complexity in one system is required to control complexity in another system.[17] This relationship is part of being an open system. Each sector in the external environment requires an internal employee or department to deal with it. The personnel department deals with unemployed people who want to work for the company. The marketing department finds customers. Procurement obtains raw materials from suppliers. The finance group deals with bankers. The legal department works with the courts and government agencies. The engineering department responds to new technological developments. Long-range planners are concerned with economic conditions, demand, and competition. The complexity of external domains increases the complexity of the organization. An organization in a complex environment will need a greater number of departments and tasks than will an organization in a simple environment.

Buffers James Thompson conceptualized the organization as a technical core surrounded by buffers.[18] **Buffers** absorb uncertainty from the environment. The technical core performs the primary activity of the organization, which is production in a manufacturing firm or research and teaching in a university. In order to make the technical core as efficient as possible, it should not be disturbed by external uncertainties. Specific departments are established to deal with environmental domains and absorb the uncertainty originating from each domain. The goal of buffer departments is to make the technical core as nearly a closed system as possible so it can function efficiently. Examples of buffer departments are shown in figure 2.3 as R & D (research and development), finance, purchasing, and sales.

A purchasing department and a warehouse can ensure a steady flow of raw materials to the production line. Even if the supply of raw materials is uncertain, a purchasing manager can stock up on scarce supplies so that the assembly line does not have to shut down from supply fluctuations. Advertising, marketing, and sales attempt to buffer the organization on the output side. They can use warehouses and inventory. If demand is uneven, the production department can produce at a steady rate for inventory, which will be sold as demand requires. Auto companies will keep up to 60 days of inventory on hand to avoid production cutbacks. The personnel department provides a steady flow of suitable personnel to work in the organization. Finance ensures accurate recordkeeping, collects payments from customers, and sees that paychecks go to employees. Nonproduction departments absorb environmental uncertainty and fluctuations, thereby enabling the technical core to be efficient. Threats, changes, and other uncertainties are absorbed by the buffer departments.

Boundary spanning **Boundary-spanning roles** link and coordinate the organization with key elements in the external environment. The boundary role establishes a relationship with individuals and organizations in the environment. By carrying information back and forth between the environment and the organization, plans and activities can be coordinated and uncertainty reduced. The organization will be better equipped to adapt to the environment, and the environment may be able to adapt to the needs of the organization.

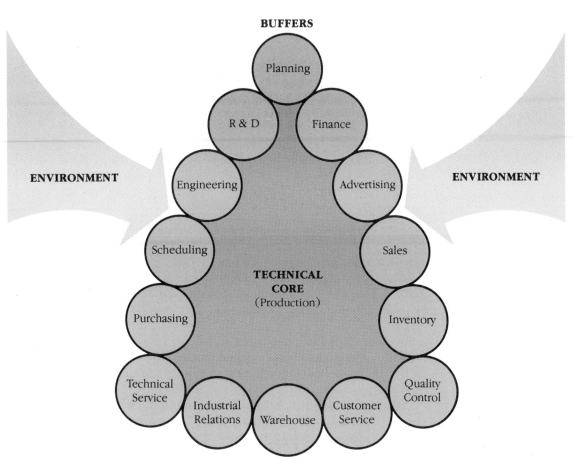

Figure 2.3. Buffer Departments Reduce Environmental Uncertainty for the Technical Core.

Boundary-spanning roles serve two purposes: (1) to detect and process information about changes in the external environment, and (2) to represent the organization to the environment.[19] The buffer departments described in figure 2.3 transfer materials, resources, services, and money between the environment and the organization. Boundary roles concentrate on information. Boundary roles are often part of buffer departments, but they process information for the organization.

Boundary personnel scan and monitor events in the environmental domain. Market research is a formalized boundary role that monitors trends in consumer taste. By scanning the environment for abrupt changes and long-term trends, boundary spanners can supply information to decision-makers. By identifying new technological developments, innovations, regulations, sources of supply, and so on, boundary personnel supply information that enables the organization to make plans and adjustments. Boundary spanners prevent the organization from stagnating and becoming out of synchronization with environmental changes.[20]

The boundary task of representation sends information out to the environment. The boundary role influences other people's perception of the organization. In the marketing department, advertising and sales-agents represent the organization to customers. Similar activities occur in other departments. Purchasers may call upon suppliers and describe purchasing needs. Accounting personnel may phone the bank or customers about payment schedules. The legal department may inform lobbyists or elected officials about the organization's needs or views on political matters. Managing the organization's image can serve to reduce uncertainty in that domain.

IN PRACTICE 2.6

Ohio State University

On a typical Monday morning, about 30 representatives of Ohio State University board commercial airliners for Washington. They will spend the day here prowling the halls of Congress and federal agencies seeking some of the $63 million in federal aid the school receives each year.

So heavy is the traffic between Columbus and the nation's capital that Edwin M. Crawford, Ohio State's vice president for public affairs—and the school's chief lobbyist—wants the school to buy its own airliner . . . .

So vital have federal dollars become in the higher education industry that Ohio State is but one of at least 100 institutions to have opened offices in Washington or hired lobbyists in the last decade to represent their interests on Capitol Hill and with federal agencies . . . .

At Princeton, where 41% of the university's $100 million annual budget comes from the federal government and 45% of the students receive federal financial aid, lobbyist Nan Wells estimates she spends one-third of her time in Washington.

Last year, when Congress was considering changes in the complex formula for distributing student aid, it was Wells who argued for language that would stretch eligibility as widely as possible. The result: an extra $1.5 million in grants and loans for Princeton's students, money that eventually found its way into the university's coffers.

At the University of Tennessee, a vice president, Walter Lambert, keeps careful track of all students receiving any part of the $9 million in federal tuition grants or loans distributed over the school's five campuses.

When it comes time to vote on such measures, he has the list broken down by congressional district and he makes sure each Tennessee congressman knows exactly how many of his constituents are receiving the federal largess . . . .

Most Washington representatives of higher education no longer quarrel with use of the term "lobbyist," but they are not required to register as such. Most agree with the University of Missouri's Sandra

Moody that the broader designation of "federal relations officer" better describes their work.

Moody spends more time tracking down grants in the federal bureaucracy than she does trying to influence legislation on the Hill. But, she said, "You can't have one without the other. It requires legislative effort to establish the grants." [21]

Federal relations officers employed by universities are boundary spanners. They scan the government domain for grants and bring the information back to the university. They also present the university's point of view to members of Congress. These activities reduce financial uncertainty for the university by increasing and stabilizing the flow of government funds into the university treasury.

Differentiation and Integration

Organizational Differentiation is "the differences in cognitive and emotional orientations among managers in different functional departments, and the difference in formal structure among these departments." [22] When the external environment is complex and rapidly changing, organizational departments become highly specialized to handle the uncertainty in their external domain. Success in each domain requires special activities. Employees in a research and development (R&D) department have unique attitudes, values, goals, and educational levels that distinguish them from employees in manufacturing or sales.

Figure 2.4. Organizational Departments Differentiate to Meet Needs of Subenvironments.

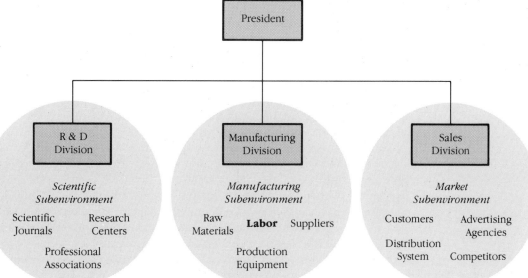

A study by Paul Lawrence and Jay Lorsch at Harvard examined three organizational departments—manufacturing, research, and sales—in ten corporations.[23] Their study found that each department evolved toward a different orientation and structure in order to effectively interact with specialized parts of the external environment. The market, scientific, and manfacturing subenvironments are illustrated in figure 2.4. Each department interacted with different external groups. The differences between departments that evolved are shown in table 2.2. In order to work effectively with the scientific subenvironment, R & D had a goal of quality work, a long time horizon (up to five years), an informal structure, and task-oriented employees. Sales was at the opposite extreme. They had a goal of customer satisfaction, were oriented towards the short term (two weeks or so), had a very formal structure, and were socially oriented.

Table 2.2. Differences in Goals and Orientations among Organizational Departments.

Characteristic	R & D Department	Manufacturing Department	Sales Department
Goals	New developments, quality	Efficient production	Customer satisfaction
Time Horizon	Long	Short	Short
Interpersonal Orientation	Mostly task	Task	Social
Formality of Structure	Low	High	High

Source: Paul R. Lawrence and Jay W. Lorsch, *Organization and Environment* (Homewood, IL: Irwin, 1969) pp. 23–39.

The implication of high differentiation is that coordination between departments is difficult. More time and resources must be devoted to achieving coordination when attitudes, goals and work orientation differ so widely. **Integration** is the quality of collaboration between departments.[24] Formal integrators are often required to span the boundary between departments. When the environment is highly uncertain, the changes require more information processing to achieve coordination, so integrators become a necessary addition to the organization structure. Integrators are assigned the responsibility of carrying information between departments and of achieving cooperation and coordination. Sometimes they are called liaison personnel. In organizations with highly uncertain environments and a highly differentiated structure, about 22% of management personnel are assigned integration activities, such as serving on committees, task forces, or in liaison roles.[25] In organizations characterized by very simple, stable environments, almost no managers are assigned to integration roles. The relationship between environment and internal integrators is summarized in table 2.3.

Table 2.3. Environmental Uncertainty and Organizational Integrators.

	Industry		
	Plastics	**Foods**	**Container**
Environmental Uncertainty	HIGH	MODERATE	LOW
Departmental Differentiation	HIGH	MODERATE	LOW
Percent Management in Integrating Roles	22%	17%	0%

Source: Jay W. Lorsch and Paul R. Lawrence, "Environmental Factors and Organizational Integration," *Organization Planning: Cases and Concepts* (Homewood, IL: Irwin and Dorsey, 1972), p. 45.

Organic versus Mechanistic Structure

Burns and Stalker observed 20 industrial firms in England and discovered that external environment was related to internal management structure.[26] When the external environment was stable, the internal organization was characterized by rules, procedures, and a clear hierarchy of authority. Organizations were formalized. They were also centralized, with most decisions made at the top. Burns and Stalker called this a "mechanistic" organization system.

In rapidly changing environments, the internal organization was much looser, free flowing, and adaptive. Rules and regulations often were not written down, or if written down were ignored. People had to find their own way through the system to figure out what to do. The hierarchy of authority was not clear. Decision-making authority was decentralized. Burns and Stalker used the term "organic" to characterize this type of management structure.

Table 2.4 summarizes the differences in organic and mechanistic structure. These structures combine several structural characteristics, including formalization, centralization, standardization, and specialization. The following case illustrates what an organic organization is like.

Table 2.4. Mechanistic and Organic Forms.

Mechanistic	**Organic**
1. Tasks are broken down into specialized, separate tasks.	1. Employees contribute to common task of department.
2. Tasks are rigidly defined.	2. Tasks are adjusted and redefined through employee interactions.
3. Strict hierarchy of authority and control. Many rules.	3. Less hierarchy of authority and control. Few rules.
4. Knowledge and control of tasks are centralized at top of organization.	4. Knowledge and control of tasks are located anywhere in organization.
5. Communication is vertical.	5. Communication is lateral.

Source: Adapted from Gerald Zaltman, Robert Duncan, and Jonny Holbek, *Innovations and Organizations* (New York: Wiley, 1973), p. 131.

Electronics Firm

[I]n the electronics industry proper . . . there is often a deliberate attempt to avoid specifying individual tasks, and to forbid any dependence on the management hierarchy as a structure of defined functions and authority. The head of one concern . . . attacked the idea of the organization chart as inapplicable in his concern and as a dangerous method of thinking about the working of industrial management. The first requirement of management, according to him, was that it should make the fullest use of the capacities of its members; any individual's job should be as little defined as possible, so that it will "shape itself" to his special abilities and initiative . . . .

. . . When the position of product engineer was created, for example, the first incumbents said they had to "find out" what they had to do, and what authority and resources they could command to do it.

In fact, this process of "finding out" about one's job proved to be unending. Their roles were continually defined and redefined. This happened through a perpetual sequence of encounters with laboratory chiefs, with design engineers, product engineers, draughtsmen, the works manager, with the foremen in charge of the production shop, with rate-fixers, buyers, and operatives. In every single case they had to determine their part and that of the others through complex, though often brief, negotiations.

"Normally," said a department manager, "management has a sort of family tree showing who is responsible for what, and what he is responsible for. It's a pity there's nothing like that here. It's rather difficult not knowing. You get an assistant to a manager who acts as though he were an assistant manager, a very different thing." Another man, a product engineer, said, "One of the troubles here is that nobody is very clear about his title or status or even his function." A foreman said that when he had first been promoted he had been told nothing of his duties and functions.

The disruptive effects of [lack of formal structure] were countered by a general awareness of the common purpose of the concern's attitudes. This awareness . . . was an essential factor in, for example, the ability of the "product engineers" to perform their tasks, dependent as they were on the cooperation of persons and groups who carried on the basic interpretive processes of the concern. Indeed, discussion of the common purposes of the organization featured largely in the conversation of groups existing among managers.[27]

The electronics firm was not managed very tightly, but Burns and Stalker concluded that the organic system was appropriate in the rapidly changing electronics industry. The definition and finding out of jobs facilitated the information-sharing needed for change and adaptation. Extensive rules, procedures, job descriptions, and centralized decisions would just get in people's way. In a rapidly changing environment, old rules no longer apply. Although managers and employees were often frustrated, they were able to coordinate changes and respond to external emergencies and crises. Everyone had to be involved.

Planning and Forecasting

When the environment is stable, the organization can concentrate on current operational problems and day-to-day efficiency. Long-range planning and forecasting are easy to do because environmental demands in the future will be the same as they are today.

Under conditions of environmental change, planning and forecasting are necessary.[28] Planning can soften the adverse impact of external shifting. A separate planning department is often established in organizations that have unstable environments. In a disturbed, reactive environment, planners must identify relevant environmental elements, and analyze potential moves and countermoves by other organizations. Planning can be very extensive and may forecast various scenarios for environmental contingencies. As time passes, plans are updated through replanning.[29] The emphasis on updated plans is consistent with the organic form of organization. Decisions are pushed down to lower organization levels where information relevant to the decision is held. There is little time for passing information to the top of the hierarchy, as would be the case in a mechanistic structure.

Texas Instruments uses an extensive planning system to anticipate and reduce the effects of environmental change. It is called the Objective, Strategies, and Tactics (OST) system. The OST planning system is unique because it ties together long-range strategic plans with short-term operational plans. Strategic decisions are made in response to anticipated environmental changes and then translated into day-to-day operational activities. The plans provide information necessary for adaptation and coordination between divisions and up and down the hierarchy. OST helps Texas Instruments cope with the high level of uncertainty in the consumer electronics industry.

CONTINGENCY FRAMEWORK FOR ENVIRONMENT AND STRUCTURE

The ways environmental uncertainty influences organization structure are summarized in figure 2.5. This framework uses the environmental dimensions of change and complexity described earlier. These dimensions each have distinct influence on organization structure and, combined, they determine the amount of uncertainty felt by managers.

In a simple environment, the organization structure is simple. As the environment becomes more complex, the organization needs a larger number of buffer departments and boundary spanners. When the environment is stable, internal structure and processes are mechanistic. When the environment is unstable, the organization structure is less formalized, and less centralized. Organic processes dominate. Moreover, planning becomes more important because the organization reduces uncertainty by anticipating future changes.

Environmental Change	Simple	Complex
Stable	*LOW UNCERTAINTY* Mechanistic Structure formal, centralized Few Departments No integrating roles Operational orientation	*LOW MODERATE UNCERTAINTY* Mechanistic Structure formal, centralized Many Departments, Buffers Few integrating roles Some planning
Unstable	HIGH MODERATE UNCERTAINTY Organic Structure informal, decentralized Few Departments Few integrating roles Planning orientation	*HIGH UNCERTAINTY* Organic Structure informal, decentralized Many departments, differentiated Many integrating roles Extensive planning, forecasting

Environmental Complexity

Figure 2.5. Contingency Framework for Environmental Uncertainty and Organization Structure.

These two dimensions in figure 2.5 produce four levels of uncertainty. The low uncertainty environment is populated by small organizations that have few departments and a mechanistic structure. Low-moderate uncertainty is more complex. More departments are needed along with more integrating roles to coordinate the departments. Some planning is used to analyze the external domains. Environments that are high-moderate uncertainty are unstable. Organization structure is organic. Planning is emphasized. The highly uncertain environment is the most difficult of all from a management perspective. The organization is large and has many departments, but is also organic. A large number of management personnel are assigned to coordination and integration, and the organization stresses planning and forecasting.

STRATEGIES FOR CONTROLLING THE EXTERNAL ENVIRONMENT

Thus far we have described several ways in which organizations adapt to external environments. Organization structure, buffer departments, boundary roles, differentiation, and planning all reflect pressures from the external environment. An organization functioning in a highly uncertain environment will have structural and management systems very different from an organization that functions in a certain environment.

The relationship between the organization and the environment is not simply one of organizational adaptation, however. Organizations can also reach out and change the external environment. As described earlier, the organization depends upon the external environment for resources vital to survival and success. It is possible to change elements in the external environment to increase the probability for survival. Two types of strategies can be adopted to manage the external environment: (1) establish favorable linkages with key elements in the environment, and (2) shape the environmental domain.[30] Techniques to accomplish each of these strategies are listed in table 2.5.

Establishing Favorable Linkages

Merger In a merger, the organization acquires an organization in the domain that is creating uncertainty. Merger is the most effective linkage strategy, because it removes all dependence on the external element. If a source of raw material is uncertain, buying the supplier removes that uncertainty. The supplier will give priority to the parent organization. Steel companies, for example, have bought iron mines, and soft drink manufacturers have purchased bottle-makers. This form of merger is called vertical integration. Vertical integration can also extend in the other direction. General Host Corporation could not sell their unprofitable Cudahy Foods Division, a producer of meat. General Host's solution was to acquire Hickory Farms, a retail chain that could be an outlet for Cudahy's meat production. In this case, uncertainty was on the market side. Hickory Farms provided a guaranteed market for Cudahy's output.

Contracts, Joint Ventures Contracts and joint ventures reduce uncertainty through a legal and binding relationship with another firm. In a joint venture, organizations share the risk and cost associated with a large innovation. Contracts can provide long-term security for both the supply of raw materials and consumption of output. By tying customers and suppliers to specific amounts and prices, risk is reduced. McDonald's contracts for an entire crop of russet potatoes to be certain of its supply of french fries. Key employees can also be tied to the company with a contract.

Cooptation, Interlocking Directorates Cooptation occurs when leaders from important domains in the environment are brought into the organization. Cooptation occurs, for example, when influential customers or suppliers are appointed to the board of directors. As a board member, they have an

Table 2.5. Organization Strategies For Controlling the External Environment.

Establishing Favorable Linkages	Controlling the Environmental Domain
1. Merger	1. Change domains
2. Joint ventures, contracts	2. Political activity, regulation
3. Cooptation, interlocking directorates	3. Trade associations
4. Executive recruitment	
5. Advertising, public relations	

interest in the organization. Community leaders are also appointed to boards of directors or to organizational committees. They are introduced to the needs of the company and are more likely to include the company's interests in their decision-making.

An interlocking directorate is similar, except that an individual is part of several organizations by being on several boards. This person becomes a communication channel at the top level between several organizations. Individuals may be selected to a board because they are on the boards of companies that are competitors or customers.

Executive Recruitment Exchanging executives also offers a method of establishing favorable linkages with external organizations. The aerospace industry each year hires retired generals and executives from the Defense Department. These generals have personal friends in the Department, so the aerospace company obtains better information about technical specifications, prices, and dates. They learn the needs of the Defense Department, and are able to represent their case for defense contracts in a more effective way. Companies without these contacts find it impossible to get a defense contract. Having channels of influence and communication between organizations serves to reduce uncertainty and dependence for the organization.

Advertising, Public Relations A traditional way of establishing favorable relationships is through advertising. Organizations spend large amounts of money to influence the taste of consumers. Advertising is especially important in highly competitive industries, and in industries that experience variable demand. A hotel that is only 50% full during the winter can use advertising to increase business during the off-season. Colleges advertise to make linkages with prospective students.

Public relations is similar to advertising, except that it is unpaid and is aimed at public opinion. Public relations people cast the organization in a favorable light in speeches, press reports, and on television. Public relations shapes the company's image in the minds of customers, suppliers, and government officials.

Controlling Environmental Domains In addition to establishing favorable linkages, organizations can often change the environment. There are three techniques for influencing external domains:

Change Domains The nine domains described earlier in this chapter are not fixed. Over a period of years, the organization has decided which business it is in, the market to enter, and the suppliers, banks, employees, and location to use. The current domain can be changed.[31] An organization can seek new environmental relationships and drop old ones. An organization may try to find a set of domains where there is little competition, no government regulation, abundant suppliers, affluent customers, and barriers to keep competitors out. Diversification and divestment are two techniques for altering the domain. An organization may buy or sell product lines.

Companies in the tobacco industry adopted this strategy after realizing the impact of public attitudes and government regulations on smoking. They acquired new companies outside the tobacco industry to make the external domain more favorable.

Political Activity, Regulation   Political activity includes techniques to influence government legislation and regulation. Organizations pay lobbyists to express their views to members of federal and state legislatures. Political strategy can be used to erect barriers against competitors, and to establish rules for the game that are favorable to extant organizations. Trucking firms support continued regulation of trucking. For thirty-five years after establishment of the civil aeronautics board in 1938, no new air carriers were started.[32] Regulatory agencies hire personnel who have experience in the regulated industry. Corporations try to influence the appointment of people to agencies who are sympathetic with their needs. For smaller companies, political activities can be used to block competition in the local domain. A large taxi company in a midwestern city persuaded the city council to pass stiff licensing and financial requirements for new taxi companies. No new cab company could meet these impossible conditions, so the existing company did not have to worry about competition.

Trade Associations   Much of the work to influence the external environment is accomplished jointly with other organizations that have similar interests. Most manufacturing companies are part of the National Association of Manufacturers, and also belong to associations relevant to their specific industry. By pooling resources, these organizations can afford to pay people full-time to carry out activities such as lobbying legislators, influencing new regulations, developing public relations campaigns, and blocking competition. Most organizations engage in external activity through trade associations. They work with the larger membership to change unfavorable elements in the external environment.

IN PRACTICE 2.8
Standard Oil

Large corporations blossomed in the rich legal and technological soil of the United States after the Civil War. The spread of railroad and telegraph networks encouraged communication and transportation on a national scale. New large-batch manufacturing and continuous-process refining methods enabled small firms to increase output dramatically. Soaring output drove down prices, so companies moved to control the environment with two strategies designed to maintain profits. The first method was to agree with other firms to control price and output—a strategy of horizontal combination. The other method was to add raw material and marketing divisions—a strategy of vertical integration.

Declining prices in the 1870s encouraged manufacturers to initiate environmental control through trade associations which could control prices and production quantities among members. Thus allocation of a specific market to each firm was one technique used to influence the market domain. The trade associations also formed money pools in which each firm was allocated a specific income.

The largest oil refinery in the 1870s was the Standard Oil Company, founded by John D. Rockefeller. In an effort to gain environmental control, Rockefeller encouraged the creation of a refiners' association, but he found that it did not provide sufficient control. Consequently, Rockefeller and his associates moved beyond the trade association to create the first legal merger of many small refiners into the Standard Oil Trust (1882). The trust provided legal control over member companies in an effort to increase profits through the concentration and centralization of production. Once the trust was formed, Rockefeller and others flexed their economic muscles. They asked the Lake Shore Railroad to reduce its rate from $2.00 to $1.35 a barrel on Standard Oil shipments. Other members of the trust received the same bargain. By this time, the alliance controlled almost 90% of the country's refining capacity. And it was willing to use its power ruthlessly. The trust could financially crush the remaining small refiners or any of its competitors producing lubricants and other specialized products.

The next step was to control the marketing of refinery products. When the long-distance pipeline proved technologically feasible, Rockefeller moved quickly. Because pipelines moved oil far more cheaply than railroads did, Standard Oil's leaders set up the National Transit Company to build and operate cross-country pipelines. They then made further marketing inroads in 1885 by establishing two sales subsidiaries—Continental Oil and Standard Oil of Kentucky—to handle the sale of oil to consumers.

In the late 1880s, Standard Oil began to produce its own crude oil, which further reduced uncertainty with respect to supply. Within three years from the time the trust began to buy oil-producing properties, it was providing 25% of the nation's crude oil.

By the early 1890s, Standard Oil was a fully integrated enterprise. What began as a simple refinery now controlled every stage of production from the wellhead to the consumer. Competitors were also controlled through their merger into the Standard Oil Trust.

New environmental developments, including the automobile, new patterns of manufacturing and marketing, and government regulation, created additional uncertainties for Standard Oil. Government regulation began to reflect the widespread belief that multienterprise trusts were too powerful for the national good. In 1890 the U.S. Congress passed the Sherman Antitrust Act in an effort to regulate trusts. But about the same time manufacturing companies persuaded the New Jersey legislature to pass a law to permit companies to purchase and hold stock in other enterprises within and without the state through a device called a holding company. Holding companies quickly became the new form of legal combination. Finally, after additional legislation and a long battle with the Federal government, the Supreme Court in 1911 ordered that the Standard Oil combination be broken up.[33]

Standard Oil was able to reduce environmental uncertainty in the oil refining industry and the broader economic domain by joining a trade association, and then by creating legal forms of merger. It also acquired sources of supply and methods of distribution and sales to control the raw material and market domains. The trust also influenced legislation (government domain) in a direction favorable to itself. By reducing uncertainty in all these domains, Standard Oil achieved enormous efficiency in the production of oil. Once Standard Oil established control over the external environment, the trust was able to achieve large size and substantial profitability.

INTERORGANIZATIONAL RELATIONSHIPS

Interorganizational Set Another perspective on the environment is to analyze the organization's set. The **organizational set** is all organizations that have a relationship with the organization under analysis. Rather than analyzing domains, this approach analyzes organizations in those domains. Competitors, customers, government, technological developments, raw materials, and financial resources are represented by other organizations. A single organization may have relationships with hundreds of organizations in the environment.

The interorganizational set is dynamic. New relationships are established and old ones are discontinued when they are no longer useful to the organization. The two most important reasons for establishing or breaking specific interorganizational relationships are resource exchange and government mandate.

Resource Exchange The principle reason for entering into a relationship with another organization is that each organization has something that the other wants. Money can be exchanged for raw materials, or a position on the board can be exchanged for legal advice. Each party to the exchange sees instrumental value in the exchange.[34] Each organization can receive some benefit. Organizations can use the exchange relationship to achieve their respective goals. A large organization will be engaged in literally hundreds of exchange relationships in order to perform effectively. When a positive exchange is not possible, the interorganizational linkage will be discontinued.

Government Mandate Some interorganizational linkages are required by law. This is frequently the case with not-for-profit organizations and government agencies. Welfare agencies in a local community are required to interact with the State Human Resources Agency and with local employment agencies, and with municipal, state, and federal departments. Every organization thus will have a number of interorganizational relationships that are required by law.

CETA

A partial organization set for a government agency is shown in figure 2.6. CETA organizations were established under the Comprehensive Employment Training Act. They are established by government mandate to identify and provide job readiness and training to underprivileged people. A CETA organization interacts with the local school district, employment commission, private businesses, the Department of Community Affairs, and the State Rehabilitation Commission. These contacts enable the CETA organization to achieve its objectives. Some of the relationships are formal. Contracts are written with school districts to provide classes in welding. Private businesses sign contracts to a certain wage and provide on-the-job training. Other contracts are informal. The CETA director occasionally visits with the Director of the Chamber of Commerce, for example. They may know one another personally and exchange information about which businesses are interested in hiring CETA employees.

Set Size   The size of an organization's set indicates the nature of the relationship between the organization and the environment. When the external environment is highly uncertain, an organization will develop as many linkages as possible.[35] Multiple linkages provide a measure of protection and certainty in domains important to the organization's survival. A large set provides substitute suppliers and consumers if they are needed.[36]

A large organization set has other benefits. It enhances the visibility and legitimacy of an organization. A large number of relationships provides wide contacts. A larger set provides a basis for a widespread positive image of the organization. A large set also reduces resource dependence. The CETA organization described above greatly increased its resource base by establishing relationships with schools, businesses, and the rehabilitation commission. The organizational set increases the scope of resources available to perform an organization's task.[37]

Organization structure is also related to the size of the organization's set. Greater organization complexity—a larger number of departments—is associated with a larger set. A larger number of departments enables the organization to establish a number of linkages in the environment. Extensive formalization and centralization is associated with a smaller set. Formalization and centralization are partly a response to environmental uncertainty, so fewer linkages are needed.[38]

Power and dependency are also reflected in the organization set. When the set is composed of just a few organizations, they are more likely to have substantial power over the focal organization. The focal organization will have only a few sources of supply, resources, or customers, and thus will be heavily dependent on each source. Organizations that have a large number of organizations to interact with tend to be relatively more dominant in the set. They are not so dependent upon any single organization.[39]

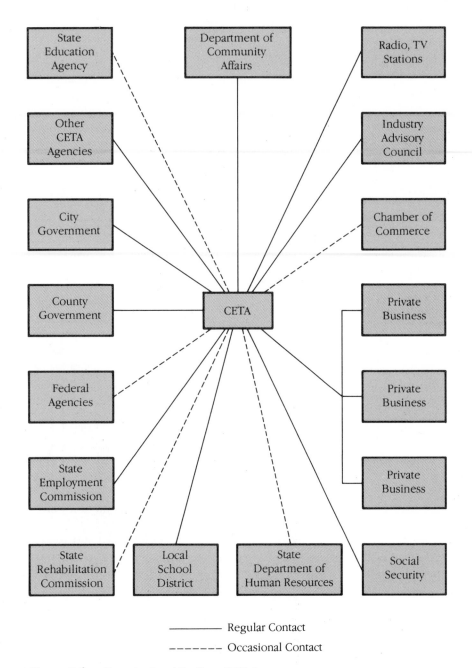

Figure 2.6. Organizational Set for a CETA Agency.
Source: Based on Ken Hogue, W. A. McIntosh, J. Steven Picou, and S. Renee Rigsby, "Model CETA and Private Sector Linkage System," Occupational Research Division, Texas A&M University, 1981.

The single most important idea in this chapter is the overwhelming impact of the external environment on management uncertainty and organization functioning. Organizations are open social systems. They are continuously involved in interactions with hundreds of external elements. The change and complexity in environmental domains has major implications for organizational design and activities. Organizational functioning cannot be understood by examining internal factors. Factors outside, as well as inside, the organization must be analyzed and managed. Most organizational decisions, activities, and outcomes can be traced to stimuli in the external environment.

Organizational environments differ in terms of uncertainty and causal texture. Organizational uncertainty is the result of the stable-unstable and simple-complex dimensions of the environment. Simple, stable environments do not create much uncertainty for managers. As complexity and change increase, uncertainty increases. Uncertainty is also influenced by the connections among elements in the external environment. These linkages create an environmental texture. Government policies, for example, may be related to economic conditions and cultural values. Customer demands may be related to changes in technology. Organizational planning and environmental analysis should consider these linkages as well as changes in single elements in each domain. Linkages mean that several domains may change simultaneously, which can cause serious problems for the organization.

Organization design takes on a logical perspective when the environment is considered. Organizations try to survive and achieve efficiencies in an uncertain world. Specific departments and functions are created to deal with specific uncertainties. The organization can be conceptualized as a technical core surrounded by departments that buffer environmental uncertainty. The technical core represents the primary purpose of the organization. The buffer department obtains needed resources so that the technical core can function under conditions of reliability and certainty. Likewise, organizations must have information on relevant external domains, and boundary-spanning roles provide that information. Decision-makers can thus respond in a timely manner and take appropriate steps to adapt to environmental contingencies.

The concepts in this chapter provide specific frameworks to understand how the environment influences structure and functioning of the organization. Environmental complexity and change, for example, have specific impact on internal complexity and adaptability. The internal structure must reflect external requirements. The causal texture framework indicates that environmental elements are themselves interconnected, which has additional implications for an organization. Thus, an organization in one environment will be very different in structure and orientation from an organization functioning in another environment. Under great uncertainty, more resources are allocated from the technical core to departments that will plan, deal with specific environmental elements, and integrate diverse internal activities.

The most recent research on organizations indicates that organizations not only respond and react to external changes, but can also exert control over the environment. Organizations command many resources. An effective strategy is to neutralize or change problematic elements rather than to continually respond to them. An important concept, then, is that the environment is not fixed. It can be influenced, and indeed should be influenced, by organizations alone or in groups.

Another important idea is the concept of organizational set. To understand an organization requires an understanding of the set in which it is embedded. Organizations have agreements and responsibilities that support one another. Organizations are interlocked, and the behavior of one influences others. The behavior and outcomes of an organization are influenced by the size of its set. Managers should consider establishing relationships with other organizations to increase available resources and to reduce external dependence.

DISCUSSION QUESTIONS

1. Define organizational environment. Is it appropriate to include only those elements that actually interact with the environment?
2. Briefly describe the nine environmental domains identified in the chapter. How does the industry domain differ from the market domain? Raw material domain from the human resource domain?
3. What is environmental uncertainty? Which has the greatest impact on uncertainty—environmental complexity or environmental change?
4. Why does environmental complexity lead to organizational complexity? Explain.
5. What is a placid, randomized environment? How does it differ from a placid, clustered environment?
6. Is changing the organization's domain a feasible strategy for reducing an uncertain or threatening environment? Explain.
7. Describe differentiation and integration. In what type of environment will differentiation and integration be greatest? Least? In which environment might differentiation occur without extensive integration?
8. Under what environmental condition is organizational planning emphasized? Under what condition is planning likely to be ignored because the organization concentrates on day-to-day operational activities? Is planning an appropriate response to a turbulent environment?
9. What is an organic organization? A mechanistic organization? How does the environment influence organic and mechanistic structures?
10. What techniques can organizations use to control the external environment?
11. Why do organizations become involved in interorganizational relationships? Do these relationships affect the organization's dependency on the external environment?
12. What advantages does a large organization set have for an organization?
13. Assume you have been asked to calculate the ratio of staff employees to production employees in two organizations—one in a simple, stable environment and one in a complex, shifting environment. How would you expect these ratios to differ? Why?

As an organization designer:

1. Scan the external environment for threats, changes, and opportunities. Organize elements in the external environment into these nine domains for analysis: industry, market, raw materials, human resources, financial resources, technology, government, economic conditions, and cultures. Focus on domains that may experience significant change at any time.
2. Match internal organization structure to the external environment. If the external environment is complex, make the organization structure complex. Reflect the rate of environmental change in the internal structure. Associate a stable environment with a mechanistic structure, and an unstable environment with an organic structure. If the external environment is both complex and changing, make the organization highly differentiated and organic, and have mechanisms to achieve coordination across departments.
3. Reach out and control external domains that are uncertain and threatening. Influence external domains by engaging in political activity, by joining trade associations and by establishing favorable linkages. Establish linkages through merger, contracts, joint ventures, interlocking directorates, advertising, and executive recruitment. Reduce the amount of change or threat from the external environment in order that the organization will not have to change internally.
4. Use connections between organizations to influence external environments. Take advantage of interdependencies to increase resources available to do the organization's task.

Consider these Guides when analyzing the following cases and when answering the questions listed after each case.

CASES FOR ANALYSIS

1. AVONDALE SHIPYARDS, INC.

Officials of Avondale Shipyards, Inc., a subsidiary of Ogden Corp., broke out champagne in 1973 after winning a $309 million, fixed-price contract to build three huge liquified natural gas tankers for El Paso Co. LNG was being promoted as an important new fuel, and Avondale envisioned the El Paso contract as the start of a brisk new business in building ships to haul it.

Since then, however, the champagne has gone flat. The Avondale tankers last year flunked U.S. Coast Guard certification tests to carry the supercold ($-250°$ F) LNG. Algeria shut off El Paso's gas supply. A group of insurance companies led by Lloyd's of London has agreed to pay out $300 million in claims to El Paso on policies covering the ships' completion. The money will go mostly to pay off federally-backed bonds sold to finance construction. The Federal Maritime Administration lost $52 million in construction subsidy payments. Now, El Paso is offering the ships for sale at bargain prices—as low as $50 million for all three—for any use, even for scrap.

Cruelest of all, Avondale's parent company needs three LNG tankers for possible shipment of Indonesian LNG to California, but instead of having Avondale build the ships, Ogden is turning to General Dynamics Corp.'s Quincy (MA) shipyard to build them. The Quincy shipyard uses a different tankage system to contain the LNG, and it has successfully built nine such ships.

A Nightmare An Ogden official crisply explains: "The [Avondale] ship-yard can be better utilized in other work." Avondale President Albert L. Bossier Jr. says only that "New York made the decision." But he adds: "I don't have any opposition to it."

Avondale's LNG affair was a seven-year nightmare. Because of the relative newness of LNG as a fuel, there was little experience with the technology for carrying it. Currently, three basic techniques are used for tankage and insulation. Two systems use rectangular tanks combined with elaborate insulation. General Dynamics uses huge aluminum spheres.

In ordering the Avondale ships, El Paso opted for a tankage system developed by Conch LNG, a company jointly owned by Conoco Inc., USY&T Industries Inc., and the Royal Dutch/Shell Group. Huge, rectangular alumi-num tanks were to be insulated with a "secret" formula of polyurethane foam developed by Kaiser Aluminum & Chemical Sales Inc. Avondale awarded Kaiser a $70 million contract to build and install the tankage system in the three ships, including applying the special polyurethane foam insulation.

Lawsuits Delays and disputes came quickly. The first tanker was com-pleted more than three years behind schedule, in the summer of 1979. Then, in July of that year, when the Coast Guard tested the ship with a partial load of LNG, tiny cracks developed in the insulation. As a result, the Coast Guard refused to certify the ships. One reason was that if the cold LNG came into contact with the ship's hull, it would cause the metal to become brittle, fracture, and crumble.

There followed a year in which experts were called in to solve the problem. Their final analysis was that any corrective measure would cost too much—on the order of $100 million per ship. That doomed the three vessels, and the insurance companies finally settled last Sept. 30.

El Paso still must sell the tankers for at least $50 million; otherwise, it is going to have to absorb the difference as a loss. Because it was costing Avondale almost $200,000 a month to keep the ships in its yard, they are now being towed to the Army terminal in Boston for storage until they are sold. Meanwhile, Kaiser has sued Avondale for $40 million, and Avondale has countersued for $169 million in what everyone expects will be a bitter, costly, drawn-out legal battle over who was at fault.[40]

1. Which environmental domains are causing problems for Avondale Shipyards?
2. Evaluate the complexity and rate of change in Avondale's environment. Where would you place Avondale on the environmental uncertainty framework in figure 2.2? Why?
3. Would the causal texture of Avondale's environment best be described as placid, random; placid, clustered; disturbed, reactive; or turbulent field? Explain.

2. THE CONSTITUTION NATIONAL BANK[41]

The Constitution National Bank was founded in 1947 and grew very rapidly during the housing boom of the 1950s and early 1960s. It became one of the largest national banks in a small but densely populated state with assets of $1.5 billion. During its early years, the top management of Constitution National was concerned with (a) how to attract and retain depositors, (b) how to gain a reputation in the community as a solid financial institution, (c) how to service the primary needs of potential borrowers, and (d) what policies and procedures it wanted to formulate for the purpose of achieving its objectives and operating efficiently and effectively.

During the late 1960s, Constitution National experienced some difficult times. Several new branch locations were opened but had to be closed because of their inability to attract depositors and borrowers and the lack of flexibility to offer the types of services required by the people in these communities. The Bank also did not participate in central city renewal and operation "face lift." The growth rate of the Bank decreased and several unsuccessful undertakings diminished Constitution National's reputation within the financial community.

One of the branches that failed was located in a large city which included a sizeable population of newly settled minority people. Another branch was located in an area populated by a large number of college students attending two universities. In both cases of failure, the principal cause was the Bank's inability to service customers who were young or newly settled in the area.

In 1970, a new group of managers was hired to run the Bank. Under the new leadership several reforms were introduced. The Board of Directors felt that it was important to bring in an entirely new group of managers so it could make a change in its image and try to overcome the reputation of inefficiency that surrounded the Bank in recent years. The new president sought to project a new image for the Constitution National Bank which would be known as a young, customer-oriented institution that was deeply concerned with needs of people and the social problems that plagued urban centers in the late 1960s. The first objective that the new president aimed at was to obtain closer relationships between the Bank and the people it served. Policies were formulated that would allow the Bank to service low-income groups in the state.

One of the branch managers proposed the formation of an advisory board at each of the five locations of Constitution National Bank. The purpose underlying the formation of advisory boards was to select a wide variety of people from the community to participate in a committee that would make recommendations to top management and serve as a liaison between their own constituency and the Bank. Each advisory board would be composed of a Bank representative who would act as the chairperson, prominent local business people, women, minority group members, college students, and others. Because these people would be conversant with the problems of their communities, they had the potential of providing useful information and suggestions to the top management of the Bank. Advisory board members could also counsel prospective customers about the services that Constitution National Bank could offer them, refer people for possible employment by the Bank, and in general promote the goodwill of the Bank. The Bank in turn would offer the advisory board members some prestige and remuneration for their services.

Another of the new managers proposed that the bank invest more heavily in local advertising and public relations. She argued that bank managers should become more involved in community groups such as the Chamber of Commerce and United Way. Another manager proposed that the bank make a contribution to the Regional Association of Bankers to support two lobbyists working at the state capital to raise the legal interest rate ceiling.

The board of directors considered these proposals but were not certain how to proceed. Would minority group members or college students act in a responsible manner? Could the bank afford to invest in advertising, public relations, or lobbying? Would managers be willing to become involved in community groups? They even wondered whether it was legitimate for a bank to be involved in these kinds of "nonbanking" activities.

Questions
1. To what extent have the bank's problems resulted from lack of control over the external environment? Which external domains are most threatening to the bank? Which of the proposed techniques do you recommend the bank should adopt? Explain.
2. Will the bank have to change its structure (assignment of responsibilities, creation of new positions or departments) to implement these proposals? Will the bank incur additional expenses, such as for new activities or new salaries? Is it appropriate for an organization to finance activities not directly related to its technical core?

NOTES

1. John Holusha, "Planning Automobiles for the Future is Manufacturers' Most Difficult Task," *Houston Chronicle,* August 3, 1981, p. 3–4. © 1981 by the New York Times Company. Reprinted by permission.
2. Jeffrey Pfeffer and Gerald R. Salancik, *The External Control of Organizations: A Resource Dependent Perspective* (New York: Harper & Row, 1978), p. 138.
3. "San Antonio Food War Hot," *Houston Chronicle,* September 18, 1981. Copyright © 1981, United Press International. Reprinted by permission.

4. Bro Uttal, "The Blumenthal Revival at Burroughs," *Fortune,* October 5, 1981, p. 134. © 1981 Time, Inc. All rights reserved.

5. James Cook, "Nothing But the Best," *Forbes,* September 28, 1981, p. 157.

6. Herman Nickel, "Dante in the Federal Inferno," *Fortune,* June 2, 1980, pp. 78–83. © 1980 Time, Inc. All rights reserved.

7. Robert B. Duncan, "Characteristics of Organizational Environment and Perceived Environmental Uncertainty," *Administrative Science Quarterly* 17 (1972): 313–327.

8. Ray Jurkovich, "A Core Typology of Organizational Environments." *Administrative Science Quarterly* 19 (1974): 380–394.

9. *Ibid.*

10. J. A. Litterer, *The Analysis of Organizations,* 2nd ed. (New York: Wiley, 1973), p. 335.

11. David P. Garino, "Rail-Car Boom Turns to Bust for Scullin," *The Wall Street Journal,* September 29, 1981, pp. 25, 31.

12. Rosalie L. Tung, "Dimensions of Organizational Environments: An Exploratory Study of Their Impact on Organization Structure," *Academy of Management Journal* 22 (1979): 672–693.

13. Fred E. Emery and Eric L. Trist, "The Causal Texture of Organizational Environments." *Human Relations* 18 (1965): 21–32. Material in this section is based on that article.

14. "Procter & Gamble's Profit Problem—Food," *Business Week,* January 26, 1981, p. 65; Carol J. Loomis, "P & G Up Against Its Wall," *Fortune,* February 23, 1981, pp. 48–54.

15. Pfeffer and Salancik, *External Control of Organizations,* pp. 50–52.

16. John P. Kotter, "Managing External Dependence," *Academy of Management Review* 4 (1979): 87–92.

17. Ross W. Ashby, *An Introduction to Cybernetics* (New York: Wiley, Science Edition, 1956).

18. James D. Thompson, *Organizations in Action* (New York: McGraw-Hill, 1967), pp. 20–21.

19. Howard Aldrich and Diane Herker, "Boundary Spanning Roles and Organization Structure," *Academy of Management Review* 2 (1977): 217–239.

20. *Ibid.*

21. Donald T. Baker and Bart Barnes, "University Lobbyists Busy Bees Keeping 'Honey Pots' Filled," copyright © 1980, Los Angeles Times-Washington Post News Service. Reprinted with permission.

22. Jay W. Lorsch, "Introduction to the Structural Design of Organizations," in Gene W. Dalton, Paul R. Lawrence, and Jay W. Lorsch, eds., *Organization Structure and Design* (Homewood, IL. Irwin and Dorsey, 1970), p. 5.

23. Paul R. Lawrence and Jay W. Lorsch, *Organization and Environment* (Homewood, IL: Irwin, 1969).

24. Lorsch, "Introduction to Structural Design," p. 7.

25. Jay. W. Lorsch and Paul R. Lawrence, "Environmental Factors and Organizational Integration," in J. W. Lorsch and Paul R. Lawrence, eds., *Organizational Planning: Cases and Concepts* (Homewood, IL: Irwin and Dorsey, 1972), p. 45.

26. Tom Burns and G. M. Stalker, *The Management of Innovation* (London: Tavistock, 1961).

27. *Ibid.,* pp. 92–94. Reprinted by permission.

28. Tung, "Dimensions of Organizational Environments," pp. 672–693; Thompson, *Organizations in Action.*

29. Tung, "Dimensions of Organizational Environments," pp. 672–693.

30. This discussion is based on Jeffrey Pfeffer, "Beyond Management and the Worker: The Institutional Function of Management," *Academy of Management Review* 1 (April, 1976): 36–46; and Kotter, "Managing External Dependence," pp. 87–92.

31. Kotter, "Managing External Dependence."

32. Pfeffer, "Beyond Management and the Worker."

33. Alfred D. Chandler, Jr., *The Visible Hand: The Managerial Revolution in American Business* (Cambridge, MA: The Belknap Press of Harvard University Press, 1977), pp. 315–326.

34. David A. Whetten and Thomas K. Lueng, "The Instrumental Value of Interorganizational Relations: Antecedents and Consequences of Linkage Formation," *Academy of Management Journal* 22 (1979): 325–344.

35. Paul M. Hirsch, "Processing Fads and Fashions: An Organization-Set Analysis of Cultural Industry Systems," *American Journal of Sociology* 72 (1972): 639–659.

36. Steven K. Paulson, "Causal Analysis of Interorganizational Relations: An Axiomatic Theory Revised," *Administrative Science Quarterly* 19 (1974): 319–337; Andrew H. Van de Ven, "On the Nature, Formation and Maintenance of Relations Among Organization," *Academy of Management Review* 1 (1976) 24–36; Whetten and Lueng, "Instrumental Value of Interorganizational Relations."

37. David A. Whetten and Howard Aldrich, "Organization Set Size and Diversity: People-Processing Organizations and Their Environments," *Administration and Society* 11 (1979): 251–281.

38. Michael Aiken and Jerald Hage, "Interorganizational Dependence and Intra-Organizational Structure," *American Sociological Review* 33 (1968): 912–930.

39. Pfeffer and Salancik, *The External Control of Organizations;* William M. Evan, "The Organization-Set: Toward a Theory of Interorganizational Relations," in James D. Thompson, ed., *Approaches to Organizational Design* (Pittsburgh: University of Pittsburgh Press, 1966).

40. "Avondale's Ill-Fated Dip into LNG Waters," *Business Week,* November 30, 1980, p. 37. Reprinted from the November 30, 1980, issue of *Business Week* by special permission, © 1980 by McGraw-Hill, Inc., New York, NY 10020. All rights reserved.

41. Adapted from John F. Veiga and John N. Yanouzas, "The Constitution National Bank," *The Dynamics of Organization Theory: Gaining a Macroperspective* (St. Paul, MN: West, 1979), pp. 139–140.

3

Goals and Effectiveness

RALSTON PURINA COMPANY

William P. Stiritz, President of the $5-billion Ralston Purina agribusiness giant, learned a lesson in the early 1960s that shapes his approach to business today.

In the early days, he was a brand manager at Pillsbury. Another bright young brand manager figured out a way to drive up sales of angel food cake mix. Prices were cut 20% in the Denver area. Volume doubled. The brand manager persuaded Pillsbury to extend the price-cutting strategy nationwide. Competitors responded with price cuts of their own. As a result, Pillsbury's profits plunged. The brand manager was fired.

The lesson Mr. Stiritz learned was to maintain profit margins, even if market share is sacrificed. "The end isn't just selling goods," Mr. Stiritz stresses, but rather to "earn an adequate return. That goal sometimes gets lost."[1]

The goal of adequate profit margins is being applied to each of Ralston's divisions. The division that sells Chicken of the Sea tuna, for example, has 30% of the market but has been only marginally profitable. The industry requires huge amounts of capital and discounts to retailers. Mr. Stiritz is moving to increase the division's profitability by eliminating its market structure, which will save several million dollars. Tuna will be sold through another division. Mr. Stiritz believes that running with marginal profits is a poor way to do business.

The board of directors approve of Mr. Stiritz's philosophy. He came to their attention during an intense domestic pet-food war that began in 1977. As vice president, he was confronted with four major competitors spending more than $100 million to introduce new dog-food products.

Pet food is the largest source of Ralston's profits. The company had more than 40% of the dog and cat food market. Instead of lowering prices to protect market share, Mr. Stiritz decided to hold prices stable and step up product development and advertising.

Market share dropped several points but profits held up. Competitors found that the pet-food market was not an easy payday. Ralston's market share quickly recovered.

The directors admired his coolness. Instead of panicking when market share dropped, he stuck to the goals he considered most important for Ralston.

Of course, Ralston Purina does not invest only in profitable undertakings. The company recently completed a transformation of the area surrounding its St. Louis headquarters from a slum into a well-manicured community. Ralston invested several million dollars. The community now has new homes, rehabilitated town houses, apartments for the elderly, churches, and light industrial facilities.

Why invest in real estate? Ralston Purina believes that attractive, safe surroundings attract the very best employees to the company. It also makes the existing land and buildings more valuable real estate assets. The investment will not show up in profit margins, but employees at the St. Louis headquarters are delighted. A textbook example of the worst type of urban decay is now an attractive community where several employees reside.[2]

An **organizational goal** is a desired state of affairs that the organization attempts to realize.[3] The desired state of affairs at Ralston Purina is composed of several elements. First, top managers want to make a profit, which seems to be the primary goal. They also want to sell goods. They want to maintain a reasonable market share. Managers are also concerned with attracting quality employees and maintaining an attractive community around Ralston's St. Louis headquarters. Moreover, Ralston has both a long- and a short-time horizon. Ralston will sacrifice profits in one period to gain larger profits later on. They will also invest in nonmarketing activities, such as real estate, to secure stability in its valued labor force. Other outcomes, such as growth, providing an adequate return to investors, and customer loyalty, may also be goals at Ralston.

What can we learn about goals from the Ralston case? First, a large organization like Ralston has many goals. Second, these goals are in competition with one another. The goal of high profits may hurt the goal of market share. The goal of being in an attractive community may work against the goal of profits. Third, managers decide upon goals. Goals are not fixed. Each manager may value different goals. One important task of management is to evaluate goals and set goal priorities. Fourth, some goals are the means to achieve other goals. Goals are linked together. The immediate goal of introducing a new product may lead to the attainment of the long-term goal of high profits.

Purpose of This Chapter

The purpose of this chapter is to explore the issues of organizational goals and effectiveness. We want to understand the types of goals that organizations pursue, and the importance of these goals to organizational performance. Organizations are goal-attainment devices. Organizations are tools that owners and managers use to achieve certain ends. The clear statement of an organizational goal is extremely important for communicating the organization's purpose to both external groups and to employees.

The first part of this chapter explores the types of goals used within organizations and the process by which goals are chosen. The latter part of the chapter examines organizational effectiveness. Goals provide an important mechanism for evaluating whether organizational performance is acceptable. Organization effectiveness is a thorny issue, and there is no single way to evaluate effectiveness. We will evaluate the relative strengths and weaknesses of the more popular approaches for measuring effectiveness.

There are two effectiveness issues covered in this book. The first issue is how to assess effectiveness, and is concerned with concepts and measurements that are needed to evaluate an organization's performance. The second issue is the cause of effectiveness. In other words, how does an organization become more effective? The material in this chapter focuses on the first issue. We explore frameworks that explain how to measure and evaluate effectiveness. In order to manage organizations well, managers need a clear sense of organizational goals, and how to measure the effectiveness of organizational efforts. The second issue—how to be more effective—is treated throughout the rest of the book. Each chapter explores a different set of organizational activities associated with organizational performance. This chapter, then, is concerned with how to evaluate effectiveness. The following chapters cover a range of ideas for making organizations more effective.

ORGANIZATIONAL GOALS

Importance of Goals Why should we care about organizational goals? Two reasons. First, goals represent the reason for an organization's existence. An organization is a goal-attainment device. Without some purpose, there is no need for the organization. Goals summarize and articulate that purpose. This is especially important in not-for-profit organizations, in which easily measured goals like profit and market share are not relevant. In a prison, for example, is the goal to rehabilitate inmates so they can return to a normal existence? Is the goal to protect society? Or is it to provide an orderly, safe life for inmates during incarceration? The purpose of a not-for-profit organization may not be obvious, so goals help provide a clear focus.

The second reason for studying goals is that the management process of identifying goals and carrying them out provides several benefits for the organization. The presence of goals provides legitimacy for the organization, a sense of direction and decision guidelines, criteria of performance, and reduction of uncertainty.

Legitimacy For corporations, legitimacy is granted in a legal charter. Corporations are given the right to produce goods and services for a profit. Not-for-profit organizations are also granted legal rights to incarcerate prisoners, provide welfare services, or to perform the myriad activities of local and federal government.

Just as important as the legal charter, the stated goals of the organization provide a symbol of legitimacy to external constituencies. Goals describe the purpose of the organization so people know what it stands for and will accept its existence. Organizations that are viewed as illegitimate, or whose goals are not accepted, will encounter resistance. Such an organization may be prosecuted by the legal system or be the target of demonstrations by consumer groups. Goals also legitimize the organization for employees. They can join and become committed to an organization when they identify with the organization's stated goals. Goals serve to legitimize the organization by signaling to both internal and external groups what the organization stands for.

Legitimization always comes from other people—consumers, suppliers, regulatory agencies, taxpayers, employees. One task of management is to establish the legitimacy of the organization's output. This is somewhat easier for economic organizations because of market mechanisms. If the product is viewed as legitimate, it will be purchased and the firm can make a profit. If not, the organization will probably fail. Organizations in the tobacco industry, for example, have continued to voice legitimacy of cigarettes, but at the same time have diversified so that they do not depend upon the acceptance of cigarettes for their organization's prosperity.

Not-for-profit organizations do not have a market to provide legitimacy. Government agencies are often established with good intentions, but must maintain goodwill of legislators, taxpayers, and users in order to survive. In recent years, the role of welfare departments has been questioned by taxpayers, and many departments are receiving fewer funds. Another example is the Farm Security Administration, which was born in the Depression to serve poor farmers. It was later eradicated because it was not perceived as legitimate by wealthy farmers who became the primary clients of the FSA.[4]

Direction and Decision Guidelines Goals give a sense of direction to organization participants. The stated end toward which an organization is striving provides information about what employees are working toward. Goals help motivate participants, especially if they help select the goals.

The goals of an organization also act as guidelines for employee work and decision-making. Organizational goals are a set of constraints on individual behavior and decisions.[5] When regional managers at Ralston understood that the primary goal was to make a reasonable profit, they could adopt behavior that enhanced this goal rather than behavior that attempted to penetrate new markets with price-cutting efforts.

Reduce Uncertainty The process of goal-setting, and agreement upon specific goals, reduces uncertainty for organization participants. This is especially true for senior managers. The desired future state of the organization involves diverse and conflicting elements. Goal-setting enables management to discuss options and to settle upon goals that are most important and should take priority. Once goals are established, there is a sense of relief and accomplishment. Uncertainty is reduced for the entire organization:

Goal-setting is attempted as a psychological means for reducing uncertainty, and when participants succeed in stating and agreeing on goals, it symbolizes a reduction in uncertainty. It is, in this case, an agreement, usually tacit, on a prediction: "This is what can be made to work out. . . ." In this state of mind, if agreement on goals could really be reached it would imply a greater likelihood of order, and this anticipated reduction in uncertainty is comforting to contemplate.[6]

Criteria of Performance   Goals provide a standard for assessment.[7] The level of organization performance, whether in terms of profits, units produced, or number of complaints, needs a basis for evaluation. Is a profit of 10% on sales good enough? The answer lies in goals. Goals reflect past experiences and describe the desired state for the future. If the profit goal is 8%, then 10% is excellent. The rating of performance on many criteria can be evaluated by comparing performance to established goals.

Types of Goals   Many types of goals exist in an organization, and each type performs a different function. One of the major distinctions is between the officially stated goals of the organization and the goals that it actually pursues.

Official Goals   **Official goals** are the formally defined outcomes that the organization states it is trying to achieve. Official goals reflect what the organization should be doing, the reason it exists, and the values that underlie its existence.[8]

Official goals are normally written down, for example, in a policy manual or in the annual report. They are also emphasized in public addresses by top officials of the organization. Upon close analysis, official goals appear abstract and vague. They describe a value system for the organization, but are often not specific or measurable. Official goals serve the purpose of legitimizing the organization. Goal statements are written or spoken to appeal to public opinion. Official goals are not used for guides to action and criteria of performance. They signal the purpose of the organization to important constituencies. Official goals are often the goals that employees identify with as they become committed to the organization. The following case describes the official goals that were written in the policy manual of a school organization.

IN PRACTICE 3.1

Plankton High School District

A fundamental premise underlying our democratic way of life is a belief in the intrinsic worth of every individual. Therefore, we believe that all members of our free society must be provided the opportunity for maximum development of their individual capabilities through education. The Plankton School District shall provide a learning environment which will encourage the students of this district to be thinking, feeling, creative, healthy, communicating, contributing members of society. Trustees, administrators, and teachers shall dedicate their efforts toward providing each student with intellectually stimulating instruction of the highest quality together with the individual guidance required to develop the student's academic, aesthetic and occupational talents.

Schools of the Plankton School District will provide experiences for students that will enable them:

GOAL I To develop intellectual curiosity, a love of learning, and skills in communication and basic subjects.

GOAL II To develop the ability to cope with problems and to seek solutions through effective use of knowledge, and the application of both logical and creative problem-solving techniques.

GOAL III To develop the capacity for self-direction and self-discipline by fostering a sense of self-worth and an awareness of one's ability to influence one's own destiny.

GOAL IV To impart a sense of historical perspective, and appreciation of the heritage of mankind and an understanding of the rights and responsibilities of citizenship which will encourage a respect for the rights of others.

GOAL V To develop the ability for the expression of ideas and emotions through participation in creative and cultural activities.

GOAL VI To become aware of career opportunities and develop skills to pursue an occupation and/or continued education.

GOAL VII To acquire an understanding of personal hygiene, nutrition, and physical exercises, develop wholesome attitudes toward competition and learn lifetime physical skills essential to the maintenance of personal health.

GOAL VIII To develop knowledge about and a positive attitude toward the structure and processes of the American Free Enterprise System[9]

Can a school district realistically expect to attain these goals? Terms such as "wholesome attitudes," "historical perspective," and "a love of learning" represent abstract concepts that cannot be measured. Yet the official goals do state the general purpose of the school district, and few people would disagree with them. These goals appeal to people in the environment (parents, taxpayers) and are consistent with the aspirations of employees (teachers).

Operative Goals Operative goals represent the "real" goals of the organization. **Operative goals** "designate the ends sought through the actual operating policies of the organization; they tell us what the organization actually is trying to do, regardless of what the official goals say are the aims."[10]

Operative goals describe desired operational activities and are often concerned with the short run. In many organizations, operative goals are not consistent with official goals.

Where operative goals provide the specific content of official goals they reflect choices among competing values. They may be justified on the basis of an official goal, even though they may subvert another official goal. In one sense they are means to official goals, but since the latter are vague or of high abstraction, the "means" become ends in themselves.... For example, where profit-making is the announced goal, operative goals will specify whether quality or quantity is to be emphasized, whether profits are to be short run and risky or long run and stable, and will indicate the relative priority of diverse and somewhat conflicting ends of customer service, employee morale, competitive pricing, diversification, or liquidity.[11]

Types of Operative Goals

Many types of operative goals exist within organizations. Below are five types of operative goals that provide direction for the day-to-day decisions and activities within organizations. Each type of goal and the purpose it serves are summarized in table 3.1.

1. Environmental goals are to satisfy the people and organizations in the external environment of the organization.[12] In one sense, this goal is met through the process of legitimizing the organization. Top administrators use official goals to win approval for the organization's activities. A key activity is simply to satisfy clients and customers. Most organizations are concerned with the feelings, attitudes, and perceptions held by various groups that interact with the organization. In profit-making organizations, customer satisfaction is crucial. In not-for-profit organizations, client satisfaction is often important, and so is the satisfaction of government regulatory agencies and legislative groups that provide resources. Environmental goals for the Plankton High School District would be to maintain the satisfaction of parents and taxpayers with educational services. Satisfying these groups is one type of operating goal, and is not listed in the "official" goal statement.

2. Output goals define the type of business the organization is in.[13] Output goals pertain to the amount and forms of output produced by the organization. How diverse should the product lines be? What markets should be entered? Managers of a local Planned Parenthood organization must decide whether to adopt the goal of only providing birth-control information to those who ask, or whether to actively reach out to schools and churches to educate members of the community. Universities have to decide how much emphasis to give to teaching versus research outputs. Output goals are related to the identification of consumer needs. The definition of an output goal has substantial implications for the allocation of personnel and resources. In the Plankton High School District, output goals will pertain to preparation for college or for jobs, and will determine to which output most resources will be allocated.

Table 3.1. Goal Type and Purpose.

Type	Purpose
OFFICIAL GOALS	Legitimacy
OPERATIVE GOALS	Directions and Decision Guidelines
Environment	Reduction of Uncertainty
Output	Standard of Performance
System	
Product	
Subunit	

3. System goals are concerned with the maintenance of the organization itself.[14] System goals reflect the desired size, form and health of the internal organization. System goals identify such things as growth versus stability, whether the structure should be centralized or decentralized, the desired level of employee job satisfaction, and internal climate. The organization itself must be maintained and renewed or it will stagnate. System goals pertain to this maintenance function. System goals at Plankton pertain to teacher autonomy and satisfaction, rate of growth, and the quality of school buildings and classrooms.

4. Product goals pertain to product characteristics—the form of the product or service given to consumers.[15] Product goals define quantity, quality, variety, styling, uniqueness. Product goals emphasize the nature of the product delivered into the hands of clients or customers. Many organizations, on the operational level, make their mark through distinctive product characteristics. They are known for high volume, for shoddy outputs at low price, for quality, or for novelty. High quality at the expense of quantity or even high profits is not unusual. A high school district like Plankton may try to stay small and make a distinctive mark on students, or it may try to turn out a large number of students from one or two standard programs.

5. Subunit goals are the goals of individual departments and work units. The operative goals of work units are the means through which the organization attains its output or system goals. The R & D goal of designing a new product is the means through which the total organization satisfies its product goal of novelty and uniqueness. The personnel department goal to create a good work climate leads to attainment of the system goal of worker satisfaction. Every organization has operative goals at lower hierarchical levels that lead to higher-level goal attainment. This is a "means-ends" goal hierarchy, because department goals are the means to achieve organizational ends. In a high school, each education department —math, science, language arts—will have goals that lead to the attainment of overall school district goals.

Daimler-Benz

A glimpse of an organization with a product goal of quality is provided by the *Fortune* story of "Daimler-Benz: Quality über Alles." The firm built the world's first practical automobile and has been building quality cars in small numbers for over 75 years. The chief engineer of the company described the 75-year-old tradition as "constant experimentation, concentration on new developments, and continuous improvement." This has meant that the Mercedes has incorporated, as standard equipment, all significant innovations as soon as they appear, whether the public demands them or not and without regard to the increase in the cost of the car. For example, Daimler-Benz introduced such innovations as four-wheel suspension, fuel injection, and joint rear swing axle long before they were adopted by other manufacturers. The company is dominated by engineers and has an adequate pool of skilled labor. Its workers have lived and worked for generations in the German towns where the cars are produced, and they take a fierce pride in their skilled craftsmanship.

American car makers begin with what they think the public wants in terms of appearance, size, features, power, and price, based upon extensive marketing research and the whims of a few top people. With frequent styling changes mistakes can be adjusted, and popular models can be imitated. The manufacturers are also in a position to manipulate consumer desires to some extent, through advertising. This is the familiar strategy of high-volume, mass-market enterprises, whether for cars or for grocery stores. Daimler-Benz has always built automobiles to the tastes of the engineers whether the public likes it or not.[16]

Daimler-Benz has adopted a product goal of high-quality cars. This goal takes precedence over other goals, and Mercedes is known worldwide as a quality automobile. Managers in American auto firms pursued another type of product goal for many years—flashy styling. By the 1980s the lack of quality in American cars began to hurt, so manufacturers began to stress quality more and styling less.

MANAGING MULTIPLE
AND CONFLICTING GOALS

An important point so far is that organizations have multiple goals. These goals are in conflict with one another. Market share and profit maximization are not compatible; success in one may mean less success in the other. The same is true for the rehabilitation versus safe-custody goals of prisons. Organizations not only have multiple goals, but they are trying to achieve goals at both departmental and organizational levels in the hierarchy. There are product goals, system goals, and output goals for the organization itself, and another set of goals may be pursued by departments. Moreover, the organization has official goals and operative goals, which are not always congruent.

How does the organization satisfy these different goals, many of which pull in different directions? Managers typically use four techniques.

1. Satisficing means that organizations accept a "satisfactory" rather than a maximum level of performance.[17] By accepting satisfactory performance across several criteria, the organization can achieve several goals simultaneously. Ralston Purina tries to attain satisfactory levels of profits, market share, and new products. It doesn't maximize any of these goals. University students also satisfice. They have multiple goals, including a livable income, good grades, and social activities. Instead of maximizing income, getting straight As, and spending large amounts of time with family and friends, which would be goal maximization, most students satisfice. They earn enough money to get through the next semester, achieve As where they can but some accept Bs and Cs, and try to see the family on weekends. Organizations use a similar process to reach acceptable levels across multiple goals.
2. Sequential attention means that organizations attend to important goals for a period of time and then turn to other goals.[18] Sequential attention enables an organization to achieve satisfactory levels of performance on one goal before going to another goal. When an organizational crisis occurs, such as a precipitous loss in market share, that goal receives attention until satisfied. During final examinations, students put more of their energy into study, but during the summer they turn to other goals, such as earning income. Organizations do likewise, perhaps sacrificing profits this year in order to increase advertising and new-product development.
3. Preference ordering means that top management establishes goal priorities. In the case of Ralston described at the beginning of this chapter, profitability was given priority over market share and sales volume. Giving priority to profit-making does not mean that other goals will not be attained. But those goals may not be as difficult to attain, or the current level of performance may be satisfactory. If market share should drop dramatically, top managers would reevaluate the goal priorities and perhaps sacrifice profits to regain competitive position. In some cases, system goals may take priority over output goals, such as when techniques of production are in bad shape or organization structure is not facilitating the appropriate level of performance.
4. Goal changes mean that goal priorities are periodically revised. Goals are not static. They are constantly being reevaluated and changed in light of new information, generally from the environment.[19] The desired state of affairs will change to reflect changes in customers, regulations, or competitor goals.

   Most goal changes are a response to external factors. A dramatic goal change was illustrated by the Foundation for Infantile Paralysis. This organization was committed to the goal of developing a cure for polio, and it succeeded. It no longer had a legitimate goal for its activities. Rather than disband, the organization developed a new goal: fighting birth defects and arthritis. Senior management redirected the efforts of the organization toward a new outcome.[20]

Goal changes are not automatic, or easy. Sometimes the organization has to be in real trouble to make top management realize the need for a new direction, as at Eastern Airlines.

IN PRACTICE 3.3
Eastern Airlines

Even though he owned only three percent of the stock (no one owned more), it was quite clear that Eddie Rickenbacker, the World War I ace, controlled Eastern Airlines from 1935 to 1959 and ran it as if he owned it all. For 25 years it had a record of uninterrupted profits; this included very large gains at a time when the other airlines were losing money. According to *Fortune,* Rickenbacker was a one-man show, and the main act was economy: "Despite his dashing war record and flamboyant exterior, he had the cautious soul of a greengrocer when it came to spending money." His frugality became an industry legend. He actually lectured his employees on the importance of saving not just pennies, but mills (a mill is one-tenth of a cent). His main goal for the company appeared to be cost reduction, and it worked for a good many years. . . .

Cutting costs meant reducing services. The airline was slow in introducing faster and more comfortable aircraft, which started to come along every three or four years. Tight scheduling, to ensure maximum use of aircraft, and careful control of maintenance saved money, but this meant that scheduling and maintenance were at the convenience of the company, not the customers, and less desirable departure and arrival times were utilized. Service aboard the plane was spartan; given the cost of a ticket, the saving on a midmorning snack was really pinching pennies. Coffee and cookies were served instead of breakfast. Seating was five abreast in contrast to four on other lines. While other airlines were hiring pretty stewardesses, Eastern retained male stewards on the grounds that they could perform a wider range of duties and would not give up their jobs to get married . . . .

Meanwhile, the competition, investing in newer planes, nonstop service conveniently scheduled, pretty girls, and good food started to cut into Eastern's near-monopoly. The final straw was the decision of the Civil Aeronautics Board to strengthen smaller lines and competition by giving them a chance at the more profitable and busy routes. This step affected all large airlines, but Eastern was already performing poorly. With old equipment, and inconvenient schedules at Eastern, the interlopers did well and Eastern started to go under. The line lost increasing amounts of money from 1960 to 1963, and its share of trunk-line traffic was cut by one-third. Rickenbacker had retired in 1959, just before the deluge . . . .

It was only after Floyd Hall took over in 1963, and Rickenbacker had left the board, that company policies and system and product goals were changed. Hall bought new planes and introduced nonstop routes, substantially increasing debt; sold off unprofitable feeder lines; stressed customer service (reducing short-run efficiency) and undertook the then unsentimental and unusual step of changing the advertising agency in order to create a new image. The "new look" at Eastern paid off, and remarkably quickly . . . . The profit in 1965 was a handsome 29.7 million dollars . . . .

The system goal pursued by Rickenbacker deserves analysis. Given the goal of maximizing profits through cost reduction, his preoccupation with frugality served the company extremely well for 25 years. The other airlines . . . pursued goals of growth and innovation. The other companies simply had different goals, and when their goals of growth and product innovation began to pay off, Eastern had to change its goals too.[21]

Eastern spent many years overcoming the image of being a penny pinching airline. Today, the goals of growth, product innovation, and customer service have paid off. Ex-astronaut Frank Borman, who is now president of Eastern, expresses the goal of customer service in frequent TV ads by stating, "We have to earn our wings every day."

Whose Goals? The final issue to be considered is who determines organizational goals. Goals are value judgments. They are not fixed or given.[22] They originate with people, and the key people are managers. Top managers set the direction of the organization and define the desired future state.[23] Organizational tasks take place at different hierarchical levels, so the managers at each level have primary responsibility for establishing the goals and direction for their respective departments.

Single Managers In a few organizations, a single person may decide upon goals. In small organizations, the owner typically decides what is to be attained. Occasionally the vision of a single person also dominates goal-setting in large corporations, as in the case of Rickenbacker at Eastern Airlines. The more typical case is that goals are decided upon by a group of managers.

Coalitions A **coalition** is an alliance among several managers who agree about organizational values. Coalitions are used because agreement is not automatic. Competing values are held by different managers. Departments have an interest in different organizational outcomes. Managers work to overcome these differences and to build a coalition for certain goals.

An example of coalition-building occurs among medical practitioners, administrators, and trustees in a hospital.[24] Trustees raise money, and want to see the hospital involved in highly visible, beneficial activities that will attract donors. Visible activities are expensive, and do not always add to the quality of health care. Physicians, on the other hand, are concerned with the quality of health care, and want to provide the most recent, up-to-date health-care techniques. Top quality patient care requires recent technology, which is so expensive that costs may be difficult to recover from patients. Administrators have different goals. They want to find efficient ways to process large numbers of patients, and to keep track of employees and doctors. They want up-to-date administrative technology, such as computers. More important, they want to decrease costs and increase revenues from patients. Administrators may try to reduce the number of charity patients, even if it conflicts with the physicians' goal of delivering medical care or upsets the trustees' goal of using charity patients as a device for raising funds.

How are these differences resolved? The goals of each group are in conflict, so they may be given a preference ordering, or be treated sequentially. The hospital may accept "satisfactory" performance on each of the competing goals. Each goal will receive some attention, although no goal will dominate completely. Managers from key subgroups (e.g., trustees, doctors, administrators) participate in discussions and meetings. A coalition will normally emerge that agrees upon goal preferences and orderings.[25] The term coalition describes the political nature of the goal-forming process. Substantial bargaining and compromise may take place. Through discussion and negotiation, most interest groups are able to attain some part of their goals.

ORGANIZATIONAL EFFECTIVENESS

Understanding organizational goals is the first step toward understanding organization effectiveness. Organizational goals represent the reason for the organization's existence, its purpose and mission. In this part of the chapter we explore the topic of effectiveness, and how effectiveness is measured in organizations.

Effectiveness and Efficiency

Goals were defined earlier as the desired future state of the organization. **Organizational effectiveness** is the degree to which an organization realizes its goals.[26] Effectiveness is a broad concept. It implicitly takes into consideration a range of factors both inside and outside the organization. The organization pursues multiple goals, and goals must be achieved in the face of competition, limited resources, and disagreement among interest groups.

Efficiency, by contrast, is a more limited concept that pertains to the internal workings of the organization. **Efficiency** is the amount of resources used to produce a unit of output.[27] Efficiency can be measured as the ratio of inputs to outputs. If one organization can achieve a given production level with fewer resources than another organization, it would be described as more efficient.[28] In many organizations, efficiency and effectiveness are not related. An organization may be highly efficient but fail to achieve its goals, because it makes a product for which there is no demand. Likewise, an organization may achieve its goals but be inefficient. Efficiency and effectiveness represent two different approaches to organizational assessment.

Effectiveness is an important concept in organization theory. It helps us understand whether organizations are performing well and achieving their goals. Society's resources are scarce, and are becoming more scarce, so we want to understand how to assess the performance of organizations consuming these resources. But the assessment of effectiveness has proven to be one of the more intractable problems in organization theory. There has been no simple solution. Organizations are large, diverse, and fragmented. They perform many activities simultaneously. They pursue multiple goals. They generate many outcomes, some intended and some unintended. A variety of frameworks has evolved to measure performance, and each examines a different criterion of effectiveness.[29]

THREE EFFECTIVENESS APPROACHES

The measurement of effectiveness has focused on different parts of the organization. Organizations bring resources in from the environment that are transformed into outputs delivered back into the environment, as shown in figure 3.1. The **goal approach** to organizational effectiveness is concerned with the output side, and whether the organization achieves its goals in terms of desired levels of output. The **system resource approach** assesses effectiveness by observing the other end of the process and evaluating whether the organization effectively obtains resources necessary for high performance. The **process approach** looks at internal activities and assesses effectiveness by indicators such as internal health and efficiency.

These three approaches are somewhat inconsistent with our earlier discussion of goals, because managers can adopt goals that pertain to either

Figure 3.1. Three Approaches to the Measurement of Organizational Effectiveness.

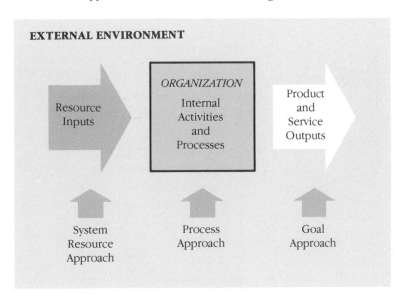

input, transformation, or output activities in their organization. The goal approach to effectiveness has evolved to reflect only those goals that pertain to output. In the next section, the goal approach is used to assess the attainment of output goals. The system resource and internal process approaches provide a means to assess other organizational activities. In the final section of this chapter, these three approaches are combined into a contingency model that considers goals for all types of organizational activities.

The Goal Approach   The goal approach to effectiveness consists of identifying an organization's output goals and assessing how well it has attained those goals.[30] This is a logical approach because organizations do try to attain certain levels of output, profit, or client satisfaction. This approach measures progress toward attainment of those goals.

The important goals to consider are operative goals. Efforts to measure effectiveness have been more productive using operative goals than using official goals.[31] Operative goals reflect activities the organization is actually performing. Identifying operative goals and measuring performance, however, present several problems. In order to accurately evaluate effectiveness, issues of multiple outputs, subjective measurement, and contextual effects must be resolved.

Multiple Outcomes   Application of the goal approach is complicated by the problem of multiple goals and outcomes. Since organizations have multiple and conflicting goals, effectiveness cannot be assessed by a single indicator. High achievement on one goal may mean low achievement on another. Moreover, there are department goals as well as overall goals. The assessment of effectiveness has to take into consideration several goals simultaneously.

One example of multiple goals is taken from a survey of U.S. business managers.[32] Their preferred goals are shown in table 3.2. Eight goals were

Table 3.2.   Organizational Goal Preferences of U.S. Managers.

Goal	% Rating Goal as Highly Important	% Indicating Goal is Significant for Corporate Success
Organizational efficiency	81	71
High productivity	80	70
Profit maximization	72	70
Organizational growth	60	72
Industrial leadership	58	64
Organizational stability	58	54
Employee welfare	65	20
Social welfare	16	8

Source: G. W. England, "Organizational Goals and Expected Behavior of American Managers," *Academy of Management Journal* 10 (1967): 108. Reprinted by permission.

listed as being important to these managers. These eight goals represent outcomes that cannot be achieved simultaneously. Table 3.3 contains the fourteen indicators of effectiveness used most frequently by researchers.[33] Several of these indicators, such as productivity, profit, and efficiency were also goals in table 3.2. The total set of outcomes in tables 3.2 and 3.3 illustrates the array of outcomes that organizations attempt to achieve. Some outcomes are interrelated. The outcome of adaptability-flexibility may lead to greater profitability, which is another outcome on the same list. The point of multiple criteria is that organizations have many goals and many outcomes. In order to assess performance, several indicators of goals have to be selected and combined. Effectiveness should not be assessed on only one dimension, because this would oversimplify organizational goals and outcomes.

Table 3.3. Frequency of Evaluation Criteria in Studies of Organizational Effectiveness.

Criteria	# Mentions
Adaptability-flexibility	10
Productivity	6
Satisfaction	5
Profitability	3
Resource acquisition	3
Absence of strain	2
Control over environment	2
Development	2
Efficiency	2
Employee retention	2
Growth	2
Integration	2
Open communications	2
Survival	2
All other criteria	1

[Source: Reprinted from "Problems in the Measurement of Organizational Effectiveness" by R. M. Steers published in *Administrative Science Quarterly* 20(4) (1975): 546–558 by permission of *The Administrative Science Quarterly.* Copyright © 1975 by Cornell University Press.]

Subjective Indicators The next issue to resolve with the goal approach is how to actually identify operative goals and measure goal attainment. For business organizations, there are often objective indicators. The stated objectives of top management and measures such as profit and market share are available in published reports. For many organizations, however, goal achievement cannot be measured objectively. The goals that are formally written down are not the real goals. Someone has to go into the organization and learn what the goals are. Since goals are the values of top management, the best informants are members of the top-management coalition.[34] These managers can report on the real goals of the organization. Once goals are identified, subjective perceptions of goal achievement can be obtained if quantitative indicators are not available. Subjective assessment is needed in business organizations for such outcomes as employee development or job satisfaction, which may be among the goals of top administrators. The subjective nature of goals and the measure of progress toward goals is a complicating factor in the assessment of effectiveness. However, these problems can be overcome, as indicated in the following example of a juvenile court.

IN PRACTICE 3.4

Juvenile Court

Richard Hall and John Clark studied youth-related welfare organizations in twelve large cities.[35] The organizations included juvenile courts, adolescent mental-health centers, juvenile detention divisions, and school social work activities.

In order to assess effectiveness, the research team visited each organization. Members and employees were asked to list the five most important tasks of the organization. From these responses they developed a long list of goals. Respondents then indicated which were the key goals for the organization. The final list of goals was approved by the organization's top administrator. This procedure was quite effective for identifying operational goals. The operative goals for one organization—the juvenile court—are as follows.

1. Determine the best disposition for each child who appears before the court.
2. Protect the civil and legal rights of minors.
3. Protect the community from those youths who pose personal threats to the community.
4. Hear and justly dispose of cases before the court.
5. Cooperate with other agencies who deal with problem youths.
6. Remove children from family situations that are damaging to their welfare.
7. Foster acceptance of an individualized rehabilitative treatment philosophy by the general public and other system agencies.
8. Develop more resources and better methods of helping problem youth.[36]

These eight goals are specific and operational. These goals were then used to evaluate effectiveness by asking each employee how well the organization performed. Objective indicators were also available for several goals. Objective indicators provided information for such things as percentage of cases closed, proportion of recommendations accepted by other agencies, and percentage of time devoted to a given goal. A positive association was found between objective and subjective indicators of effectiveness. The identification of goals and assessment of performance through interviews with employees was a useful technique for assessing goal effectiveness in the juvenile court.

Contextual Effects The third issue when assessing organizational effectiveness on the basis of goal achievement concerns the organizational environment and context. Some organizational settings are more conducive to high performance than others. Each organization functions in an environmental niche that is unlike any other. Resource availability, consumer demand, quality of employees, government regulations, and the like, differ by industry, town, and location.

One of the most dramatic examples of contextual effects was reported in a study of pharmaceutical manufacturing firms and phonograph record companies.[37] Effectiveness was measured by profits and rates of return. Despite many similarities between the two types of companies, phonograph record manufacturers were much less profitable. The average rate of return for the record industry was about 7%. Pharmaceutical manufacturing was one of the most profitable industries in the United States, with return on investment averaging from 16.7% to 20.3%. The reasons were that factors in the general environment—pricing and distribution, patent and copyright law, and external opinion leaders—placed constraints on firms in each industry. The external constraints on the record industry had substantial bearing on the ability of any single organization to attain a high standard of performance.

Factors outside the organization's control may influence goal achievement. Measuring differences in external factors can be important if the organizations have similar goals but are in different industries.[38] Another way to allow for external differences is to include measures of efficiency in the assessment of effectiveness. This would indicate how efficiently resources are used within the organization, regardless of environmental differences.

Evaluation The goal approach is a logical way to assess organizational effectiveness. Effectiveness is defined as the ability of an organization to attain its goals. But the actual measurement of effectiveness is a complex problem. Organizations have many goals, so there is no single indicator of effectiveness. Goals are often subjective and have to be identified by employees within the organization. The rating of the organization's performance is often subjective and must be provided by people familiar with the organization's activities. Moreover, the attainment of goals may be influenced by factors outside the organization's control. The assessment of organizational effectiveness using the goal approach requires that the evaluator be aware of these issues and allow for them in the final evaluation of effectiveness.

System Resource Approach   The system resource approach looks at the input side of the transformation process shown in figure 3.1. Organizations must be successful in obtaining resource inputs and in maintaining the organizational system in order to be effective. The system resource approach is based on open-systems theory, which was discussed in chapters 1 and 2. Organizations have an exchange relationship with the external environment. Resources in the external environment are scarce and valued. Organizational effectiveness from a systems view is defined as "the ability of the organization, in either absolute or relative terms, to exploit its environment in the acquisition of scarce and valued resources."[39] Obtaining resources to maintain the organization system is the criterion by which organizational effectiveness is assessed. In a narrow sense, the amount of resources acquired from the environment would be the criterion of effectiveness. In a broader sense, the system resource model encompasses the following dimensions.

1. Bargaining position—the ability of the organization to exploit its environment in acquisition of scarce and valued resources.
2. Ability of the system decision-maker to perceive and correctly interpret the real properties of the external environment.
3. Ability of the system to use resources to produce a specified output.
4. Maintenance of internal day-to-day organizational activities.
5. Ability of the organization to respond to changes in the environment.[40]

One important reason for the development and use of the system resource approach is that it provides a unique basis of comparison, and hence overcomes some problems in the goal approach. A school district and a juvenile court, for example, pursue different goals, so how can their relative effectiveness be assessed? One solution is to look at their ability to acquire resources. Each organization must obtain financial and human resources, office space, and physical facilities. The ability to obtain common resources is one way to compare effectiveness, even if the organizations do not have similar goals.

The first criterion of system effectiveness is survival. Those that survive are more effective than those that do not. If the organization obtains sufficient inputs to stay alive, one level of effectiveness is achieved. Beyond survival, effectiveness can be assessed by the dollar value of scarce resources obtained from the environment. Organizations can be compared on the same criteria when output goals differ.

Evaluation   The value of the system resource approach is threefold: it takes the entire organization as a frame of reference, it considers the relationship of the organization to the external environment, and it can be used to compare organizations that have different goals. However, the system resource approach has not been used extensively to measure effectiveness. Part of the problem is that it provides a limited perspective on organizations. One study assessed public agencies in Iowa counties.[41] The agencies included the Soil Conservation Service, Extension Service, Farmer's

Home and Administration. These were different types of organizations with different goals, so the system resource approach was used to assess resource inflows. Resources such as personnel, equipment, meeting rooms, or funds received from other organizations were indicators of effectiveness. The investigators found that organizational characteristics were related to resource differences. They also assessed goals, and found that resource inflows were not correlated with goal attainment.

The findings from county agencies raise the question of whether acquisition of resources is as important as the utilization of these resources. Utilization is measured by looking at goal achievement or efficiency. Moreover, exploiting a large number of resources, if they are not used, might not be considered effective. A college football team with so many star players that several sit on the bench might not be considered effective if the team loses its game.

The system resource approach does offer an alternative perspective on organizational effectiveness. It is especially useful when goals are different because outputs cannot be used as the measure of effectiveness.

Internal Process Approach

In the internal process approach, effectiveness is measured as internal organizational health and efficiency. The effective organization has a smooth, well-oiled internal process. Employees are happy and satisfied. Departmental activities mesh with one another to ensure high productivity. This approach is not concerned with the external environment. The important element in effectiveness is what the organization does with the resources it has, which is reflected in internal health and efficiency.

The best-known proponents of a process model are from the human relations approach to organizations. Writers such as Argyris, Bennis, Likert, and Beckhard have all worked extensively with human resources in organizations and emphasize the connection between human resources and effectiveness.[42] Components of an effective organization, as seen from this viewpoint, are listed below. Each of these dimensions can be assessed by interviewing organizational employees.

1. Supervisor interest and concern for workers.
2. Team spirit, group loyalty, and teamwork.
3. Confidence, trust, and communication between workers and management.
4. Decisions are made near sources of information, regardless of where these sources are on the organizational chart.
5. Communication laterally and vertically is undistorted. People share relevant facts and feelings.
6. The total organization and individuals manage their work against goals and plans.
7. The reward system rewards managers for performance, growth and development of subordinates, and creating an effective working group.
8. The organization and its parts interact with each other. Conflict will occur over projects but will be resolved in the interest of the organization.[43]

A second approach to internal processes is to measure economic efficiency. William Evan developed a method that uses quantitative measures of efficiency.[44] He proposed that three variables could be measured: "inputs" of resources, "transformation" of resources into outputs, and "outputs" that are delivered to consumers outside the organization.

This approach is relevant to internal processes because Evan developed a series of ratios that measure efficiencies within organizations. The first step is to identify the financial cost of inputs (I), transformation (T), and outputs (O). Next, the three variables can be combined in ratios to evaluate various aspects of organizational performance. The most popular assessment of efficiency is O/I. For business organizations, this would be return on investment. For a hospital, the O/I ratio is the number of patients/annual budget. For a university, it is the number of students graduated divided by the resource inputs.

Other ratios, such as T/O, indicate the amount of transformation required to provide a given level of output. In a business organization, this might be indicated by the size of research and development divided by the volume of sales. In a hospital, T/O is the investment in medical technology divided by number of patients treated. Managers interested in assessing organizational efficiency can measure the cost of inputs, transformation processes, and outputs. Quantification of these variables enables the calculation of several aspects of efficiency.

Evaluation   The internal process approach is important because the efficient use of resources and harmonious internal functioning is one way to measure effectiveness. The internal process approach can be used to compare organizations if goals are not the same or are not identifiable. This approach also controls for environmental differences to some extent so that organizational efficiency is compared on a similar basis.

The internal process approach also has shortcomings. Internal efficiency is a very limited view of organizational effectiveness. The goals that resources are used to attain, and the organization's relationship with the external environment are not evaluated. Evaluations of internal health and functioning are often subjective. Like the other approaches to organizational effectiveness, the internal process approach has something to offer. But managers should be aware of and allow for possible shortcomings.

Combined Approach   A reasonable approach to organizational effectiveness is to measure organizational characteristics that pertain to all three approaches, if they are available. The shortcomings of one approach can be offset by measuring other characteristics. Organizational assessment might include measures of resource inputs, the efficiency of the transformation process, and the achievement of output goals by evaluating performance on each dimension. In the following case, measures from all three approaches were obtained to provide a valuable assessment of the relative effectiveness of municipal fire departments.

Fire Departments

How would you measure the effectiveness of fire departments? Measuring the effectiveness of public sector organizations is always difficult because services are not sold for a profit. Philip Coulter assessed fire department effectiveness by including elements of each effectiveness approach described above.[45] His first step was to develop four performance measures for fire departments. He assumed that all fire departments had the twin goals of preventing fires and of responding quickly to fires when they occur. These measures represent the goal approach to organizational effectiveness. He also looked at resource inputs to the fire department, which reflects the system resource approach. He analyzed internal efficiency by measuring the utilization of resources to reduce fire loss.

Measures of Fire Department Effectiveness.

Approach	Variable	Measure
Goal	Fire prevention	Number of fires per population
Goal	Fire suppression	Dollars of fire property loss per 1000 population
System resource	Total revenues expended	Annual fire department budget per capita
Internal process	Efficiency	Total cost (fire loss plus department budget) per capita

Coulter obtained data on fire department performance in 324 municipalities with a population of 25,000 or more. Analysis of his data provided three interesting conclusions. First, effectiveness can be measured in public sector organizations. Second, the fire departments differed widely on each effectiveness variable. Municipalities across the nation are not receiving the same levels of fire department performance on any of the four measures. Third, organizations that scored high on one dimension did not necessarily score high on other dimensions. Goal attainment, resource acquisition, and efficiency were not related in the same department. Multiple criteria of effectiveness were important to determine what each fire department did well.

The findings also showed that effectiveness may be a combination of both internal performance and environment context. Departments that maximized the goal of fire prevention were in upper-middle and middle-class communities that emphasized prevention and contained few fire hazards. Departments that maximized the goal of fire suppression were in small cities that had shorter travel distances and fewer large buildings, so losses were minimal. Departments that maximized resource acquisition had mostly full-time paid firefighters (rather than volunteers) and were unionized. Finally, departments that were most efficient internally had greater specialization, smaller administrative staffs, and quicker response times.

The importance of the study of fire departments is that it shows how relative effectiveness can be measured. None of the measures was perfect by itself, but by combining several measures and comparing several organizations of the same type, overall effectiveness was assessed. Organizations do not excel on all dimensions simultaneously, so the combination of effectiveness approaches provides a balanced approach. Moreover, some of the factors measured in the above study were within the control of fire department managers. The managers can take advantage of these findings to improve effectiveness in their organization.

MULTIPLE DOMAINS OF EFFECTIVENESS

The three approaches—goal, system resource, internal process—to organizational effectiveness described above all have something to offer and all have shortcomings. Each approach tells only part of the story. An organization may be good at exploiting resources, but may squander them and thus fail to achieve its goals. Or an organization may have excellent internal working relationships, but is going broke and will fail to survive. The conclusion from the three approaches is that there is no ultimate criterion of effectiveness. There is no single measure, no single theory, that will allow us to arrive at an unequivocal measurement of performance.

Recently, integrative approaches to organizational effectiveness have been introduced. These new approaches acknowledge that organizations do many things and have many outcomes. No single criterion of effectiveness is appropriate. Managers in organizations performing similar tasks may select different activities to emphasize. One college coach may emphasize winning at all costs (goal approach), while another emphasizes character building of athletes (process approach). The assessment of effectiveness to some extent has to be tailored to the goals and the situation of the organization under study.

Constituencies One proposed approach that integrates diverse organizational activities focuses on organizational consituencies. A **constituency** is any group within or outside the organization that has a stake in the organization's performance. Stockholders, suppliers, employees, and owners are all constituencies, and effectiveness can be assessed by determining how satisfied each group is with the organization.[46] Each constituency will have a different criterion of effectiveness because it has a different interest in the organization. Each constituency has to be surveyed to learn whether the organization performs well from its viewpoint.

The initial work on evaluating effectiveness on the basis of constituencies included ninety-seven small businesses in Texas. Seven constituencies relevant to these businesses were surveyed to determine the perception of effectiveness from each viewpoint.[47] Each constituency and the criterion of effectiveness are as follows:

Constituency	Effectiveness Criteria
1. Owners	Financial return
2. Employees	Work satisfaction, pay, supervision
3. Customers	Quality of goods and services
4. Creditors	Credit worthiness
5. Community	Contribution to community affairs
6. Suppliers	Satisfactory transaction
7. Government	Obedience to laws, regulations

The survey of constituencies discovered that the small business found it difficult to simultaneously fulfill the demands of all groups. One organization may have high employee satisfaction, but satisfaction of other groups may be lower. Nevertheless, measuring all seven constituencies provides a more accurate view of effectiveness than any single measure. Evaluating how organizations perform across each constituency offers an overall assessment of effectiveness.

IN PRACTICE 3.6

Levi Strauss

Levi Strauss and Company is a $2-billion apparel company that has manufacturing facililties in thirteen countries. Levi Strauss distributes jeans to consumers through retail chain stores. They have been responsible for several technological breakthroughs, such as Sta-Prest, which keeps clothing wrinkle-free and helped create a new market for casual wear fashion. Levi is known for a quality product and as a good place to work. An assessment of organizational effectiveness using the constituency approach produced the following analysis.

Constituency	Effectiveness Criteria
1. Owners	Net profit of $145 million based on sales of $1.68 billion in 1978. By 1982, non-jean apparel will account for one-half of $2 billion in gross sales. Earning rate for last five years has exceeded 30%.
2. Employees	The slogan "Levi's is people" shows what the company thinks of its employees; namely, that people come first at Levi.

3. Customers	Levi Strauss means quality and durability at a reasonable cost. Levi keeps young people in mind and develops new products to suit them.
4. Creditors	Paid when the bill is due. The company is financially sound.
5. Community	Levi supports local charity with 1.5% of pre-tax profits. This was over $1,450,000 in 1978.
6. Suppliers	Suppliers see Levi as the largest buyer of denim. They see no end to the popularity of jeans, and they know that Levi Strauss will lead the market.
7. Government	Antitrust lawsuit in California charged price fixing in collaboration with retailers. Refunds made in 1980 to customers who purchased jeans from 1972–1975.

On the basis of the constituency approach, Levi Strauss would be considered an effective company. Most constituents are highly satisfied with their stake in the corporation. Levi Strauss did have problems with the government over price fixing, and would be rated somewhat lower with that constituency. But the average across constituencies is quite high.[48]

Evaluation The strength of the constituency approach is that it takes a broad view of effectiveness and examines factors in the environment as well as within the organization. It also handles several criteria simultaneously—inputs, internal processing, outputs—and acknowledges that there is no single measure of effectiveness. The well-being of employees is just as important as achievement of the owner's goals.

The constituency approach is gaining in popularity, based on the view that effectiveness is a complex, multi-dimensional concept that has no single measure.[49] A valid approach is to evaluate organizations across several criteria that represent outcomes to relevant interest groups. Each group makes different demands on the organization. It is impossible to excel on all demands simultaneously, but overall performance can be evaluated.

Goal Domains An approach that integrates the idea of goals described earlier in this chapter with the idea of multiple organization activities and outcomes looks at organizational domains.

Multiple Domains Organizational activities can be divided into domains, and performance in each domain assessed along with the goal priority given that domain by the organization. Kim Cameron identified domains in universities.[50] Some universities emphasized the teaching domain. These schools were located in urban areas and attracted disadvantaged students. Extensive resources were allocated to training students who could graduate from college and get good jobs. Choosing goals in the teaching domain and allocating resources to teaching activities meant that other areas, such as scientific research, suffered. Other universities emphasized the research domain, in which case disadvantaged students were not helped at all. Cameron found that universities that emphasized one domain did not perform well in other domains, and should not be expected to. This approach is important because it integrates the goals selected by managers with the various domains that may be relevant to organization performance.

Domain Framework A useful framework for understanding organizational domains was proposed by Kilmann and Herden.[51] They distinguished between efficiency and effectiveness and whether organizational goals focus on internal or external domains. They proposed the four general domains shown in figure 3.2. The framework in 3.2 is especially valuable because each domain is similar to one of the effectiveness approaches described in this chapter. This framework integrates several approaches to evaluating effectiveness.

Internal efficiency is concerned with the effective utilization of scarce resources. This domain is similar to the internal efficiency approaches to effectiveness. One measurement is to calculate outputs divided by inputs.

Figure 3.2.   Domains of Organizational Effectiveness.
Source: Ralph H. Kilmann and Richard P. Herden, "Towards a Systematic Methodology for Evaluating the Impact of Interventions on Organizational Effectiveness," *Academy of Management Review* 1 (1976): 87–98. Reprinted by permission.

	Internal	**External**
Efficiency	*INTERNAL EFFICIENCY* Focus: Output/Input Measures: Units produced per work hour Rate of return on invested capital Cost of goods sold Scrap material per unit Sales per advertising dollar	*EXTERNAL EFFICIENCY* Focus: Bargaining Position with Environment Measures: Cost of capital Market share Cost of raw materials Labor cost New market development Profit
Effectiveness	*INTERNAL EFFECTIVENESS* Focus: Employee Satisfaction Measures: Employee turnover Employee attitudes Organizational climate Employee commitment Interpersonal relationships	*EXTERNAL EFFECTIVENESS* Focus: Societal (constituent) Satisfaction Measures: Community satisfaction with organization Satisfaction of supplier with organization Consumer satisfaction Social responsibility Quality of life

Internal efficiency is concerned with mechanical activities, and focuses on costs of inputs, transformation, and outputs.

External efficiency deals with the acquisition of resources needed by the organization. This domain is similar to the system resource approach to organizational effectiveness. Relationships with external groups are emphasized. Acquisition of supplies and other resources are in this domain, as well as relationships with customers and market share. Other factors that influence resource exchange, such as pricing and identification of markets, are also included here.

Internal effectiveness stresses outcomes for employees. This domain is similar to the internal process approach to effectiveness. Measures in this domain pertain to employee motivation and fulfillment, job design, reward systems, coordination, and personnel training and development.

External effectiveness refers to external constituencies and their satisfaction. This approach is similar to the constituency approach described above. Many people, including owners, customers, and suppliers, have a stake in the organization. Ultimate achievement of goals and profitability are a function of satisfying these constituencies. External effectiveness considers the relationship between the organization and its environment in a global sense. The organization must build linkages to several external constituencies and satisfy them to be effective.

Contingency Framework

The selection of a domain is part of the goal-setting process described earlier in this chapter. Goals reflect the value judgments and preferences of managers. Top managers may choose to emphasize the domain of external effectiveness, for example, because of special organizational needs perceived by managers.

Organizational characteristics also influence which domains tend to be emphasized. The contingency framework proposed in figure 3.3 identifies organizational circumstances in which each domain will be used to evaluate effectiveness. This framework is based upon the work of James Thompson.[52]

The two dimensions that influence domain selection in figure 3.3 are clarity of output standards and knowledge of cause and effect relationships. **Clarity of output standards** means whether standards for the assessment of goal attainment are measurable. When outcomes are clear and measurable, the organization can assess them accurately. When they are not clear, the organization will consider another strategy to assess effectiveness. **Cause-effect relationships** pertain to the degree of understanding about the organization's internal transformation process. When these processes are well understood, managers know exactly what to do to achieve desired outcomes. An assembly line is an example of a well-understood conversion process. In other organizations, the conversion process is not well understood. Factors that lead to high performance cannot be identified, perhaps because they are qualitative or intangible, or because the organization lacks experience in a new activity. The combination of outcome clarity and cause-effect knowledge will influence the effectiveness domain selected by top managers.

Clarity of Output Standards	Knowledge of Cause-Effect Relationships: Complete	Knowledge of Cause-Effect Relationships: Incomplete
Clear	*EFFICIENCY CRITERIA* Cost to achieve output goals	*OUTPUT CRITERIA* Achievement of output or profit goals
Ambiguous	*INTERNAL PROCESS CRITERIA* Climate and Satisfaction	*SOCIAL CRITERIA* Satisfaction of External Constituencies

Figure 3.3. Contingency Effectiveness Framework Based Upon Goal Domains and Organizational Circumstances.
Source: Adapted from James Thompson, *Organizations in Action* (New York: McGraw-Hill, 1967), p. 85.

The two dimensions combine into four categories of goal domains and effectiveness criteria. When senior management knows exactly what the outcomes are to be and they have complete knowledge of internal processes, they will normally select the *efficiency* domain of effectiveness. Managers will emphasize the cost efficiency of each increment of goal attainment. This is perhaps the easiest situation in which to measure effectiveness. Managers know what the desired result is, and the best way to achieve it, so that can verify if resources are efficiently used. The Ralston case at the beginning of the chapter is an example. The desired outcome (profitability) is clear and they know how to attain it (market share and price).

In organizations in which standards of output are clear, but knowledge of the conversion process is poor, the criterion will be attainment of *output goals*. Rather than calculate internal efficiency, managers will consider whether they are achieving their goals in relation to the environment. This is part of the external efficiency domain. So long as outcomes are achieved, regardless of efficiency, the organization will be successful. An example is a college basketball team. The exact process needed to create a winning team is not known. Various coaching techniques might be used to achieve a winner. The techniques may vary in cost and efficiency. So an internal efficiency test that relates costs to victories is seldom used. The coach and alumni know they want a winning team (standard of output is clear), and the test of effectiveness is whether the team wins games. The correct effectiveness domain involves the assessment of organizational outputs.

In the third category of figure 3.3 there is lack of clarity about goals, but internal processes are well understood. In this situation, the domain will reflect an *internal process* criterion of effectiveness. Managers will be oriented toward internal activities and will work to enhance employee behavior and the internal processes that will eventually lead to effectiveness. Satisfaction of employees and internal working relationships hold the key to effectiveness because desired outputs are not agreed upon or cannot be identified. This domain would be used in a basic research organization when outputs of research won't be known for years in the future. Effectiveness is evaluated by evaluating internal process.

Finally, a few organizations are in the position of not knowing exactly what outcomes to achieve or even how to achieve outcomes. This is often the case in public organizations in which there is substantial disagreement about the organization's purpose. In human service organizations, the best internal process to achieve outputs (e.g., how to get people off welfare) is not known. Moreover, organization members do not even agree upon goals (are we to provide welfare benefits or break the welfare cycle?). In these organizations, *external constituencies* and reference groups become the domain of effectiveness measurement. Measuring effectiveness by output achievement is not logical because specific outputs are not defined. Assessing effectiveness on the basis of internal processes or efficiency is not appropriate either because the techniques for reaching output goals are not well understood. The best indicator of effectiveness is to determine whether constituencies are satisfied with the organization's performance. In a study of juvenile agencies, the investigators found that constituent groups (other agencies, parents, community leaders) could report on effectiveness.[53] By measuring satisfaction of other organizations with the performance of the juvenile unit, overall effectiveness could be determined. Senior managers in this organization will be oriented toward the domain of external constituencies rather than toward tests of internal efficiency or goal achievement.

Manager Preferences James Thompson argues that organizations prefer the more precise criteria of performance when available.[54] Managers first prefer efficiency criteria, then goal outcomes, then internal process criteria, and finally criteria of social reference groups and constituencies. The latter criteria are hardest to define and the most difficult to measure. Many organizations do not have the luxury of well-defined goals and conversion processes, however, so other, more complicated forms of effectiveness measurement are required. The characteristics of output clarity and cause-effect knowledge will be an important factor in managers' selection of goals and effectiveness domains in which the organization tries to excel.

IN PRACTICE 3.7

Montreal Psychiatric Hospital

The nurses had never witnessed anything like it. The psychiatrists were split down the middle, polarized, about how to deliver psychiatric care at Montreal. Several of the psychiatrists wanted to adopt the milieu approach to therapy that had been developed in England. Milieu therapy engaged the entire hospital environment in the therapeutic process. Patients would interact with nurses, support staff, and each other in structured group activities. Patients' idle time was converted to therapeutic encounters. Private sessions with doctors were also retained as needed.

The other psychiatrists believed in the traditional approach to therapy. Mental illness was perceived by them as a disease that must be fought by physicians. The doctor is the primary expert in the fight, and he should use drugs or other techniques to combat the illness. The physician's skill was the primary ingredient in helping the psychotic patient recover. Nonexperts should not be involved in so difficult a task.

All the psychiatrists could agree on one thing: they wanted to deliver higher quality therapeutic care to both private and public patients in the Montreal area. But they could not agree on the best techniques for providing this care. The hospital staff committee (made up of twelve physicians and the directors of nursing and support staff) made policy decisions about therapeutic care. Their decisions usually reflected the consensus among medical staff. As one member described the decision-making process: "It is impossible to reduce things down to solely hard facts and rigid rules: psychiatry is not an exact science."

Dr. Macintosh, head of the hospital, was concerned with overall effectiveness. Everyone agreed with the goals the hospital was trying to accomplish (quality care), but they were severely split about how to achieve the appropriate level of effectiveness. Calculations of efficiency based upon cost-benefit analyses had little impact. Milieu therapy was somewhat cheaper because physician time was reduced, but that had no sway on decision-makers. Doctors would not use a technique because it was cheaper or more efficient. They wanted to deliver quality care.

The dilemma was finally resolved on a temporary basis by conducting an experiment. Facilities would be made available for both types of therapy over a period of two years. Patients would be randomly assigned to each type of therapy by a subcommittee of psychiatrists representing both factions. The best test of effectiveness, they decided, was to learn which form of therapy had the most positive impact on the mental health of patients.[55]

In the psychiatric hospital, an internal efficiency goal was not appropriate because the process of converting mentally ill people into a mentally healthy state was not well understood. The primary test of effectiveness became one of outcomes—which form of therapy enabled the organization to achieve its output goal of providing the best mental-health care. Whichever technique achieved that goal would be considered most effective and would be adopted.

SUMMARY AND INTERPRETATION

This chapter discussed organizational goals and ways to measure organizational effectiveness. Goal-setting specifies the mission or purpose of the organization and its desired future state. Effectiveness indicates how well the organization realizes its purpose and attains its desired future state.

Goals and effectiveness are important topics because organizations exist for a purpose. They have a specific mission or task to be accomplished. Sometimes this mission is taken for granted by people within the organization. They become involved with day-to-day activities, and forget the direction in which they are headed. The importance of organizational goals is that they make explicit the purpose and direction of the organization. Organizational goals are not given or fixed. They change over time, and new goals must be sequenced and given priority. Goals are a key element in organizations because they meet several needs—establishing legitimacy with external groups, reducing uncertainty, and setting standards of performance for participants. Goals must be explicit, and they must be updated. Understanding the diverse and critical roles of goals in organizations is one of the most important ideas in this chapter.

A second important idea is the complexity of measuring organizational effectiveness. There is no easy, simple, guaranteed measure that will provide an unequivocal assessment of performance. The complexity of effectiveness measurement reflects the complexity of organizations as a topic of study. Organizations do many things. They have many outcomes, and they must perform diverse activities well—from obtaining resource inputs to delivering outputs—in order to be successful. Traditional approaches used output goals, resource acquisition, or internal health and efficiency as the criteria of effectiveness. New approaches stress a broad-based view of effectiveness that considers multiple activities simultaneously. Organizations can be assessed by surveying several constituencies that have a stake in organizational performance or by evaluating selected domains. The variety of approaches to organizational effectiveness has evolved to help solve the problem of measurement. One approach may be suitable in one organization but not in another. No framework is perfect, but each offers some advantage that the others may lack.

From the point of view of managers, the goal approach to effectiveness and measures of internal efficiency are appropriate, when they are available. The attainment of goals reflects the purpose of the organization, and efficiency reflects the cost of attaining those goals. In a few organizations, the goals may not be agreed upon or internal efficiency may not be measurable, in which case alternative means of assessment will have to be used. Evaluating such criteria as the ability to obtain necessary resources or the satisfaction of constituencies would then be used. These measures can also be used in addition to measures of goals and efficiency if managers feel they are relevant to performance.

From the point of view of people outside the organization, such as academic investigators or government researchers, the constituency and domain approaches to organizational effectiveness are preferable. The constituency approach evaluates the organization's contribution to society. The domain approach acknowledges different areas of activity (internal, external, input, output) and allows for managers to choose one domain to emphasize.

Both the diversity of organizational domains and the preference of managers for one domain is acknowledged in these approaches.

DISCUSSION QUESTIONS

1. What is the purpose of official goals in organizations? Of operational goals?
2. How do output goals differ from product goals?
3. Hurco Manufacturing Company produces high-technology machine tools. Hurco's president is a religious person, and senior management has pledged Hurco to "create products which contribute to the benefit of mankind; provide a stimulating, stable and safe working environment which fairly rewards each employee in proportion to his or her contribution of talent and effort; be an example in society as a company which serves the living God, believes only in fair and ethical practices, recognizes its responsibility to help preserve the free enterprise system." Based upon the contingency framework in figure 3.3, which domains are Hurco pursuing? How will effectiveness be measured for each of these goals? Do you expect management to also look at more traditional criteria such as profits and market share? Discuss.
4. In Practice 3.4 described eight goals pursued in a juvenile organization. How is it possible for an organization to pursue this many goals simultaneously?
5. Who is responsible for goal-setting in the organization? Discuss.
6. Define effectiveness versus efficiency. Are they related in organizations?
7. Is it appropriate to use the subjective judgments of managers to identify organizational goals and measure effectiveness? Why?
8. You have been asked to evaluate the effectiveness of the police department in a medium-sized community. Where would you begin and how would you proceed? What effectiveness approach would you prefer?
9. What are the advantages and disadvantages of the system resource approach versus the goal approach for measuring organizational effectiveness?
10. What are the similarities and differences between assessing effectiveness on the basis of domains versus constituencies? Explain.
11. A noted organization theorist once said, "Organizational effectiveness can be whatever top management defines it to be." Discuss.
12. James Thompson argued that in selecting domains for performance measurement, managers prefer those that are precise and easily measured. Managers would measure efficiency domains first, then outputs, internal processes, and finally the social domain. Examine the goals listed in table 3.2. In which domain is each goal? Does the ordering of goals support Thompson's suggestion that managers prefer efficiency, then output, internal process, and finally social tests of effectiveness? Discuss.

As an organization manager:

1. Establish and communicate organizational goals. Communicate official goals in order to provide a statement of the organization to external constituents. Communicate operational goals in order to provide internal direction, guidelines, and standards of performance for employees.
2. Sort out the many competing goals of an organization and establish priorities. Identify the domain in which the organization truly wants to succeed. Achieve multiple goals through the processes of satisficing, sequential attention, priority setting, and goal changing.
3. Do not set goals alone. Discuss goals widely with other managers, and develop a coalition that agrees on which goals to emphasize.
4. Assess the effectiveness of the organization. Use the goal approach, internal process approach, and system resource approach to obtain specific pictures of effectiveness. Assess constituency satisfaction or performance in several goal domains to obtain a broader picture of effectiveness.
5. Combine several techniques to provide a perspective on effectiveness. Use efficiency tests when both inputs and outputs are measurable. Use attainment of output goals when internal transformation processes are difficult to analyze. Use internal health and functioning, and the constituent approaches when measurements of goal attainment are not feasible. Clearly articulate the goal domain in which the organization is trying to succeed, and then assess whether the desired level of performance has been achieved.

Consider these guides when analyzing the following case and when answering the questions listed after the case.

CASE FOR ANALYSIS

THE PARADOXICAL TWINS: ACME AND OMEGA ELECTRONICS[57]

Part I   In 1955, Technological Products of Erie, Pa., was bought out by a Cleveland manufacturer. The Cleveland firm had no interest in the electronics division of Technological Products and subsequently sold to different investors two plants that manufactured printed circuit boards. One of the plants, located in nearby Waterford, Pa., was renamed Acme Electronics and the other plant, within the city limits of Erie, was renamed Omega Electronics, Inc. Acme retained its original management and upgraded its general manager to president. Omega hired a new president, who had been a director of a large electronics research laboratory, and upgraded several of the existing personnel within the plant. Acme and Omega often competed for the same contracts. As subcontractors, both firms benefited from the electronics boom of the early 1960s and both looked forward to future growth and expansion. Acme had annual sales of $10 million and employed 550 people. Omega had annual sales of $8 million and employed 480 people. Acme regularly achieved greater net profits, much to the chagrin of Omega's management.

Inside Acme   The president of Acme, John Tyler, credited his firm's greater effectiveness to his manager's abilities to run a "tight ship." He explained that he had retained the basic structure developed by Technological Products because it was most efficient for high volume manufacture of printed circuits and their subsequent assembly. Tyler was confident that had the demand not been so great, its competitor would not have survived. "In fact," he said, "we have been able to beat Omega regularly for the most profitable contracts thereby increasing our profit." Acme had detailed organization charts and job descriptions. Tyler believed that everyone should have clear responsibilities and narrowly defined jobs, which would lead to efficient performance and high company profits. People were generally satisfied with their work at Acme; however, some of the managers voiced the desire to have a little more latitude in their jobs.

Inside Omega   Omega's president, Jim Rawls, did not believe in organization charts. He felt that his organization had departments similar to Acme's, but he thought the plant was small enough that things such as organization charts just put artificial barriers between specialists who should be working together. Written memos were not allowed, since, as Jim expressed it, "The plant is small enough that if people want to communicate they can just drop by and talk things over." The head of the mechanical engineering department said: "Jim spends too much of his time and mine making sure everyone understands what we're doing and listening to suggestions." Rawls was concerned with employee satisfaction and wanted everyone to feel part of the organization. The top management team reflected Rawls' attitudes. They also believed that employees should be familiar with activities throughout the organization so that cooperation between departments would be increased. A newer member of the industrial engineering department said, "When I first got here, I wasn't sure what I was supposed to do. One day I worked with some mechanical engineers and the next day I helped the shipping department design some packing cartons. The first months on the job were hectic but at least I got a real feel for what makes Omega tick."

Questions   1. What are the goals at Acme? At Omega?
2. Who chooses these goals?
3. Do these goals reflect different effectiveness domains? Explain.

Part II   In 1966, integrated circuits began to cut deeply into the demand for printed circuit boards. The integrated circuits (I.C.) or "chips" were the first step into micro-miniaturization in the electronics industry. Because the manufacturing process for I.C.s was a closely guarded secret, both Acme and Omega realized the potential threat to their futures and both began to seek new customers aggressively. In July 1966, one of the major photocopy manufacturers was looking for a subcontractor to assemble the memory unit for their new experimental copier. The projected contract for the job was estimated to be $5 to $7 million in annual sales. Both Acme and Omega were geographically close to this manufacturer and both had submitted highly competitive bids for the production of one hundred prototypes. Acme's bid was slightly lower than Omega's; however, both firms were asked to produce one hundred units. The photocopy manufacturer told both firms that speed was critical because their president had boasted to other manufacturers that they would have a finished copier available by Christmas. This boast, much to the designer's dismay, required pressure on all subcontractors to begin prototype production before final design of the copier was complete. This meant that Acme and Omega would have at most two weeks to produce the prototypes or delay the final copier production.

Question 1. Which firm do you think will produce the best results? Why?

Part III ***Inside Acme*** As soon as John Tyler was given the blueprints (Monday, July 11, 1966), he sent a memo to the purchasing department requesting them to move forward on the purchase of all necessary materials. At the same time, he sent the blueprints to the drafting department and asked that they prepare manufacturing prints. The industrial engineering department was told to begin methods design work for use by the production department supervisors. Tyler also sent a memo to all department heads and executives indicating the critical time constraints of this job and how he expected that everyone would perform as efficiently as they had in the past.

The departments had little contact with one another for several days, and each seemed to work at its own speed. Each department also encountered problems. Purchasing could not acquire all the parts on time. Industrial engineering had difficulty arranging an efficient assembly sequence. Mechanical engineering did not take the deadline seriously, and parceled its work to vendors so the engineers could work on other jobs scheduled previously. Tyler made it a point to stay in touch with the photocopy manufacturer to let them know things were progressing and to learn of any new developments. He traditionally worked to keep important clients happy. Tyler telephoned someone at the photocopy company at least twice a week and got to know the head designer quite well.

On July 15, Mr. Tyler learned that mechanical engineering was way behind in its development work, and he "hit the roof." To make matters worse, purchasing did not obtain all the parts so the industrial engineers decided to assemble the product with one part missing, which would be inserted at the last minute. On Thursday, July 21, the final units were being assembled, although the process was delayed several times. On Friday, July 22, the last units were finished while John Tyler paced around the plant. Late that afternoon, Tyler received a phone call from the head designer of the photocopy manufacturer who told Tyler that he had received a call on Wednesday from Jim Rawls of Omega. He explained that Rawls' workers had found an error in the design of the connector cable and taken corrective action on their prototypes. He told Tyler that he checked out the design error and that Omega was right. Tyler, a bit overwhelmed by this information, told the designer that he had all the memory units ready for shipment and that as soon as they received the missing component, on Monday or Tuesday, they would be able to deliver the final units. The designer explained that the design error would be rectified in a new blueprint he was sending over by messenger and that he would hold Acme to the Tuesday delivery date.

When the blueprint arrived, Tyler called in the production supervisor to assess the damage. The alterations in the design would call for total disassembly and the unsoldering of several connections. Tyler told the supervisor to put extra people on the alterations first thing Monday morning and to try to finish the job by Tuesday. Late Tuesday afternoon the alterations were finished and the missing components were delivered. Wednesday morning, the production supervisor discovered that the units would have to be torn apart again to install the missing component. When John Tyler was told this, he again "hit the roof." He called industrial engineering and asked if they could help out. The production supervisor and the methods engineer couldn't agree on how to install the component. John Tyler settled the argument by ordering that all units be taken apart again and the missing component installed. He told shipping to prepare cartons for delivery on Friday afternoon. On Friday, July 29, fifty prototypes were shipped from Acme without final inspection. John Tyler was concerned about his firm's reputation so he waived the final inspection after he personally tested one unit and found it operational. On Tuesday, August 2, Acme shipped the last fifty units.

Inside Omega   Jim Rawls called a meeting on Friday, July 8, that included department heads to tell them about the potential contract they were to receive. He told them that as soon as he received the blueprints, work could begin. On Monday, July 11, the prints arrived and again the department heads met to discuss the project. At the end of the meeting, drafting had agreed to prepare manufacturing prints while industrial engineering and production would begin methods design.

Two problems arose within Omega that were similar to those at Acme. Certain ordered parts could not be delivered on time. The assembly sequence was difficult to engineer. The departments proposed ideas to help one another, however, and department heads and key employees had daily meetings to discuss progress. The head of electrical engineering knew of a Japanese source for the components that could not be purchased from normal suppliers. Most problems were solved by Saturday, July 16th.

On Monday, July 18, a methods engineer and the production supervisor formulated the assembly plans and production was set to begin on Tuesday morning. On Monday afternoon, people from mechanical engineering, electrical engineering, production, and industrial engineering got together to produce a prototype just to ensure that there would be no snags in production. While they were building the unit, they discovered an error in the connector cable design. All the engineers agreed, after checking and rechecking the blueprints, that the cable was erroneously designed. People from mechanical engineering and electrical engineering spent Monday night redesigning the cable and on Tuesday morning the drafting department finalized the changes in the manufacturing prints. On Tuesday morning, Jim Rawls was a bit apprehensive about the design changes and decided to get formal approval. Rawls received word on Wednesday from the head designer at the photocopier firm that they could proceed with the design changes as discussed on the phone. On Friday, July 22, the final units were inspected by quality control and were then shipped.

Questions
1. Which organization was more effective at developing the prototype and meeting the deadlines? Was their level of effectiveness due to the goals chosen by top management?
2. Predict which organization will get the final contract. Why?

Part IV Ten of Acme's final memory units were defective while all Omega's units passed the photocopier firm's tests. The photocopier firm was disappointed with Acme's delivery delay, and incurred further delays in repairing the defective Acme units. However, rather than give the entire contract to one firm, the final contract was split between Acme and Omega with two directives added: (1) maintain zero defects, and (2) reduce final cost. In 1967, through extensive cost-cutting efforts, Acme reduced its unit cost by 20% and was ultimately awarded the total contract.

Questions
1. How can Acme's success be explained? Did Acme's goals seem more appropriate? Did constituent satisfaction play a role?
2. Overall, who was more effective, Acme or Omega? Explain.

NOTES

1. David T. Garino, "New Ralston Chief Says He'll Sacrifice Sales to Keep Company's Profit Margins High," *Wall Street Journal,* July 2, 1981, p. 21.
2. *Ibid,;* "Ralston's Urban Commitment," *Dun's Business Month,* p. 98–100.
3. Amitai Etzioni, *Modern Organizations* (Englewood Cliffs, NJ: Prentice-Hall, 1964), p. 6.
4. Charles Perrow, *Organizational Analysis: A Sociological View* (Belmont, CA: Wadsworth, 1970), p. 99.
5. Herbert A. Simon, "On the Concept of Organizational Goal," *Administrative Science Quarterly* 9 (1964): 1–22.
6. Donald N. Michael, *On Learning to Plan—And Planning to Learn* (San Francisco: Jossey-Bass, 1973), p. 149.
7. James D. Thompson, *Organizations in Action* (New York: McGraw-Hill, 1967), pp. 83–98.
8. Charles Perrow, "The Analysis of Goals in Complex Organizations," *American Sociological Review* 26 (1961): 854–866.
9. The school district that provided the official goal statement wishes to remain anonymous.
10. Perrow, "Analysis of Goals," p. 855.

11. *Ibid.*
12. Perrow, *Organizational Analysis,* p. 135
13. *Ibid.*
14. *Ibid.*
15. *Ibid.*
16. *Ibid.,* pp. 168–169.
17. James G. March and Herbert A. Simon, *Organizations* (New York: Wiley, 1958); Richard M. Cyert and James G. March, *A Behavioral Theory of the Firm* (Englewood Cliffs, NJ: Prentice-Hall, 1963); Thompson, *Organizations in Action.*
18. Cyert and March, *Behavioral Theory of the Firm,* p. 118.
19. Etzioni, *Modern Organizations.*
20. David L. Sills, *The Volunteers* (New York: The Free Press, 1957).
21. Perrow, *Organizational Analysis,* pp. 147–150.
22. Simon, "On the Concept of Organizational Goal," pp. 1–22.
23. Perrow, *Organizational Analysis.*
24. Perrow, "Analysis of Goals," pp. 859–864.
25. Cyert and March, *Behavioral Theory of the Firm,* pp. 114–127.
26. Etzioni, *Modern Organizations,* p. 8.
27. *Ibid.*
28. Richard M. Steers, *Organizational Effectiveness: A Behavioral View* (Santa Monica, CA: Goodyear, 1977), p. 51.
29. Karl E. Weick and Richard L. Daft, "The Effectiveness of Interpretation Systems," in Kim S. Cameron and David A. Whetten, eds., *Organizational Effectiveness: A Comparison of Multiple Models* (New York: Academic Press, 1982).
30. James L. Price, "The Study of Organizational Effectiveness," *The Sociological Quarterly* 13 (1972): 3–15.
31. Richard H. Hall and John P. Clark, "An Ineffective Effectiveness Study and Some Suggestions for Future Research," *The Sociological Quarterly* 21 (1980): 119–134; Price, "Study of Organizational Effectiveness"; Perrow, "Analysis of Goals."
32. George W. England, "Organizational Goals and Expected Behaviors in American Managers," *Academy of Management Journal* 10 (1967): 107–117.
33. Richard M. Steers, "Problems in the Measurement of Organizational Effectiveness," *Administrative Science Quarterly* 20 (1975): 546–558.
34. Johannes M. Pennings and Paul S. Goodman, "Toward a Workable Framework" in Paul S. Goodman, Johannes M. Pennings, and associates, *New Perspectives on Organizational Effectiveness* (San Francisco: Jossey-Bass, 1979), p. 152.
35. Hall and Clark, "An Ineffective Effectiveness Study," p. 39.
36. *Ibid.,* pp. 129–130.
37. Paul M. Hirsch, "Organizational Effectiveness and the Institutional Environment," *Administrative Science Quarterly* 20 (1975): 327–344.
38. Michael T. Hannan and John Freeman, "Obstacles to Comparative Studies," in Goodman, Pennings, and associates, *New Perspectives,* pp. 106–131.

39. Ephraim Yuchtman and Stanley E. Seashore, "A System Resource Approach to Organizational Effectiveness," *Administrative Science Quarterly* 12 (1967): 377–395.

40. J. Barton Cunningham, "A Systems-Resource Approach for Evaluating Organizational Effectiveness," *Human Relations* 31 (1978): 631–656.

41. Joseph J. Molnar and David C. Rogers, "Organizational Effectiveness: An Empirical Comparison of the Goal and System Resource Approaches," *The Sociological Quarterly* 17 (1976): 401–413.

42. Chris Argyris, *Integrating the Individual and the Organization* (New York: Wiley, 1964); Warren G. Bennis, *Changing Organizations* (New York: McGraw-Hill, 1966); Rensis Likert, *The Human Organization* (New York: McGraw-Hill, 1967); Richard Beckhart, *Organization Development: Strategies and Models* (Reading, MA: Addison-Wesley, 1969).

43. J. Barton Cunningham, "Approaches to the Evaluation of Organizational Effectiveness," *Academy of Management Review* 2 (1977): 463–474; Beckhart, *Organization Development.*

44. William M. Evan, "Organization Theory and Organizational Effectiveness: An Exploratory Analysis," *Organization and Administrative Sciences* 7 (1976): 15–28.

45. Phillip B. Coulter, "Organizational Effectiveness in the Public Sector: The Example of Municipal Fire Protection," *Administrative Science Quarterly* 24 (1979): 65–81.

46. Terry Connolly, Edward J. Conlon, and Stuart Jay Deutsch, "Organizational Effectiveness: A Multiple-Constituency Approach," *Academy of Management Review* 5 (1980): 211–217; Michael Keely, "A Social-Justice Approach to Organizational Evaluation," *Administrative Science Quarterly* 23 (1978): 272–292.

47. Frank Friedlander and Hal Pickle, "Components of Effectiveness in Small Organizations," *Administrative Science Quarterly* 13 (1968): 289–304.

48. Kevin Flack, Pat Bailey, and Doug Simmons, "Levi Strauss & Co.," unpublished manuscript, Texas A & M University, 1981.

49. Connolly, Conlon, and Deutsch, "Organizational Effectiveness"; Robert H. Miles, *Macro Organizational Behavior* (Santa Monica, CA: Goodyear, 1980).

50. Kim F. Cameron, "Domains of Organizational Effectiveness in Colleges and Universities," *Academy of Management Journal* 24 (1981): 25–47.

51. Ralph H. Kilmann and Richard P. Herden, "Towards a Systematic Methodology for Evaluating the Impact of Interventions on Organizational Effectiveness," *Academy of Management Review* 2 (1976): 87–98.

52. Thompson, *Organizations in Action*, p. 86.

53. Hall and Clark, "An Ineffective Effectiveness Study."

54. Thompson, *Organizations in Action.*

55. This case was inspired by Danny Miller, "Davidson Psychiatric Hospital," distributed by the Intercollegiate Case Clearing House, Soldier's Field, Boston, MA 02136, 1976.

56. John Halbrooks, "Making Money Isn't the Religion at Hurco," *Inc.,* April 1981, pp. 104–110.

57. Adapted from John F. Veiga, "The Paradoxical Twins: Acme and Omega Electronics," in John F. Veiga and John N. Yanouzas, *The Dynamics of Organization Theory* (St. Paul, MN: West, 1979), pp. 132–138.

PART III

Organization Structure and Design

4

Organization Bureaucracy, Size, and Growth

A GYPSUM PLANT

Several miles from a medium-sized city near one of the Great Lakes there was a company which mined gypsum rock, crushed it, mixed it with bonding and foaming agents, spread it out on a wide sheet of paper, covered it with another sheet, let it set a bit, sliced it into large but inedible sandwiches, and then dried them. The resulting material was sold as wallboard, used for insulation and for dividing up rooms in buildings.

The gypsum plant fitted comfortably into the style of life in the area. Most of the men working at the plant, some 255 including the miners, had worked there for many years. They knew one another well on the job and visited outside of the plant in the surrounding hamlets. Indeed, perhaps as many as one-half of the workers were related to others employed in the plant. The personnel man who hired and fired people argued that it was good to learn something about a prospective employee by asking others in the plant or community about him and his family. He also preferred farm boys over city boys. The personnel man had few other rules for hiring, firing, or other matters with which he had to deal. He disliked paperwork and, as one employee said, "He regarded everything that happened as an exception to the rule." He had only an eighth-grade education, but since he relied so heavily upon the community norms and his own rule-of-thumb methods, not much education seemed to be required.

In the plant itself, the workers had considerable leeway. The men were able to try different jobs until they found one that they liked, as long as they did it within the general limits of their union regulations. Moreover, they stretched out their lunch hours, were allowed to arrive late as long as they had some excuse, and were not required to keep busy. As long as their work was done, their time was their own. Production records were kept informally.

Many employees used the plant materials and services freely. Men took dynamite home with them to explode in ponds (an easy way to fish), and for construction. They appropriated quantities of wallboard, even truckloads, for their personal use. They brought in broken items such as furniture to be fixed by the carpenters. And both employees and farmers in the area brought in broken parts for free welding. For the workers, the plant was a pleasant and comfortable operation.

But for other interested parties, the plant was not all that satisfying. A jobseeker found it difficult to get work if he was not well known, did not have relatives in the plant, or did not measure up to the vague standards of the personnel man—which had little to do with the ability to do the job. The customer found deliveries erratic. He might also suspect that if all gypsum plants were run this way, he would be paying a surcharge to cover the purloined materials, repair work, and general laziness. Top managers in the company headquarters, faced with intense postwar competition from other companies and competing products, were apparently climbing the walls.

When the plant manager died, headquarters sent in an aggressive new manager with orders to tighten things up—increase productivity and cut costs . . . . This man was not blessed with bountiful tact and insight, even though he was an otherwise efficient manager. He cracked down rather hard and accumulated much ill will. He activated dormant rules, instituted new ones, demoted the personnel man, and brought in one who applied a "universalistic" standard—the only thing that counted was a man's ability to do the job.[1]

Under the old manager, workers in the gypsum plant experienced an easygoing, nonbureaucratic atmosphere. Workers could come and go as they pleased. They could take supplies and equipment for themselves. Hiring decisions were based upon friendship and family ties. Rules and regulations were not enforced, and paperwork was practically nonexistent.

The new plant manager made the gypsum plant more bureaucratic. He instituted and enforced rules, restricted the discretion of employees to do as they pleased, and tried to treat employees and potential employees on an equal basis. Technical ability became the important criterion for hiring or promotion. Employees did not like the change initially, but the plant became more orderly and efficient.

Although the gypsum plant became bureaucratic practically overnight, the bureaucratic form of organization came into being over hundreds of years.[2] During the 20th century, bureaucratic organizations have become widespread, and over the last thirty years bureaucracy has been a major topic of study in organizational sociology. Today, most large organizations are bureaucratic in nature. They provide us with abundant goods and services, and they surprise us with astonishing feats—men to the moon, thousands of airline flights daily without an accident—that are testimony to their effectiveness. On the other hand, bureaucracy is also accused of many sins, including inefficiency, irresponsibility, and the creation of demeaning, routinized work that alienates both employees and the people the organization tries to serve.[3]

Purpose of this Chapter   The purpose of this chapter is to explore the nature of bureaucracy and its role in the design and control of today's large organizations. In the next section, the concept of bureaucracy is defined. Then the relationship between bureaucratic characteristics and organization size is discussed. The impact of growth and decline on bureaucracy is also analyzed. Finally, the economic and social outcomes of bureaucratic organizations is explored. By the end of this chapter, students should understand the nature of bureaucracy, its strengths and weaknesses, and when to use bureaucratic characteristics to make an organization effective.

BUREAUCRACY

The bureaucratic model of organizations was proposed originally by Max Weber.[4] Weber, a sociologist, was concerned with the role of organizations in the larger society. The question he asked was: What form of organization would serve the increasingly industrialized society he observed in Europe at the turn of the century.

His answer was bureaucracy. Bureaucracy seemed to have the characteristics needed to ensure efficient functioning in both government and business settings. Bureaucracies, as Weber envisioned them, would facilitate the allocation of scarce resources in an increasingly complex society. He identified seven characteristics that could be found in bureaucratic organizations.

1. "A continuous organization of official functions bound by rules."[5] Rules and standard operating procedures enable organizational activities to be performed in a predictable, routine manner. Organization personnel thus could depend upon each other, and clients could depend upon the organization for reliable service.
2. "A specified sphere of competence."[6] Specific duties should be divided among people in a clear division of labor, and the job holder should be given the necessary authority to do those duties.
3. "The organization of offices follows the principle of hierarchy; that is, each lower office is under the control and supervision of a higher one."[7] This is what we now call the hierarchy of authority, or chain of command.
4. "Only a person who has demonstrated an adequate technical training is qualified to be a member of the administrative staff . . . and hence only such persons are eligible for appointment to official positions."[8] Technical competence was the basis by which people were hired and assigned to jobs within the organization. Friendship, family ties, and favoritism were not the basis for hiring or promoting people in a bureaucracy.

5. "Members of the administrative staff should be completely separated from ownership of the means of production or administration."[9] Weber felt that separation of ownership maintained the impersonal aspects of organization that were important to production efficiency.
6. "There is a complete absence of appropriation of his official position by the incumbent."[10] Individuals do not take over the rights or property of the office. Weber wanted the conduct of the office to be completely objective and oriented to relevant tasks rather than to serving the personal needs of employees.
7. "Administrative acts, decisions, and rules are formulated and recorded in writing."[11] Recordkeeping provided an organizational memory, and written documents provided continuity over time. Written documents also made up part of the functions and knowledge base for specific jobs.

Ideal Type Today, many of Weber's dimensions seem to be stating the obvious. The organizations we see all around us have rules, a division of labor, written documents, and a hierarchy of authority. Moreover, if Weber's ideas were adopted literally—e.g., everything was written down—the organization would probably bog down under the weight of its own paper, and it would be rigid and inflexible.

Weber was describing an ideal type of organization. Organizational forms prior to industrialization—even today in many non-industrialized countries—seemed improper for the needs of an increasingly complex society. These other forms of organization were based upon favoritism, social status, family connections, personal friends, or some type of feudalism. Graft was also a problem. Office holders often tried to benefit from their position by selling organization services for personal profit. These activities were extremely inefficient and were not in society's interest. By comparison, the logical and rational form of organization described in Weber's ideal model had great potential. Work would be conducted efficiently, and employees would not squander valuable resources.

Bases of Authority The ability of an organization to function efficiently depends upon the authority structure. Authority is the basis for making decisions. Weber argued that legitimate, rational authority was preferred over other types of authority (e.g., payoffs, favoritism) as the basis for internal decisions and activities. Within the larger society, however, Weber identified three types of authority that could explain the creation of an organization and its leadership.[12]

1. Rational-legal authority is based on employees' beliefs in the legality of rules, the division of labor, and the right of those elevated to authority to issue commands. Rational legal authority is the basis for most government organizations.
2. Traditional authority is the belief in the sanctity of traditions and the legitimacy of the status of people exercising authority through those traditions. Traditional authority is the basis for monarchies and churches.

3. Charismatic authority is based upon devotion to the exemplary character or heroism of an individual person and the order defined by him. Revolutionary military organizations are often based on the leader's charisma.

The internal activities of organizations require rational-legal authority. But the reason for the organization's existence could be tradition or charisma. A religious or a military organization may exist because of tradition or charisma, but rational-legal authority would govern internal work activities and decision-making.

The important outcome of Weber's work is his specification of organizational characteristics that provide rationality in the pursuit of an organization's goals. Table 4.1 summarizes the seven dimensions of bureaucracy and the three types of authority envisioned by Weber. The bureaucratic model had the potential for objectivity and impersonality in the hiring, firing, and promotion processes. Technical competence was preferable to family ties or social status as the basis for holding a position. Rules and the division of labor promoted efficiency. Nonbureaucratic forms of organization seemed wasteful and inefficient compared to Weber's model.

Table 4.1. Weber's Dimensions of Bureaucracy and Bases of Organizational Authority.

Bureaucracy	Legitimate Bases of Authority
1. Rules and procedures	1. Rational-legal
2. Specialization and division of labor	2. Tradition
3. Hierarchy of authority	3. Charisma
4. Technically qualified personnel	
5. Position and incumbent are separate	
6. Impersonality	
7. Written communications and records	

IN PRACTICE 4.1

United Parcel Service

United Parcel Service has taken on the United States Post Office at its own game, and won. UPS specializes in the delivery of small packages. It can deliver a package anywhere in the United States for $2–$3. UPS sees itself in price competition with the Post Office so it sets prices below Post Office rates. Unlike the Post Office, UPS pays taxes on real estate, income, and fuel, and cannot subsidize packages with revenue from first-class letters. UPS still makes an excellent profit.

Why has UPS been so successful? There are several reasons, but two important ones are automation and bureaucracy. Automation is visible in the 100 mechanized hubs that can sort 40 thousand packages per hour. A new center under construction will sort 60 thousand packages per hour. UPS handles 6 million packages a day. UPS is so efficient that it can send a truck to pick up packages from a home or business, deliver packages door-to-door, and still make money.

Many efficiencies are realized through adoption of the bureaucratic model of organization. UPS is bound up in rules and regulations. There are safety rules for drivers, loaders, clerks, and managers. Strict dress codes are enforced—no beards, hair cannot touch the collar, no side-burns, mustaches must be trimmed evenly and cannot go below the corner of the mouth, etc. Rules specify the cleanliness of buildings and property. All UPS delivery trucks must be washed inside and out at the end of every day. Each manager is given bound copies of policy books with the expectation of regular use.

Jobs are broken down into a clearly defined division of labor. UPS plants consist of specialized drivers, loaders, clerks, washers, sorters, and maintenance personnel. The hierarchy of authority is clearly defined and has eight levels, extending from a washer at the local UPS plant up to the president of the national organization.

Technical qualification is the criterion for hiring and promotion. The UPS policy books says, "A leader does not have to remind others of authority by use of a title. Knowledge, performance, and capacity should be adequate evidence of position and leadership." Favoritism is forbidden. Each person sets performance goals and has equal opportunity to succeed. Promotions and salary increments are based on rational criteria, not on a person's background or position in the organization.

Finally, UPS thrives on written records. Daily worksheets that specify performance goals and work output are kept on every employee and department. Operating costs and production runs are recorded and compared to competitors'. Daily employee quotas and achievements are accumulated on a weekly and monthly basis. Computer systems have been installed to facilitate the recordkeeping process.[13]

UPS is a living example of Weber's bureaucracy. Rational-legal authority is the basis for UPS's bureaucratic design. In this organization, bureaucratic structure is an important reason for an excellent record of performance and growth.

ORGANIZATION SIZE AND BUREAUCRACY

Large organizations typically have bureaucratic characteristics such as rules, division of labor, and a clear hierarchy of authority. One question of interest to both organization managers and scholars is the effect of organization size. Should the organization become more bureaucratic as it grows larger? When are bureaucratic characteristics most appropriate?

Over one hundred studies have attempted to answer these questions.[14] Most of these studies indicate that large organizations are very different from small organizations along several dimensions of structure.

Formalization Formalization, as described in chapter 1, refers to rules, procedures, and written documentation such as policy manuals and job descriptions. The evidence supports the conclusion that large organizations are more formalized. The reason is that large organizations rely on rules, procedures, and paperwork to achieve standardization and control across the large number of employees and departments. Personal supervision by top management can be used to control a small organization. In large firms, formalization of procedures allows top administrators to use impersonal means of control. Rules take the place of personal surveillance.[15]

IN PRACTICE 4.2

Johns-Manville

Major companies all over the United States are inserting new pages into their rule books and policy manuals. Why? Sexual harassment. Company surveys have shown that unwelcome physical or verbal advances pervade the workplace and increase employee absenteeism and turnover. Companies are also learning about the problem from the increase in complaints by women at all levels. Another corporate eye opener has been the sting of lawsuits. The federal government and the courts have ruled that sexual harassment is illegal discrimination in employment. Several major employers have lost lawsuits charging them with failure to act against harassment.

The courts became involved when a vice president of Johns-Manville Corporation pressured Mary K. Heelan to have an affair with him. As her refusals became more adamant, he began sabotaging her work. Finally, the vice president threatened to dismiss her. Heelan refused to go along and found herself out of a job. She sued Johns-Manville. In a landmark decision, the district court awarded in her favor. Johns-Manville made an out-of-court settlement for a reported $100,000.

Until a few years ago, most companies did not have official policies on sexual harassment. Now, almost all large companies are updating policy manuals. General Motors, General Electric, Bank of America, IBM, GTE, and numerous city, state, and federal agencies are acting to curb harassment in their organizations.

These companies are large and diverse so that specific guidance is needed to standardize behavior. Most policies spell out no-nos. American Telephone and Telegraph Company's policy says employees can be fired for "repeated, offensive flirtations," or for using "sexually degrading words" to describe someone. The U.S. Army goes even further. It recently ordered an end to soldiers' cat calls, whistles, terms such as "honey" or "baby" around women, and the wearing of T-shirts imprinted with sexual language.[16]

In the cases of AT&T and the U.S. Army, which are huge organizations, rules specify behavior down to very small details. Management uses rules and policies to achieve an acceptable standard of behavior across a large number of people. The example of sexual discrimination also suggests that rules have two sides—rules restrict the freedom of employees to engage in certain behavior, but rules also protect employees and encourage equal treatment for everyone.

Decentralization Decentralization refers to the level of hierarchy that has authority to make decisions. In centralized organizations, decisions tend to be made at the top. In decentralized organizations, similar decisions would be made at a lower level. The research on organization size indicates that large organizations (e.g., IBM, Burroughs) permit greater decentralization.[17] The explanation is that large organizations have longer chains of command and a greater number of people and departments. Decisions simply cannot be passed to the top of the hierarchy, or senior managers would be overloaded. In addition, greater formalization reduces variability within the organization so that decisions can be made at a lower level without loss of control.

Complexity As discussed in chapter 1, complexity refers to both the number of levels in the hierarchy (vertical complexity) and the number of departments or jobs (horizontal complexity). Large organizations show a definite pattern of greater complexity.[18] The explanation for the relationship between size and complexity is straightforward. First, the need for additional specialties occurs more often in large organizations. For example, a study of new departments reported that new administrative departments were often created by problems of large size.[19] A planning department was established in a large organization because a greater need for planning arose after a certain size was reached.

Second, a large organization can add a new specialty at a much smaller proportional expense than can a small organization. Hiring two new planners to work in a new department is a trivial expense in an organization with a $100,000,000 budget, but will be a substantial expense when the budget is $100,000 or so. Third, as departments within the organization grow in size, pressure to subdivide arises. Departments eventually get so large that managers cannot control them effectively. At this point, subgroups will lobby to be subdivided into separate departments.[20]

The creation of new departments also adds to size.[21] The addition of a new department reflects a commitment to the new activity, so new employees are hired to perform that activity. Size and horizontal complexity thus influence one another.

Finally, vertical complexity is needed to maintain control over a large number of people. As the number of employees increases, additional levels of hierarchy keep spans of control from becoming too large. In both vertical and horizontal directions, then, large organizations are vastly more complex than small organizations.

Administrative Ratio The most frequently studied structural variable is the administrative ratio. In 1957, C. Northcote Parkinson published *Parkinson's Law,* which argued that work expands to fill the time available for its completion.[22] He developed an argument to show that there was no relationship between the amount of work to be done within an organization and the number of administrators required to perform that work. Parkinson argued that administrators were motivated to add more administrators for a variety of reasons, including the enhancement of their own status through empire-building. Parkinson used his argument to make fun of the British Admiralty. During a fourteen-year period from 1914 to 1928, the officer corps increased by 78%, although the total navy personnel decreased by 32% and the number of warships in use decreased by approximately 68%. Parkinson's book made large organizations seem very inefficient, and provided the impetus for scholars to survey organizations to learn whether cumbersome administrative ratios were widespread.

In the years since Parkinson's book, the administrative ratio has been studied in school systems, churches, hospitals, employment agencies, and other business and voluntary organizations.[23] Two clear patterns have emerged.

The first pattern is that the ratio of top administration to total employment is smaller in large organizations.[24] This is exactly the opposite of Parkinson's argument, and indicates that organizations may experience administrative economies as they grow larger. Large organizations have larger departments, more regulations, and a greater division of labor. These mechanisms require less supervision from the top. Increasing bureaucratization is a substitute for personal supervision. The ratio of top administrators to workers is actually smaller in large organizations.

The second pattern concerns other personnel support components. Recent studies have subdivided support personnel into subclassifications such as clerical, maintenance, and professional staff.[25] These support groups tend to increase in proportion to organization size. The clerical ratio increases in size because of the greater communication (memos, letters) and paperwork requirements (policy manuals, job descriptions) in large organizations. Plant maintenance also increases with organization size, and so do professional staff support groups.[26] The increase in these specialties is explained by the division of labor. In a small organization, an individual may be a "jack of all trades." In a large organization, people spend full time on specific activities.

IN PRACTICE 4.3

Cook County School Districts

The administrative and support ratios for small and large organizations are plotted graphically in figure 4.1 for school districts in suburban Cook County, Illinois. Figure 4.1 indicates that from the smallest school district (500 students) to the largest school district (over 16,000 students),

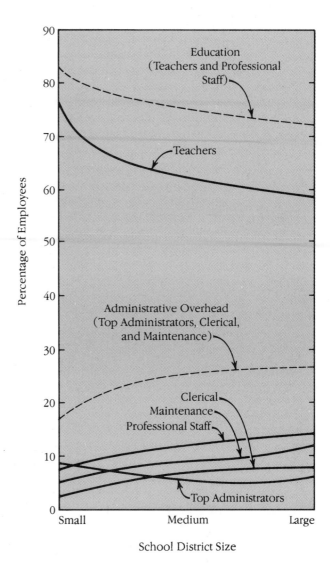

Figure 4.1. Percentage of Personnel Allocated to Teaching and Support Activities. Source: Richard L. Daft and Selwyn W. Becker, "District Size and the Deployment of Personnel Resources," *The Alberta Journal of Educational Research* 24 (1978): 181, with permission.

the administrative ratio declined from about 9% to 7% of total employment. Other support groups, such as clerical (3% to 8%), building maintenance (6% to 13%), and professional staff (8% to 15%) all were a much larger percentage of employment in large districts. The net effect for teachers is that they declined from 74% of employees in the smallest district to 57% in the largest district.

To learn whether large organizations require more total support personnel, the administrative, clerical, and maintenance groups were combined. These personnel represent total administrative overhead. Professional staff provide counseling services to students and other people in the community, so they were combined with teachers to reflect the number of people assigned to the educational task. As shown in figure 4.1 (broken line), all education-related staff decreased from 82% to 72% of employees from small to large districts. For support personnel, the finding was the opposite. The percentage decline in top administrators was more than offset by increases in the clerical and maintenance areas. All support personnel increased from 18% to 28% of employees when comparing small and large school districts.[27]

The literature on administrative ratio both supports and disconfirms intuitive ideas that were the basis for this research. Top administrators do not increase their own number disproportionately in large organizations; in fact, they decrease as a percentage of total employment. Top administrators do not build empires, as proposed by Parkinson. However, the idea that proportionately greater administrative overhead is required in large organizations is supported. People in clerical and maintenance departments increase at a faster rate than people who work in the technical core of the organization.

RELATIONSHIPS AMONG BUREAUCRATIC DIMENSIONS

The previous discussion indicates that large organizations are structured differently than small organizations. Students can observe these differences in their own university. Students at large state universities have had lots of experience with bureaucratic structure. Often they have to wait in line to register or see an advisor and they have to wade through all kinds of red tape to enroll in class or to graduate. Certain forms have to be filled out in certain ways to get things done. These students have experienced the "run around" to get a task accomplished or to obtain information. Because of extreme specialization, they have to search through the bureaucracy until they find just the right person to help them.

Procedures in small colleges are quite different. Students might have many things handled on a casual basis. A request might be granted without ever being written down. Red tape is nonexistent. University employees may have experience with a variety of tasks and be able to help students with a number of problems or tasks.

The differences between small and large organizations are summarized in table 4.2. Larger organizations have many characteristics that distinguish them from small organizations: more rules and regulations; more paperwork, written communication, and documentation; greater specialization; more decentralization and delegation; a lower percentage of people devoted to administration; and a larger percentage of people allocated to clerical, maintenance, and professional support staff.

Table 4.2.   Relationship Between Size and Other Organization Characteristics.

Greater organization size is associated with:
1. Increased number of management levels (vertical complexity).
2. Greater number of jobs and departments (horizontal complexity).
3. Increased specialization of skills and functions.
4. Greater formalization.
5. Greater decentralization.
6. Smaller percentage of top administrators.
7. Greater percentage of technical and professional support.
8. Greater percentage of clerical and maintenance support.
9. Greater amount of written communications and documentation.

An important additional point is that size does not cause variables by itself. As organizations increase in size, bureaucratic characteristics tend to influence each other as well as being influenced by size. Figure 4.2 summarizes several relationships among structural characteristics.[28] This figure illustrates that an increase in size has its greatest impact on division of labor and hierarchy of authority (complexity). Division of labor requires greater supervision and coordination to ensure that separate parts of the organization work together. The multilevel hierarchy of authority requires greater decentralization because people at the top become overloaded. Decentralization, in turn, increases formalization, which is a substitute for personal supervision and helps provide uniformity and standardization across the organization. The increased division of labor also leads to greater support staff because staff jobs are now separate from the technical core. Formalization and decentralization reduce the need for top administrators. Rules take the place of personal surveillance, and middle managers take over some decision-making. Size is thus a major cause of organizational bureaucracy. Bureaucratic characteristics also influence each other so that large organizations become more bureaucratic along several dimensions. Bureaucracy helps meet the great need for coordination and administrative control in large organizations.

IN PRACTICE 4.4

Sears, Roebuck and Co.

During its 92-year history, Sears has been the envy of the retail industry. It has built stores in excellent suburban locations, and has found innovative products to sell at low cost. Sears has brought novel product lines (Allstate Insurance, optometrists) into its stores, and has been consistently profitable.

No one envies Sears today. Sears has become known as a high-cost operator. With its huge size and cumbersome cost structure, Sears needs a 50% markup to make a profit on items when competitors need a

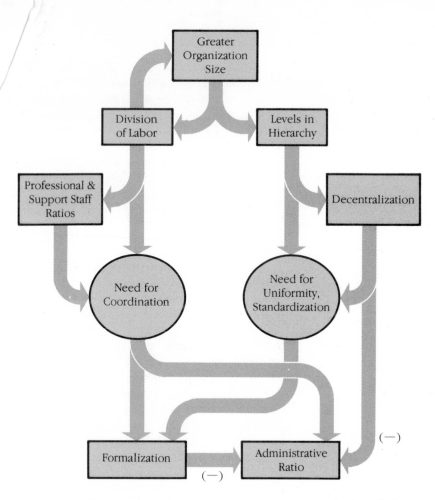

Figure 4.2. Negative and Positive Relationships among Size and Selected Elements of Bureaucratic Structure.

markup of only 35%. Its huge size seems to have gotten the better of Sears. Management is trying to gain control over the layers of managers and the huge support staffs that have grown up in an empire of 900 stores, 12,000 suppliers, and 400,000 employees.

Sears may have reached the size where it can no longer compete on price with smaller retail chains. Sears tries to be efficient, and has excellent internal systems, such as for inventory control. But overhead expenses are eating them up. Sears has the highest cost in the business. Overhead and administrative expenses siphon off 29.9% of Sears' sales dollar (on $25 billion sales). By comparison, K-Mart has 23% overhead expenses ($14 billion sales) and Walmart 15.3% ($1.6 billion sales).

Sears' top management is trying to streamline its operation, but will have to weed out at least $100 million a year in overhead expenses to be competitive in a low-cost market. Top management at this point is directing Sears' retail business toward middle- and upper-middle-class consumers where price is less important. In the meantime, new growth and profits are expected to come from ventures into non-retail areas, such as insurance and financial services.[29]

Sears is a giant corporation. Its structure reflects a combination of bureaucratic characteristics. Top management is beginning to realize that Sears is intrinsically different from smaller retail chains. Sears no longer can compete on the basis of low overhead costs or a flexible structure. Sears will do best in competition for a more affluent retail customer.

ORGANIZATIONAL GROWTH AND BUREAUCRACY

Reasons for Growth Why do organizations grow? Why should they grow? The material described so far in this chapter has compared large organizations to small organizations. A few investigators have tried to understand the gradual growth and evolutionary processes that take place within an organization. This type of research traces the organization's development over time. The impact of growth on bureaucracy and structure is observed directly. The evidence indicates many reasons why organizations grow. The following reasons are most important.

Organizational Self-Realization Self-realization refers to managers' beliefs that the organization should become complete, carry out new functions, and make progress.[30] Customers may want a complete service or product line from a single company. Managers also feel pressure to face and conquer new challenges. Those are the reasons for growth at Campbell Taggart.

Campbell Taggart, Inc. bakes bread. They bake a lot of it, and are the second largest producer in the country (after Wonder Bread). White bread, Campbell Taggart's major product, has hit a wall. The demand for white bread is no longer growing. Top management wants to grow larger and round out the line with related products. Over the last few years, Campbell Taggart moved into dinner and sweet rolls, and have begun producing a high-quality, high-priced line of pastries, cookies, and cakes. They have also started baking for ethnic tastes. The major ethnic line is bread for Spanish tastes in the Southwest. The Earth Grain bread line was added to satisfy demand for natural foods. More recently, Campbell Taggart has moved further afield into other food lines, including salad dressings and sandwiches for institutional use. The most recent venture was to acquire El Chico restaurants, a full-service restaurant chain. Executives now feel that Campbell Taggart is a well-rounded company, and has the strength for continued success. A soft spot in one product line can be offset by strength in other lines.[31]

Executive Mobility A record of growth is often necessary to attract and keep quality managers. A growing organization offers greater prestige and better salaries than a stagnating one. Growing organizations are an exciting place to work. There are many challenges and opportunities for advancement when the number of employees is expanding. If an organization were stable or declining, the best executives may go elsewhere.[32]

Economic Factors   Organizational growth has many financial benefits. Costs can be reduced because economies of scale in manufacturing or production are possible. Revenues can be increased, especially if greater size gives the organization additional power in the marketplace. Growth through vertical integration or acquisition of other firms can ensure stability, long life, and high profits for the organization.[33]

Survival   Survival may be the most important reason of all to grow. A survey of executives found that, "If firms do not expand, they contract; they cannot stand still."[34] Competitors develop new products and try to increase their share of the market at the expense of your organization. To be stable, to relax, or to accept decline may signal the ultimate demise of the organization. The administrator of a hospital said that he could not restrict growth. If the hospital turned away patients for any reason, they would feel unwanted and go elsewhere. If a large number of patients went elsewhere, the hospital would be in severe trouble. Hospital administrators have to anticipate and increase facilities sufficient to meet the demand for their services.

Hence, there are many motives for growth. Growth is a goal for most organizations. But the process of growth is not easy. Organizations have growing pains. Growth is associated with a series of crises that must be met and solved if growth is to continue.

Stages of Growth   A useful model of organizational growth was proposed by Larry Greiner.[35] Greiner observed that organizations often got into trouble when their specific structure was not appropriate to the organization's stage of growth and development. A small research organization that had a complicated and formalized structure, for example, was too bureaucratized to adapt to changing needs. Greiner examined historical studies of organizations, and combined those findings with his own research to identify the dominant issues and crises that faced growing organizations. He called the period before and after each crisis a new phase of development. The series of crises are summarized in figure 4.3.

Phase One: Creativity   The organization is born, and the emphasis is on creating a product and surviving in the marketplace. The founders are entrepreneurs, and they devote full energies to the technical activities of production and marketing. The organization is informal and nonbureaucratic. The hours of work are long. Control is based on the owner's personal supervision.

- *Leadership Crisis:*   As the organization starts to grow, the larger number of employees causes problems. The technically oriented owners have to deal with management issues, but they prefer to be involved with making or selling the product. The organization enters a crisis because the founders are not skilled or interested in management activities. They may restrict growth. If the organization continues to grow, it may flounder. A strong manager is needed who can introduce management techniques.

Phase Two: Direction If the leadership crisis is resolved, strong leadership is obtained and the organization begins to develop clear goals and direction. Departments are established along with a hierarchy of authority, job assignments, and a beginning division of labor. Management systems for accounting, budgets, inventory, and purchasing may be introduced. Communication may become more formal. Elements of bureaucracy are becoming apparent.

- *The Autonomy Crisis:* If the new management techniques have been successful, lower-level employees gradually find themselves restricted by the strong leadership and increasing bureaucracy. Lower-level managers begin to acquire confidence in their own functional areas and want more discretion. The autonomy crisis occurs when top managers, who were successful by strong leadership and vision, do not want to give up responsibility. Lower-level managers may not be used to decision-making, even though they desire it.

Figure 4.3. Five Stages of Growth.
Source: Reprinted by permission of the *Harvard Business Review.* Exhibit from "Evolution and Revolution as Organizations Grow" by L. E. Greiner, July–August, 1972, p. 41. Copyright © 1972 by the President and Fellows of Harvard College; all rights reserved.

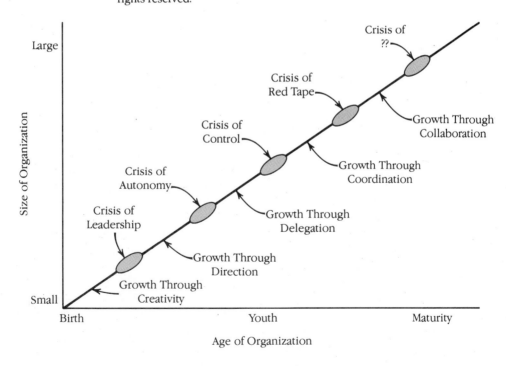

Phase Three: Delegation   The next phase involves formal delegation and decentralization by top management. Greater responsibility is given to middle managers who may be in charge of plants or market territories. Top management becomes concerned with top management issues such as strategy and planning, and leaves the operation of the firm to lower-level management. Internal control and information systems are installed and used. Communication is less frequent and more formal. New products and new employee specialists may be added.

- *The Control Crisis:*   As middle- and lower-level managers become more autonomous, top executives often sense that the organization is going in several directions at once. Top management needs to make sure that all parts of the organization are pulling in the same direction. Too much autonomy can result in decreased performance. In order to surmount this crisis, the organization needs to find new techniques to coordinate the increased number of departments and activities.

Phase Four: Coordination   The response to the control crisis is sophisticated techniques of coordination. Staff personnel and specialists may be hired to review company-wide programs. Product groups or other decentralized units may be formed to improve coordination. Incentive systems, based upon profits, may be implemented to ensure that managers work toward what is best for the overall company. The new coordination systems, when effective, enable the organization to continue growing by establishing linkage mechanisms between top management and field units.

- *The Red-Tape Crisis:*   At this point in the organization's development, the proliferation of systems and programs may begin to strangle middle-level executives. The organization seems over-bureaucratized. Middle management may resent the intrusion of staff people and top management. Innovation may be restricted. The organization seems too large and complex to be managed through formal programs.

Phase Five: Collaboration   The solution to the red-tape crisis is a new sense of collaboration and cooperation. Throughout the organization, managers develop skills for confronting problems and resolving interpersonal differences. Bureaucracy may have reached its limit. Social control and self-discipline reduce the need for additional formal controls. Managers learn to work within the bureaucracy without adding to it. This learning process may require the assistance of outside consultants. In order to achieve collaboration, teams may be formed across functions or divisions of the company. Formal systems may be simplified and partially replaced by manager conferences and task forces.

Generations of employees may pass by the time the organization reaches its final stage of development. Over that period of time, the stages of development reflect patterns similar to those observed in the earlier discussion of size and bureaucracy. As the organization grows, there is movement toward formalization and decentralization. Additional complexity arises from new product lines and specialties. Acquisition of staff personnel increases the clerical and staff ratios. The work by Greiner provides insight into the incremental processes that lead to increased bureaucratization in large organizations.

IN PRACTICE 4.5

Bill Sauey of Flambeau Corp.

"I was killing myself trying to manage 500 employees spread out in five plants around the country, running three shifts a day," says Bill Sauey, sitting in an office cluttered with plastic toys, housewares, sporting goods, and industrial parts. "After 25 years of keeping everything under my control, I decided there had to be a better way."

The better way Sauey found was to chop his company, Flambeau Corp., into pieces and turn over control of the pieces to a group of independent general managers. Before Sauey made the change at the beginning of 1979, Flambeau was highly centralized. The company, which manufactures plastic products, had grown steadily to $24 million with Sauey running the whole show. But as Flambeau got larger and larger, the pressure to continue that growth became too much for one man to handle. Today, Sauey presides over a company with six independent divisions under six managers—and sales have jumped to $35 million.

Sauey started Flambeau Corp. in 1947. From that point on, he guided Flambeau singlehandedly. By 1965, it had reached $10 million in sales. Sauey signed all the checks, bought all the plant equipment, interviewed all potential employees, and played a role in developing and selling all Flambeau's products. The company was a testament to his persistence and his conviction that he could solve any business problem. So he continued to manage the company in his own tightly controlled way even though there were signs that this style wasn't working so well anymore . . . .

"I didn't want to decentralize authority," says Sauey, "because I thought I'd lose the ability to get my message across and get the job done effectively." Sauey continued to make all important budgetary, sales, marketing, and production decisions for both the Georgia and Wichita plants, and he couldn't find a manager who wanted to work under those conditions.

It was the sheer weight of details Sauey wanted to keep under his control that finally led to an uncharacteristic decision—he gave up control over one part of the company. This happened in 1977 when Flambeau acquired Vlchek Plastics Co. in Middlefield, Ohio. In the past, Sauey had always merged acquisitions into the central organization. "But I didn't this time," he says, "because I was so busy with the rest of the company—which by now had 500 employees working in five plants—that I knew if I brought it into our system, I'd screw it up."

Two things happened. Vlchek's sales began doubling annually, and for once, Sauey didn't feel insecure about his lack of direct control. "I was really surprised at how little I worried about what went on at Vlchek," he says, his voice still registering amazement.

Unlike the early days, Sauey couldn't just work harder to make things go; he was already overworked and tired, and he was feeling the pressure of trying to hold the company together while the forces of growth were pulling things apart.

"I was sitting at home one night after a frantic day at work, and I made up my mind. I just said to myself, 'By God, I've got to do it.'"

Things moved very fast after that. Sauey wrote up a reorganization manual that spelled out how he was going to decentralize Flambeau and give authority to general managers who would report to him but have the freedom to run their division as they saw fit. It had taken him seven years, though, to decide that it was fundamental to Flambeau's growth.[36]

The Bill Sauey example illustrates how difficult it is for an owner/manager to let go and delegate after having been solely responsible for building a successful organization. But refusing to adapt to the structural needs of the organization as it entered a new stage of development would create a genuine crisis, which could have caused the stagnation of Flambeau Corp.

Summary of Structural Conditions and Growth The crises identified by Greiner may occur at different times for each organization, depending upon rate of growth, industry, and management style. Most organizations evolve through three major cycles in their life, within which the crises occur. These major stages in the life cycle are birth, youth, and maturity. Each stage is associated with distinct organization structure and internal conditions, which are summarized in table 4.3.

Birth Initially, the organization is small, nonbureaucratic, and a one-man show. The top manager provides the structure and control system. Organizational energy is devoted toward survival and the production of a single product or service.

Youth During organizational youth, bureaucratic characteristics emerge. The organization adds staff support groups, formalizes procedures, and establishes a clear division of labor. Top management has to provide some delegation, but also implements formal control systems. The organization may develop complementary products to offer a complete product line.

Maturity The mature organization is large and bureaucratic, with extensive control systems, rules, and procedures. Organization managers attempt to develop a team orientation within the bureaucracy and prevent further bureaucratization. Top managers are concerned with establishing a complete organization. Organizational stature and reputation are important. Change procedures are institutionalized through an R&D department. Management is no longer concerned with survival and may be frustrated with the bureaucracy.

Table 4.3. Organization Characteristics During Three Stages of Life Cycle.

Characteristic	I Birth	II Youth	III Maturity
	Nonbureaucratic	Bureaucratic	Very Bureaucratic
Structure	Informal, one-man show	Formal procedures, division of labor, add new specialties	Teams work within bureaucracy
Products/ Services	Single product/ service	Product/ service line	Multiple lines
Reward and Control Systems	Personal, paternalistic	Impersonal, formalized systems	Extensive, tailored to product and department
Innovation	By owner/ manager	Separate innovation group	Institutionalized R & D
Strategic Issue	Survival	Reputation, stability, expand market	Uniqueness, complete organization
Top Management Style	Individualistic, entrepeneurial	Delegation with control	Participation, team approach

Source: Adapted from Larry E. Greiner, "Evolution and Revolution as Organizations Grow," *Harvard Business Review,* 50 (July-August, 1972): 37–46; and G. L. Lippitt and W. H. Schmidt, "Crises in a Developing Organization," *Harvard Business Review,* 45 (Nov.–Dec., 1967): 102–112; B. R. Scott, "The Industrial State: Old Myths and New Realities," *Harvard Business Review,* 51 (March-April, 1973): 133–148.

BUREAUCRACY AND PERFORMANCE

Economic Performance

An important question for organizational design is whether bureaucratic characteristics are associated with organizational performance. John Child surveyed business corporations in England.[37] He measured their bureaucratic characteristics and controlled for size. We would expect bureaucracy to be associated with high performance in large corporations because bureaucracy is needed for coordination and control. Child's findings are summarized in figure 4.4. The sloped lines indicate that as organizations grow larger, higher performance is indeed related to degree of bureaucracy. Corporations that stay informal do less well if they are large. For small organizations (less than 2,000 employees), the high performing companies were less bureaucratized. This evidence supports a positive relationship among size, bureaucracy, and performance.

Criticisms of Bureaucracy

Child's analysis of bureaucracy and performance was concerned with profit and other economic indicators. Organizational performance as discussed in chapter 2 includes many dimensions, such as employee satisfaction and internal health and well-being. Large, bureaucratic organizations have come under criticism for noneconomic dimensions of performance. Bureaucratic

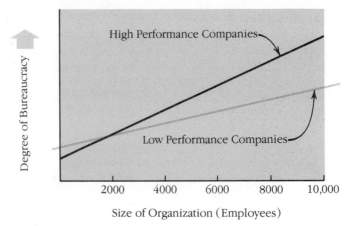

Figure 4.4. Size of Organization, Bureaucracy, and Performance.
Adapted from John Child, "Managerial and Organizational Factors Associated with
Company Performance—Part II. A Contingency Analysis," *Journal of Management
Studies* 12 (1975): 12–27.

organizations, with their rules, paperwork, and impersonality, are often seen
as a problem for society, not as a solution. Specific criticisms usually pertain
to employee dissatisfaction, resistance to change, and poor system management. A summary of these criticisms, as well as arguments in defense of
bureaucracy, are given in table 4.4.

Employee Satisfaction One of the most compelling arguments against
bureaucracy is that extensive rules, standardization, and specialization stifle
spontaneity, freedom, and the opportunity for challenging work. Bureaucracy
does not take advantage of human potential. Bureaucracy does not allow for
personal growth. Employees are dehumanized, and the result is job dissatisfaction and alienation.[38]

Bureaucracies are sometimes guilty of creating work that is not challenging. In many cases, however, bureaucracy actually has advantages for employees. Rules and regulations reduce uncertainty and protect employees
from management whims and arbitrary decisions. An example is the rule
against sexual discrimination described in In Practice 4.2. Regulations are
a two-edged sword, and employees can invoke rules for their own protection.[39] The absence of rules, such as in the gypsum plant described at the
beginning of this chapter, can cause as many problems as too many rules.
Furthermore, the bureaucratic division of labor into specialized tasks enables
employees to acquire skills and technical competence needed for successful
performance and career development.[40]

Change The second criticism is that bureaucratic characteristics act as a
barrier to performance. The world is changing rapidly, and bureaucracies
are unable to keep up. Bureaucratic characteristics promote rigidity, lack of
response, and poor adaptation.[41]

Table 4.4. Criticism and Defense of Bureaucracy.

Criticism	Defense
Employee Satisfaction	
Rules stifle spontaneity and restrict freedom. Rules reduce discretion.	Rules reduce uncertainty and capriciousness, and protect employees. Absence of rules causes more problems than too many rules.
Small jobs do not challenge people, and alienation results.	Specialization often enables in-depth skill acquisition and opportunity for professionalism.
Change	
Bureacracy causes rigidity, slow response, and lack of innovation.	Bureaucracy guarantees uniform behavior and responses. Security and tenure encourage risk-taking.
Management	
Bureaucracies are too complex. No one can comprehend them.	Strength of bureaucracy is that it overcomes cognitive limits of individuals. Can perform tasks far too complex for individuals.
Control and coordination of system is difficult.	Bureaucratic structure (rules, hierarchy of authority, etc.) provide control and coordination.

Again, there is merit to this argument, especially in the case of rapidly changing environments. The defense of bureaucracy is that they provide uniformity and predictability of behavior within the organization. Sometimes innovation may be slow, but in return the organization gains efficient and reliable performance. In addition, the security and tenure associated with bureaucracy may encourage risk-taking.[42] Bureaucracy is best suited to stable and moderately changing environments.

Management Large bureaucracies seem unmanageable. They are incredibly complex. No single person can comprehend them. One department does not know what other departments are doing. Coordination and control from a central source are difficult. Top managers must rely on staff experts and support personnel who themselves may not comprehend more than a small piece of the total system.[43]

Proponents of bureaucracy argue that the complexity of the system, far from being a disadvantage, is the true strength of bureaucracy. Individuals have limited cognitive ability. The division of labor in organizations enables bureaucracies to achieve outcomes far beyond the comprehension and ability of individual managers.[44] Moreover, bureaucratic characteristics hold the system together. Rules, hierarchy of authority, and division of labor are mechanisms that enable managers to coordinate and control the entire system.

McDonald's

McDonald's Corporation has experienced a Cinderella story of growth and profits. According to McDonald's executives, the reason for McDonald's corporate success is product consistency and uniformity. A person buying a McDonald's hamburger will receive the same product whether it is purchased in College Station, Texas, or College Park, Maryland. A customer can also expect the same level of quality from one purchase to the next at the local McDonald's store. To achieve this uniformity, each store must be stamped from the same mold. The McDonald's mold was designed and maintained through the use of professional staff specialists and extensive bureaucracy. Equally important, McDonald's takes care of its employees, and adapts to changes in the environment. McDonald's has taken advantage of size and bureaucracy without succumbing to organizational rigidity or employee dissatisfaction.

Rules and regulations are the gospel at McDonald's. The company's operating bible has 385 pages describing the most minute activities in each outlet. The manual prescribes that certain equipment—cigarettes, candy, and pinball machines—is not permitted in the stores. It also prescribes strict standards for personal grooming. Men must keep their hair short and their shoes black and highly polished. Women are expected to wear hair nets and to use only very light makeup. The store manager is even provided with a maintenance reminder for each day of the year, such as "Lubricate and adjust potato-peeler belt."

McDonald's has a passion for standardization of products and work activities. The basic hamburger patty must be a machine-cut, 1.6-ounce chunk of pure beef—no lungs, hearts, cereal, soybean, or other fillers—with no more than 19% fat content. Hamburger buns must have 13.3% sugar in them. Milkshakes must be thick enough to stand a straw in them. French fries are kept under the light for only seven minutes. A flashing light cues the cook to the exact moment to flip the hamburger patties. Specially designed scoops determine the precise number of fries to fit in each pouch. The standardization of work reduces discretion of employees, but provides uniformity and consistency of products for consumers.

McDonald's employs a large number of staff specialists. Field service managers visit each store regularly. An inspector will observe each store for three days, timing the counter and drive-through operations, and checking cooking procedures. Grades of A through F are given for cleanliness, quality, and service. If low grades are received, the inspector will come back unannounced and check again. If problems persist, the franchise may be taken away from the owner.

Each store has a refined division of labor. Assistant managers are assigned to cover each shift, and crew leaders are responsible for specific periods, such as breakfast or lunch. Cooks and waitresses know exactly what to do. Trainers teach new employees the exact procedure for greeting customers and taking orders. Hostesses are assigned the task of helping young children and old people, and they coordinate birthday parties and make sure customers are comfortable. Stores also have a community relations representative who coordinates McDonald's activities in the community.

McDonald's wants each employee to be happy, cheerful, and friendly toward customers. Employees are given the opportunity to move up quickly within the organization, and are encouraged to do so. Motivational programs include employee contests, crew member of the month recognition, incentive pay for crew productivity, and monetary bonuses for outstanding service.

Research and marketing departments gently push innovation and change. Gradual environmental change takes place in two environmental domains: competition and population migration. McDonald's adapts to migration by building new stores. It adapts to the competition by introducing new products, and by advertising. Chicken McNuggets were tested for six years and were recently released to stores. The chain's image and competitive position are maintained through extensive, high-quality advertising that has won several awards.[45]

McDonald's is a bureaucracy without the disadvantages. Rules, standardization, and division of labor lead to efficient and reliable performance. Top management also pays attention to employee well-being and to innovation. Special programs overcome the disadvantages that might occur in such a large, bureaucratic organization.

WHEN TO BE NONBUREAUCRATIC

Performance is not always improved by increasing bureaucratic characteristics. Bureaucracy certainly has its benefits, but should not be used when organizations are small, when employees are highly professional, or when the environment is unstable.

Small Size The theme throughout this chapter has been that bureaucratic characteristics are associated with large size. Small organizations should be nonbureaucratic. Small organizations should be informal and have minimum rules and paperwork. Managers can control the organization through personal supervision and face-to-face interaction with employees. Maintaining bureaucracy would waste employees' time. As Child's study of the relationship between size and performance indicated, small organizations were more effective when they were less bureaucratic.

Professional Employees Professionalism was defined in chapter 1 as the length of formal training and experience of employees. Through extensive training, professionals are socialized toward high standards of performance. They have extensive knowledge and are able to work without close supervision or extensive rules and regulations. In recent years, large numbers of young professionals have joined organizations. It is common to see departments of attorneys, researchers, or doctors at General Motors, K-Mart, and other organizations that would be considered nonprofessional.

The mixing of professionals and bureaucracy causes a conflict, because professionals desire freedom from bureaucratic rules and authority. Studies of professionals show that formalization and professionalization do the same thing—organize and regularize behavior of the members of the organization.[46] The experience, training, and socialization of professionals act as a substitute for bureaucracy. Professionals respond better in departments that have fewer rules and regulations. A research and development group, for instance, should have fewer hierarchical levels, fewer rules, and a more collegial atmosphere than other departments in the organization. By debureaucratizing professional departments, the needs of professionals can be met while maintaining the advantage of bureaucratic structure for the overall organization. When the entire organization is made up of professionals, such as in a consulting firm or a medical practice, managers should consciously downplay bureaucratic characteristics.

Unstable Environment The discussion of external environments in chapter 2 indicated that the rate of environmental change influenced internal organization characteristics. Under conditions of rapid change, organizations are more organic. When the organization must be free flowing and flexible, extensive bureaucracy is inappropriate. When environments are moderately stable, the efficiencies of bureaucratic structure can be realized, as at McDonald's. When an organization must change frequently and rapidly, the absence of bureaucracy will promote better performance.

ORGANIZATIONAL DECLINE

The concern with growth and large organization size reflects the preoccupation with these issues in society. Western countries have experienced unprecedented economic growth since 1940, and organizations have adapted to an environment of growth and expansion. The belief that growth and large size are symbols of success is deeply rooted in the psychology of management.

One of the realities facing today's organizations is that the rate of growth and expansion experienced since the 1940s may not continue. All around us we see evidence that some organizations are having to stop growing. Many are declining. Schools have had decreasing enrollments, churches have closed their doors, municipal services have been curtailed, and certain industries, such as automotive, have laid off record numbers of employees in response to recession.[47]

Decline has been a small part of organizational life, so it has not been studied extensively. Our understanding of the relationship between bureaucracy and decline is far from complete. The ideas concerning organizational decline that follow were consolidated by David Whetten of the University of Illinois.[48]

Definition   The term **decline** is normally used to "denote a cutback in the size of an organization's workforce, profits, budget, or clients."[49] Decline may occur because an organization's command over environmental resources has been reduced (e.g., smaller share of market) or because the environment itself has become poorer (e.g., erosion of a city's tax base). A key management issue in these circumstances is to understand the reasons for downturn and to reduce the element of crisis through forecasting and planning.

Why decline?   Whetten identified four reasons why organizations decline:[50]

1. *Organizational Atrophy.*   Atrophy occurs when organizations grow older, become inefficient, and lose muscle tone. The organization gets used to success and no longer has a sharp edge.
2. *Vulnerability.*   Vulnerability reflects the inability of the organization to prosper in its environment. Often this happens because the organization is small and has not become fully established. It is vulnerable to changes in consumer tastes or in the economic health of the larger society.
3. *Loss of Legitimacy.*   Certain services or resources may lose legitimacy. Prisons have received a declining share of resources because they do not produce something valued by the mainstream of society. The same thing can happen when profit-making organizations are out of step with the values and attitudes of the buying public. This has happened with manufacturers of cigarettes and certain toys.
4. *Environmental Entropy.*   This refers to the reduced capacity of the environment to support the organization; external resources are simply insufficient. The organization either has to scale down operations or find another product niche. This is the circumstance faced by organizations in a stagnating economy. The external resource base is no longer growing, so organizations have to divide up a stable or shrinking pie. Organizations in this context will inevitably decline.

Managing the Effects of Decline   Decline represents change, perhaps a change that the organization doesn't want, but nevertheless a change that has to be managed. There are positive ways for organizations to manage decline.[51] The most positive approach is to simply embrace the change and try to make the best of it. Harm is minimized, and the best is made of a potentially negative situation. If people understand and are informed of the need for decline, resources can be allocated in a way to minimize the negative effects. Strategies such as selectively dropping entire product lines or departments may also be appropriate.[52] A tight bureaucratic structure makes it easier to implement these cutbacks.

In all cases of decline, managers should be prepared for conflict. The most serious and difficult aspect of decline is the difference of opinion and fear of loss within the organization. Resource cutbacks sharply increase conflict and force people into win-lose situations.[53] Research on this topic has not been extensive, but heightened conflict among groups about who has to give up resources is one of the major issues that has to be resolved.

Another problem is simply the agonizing issue of who should suffer most from the decline. Should all subunits suffer equally or should certain individuals and groups be penalized more heavily in order for the organization to suffer least? Decline tends to penalize most those who can least afford it.[54] The first employees to be dismissed are the low-skilled, low-income, young or old staff members. These people have the most difficult time finding new jobs.

Finally, the process of decline increases the rate of change to which management must respond.[55] Innovations adopted in response to decline should be designed to increase efficiency and make better use of scarce resources. Some city governments have rescheduled janitors to work during the day in order to save the light bill from working at night.[56] The size of police cars has been reduced, and one city even used taxi-style Checker sedans as police cruisers to save money. Managers may be able to decrease the negative effect of decline by encouraging an innovative climate.

IN PRACTICE 4.7

Acme-Cleveland Corp.

In today's economic climate, two reasons account for most organizational cutbacks. The first is government. Organizations that depend on federal or state governments are experiencing rising costs and reduced budgets. Cutbacks are inevitable. Eight years ago Duke University built a brand-new School of Nursing building. Duke no longer accepts nursing students. As soon as current students graduate, the nursing program will be discontinued. It is closing the Department of Education as well.

The other reason for cutting back is the appearance of red ink on corporate profit and loss statements. Acme-Cleveland Corp. saw earnings plunge last year, but corporate overhead remained constant. Unless costs can be cut, profits will be eroded even further. During the good years, Acme-Cleveland became overloaded with corporate and staff support personnel. Top management decided to perform radical surgery. The first cuts were amputations at the corporate level of the entire departments of advertising, promotion, and market research. Cutting entire departments is the same strategy used at Duke, and prevents the anguish of deciding among people within departments. Acme-Cleveland also made selective cuts, including corporate accountants, computer programmers, and many assistant managers in manufacturing, research, sales, and finance. Nearly 900 persons were dismissed.

Corporations need time to recover from surgery just as people do. The amputation of entire departments seems to be the easiest form of surgery, but it has costs. The morale of employees who remain often takes a nosedive, and so does productivity. The most difficult part for employees is the uncertainty. They are uncertain about whether they will be fired, and they are uncertain about new jobs and careers. Employees feel disappointment, anger, depression, and emptiness. Many resist. Some employees respond with lawsuits, which creates a hostile climate. Others fight internally, or simply raise a ruckus. Managers who perform surgery also experience stress. "You have to be tough-minded to make it stick," said one manager. "If you have doubts, you either fail to make the decision or you regret it afterward."[57]

SUMMARY AND INTERPRETATION

The material covered in this chapter contains several important ideas about organizations. One of the most important is that Weber's model of bureaucracy has been found to make sense. Bureaucracy becomes important as organizations grow large and complex. Bureaucracy enables organizations in a complex society to use scarce resources productively. The need for greater bureaucracy in large organizations means that the informal atmosphere associated with small size cannot be maintained as size increases.

Parkinson's notion of empire building and inefficiencies by top administrators is not supported by the majority of organizations. Greater overhead support is required from clerical, maintenance, and other technical staff groups in large organizations. This is a logical outcome of employee specialization and the division of labor. By dividing up tasks, each subgroup can become more efficient, especially the production employees.

Organizations evolve through distinct stages as they grow and mature. Organization structure, internal systems, and management issues are different for each stage of development. Growth causes many stresses and strains. There are many crises and revolutions along the way toward large size. The same is true for decline. The crises for management are intense.[58] We don't yet know very much about decline, but bureaucratic characteristics do not seem to reverse themselves toward less bureaucracy when organizations get smaller. Conflict, redeployment of resources, laying off employees, and new types of innovation are all important issues in the declining organization.

Finally, bureaucracy has advantages, but it also has shortcomings. The dilemma of bureaucracy versus nonbureaucracy has not been completely resolved. Bureaucracy is not appropriate in small, professional, or rapidly changing organizations. Even in large, stable organizations, bureaucratic characteristics may have unanticipated and undesirable consequences. Bureaucratic characteristics are intended to benefit the organization, but they often frustrate employees. From the point of view of management, bureaucracy and formalization are essential if the organization is to be efficient as it grows larger. But employees may feel distant from the organization, perhaps as cogs in a large machine. In the final analysis, bureaucracy is and will continue to be the dominant form of organization in industrial societies. As a tool of mankind, bureaucratic structures have enabled us to master complex tasks and produce a volume of goods and services never before equaled in our history. In actual use, however, bureaucracies do not live up to the ideal expectations of Weber. Paperwork, routine jobs, and silly rules sometimes get to all of us. But for most large organizations, bureaucracy seems to be the best bet. Bureaucracy may get even better as researchers and managers find ways to make them more satisfying for employees and more useful to clients while maintaining the efficiencies that bureaucratic structure provides.[59]

DISCUSSION QUESTIONS

1. Describe the three bases of authority identified by Weber. Is it possible for each of these types of authority to function within departments in an organization?
2. What are the negative consequences of bureaucracy for employees? From society's point of view, is the efficiency and productivity of large organizations sufficiently important that we can sacrifice some employee satisfaction?
3. How would you define size? What problems can you identify with using number of employees as a measure of size?
4. The manager of a medium-sized manufacturing plant once said, "We can't compete on price with the small organizations because they have lower overhead costs." Based upon the discussion in this chapter, would you agree or disagree with that manager? Why?
5. Why do large organizations tend to be more formalized?
6. If you were the manager of a department of college professors, how might you structure the department differently than if you were managing a department of bookkeepers? Why?
7. Reread the example of Bill Sauey in the chapter. What stage of development is his organization in, and what crisis did it pass through?
8. Assume you are the manager of an organization that is experiencing decline. What problems should you be prepared to cope with?
9. Organizational researchers typically measure professionalism by amount of formal education. People with fourteen years of education are considered more professional than those with nine years of education. Do you agree that this is an appropriate measure of professionalism?
10. Discuss the advantages and disadvantages of rules and regulations.
11. Should a "no-growth" philosophy of management be taught in business schools? Is a no-growth philosophy more realistic for today's economic conditions?

As an organization designer:

1. Introduce greater bureaucratization to an organization as it increases in size. As it becomes necessary, add more rules and regulations, greater written documentation, increased job specialization, a longer chain of command, greater impersonality, the criterion of technical competence in hiring and promotion, the subdivision of the organization into a larger number of departments, and decentralization. Increase the efficiency of a large organization by increasing the bureaucratic dimensions of structure as the organization grows.

2. With the growth of the organization, decrease the percentage of top administrators and increase the percentage of support personnel. Large support ratios do not necessarily reflect inefficiency, but reflect the division of labor and greater organizational need for written communication, documentation, and technical support.

3. Do not increase bureaucracy when the organization is small, when employees are highly professional, or when the environment is rapidly changing.

4. Grow when possible. With growth you can provide opportunities for employee advancement and greater profitability and effectiveness. Apply new management systems and structural configurations at each stage of the organization's development. Interpret the needs of the organization and respond with the management and internal systems that will carry the organization through to the next stage of development.

5. When an organization is in decline, mediate intense conflicts among departments that do not want to give up resources, make difficult decisions about reductions in people and products/services, and promote innovations and changes that can effectively utilize limited resources and reduce the negative consequences of decline.

Consider these Guides when analyzing the following case and when answering the questions listed after the case.

CASE FOR ANALYSIS

HOUSTON OIL AND MINERALS CORP.

Part I   Houston Oil and Minerals Corp. is an independent oil company. Oil exploration and production are its primary businesses. Like other small independent oil companies, HOM has kept overhead lower than the majors, and can move quickly when an opportunity presents itself.

Houston Oil's chairman and president, Joseph C. Walter, Jr., has very firm ideas about organization structure. He wants to maintain a "swashbuckling" approach to exploration. This means a minimum of bosses and a maximum of autonomy for geologists exploring in the field. "As far as possible I try to run the place with no bosses at all." Of course, every organization has to have bosses, and along with five other managers, Walter supervises the work of fifty-three geologists and geophysicists. The small number of bosses partly explains the low overhead. Houston Oil spends an average of $2.50 to find a barrel of oil, compared to $5 for the industry as a whole.

The company increased its growth to 500 employees in 1977, and continued to add new ones. The development budget is similar to the budgets of many major oil companies, where several layers of management are involved. These layers of management are not present in Houston Oil. Avoiding layers of management is difficult, but Walter says, "The only way I know how to do it is to push decision-making down as far as it can go." This gives geologists almost complete autonomy over how to spend the budgeted resources.

Formal committees are avoided at Houston Oil. Ad hoc task forces are used to solve problems that involve more than one department. The company does have a weekly meeting of officers, but their goal is to suppress formalized procedures in order to retain flexibility.

Questions

1. How would you rate (high or low) the formalization, centralization, administration ratio, and professionalism at Houston Oil and Minerals Corp.?
2. Will the company be able to maintain its informality as it grows larger? Is the amount of bureaucracy appropriate to the level of professionalism? Explain.
3. Predict whether the informal "swashbuckling" approach to management will lead to successful performance.

Part II Houston Oil and Minerals Corp. developed an astonishing performance record. Houston Oil's geologists seemed to be able to pick successful drilling sites at will. Earnings increased eight-fold during a period (1970–1976) in which domestic oil and gas production fell 15%. From 1973 to 1980, the price of its stock jumped almost 5,000%. Revenues spurted from $1.5 million in 1970 to over $400 million in 1980.

One reason for this success was the absence of bureaucracy. The free-wheeling approach to structure enabled Houston Oil to assemble an excellent team of exploration geologists (called explorationists in the trade). The head of exploration for another oil company said: "They manage to attract some of the more inventive geologists who feel straight-jacketed in the environment of a large corporation. It's the opposite extreme in other independents. The top guy calls all of the shots. Joe [Walter] turns his geologists loose."

Houston Oil in just a few years became an oil-patch legend. Houston Oil grew so big, so fast, that it also became overextended financially. Huge Tenneco Corp. was searching for ways to increase its reserves and new discoveries. Late in 1980, Tenneco purchased Houston Oil. Tenneco can provide the financial resources for increased oil exploration around the world. Houston Oil and Minerals Corp., the oil-patch legend, is now part of a giant corporation.

Questions
1. Will Houston Oil be able to maintain its nonbureaucratic structure as part of a giant corporation?
2. Do you think Houston Oil would be better off with some of the efficiencies of bureaucratic structure? Discuss.
3. Will the professional explorationists be happy under the umbrella of a large corporation? Predict whether they will stay or leave the company.

Part III
Within a few months after the merger, 34% of Houston Oil's management and 25% of its explorationists quit. Within a year, nearly all the managers and over half its explorationists were gone. People are still leaving.

Tenneco anticipated a problem and offered lucrative salary increases and other financial inducements to Houston Oil's personnel. But it just didn't work. The professionals were entrepreneurial types who could not stand the constraints of a rigid bureaucracy. Tenneco responded by proposing a smaller corporate division with greater autonomy. But Tenneco still had a long chain of command, and emphasized things like budgeting and forecasting. It also generated an avalanche of paperwork, which Houston Oil staffers couldn't tolerate. Tenneco couldn't treat the Houston Oil division too differently from other divisions, or it would have problems of equity across the entire corporation. Some standardization was essential.

One staff member complained that it took eight weeks to get a work order approved to move a telephone. Previously, he could spend $50,000 on his own. Now he doesn't have the authority to approve a box of pencils.

The hemorrhaging of Houston Oil's staff is causing problems for Tenneco. Tenneco picked up 1.4 million acres of unexplored land, but the people who did the preliminary evaluation of the property are gone. Tenneco has to start from scratch in reevaluating the acreage—a slow process. Oil and gas leases on about 60,000 acres are beginning to expire. Tenneco is either going to have to farm out leases to other oil companies or give them up. Without professional staff, they can't evaluate and drill on time.[60]

Questions
1. How can the dramatic turnaround at Houston Oil be explained? Would it ever be possible to mix independent-minded explorationists with an organizational bureaucracy? Explain.
2. What would you recommend to large corporations like Tenneco, Mobil, Getty Oil, and Standard Oil to help them retain their first-rate exploration professionals?

NOTES

1. Charles Perrow, *Complex Organizations: A Critical Essay* (Glenview, IL: Scott, Foresman: 1979), pp. 1–3.

2. Reinhard Bendix, "Bureaucracy," *International Encyclopedia of the Social Sciences* (New York: The Free Press, 1977); Perrow, *Complex Organizations,* p. 4.

3. Perrow, *Complex Organizations,* ch. 1.

4. Max Weber, *The Theory of Social and Economic Organizations,* translated by A. M. Henderson and T. Parsons (New York: Free Press, 1947).

5. *Ibid.,* p. 330.

6. *Ibid.*

7. *Ibid.,* p. 331.

8. *Ibid.*

9. *Ibid.*

10. *Ibid.,* p. 332.

11. *Ibid.*

12. *Ibid.,* pp. 328–340.

13. Kathy Goode, Betty Hahn, and Cindy Seibert, "United Parcel Service: the Brown Giant," unpublished manuscript, Texas A & M University, 1981.

14. John R. Kimberly, "Organizational Size and the Structuralist Perspective: A Review, Critique, and Proposal," *Administrative Science Quarterly* (1976): 571-597; Richard L. Daft and Selwyn W. Becker, "Managerial, Institutional, and Technical Influences on Administration: A Longitudinal Analysis," *Social Forces* 59 (1980): 392-413.

15. Bernard Reimann, "On the Dimensions of Bureaucratic Structure: An Empirical Reappraisal," *Administrative Science Quarterly* 18 (1973): 462-476; Richard H. Hall, "The Concept of Bureaucracy: An Empirical Assessment," *American Journal of Sociology* 69 (1963): 32-40; William A. Rushing, "Organizational Rules and Surveillance: A Proposition in Comparative Organizational Analysis," *Administrative Science Quarterly* 10 (1966): 423-443.

16. Joanne S. Lublin, "Employers Act to Curb Sex Harassing on Job; Lawsuits, Fines Feared," *Wall Street Journal,* April 24, 1981, p. 1; "Sexual Harassment Lands Companies in Court," *Business Week,* October 1, 1979, pp. 120-122.

17. Jerald Hage and Michael Aiken, "Relationship of Centralization to Other Structural Properties," *Administrative Science Quarterly* 12 (1967): 72-91.

18. Robert Dewar and Jerald Hage, "Size, Technology, Complexity, and Structural Differentiation: Toward a Theoretical Synthesis," *Administrative Science Quarterly* 23 (1978): 111-136.

19. Richard L. Daft and Patricia J. Bradshaw, "The Process of Horizontal Differentiation: Two Models," *Administrative Science Quarterly* 25 (1980): 441-456.

20. Peter M. Blau, *The Organization of Academic Work* (New York: Wiley-Interscience, 1973).

21. Daft and Bradshaw, "Horizontal Differentiation"; Eugene Haas, Richard H. Hall, and Norman J. Johnson, "The Size of the Supportive Component in Organizations: A Multiorganizational Analysis," *Social Forces* 43 (1963): 9-17; Norman P. Hummon, Patrick Doreian, and Klaus Teuter,

"A Structural Control Model of Organizational Change," *American Sociological Review* 40 (1975): 813–824.

22. C. Northcote Parkinson, *Parkinson's Law* (New York: Ballantine Books, 1964).

23. Jeffrey D. Ford and John W. Slocum, Jr., "Size, Technology, Environment and the Structure of Organizations," *Academy of Management Review* 2 (1977): 561–575; John D. Kasarda, "The Structural Implications of Social System Size: A Three-Level Analysis," *American Sociological Review* 39 (1974): 19–28.

24. Peter M. Blau, "Interdependence and Hierarchy in Organizations," *Social Science Research* 1 (1972): 1–24; Peter M. Blau and R. A. Schoenherr, *The Structure of Organizations* (New York: Basic Books, 1971); A. Hawley, W. Boland, and M. Boland, "Population Size and Administration in Institutions of Higher Education," *American Sociological Review* 30 (1965): 252–255; Richard L. Daft, "System Influence on Organization Decision-Making: The Case of Resource Allocation," *Academy of Management Journal* 21 (1978): 6–22; B. P. Indik, "The Relationship Between Organization Size and the Supervisory Ratio," *Administrative Science Quarterly* 9 (1964): 301–312.

25. T. F. James, "The Administrative Component in Complex Organizations," *The Sociological Quarterly* 13 (1972): 533–539; Daft, "System Influence on Organizational Decision-Making"; E. A. Holdaway and E. A. Blowers, "Administrative Ratios and Organization Size: A Longitudinal Examination," *American Sociological Review* 36 (1971): 278–286; John Child, "Parkinson's Progress: Accounting for the Number of Specialists in Organizations," *Administrative Science Quarterly* 18 (1973): 328–348.

26. Child, "Parkinson's Progress"; Daft, "System Influence on Resource Allocation."

27. Richard L. Daft and Selwyn Becker, "School District Size and the Deployment of Personnel Resources," *The Alberta Journal of Educational Research* 24 (1978): 173–187.

28. Peter M. Blau, "A Formal Theory of Differentiation in Organizations," *American Sociological Review* 35 (1970): 201–218.

29. "Can Sears Come Back," *Dun's Review,* February, 1979, pp. 68–70; "How Sears Became a High Cost Operator," *Business Week,* February 16, 1981, pp. 52–57; Jeremy Main, "K-Mart's Plan to Be Born Again," *Fortune,* September 21, 1981, pp. 78–85.

30. William H. Starbuck, "Organizational Growth and Development," in James G. March, ed., *Handbook of Organizations* (New York: Rand McNally, 1965), pp. 451–522.

31. Ann M. Morrison, "A Big Baker That Won't Live By Bread Alone," *Fortune,* September 7, 1981, pp. 70–76.

32. Starbuck, "Organizational Growth and Development"; Child, *Organizations,* ch. 7.

33. Starbuck, *ibid.*

34. W. H. Newman and J. P. Logan, *Management of Expanding Enterprises* (Columbia: Columbia University Press, 1955); Starbuck, "Organizational Growth and Development."

35. Larry E. Greiner, "Evolution and Revolution as Organizations Grow," *Harvard Business Review* 50 (July–August, 1972): 37–46.

36. From David DeLong, "They All Said Bill Sauey Couldn't Let Go," *Inc.,* May, 1981, pp. 89–91. With special permission of author David DeLong.

37. John Child, *Organizations* (New York: Harper and Row, 1977), ch. 7.

38. Chris Argyris, *Personality and Organizations* (New York: Harper, 1956); Warren G. Bennis, *Changing Organizations* (New York: McGraw-Hill, 1966).

39. Perrow, *Complex Organizations,* ch. 1.

40. Peter M. Blau, *The Dynamics of Bureaucracy* (Chicago: University of Chicago Press, 1973).

41. Victor Thompson, "Bureaucracy and Innovation," *Administrative Science Quarterly* 10 (1965): 1–20.

42. Blau, *Dynamics of Bureaucracy.*

43. Dwayne S. Elgin and Robert A. Bushnell, "The Limits to Complexity: Are Bureaucracies Becoming Unmanageable?" *The Futurist,* December, 1977, pp. 337–349.

44. James March and Herbert Simon, *Organizations* (New York: Wiley, 1958), ch. 1.

45. A. Lucas, "As American as McDonald's Hamburger on the Fourth of July," *New York Times Magazine,* July 4, 1971; Melinda Culver, Lisa Mewis, and John Vaughn, "McDonald's Case Study," unpublished manuscript, Texas A & M University, 1981.

46. Richard H. Hall, *Organizations: Structure and Process* (Englewood Cliffs, N.J.: Prentice-Hall, 1977), p. 170.

47. David A. Whetten, "Sources, Responses, and Effects of Organizational Decline," in John R. Kimberly and Robert H. Miles, eds., *The Organizational Life Cycle* (San Francisco: Jossey-Bass, 1980), pp. 342–374.

48. David A. Whetten, *ibid.;* David A. Whetten, "Organizational Decline: A Neglected Topic in Organizational Science," *Academy of Management Review* 5 (1980): 577–588.

49. Whetten, "Sources, Responses, and Effects of Organizational Decline," p. 345.

50. *Ibid.*

51. *Ibid.*

52. Kathryn Rudie Harrigan, "Strategy Formulation n Declining Industries," *Academy of Management Review* 5 (1980): 599–604.

53. C. H. Levine, "Organizational Decline and Cut Back Management," *Public Administration Review* 38 (1970): 316–325.

54. Whetten, "Sources, Responses, and Effects of Organizational Decline."

55. *Ibid.*

56. Brooks Jackson, "Janitors Work Days and Cops Ride Bikes to Save Tax Dollars," *Wall Street Journal,* May 1, 1981, p.

57. Roger Ricklefs, "Some Colleges Drop Whole Departments to Meet Fiscal Crunch," *The Wall Street Journal,* September 11, 1981; p. 1, 17; "A New Target: Reducing Staff and Levels," *Business Week,* December 21, 1981, pp. 69–73.

58. Whetten, "Sources, Responses, and Effects of Organizational Decline"; Jeffrey D. Ford, "The Occurrence of Structural Hysteresis in Declining Organizations," *Academy of Management Review* 5 (1980): 589–598.

59. "Special Report: The New Industrial Relations," *Business Week,* May 11, 1981, pp. 85–98; Larry L. Cummings and Chris J. Berger, "Organization Structure: How Does It Influence Attitudes and Performance?" *Organizational Dynamics,* Autumn, 1976, pp. 34–49.

60. This case was based on "Houston Oil's Freehand Approach to Growth," *Business Week,* June 13, 1977, pp. 97–99; Todd A. Cohen, "We grew so big so fast . . ." *Forbes,* Dec. 8, 1980, pp. 90–92; Alexander Stuart, "Why an Oil-Patch Legend Joined Tenneco," *Fortune,* January 12, 1981, pp. 48–52; George Getschow, "Loss of Expert Talent Impedes Oil Finding by New Tenneco Unit," *Wall Street Journal,* February 9, 1982, pp. 1, 23.

5

Organizational Technology

THE COTTON-TEXTILE INDUSTRY

The two basic processes in the cotton-textile industry are spinning and weaving. In the spinning room, spindles convert cotton fiber into threads or yarn. In the weaving room, looms weave the yarn into cloth. Plants vary in the number of processes carried out. An increasing number of mills, especially the largest ones, carry out every process from the cleaning of the cotton bale to the packaging of finished articles ready for the consumer.

. . . A fully integrated mill requires a large plant and at least several hundred workers. There are more than a dozen rooms through which the product moves, in each of which different machinery carries out a particular phase of the manufacturing process.

In the first, the breaker room, three things take place. The cotton, which has been tightly packed into bales at the gin, is loosened. A great deal of the dirt and trash which has accumulated is shaken out. And cotton from dozens of bales is mixed, in order to begin averaging out the differences in the fiber caused by variations in soil and growing conditions. Only a few workers are required on those machines; their work handling the bales is heavy, dirty, and unskilled.

From the breaking room, a mechanical conveyer moves the loose cotton to the picking room, where machines further clean it, form it into sheets, and roll these into "laps" for carding. The work of handling the laps is also heavy and dirty, though less so than the jobs in the breaking room. It requires somewhat higher skill, since it involves the operation of more elaborate machines and controls.

The tasks more characteristic of textile technology and work operations start in the carding room, where the process of straightening the fibers begins. On the carding machine, the lap from the picker is passed over a surface thickly set with bent wires, which comb it, removing noils and aligning the fibers into a sheer, fragile sheet; gather the sheet into a soft roll; and coil it into a deep container or can. Only a few workers are needed to attend many carding machines. The operator feeds the lap into the machine or, more commonly, joins a new one to the old just before it is exhausted. Besides keeping the card supplied with material, he removes or "doffs" the filled cans. He must also patrol all the machines assigned to him, watching for malfunctions. If something goes wrong with the mechanism for gathering and coiling the delicate veil-like sheet of cotton, it spills off the card like a heavy snowfall. . . .

In the spinning room, fibers are spun into thread through a twisting process which increases their strength. Here, row on row of spinning frames containing thousands of spindles move incessantly up and down, filling the air with a droning hum. These machines are largely automatic. The spinner starts the process by attaching the roving between rollers which attenuate it to a narrow, filmy sliver and deliver it to the fast-turning spindle. The spindle twists the sliver into yarn and winds the yarn onto a bobbin. When this automatic process fails, slivers of cotton accumulate on a waste roll and are visible up and down the alleys between the spinning frames. Reacting to this signal that an "end is down," the spinner hurries to the trouble spot, unwinds a bit of yarn from the bobbin, and "pieces it up," touching the yarn to the sliver to restore the twisting. She then clears the accumulated cotton from the waste roll. A spinner tends many long frames and must keep on the move, looking for such breaks and stoppages. The work is light and requires only a quick, facile movement in the piecing up, which is readily learned . . . .

In the weaving room, hundreds or thousands of identical automatic looms weave the yarn into cloth. This is the largest and the noisiest place in a cotton mill. The atmosphere is almost bizarre: the constant back-and-forth motion of the shuttles creates a considerable din, and the striking red and green colors of the looms contrast with the whiteness of the lint settling on everything with a light film.[1]

Technology is the knowledge, tools, techniques, and actions used to transform inputs into outputs.[2] Technology is the organization's transformation process, and includes machinery, employee education and skill, and work procedures used in that transformation process. In Robert Blauner's description of technology in an integrated cottonmill above, the input was bales of raw cotton direct from farmers, and output was finished bedsheets and pillowcases for sale to consumers. The transformation process consisted of breaking up the bales, picking the cotton, cording it, winding thread, and weaving cloth. The tools, machines, and worker activities are the technology used to transform cotton into finished linen.

Technologies cover an enormous range of activities. One organization might write stories for television shows. Others might produce cardboard boxes, design blueprints for building construction, or manufacture specialized fluids (muds) used for drilling oil wells. Technology also includes cancer research, coaching a football team, and fighting a war. All forms of technology begin with raw materials of some type (e.g., paperwork in a government agency, steel castings in a valve manufacturing plant, students in a university). Employees take action on the raw material to make a change in it (e.g., paperwork is filed, steel castings are machined, students are taught), which transforms the raw material into the output of the organization (e.g., an orderly filing system, control valves ready for shipment to oil refineries, knowledgeable university graduates).

Technology can be analyzed at both organizational and departmental levels. In terms of the systems theory described in chapter 1, the organization's technology is the transformation process that takes place in the production subsystem. Organizational technology is used to produce the principal products or services of the organization. The case above described the organizational technology for a mechanized textile manufacturing process. Other organizational technologies would include the transformation of crude oil into gasoline, manufacture of chemicals, and the assembly of automobiles.

In today's large, complex organizations, different technologies are used in different parts of the organization. Each department or subsystem of the organization transforms inputs into outputs. Research and development transforms ideas into new products. Marketing transforms inventory into sales. These departments are not responsible for the primary production process of the organization, but each department uses a technology to perform its own work.

The activity of an individual employee is called a task. Throwing a bale of cotton into the breaking machine is a task. Individual tasks aggregate into department and organization technologies. The relationship between individual tasks and the production technology of an organization is illustrated in figure 5.1. Raw materials flow into and through the organization's production process in a logical sequence, and work activities are performed with a variety of tools, techniques, or machines to transform the material into useful outputs.

Purpose of This Chapter

The purpose of this chapter is to explore the nature of organizational technologies and the relationship between technology and organization structure. Previous chapters have described how environment and size influence the organization. A complex environment typically leads to a more complex structure. Large organizations have greater problems of coordination, control, and supervision, which lead to greater formalization, standardization, and decentralization. This chapter looks at structure based on an internal view of organization. The question addressed is: How should organization structure and management systems be designed to accommodate internal work activities? An analogy is the structure of a building. The building's structure reflects both environmental and size considerations. But it also reflects the nature of activities performed within the building, as shown in figure 5.2. The organization structure of a textile plant would differ from the organization structure for a university or for an oil refinery.

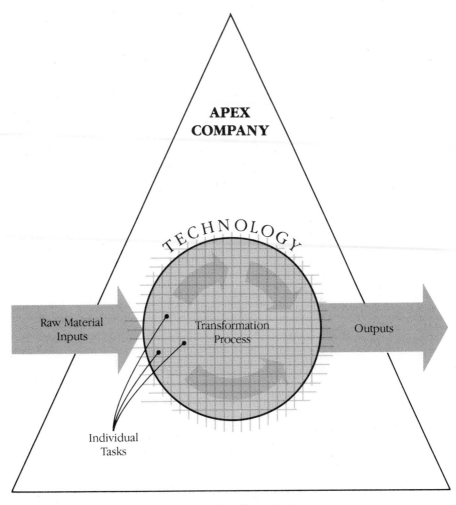

Figure 5.1. An Organization's Transformation Process.

Technologies vary so widely that different measures and definitions sometimes reflect different parts of the transformation process. Technology can be assessed by examining the raw materials flowing into the organization,[3] the variability of work activities,[4] the degree of mechanization in the transformation process,[5] the use of mechanical aides,[6] the extent to which one task depends upon another in the work flow,[7] and the number of new product outputs.[8] The focus on different parts of the transformation process can be confusing, so it is best to remember that each measure deals with some part of the input-transformation-output process. It is the general nature of the transformation process at either the organization or department level that is important to organization structure.

The next section describes organization-level technology and the ways in which the production technology influences overall structure and design.

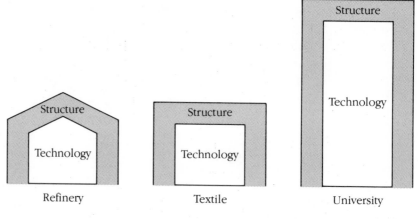

Figure 5.2. Hypothetical Relationship between Technology and Organization Structure.

Then department technology is analyzed to discover how structure and management process should be tailored to tasks of individual departments. Departments within a single organization may have wide variation in structure, depending upon their technology. The last section of the chapter examines technological interdependency between departments. The extent to which departmental activities are tightly connected to each other also has substantial impact on organization design.

ORGANIZATIONAL TECHNOLOGY

Manufacturing Firms

South Essex Study The most influential study of technology was conducted by Joan Woodward, a British industrial sociologist. Her research began as a field study of management principles in south Essex. The prevailing management wisdom at the time (1950s) was contained in what was known as universal principles of management. These principles offered prescriptions that effective organizations were expected to adopt. Each manager should have a certain span of control, each organization should have a similar structure, and so on. Scientists often question established principles, so Woodward surveyed 100 manufacturing firms firsthand to learn how they were organized.[9] She and her research team visited each firm, interviewed managers, examined company records, and observed the manufacturing operations. Her data included a wide range of structural characteristics (span of control, levels of management, management and clerical ratios, worker skill level). Her data also included dimensions of management style (written versus verbal communications, use of sanctions) and the type of manufacturing process. Data that reflected commercial success of the firm were also obtained.

Analysis Initially, her data was a mess. Firms varied widely on such things as span of control, number of hierarchical levels, administrative ratio, and amount of verbal communications. No support was given to the "one best way" principles of management. Her challenge was to determine whether the organization structures reflected random choices of managers or whether previously undiscovered factors could explain the unexpected differences that were observed.

Reanalysis Woodward developed a scale and organized the firms according to technical complexity of the manufacturing process. Technical complexity represents the mechanization and the predictability of the manufacturing process. Her scale had ten categories that were grouped into three production types, as summarized in figure 5.3.

Figure 5.3. Woodward's Classification of 100 British Firms according to Their System of Production.
Source: J. Woodward, *Management and Technology* (London: Her Majesty's Stationery Office, 1958). Reproduced with the permission of her Britannic Majesty's Stationery Office.

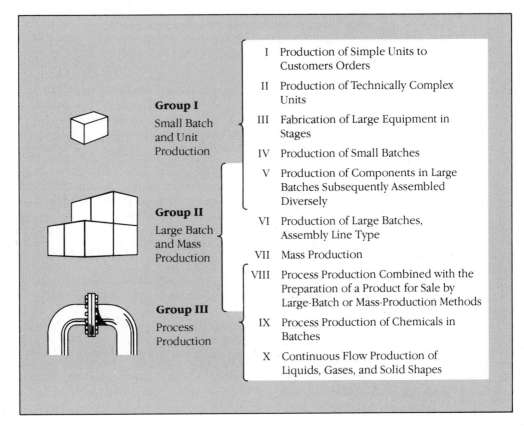

Group I		
Small Batch and Unit Production	I	Production of Simple Units to Customers Orders
	II	Production of Technically Complex Units
	III	Fabrication of Large Equipment in Stages
	IV	Production of Small Batches
Group II	V	Production of Components in Large Batches Subsequently Assembled Diversely
Large Batch and Mass Production	VI	Production of Large Batches, Assembly Line Type
	VII	Mass Production
Group III	VIII	Process Production Combined with the Preparation of a Product for Sale by Large-Batch or Mass-Production Methods
Process Production	IX	Process Production of Chemicals in Batches
	X	Continuous Flow Production of Liquids, Gases, and Solid Shapes

Group I: Small-Batch and Unit Production   These firms tend to be job shop operations that manufacture and assemble small orders to meet specific needs of customers. Custom work is the norm. This technology relies heavily on the human operator; it is thus not highly mechanized, and predictability of outcome is low. Examples include many types of made-to-order manufactured products, such as specialized construction equipment or custom electronic equipment.

Group II: Large-Batch and Mass Production   This manufacturing process is characterized by long production runs of standardized parts. Output often goes into inventory from which orders are filled because customers do not have special needs. Examples would include most assembly lines, such as for automobiles or trailer homes. The integrated cotton mill described at the beginning of this chapter is a mass production technology.

Group III: Continuous-Process Production   In this technology, the entire process is mechanized. There is no starting and stopping. This represents mechanization and standardization one step beyond an assembly line. The organization has high control over the process, and outcomes are highly predictable. Examples would include chemical plants, oil refining, and liquor production.

Using this classification of technology, Woodward's data fell into place. A few of her key findings are given in table 5.1. Number of management levels and manager/total personnel ratio, for example, show definite increases as technical complexity increases from unit production to continuous process. Direct/indirect labor ratio decreases with technical complexity, because more indirect workers are required to support the more complex transformation processes. Other characteristics, such as span of control, formalized procedures, and centralization are high for mass-production technology but low for other technologies. The number of skilled workers and the use of verbal versus written communication also depend upon manufacturing technology. Overall, the management system in both unit-production and continuous-process technology are characterized as organic. They are free-flowing and adaptive, with fewer procedures and less standardization. Mass production, however, is mechanistic, with standardized jobs and formalized procedures. Woodward's discovery of production technology was thus a critical variable that provided substantial new insight into organization structure. In Joan Woodward's own words, "Different technologies impose different kinds of demands on individuals and organizations, and those demands had to be met through an appropriate structure."[10]

Technology and Performance   Another portion of Woodward's study examined the success of the firms along dimensions such as profitability, market share, stock price, and reputation. The discussion in chapter 3 indicated that the measurement of effectiveness is not simple or precise, but she was able to rank firms on a scale of commercial success that represented above-average performance, average performance, and below-average performance.

Table 5.1. Relationship Between Technical Complexity and Structural Characteristics.

Structural Characteristic	Technology		
	Unit Production	Mass Production	Continuous Process
Number of management levels	3	4	6
Supervisor span of control	23	48	15
Direct labor/indirect labor ratio	9 : 1	4 : 1	1 : 1
Manager/total personnel ratio	Low	Medium	High
Number "skilled" workers	High	Low	High
Formalized procedures	Low	High	Low
Centralization	Low	High	Low
Amount of verbal communication	High	Low	High
Amount of written communication	Low	High	Low
Overall structure	Organic	Mechanistic	Organic

Source: Joan Woodward, *Industrial Organization: Theory and Practice* (London: Oxford University Press, 1965), with permission.

Woodward compared the structure-technology relationship to commercial success, and discovered that successful firms tended to be those that had complementary structures and technologies. Many of the organizational characteristics of the successful firms were near the median of their production category in table 5.1. Below-average firms tended to depart from the median of the structural characteristics for their technology type. Another important conclusion was that structural characteristics could be interpreted as clustering into organic and mechanistic management systems. Successful small-batch and continuous-process organizations had organic structures, and successful mass-production organizations had mechanistic structures.

U.S. Studies   Two studies in the United States have confirmed Woodward's findings. A direct replication of Woodward's research was conducted by William Zwerman on fifty-five firms in the Minneapolis-St. Paul area.[11] Most of the structural dimensions Zwerman measured showed a similar relationship to technology. Zwerman also examined whether management systems were organic or mechanistic. The large majority of small-batch and continuous-process firms had organic management systems, and the large majority of mass-production organizations had mechanistic systems. Finally, as in the Woodward study, structure was related to organizational success. Those firms that had the appropriate structure for the technology tended to experience higher performance levels.

The other major study was by Edward Harvey, and investigated the relationship between technology and structure in forty-three industrial organizations.[12] Harvey argued that it was important to take into account the amount of change taking place within a given form of technology. Frequency of change is similar to Woodward's concept of technical complexity. Frequent changes take place in small-batch technologies, and only a few in continuous-process technologies. Harvey's findings support the relationship between manufacturing technology and organizational structure. He found, for example, that as product changes increased (similar to Woodward's small batch), the extent of formalization and bureaucracy decreased. More change was associated with a fewer number of separate subunits, fewer levels of authority, smaller management ratios, and less formalization of structure.

Conclusion The general conclusion from the research into manufacturing firms is that production technology has a systematic relationship with structure and management characteristics. Woodward's discovery was extremely important to the development of organization theory. Her findings spelled the beginning of the end for the universal principles of management, and opened up the new horizon called contingency theory. Such things as organizational structure, management style, and commercial success are all contingent upon factors such as production technology.

IN PRACTICE 5.1

Corrugated Containers

Cardboard boxes are manufactured by a transformation process that converts mill paperboard into specialty corrugated containers. The technology typically used in this manufacturing process is fairly simple, and is illustrated in figure 5.4. The technology is capital-intensive, with large machines doing most of the work. Each customer order has its own specifications regarding size, folding, and printing. These specifications are set into the corrugating machine and printer. A few orders do not require printing, so after corrugating they are cut and banded for shipment. Other orders are run through a more complicated process that includes printing and finishing. The finishing glues and stitches the paperboard to the manufacturer's specification. After finishing, they are packaged and banded for shipment.

Corrugated container technology is designed for long production runs, but customers often demand immediate production and delivery of urgent orders. A company frequently runs large batches of standard boxes for inventory, but also produces short runs of paperboard that are assembled diversely for delivery to specific customers.

The labor force in a container plant is typically unskilled or semiskilled. Employees can be trained in a few days to do their work, and only a few skilled employees are needed to oversee the operation. Procedures tend to be formalized. Most important decisions are centralized

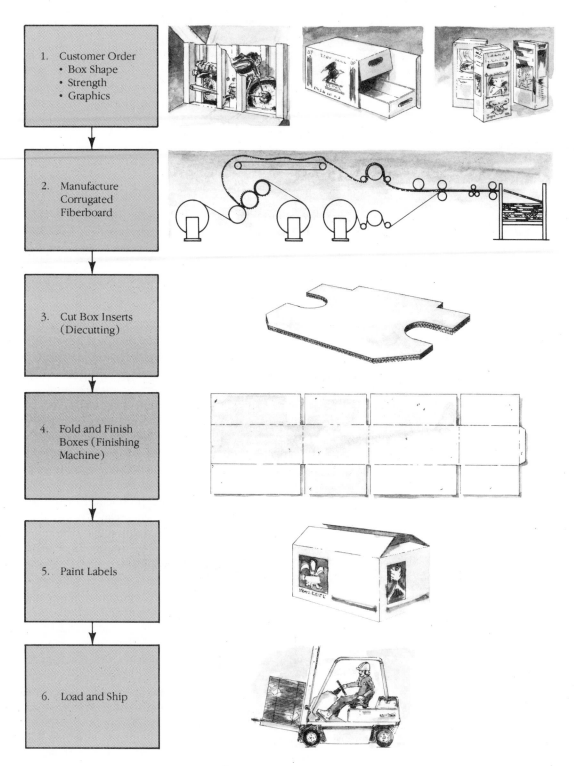

1. Customer Order
   • Box Shape
   • Strength
   • Graphics

2. Manufacture Corrugated Fiberboard

3. Cut Box Inserts (Diecutting)

4. Fold and Finish Boxes (Finishing Machine)

5. Paint Labels

6. Load and Ship

Figure 5.4. Conversion Process for Making Corrugated Boxes from Paperboard.

with the plant manager. The typical plant has three to four management levels, and the span of control is medium to large.

The technology for corrugated containers is characteristic of large-batch production (Group II) in Woodward's classification. Since these firms often have to do short- and medium-length runs to meet special needs of customers, they are unable to run continously as a mass-production operation, and are located at level V on Woodward's ten-level scale in figure 5.3.

NONMANUFACTURING FIRMS

Technology and Environment

Another pioneer in the technology arena was James Thompson.[13] Unlike Woodward, Thompson's work was not based on field research. His contribution was theoretical—he drew from a variety of sources and proposed new ideas and frameworks about organizations, several of which appear throughout this book. In Thompson's view, organizations are open systems, and technology reflects the environment outside the organization as well as internal task activities. He proposed three categories of technology that reflect relationships with clients as well as the internal transformation process.

1. *Mediating Technology.* Mediating technologies involve the mediation or linking of clients from the external environment. Typically, these clients cannot deal with each other because of costs or complexities involved in face-to-face transactions. A stockbroker, for example, mediates between sellers and buyers. So does a real-estate firm. Employment agencies bring together clients who are jobless with clients who have job openings. Banks and retail stores also mediate between clients in the environment.
2. *Long-Linked Technology.* The concept of long-linked technology "refers to the combination in one organization of successive stages of production; each stage of production uses as its inputs the production of the preceding stage and produces inputs for the following stage."[14] Organizational activities occur in sequence in long-linked technologies: the output of operation 1 becomes the input to operation 2, the output of operation 2 becomes the input to operation 3, and the finished product is then available to customers. Large-scale organizations that use assembly-line production to produce goods or services through a sequence of activities, as in the automobile industry, are examples of long-linked technologies.
3. *Intensive Technology.* Intensive technologies are characterized by the collection of specialized services for clients. A variety of activities can be brought to bear on the client and have substantial impact on the client. Intensive technologies generally go beyond providing a simple service and are designed to bring about change in the client. Hospitals are an excellent example, because they represent a collection of specialized skills to bring about therapeutic change in patients. A university is another example—a wide variety of disciplines and support services are available to facilitate educational development of students. Figure 5.5 illustrates the three types of technology.

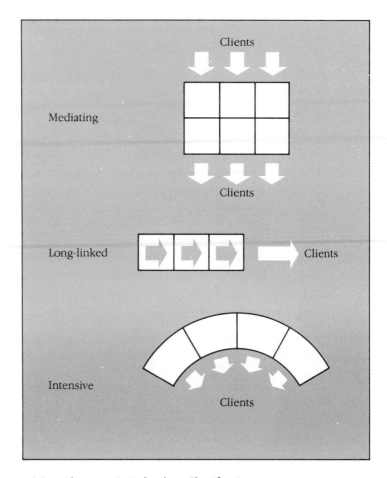

Mediating

Clients

Clients

Long-linked

Clients

Intensive

Clients

Figure 5.5. Thompson's Technology Classification.

Aston Studies A research team from the University of Aston in Birmingham, England, surveyed a wide range of organizations to develop a scale for classifying technologies.[15] The inclusion of diverse manufacturing and nonmanufacturing organizations meant they had to develop a scale of technology different from Woodward's or Thompson's. The Aston team identified three primary variables that seemed pertinent to workflow operations across organizations.

1. *Automation of Equipment.* This represents the amount of activity performed by machines in self-acting capacities rather than by humans.
2. *Workflow Rigidity.* This represents the extent to which operational knowledge, skills, and equipment are rigid rather than adaptable in their uses. A single-purpose machine would be considered rigid. A semiskilled employee would be adaptable to several uses. Workflow rigidity also reflects the extent to which the sequence of operations is tightly connected.

3. *Specificity of Evaluation.* The means of assessing operational activities can range from precise, quantitative measurement to nonspecific, personal opinions of managers.

These technology concepts have a thread of connection to other research. Automation of equipment is similar to Woodward's notion of increasing complexity and mechanization. Workflow rigidity is similar to the rate of change in technology that was measured by Harvey.

The Aston group visited and interviewed participants in fifty-two organizations to gather data about technology and structural characteristics. Their first discovery regarding technology was that the three technology variables were highly associated with each other. So they combined their data on technology into a single scale called *Workflow Integration.* Table 5.2 shows firms from their study and the workflow integration score for each firm. A higher score in table 5.2 means that the firm's technology is characterized

Table 5.2. Examples of Workflow Integration Scores for a Sample of Manufacturing and Service Firms.

Workflow Integration Score	Organization Description	Organization Type	
		Manufacturing	Service
17	Vehicle manufacturer	✓	
16	Food manufacturer	✓	
15	Packaging manufacturer	✓	
14	Metal-goods manufacturer	✓	
13	Commercial-vehicle manufacturer	✓	
12	Vehicle-tire manufacturer	✓	
11	Printer		✓
10	Local authority water department	✓	
9	Nonferrous metal processor	✓	
8	Toy manufacturer		✓
7	Local authority civil engineering department		✓
6	Insurance company		✓
5	Research division		✓
4	Savings bank		✓
3	Chain of shoe-repair stores		✓
2	Department stores		✓
1	Chain of retail stores		✓

Source: David J. Hickson, D. S. Pugh, and D. C. Pheysey, "Operations Technology and Organization Structure: An Empirical Reappraisal," *Administrative Science Quarterly* 14 (1969): 385, with permission.

by greater automation of equipment, greater rigidity of workflow, and more precise measurement of operations. Manufacturing firms tend to have higher scores than nonmanufacturing firms. Manufacturing technologies are characterized by more automation, rigidity, and precise measurement.

The general pattern of findings across their organizations indicated that structure was related to technology. They found that as the workflow integration increased, so did bureaucratic characteristics. More specifically, the extent of specialization, overall standardization of procedures, and decentralization of authority to lower management all increased with workflow integration, and supervisory ratio was smaller.[16]

IN PRACTICE 5.2

Bay Chemical Company

A continuous-process plant is quite different from a typical factory. There are no recognizable machines and very few workers visible. Except for a few maintenance workers in colored helmets welding or painting pipes, you see very few people doing anything and nobody making anything. Instead, one sees a large number of individual buildings with vast areas of open space between them, huge networks of pipes, and large towers and other equipment which one later learns are various types of distillation units or chemical reactors. The chemicals that are made and the oils which are refined flow through these pipes from one state of their processing to another, usually without being handled at all by the workers. They are processed in large reactors where raw materials are combined or separated. Generally, oils and chemicals must pass through a number of reaction operations before the product is completed. The flow of materials, the combination of different chemicals, and the temperature, pressure, and speed of the processes are regulated by automatic control devices. The automatic controls make possible a continuous flow in which raw materials are introduced at the beginning of the process and a large volume of the product continually emerges at the end stage.

Decentralization is a decisive feature of the continuous-process industries, expressed not only by the distribution of the plants in a single company but also by the organization of individual plants. Chemical and oil-refining operations are divided among many buildings or subplants, with large stretches of open space between the buildings. In a sense, a chemical factory or a refinery does not consist of one plant, but of a large number of plants, in each of which a particular product or a particular reaction is processed. The 400 blue-collar employees of the Bay Chemical Company are dispersed throughout the ammonia plant, the caustic plant, the chlorination plant, the methionine plant, the xanthate plant, the mercaptan plant, and the electrolytic-cell plant, in addition to several maintenance buildings. The danger of fire and other hazards, as well as the range of products and processes, makes such decentralization necessary . . . .

Continuous-process technology is the most highly mechanized of the various forms of manufacturing. Capital investment is enormous. So much of the process is carried out by the machine system that relatively few workers are required . . . .

The developing mechanization in continuous-process technology results in an internal distribution of the blue-collar labor force that is different from the assembly-line mass-production industries. The most dramatic change is the reduction in the number of semiskilled operatives, since automatic processes do the work which these men would do in other technological situations. There is also a striking increase in the number of skilled craftsmen, who are needed to maintain and repair the expensive, delicate automatic machinery. In the Bay chemical plant, pipe fitter-welders, machinists, millwrights, construction men, electricians, instrument repairmen, and other maintenance workers make up 40% of the blue-collar force . . . .

Very little of the work of chemical operators is physical or manual, despite the blue-collar status of these factory employees. Practically all physical production and materials-handling is done by automatic processes, regulated by automatic controls. The work of the chemical operator is to monitor these automatic processes: his tasks include observing dials and gauges; taking readings of temperatures, pressures, and rates of flow; and writing down these readings in log data sheets. Such work is clearly of a non-manual nature.

The extreme rationalization and division of labor in a textile mill and on an automobile assembly line result in jobs which are the ultimate in repetition and routine. The variety of the jobs of chemical workers in a continuous-process plant is considerably greater . . . .

Jobs are not as limited in scope in the continuous-process industries because chemical processes cannot be subdivided to the extent that the mechanical operations in assembly can be. Chemicals are not discrete units upon which a number of operations can be performed very quickly, but liquids and gases that flow continuously through a series of automatic operations, each of which takes a considerable amount of time. Job design must be organized around the entire process the chemical undergoes in its production.[17]

Bay Chemical Company illustrates many of the concepts described so far in this chapter. It would be classified as a continuous-process technology in Woodward's framework. It is a long-linked technology in Thompson's framework because the conversion process operates sequentially. Bay Company would receive a very high workflow integration score in the Aston framework because the equipment is automated, it cannot be converted to other uses, and measurement by gauges and dials is very specific.

Bay Chemical also illustrates many of the structure and design outcomes of technology. The continuous-process activities cannot be subdivided and the machinery does the work of unskilled labor, so highly skilled employees are required. A high percentage of support personnel are needed because maintaining automated equipment is a complex task. Decentralization is necessary because workers are skilled and move from area to area to monitor production activities. The overall management system is quite organic because employees are not constrained by rigid rules or procedures and are free to adapt to changing circumstances.

Structure Centered on the Production Workflow Further analysis of the Aston Group's data led to the conclusion that technology is only one factor influencing structure, and it may be less important than other variables, especially size. Size was discussed in chapter 4, and the Aston research suggested that size may be more strongly associated with structural variables than is technology.

An important idea introduced by the Aston group to explain size versus technology was that production technology has its primary effect on those structural variables centered on the workflow.[18] For example, Woodward's firms were smaller in size than the Aston group's sample, hence technology could be expected to have more effect in the Woodward sample because the structural dimensions were located closer to the production workflow. In large, diverse organizations, size may be more important to structural design because upper-management activities are several levels removed from the production workflow. When organizations are small, structures will be more heavily influenced by technology. In addition, technology will have a strong effect in small departments because personnel in small departments are located close to the technical activities of that unit. The relationship between technology and structure in departments will be examined in the next section.

DEPARTMENTAL TECHNOLOGY

The framework that has had the greatest impact on our understanding of departmental technologies was developed by Charles Perrow.[19] His model has been useful for measuring both manufacturing and nonmanufacturing technologies, which made it ideal for research into diverse departmental activities.

Variety Perrow specified two dimensions of work activities that were relevant to organizational structure and process. The first is number of exceptions in the work. This refers to task variety, which is the frequency of unexpected and novel events that occur in the conversion process. When individuals encounter a large number of unexpected situations, with frequent problems, variety is considered high. When there are few problems, and when day-to-day job requirements are repetitious, technology contains little variety. Variety in departments can range from the repetition of a single act, such as on an assembly line, to work that is a series of unrelated problems or projects.

Analyzability The second dimension of technology concerns the analyzability of work activities. When the conversion process is analyzable, the work can be reduced to mechanical steps, and participants can follow an objective, computational procedure to solve problems. Problem solution may involve the use of standard procedures such as instructions and manuals, or technical knowledge such as in a textbook or handbook. On the other hand, some work is not analyzable. Cause-effect relationships characterizing the conversion process are unclear. When problems arise, it is difficult to identify the correct solution. There is no store of techniques or procedures to tell a person exactly what to do. Employees rely on accumulated experience, intuition, and judgment. The final solution to a problem is often the result of wisdom and experience, and is not the result of standard procedures. Quality-control departments at Blue Bell Creameries and Heineken Brewery have unanalyzable technologies. Inspectors taste each batch of product to identify the mix of ingredients and to see whether it fits within acceptable flavor limits. These quality-control tasks require years of experience and practice. Standard procedures will not tell a person how to do this task.

Framework The two dimensions of technology and examples of departmental activities on Perrow's framework are shown in figure 5.6. The dimensions of variety

Figure 5.6. Perrow's Technology Framework.
Adapted with permission from Richard Daft and Norman Mcintosh, "A New Approach to Design and Use of Management Information," *California Management Review* 21 (1978): 82–92. Copyright © 1978 by the Regents of the University of California. Reprinted by permission of the Regents.

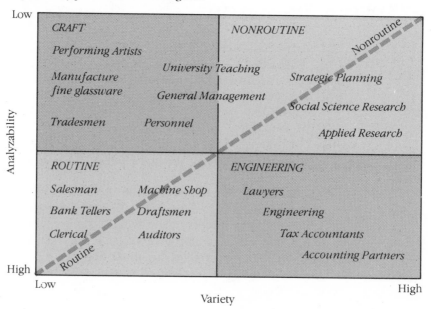

and analyzability form the basis for four major categories of technology—routine, craft, engineering, and nonroutine.

Routine Routine technologies are characterized by little task variety and the use of objective computational procedures. The tasks are formalized and standardized. Examples include an automobile assembly line and bank tellers.

Craft Craft technologies are characterized by a fairly stable stream of activities, but the conversion process is not analyzable or well understood. Tasks require extensive training and experience because employees respond to intangible factors on the basis of wisdom, intuition, and experience. Glassmakers at Corning's glass plant in upstate New York are an example. It takes twenty years to reach the highest skill level.

Engineering Engineering technologies tend to be complex because there is substantial variety in the tasks performed. But the various activities are usually handled on the basis of established formulas, procedures, and techniques. Employees normally refer to a well-developed body of knowledge to handle problems. Engineering and accounting tasks usually fall in this category.

Nonroutine Nonroutine technologies have high task variety, and the conversion process is not analyzable or well understood. In nonroutine technologies, a great deal of effort is devoted to analyzing problems and activities. Several equally acceptable options typically can be found. Experience plus technical knowledge are used to solve problems and perform the work. Basic research, strategic planning, and other work that involves new projects and unexpected problems are nonroutine.

Figure 5.6 also illustrates that variety and analyzability can be combined into a single dimension of technology. The dimension is called routine versus nonroutine technology, and is the diagonal line in figure 5.6. Perrow hypothesized that the analyzability and variety dimensions would be positively correlated, and suggested that the diagonal would capture differences in both dimensions. Routine versus nonroutine characteristics can be used to analyze departmental technology.

IN PRACTICE 5.3

Measuring Department Technology

Departmental technologies vary widely across Perrow's technology framework, and identifying the correct technology can be difficult. Organization researchers have tried various techniques for measuring technology, such as having experts assign departments to specific categories and asking employees to describe their activities on questionnaires. Questionnaire scales have been the most successful approach. The two questionnaire scales below have psychometric validity and can be used to measure department technology.[20] Employees normally circle a number from one to seven in response to each question.

Variety
1. How many of these tasks are the same from day-to-day?
2. To what extent would you say your work is routine?
3. People in this unit do about the same job in the same way most of the time.
4. Basically, unit members perform repetitive activities in doing their jobs.
5. How repetitious are your duties?

Analyzability
1. To what extent is there a clearly known way to do the major types of work you normally encounter?
2. To what extent is there a clearly defined body of knowledge or subject matter that can guide you in doing your work?
3. To what extent is there an understandable sequence of steps that can be followed in doing your work?
4. To do your work, to what extent can you actually rely on established procedures and practices?
5. To what extent is there an understandable sequence of steps that can be followed in carrying out your work?

The questions in each scale help explain the content of the variety and analyzability dimensions of Perrow's framework. Employee responses to these questions were used to place the departments on the grid in figure 5.6. Try completing the questions for work activities in a department where you have been employed.

TECHNOLOGY AND DEPARTMENT DESIGN

Department technology tends to be associated with a cluster of other department characteristics, such as the qualification of employees, formal structure, and patterns of communication. It is an oversimplification to argue that technology "causes" these other variables, but definite patterns do exist in the relationship between work unit technology and other characteristics. Key relationships between technology and other dimensions of departments are described below. The strongest relationships have been observed between routine and nonroutine departments along the diagonal in figure 5.6. Routine versus nonroutine technology combines the effect of the variety and analyzability dimensions.

Organic versus Mechanistic   The single most persistent pattern is that routine technologies are characterized by mechanistic structure and processes and nonroutine technologies by organic structure and processes. Traditional rules and tightly centralized management apply to routine units. When work is nonroutine, department administration is characterized as more organic and free flowing. Differences in management systems are very visible and can be observed by simply walking through different departments, such as production or finance or research and development. Atmosphere, dress, work habits, and autonomy all seem to be related to technology.

Qualifications of Staff   Staff in routine technologies typically require little education or experience, which is congruent with repetitive work activities. In work units with greater variety, staff are more qualified, and often have formal training in technical schools or universities. Training for craft activities, which are less analyzable, is more likely to be through job experience. Nonroutine activities require both formal education and job experience.[21]

Formal Structure   Routine technology is characterized by extensive standardization, division of labor into small tasks, and formalization. For tasks that are less routine, the structure is less formal and less standardized. When variety is high, for example, fewer activities are covered by formal procedures.[22]

Span of Control   Span of control is the number of employees who report to a single manager or supervisor. Span of control is normally influenced by task complexity and employee professionalism. The more complex and nonroutine the task, the more problems arise in which the supervisor becomes involved. The span of control should be smaller for complex tasks because supervisor and subordinate must interact frequently. Highly professional employees, however, do not require close supervision. They have expert knowledge and internal standards of performance, so the span of control can be larger.

For department technology, nonroutine tasks and professionalism have the opposite impact on span of control. Nonroutine tasks have more highly professional employees. The net effect is that the span of control is usually smaller as the work becomes more nonroutine. The frequency of problems is so great that interaction is required even when employees are highly professional. The largest spans of control usually appear in routine departments.[23]

Decentralization, Power, and Discretion   Power and discretion for lower employees is very small in routine technologies. Most power is centralized to management.[24] In engineering technologies, employees with technical training tend to acquire moderate power and discretion because technical knowledge is important to task accomplishment and decision-making. Production employees who have extensive experience obtain substantial discretion in craft technologies. Decentralization of power to employees is greatest in nonroutine settings, where many decisions are made by employees.

Communication   Communication activity and frequency increases as task variety increases.[25] Frequent problems require more information-sharing to solve problems and ensure proper completion of activities. The direction of communication is typically horizontal in nonroutine work units and vertical in routine work units.[26] The form of communication varies by task analyzability.[27] When tasks are highly analyzable, statistical and written forms of communication (memos, reports, rules, and procedures) are frequent. When tasks are less analyzable, information typically is conveyed face-to-face, for example, over the telephone or in group meetings.

Coordination and Control   Coordination mechanisms reflect a pattern similar to communication activities. In nonroutine technologies, lower-level employees participate in decisions and activities as a result of group meetings and horizontal processes. In routine departments, vertical processes dominate. Supervisors use their greater influence and rules and procedures to make decisions and control activities.[28]

Production Emphasis   In routine technologies, activites are standardized and routinized and the emphasis is on efficiency and quantity of output. In engineering technologies, reliability is often the primary production emphasis. In both craft and research technologies, quality of output is more important than quantity, efficiency, or reliability.[29]

Conclusion   The relationship between technology and other department characteristics is summarized in figure 5.7. These relationships are patterns that have been found to exist across departments. Managers should design their departments so that requirements based on technology can be met. Design problems are most visible when the design is clearly inconsistent with technology. One study, for example, found that when structure and communication characteristics did not reflect technology, departments tended to be less effective.[30] Employees could not communicate with the frequency needed to solve problems. Well-intentioned managers who impose a tight, mechanistic structure on nonroutine activites are working against the requirements of the technology.

IN PRACTICE 5.4

Creative Industries

In Creative Industries, Inc.'s modern New York City offices, Samuel E. Powell, a conservatively clad executive vice-president, rides up in an elevator with a woman wearing jeans, a sweat shirt, and a large button which reads "I am woman." Powell, pointedly, says nothing. Later he explains that the woman was a motion picture executive. Powell goes on to discuss his problems with managing people in the creative fields of recording, movie making, and the like:

  . . . "this industry requires different rules. My B-school training simply did not prepare me to deal with this environment. None of the sophisticated marketing or sales projection techniques really work. The best ideas are often a shot in the dark—a gut feeling. Moreover, the artists have, at best, peculiar work habits and outsized egos. The creative staff will not follow orders, constantly demand artistic freedom, and must be persuaded to follow a profitable path. If you push them too hard, there

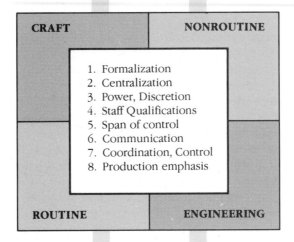

CRAFT

1. Moderate
2. Moderate
3. Craftsmen
4. Work Experience
5. Moderate to wide
6. Horizontal, Verbal
7. Training, Meetings
8. Quality

NONROUTINE

1. Low
2. Low
3. Employees
4. Training plus experience
5. Moderate-Narrow
6. Horizontal, Meetings
7. Group meetings, Norms
8. Quality

1. Formalization
2. Centralization
3. Power, Discretion
4. Staff Qualifications
5. Span of control
6. Communication
7. Coordination, Control
8. Production emphasis

ROUTINE

1. High
2. High
3. Management
4. Low
5. Wide
6. Vertical, Written
7. Rules, Budgets, Reports
8. Quantity, Efficiency

ENGINEERING

1. Moderate
2. Moderate
3. Technical Specialists
4. Formal training
5. Moderate
6. Written and Verbal
7. Reports, Meetings
8. Reliability

Figure 5.7. Relationship of Department Technology to Structural and Management Characteristics.

are plenty of other rivals ready to hire them, especially the really creative ones. Sometimes staff members will work on an idea until 2:00 a.m. and then not show up for work until 11:00. Sometimes they hit a creative roadblock and need a walk in Central Park."[31]

Creative Industries is an example of a craft technology in which creative work is not analyzable. Employees have substantial power and discretion, and formalization is low. The production emphasis is on quality—developing a really great idea—rather than on production quantity or efficiency. Most communication and coordination is horizontal through face-to-face discussion.

THE TECHNOLOGICAL IMPERATIVE

The discovery of technology as an important variable in the design of organization structure began with Woodward's findings from manufacturing firms. The notion that technology had a compelling influence on structure quickly took hold, and became known as the "technological imperative." The Aston studies did not support the notion of technology as an "imperative" because other variables, such as size or the environment, also influenced structure, perhaps more so than technology in some organizations. Technology appeared to have greatest influence in small organizations or in specific departments of large organizations.

A substantial amount of additional research was undertaken over the next several years to sort out the relationship of technology to structure in a variety of organizational settings. For example, John Child gathered data on eighty-two British business organizations using the same variables and procedures as the Aston group.[32] Child concluded that the findings of the Aston group were correct. Size was a better predictor of most structural charactristics than was production technology. However, technology did have a relationship with specialization, standardization, formalization, and centralization, and, most important, technology had a stronger relationship in smaller firms.

Other studies followed. Pradip Khandwalla mailed questionnaires to presidents of seventy-nine American manufacturing firms.[33] Peter Blau and others compared technology and size to several structural dimensions in 110 manufacturing organizations in New Jersey.[34] They used measures similar to Woodward's for technology, but they also studied the use of computers as an additional form of technology. The Khandwalla and Blau et al. findings in general supported the influence of technology as *selective*—it depended on the specific structural variable under consideration. Technology, for example, was related to decentralization of operating decisions, and had greater influence in profitable firms.

Most technology research thus reveals a similar pattern. In large organizations, technology has a limited relationship with structure.[35] The logic of the technological imperative was perhaps best captured in a recent paper that distinguished between organization-wide and workflow measures of technology and structure.[36] Organization-wide technologies tend to be related to organization-wide structural variables, and workflow technologies tend to be related to workflow structures.

It is appropriate to conclude that technology does influence the design of organization structure, but with limitations. Organization structure in giant corporations is the result of many influences. The exact structure and design will reflect the influence of technology, size, and environment. The effect of technology is greatest when a firm is small and for structural characteristics (e.g., supervisor span of control) that are close to workflow technology. The effect of technology is also greater at the department level. The application of technology to the design of large organizations is most helpful if managers think of large organizations as a series of separate departments, and design the structure of each department to fit its technology.

Is Technology Fixed?

An issue that is related to the technological imperative contains a puzzlement for managers that has yet to be resolved. The issue is whether technology is fixed and hence the structure has to be designed to fit it, or whether technology can be altered so that other structures might be appropriate. Several theorists have recently argued that technology is not fixed, but is the result of the interpretation and choice of managers.[37] In other words, managers interpret the technology. Does the interpretation or the underlying technology determine the appropriate structure? Consider the following case.

IN PRACTICE 5.5

Reform School

Street, Vinter, and Perrow described two very different structures for what appeared to be the same technology—changing delinquent boys into nondelinquent boys.[38] In Institution A, delinquent boys were handled with rigid regulation and discipline. They were constantly watched, marched about, and taught to say "Yes, sir" and "No sir," and they were frequently counted and inspected. The boys had to ask permission for small requests, such as going to the bathroom. There were strict rules for all behavior. They were not allowed to talk during meals. Punishment for rule infractions was frequently physical, such as paddling in front of other boys. Runaways had their heads shaved, and they were sentenced to a diet of bread and water and put in isolation. This style for working with delinquent boys was compatible with the managers' beliefs about the transformation process. They believed that boys were delinquent because they lacked respect and obedience, and that respect and obedience could be taught through rigid regulation and discipline. Delinquent boys were all the same (low variety) and the task was highly analyzable. Organization members perceived they knew exactly how to straighten the boys out. The structure and management style could be characterized as centralized and mechanistic and were perfectly suited to a routine technology.

Institution B approached the task quite differently. Delinquents were free to talk at mealtime, and they frequently griped about the food. The boys were permitted to horse around at bedtime, and they were allowed to resolve many of their own problems with the other boys, so that quarrels would occasionally erupt. Rules and regulations were minimized. Supervision was also minimal. There were few sanctions for misbehavior. Treats might be withdrawn, but some infractions were not punished at all. Once again, this style of handling delinquent boys was compatible with the perception of the task. Members believed that the delinquent's problems were psychological. Staff members saw each delinquent as unique. They had to learn about each boy in detail, and necessary changes could be brought about only through understanding, empathy, and a permissive environment. Each boy was considered different (high variety) and the task of rehabilitation was not analyzable. Thus a highly organic management approach was developed to fit this nonroutine technology.

In each of the institutions, the management structure fit the technology as perceived by organization managers. The puzzling issue is whether the technology was indeed routine or nonroutine. Most people would agree that the technology for rehabilitating delinquent boys is nonroutine. The managers at Institution A made a mistake, and hence adopted the wrong structure. In the case of manufacturing organizations, technologies are typically fixed and there is little leeway for differences in interpretation. For other types of departments there may be leeway in how technology is perceived, which makes the diagnosis and application of management concepts more complicated. Organization theorists don't have a precise answer to this problem. Questionnaires like the one in In Practice 5.3 help. Fortunately, substantial agreement does exist in most organizations about the nature of the underlying technology.

TASK INTERDEPENDENCE

The final characteristic of technology is interdependence. James Thompson proposed that structure and workflow within organizations is based upon task interdependence.[39] Interdependence means the extent to which employees or departments depend upon each other to accomplish their tasks. Low interdependence means that departments can do their work independently of each other and have little need for interaction, consultation, or exchange of materials.

Pooled Interdependence Pooled is the lowest form of interdependence departments can have and still be a part of the same organization. Work does not flow between units. Each department is part of the organization and contributes to the common good of the organization, but works independently. McDonald's stores are an example of pooled interdependence.

Branch banking is another example. A branch in Chicago does not need to interact with a branch in Urbana. The only connection between branches is that they share financial resources from a common pool, and the success of each branch contributes to the success of the organization.

The management implications associated with pooled interdependence are quite simple. Thompson argued that managers should standardize across departments. Each department should use the same procedures and financial statements so their outcomes can be measured and pooled. Very little day-to-day coordination is required among units.

Sequential Interdependence When interdependence is of serial form, with parts produced in one plant becoming inputs to another plant, then the interdependence is called sequential. The first plant must perform correctly in order for the second plant to perform correctly. This is a higher level of interdependence than pooled, because some plants depend upon others to perform well.

The management requirements are more demanding than they are for pooled interdependence. Coordination among plants is required. Since the interdependence implies a one-way flow of materials, extensive planning is generally needed. Plant B needs to know what to expect from Plant A so both can perform effectively. Some day-to-day communication among plants is also needed to ensure that exceptions to plans are handled satisfactorily.

Reciprocal Interdependence The highest level of interdependence is reciprocal. Output of operation A is the input to operation B, and the output of operation B is the input back again to operation A. The output of departments influences one another in reciprocal fashion. An airline that contains both operations and maintenance units is an example. The output of production is serviceable aircraft that are ready for operations, and the output of operations is aircraft in need of maintenance. Each unit is influenced by the other.

Management requirements are greatest in the case of reciprocal interdependence. The structure must allow for frequent communication and adjustment. Extensive planning is required, but plans generally will not anticipate or solve all the problems. Continuous interaction and mutual adjustment are required. Managers are heavily involved in coordination and decision-making. Reciprocal interdependence is the most complex interdependence for organizations to handle.

Structural Implications Since decision-making, communication, and coordination problems are greatest for reciprocal interdependence, it should receive priority in organization structure. Activities that are reciprocally interdependent should be grouped together (clustered) in the organization so they have easy access to one another for mutual adjustment. These units should report to the same person on the organization chart and be physically close so coordination costs can be minimized. Poor coordination will result in poor performance for the organization. If the reciprocally interdependent units cannot be grouped together, the organization should build in additional mechanisms for coordination, such as daily meetings between departments.

After grouping units to allow for reciprocal interdependencies, the next priority is given to sequential interdependencies, and finally to pooled interdependencies. If no reciprocal interdependencies exist within the organization, sequential interdependencies take priority. This strategy of organizing keeps the communication channels short where coordination is most critical to organizational success. The types of interdependencies and their implications for communication, coordination, and structure are summarized in figure 5.8.

The impact of interdependency on coordination methods was investigated by Van de Ven, Delbecq, and Koenig for 197 departments in a large state employment security agency.[40] They found strong support for the relationship between interdependency and coordination. The relationship between workflow interdependence and types of coordination used within the departments in the employment agency is summarized in figure 5.9. Lesser amounts of task interdependence were handled by rules (standardization) and plans, and greater levels of interdependence were handled by face-to-face meetings and other forms of mutual adjustment.

Figure 5.8. Thompson's Classification of Interdependence and Management Implications.

Form of Interdependence	Demands on Communication, Decision Making	Type of Coordination	Priority in Structural Grouping
Pooled 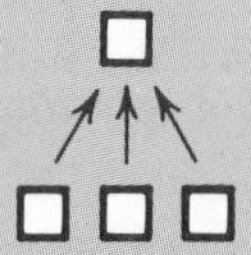	Low	Standardization	Low
Sequential 	Medium	Plan	Medium
Reciprocal 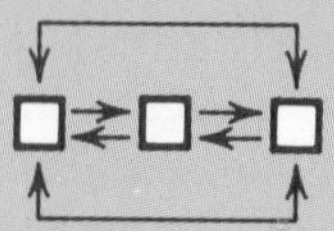	High	Mutual Adjustment	High

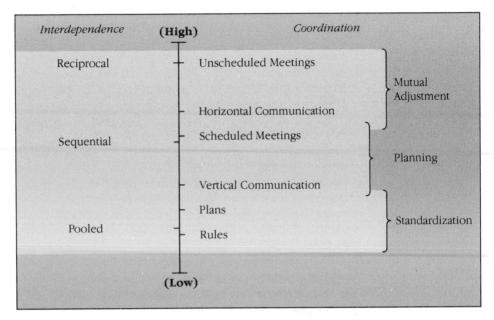

Figure 5.9. Primary Means to Achieve Coordination for Different Levels of Task Interdependence.
Adapted from Van de Ven, Delbecq, and Koenig, "Determinants of Communication Modes Within Organizations," *American Sociological Review* 41 (1976): 330.

IN PRACTICE 5.6

Putnam Plastics, Inc.

Putnam Plastics manufactures and sells plastic materials across a wide geographical area in the eastern United States. Six months ago, Putnam installed a computerized system that gave the sales managers an up-to-date readout of availability of goods. Sales personnel in the field can have their inquiries answered in a few minutes and this has stimulated sales. At the point of sale, the sales person can place a telephone call to the sales clerk in the Sales Processing Department to obtain up-to-date information on prices and availability and delivery dates. The pricing information is provided by the sales clerk who obtains availability information from the order clerk in the Production Department. The order clerk interrogates the computer for a readout on the availability of the goods and probable delivery date. Sales people can thus respond very quickly to customer inquiries about the availability and anticipated delivery date of an order.

Sales people like this quick access to information, but some customers have complained about subsequent treatment. Once the order is taken, the sales clerk in the Sales Department requests a credit clearance from the Finance Department. Most orders are then written up by the sales clerk and processed through to the warehouse clerk, while other orders have to be altered or cancelled because of credit limitations on a particular customer or unacceptable credit ratings. This subsequent treatment occurs to about 10% of the orders and has resulted in bad relations with prospective customers. It has also created some internal tension between the Sales Manager and Credit Manager, as well as the sales clerks and the credit analysis personnel.

Using a task interdependence approach to analyze Putnam's sales-credit problem, figure 5.10 shows how the work moves through the organization. Interactions numbered 1, 2, 3, and 4 show the initial inquiry to obtain pricing and availability of goods, interaction 5 involves the request for credit clearance, interaction 6 depicts those cases in which the credit check results in an alteration or a cancellation of a customer order, and interaction 7 indicates the processing of an order through the warehouse. Three departments are involved in one unit of work that includes order processing.

Using the interdependence criterion, a reorganization of order processing would group all the reciprocal activities and personnel involved in the ordering process into one unit with one supervisor. Figure 5.11 shows the workflow under the revised organization design. The Sales Clerk, Credit Analysis Clerk, and Order Clerk functions are grouped into one work unit under the direction of an Order Process Supervisor. The broken lines connecting the functional manager to respective clerks represent functional relationships.

Figure 5.10. Task Interdependencies and Workflow at Putnam Plastics. Based on "The Sales-Credit Controversy," in *The Measure of Management*, by Eliot D. Chapple and Leonard R. Sayles (New York: MacMillan, 1961), p. 23, as adapted by John F. Veiga and John N. Yanouzas, in Veiga and Yanouzas, eds., *The Dynamics of Organization Theory* (St. Paul: West, 1979), p. 218.

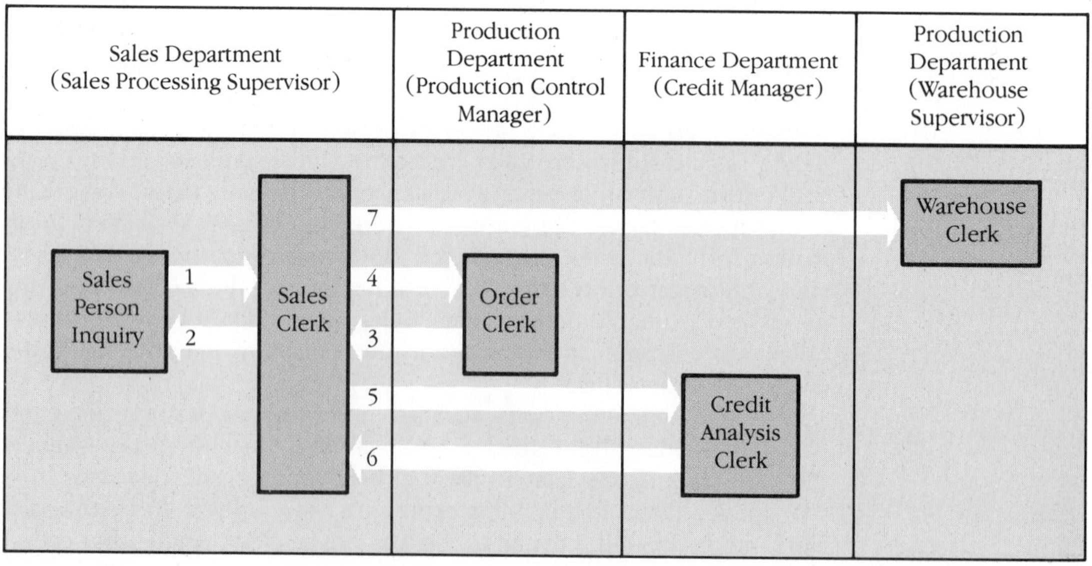

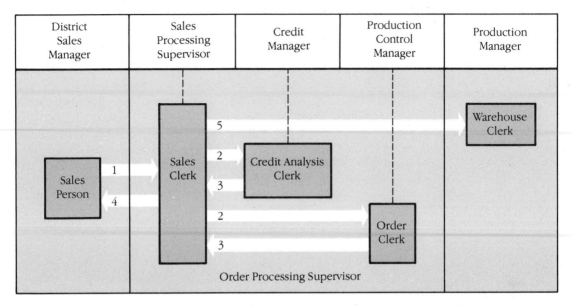

District Sales Manager	Sales Processing Supervisor	Credit Manager	Production Control Manager	Production Manager

Figure 5.11. Reorganization that Groups Highly Interdependent Functions Together.
Based on "The Sales-Credit Controversy," in *The Measure of Management*, by Eliot D. Chapple and Leonard R. Sayles (New York: MacMillan, 1961), p. 26, as adapted by John F. Veiga and John N. Yanouzas, in Veiga and Yanouzas, eds., *The Dynamics of Organization Theory* (St. Paul: West, 1979), p. 220.

The sales person still makes inquiries to the sales clerk, and will receive feedback after a decision is made. Reciprocal functions requiring mutual adjustment for order processing are handled in one unit supervised by the same person. Coordination under the workflow pictured in figure 5.11 is much more effective because communication and mutual adjustment are easier.[41]

SUMMARY AND INTERPRETATION

This chapter has reviewed several frameworks and key research findings on the topic of organizational technology. The potential importance of technology as a factor in organizational structure was discovered during the 1960s. During the 1970s, a flurry of research activity was undertaken to understand more precisely the relationship of various technology dimensions to other characteristics of organization. In the 1980s, the number of technology studies is declining somewhat. Technology is understood quite well, and no new technology frameworks have been developed. The field of research is now in a period of consolidation, with several attempts being made to draw out key findings and relationships from the available research.

There are three concepts in the technology literature that stand out as especially important. The first is Woodward's research into manufacturing technology. Her work is a model for how organizational research should be undertaken. Woodward decided to explore the validity of established principles, and was willing to modify her thinking based upon what she learned from her data. She went into organizations and collected large amounts of practical data, including administrative ratio, hierarchical levels, span of control, direct/indirect labor ratio, formalization, centralization, and the use of verbal and written communication. She sought basic underlying relationships, and reported her findings in a simple and straightforward manner. She presented each characteristic of organizations in each technology category. Her findings are so clear and informative that managers without training in organization theory can use them. Managers can analyze how their own organizations compare on the same dimensions of management structure.

The second significant concept is Perrow's framework applied to department technologies. Understanding the variety and analyzability of a technology tells us about the management style, structure, and process that should characterize that department. For people who do not wish to use these two dimensions separately, the simple notion of routine versus non-routine work can be very informative. Department technology is an important idea because applying the wrong management system to a department will result in dissatisfaction and less than optimum efficiency.

The third important concept is interdependence. The extent to which departments depend on each other for materials, information, or other resources determines the amount of coordination required between them. As interdependence increases, demands on the organization for coordination increase. Interdependence is thus an important basis for determining organizational design. The concept of interdependence will be used again in later chapters to explain organization structure and manager behavior.

Two other models of technology were also covered in this chapter. The first is Thompson's classification of technologies as mediating, long-linked, and intensive. Thompson's contribution with this classification was to link technology with customers in the environment. A bank, for example, could be considered a mediating technology because it brings together savers and borrowers from the environment. Thompson's purpose was not to describe internal technology but to understand how the organization's task is related to the external environment. For this reason, his framework is not as easy to apply to the structure and design of specific organizations. The implications of Thompson's classification have yet to be fully explored by organization scholars.

The concept of workflow integration developed by the Aston group is the final framework. This framework was developed to measure technology in all types of organizations. Since the scale is generalizable to all organizations, the practical implication for any single organization is not always clear. Specifying the appropriate structure can be difficult because research has not yet connected specific structural variables to specific technology characteristics.

Why include several models of technology if some do not have immediate practical application? The answer is that the models are useful for developing an understanding of organizations. Both the Thompson model and the technology measures developed by the Aston group help us map out and think about organizations. Only by exploring different conceptualizations, some of which are practical and some not so practical, can people come away with a set of ideas and models that will be useful to future analysis and applications. The Aston group showed how size and technology both influence structure. They also discovered that the impact of technology is greater in small organizations and on structures located close to the workflow. These general relationships are important to the design of organizations.

DISCUSSION QUESTIONS

1. Where would your university department be located on Perrow's technology framework? Try to look for the underlying variety and analyzability characteristics when making your assessment. Would a department devoted exclusively to teaching be put in a different quadrant from a department devoted exclusively to research?

2. Explain Thompson's levels of interdependence. Identify an example of each level of interdependence in the university setting. What kinds of coordination mechanisms should management develop to handle each level of interdependence?

3. Describe Woodward's classification of organizational technologies, and provide an example of each type.

4. How do you reconcile the separate influences of technology and size on organization structure? Under what circumstances would one or the other be more important?

5. What does it mean to say that technology has influence on structure that is centered on the workflow?

6. What was the relationship Woodward discovered between supervisor span of control and technological complexity? Would this be called a linear or curvilinear relationship? Are there factors other than technology (e.g., educational level of employees) that might account for this relationship?

7. Manufacturing versus service firms tend to be located on opposite ends of the Aston group's technology continuum (table 5.2). What does this mean? Does the transformation process for service organizations seem different from that for manufacturing organizations?

8. Edna Peterson retired from the Air Force as a colonel in charge of the finance section of an air base in New Mexico. Financial work in the military involves large amounts of routine matters and paperwork, and Edna gradually developed a philosophy of management that was fairly mechanistic. She believed that all important decisions should be made by administrators, that elaborate rules and procedures should be developed and followed, and that subordinates should have little discretion and be tightly controlled. After retiring, Edna obtained a job as administrator of a small hospital in Texas. In this administrative capacity she had to deal extensively with physicians and other professional groups

(nurses, technicians) within the hospital. This hospital also had the only 24-hour emergency room in the area. What do you think will happen when Edna applies her management philosophy to the hospital setting? Will she be successful? Should her management style be contingent upon the type of work the organization performs?

9. A top executive claimed that top-level management is a "craft" technology because the work contains intangibles such as handling personnel, interpreting the environment, and coping with unusual situations that have to be learned through experience. If this is true, is it appropriate to teach management in a business school? Does teaching management from a textbook assume that the manager's job is analyzable, and hence that formal training rather than experience is most important?

10. In which quadrant of Perrow's framework would a mass-production technology be placed? Where would small-batch and continuous-process technologies be placed? Why? If you have work experience in any of the manufacturing technologies described by Woodward, complete the questions in In Practice 5.3 and see where they are located on Perrow's framework. Would Perrow's framework lead to the same recommendation about organic versus mechanistic structures that Woodward made?

GUIDES TO ACTION

As an organization manager:

1. Relate organization structure to technology. Technology has its greatest impact in small organizations and individual departments. Use the two dimensions of variety and analyzability to discover whether the work in a department is routine or nonroutine. If the work in a department is routine, use a mechanistic structure and process. If the work in a department is nonroutine, use an organic management process. Figure 5.7 illustrates this relationship between technology and organization structure.

2. Use the categories developed by Woodward to diagnose whether the primary production activities in a major manufacturing unit are small batch, mass production, or continuous process. Use an organic structure with small batch or continuous technologies. Use a mechanistic structure with mass production technologies.

3. Evaluate the interdependencies between organizational departments. Using the general rule that as interdependencies increase, mechanisms for coordination must also increase.

4. Analyze actual conditions or circumstances in an organization using technology. As an example let us analyze a greeting card company (figure 5.12) that produces about ten million cards a year with five hundred designs. Department technologies as well as interdependencies between departments should be considered in the design of an appropriate organization structure. Thus in the marketing function, planning and forecasting is nonroutine, and should have an organic structure.

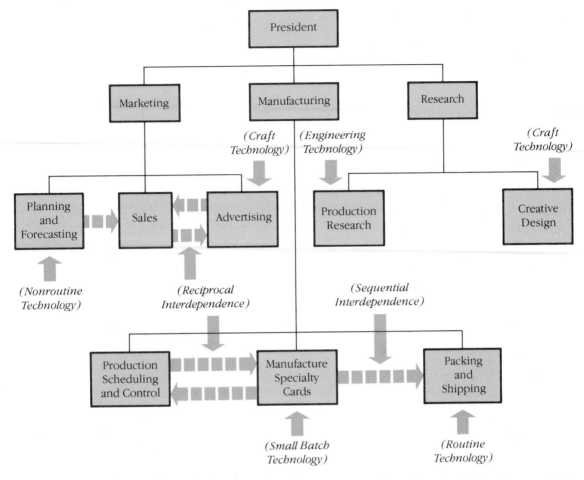

Figure 5.12. Examples of Departments and Interdependencies in a Greeting Card Company.

Interdependence with other units is sequential, so they would send written reports to other departments as a result of their studies into future trends. The sales and advertising departments have craft characteristics, and they are highly interdependent with one another. Amount of sales influences advertising strategy and vice versa. Mechanisms are needed for continuous mutual adjustment, so frequent meetings would be required.

The shop activity in manufacturing is small batch, and should have the management system described by Woodward (organic, small number of levels, medium span of control, little indirect labor, small administrative ratio). Shipping is very routine, and should have a mechanistic structure. The interdependence between manufacturing and shipping is sequential because materials move in one direction to shipping. Planning would be a satisfactory way to coordinate these two units.

Production scheduling is reciprocally interdependent with manufacturing. Scheduling decides the flow of work through the manufacturing process. Any completed job or delay is an input back to scheduling, which may change the scheduling of other orders. Mutual adjustment is required between the scheduling and manufacturing departments. Production schedulers will go out on the shop floor and talk directly to supervisors.

Production engineering is an engineering technology, and creative design is a craft technology. Engineering personnel would have more formal education, while creative personnel would rely on experience and intuition for their work. The interdependence between the two departments is low, so employees would not need regular meetings. An occasional exchange of technical information would be all that is required. Each of these departments provides services to other parts of the organization, however, so for specific projects they would need regular meetings and horizontal communication to coordinate with users.

Consider these Guides when analyzing the following case and when answering the questions listed after the case.

CASE FOR ANALYSIS

OLSON'S LOCKER PLANT[42]

Olson's Locker plant is located in Grand Island, Nebraska, a city of about 50,000 people. The locker plant was started in 1952 by Herb Olson when he came out of early retirement. He had been co-owner and manager with his wife of a successful downtown hotel and restaurant until she died. He sold the business in 1950 at the age of 40. Two years later he decided to buy a small locker plant as a way to keep busy and increase his knowledge of the meat business.

For the first two years, all work was completed by Mr. Olson and an assistant who helped with the butchering. His clients were people who wished to have a hog or steer butchered, cut, and wrapped to order. The plant also had a small counter and meatcase in the front from which Mr. Olson sold meat to walk-in customers.

Olson's reputation for selling good meat at a fair price quickly spread. The business grew steadily. After ten years he had twenty-two employees, and after twenty-five years he employs seventy people. The locker plant still does custom orders, but 70% of its business in 1978 is supplying meat to independent grocery stores, restaurants, and small markets in central Nebraska. Beef products account for 60% of the volume, pork the other 40%. The locker plant now handles about 35,000 lbs. of meat a day.

Plant and Equipment   As the volume of business increased, the locker plant became more mechanized. The plant is located in a single-story building with 7,000 square feet of work space. The building is divided into two parts. One side is used to kill and dress animals. The other side is used to cut and prepare finished meats for delivery to customers.

Mechanization has developed to the point where carcasses are now transported through the plant entirely by hooks and overhead rails. Workers use mechanical tools for several operations, such as power saws for splitting carcasses and a hydraulic winch to pull the skin from the carcass.

Employees range in age from eighteen to sixty-two. Workers on the shop floor are considered semiskilled and paid an hourly wage. The company is not unionized. Turnover is low. Many employees have been with the company several years. Most do not have formal education beyond high school.

Organization

Olson's locker plant has a simple organization structure. Herb Olson is president. The management team includes a treasurer, who also helps with the purchase of pigs and cattle. A sales manager has two salespeople reporting to him. The sales manager and one sales representative handle outside sales. The other salesperson handles sales over the counter. Other management personnel include an industrial engineer, a personnel director, and the plant superintendent. All workers involved in the conversion of live animals to packaged meat report to the plant superintendent. The managers meet every Thursday evening to review their respective activities and to share information. This meeting is used to coordinate activities and to discuss solutions to unexpected problems.

The Pork Conversion Process

The process for converting live pigs into bacon and ham normally requires fourteen operations. The dressing sequence begins by stunning the pig electrically. A rear limb is shackled, and the pig is elevated to an overhead rail where it is stuck and bled. The carcass is then dipped mechanically into a scalding tank for up to five minutes, where the hair is loosened. After scalding, pigs are moved mechanically to the dehairing area where the carcasses are scraped clean. The scraping process is partly accomplished by hand. After dehairing, the carcass is transferred to the singeing area. Singeing darkens the meat's outer edge and produces skin that has good leather quality. The carcass is then eviscerated. Next the carcass is skinned and the head is removed. Finally, the carcass is split in half with a handheld electric saw. At this point the carcass is inspected for disease and sent to the chilling room.

Pig halves are taken from the chilling room as needed by the meat-cutting operation. In this area, meat is thawed, cut into hams, bellies, and shoulders, injected with brine, boned, smoked, packed for sale or shipment, and rechilled.

A more detailed description of selected steps in the pork conversion process follows.

Skinning Skinning is next to the last operation in the butchering and dressing process. The pig carcass hangs from the overhead rail, and the lower end is anchored by a hook in the jaw cavity to secure the carcass. The skin is cut open down the back of the front legs, down the back of the back legs, and down the middle of the belly. The legs are skinned out by hand with a sharp knife. An employee also loosens a fold of skin about three inches wide along each side of the belly cut. The knife should be used carefully and kept tight against the skin at all times. The fat is soft and easily cut. Gashes made by uncontrolled strokes of the knife do considerable damage to hams and bacons that are to be cured. A mechanical winch is then hooked to a fold of skin behind the neck, and it pulls the skin up-ward in a rapid motion, peeling it from the carcass. The carcass is then washed and moved to the next work station for splitting.

Brine Injection Brine injection is the third procedure in the meat-cutting operation. After warming the carcass and cutting it into hams and shoulders, brine is injected into the meat. The purpose of the brine injection is to introduce a solution of salt, sugar, and nitrates into the meat. The salt acts as a preservative while the nitrates are used to retain the reddish color of the meat. The brine is injected by hand using a series of injection needles that are connected to a pumping machine. The brine ensures a more uniform cure and reduces the curing time to two or three days. Bellies are injected twice, once in the morning and again in the evening.

The injection requires modest skill. Operators are responsible to see that the quantity of solution does not exceed the limit set by federal law. They must also see that the brine is injected uniformly throughout the meat, and see that the needles are inserted into the arteries. The rate and pressure of the brine injection is controlled by the pumping machine.

Smoking All pork products at Olson's Locker Plant are smoked during the conversion process. The purpose of smoking is to cook the raw meat and thus convert it to an edible product. The combination of heat and smoke causes a significant reduction in surface bacteria, so it is an important health item. Smoking also imparts a smoky flavor to the meat, which makes it more appealing to the customer. Smoking in the locker plant takes place in a separate smokehouse, which is actually an insulated room in which steam and smoke are introduced through a system of pipes. The smoke flavor is caused by the insertion of hickory, maple, and mahogany shavings in the fire that produces smoke. The minimum temperature for smoking a product can vary widely, depending upon the time available. Smoking at Olson's Locker Plant usually takes place at about 130° F and lasts two days.

Smokehouse operators are responsible for deciding when a product is properly cooked. The final decision rests on the operator's judgment and is based on touch and appearance. Temperature, humidity, and other weather factors influence the required smoking time. There are many devices for measuring smokehouse conditions, but the final decision is based on personal experience and judgment.

Boning The boning operation consists of trimming excess fat and cutting out the bones from hams and shoulders. Five employees are assigned to this task. They work around a large rectangular table. Boning the meat typically takes three times as long as trimming the fat and is the most difficult task. The workers along the boning platform are considered to be among the most skilled in the plant. Great dexterity is required to trim the fat and remove the bone with a minimum of waste. It takes a new person at least six months to gain proficiency in this task. Eight different methods of trimming and boning have to be learned to handle the various cuts of meat. Each ham within any category can present specific problems, depending upon size and the amount of fat and skin remnants. An experienced operator can tell immediately whether a ham will be difficult to work with. The criteria for assigning people to the boning operation are two years of experience working with meat and excellent manual dexterity.

Other Tasks **_Industrial Engineering_** In 1976, Mr. Olson hired an industrial engineer to improve internal efficiency. The industrial engineer works to establish production standards to control costs. He is also involved with production planning. The work includes studying the production operation throughout the plant, time and motion studies of each task, and suggesting new work procedures. The industrial engineer is also responsible for evaluating new equipment with respect to cost and labor savings. A monthly labor analysis report is also prepared for Olson and the plant superintendent.

The industrial engineering function encompasses several activities that require an engineering background. The industrial engineer's most important task is to develop production standards that measure productivity. Accurate production standards also help management schedule the flow of meat through the plant.

Purchasing and Selling Herb Olson spends most of his time purchasing live animals and making sales to area stores. The company has two people making outside sales, but many buyers want to deal directly with Mr. Olson.

Livestock purchasing is tricky because there is no organized commodity market for meat in the area. Meat prices in the major centers (Omaha) fluctuate daily. Seventy percent of the cost of the finished product is the value of the livestock, so purchase price directly influences profit margins. Mr. Olson usually talks daily with meat brokers, local farmers, sale barns, and other sources of price information. He also negotiates directly with area farmers to buy livestock at a fixed price to reduce the risk for both sides. These purchases require Mr. Olson to visit farms and inspect the pigs.

Purchasing decisions are made quickly and informally. Formal confirmation is usually by letter, but the meat is often already shipped. Buyer and seller have to trust each other. Extensive experience is required to handle the purchase of livestock. Carcasses are also purchased from area slaughtering plants to handle unusual fluctuations in the demand for cut meat.

Mr. Olson stays in telephone contact with many buyers of his company's meat products. He visits stores on the way to visiting farms for the purchase of pigs and cattle. His salespeople also spend time telephoning and calling on local store buyers. An inside salesperson handles the sales paper work, and sells meat to customers over the counter. Mr. Olson stresses to the salesforce that they are to provide service to the customer no matter what the cost. He believes that as long as the company strives for perfection and customer satisfaction, the company will continue to grow and prosper.

Mr. Olson told an interviewer, "The most difficult part of my job is forecasting meat prices in the future. About 70% of the time I can predict whether prices will increase or decrease and make purchase contracts accordingly."

Order Assembly   The last step in the production sequence is the assembly of customer orders. Three people perform this operation. They assemble items from finished stock, move them to the packing area, check the assembled order against the customer's order, and arrange for shipment.

Questions

1. How would you classify Olson's Locker Plant in the Woodward, Thompson, and Aston group frameworks? Explain.
2. Do the different tasks in the organization reflect different types of department technologies as described by Perrow? How would you classify them?
3. What structure and management characteristics would you recommend for Olson's Locker Plant? Discuss.

NOTES

1. Robert Blauner, *Alienation and Freedom* (Chicago: The University of Chicago Press, 1964), pp. 62–64, with permission.
2. Charles Perrow, "A Framework for the Comparative Analysis of Organizations," *American Sociological Review* 32 (1967): 194–208; Denise M. Rosseau, "Assessment of Technology in Organizations: Closed versus Open Systems Approaches," *Academy of Management Review* 4 (1979): 531–542.
3. Charles Perrow, *Organizational Analysis: A Sociological Approach* (Belmont, CA: Wadsworth, 1970): William Rushing, "Hardness of Material as Related to the Division of Labor in Manufacturing Industries," *Administrative Science Quarterly* 13 (1968): 229–245.
4. Lawrence B. Mohr, "Organizational Technology and Organization Structure," *Administrative Science Quarterly* 16 (1971): 444–459; David Hickson, Derek Pugh, and Diana Pheysey, "Operations Technology and Organization Structure: An Empirical Reappraisal," *Administrative Science Quarterly* 14 (1969): 378–397.
5. Joan Woodward, *Industrial Organization: Theory and Practice* (London: Oxford University Press, 1965); and *Management and Technology* (London: Her Majesty's Stationary Office, 1958).
6. Pradip Khandwalla, "Mass Output Orientation of Operations Technology and Organization Structure," *Administrative Science Quarterly* 19 (1974): 74–97.
7. Hickson, Pugh, and Pheysey, "Operations Technology and Organization Structure"; James D. Thompson, *Organizations in Action* (New York: McGraw-Hill, 1967).
8. Edward Harvey, "Technology and the Structure of Organizations," *American Sociological Review* 33 (1968): 241–259.

9. This discussion is based on Woodward, *Industrial Organizations* and *Management and Technology.*

10. Woodward, *Industrial Organizations,* p. vi.

11. William L. Zwerman, *New Perspectives on Organizational Theory* (Westport, CN: Greenwood Publishing Co., 1970).

12. Harvey, "Technology and the Structure of Organizations," pp. 241–259.

13. Thompson, *Organizations in Action.*

14. Thompson, *Organizations in Action,* p. 40.

15. Hickson, Pugh, and Pheysey, "Operations Technology and Organization Structure"; Derek Pugh, David Hickson, and C. Turner, "The Context of Organization Structure," *Administrative Science Quarterly* 14 (1969): 91–114.

16. Derek Pugh, David Hickson, and C. Turner, "Dimensions of Organization Structure," *Administrative Science Quarterly* 8 (1968): 289–315.

17. Blauner, *Alienation and Freedom,* pp. 124–134.

18. Hickson, Pugh, and Pheysey, "Operations Technology and Organization Structure,"

19. Perrow, "Framework for Comparative Analysis," pp. 194–208, and *Organizational Analysis.*

20. Michael Withey, Richard L. Daft, and William C. Cooper, "Measures of Perrow's Work Unit Technology: An Empirical Assessment and a New Scale," *Academy of Management Journal* 25 (1982), in press.

21. Patrick E. Connor, *Organizations: Theory and Design* (Chicago: Science Research Associates, 1980); Richard L. Daft and Norman B. Macintosh, "A Tentative Exploration into Amount and Equivocality of Information Processing in Organizational Work Units," *Administrative Science Quarterly* 26 (1981): 207–224.

22. Charles A. Glisson, "Dependence of Technological Routinization on Structural Variables in Human Service Organizations," *Administrative Science Quarterly* 23 (1978): 383–395; Gerald Hage and Michael Aiken, "Routine Technology, Social Structure and Organizational Goals," *Administrative Science Quarterly* 14 (1969): 368–379.

23. Gerald D. Bell, "The Influence of Technological Components of Work Upon Management Control," *Academy of Management Journal* 8 (1965): 127–132; Peter M. Blau and Richard A. Schoenherr, *The Structure of Organizations* (New York: Basic Books, 1971).

24. A. J. Grimes and S. M. Kline, "The Technological Imperative: The Relative Impact of Task Unit, Modal Technology, and Hierarchy on Structure," *Academy of Management Journal* 16 (1973): 583–597; Lawrence G. Hrebiniak, "Job Technologies, Supervision and Work Group Structure," *Administrative Science Quarterly* 19 (1974): 395–410; Jeffrey Pfeffer, *Organizational Design* (Arlington Heights, IL: AHM, 1978), ch. 1.

25. Daft and Macintosh, "Tentative Exploration into Amount and Equivocality of Information Processing"; Michael L. Tushman, "Work Characteristics and Subunit Communication Structure: A Contingency Analysis," *Administrative Science Quarterly* 24 (1979): 82–98.

26. Andrew H. Van de Ven and Diane L. Ferry, *Measuring and Assessing Organizations* (New York: Wiley, 1980).

27. Richard L. Daft and Norman B. Macintosh, "A New Approach to Design and Use of Management Information," *California Management Review* 21 (1978): 82–92. Daft and Macintosh, "Tentative Exploration in Amount and Equivocality of Information Processing"; W. Allen Randolph, "Organizational Technology and the Media and Purpose Dimensions of Organizational Communication," *Journal of Business Research* 6 (1978): 237–259.

28. Andrew H. Van de Ven and Andre Delbecq, "A Task Contingent Model of Work Unit Structure," *Administrative Science Quarterly* 19 (1974): 183–197.

29. Perrow, *Organizational Analysis,* p. 81.

30. Michael L. Tushman, "Technological Communication in R & D Laboratories: The Impact of Project Work Characteristics," *Academy of Management Journal* 21 (1978): 624–645.

31. John F. Veiga and John N. Yanouzas, "B-Movies and B-Schools," in John F. Veiga and John N. Yanouzas, eds., *The Dynamics of Organization Theory* (St. Paul, MN: West Publishing Co., 1979), p. 234, with permission.

32. John Child, "Organization Structure and Strategies of Control: A Replication of the Aston Study," *Administrative Science Quarterly* 17 (1972): 163–177; John Child, "Predicting and Understanding Organization Structure," *Administrative Science Quarterly* 18 (1973): 168–185; John Child and Roger Mansfield, "Technology, Size and Organization Structure," *Sociology* 6 (1972): 369–392.

33. Khandwalla, "Mass Output Orientation."

34. Peter Blau, C. M. Flabe, W. McKinley, and P. K. Tracy, "Technology and Organization in Manufacturing," *Administrative Science Quarterly* 21 (1976): 20–40.

35. Richard C. Reimann, "Dimensions of Organizational Technology and Structure," *Human Relations* 30 (1977): 545–566.

36. Richard C. Reimann, "Organization Structure and Technology in Manufacturing: System Versus Workflow Level Perspectives," *Academy of Management Journal* 23 (1980): 61–77.

37. Randolph H. Bobbitt, Jr., and Jeffrey D. Ford, "Decision Maker Choice as a Determinant of Organizational Structure," *Academy of Management Review* 5 (1980): 13–23; John R. Montanari, "Managerial Discretion: An Expanded Model of Organization Choices," *Academy of Management Review* 3 (1978): 231–241; Pfeffer, *Organizational Design;* Rousseau, "Assessment of Technology in Organizations."

38. David Street, Robert Vinter, and Charles Perrow, *Organization for Treatment* (New York: The Free Press, 1966), pp. 155–158.

39. Thompson, *Organizations in Action.*

40. Andrew H. Van de Ven, Andre Delbecq, and Richard Koenig, "Determinants of Coordination Modes Within Organizations," *American Sociological Review* 41 (1976): 322–338.

41. This case is based on "The Sales-Credit Controversy," in *The Measure of Management*, by Eliot D. Chapple and Leonard R. Sayles (New York: MacMillan, 1961), pp. 21–27, as adapted by John F. Veiga and

John N. Yanouzas, "Bottom-Up Approach to Organization Design," in Veiga and Yanouzas, eds., *Dynamics of Organization Theory,* pp. 217–220, with permission.

42. This case is based on materials from Horace Thornton and J. F. Gracey, *Textbook of Meat Hygiene,* 6th ed. (London: Bailliére Tindall, 1974), pp. 517–522; John R. Romans and P. Thomas Ziegler, *The Meat We Eat* (Danville, IL: The Interstate Printers and Publishers, 1977), pp. 94–102; and "Pioneer Company (A) and (B)," in Gene W. Dalton, Paul R. Lawrence, and Jay W. Lorsch, eds., *Organization Structure and Design* (Homewood, IL: Irwin and Dorsey, 1970), pp. 165–199.

6

Functional, Product, and Matrix Structures

David C. Dawson recently became president of ESB Ray-O-Vac Corporation, the second largest battery manufacturer in the country. Dawson was a vice-president of the parent company, Inco., Ltd., when he was sent to Ray-O-Vac to turn its slumping battery business around and to untangle what was termed "an organizational Gordian knot."[1]

After spending his first few months visiting some 300 of the company's managers, Dawson identified the root of the problem as the inability to develop and market new products fast enough to keep up with major competitors. Union Carbide Corp., whose Eveready division is the nation's largest battery maker, Gould Inc., and P. R. Mallory and Co. were gaining market share at Ray-O-Vac's expense. To solve this problem, Dawson launched a major corporate reorganization aimed directly at those factors that were stifling new product introduction.

To accomplish this goal, Dawson first eliminated a layer of corporate vice presidents that he saw as a major stumbling block for new products. Then he reorganized the company on a decentralized, product-oriented basis into four major divisions: Ray-O-Vac for dry cell batteries, Exide Co. for auto batteries, Systems and Electronics Co. for products such as pacemakers and emergency lighting systems, and Universal Electric Co. for small electric motors. These companies are now autonomous operating units with their own research, product development, and marketing responsibilities. By contrast, research and development had been centralized in the previous structure. Dawson has given his managers in the field much greater responsibility and autonomy than before.

The vice-presidential layer that Dawson eliminated was originally created with the expressed purpose of linking field operations to corporate management. But each vice president was put in charge of an odd assortment of products, corporate functions, and geographical areas. These reporting relationships did not facilitate innovative product introduction, because no one in upper management was concerned with a specific product or product line. The vice presidents were overly cautious. They added a layer of approval for each innovation. Slow decision-making caused Ray-O-Vac to fall behind with new growth products, like the maintenance-free auto battery and long-life alkaline dry cells. The irony was that ESB's scientists had developed these products early but the go-ahead was bogged down in the bureaucracy. Without top management support, introduction was stalled and the competition gained the edge.

Dawson has assigned responsibility for their own operations to each division manager who reports directly to Dawson. With this new organization structure, division bosses have more impetus to develop and market products to improve division performance. Divisions can introduce products without gaining approval of headquarters. After decentralization, most of the company's top executives are still around. No one has been fired. They have just been rearranged into a new divisional structure.[2]

The president of ESB Ray-O-Vac sensed things weren't working correctly so he changed the structure, hoping internal activities, especially those concerning product innovation, would improve. Most organizations face similar circumstances at one time or another. Managers realize things aren't going very well, and they believe that reorganization may lead to improvement. The appropriate structure is often found through a process of trial and error, with reorganizations coming every few years.

Purpose of This Chapter   The concept of organization structure has been discussed in previous chapters. An organization's environment, size, technology, and goals all influence its structure. These characteristics determine such things as the number of departments in an organization and the extent to which the organization is formalized and standardized. The purpose of this chapter is to consolidate the ideas about structure and to show how they appear on the organization chart. This chapter focuses on the design of the overall organization and on the way diverse organization segments are held together.

The material on structure is presented in the following sequence. First, the four basic elements of structure are defined. Second, designing the organization chart to identify tasks and reporting relationships is covered. Third, after the basic concept of an organization chart is understood, vertical and horizontal linkages are explored. Organizations use a variety of linking mechanisms to coordinate each part of the organization into a coherent whole. Fourth, strategies for grouping organizational activities into either functional or product structures will be discussed. Finally, the matrix, which is a unique structure designed to meet special circumstances, will be analyzed. By the end of this chapter, students will be able to decide whether David Dawson made the correct choice in reorganizing ESB Ray-O-Vac into decentralized product divisions.

DEFINITION OF STRUCTURE

Organization structure is reflected in the organization chart. The organization chart represents a whole set of underlying activities and processes in an organization. The four key components in the definition of organization structure are:

1. Organization structure describes the allocation of tasks and responsibilities to individuals and departments throughout the organization.
2. Organization structure designates formal reporting relationships, including the number of levels in the hierarchy and the span of control of managers and supervisors.
3. Organization structure identifies the grouping together of individuals into departments and the grouping of departments into the total organization.
4. Organization structure includes the design of systems to ensure effective communication, coordination, and integration of effort in both vertical and horizontal directions.[3]

The first three elements of structure in the above definition are typically easiest to design. They are the "static" elements of structure that are visible on the organization chart. The fourth element is more difficult to design and implement, especially the mechanisms to achieve horizontal coordination. These are "dynamic" characteristics of structure. The next section describes how to allocate tasks and designate formal reporting relationships, and is followed by a discussion of mechanisms to achieve integration and coordination across departments and hierarchical levels.

TASKS, REPORTING RELATIONSHIPS, AND GROUPING

An ideal organization chart provides employees with information about their place in the organization, their relationship to others, their tasks and responsibilities, and to whom they report. Figure 6.1 is the organization chart for a printing company in Southern California. Each management title is listed on the chart along with the job titles that report to each manager. This organization chart illustrates reporting relationships, tasks, and groupings.

Reporting Relationships The reporting relationships in the hierarchy of authority are represented by the vertical lines in figure 6.1. The lines show who reports to whom and identify the responsibility domain for each manager and supervisor. In a large organization like Standard Oil, 100 or more charts would be required to identify all reporting relationships.

Task and Responsibility Allocation The organization chart for the printing company in figure 6.1 provides information about tasks and responsibilities. Job titles and lines of authority indicate general areas of

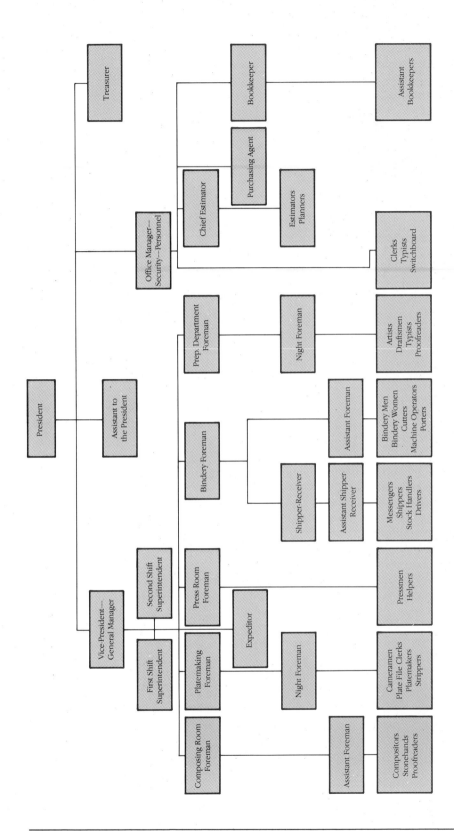

Figure 6.1. Organization Chart for a Printing Company.

responsibility. Additional charts or job descriptions could be developed that list departmental and employee responsibilities.

Functional Grouping   Employees in the printing company are grouped together by function, which means that employees who do similar jobs are grouped together and report to a common supervisor. Each employee involved in the making of printing plates reports to the platemaking supervisor. Each production supervisor reports to the vice president and general manager who is in charge of all printing activities. The administrative functions of bookkeeping, typing, and purchasing all report to the office manager.

Each organization develops its own system of organization charts and backup documents to allocate tasks and responsibilities, identify reporting relationships, and organize people into groups and departments. This documentation is part of the formalized paperwork of the organization. In a small, informal organization, organization charts may be sketchy and indicate only general departments and responsibilities. In rapidly changing organizations, the paper documentation often lags behind the actual allocation of responsibilities. In stable organizations, the charts provide a very precise and up-to-date representation of organization structure. An example of organization charts and supporting documentation is provided below for Oilfield Service Company.

IN PRACTICE 6.1

Oilfield Service Company

Oilfield Service Company is a $300-million company that markets equipment and support services for oil-drilling rigs worldwide. Oilfield Service is based in New Orleans and has about 4,000 employees. As a marketing company, most goods are purchased from other suppliers. Oilfield provides engineering expertise and service at the wellhead to make sales. Products include drilling bits, seismic & logging equipment, valves, and drilling lubricants.

The organization chart for the senior management at Oilfield Services is shown in figure 6.2. The company is large so organization charts for the areas reporting to each vice president and general manager are developed separately. The chart in figure 6.2 indicates the reporting relationships among senior management, and includes the name of each executive.

Figure 6.3 shows a responsibility chart developed for the Marketing and Sales Division at Oilfield Services. This chart specifies the tasks that people within each department are expected to perform. For example, marketing analysis is expected to do market evaluations, monitor and audit sales by area and affiliate, collect data on the competition, and analyze customer requirements.

Oilfield Services also provides position descriptions for each executive. An example of a position description for the Vice President for Marketing

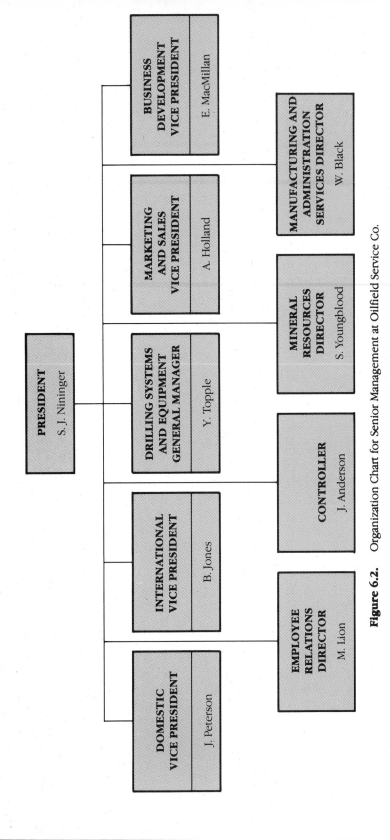

Figure 6.2. Organization Chart for Senior Management at Oilfield Service Co.

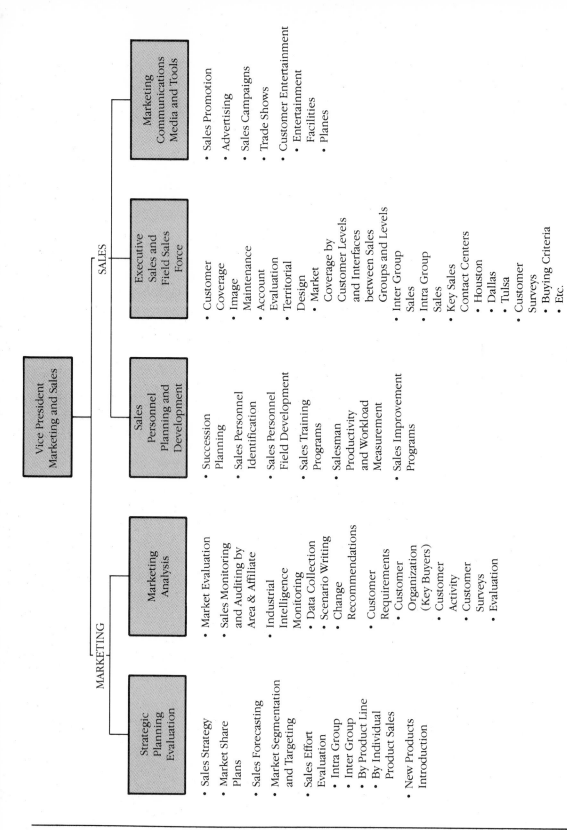

Figure 6.3. Departmental Responsibility Chart for Oilfield Services Co.

and Sales is given in figure 6.4. Responsibility charts, position descriptions, and organization charts are developed by the personnel department. Oilfield Services has a complete set of documents that specify the position in the hierarchy and task responsibilities for each employee.

VERTICAL AND HORIZONTAL STRUCTURAL LINKAGES

The organization charts described above identify tasks, responsibilities, and formal reporting relationships. Another important purpose of organization structure is to link together diverse employees, departments, and hierarchical levels. **Linkage** is defined as the extent of coordination between organizational elements. Employees located at various departments and levels are physically separated; they may not see or interact with each other on a regular basis. Yet mechanisms must be in place to ensure adequate coordination and integration of effort.

Vertical Linkages   Vertical linkages are used to coordinate activities between the top and bottom of the organization. Employees at lower levels should carry out activities consistent with top-level goals. People at the top of the organization must be informed about activities and accomplishments at the lower levels. Linkage is also required horizontally across the organization. Without horizontal linkages, decisions and activities in departments could undercut each other. Horizontal linkage ensures that the right and left hands of the organization know what the other is doing.

Figure 6.4.   Position Description Used at Oilfield Services Co.

POSITION DESCRIPTION

POSITION TITLE: Vice President Marketing and Sales

REPORTS TO: Group President

MAJOR AREAS OF RESPONSIBILITY:

Marketing Responsibility

Strategic planning and evaluation of the marketing effort.

Marketing analysis evaluation and monitoring of sales organization. Industrial intelligence, and customer requirements.

Critical sales interface between marketing and other Oilfield Service departments.

Sales Responsibilities

Sales personnel planning, development, productivity.

Executive sales and field sales force, customer coverage and territorial design. Image maintenance, account evaluation, and customer surveys.

Marketing communications, advertising, sales campaigns, trade shows, and customer entertainment.

The essence of linkage is coordination and communication. Linkage mechanisms enable diverse organization groups to communicate with each other and to coordinate their activities so that organization performance is enhanced. The discussion that follows specifies when linkages are required and the specific techniques that can be used to achieve needed coordination.

Linkage Requirements Two factors—size and uncertainty—determine the extent of vertical linkage required in the organization. When an organization is large and complex, the vertical hierarchy is longer and there are a larger number of departments that must be linked into the organizational whole. Uncertainty is the unpredictability and variability in both the organization's environment (chapter 2) and technology (chapter 5). When uncertainty is high, change will occur more frequently at both the top and bottom of the organization. Goals may change or work requirements may change. Greater linkage enables the changes to be coordinated up and down the hierarchy.

Linkage Devices Organizations may use any of a variety of structural devices to achieve vertical linkage. These structural devices include hierarchical referral, rules and procedures, plans and schedules, adding positions or levels to the hierarchy, and formal management information systems.[4] When organization size and uncertainty are great, more linkage mechanisms will be used.

Hierarchical Referral The first vertical device is the hierarchy or chain of command. If a problem arises that employees don't know how to solve, they refer it up to the next level in the hierarchy. When a cashier in a grocery store encounters an unusual situation, the correct response is to refer it to the assistant manager. When the problem is solved, the answer is passed back down to the cashier. In hierarchical referral, the lines of the organization chart act as communication channels. Information is passed up or down the hierarchy to achieve linkage.

In a new, small organization, hierarchical referral is the dominant form of vertical coordination. Whenever people have problems, they refer them to the owner/manager. As the organization becomes larger and more complex, the owner/manager will be overwhelmed with information and decisions. A single person cannot be the sole means of vertical coordination, so other mechanisms are put in place.

Rules and Procedures The next linkage device is the use of rules and procedures. To the extent that problems and decisions are repetitious, a procedure can be established so that employees know how to respond without communicating directly with their manager. Rules and procedures standardize tasks and thus eliminate the need to process information up and down the hierarchy. Rules and procedures link upper- and lower-level employees so that decisions can be made at lower levels. Rules and procedures enable the cashier and assistant manager in a grocery store to be coordinated without actually communicating about every cash transaction.

Planning and Scheduling   Another device for achieving vertical linkage is planning and scheduling. In the previous chapter about technology, planning was described as a coordination device. The most widely used plan is the budget. By establishing carefully designed plans and schedules, employees at lower levels can be left on their own to perform activities so long as the plan is met. Plans take into consideration the goals of top management and the needs of other departments. Planning and scheduling reduce the amount of information flowing up and down the hierarchy on a day-to-day basis, yet link managers along the hierarchy to each other. If a problem occurs so that the plan will not be met, managers can be informed by hierarchical referral.

Add Levels or Positions to Hierarchy   When many problems occur, planning and hierarchical referral may overload certain managers. In growing organizations or organizations experiencing high uncertainty, additional vertical linkage mechanisms may be required. One technique is to add positions to the hierarchy. In some cases, an assistant-to will be assigned to help an overloaded manager. Normally used at the top of the hierarchy where several lines of authority converge, the assistant-to acts in place of the executive and may attend meetings or establish plans in the executive's place.

As the organization grows, additional levels or positions in the direct line of authority may be added, which reduces the span of control. One position can be subdivided into two positions, which report to the same supervisor. Responsibilities are divided between the two positions. The addition of positions provides sufficient managers to handle problems and make decisions relevant to vertical responsibilities.

Vertical Information Systems   Vertical information systems are another strategy for providing vertical linkages. The purpose of information systems is to make information processing up and down the hierarchy more efficient. Vertical information systems increase the capacity to process information so that top managers do not become overloaded. Vertical information systems may reduce the need to add new positions. However, information systems normally require additional clerical and support staff to produce them. Many corporations computerize the information system. Computerized vertical information systems summarize data and compare performance to plans and schedules. These periodic reports link top management to activities at lower levels.

Summary   The structural mechanisms for achieving vertical linkage are summarized in figure 6.5. These structural mechanisms represent alternatives managers can use in designing an organization. Once the organization chart identifies the tasks and responsibilities for each employee and department, a means of achieving vertical integration is required. Depending upon the extent of coordination needed in the organization, several of the structural mechanisms shown in figure 6.5 may be used.

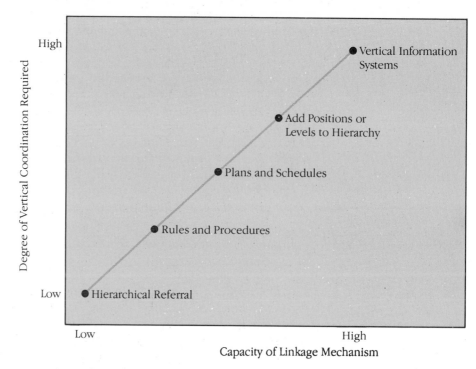

Figure 6.5. Mechanisms for Vertical Linkage and Coordination.

IN PRACTICE 6.2

Atlas Manufacturing Company

Atlas Manufacturing Company manufactures electrical and mechanical parts for home appliances. They also have a small division that specializes in heating elements. Most products are sold directly to appliance manufacturers.

The manufacturing facilities are located in Ohio, with regional sales offices located in New York and Northern California. The organization chart, including proposed additions for the future, is given in figure 6.6. Atlas Manufacturing uses several vertical linkage mechanisms to achieve coordination.

The Manufacturing General Manager established rules for materials that can be acquired in the purchasing department. Each purchasing agent has a dollar limit for certain categories of raw material and equipment. Rules and procedures guide the purchasing process. Exceptionally large or nonstandard purchases are referred up to the Manufacturing General Manager. Plans and schedules are also used. The Manufacturing General Manager works with the production department to establish specific targets, and sufficient resources are allocated to meet the plan. Forty units will be delivered to assembly each Monday. Purchasing also

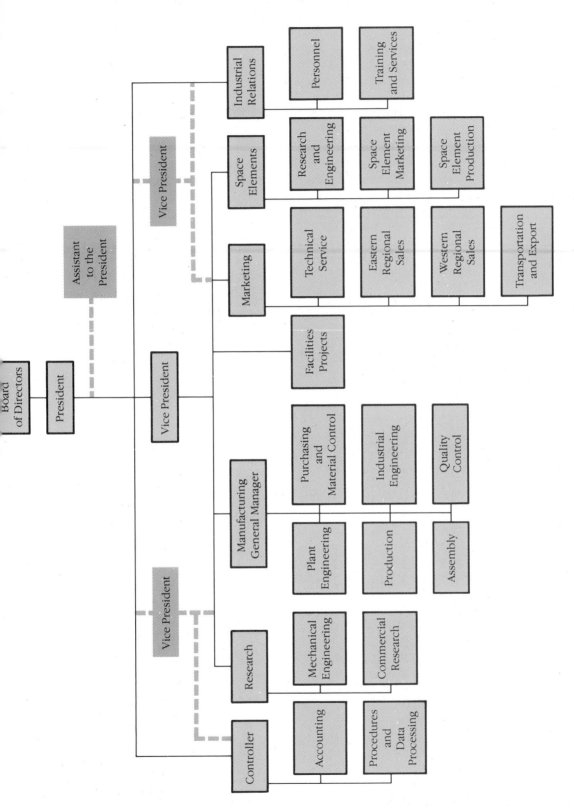

Figure 6.6. Atlas Manufacturing Co. with the Addition of Positions for Vertical Coordination.

uses plans to specify the number of parts that have to be ordered for the manufacturing process. Whenever a problem occurs, it is passed up the hierarchy. Rules and planning provide coordination for most day-to-day activities.

Rapid growth at Atlas caused the president to ask the personnel department to propose new organization charts. Both the president and executive vice president are overloaded. The personnel department proposed the addition of an assistant to help the president process information up and down the hierarchy. The assistant-to could stand in for the president for certain meetings. Another proposal was to divide the executive vice president position into three vice presidents. The two new vice presidential positions are indicated by dotted lines in figure 6.6. One vice president would be in charge of industrial relations and marketing. Another would be in charge of research and finance. The current vice president would have responsibility for manufacturing.

The addition of vice presidents may be postponed because the data processing department developed an on-line system for use by senior executives. The on-line computer system records each order received by the company, and follows its progress through manufacturing. As each stage is completed, the result is signaled to the computer. Each morning senior executives receive a report on the number of orders that are behind schedule and the progress of urgent orders. Each executive has a computer terminal and can request information on any order for which they receive an inquiry. The information provided by the computer replaces the need for direct contact with managers at lower levels. The linkage between upper and lower levels is improved because the flow of vertical information is more efficient.

Horizontal Linkages

When vertical coordination devices are in place, an organization still may not perform as a coordinated whole. This is especially true when organizations work in extremely uncertain environments. Chapter 2 described how environmental uncertainty led to differences in goals and orientation among organizational departments. Each department interacts with a specialized subenvironment that requires different skills, goals, and values. The organization must find ways to achieve horizontal integration across departments despite the difference in orientations of employees. The material in this section specifies when horizontal linkages are required, and the array of devices that can be used to meet coordination needs.

Linkage Requirements

Three factors—uncertainty, interdependence, and goals—normally determine the amount of horizontal coordination required between departments. Uncertainty, as defined in a previous section, is the amount of change and unpredictability facing managers in the organization. As uncertainty increases, the need for information processing and horizontal coordination increases. Interdependence was defined in the previous chapter on technology. The three levels of interdependence between departments are pooled, sequential, and reciprocal. Higher interdependence between departments requires greater coordination. Horizontal linkage devices should be implemented between departments that are interdependent.

Organizational goals are derived from the dominant competitive issue. The dominant competitive issue originates in the environment and is defined as the behavior required by the organization to succeed.[5] The **dominant competitive issue** represents what the organization has to do to satisfy its customers, to stay ahead of competitors, and to earn economic profits. Top managers interpret the dominant competitive issue in their industry, and derive goals from it. In an industry such as the manufacture of electronic calculators, the dominant competitive issue is new product innovation. In the trucking industry, the dominant competitive issue is timely and reliable service. Customers choose a trucking firm based on its ability to provide service when needed. Organizational goals will thus reflect the desire to provide this service to customers. The dominant competitive issue and goals depend on the environment of the firm, and may include such things as low prices, production efficiency, innovation, marketing, product quality, or a combination of several factors.

In a firm that manufactures electronic calculators, the goal is to be innovative. Horizontal linkages are needed between the research department and other departments, as shown in figure 6.7. Research is responsible for innovation. It is the primary department for achieving organizational goals and has to be closely linked with both production and marketing. Linkage with marketing provides information to R & D about customer requirements and competitor activities. Linkage with production provides information about production limitations that may constrain new products. The organization structure for a firm in the electronic calculator industry must facilitate coordination between research and other departments.

In an organization producing cardboard boxes, the dominant competitive issue is quick delivery at reasonable prices.[6] Product innovations in the cardboard box industry are rare. Coordination is needed between production and sales. As illustrated in figure 6.7, these two departments must be closely linked to coordinate the acceptance of new orders with current production runs. Orders are accepted only if they can be delivered in time to satisfy customers without destroying the efficiency of production. The research department is relatively unimportant, and is only concerned with an occasional change in the production process.

Linkage Mechanisms   Each of the following devices is a structural alternative that improves horizontal coordination and information flow.[7] Each device enables people to exchange information. Horizontal linkage mechanisms are often not drawn on the organization chart, but they are an important part of organization structure.

Paperwork—Memos, Reports   One form of horizontal linkage is simply to exchange paperwork about a problem or decision or to put other departments on a mailing list so they will be informed about activities relevant to them. Other departments may receive copies of correspondence or have

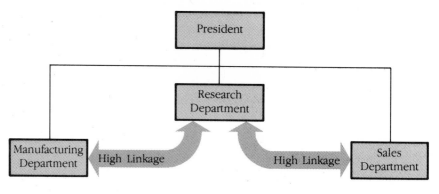

(a)   Electronic Instruments Co.

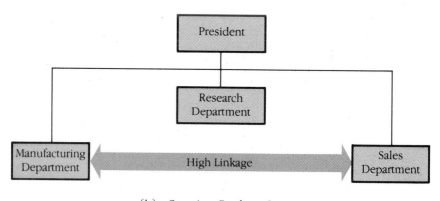

(b)   Container Products Co.

Figure 6.7.   Horizontal Linkages Between Departments Depend Upon Each
Company's Goals and Dominant Competitive Issue.
Adapted from Jay W. Lorsch, "Introduction to the Structural Design of Organizations,"
in Gene W. Dalton, Paul R. Lawrence, and Jay W. Lorsch, eds., *Organization Structure
and Design* (Homewood, IL: Irwin and Dorsey, 1970), pp. 8–9.

reports forwarded to them. Linkage through paperwork normally provides
only a low level of coordination and does not permit joint decisions to be
made or a large volume of information to be processed.

Direct Contact   A somewhat higher level of horizontal linkage is direct
contact between managers affected by a problem. A possible disadvantage
of direct contact is that top managers may not know about certain problems,
or lower managers may resolve a problem in a way that is not in the
interests of the overall organization.

Liaison Role   Creating a special liaison role is the next alternative. Liaison
roles often exist between engineering and manufacturing departments be-

cause engineering has to develop and test products to fit the limitations of manufacturing facilities. A liaison person is located in one department but has the responsibility for communicating and achieving coordination with another department. These people normally deal with the other department as part of their full-time job.

Task Forces Direct contact and liaison roles usually link two departments. When linkage involves several departments, a more complex linkage device is required. A task force is a temporary committee composed of representatives from each department affected by a problem. Each member represents the interest of a department and can carry information from the meeting back to their respective departments.

Task forces are an effective horizontal linkage device for temporary issues. Task forces are used in book publishing companies to coordinate the editing, production, advertising, and distribution of a special book. Business firms use task forces to study the possibility of acquiring a subsidiary and how to integrate the subsidiary into the corporation after it is purchased. Task forces solve problems by direct horizontal coordination and reduce the coordination load on the vertical hierarchy. Task forces are disbanded after the problem is solved.

IN PRACTICE 6.3

College of Business

A partial organization chart for a College of Business Administration is shown in figure 6.8. The college has five academic departments. The management and accounting departments each have thirty professors, and the other three departments have approximately fifteen professors each.

Coordination between departments is needed for several activities. Agreement has to be reached for course sequencing, class scheduling so the students can get necessary courses to graduate, prerequisities, and course content. Departments also have to agree on standards for promotion and tenure of professors. Most horizontal linkages take place at the department head level. Whenever department heads make a change in procedures, they use memos or copies of letters to inform other department heads. Direct contact between department heads is also used. The heads of accounting and finance often get together to resolve questions of course content. The Dean becomes involved when problems cannot be resolved by direct contact between department heads.

The business college recently created an "Undergraduate Business Program Task Force" to develop and implement a new undergraduate curriculum. The task force has two members from management and accounting and one member from each of the other departments. The associate dean chairs the meeting. The task force meets once a week

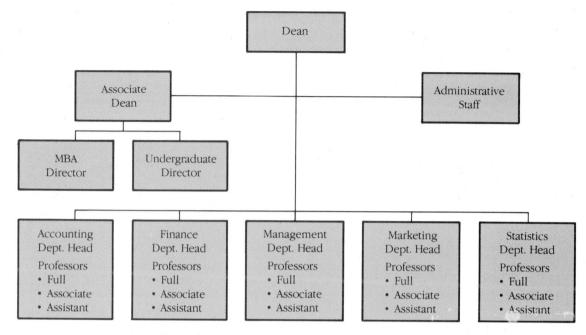

Figure 6.8. Organization Chart for a College of Business Administration.

to study the current curriculum and develop a new proposal. The task force provides an excellent linkage among departments. Representatives from each department carry information back and forth between the task force and people in their respective departments. The horizontal linkage and coordination is handled by several members of the college. They are able to process information to resolve the interests and problems throughout the five departments. When a new curriculum is eventually implemented, the task force will be disbanded.

Teams Permanent committees and project teams are yet a stronger horizontal linkage mechanism. Teams are permanent task forces, and are used when coordination requirements are permanent. When activities between departments require continuous coordination, a team is often the solution.

Special project teams are used when organizations have a large-scale project, such as a major innovation or new product line. A new product may require extensive coordination between research, sales, marketing research, manufacturing, and engineering for several years. Thousands of complex problems have to be worked out, so people from each department are full-time members of the project team. In the aerospace industry, employees from industrial engineering, production control, manufacturing, and design engineering all work full-time on the development of a single innovation such as a guidance system. These teams provide the coordination necessary to integrate the resources from each department into the design and manufacture of the new product.

Rodney Hunt Company

Rodney Hunt Company develops, manufactures, and markets heavy industrial equipment. Customer requirements are continuously changing, so effective coordination between manufacturing, engineering, and marketing is crucial to customer satisfaction. Rodney Hunt has solved the problem by establishing permanent teams for each major product line. These teams are illustrated by the shaded areas in figure 6.9. Members from each team meet daily or weekly as needed to resolve problems concerning customer needs, backlogs, engineering changes, scheduling conflicts, and any other problem with the product line. These teams foster an atmosphere of cooperation across departments. The teams of Rodney Hunt are composed of middle managers, but they could be formed at any level in an organization. A top-level team might meet regularly to consider problems of special customer requirements, new product lines, or government regulations. Teams of foremen and supervisors could deal with scheduling and production problems.

Full-Time Integrator An even stronger horizontal linkage device is to create a full-time position or department. A full-time integrator frequently has a title such as product manager, project manager, program manager, or brand manager. Unlike the liaison role described earlier, the integrator does not report to management in one of the functional departments being coordinated. The integrator is located outside the departments and has the responsibility of coordinating between two or more departments.

Examples of full-time integrators in a business college are the undergraduate program director and the MBA director. Integrating roles can be emphasized to organization members by drawing them to the side of the organization chart, and using dotted lines to show their area of responsibility, as in figure 6.10. The undergraduate program director has responsibility for coordinating the undergraduate requirements and course offerings in each of the departments, but does not have formal authority over department heads or professors. If the undergraduate program is not coordinated properly, students will experience problems getting enrolled in needed courses, keeping up with the amount of homework assigned, scheduled exams, and sequencing their coursework. The role of the undergraduate program director is to work with professors in each department to see what courses and teaching techniques fit together into a coherent program for each student taking a business major.

Integrating roles requires special skills. Integrators typically have a lot of responsibility but little authority. The integrator has to use expertise and persuasion to achieve coordination. The integrator spans the boundary between departments, and must be able to get people together, maintain their trust, confront problems, and resolve conflicts and disputes in the interest of the organization.[8] The integrator must be forceful in order to achieve coordination, but must stop short of alienating people in the line departments.

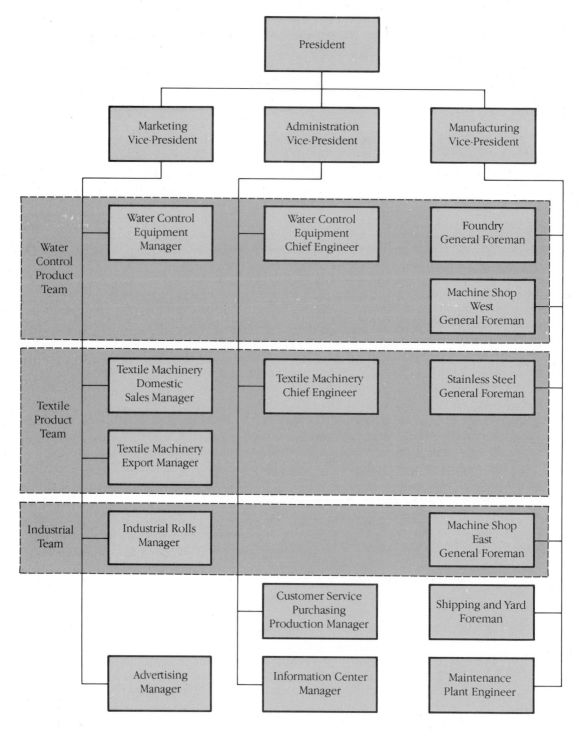

Figure 6.9. Teams Used for Horizontal Coordination at Rodney Hunt Company. Adapted from Joseph J. Famularo, *Organizational Planning Manual: Charts, Descriptions, Policies,* revised edition (New York: AMACOM, a division of American Management Association, 1971), p. 125.

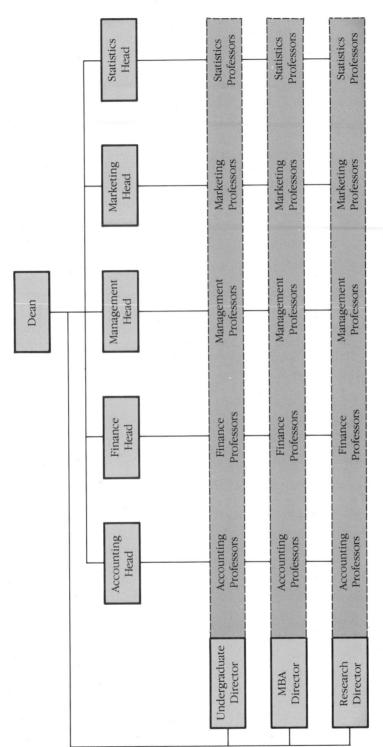

Figure 6.10. Full-time Integrating Roles in a Business College.

Integrators are used when the organization has a strong need for continuous horizontal coordination. The organization makes a major investment by assigning people full-time to coordination. An organization may have several integrators working simultaneously, as at General Mills.

IN PRACTICE 6.5

General Mills

"When General Mills completed a ten-story tower at its suburban Minneapolis headquarters last summer, the company discovered that not all the telephones could be installed at once. 'Hook up the product managers first,' the senior executive ordered. 'The business can't run without them.'"[9]

General Mills assigns a product manager to each of the more than twenty-five products in its line, including Cheerios, Wheaties, Bisquick, Softasilk Cake Mix, Stir-n-Frost Icing, Hamburger Helper, and Gold Medal Flour. Brand managers are also assigned to develop new products, name them, and test them in the marketplace.

At General Mills, product managers have the responsibility of business managers—setting marketing goals and plotting strategies to achieve those goals. The annual cycle begins with a three-month planning process. The status of the products and key issues are analyzed. Research data on the brand and its competition for several years is analyzed. A sales forecast, an itemized list of costs to meet the forecast, and advertising, pricing, and competitive tactics are laid out. The plan must be approved by the marketing director and the division general manager. Product managers are responsible for the product's profit. They get involved in any area that affects profit, which can include manufacturing productivity, ingredient substitution, competitive advertising, and commodity pricing.

Product managers at General Mills act as if they are running their own businesses. They are responsible and accountable for product success, but they have no authority. Product management is management by persuasion. If the product manager for Cocoa Puffs needs special support from the sales force and additional output from the plant for a big advertising campaign, she has to sell the idea to people who report to managers in charge of sales and manufacturing. Product managers work laterally across the organization rather than within the vertical structure. When the product manager for Crispy Wheats 'n Raisins decides the product needs different packaging, a new recipe, a more focused commercial, or new ingredients, he must convince the support groups to pay attention to his brand. The product manager can also expect to work with the procurement department, a controller, and the research lab at some point during the year.

A good product manager is vibrant, challenging, and a little abrasive. A good product manager gets things done without the aid of formal authority. The General Mills product managers are in their early thirties, and they have responsibilities as big as their ambitions. The young product manager for Crispy Wheats 'n Raisins was given responsibility for a $10 million introductory budget for the new product. The money was spent on a combination of direct mailing of trial packages and T.V. ads.[10]

The product managers at General Mills are full-time integrators. They integrate marketing, manufacturing, purchasing, research, and other functions relevant to their product line. They provide horizontal linkages within the company by persuading diverse groups to focus on the needs of each product. General Mills has been very profitable in a highly competitive industry, and an important reason is the role played by product managers.

Summary The mechanisms for achieving horizontal linkages in organizations are summarized in figure 6.11. These devices represent the range of alternatives that managers can select to achieve lateral coordination. The higher-level devices provide more effective horizontal linkages, but are also more expensive and time-consuming for the organization. Each organization must have devices to achieve horizontal linkages consistent with its goals and the interdependencies between departments. If coordination is insufficient, departments will find themselves out of synchronization, and they will not contribute to the overall goals of the organization.

Figure 6.11. Mechanisms for Horizontal Linkages and Coordination.

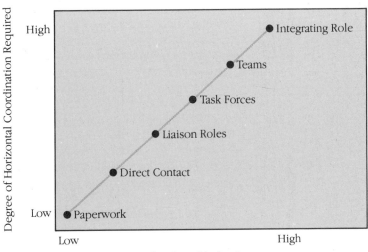

The vertical and horizontal linkage mechanisms described above complement one another and work together to achieve coordination in the organization. Rules, procedures, planning, and scheduling along the vertical structure indirectly help managers coordinate horizontally across departments. The horizontal mechanisms of direct contact, task forces, and integrating roles reduce the need for referral up the vertical hierarchy. The use of linkage mechanisms in one direction influences the use of linkage mechanisms in the other direction.

A problem faced by many medium-sized and large organizations is that they have excellent vertical linkages, but coordination across functional departments is inadequate. These organizations are getting quite complex, and may produce several product lines and reach several markets. Coordination vertically within marketing, engineering, and manufacturing may be excellent, but the differences between marketing, engineering, and manufacturing are not being integrated. Even the use of task forces, teams, or full-time integrators may not provide sufficient linkage to achieve the goals for each product.

Another alternative is for organizations to reorganize into smaller, self-contained units.[11] This type of reorganization is illustrated in figure 6.12. The organization is literally redesigned into separate product groups, and each group contains the functional departments that have to be coordinated horizontally. This reorganization occurs when product goals and interdependencies cannot be accomplished with traditional horizontal linkage devices.

Structural self-containment is similar to grouping organization departments according to interdependencies, which was discussed in the technology chapter. Departments and functions that must work closely together are grouped together on the organization chart. This realigns the vertical and horizontal linkage devices. By locating departments together under a common manager, face-to-face coordination, planning, and hierarchical referral can be used to achieve coordination. This reorganization actually gives product managers vertical authority. Each function needed to produce a product is now linked directly with the product manager.

Reorganization does not do away with the need for horizontal coordination. It simply realigns the structure to engage vertical linkage mechanisms for each product line. After reorganization, horizontal coordination will still be needed across product lines. Top management may establish an engineering task force, for example, to encourage weekly contact between engineers from each product line. Developments in one engineering group can be utilized by engineers in other product lines. Engineering task forces are used by General Motors to coordinate the engineering and design of cars in each automobile division. The effectiveness of GM's coordination is reflected in the similarity of automobile design for each division, and GM's ability to interchange standard parts. In addition, similar rules and procedures

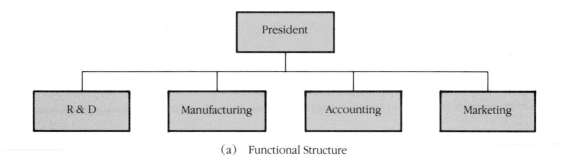

(a) Functional Structure

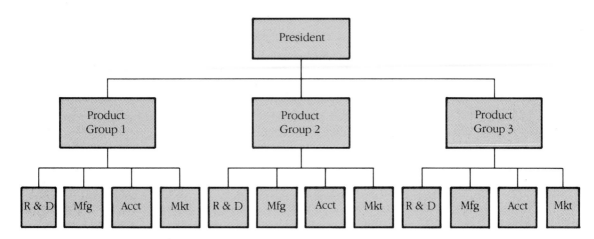

(b) Organization into self-contained product groups.

Figure 6.12.   Reorganization from Functional Structure to Self-Contained Units.

for accounting, finance, and law must be adhered to by all product groups in an organization. The shift to self-contained units does not eliminate the need for horizontal coordination. The reorganization simply gives primary emphasis to coordination within each product line.

IN PRACTICE 6.6

Bonanza International

Bonanza International is based in Dallas, Texas. Bonanza specializes in budget steakhouses, of which there are approximately 672 in nearly 600 cities across forty states. These steakhouses are operated by more than 200 individual franchise owners. The function of Bonanza International is to support these franchises with marketing, operational, and administrative programs to help them succeed as independent entrepreneurs. Bonanza also supplies most products sold in the restaurants.

A partial organization chart for Bonanza's previous structure is shown in figure 6.13. Activities were grouped according to function. Franchise owners are the customers of Bonanza International. Franchise owners worked directly with corporate personnel for help in marketing, real estate, finance, supplies, or legal advice.

The last few years have not been profitable for Bonanza. Competition from new restaurant chains and poor economic conditions have reduced the flow of the predominately blue-collar traffic on which they depend. To offset the decline in the traditional steakhouse business, Bonanza has adopted two new lines. Restaurants are being converted into the New Bonanza product line, or "B-80" as it is called within the organization. The B-80 transformation includes refurbished stores, new store fronts, and cosmetic changes. The kitchen is separate from the eating area, a salad bar is used, and waitresses take customer orders. The menu includes fish and chicken as well as steak.

The second line is a new restaurant concept called "People's." People's is still in the experimental stage. Four restaurants have been test-marketed. They stick to the family dining concept with the addition of a bar. The results are promising because the average dollar volume generated in a People's is three times that of the average Bonanza.

Coordination problems have surfaced with the introduction of B-80 and People's restaurants. Owners of separate restaurant lines have no special contact point at Bonanza International. Employees within each corporate department were trained on the traditional Bonanza concept, and do not allocate time or resources to the new product lines. The worst problem is that personnel in departments sometimes countermand each other. Finance people push investment in B-80 and People's restaurants, but real-estate people still buy property in terms of traditional budget steakhouses. There is not sufficient coordination across headquarters' functions to provide unique service to franchise owners in

Figure 6.13. Previous Functional Structure at Bonanza International.

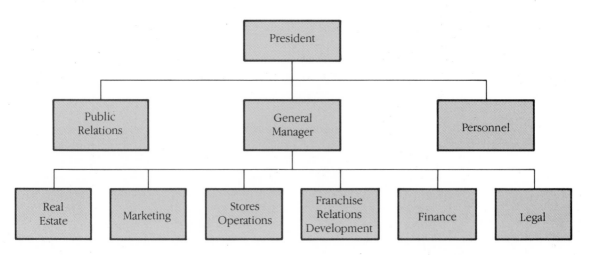

each restaurant line. Bonanza tried task forces and integrators, but franchise owners complained that the headquarters' departments were not coordinated.

Bonanza is reaching a point where traditional horizontal linkages do not suffice. They should now consider reorganization into self-contained units, similar to those in figure 6.14. Personnel could specialize and focus their attention on a single restaurant line. Employees from operations, marketing, finance, and franchise relations for each type of restaurant would be grouped together in the same set of offices and report to the same general manager. This would increase coordination within product lines. The legal and marketing research departments could be left as a small department because they provide the same service to all three

Figure 6.14. Proposed Product Structure for Bonanza International.

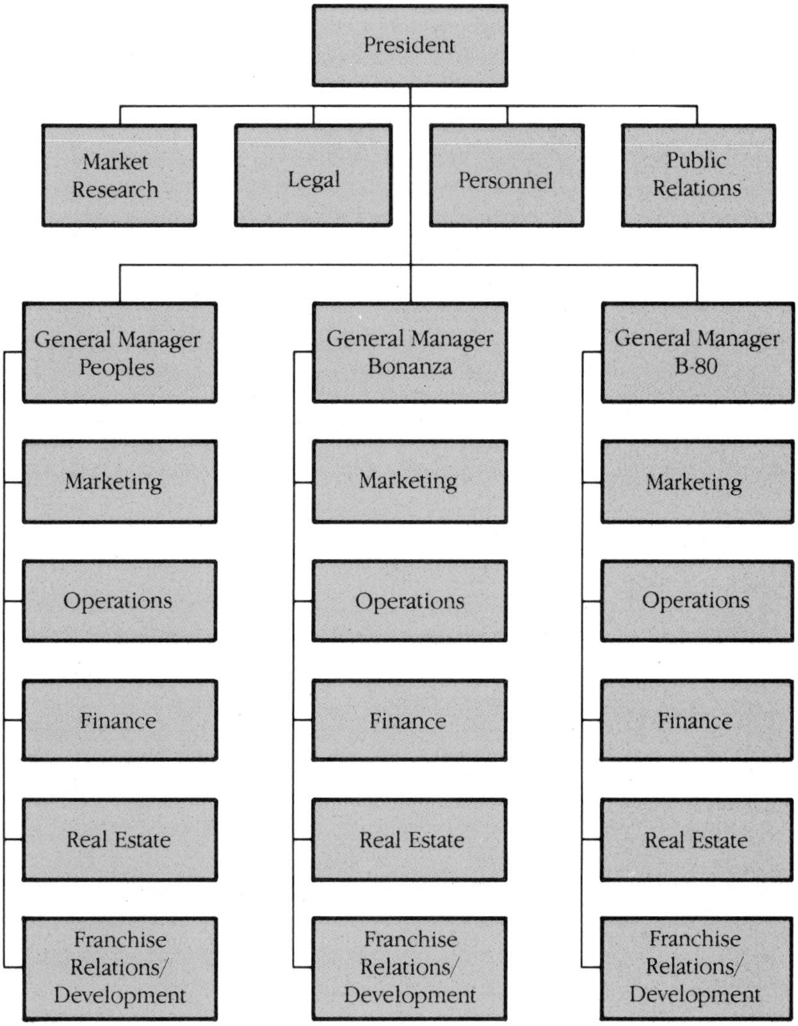

restaurant lines. Top management could institute weekly meetings among representatives from advertising, or finance, or operations to achieve horizontal linkage across the three restaurant lines.[12]

FUNCTIONAL VERSUS PRODUCT STRUCTURES

The approach to organization design covered so far in this chapter is to divide up the organization's tasks, specify a hierarchy of authority, and design vertical and horizontal linkages to achieve required coordination. Classical organization theorists stressed that organizational activities should be grouped by common function. Rules, plans, and hierarchical referral were the basic mechanisms for achieving coordination.[13] Recent approaches to organization design stress horizontal linkage devices such as cross-functional teams and full-time integrators. Organizations can also be restructured into self-contained units to facilitate coordination.

The two basic organization forms are function and product (self-contained units). The issue of whether organizational departments should be grouped by function or in self-contained units is a major dilemma for organizations. Many large organizations have switched back and forth and still are not sure which design should be used. At this time, over 75% of large corporations are in some form of self-contained units.[14]

The dilemma of functional versus product structure is a key problem for organizations to solve. The purpose of this section is to look closely at the implications of each structural form. A hybrid structure that incorporates elements of both function and product structures is also examined.

Functional Organization Structure

In a functional organization structure, activities are grouped together by common function, from the bottom to the top of the organization. All engineers are located in the engineering department and the vice president of engineering is responsible for all engineering activities. The same is true in marketing, research and development, and manufacturing.

The **functional structure** groups people and activities by resources. Each functional department provides resources (e.g., engineering, marketing, etc.) to the overall production process of the organization. Examples of purely functional organization structure are Atlas Manufacturing Company (figure 6.6), Oilfield Services (figure 6.2), The College of Business Administration (figure 6.8), and the Rodney Hunt Corporation (figure 6.9).

The functional form of organization is best when the dominant competitive issue and goals of the organization stress functional expertise, efficiency, and quality. Recall from the discussion of differentiation and integration in chapter 2 that employees in each department adopt similar values, goals, and orientations. Similarity encourages collaboration, efficiency, and quality within the function, but makes coordination and cooperation with other departments more difficult. The functional structure places the emphasis on expertise within functions rather than on horizontal coordination. Even with task forces and integrators, the primary allegiance of employees will be toward the goals of their own departments rather than toward cooperation with other departments.

Table 6.1 summarizes organization characteristics associated with the functional structure. The functional structure is most effective in a relatively stable environment. Vertical mechanisms provide coordination and integration. Within the organization, employees are committed to achieving the goals of their respective functional departments. Planning and budgeting is by function and reflects the cost of resources used in each department. Promotion up the hierarchy is normally on the basis of experience and expertise within the function (e.g., marketing, engineering). The information and linkage processes are mostly vertical, and include the hierarchy, rules, and planning.

One strength of the functional structure is that it promotes economy of scale within functions. Economy of scale means that all employees are located in the same place and can share facilities. Producing all products in a single plant, for example, enables the plant to acquire the latest machinery. Constructing only one facility instead of a separate facility for each product line reduces duplication and waste. The functional structure also promotes in-depth skill development of employees. Employees are exposed to a range

Table 6.1.   Summary of Functional Organization Characteristics.

ENVIRONMENT
Environmental uncertainty: Low to moderate
Dominant competitive issue: Technical specialization, efficiency, quality

INTERNAL SYSTEMS
Sub-goals: Functional subgoal emphasis
Planning and budgeting: Cost basis—budget, statistical reports
Influence: Functional heads
Promotion: On basis of functional expertise
Information and linkages: Vertical processes, hierarchy, rules and procedures

STRENGTHS
1. Best in stable environment
2. Economies of scale within functions
3. In-depth skill development
4. Accomplish functional goals
5. Best in small to medium-size organizations
6. Best when only one or a few products

WEAKNESSES
1. Slow response time to environmental changes
2. Decisions may pile on top, hierarchy overload
3. Poor interunit coordination
4. Less innovation
5. Restricted view of organization goals

Adapted from Robert Duncan, "What is the Right Organization Structure?: Decision Tree Analysis Provides the Answer," *Organizational Dynamics*, Winter, 1979 (New York: AMACOM, a division of American Management Associations, 1979), p. 429.

of functional activities within their own department. The functional form of structure is best for small to medium-sized organizations when there is only one or a few products produced.

The weakness of the functional structure is the slow response to environmental changes that require coordination between departments. The ESB Ray-O-Vac case at the beginning of the chapter was an example. The vertical hierarchy was overloaded. Decisions piled up and top managers were not responding fast enough. Other disadvantages of the functional structure are that interdepartmental coordination is poor, and each employee has a restricted view of overall goals.

IN PRACTICE 6.7

Blue Bell Creameries, Inc.

In an unmistakable country voice, the old timer on the radio told the story about the good times in rural Texas. Within seconds he had taken listeners out of their bumper-to-bumper world and placed them gently in Brenham, with its rolling hills, the country fair, and the time the town got its first traffic light.

"You know," he says, "that's how Blue Bell Ice Cream is. Old fashioned, uncomplicated, homemade good." He pauses. "It's all made in that little creamery in Brenham."

That little creamery isn't little anymore, but the desire for first quality homemade ice cream is stronger than when Blue Bell started in 1907. Blue Bell today employs over 600 employees and will sell over $60 million of ice cream. Each week the creamery consumes the output of 9,600 cows and several truckloads of peanuts, pecans, eggs, cane sugar, fresh fruit, and real Nabisco Oreo cookies (which are ground into Cookies 'N Cream Ice Cream).

The company cannot meet the demand for Blue Bell Ice Cream. It doesn't even try. People outside selected counties in the state of Texas and Louisiana cannot buy Blue Bell. It is not even distributed throughout Texas, its home state. The reason is the company's unwavering dedication to product quality. Management refuses to expand into regions that cannot be adequately serviced, or to grow so fast that they can't adequately train employees in the art of making ice cream. The goal of Blue Bell Creameries is a quality product. The managers will not undertake any activity that will endanger that quality. Customers expect quality, and they know they will receive it.

Customer loyalty pays off for Blue Bell. A recent survey found that fifty-eight cents of every ice cream dollar spent in Houston went to Blue Bell.

The approximate organization structure of Blue Bell is shown in figure 6.15. The major departments are sales, quality control, production, maintenance, and distribution. There is also an accounting department and a small research and development group. Product changes are infrequent

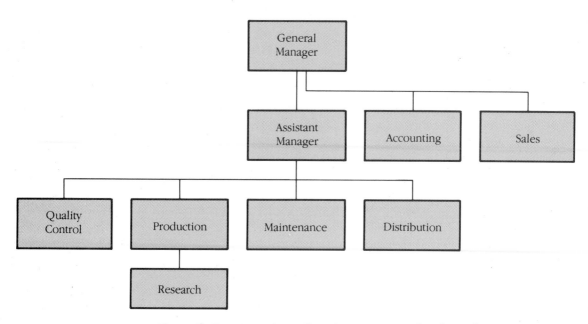

Figure 6.15. Approximate Organization Structure for Blue Bell Creameries, Inc.

because the orientation is toward tried and true products. The environment is stable. The customer base is well established. The only change has been the increase in demand for Blue Bell Ice Cream.

Blue Bell's quality control department tests all incoming ingredients to ensure that only the best products go into their ice cream. Quality control also tests all ice cream products made by Blue Bell. Every single batch is tested. Percent butterfat is measured along with acidity and alkalinity. Of course, the most important quality control test is taste. Blue Bell employs workers whose only job is to taste the ice cream. After years of experience they can spot the slightest deviation from expected quality. It's no wonder that Blue Bell has successfully maintained the image of a small-town creamery making homemade ice cream.[16]

The functional organization structure is just right for Blue Bell Creameries. They have a stable environment. The primary goal is product quality. Employees are oriented toward the goals and values of their respective departments, which add up to quality ice cream. Extensive experience and training is required, which is possible when employees are grouped together on a functional basis. The dominant competitive issue is product quality, which means that the quality control department must be closely coordinated with production. Management achieves high collaboration between these two groups. Quality control inspectors are often drawn from production employees. Quality control personnel freely interact with production personnel when testing ingredients. Blue Bell has chosen to stay medium-sized and to produce only ice cream products. The functional structure provides the coordination needed for this organization.

Product Organization Structure

The term "product structure" is used here as the generic term for self-contained units. Self-contained units can be organized according to individual products, product groups, services, markets, customers, or major programs. The term used to describe the organization structure for any of these classifications will be product structure.

The product structure is distinguished from the functional structure by grouping diverse functions into a single division or department. The functional structure was organized according to resource inputs. The **product structure** is organized according to organizational outputs. For each product output, all necessary resources such as manufacturing, research and development, and markting are contained within the department structure. Coordination across functions within each product unit is maximized. The product structure promotes flexibility and adaptability within each of the organization's product lines.

The product structure has several implications for organizations, which are summarized in table 6.2.[17] The product form of structure is excellent when the dominant competitive issue and goals of the organization emphasize coordinated action to innovate, satisfy clients, or to maintain a market

Table 6.2. Summary of Product Organization Characteristics.

ENVIRONMENT

Environmental uncertainty: Moderate to high

Dominant competitive issue: Market segment, client satisfaction, coordinated action within product line

INTERNAL SYSTEMS

Sub-goals: Product line emphasis

Planning and budgeting: Profit center basis—cost and income

Influence: Product heads

Promotion: On basis of integration and management skills

Information and linkages: Lateral as well as vertical processes

STRENGTHS

1. Suited to fast change in unstable environment
2. Client satisfaction because product responsibility and contact points are clear
3. High coordination across functions
4. Units adapt to differences in products, regions, clients
5. Best in large organizations
6. Best when several products

WEAKNESSES

1. Lose economies of scale in functional departments
2. Poor functional coordination across product lines
3. Lose in-depth competence and technical specialization
4. Integration and standardization across product lines is difficult

Adapted from Robert Duncan, "What is the Right Organization Structure?: Decision Tree Analysis Provides the Answer," *Organizational Dynamics*, Winter, 1979 (New York: AMACOM, a division of American Management Associations, 1979), p. 431.

segment. Environmental uncertainty is moderate to high. Since the self-contained units are often quite small, employees identify with the product line rather than with their own function. Budgeting and planning is on a profit basis, because each product line can be run as a separate business with both costs and income calculated. Managers with influence are those who lead the product division. Promotion into higher management is typically on the basis of management and integration skills rather than on the basis of functional expertise. Managers must be able to achieve coordination across functions rather than to be an expert in any single function. The product structure stresses horizontal as well as vertical coordination.

The product structure has several strengths. It is suited to fast change in an unstable environment, and provides high product visibility. Since each product is a separate division, clients are able to contact the right division and achieve satisfaction. Coordination across functions is excellent. Each product can adapt to requirements of individual customers or regions. The product structure typically works best in large organizations that have multiple products or services and enough personnel to staff separate functional units.

One disadvantage is that the organization loses economies of scale. Instead of fifty research engineers sharing a common facility in a functional structure, ten engineers may be assigned to each of five product divisions. The critical mass required for in-depth research is lost, and physical facilities have to be duplicated for each product line. Another problem is that product lines become separate from each another, and coordination across product lines can be difficult. In-depth competence and technical specialization are lost in this structure. Employees identify with the product line rather than with a functional specialty. R & D personnel, for example, tend to do applied research to benefit the product line rather than basic research to benefit the entire organization.

ESB Ray-O-Vac Referring back to the ESB Ray-O-Vac case described at the beginning of this chapter, Dawson's solution was to reorganize into self-contained units. In the previous structure, functional activities were performed autonomously. Research was developing new products. Manufacturing was producing products. But horizontal coordination between these departments was not sufficient to enable new products to be manufactured and marketed in a timely manner. By restructuring into separate product groups with their own R & D, manufacturing, and marketing functions, coordination between the functions will be much better. ESB Ray-O-Vac will adapt much more quickly to changing developments in the environment. Based upon our theories of organization structure, Dawson's move was correct. The dominant competitive issue for ESB Ray-O-Vac was product innovation. Without innovation, market share and profits were lost. The previous functional structure was not adequate. Even with horizontal linkage devices, it could not provide the coordination needed to be competitive in new products. We can predict that ESB Ray-O-Vac will respond more quickly with new products in the future because of the new organization structure.

Geographical Structure Large corporations that distribute products nationally often cannot coordinate all regions from a central location. Each region of the country has distinct tastes, needs, and facilities that require coordination. Another form of the self-contained unit is to divide the organization by geography. Each geographical unit includes all functions required to produce and market products in that region. For multi-national organizations, self-contained units are created for different countries and parts of the world. A geographical structure for a Canadian retail department store chain is given in figure 6.16. Customers in Quebec are physically smaller, use a different language, and have different

Figure 6.16. Geographical Structure for a Canadian Retail Chain.

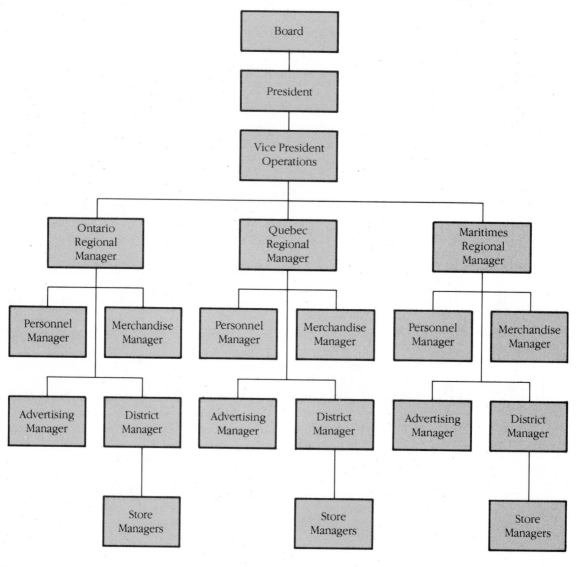

tastes than customers in Ontario or the Maritimes. The regional structure groups together the functions that can serve each region's needs.

The strengths and weaknesses of geographical structures are similar to the product organization characteristics listed in table 6.2. The organization is able to adapt to specific needs of its own region, and employees identify with regional goals rather than with national goals. Horizontal coordination within region is emphasized rather than vertical linkages to the national office.

Hybrid Structures   Most large corporations do not have either a pure product structure or a pure functional structure. When a corporation grows large and has several products or markets, it typically is organized into self-contained units of some type. Functions that are important to each product or market are decentralized to the self-contained units. However, some functions are also centralized and located at headquarters. Headquarters' functions are relatively stable and require economies of scale and in-depth specialization. By combining characteristics of both functional and product structures, corporations can take advantage of both forms of structure and avoid some of the weaknesses listed in tables 6.1 and 6.2.

An example of an oil company conglomerate that has a hybrid structure is shown in figure 6.17. This company is organized into three product groups— oil, manufacturing, insurance—and self-contained companies operate in each group. Each company contains relevant functions and operates as an autonomous business unit. But not all functions are located in the product companies. The legal department, employee relations, planning and development, and finance are centralized in a functional structure at headquarters. Industrial relations, which is responsible for bargaining with all unions, is one department so the corporation can take advantage of in-depth expertise, and be sure that employees throughout the organization are treated uniformly. Wide differences in employee benefits, pension plans, and union contracts across product divisions could eventually cause lawsuits and other labor problems for the corporation. Each business unit may have a small industrial relations department to work with its own union and employees, but the primary responsibility for bargaining is at corporate headquarters. The industrial relations people within each business unit have to coordinate their activities and take advice from the headquarters group.

Most large companies strike a balance between the pure product and pure functional structures. They deploy to the product group all functions that need close coordination within the product line. They also have functional departments for activities that require extensive training or have to be applied uniformly across the whole company.

IN PRACTICE 6.8

Levi Strauss USA

Levi Strauss USA has enjoyed rapid growth and widespread acceptance since its founder, a European immigrant named Levi Strauss, created

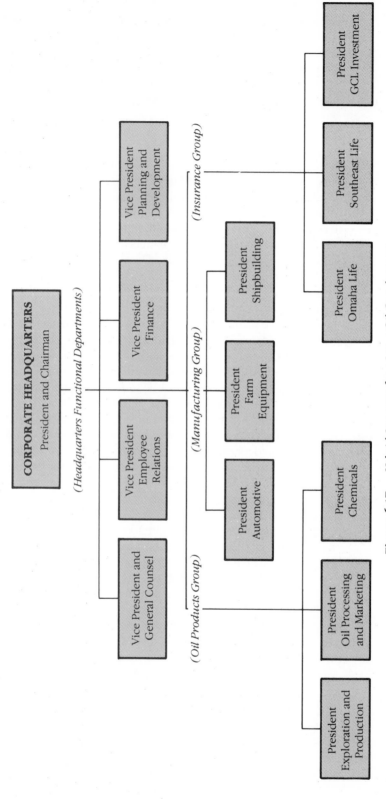

Figure 6.17. Hybrid Structure for a Large Oil Conglomerate.

Boxes in figure:

CORPORATE HEADQUARTERS
President and Chairman

(Headquarters Functional Departments)

Vice President and General Counsel

Vice President Employee Relations

Vice President Finance

Vice President Planning and Development

(Oil Products Group)

President Exploration and Production

President Oil Processing and Marketing

(Manufacturing Group)

President Chemicals

President Automotive

President Farm Equipment

President Shipbuilding

(Insurance Group)

President Omaha Life

President Southeast Life

President GCL Investment

pairs of sturdy pants out of tent canvas for goldminers in 1853. These pants immediately became known as "Levi's," and today's style is basically unchanged from the early jeans made for California goldminers. Bluejeans today occupy a unique place in American culture.

Although jeans are basically unchanged from those early days, the company that produces most of them has changed significantly. Levi Strauss is a huge corporation, reaching toward $3 billion in sales. It is a world-wide corporation with several product lines.

A partial organization chart for Levi Strauss USA is similar to that shown in figure 6.18. There are eight product divisions, which are formed into three major product groups. Each product division contains its own manufacturing and marketing facilities and engages in some product development work. Group I includes the Jeanswear, Youthwear, and

Figure 6.18.   Partial Organization Chart for Levi Strauss USA.

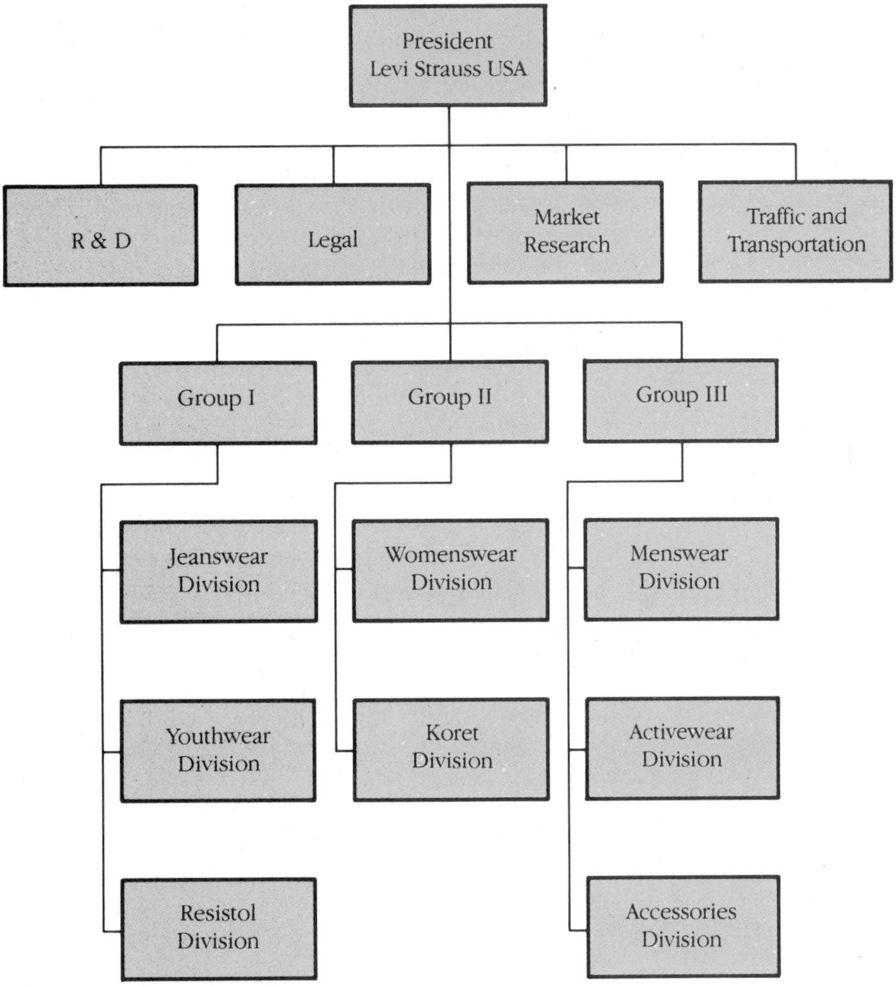

Resistol divisions, which are the biggest product lines. Jeanswear is the largest and most profitable division and produces straight-leg and boot jeans, corduroy blazers, and shirts. This division experienced a 26% increase in sales in 1980 alone. The Youthwear division markets girlswear, activewear and attire for toddlers. The Resistol division is the world's largest source of western and dress hats.

Group II is concerned solely with women's clothing. These divisions produce skirts, pants, sweaters, blouses, and blazers. Group III includes the Menswear, Activewear, and Accessories divisions. Menswear includes sportswear for men and tailored classics. The Activewear line produces attire for sports participation, including ski, tennis, racquetball, running apparel, and active outerwear. The Accessories division produces belts, wallets, casual hats, and gloves.

Several corporate functions are centralized at corporate headquarters to service the entire corporation. The legal department handles trademark infringements and counterfeits of Levi products. The company registers trademarks in foreign countries and in the last twenty years has begun a massive program of protecting its trademarks. Levi Strauss is normally involved in over fifty trademark cases at a given time.

Research and Development and Market Research also provide services for all divisions. Research does basic research for both new products and new production machines. Over 1,000 patents have been granted to the company. Market research gathers information about the marketplace, retailers, consumers, and economic trends. Each product division has development and market research groups, but the departments are small and their activities are coordinated with headquarters.

The corporate traffic and transportation office coordinates shipments within the United States. The corporate office handles negotiations with regulatory agencies and major shippers to obtain best prices for all divisions. This department also provides a trucking fleet, made up of ninety drivers and 200 trailers that service all divisions.[18]

The hybrid organization structure is well suited to Levi Strauss. The organization is large and has multiple product lines that could not be effectively coordinated in a pure functional structure. Each division can concentrate on its own product line and provide service to its own customers and clients. Each product line can also adapt to rapid changes in the marketplace. The designer label jeans of Calvin Klein, Jordache, Gloria Vanderbilt, and others recently came on the scene as important competition. The truth is, Levi's have held off the competition and maintained close to 40% of the market. Designer jeans together have only about 5% of the market.[19] Fads and fashions change in all lines of clothing. Each Levi Strauss division is able to make changes efficiently and quickly.

The functional departments provide in-depth experience and support to product divisions. The experience in fighting patent infringement applies to all divisions and should be centralized at the corporate level. The same is true for basic research and development. Research facilities are enormously expensive. It would not be efficient to duplicate them for each product division. Levi Strauss is basically a product form of organization, but has developed a hybrid structure to gain the advantages of a functional structure in the legal, research, market research, and transportation areas.

MATRIX STRUCTURE

Most organizations find that some variation of either the functional or product structure provides the best reporting relationships and horizontal linkages to achieve organizational goals. In a few situations, however, organizations face a special dilemma. They need the benefits of both the functional and product structures. They need an organization chart that gives priority to both functional activities and product lines simultaneously. The organization needs both technological expertise within functions and horizontal coordination by product line. One sector of the environment may require technological expertise as the dominant competitive issue, and another sector may require innovation within each product line. In addition, the uncertainty and rate of change in the external environment may be great so that continuous information-processing and coordination in both vertical and horizontal directions are necessary within the organization.

The matrix organization structure is often the answer when organizations find that neither the functional nor product structure combined with horizontal linkage mechanisms will work. The unique characteristic of the matrix organization is that both product and functional structures are implemented simultaneously, as shown in figure 6.19. The product managers and functional managers have equal authority within the organization, and employees report to both of them.

Conditions for the Matrix

The dual hierarchy may seem an unusual way to design an organization, but the matrix is the correct structure when the following conditions are met.[20]

Condition 1 Environmental pressure (dominant competitive issue) is from two or more critical sectors, such as for function and product, or function and region. This pressure means that a balance of power is required within the organization, and that a dual-authority structure is needed to reflect the environmental pressure.

Condition 2 The task environment of the organization is both complex and uncertain. Frequent external changes and high interdependence between departments require extremely effective linkages in both vertical and horizontal directions.

Condition 3 Economy of scale in the use of internal resources is needed. The organization is typically medium-sized and has a moderate number of product lines. It feels pressure for the shared and flexible use of people and equipment. For example, the organization may not be large enough to have sufficient engineers to be assigned to each product line, so engineers

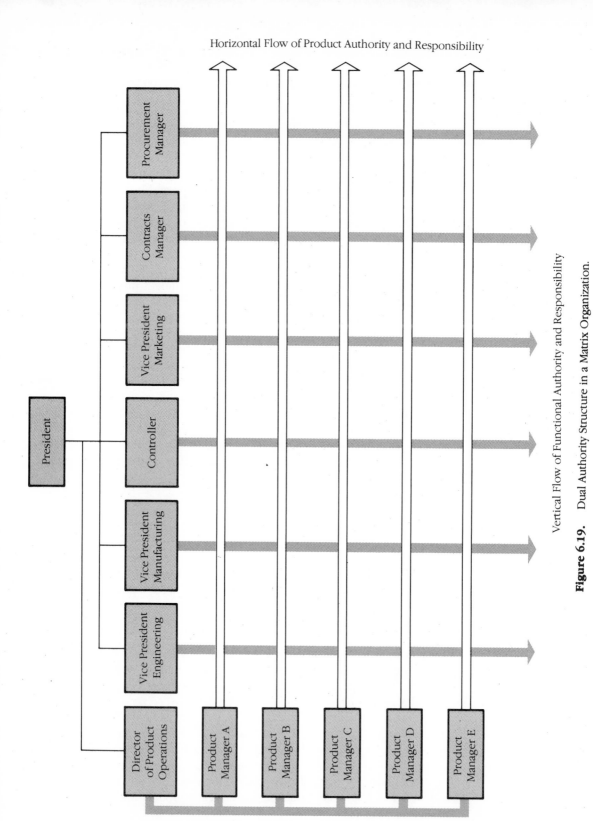

Horizontal Flow of Product Authority and Responsibility

Vertical Flow of Functional Authority and Responsibility

Figure 6.19. Dual Authority Structure in a Matrix Organization.

are allocated temporarily across several products depending upon environmental demand.

Under these three conditions, neither the functional nor the product structure is sufficient, even when horizontal coordinating devices are implemented. Both the vertical and horizontal lines of authority must be given equal recognition. A dual-authority structure is thereby created and the balance of power between them is equal.

An example of a matrix organization is described in figure 6.20. The matrix organization chart is often drawn in a diamond shape to indicate the equality of the two authority structures. The organization in figure 6.20 is a clothing manufacturer. It has three product lines that represent different markets and customers. As a medium-sized organization, it must effectively utilize the functions of manufacturing, design, and marketing. The manufacturing, design, and marketing departments require in-depth expertise and sufficient people to perform effectively. If functional departments are subdivided by product line, the critical mass and efficiencies of scale would be lost.

The unique aspect of matrix structure as reflected in figure 6.20 is that some employees have two bosses, which violates the classic principles of management. The manager of the shoe manufacturing plant reports to the vice president for manufacturing and to the director of the footwear product line. The plant manager will be subjected to conflicting pressures. The manufacturing vice president will push for manufacturing quality, uniformity, and efficiency. The product director will be concerned with customer satisfaction and a timely response to fashion changes, even if it means losing efficiency or quality in production. Each person who reports to two bosses is caught in a conflict, and is the person who performs the job of integration within the organization. Whenever conflicts arise, the manager and both bosses have to resolve the conflict. People in a matrix spend a great deal of time in meetings. The conflict built into the matrix forces discussion and coordination in both vertical and horizontal directions to resolve issues that pertain to both functions and products.

A common misperception about the matrix is that most employees report to two bosses, which is not the case. Although layered or multiple matrices do exist in theory,[21] they are rare in practice. Normally, the matrix is at the top of the organization, or at the top of the specific division that has adopted a matrix, as illustrated in figure 6.21. If a research department adopts a matrix, the research director is at the top of the matrix, and both functional and product directors report to him or her.

Key Matrix Roles   Working within a matrix structure is difficult for most managers because it requires a new set of skills compared to a single-authority structure. In order for the matrix to succeed, managers in key roles have specific responsibilities. The key roles are top leadership, matrix bosses, and the two-boss managers, as illustrated in figure 6.20.[22]

Top Leader   The top leader is the head of both command structures. The primary responsibility for this person is to maintain a power balance between

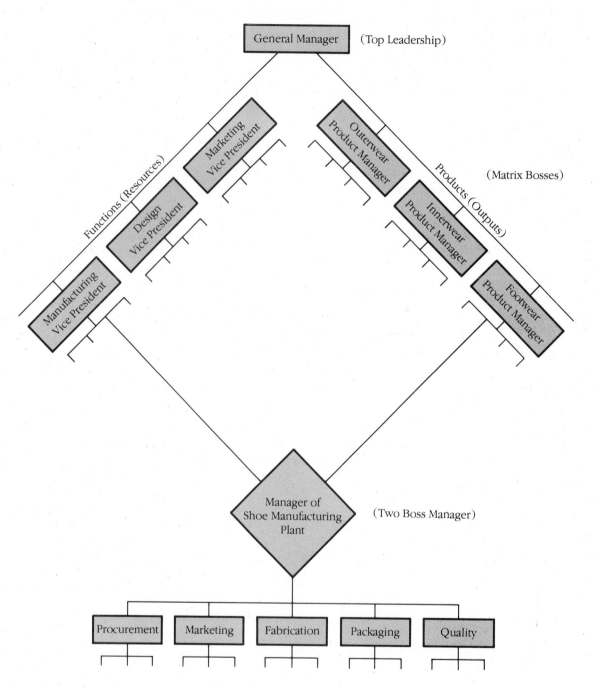

Figure 6.20. Example of a Matrix Design for a Clothing Manufacturer.
Source: Adapted from Stanley M. Davis and Paul R. Lawrence, *Matrix* (Reading, MA: Addison-Wesley, 1977), p. 22.

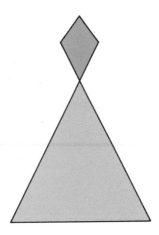

Figure 6.21. Dual-Authority Structure Is Typically at the Top of the Organization. Source: Stanley M. Davis and Paul R. Lawrence, *Matrix* (Reading, MA: Addison-Wesley, 1977), p. 24.

the functional and product managers. If either side of the matrix dominates, the organization will gradually evolve into either a functional or product form, and the benefits of the matrix will be lost. Top leaders must also be willing to delegate decisions and encourage direct contact and group problem-solving at levels beneath them, which will encourage information sharing and coordination.

Matrix Boss The problem for matrix bosses is that they do not have complete control over their subordinates. Matrix bosses must work with each other to delineate activities over which they are responsible. The functional manager's responsibilities pertain to functional expertise, rules, and standards. The product manager is responsible for coordinating the business whole. This person has the authority over subordinates for activities that achieve product goals. Matrix bosses must be willing to confront one another on disagreements and conflicts. They must also collaborate on such things as promotion and salary increases, since subordinates report to both of them. These activities require a great deal of time, communication, patience, and skill at working with people, which are all part of matrix management.

Two-Boss Managers The two-boss manager often experiences a great deal of anxiety and stress. Conflicting demands are imposed by the matrix bosses. Demands from the functional manager and from the product manager may be legitimate, but in direct contradiction. The two-boss manager must confront senior managers on conflicting demands, and reach joint decisions with them. They must maintain effective relationships with both managers, even though they may occasionally feel that their own interests are not being met. Two-boss managers also need a dual loyalty to both their function and their product.

Strengths and Weaknesses The matrix structure is best when environmental uncertainty is high and when the dominant competitive issue and goals reflect a dual requirement, such as between product and function. The matrix structure enables an organization to achieve a dual focus. The matrix enables the organization to be flexible yet have functional depth. Strengths and weaknesses are summarized in table 6.3.[23]

Internal systems reflect the dual organization structure. Two-boss employees are aware of and adopt subgoals for both their function and product. Dual planning and budgeting systems should be designed, one for the functional hierarchy and one for the product line hierarchy. Power and influence is shared equally by functional and product heads. Promotion up through the ranks can be on the basis of functional expertise or general management skills. Linkage processes are needed in both vertical and horizontal directions.

The strength of the matrix is that it enables the organization to meet dual demands from the environment. Resources can be flexibly allocated across different products, and the organization can adapt to changing external requirements. It also provides an opportunity for employees to acquire

Table 6.3. Summary of Matrix Organization Characteristics.

ENVIRONMENT
Environmental uncertainty: High
Dominant competitive issue: Dual—Product/function, geography/function

INTERNAL SYSTEMS
Sub-goals: Product and function
Planning and budgeting: Dual systems—by function and product line
Influence: Joint between functional and product heads
Promotion: On basis of functional expertise or integration skills
Information and linkages: Direct contact among matrix personnel

STRENGTHS
1. Achieves coordination necessary to meet dual demands from environment
2. Flexible use of human resources across products
3. Suited to complex decisions and frequent changes in unstable environment
4. Provides opportunity for functional and integration skill development
5. Best in medium-size organizations with multiple products

WEAKNESSES
1. Participants experience dual authority, which can be frustrating and confusing
2. Participants need good interpersonal skills; extensive training required
3. Time consuming—frequent meetings and conflict-resolution sessions
4. Will not work unless participants understand it and adopt collegial rather than vertical-type relationships
5. Requires dual pressure from environment to maintain power balance

Adapted from Robert Duncan, "What is the Right Organization Structure?: Decision Tree Analysis Provides the Answer," *Organizational Dynamics,* Winter, 1979 (New York: AMACOM, a division of American Management Associations, 1979), p. 429.

either functional or general management skills depending on their interests. The matrix structure works best in a medium-sized organization that has a small or moderate number of products.

One disadvantage of the matrix is that some employees experience dual authority, which is frustrating and confusing. They have to have excellent interpersonal and conflict-resolution skills, which may require specialized training in human relations. The matrix also forces managers to spend a great deal of time in meetings. If managers do not adapt to the information- and power-sharing required by the matrix, it will not work. They must collaborate with one another rather than rely on vertical authority in decision-making.

IN PRACTICE 6.9
Business College

Most colleges of business have a functional organization structure. Heads of respective academic departments report to the dean. The functional structure has several advantages: it encourages in-depth skill development for teaching and research, faculty members identify with departmental needs and goals, and faculty are free to concentrate on their functional specialties. A problem with the functional structure is that coordination across departments is often poor. Students may feel that faculty members are not coordinated in the amount of homework they assign, and similar content may be repeated in different courses.

Colleges of business can use various horizontal linkage devices to achieve integration in an undergraduate or graduate program. The most frequent device is to appoint program directors to serve as full-time integrators. One director might be in charge of the MBA program, another in charge of the undergraduate program, the research function, and so on. These directors would not have direct authority over faculty members, but would work with faculty to coordinate their activites.

Since program directors do not have formal authority, faculty members may not do as the directors request. The primary allegiance of faculty will be toward excellence in their functional activities and not toward coordination with other departments. To overcome this problem, a few schools have elevated the directors to program manager status. A matrix is thus created with dual lines of authority, as in figure 6.22. Individual faculty members report to both a program manager and a department head. Some professors may work in more than one program, which is an example of shared resources. Faculty promotions, tenure and salary increases are based on satisfying both managers. The advantage of the matrix is that effective coordination across functions is achieved. The disadvantage is that functional specialists (professors) are now involved in coordination and conflict-resolution activities that leave less time for teaching and research. But if the dominant competitive issue facing the business college is to achieve coordination for each program, then the

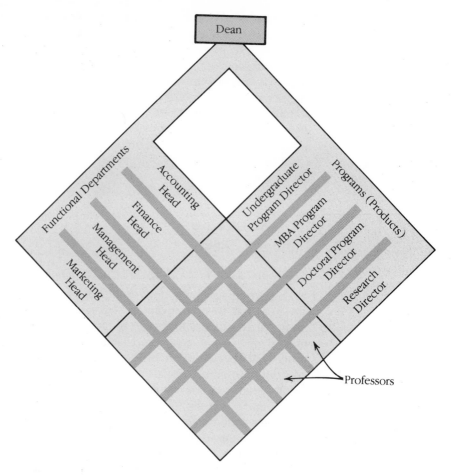

Figure 6.22. Matrix Organization Structure in a Business School.
Adapted from Don Hellriegel and John W. Slocum, *Organizational Behavior* (St. Paul: West, 1979), p. 127.

allocation of time to coordination is worthwhile. If the dominant competitive issue for the business college is functional specialization and research, the matrix would not be appropriate, and the organization should stay with the functional structure.

MATRIX VERSUS FUNCTIONAL AND PRODUCT STRUCTURES

All kinds of organizations have experimented with the matrix, including consulting firms, hospitals, banks, insurance companies, government, and many types of industrial firms.[24] Although widely adopted, the matrix is not a cure-all for structural problems. Many organizations have found that the matrix is difficult to install and maintain. When the matrix fails, it is usually because one side of the authority structure dominates, or employees have not learned to work in a collaborative relationship. In these organizations, a single authority structure with horizontal linkage mechanisms is better than a matrix.

Most organizations begin with a functional organization structure. As they become larger and more complex, they reorganize into some form of product structure, perhaps with a few centralized functional departments. If the product structure does not work, they may try a matrix. The matrix is located in the middle between functional and product structures, as illustrated in figure 6.23.[25]

The functional structure gives formal authority to functional departments, and groups departments together according to function. Horizontal linkage

Figure 6.23. Relationship Among Structural Alternatives.
Adapted from Jay R. Galbraith, "Matrix Organization Designs: How to Combine Functional and Project Forms," *Business Horizons,* February 19, 1971, p. 38.

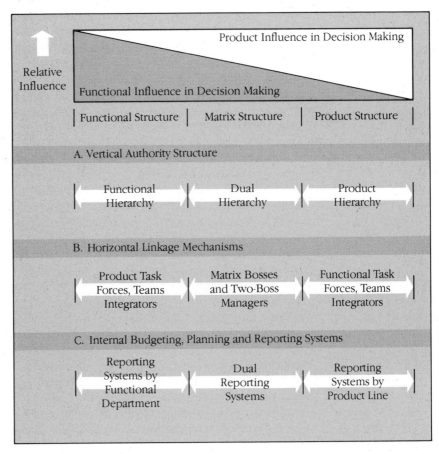

devices such as cross-functional teams can be used to achieve horizontal integration for each product line. The formal budgeting and reporting system is designed to fit each functional department.

The other extreme is the product structure, in which formal authority is given to product lines. Horizontal linkages across product lines can be achieved through the use of functional task forces, or integrators who coordinate people engaged in the same function. A formal budgeting and reporting system is designed for each product line.

The matrix organization is in the middle ground between functional and product structures (figure 6.23). A dual-authority structure gives equal importance to both functional and product hierarchies. The dual-authority structure achieves integration through convergence of the hierarchy on the two-boss managers. The matrix has dual budgeting and reporting systems. The dual-reporting system is important because it reinforces the dual hierarchy.

IN PRACTICE 6.10

Pittsburgh Steel Company

As far back as anyone can remember, the steel industry in the United States was stable and certain. If steel manufacturers could produce quality steel at a reasonable price, it would be sold. The U.S. market was growing steadily, and everything that could be made was sold. No more. Inflation, the national economic downturn, reduced consumption of autos, and competition from steelmakers in Germany and Japan has forever changed the steel industry. Today steelmakers have shifted to specialized steel products. They must market aggressively, make efficient use of internal resources, and adapt to rapid-fire changes.

Pittsburgh Steel employs 2,500 people, makes 300,000 tons of steel a year, and is 170 years old. For 160 of those years the functional structure similar to figure 6.24 worked fine. As the environment became more turbulent and competitive, Pittsburgh Steel managers discovered they were not keeping up. Fifty percent of Pittsburgh's orders were behind schedule. Profits were eroded by labor, material, and energy cost increases. Market share declined.

In consultation with outside experts, the president of Pittsburgh Steel decided that the solution was a matrix organization structure. Pittsburgh Steel had four product lines—open-die forgings, ring-mill products, wheels and axles, and steel-making. A business manager was given responsibility and authority for each line. Department heads in each of the functional departments now reported to business managers as well as to their respective functional vice presidents. The business managers had clearly defined responsibility, which included preparing a business plan for each product line, and developing targets for production costs, product inventory, shipping inventory, and gross profit. They were expected to meet those targets. Functional vice presidents were responsible

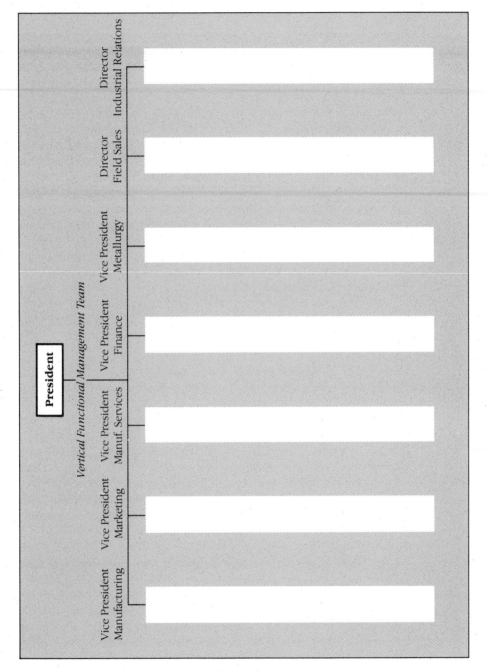

Figure 6.24. Functional Structure for Pittsburgh Steel Co.

for technical decisions relating to their function. Two functional departments, field sales and industrial relations, were not included in the matrix because they worked independently. The final design was a hybrid structure, with both matrix and functional responsibilities, as illustrated in figure 6.25.

Implementation of the matrix was slow. Middle managers were confused. Meetings to coordinate across functional departments seemed to be held every day. One manager said, "How can we have time for our normal responsibilities and still have meetings all the time? These procedures are disturbing everything we've always done."

After about a year of training by external consultants, Pittsburgh Steel is back on track. Ninety percent of the orders are now delivered on time. Market share has recovered. Both productivity and profitability are increasing steadily, despite a sluggish economy and continued foreign competition. The managers thrive on matrix involvement. Meetings to coordinate product and functional decisions have provided a growth experience. Middle managers now want to include younger managers in the matrix discussions as training for future management responsibility.[26]

SYMPTOMS OF STRUCTURAL DEFICIENCY

Managers periodically evaluate organization structure to determine whether it is appropriate to changing organization needs. David Dawson's evaluation of ESB Ray-O-Vac, for instance, led to a complete reorganization. As a general rule, when organization structure is out of alignment with organization needs, one or more of the following symptoms appear.[27]

Decision-Making Is Delayed or Lacking in Quality Decision-makers may be overloaded because the hierarchy funnels too many problems and decisions to them. Delegation to lower levels may be insufficient. Another problem is that information may not reach the correct people. Linkages in either the vertical or horizontal direction may be inadequate to ensure decision quality. Finally, decision-makers may be too segmented. The organization structure may not integrate diverse interests into the decision-making process.

The Organization Does Not Respond Innovatively to a Changing Environment One important reason for lack of innovation is that departments are not coordinated horizontally. The identification of customer needs by the marketing department and the identification of technological developments in the research department must be coordinated. Organization structure also has to specify departmental responsibilities that include environmental scanning and innovation.

Too Much Conflict Is Evident Organization structure should allow conflicting goals to combine into a single set of objectives for the organiza-

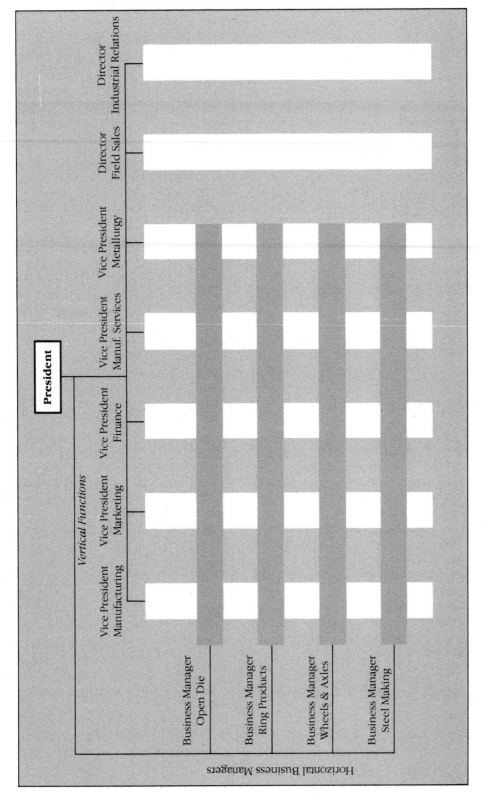

Figure 6.25. Matrix Structure for Pittsburgh Steel Co.

tion. When people act at cross purposes or are under pressure to achieve departmental goals at the expense of organizational goals, the structure is often at fault. Horizontal linkage mechanisms are not adequate. Vertical breakdowns occur when people at the operational level who see changing contingencies cannot feed information into the planning and objective setting at upper levels.

SUMMARY AND INTERPRETATION

Organization structure must accomplish two things for the organization: (1) provide a map of tasks, responsibilities, reporting relationships, and groupings, and (2) provide mechanisms for linking and coordinating organizational elements into a coherent whole. The map is relatively easy to develop and is reflected on the organization chart. Linking the organization into a coherent whole is more difficult.

The single most important idea in this chapter is to understand how to manage the need for vertical and horizontal linkage mechanisms in organizations. Each department and hierarchical level has its own goals and personnel, yet must work as part of the larger organization. Classical organization theorists stressed vertical design, and relied upon vertical linkages to provide integration. While vertical linkages are a powerful means of coordination, they are not sufficient for most organizations in today's complex and rapidly changing world. In recent years, attention has been focused on the need for horizontal coordination. Departments must solve mutual problems and share information if the organization is to be effective. Organization charts appearing in organizations today often show horizontal lines (dotted) as well as vertical lines to describe expected working relationships.

The best organization structure achieves the correct balance between vertical and horizontal coordination processes. Vertical structure and formal authority are stronger than horizontal relationships. The choice between functional and product structure determines vertical priority, and hence determines where coordination and integration will be greatest. Horizontal linkage mechanisms complement the vertical dimension to achieve the integration of departments and levels into an organizational whole. The matrix organization implements an equal balance between the vertical and horizontal dimensions of structure.

Finally, an organization chart is only so many lines and boxes on a piece of paper. A new organization structure will not necessarily solve an organization's problems. The organization chart simply reflects what people should do and what their responsibilities are. The purpose of the organization chart is to encourage and direct employees into activities and coordination processes that enable the organization to achieve its goals. The organization chart provides the structure, but employees provide the behavior. The chart is a guideline to encourage people to work together, but management must implement the structure and carry it out.

DISCUSSION QUESTIONS

1. What is the definition of organization structure? Does organization structure appear on the organization chart? Explain.
2. What factors influence span of control?
3. How do rules and plans help an organization achieve vertical integration?
4. When is a functional structure preferable to a product structure?
5. Large corporations tend to use hybrid structures. Why?
6. How does dominant competitive issue differ from the concept of goals? What is the dominant competitive issue for a McDonald's hamburger store, a coal mine, a manufacturer of electronic toys?
7. What is the difference between a task force and a team? Between liaison role and integrating role? Which of these provides the greatest amount of horizontal coordination?
8. What conditions usually have to be present before an organization should adopt a matrix structure?
9. The manager of a consumer products firm said, "We use the brand manager position to train future executives." Do you think the brand manager position is a good training ground? Discuss.
10. In a matrix organization, how do the role requirements of the top manager differ from the role requirements of the matrix bosses?
11. An organizational consultant argued that, "The matrix structure is intermediate between the functional and product structures, and combines the advantages of both." Do you disagree or agree with this statement? Why?

GUIDES TO ACTION

As an organization designer:

1. Develop organization charts that describe the allocation of tasks and responsibilities, vertical reporting relationships, the grouping of individuals into departments, as well as supplementary documentation such as responsibility charts and position descriptions. Provide sufficient documentation that all persons within the organization know their tasks, responsibilities, to whom they report, and how they fit into the total organization picture.
2. Provide vertical and horizontal linkages to integrate diverse departments into a coherent whole. Greater linkage is required in a large, complex organization in an uncertain environment than in a small organization and stable environment. Achieve vertical linkage through hierarchy referral, rules and procedures, planning and scheduling, adding levels to the hierarchy, and vertical information systems. Achieve horizontal linkage through paperwork, direct contact, liaison roles, task forces, and full-time integrators.

3. Choose between functional or product (self-contained units) structures when designing overall organization structure. Use a functional structure in a small or medium-sized organization that has a stable environment. Use a product structure in a large organization that has multiple product lines, and when you wish to give priority to product goals and to coordination across functions.

4. Implement hybrid structures, when needed, in large corporations by dividing the organization into self-contained product groups and assigning each function needed for the product line to the product division. If a function serves the entire organization rather than a specific product line, structure that function as a single functional department. Use a hybrid structure to gain the advantages of both functional and product design while eliminating some of the disadvantages.

5. Consider a matrix structure in certain organization settings if neither the product nor the functional structure meets coordination needs. For best results with a matrix structure, use it in a medium-sized organization with a small number of products or outputs that has a changing environment, and which needs to give equal priority to both products and functions because of dual issues from the environment. Do not use the matrix structure unless there is truly a need for a dual hierarchy and employees are well trained in its purpose and operation.

6. Consider a structural reorganization whenever the symptoms of structural deficiency are observed. Use organization structure to solve the problems of poor quality decision-making, slow response to the external environment, and too much conflict between departments.

Consider these Guides when analyzing the following cases and when answering the questions listed after each case.

CASES FOR ANALYSIS

I. CANCON COMPANY

CanCon is a large container corporation located in Toronto, Canada. It manufactures glass, paper, and tin containers for use throughout Ontario and Quebec. CanCon has hired a consultant and is considering a major reorganization. In the current organization, each container division has the same organization structure, as reflected in figure 6.26. The structure proposed by the consultant is shown in figure 6.27.[28]

Questions
1. What type of organization structure did the consultant propose? What factors do you think the consultant was responding to in proposing this change?

2. Under which organization structure will the organization's functions be most widely differentiated? In which organization will research and development tend to do research on applied problems relevant to a product line? Under which structure will research and development do

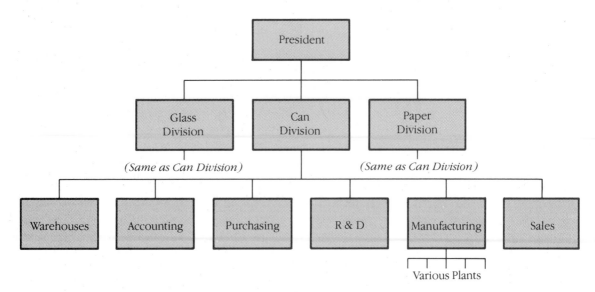

Figure 6.26. CanCon's Current Structure.

Figure 6.27. CanCon's Proposed Structure.

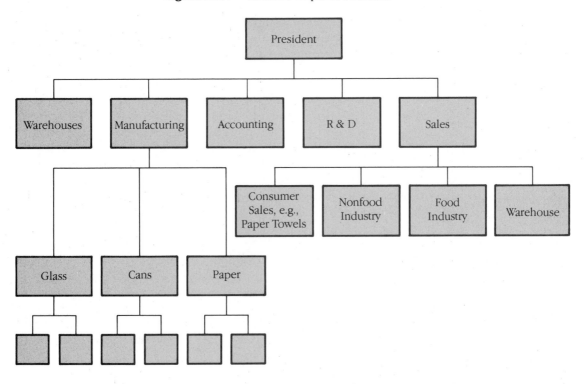

more basic research that is not immediately useful to the manufacturing or marketing of a product?

3. Which form of organization would adjust most quickly to technological change and new products? Why?

4. Which organization structure do you think would be most effective for the container industry? Why?

2. AQUARIUS ADVERTISING AGENCY

The Aquarius Advertising Agency is a middle-sized firm that offered two basic professional services to its clients: (1) customized plans for the content of an advertising campaign, e.g., slogans, layouts, and (2) complete plans for media such as radio, TV, newspapers, billboards, magazines, etc. Additional services included aid in marketing and distribution of products, and marketing research to test advertising effectiveness.

Its activities were organized in a traditional manner. The formal organization is shown in figure 6.28. Each of the functions includes similar activities, and each client account was coordinated by an account executive who acted as a liaison between the client and the various specialists on the professional staff of the Operations and Marketing Divisions. The number of direct communications and contacts between clients and Aquarius specialists, clients and account executives, and Aquarius specialists and account executives is indicated in figure 6.29. These sociometric data were gathered by a consultant who conducted a study of the patterns of formal and informal communication. Each intersecting cell of Aquarius personnel and the clients contains an index of the direct contacts between them.

Although an account executive was designated to be the liaison between the client and specialists within the agency, communications frequently occurred directly between clients and specialists and bypassed the account executive. These direct contacts involved a wide range of interactions such as meetings, telephone calls, letters, etc. A large number of direct communications occurred between agency specialists and their counterparts in the client organization. For example, an art specialist working as one member of a team on a particular client account would often be contacted directly by the client's in-house art specialist, and agency research personnel had direct communication with research people of the client firm. Also, some of the unstructured contacts often led to more formal meetings with clients in which agency personnel made presentations, interpreted and defended agency policy, and committed the agency to certain courses of action.

Both a hierarchical and professional system operated within the departments of the Operations and Marketing Divisions. Each department was organized hierarchically with a director, an assistant director, and several levels of authority. Professional communications were widespread and mainly concerned with sharing knowledge and techniques, technical evaluation of work, and development of professional interests. Control in each professional department was exercised mainly through control of promotions and supervision of work done by subordinates. Many account executives felt the need for more control and one commented:

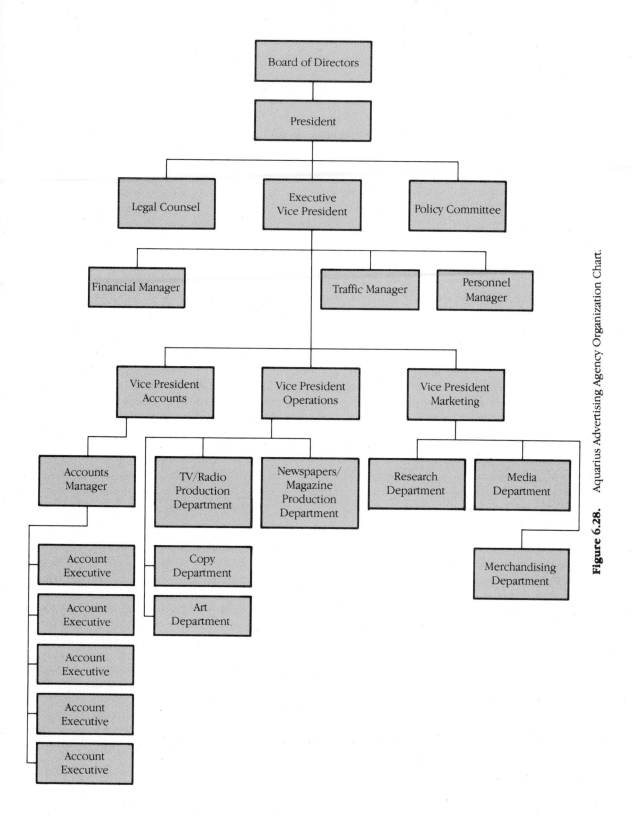

Figure 6.28. Aquarius Advertising Agency Organization Chart.

	Clients	Account Manager	Account Executives	TV/Radio Specialists	Newspaper/Magazine Specialists	Copy Specialists	Art Specialists	Merchandising Specialists	Media Specialists	Research Specialists	Traffic
Clients	X	F	F	N	N	O	O	O	O	O	N
Account Manager		X	F	N	N	N	N	N	N	N	N
Account Executives			X	F	F	F	F	F	F	F	F
TV/Radio Specialists				X	N	O	O	N	N	O	N
Newspaper/Magazine Specialists					X	O	O	N	O	O	N
Copy Specialists						X	N	O	O	O	N
Art Specialists							X	O	O	O	N
Merchandising Specialists								X	F	F	N
Media Specialists									X	F	N
Research Specialists										X	N
Traffic											X

F = Frequent—daily
O = Occasional—once or twice per project
N = None

Figure 6.29. Sociometric Index of Contacts of Aquarius Personnel and Clients.

Creativity and art. That's all I hear around here. It is hard as hell to effectively manage six or seven hot shots who claim they have to do their own thing. Each of them tries to sell his or her idea to the client and most of the time I don't know what has happened until a week later. If I were a despot I would make all of them check with me first to get approval first. Things would sure change around here.

The need for reorganization was made more acute by the changes in the environment. Within a short period of time, there was a rapid turnover in the major accounts handled by the agency. It was typical for advertising agencies to gain or lose clients quickly, often with no advance warning as consumer behavior and lifestyle changes emerged and product innovations occurred.

An agency reorganization was one of the solutions proposed by top management to increase flexibility in this subtle and unpredictable environment. The reorganization was aimed at reducing the agency's response time to environmental changes and increasing cooperation and communications among specialists of different types.[29]

Questions:
1. What type of organization structure now exists at Aquarius?
2. What is the dominant competitive issue? Where is integration required within Aquarius?
3. Design an organization structure that takes into consideration the information flows (figure 6.29) within Aquarius Advertising.
4. Would a matrix structure be feasible for Aquarius? Why?

NOTES

1. "ESB Ray-O-Vac: Decentralizing to Recharge Its Innovative Spirit," *Business Week,* March 12, 1979, pp. 116–117.
2. *Ibid.,* "Inco Ltd.," *Wall Street Journal,* January 5, 1979, p. 23.
3. John Child, *Organization* (New York: Harper & Row, 1977): p. 10.
4. This discussion is based on Jay R. Galbraith, *Designing Complex Organizations* (Reading, MA: Addison-Wesley, 1973) and *Organization Design* (Reading, MA: Addison-Wesley, 1977), pp. 81–127.
5. Jay W. Lorsch, "Introduction to the Structural Design of Organizations," in Gene W. Dalton, Paul R. Lawrence, and Jay W. Lorsch, eds., *Organization Structure and Design* (Homewood, IL: Irwin and Dorsey, 1970), pp. 1–16.
6. *Ibid.*
7. This discussion is based on Galbraith, *Designing Complex Organizations.*
8. Paul R. Lawrence and Jay W. Lorsch, "New Managerial Job: The Integrator," *Harvard Business Review* (November–December, 1967): 142–151.
9. Ann M. Morrison, "The General Mills Brand of Managers," *Fortune,* January 12, pp. 99–107.
10. *Ibid.;* Daniel Rosenheim, "The Metamorphosis of General Mills," *Houston Chronicle,* April 1, 1982, section 3, p. 4.
11. Galbraith, *Designing Complex Organizations.*
12. Mary S. McCarthy, "Bonanza International," unpublished manuscript, Southern Methodist University, 1981.
13. Henry Fayol, *Industrial and General Administration* (Paris: Dunod, 1925); Luther Gulick and Lyndall F. Urwick, eds., papers on the *Science of Administration* (New York: Institute of Public Administration, Columbia University, 1937).
14. Richard T. Rumelt, *Strategy, Structure, and Economic Performance* (Cambridge: Harvard University Press, 1974), p. 111.

15. This discussion is based upon Robert Duncan, "What is the Right Organization Structure?" *Organizational Dynamics,* (Winter, 1979): 59–80.

16. David Abdalla, J. Doehring, and Ann Windhager, "Blue Bell Creameries, Inc.: Case and Analysis," unpublished manuscript, Texas A & M University, 1981; Jorjanna Price, "Creamery Churns its Ice Cream into Cool Millions," *Parade,* February 21, 1982, pp. 18–22.

17. This discussion is based upon Duncan, "What is the Right Organizational Structure?"

18. Sheri Aldridge, Jeff Jenkins, and Barry Jones, "Levi Strauss & Company," unpublished manuscript, Texas A & M University, 1981.

19. *Ibid.*

20. Stanley M. Davis and Paul R. Lawrence, *Matrix* (Reading, MA: Addison-Wesley, 1977), pp. 11–24.

21. Harry E. Peywell, "Engineering Management in a Multiple (Second- and Third-Level) Matrix Organization," IEEE *Transactions on Engineering Management* 26 (1979): 51–55.

22. Davis and Lawrence, *Matrix,* pp. 46–52.

23. This discussion is based upon Duncan, "What is the Right Organization Structure?"

24. Davis and Lawrence, *Matrix,* pp. 155–180.

25. This discussion is based upon Jay R. Galbraith, "Matrix Organization Designs: How to Combine Functional and Project Forms," *Business Horizons* 14 (1971): 29–40.

26. This case was inspired by John E. Fogerty, "Integrative Management at Standard Steel," unpublished manuscript, Latrobe, Pennsylvania, 1980, and John M. Starrels, "Steel's Stiff Competition," *Wall Street Journal,* July 9, 1982, p. 12.

27. This discussion is based upon Child, *Organization,* ch 1.

28. This case is based on "Container Company," in *Personnel: The Human Problems of Management,* by George Strauss and Leonard R. Sayles (Englewood Cliffs, N.J.: Prentice-Hall, 1972), pp. 346–347.

29. Adapted from John F. Veiga and John N. Yanouzas, "Aquarius Advertising Agency," in John F. Veiga and John N. Yanouzas, *The Dynamics of Organization Theory* (St. Paul, MN: West, 1979), pp. 225–230, with permission.

PART IV
Structural Influence on Dynamic Processes

7

Organizational Change

A LOOK INSIDE

VALLEY FOODS

Executives at Valley Foods, a medium-sized grocery chain in the Northwest United States, wanted to adopt a new technology for computer-assisted checkouts. Computer-assisted checkout systems could be acquired in several variations, but senior executives at Valley Foods were interested in laser scanners. By the mid-1970s, the universal product code was printed on all grocery items. The laser scanner worked by reading the universal product code symbol when the checker passed the item over the laser beam. The symbol was fed into the store computer, which identified the item and inserted the price into the cash register. The name and price were automatically printed on the display screen and receipt tape. Reading and displaying the price took only a fraction of a second.

Front-end labor accounted for approximately 40% of supermarket labor costs. Because of this labor intensity, most grocery chains were interested in automated checkout systems. The laser scanner was the most advanced checkout technology and had the potential to reduce front-end labor by as much as 20%. Savings were realized from reduced checkout time, reduced ringing errors, and time lost checking for prices. Another big savings was from not manually pricing each item on the shelf because prices were stored in the computer. The computer system also had many other advantages. It provided up-to-date inventory information that could be used for planning and reordering. The system provided minute-by-minute information on how many customers used each lane, the rate of sales for any line of merchandise—especially those that were advertised to draw customers into the store—and the amount of business handled by each checker. The computer stored check-cashing and credit information. Management could review a profile of each store's activity at the end of each day.

Most senior managers were enthusiastic about the laser scanning system. The Vice President for Public Affairs, however, inserted a note of caution. He had studied consumer concerns and discovered substantial resistance. Consumers believed that laser scanners would make stores more efficient, but were afraid the efficiencies would not be passed on in the form of lower prices. An even more serious problem was the issue of item pricing. The new technology would mean that supermarkets did not have to price each item. The price would be marked on the super-market shelf, but the consumer would not be able to compare the price on the item to the price that was flashed on the computer screen. Consumers were afraid that without prices on each item they would be taken advantage of. This attitude could be a problem because one of the biggest savings to the store was the labor saved by not pricing each item.

The Director of Personnel noted that labor unions were objecting to the system. Union officials were afraid that long-term job security and employment levels would be reduced. Valley Foods assured the unions that no clerks or checkout personnel would be laid off, but the union was still concerned.

After a series of discussions, Valley Food executives were divided over the best course of action. Several wanted to try a gradualist approach. The strategy would be to go slow and leave prices on items for the first few months until consumers became used to the system. After consumers trusted the system, item pricing could be withdrawn.

Other managers felt that the objections by consumer groups and the labor union were not valid. After all, Valley Foods did not plan to take advantage of anyone. These managers wanted to push ahead with the new system and educate each group as needed. They proposed the strategy of introducing the new technology with great fanfare. Consumer groups would be invited to see the technology and have it explained to them on one night, employees the next night, and the public the next night, to show the advantages of the new system. In less than a week, everyone would be educated and the benefits of the new system could be realized.

Valley Foods was opening a new superstore in the Portland area. Management's final decision was to use the fanfare approach. Valley Foods would install the laser technology and confront relevant groups in a series of educational sessions. One year later, the laser scanning checkout system was sitting idle in the Portland superstore. Consumer groups and labor unions raised so much protest that the technology could not be used. All items were priced by hand, and each item was rung into the computer by hand. The expensive new laser scanning system sat idle.[1]

Why did this efficient new technology fail to be implemented? The causes of failure are multiple and complex. The managers at Valley Foods did not fully understand how to manage the change process. If they did, they would have used a different strategy to implement the laser-scanning technology.

Laser scanning is just one of thousands of changes taking place in organizations. It has become commonplace to suggest that change is important, that every organization must cope with change in order to survive. Organizations are open systems. They cannot completely buffer themselves from environmental instability. Organizations must respond to internal and external pressures for change. The unprecedented pace of change in recent years prompted one writer to describe change as a fire storm that continues to gather force.[2] The characterization of change as a raging inferno seems extreme, but most people agree that one thing that organizations can be sure of is that things will not remain the same.

Many visible and tangible changes are in the technological domain. New discoveries and inventions quickly replace standard ways of doing things. Computer technology, for instance, has had significant impact on many organizations. Computers do much of the accounting and routine paperwork. Computers have replaced methods of hand calculation for the research projects of most college professors. Electronic calculators have replaced slide rules for most college students. One slide rule company reported a drop in sales of 75% in two years. The parents of today's college students grew up without television, crease-resistant clothing, stereo sets, jet aircraft, and detergents, all of which we take for granted today.

Purpose of This Chapter The purpose of this chapter is to explore how organizations adapt to change, and how managers influence the change process. The concepts covered in previous chapters, such as bureaucratic characteristics and functional versus product structures, are related to change. The structure necessary to achieve change is explored more fully in this chapter. The next section defines the sequence of steps associated with successful change. Then four types of change—technology, product, administrative, people—are analyzed. Frameworks for handling each type of change are covered. Management techniques for influencing both the initiation and implementation of change are also covered. By the end of this chapter, students should be able to address the following issues: What type of organization structure is associated with change? Should changes be imposed downward from the top of the organization, or should they trickle up from the bottom? When should people participate in the change process? But before dealing with these issues, let's determine what change is.

ELEMENTS IN THE CHANGE PROCESS

Organizational change is the adoption of a new idea or behavior by an organization.[3] In order for the new idea or behavior to be adopted, a series of activities has to be completed. If one of these elements is missing, the change process will fail.[4]

1. *Need.* A need for change occurs when managers are dissatisfied with current performance. A perceived problem exists in the form of a gap between actual performance and desired performance. Organizational

goals are not being met. Dissatisfaction may arise when managers learn that customers are complaining about product quality, or when a competitor develops a technology to manufacture goods more cheaply. Dissatisfaction is necessary to unfreeze managers from the current way of doing things so they can adopt new behaviors.

2. *Idea.* An idea is a new way of doing things. The idea may be a model, concept, or plan that can be implemented by the organization. The idea may be a new machine, a new product, or a new technique for managing employees. Normally an idea has to be matched to a need before it will be adopted. The idea should have the potential to reduce the dissatisfaction felt by managers about performance. The transistor, open classrooms in high school education, assembly lines, and semiconductors were at one time somebody's idea.

3. *Proposal.* A proposal occurs when someone within the organization requests the adoption of a new behavior, idea, or technique. For many changes, employees provide a formal, written proposal with supporting documentation. For other changes, the proposal may be handled by an informal memo or request. The proposal is important because it crystalizes the idea and shows how it will solve a problem and improve performance. The proposal gives the organization the opportunity to decide if it wants to try the change.

4. *Decision to Adopt.* A decision occurs when the organization makes a choice to adopt the proposed change. For a large change, the decision might require the signing of the legal document by the board of directors. For a small change, the decision might be informal approval by a supervisor to try a modification, such as in the assembly sequence.

5. *Resources.* Human force and activity are required to bring about change. Change requires resources. Change does not happen on its own. An employee has to perceive both the need and the idea to meet that need. Someone must develop a proposal and provide the time and effort to implement it. Managers often take it upon themselves to provide the energy to bring about change. Sometimes they delegate the responsibility to a specific employee. Committees and task forces as described in chapter 6 are also effective ways to focus resources on a change. Organizations do not have enough time and human resources to do everything. In order for a change to be successfully proposed and implemented, resources must be allocated to it.

Figure 7.1 indicates the sequence in which the change elements occur. Many needs for change and ideas originate in the external environment. Environments are never perfectly stable, so the organization must adapt. Organization boundary-spanning units will discover problems to be solved and ideas that may improve performance. Needs and ideas are listed simultaneously at the beginning of the change sequence. Either may occur first. Sometimes a problem arises that precipitates search procedures to uncover an appropriate solution. Sometimes employees learn about a new idea and realize that it may be a more efficient way to do things. They propose it as a means of increasing performance. Many organizations adopted the

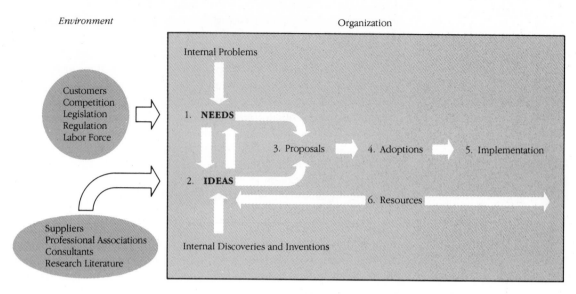

Environment

Organization

Figure 7.1.   Typical Sequence Among Ingredients of Successful Change.

digital computer, for example, not because they had a specific need for it, but because it seemed like a good way to improve performance. The search for polio vaccine, on the other hand, was stimulated by a severe need. Either the need or the idea may occur first, but in order for the change to be accomplished, each of the steps in figure 7.1 must be completed.

IN PRACTICE 7.1

Swearingen Aviation Corporation

Ed Swearingen started Swearingen Aviation in the 1960s to modify airplanes. Ed Swearingen was a great inventor, and he developed several modifications for existing aircraft. Initial operations were designed to modify the Beechcraft Queen Air into a high performance Queen Air 800, and to convert the D-50 Twin Bonanza into the Excalibur. Other inventions included a pressurized fuselage to go on top of the wings and new wing designs. He finally integrated his designs into a single new aircraft called Merlin II in 1966.

The Merlin II brought success to the company. Within two years it was modified and the Merlin IIB was introduced. Swearingen Aviation was now selling aircraft throughout the United States, Canada, and Mexico. By the late 1960s, business jets were in high demand so Swearingen began to design an executive jet. At that point, the company began to find itself in trouble. The executive jet required more resources than were available. Moreover, other new modifications to the Merlin were introduced. Five aircraft versions were being produced at the same time. The production process could not keep up with the modifications. In

1969, only fifty-one aircraft were produced. In 1970, only sixteen planes came off the line. The company was in crisis. Customers were cancelling orders, cash was being siphoned off into jet aircraft development, and production was almost at a standstill. One thousand employees were furloughed. The company was moving toward bankruptcy.

Swearingen Aviation found a solution to its problem in the form of "Tiger Teams." These teams were production engineers who were given responsibility to study the production process and to develop ideas for smoothing and coordinating each step in production. These teams came up with hundreds of ideas that were integrated into a new assembly sequence with ten control points. The control points enabled management to monitor the movement of aircraft through the assembly sequence. The reorganization took approximately one year, and it was an outstanding accomplishment. The tiger teams made major changes in tooling, and even instituted a new manufacturing accounting system. They trained new personnel and spent long hours retraining current personnel. Airplanes are now assembled in a logical, coordinated sequence that is faster and provides higher quality construction than before.

As a finishing touch, the assembly line was moved farther back in the hangar. Engines on assembled planes are started directly outside the hangar door at the end of the assembly area. The thunder of a turboprop engine provides motivation and feedback for employees. They know their jobs were successful.[5]

Each of the required change elements occurred at Swearingen Aviation. When the assembly process bogged down, managers felt a strong need for change from cancelled orders and lost profits. They did not have a solution, but they wisely allocated resources to the problem in the form of tiger teams. These teams analyzed the problem, developed ideas, proposed them, and even implemented the solution. The change was successful.

The change process at Swearingen was not always managed correctly. When Ed Swearingen was developing frequent modifications for his aircraft, the number of ideas was too great. Not all ideas met a specific need and resources were not available to implement each idea in an orderly way. Resources were spread too thin. The organization lost its change focus. The handling of too many aircraft changes was one reason for the production problem. Fortunately, the tiger teams were able to solve this problem. The change process can be managed successfully when sufficient resources are allocated and each change step is completed.

TYPES OF CHANGE

The four types of change in organizations are technology, product, administrative, and people, as shown in figure 7.2. Organization structure and management techniques are often designed to facilitate one type of change. In a rapidly changing industry, the organization may have to introduce frequent new products. In a highly competitive environment, changes in the

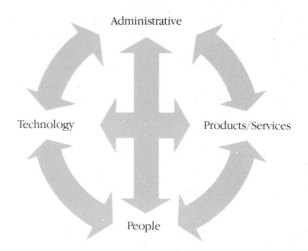

Figure 7.2.   Four Types of Change in Organizations.

production process may be needed to squeeze out increased efficiency. Government organizations often have to make administrative changes in policies and procedures. Managing the six steps described above and the correct organization structure depends upon the type of change needed by the organization.

Technology changes pertain to the organization's production process. These changes are designed to make the transformation process more efficient or to produce greater volume. Changes in technology involve new techniques for making products or services. In a university, technology changes are changes in the type of courses taught or in techniques for teaching courses. Redesigning the assembly sequence at Swearingen Aviation was a change in technology. The laser-scanning checkout system described at the beginning of this chapter was a change in the production process of a grocery store. That was a change in technology also.

Product changes pertain to the product or service outputs of the organization. New products include small adaptations of existing products, or entirely new product lines. New products are normally designed to increase the market share or to develop new markets, customers, or clients. The jet aircraft at Swearingen Aviation was a product change. A product change in a university would be non-credit evening courses for adults in the community.

Administrative changes pertain to the administrative domain in the organization. The administrative domain involves the supervision and management of the organization. Administrative changes include changes in organization structure, goals, policies, reward systems, labor relations, linkage devices, management information systems, and accounting and budgeting systems. In a university, administrative change would include a new merit pay system, or a new organizational structure.

People changes refer to changes in the attitudes, skills, expectations, and behavior of employees. An organization may wish to upgrade the leadership ability of key managers. This would be a people change. Other types of people changes include improvements in communications, problem-solving, and planning skills of managers. Increased technical skills for production employees would also be a people change. Overcoming a personal problem, such as alcoholism, is a people change. If management professors do not get along with accounting professors, the lack of cooperation could hurt the teaching mission of the business school. A people change would help the professors develop positive attitudes and behavior patterns that would lead to cooperation and work harmony.

The arrows in figure 7.2 indicate that each type of change often influences the others. A new product may require changes in the production technology. Or a change in administrative policy may influence the attitudes and skills of employees. When a state finance department established a new hiring and promotion policy that gave priority to women and minority groups (an administrative change), the attitudes of current employees were affected. Many employees were upset. Although changes affect each other, most changes can be classified as either technology, administrative, people, or product, depending upon the primary target. In many large organizations, all four types of change may be occurring simultaneously, as illustrated in the following example of General Telephone and Electronics Corporation.

IN PRACTICE 7.2

GTE

General Telephone and Electronics Corporation is now the largest independent telephone operating system in the United States. GTE employs almost 200,000 persons and is the thirtieth largest industrial and utility corporation. GTE is responsible for nineteen operating companies that provide communication services ranging from home phone service to highly complex data services for industry and national defense. Telephone markets have become increasingly dynamic, competitive, and technology-based. GTE has taken organizational steps to be innovative and take advantage of opportunities created by a changing environment. GTE manages change both aggressively and intelligently.

GTE has undertaken programs of change in the areas of technology, new products, administration, and people. Key changes from recent years are summarized in figure 7.3. New products produced by GTE companies include the GTD-5 Electronic Automatic Exchange, which offers computer-based switching systems tailored to business customers' specific needs. The Flip Phone has proved to be a popular item for home telephone users. Telemail is a nationwide electronic mail service that provides instantaneous delivery of messages anywhere in the U.S. The Micro-Fone is a credit authorization terminal used by businesses to provide quick credit checks at the point of sale. Other new products include halogen sealed-beam headlamps for automobiles that offer greatly increased life span and that are now standard on Ford cars. GTE has also developed microprocessor control systems. The control system can sense temperature, time, position, and switch closure, and can issue control commands. Initial applications have been used for automotive manufacturing, materials handling, and air conditioning applications.

Changes in technology are increasing the efficiency and scope of GTE activity. One need is for greater intercity communications capacity. Fiberoptics uses light inside extremely fine glass wires to transmit communications more efficiently than metal wires. Laser switching and transmission systems have also been developed to increase transmission efficiency. GTE uses satellites to achieve a more efficient world-wide transmission system. Within GTE offices, many departments are adopting word processors and other labor-saving devices in day-to-day operations.

Administrative changes at GTE include new equal opportunity programs. All employees are evaluated on the basis of qualification rather than on race, religion, sex, national origin, or age. Policies of affirmative action, which seek to employ minorities, women, handicapped indi-

Figure 7.3. Examples of Changes at General Telephone and Electronics Corp.

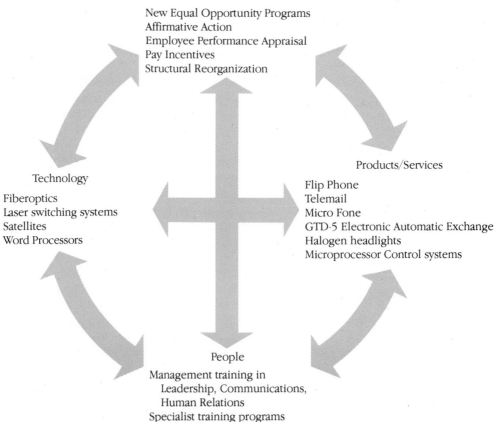

Administrative
New Equal Opportunity Programs
Affirmative Action
Employee Performance Appraisal
Pay Incentives
Structural Reorganization

Products/Services
Flip Phone
Telemail
Micro Fone
GTD-5 Electronic Automatic Exchange
Halogen headlights
Microprocessor Control systems

Technology
Fiberoptics
Laser switching systems
Satellites
Word Processors

People
Management training in
    Leadership, Communications,
    Human Relations
Specialist training programs

viduals, and disabled veterans, have also been established. Another important policy change is the requirement for frequent and insightful employee performance appraisal. GTE also implemented a pay-incentive system, and has periodically reorganized as necessary to maintain structural efficiency.

Programs for people change center on training opportunities. GTE recently finished a multimillion-dollar advanced management training center that will be used for workshops, seminars, and training sessions. Managers will receive training in leadership, communication, and human relations skills. Problem-solving and decision-making skills are also developed through formal training programs. Other programs focus on training of technical specialists so that employees in all activities can advance in their professional occupation.[6]

GTE is a huge corporation made up of several small organizations. Under this corporate umbrella are examples of changes in products, technology, administration, and people. Most organizations at one point or another will make changes in each of these areas. Immediate organizational needs, however, often indicate that one type of change is more important to the organization. The following sections describe the types of structures and management policies that are appropriate for changes in technology, administration, products, and people.

TECHNOLOGY CHANGE

Two models of organizational design provide guidelines about how to influence the amount of change in an organization's production technology. The two models are called the organic and ambidextrous models of organization change.

The Organic Model   Burns and Stalker proposed two types of organization systems—the organic and the mechanistic.[7] As described in chapter 2, the organic organization is typically associated with change, and is considered a better organizational form for adaptation. Procedures, techniques, and technologies can be quickly adapted to changes in the external environment.

The popular image of an innovative organization today is characterized by organic internal processes, including flexibility, decentralization, and the absence of rules and regulations. Mechanistic structures are believed to inhibit innovation. Mechanistic structures are fine for large organizations in a stable environment. But when organizations have to be innovative, they should be smaller and more organic.

The success of the organic organization is attributed to its ability to create and introduce new ideas into the organization.[8] Horizontal communications facilitate cross-fertilization of ideas from different perspectives. Less emphasis on control and authority enables lower-level employees to develop and initiate changes. The lesson from the organic model is that decentralization, participation, expertise, minimal control, lateral communication, and other organic characteristics are conducive to innovation and change in production technology.

IN PRACTICE 7.3

Sunny Life Insurance Company

Sunny Life Insurance Company is a medium-sized organization in western Canada. The company has very high performance goals. Management believes that insurance sales representatives are professionals, who have to be adaptive in dealing with customers. Sunny managers maintain high performance by keeping local offices small, usually with no more than twelve to fifteen agents. All employees are treated equally. Indeed, the supervision is more by the group than by the general agent. Group members meet frequently and exchange ideas in open meetings. Successful sales representatives describe their selling techniques, which can be analyzed and adopted by other agents. In subsequent meetings, other sales representatives report on their activities. Members provide feedback and assistance to each other.

A positive work climate has been established. Sales people coach one another and share knowledge and skills, when the opportunity arises. New techniques are tried and, if successful, are quickly adopted by the group. When any member attends a sales convention or reads about a new sales method, it is quickly passed among everyone in the office. People soon report whether the technique is effective and how they were able to use it. Total sales per agent is higher in these offices than in any company in the industry.[9]

Managers at Sunny Life designed an organic organization. Each office was decentralized, and the general agent had minimum control. Frequent meetings encouraged lateral communication. As a result, changes in the technology of selling insurance occurred often. New techniques were adopted quickly. The organic structure worked for Sunny, because frequent change led to increased sales.

The Ambidextrous Model

In 1966, James Q. Wilson proposed an intriguing idea.[10] He said that an organization structure that generates innovative ideas is in conflict with the structure that ultimately secures implementation. Wilson suggested that the initiation and the implementation of change are two distinct processes. Organic characteristics such as professional employees, decentralization, and low formalization are excellent for initiating ideas and proposals. But these same conditions often make it hard to implement change because employees do not have to comply. They can ignore the innovation because of decentralization and a generally loose structure.

How does the organization solve the dilemma? Robert Duncan suggested that organizations must be ambidextrous—they must incorporate structures that are appropriate to both the initiation and implementation of innovation.[11] The organization should behave in an organic way when the situation calls for the initiation of new ideas, and in a mechanistic way when implementation is required. The organization must be able to switch between organic and mechanistic structures as needed. The differences in structure for initiation and implementation are summarized in table 7.1.

An example of an ambidextrous organization was a small auto parts (100 employees) manufacturing plant that faced severe financial losses. Management created organic conditions by asking employees to participate and make suggestions for production changes. The manager of the plant shut down the plant for a day to talk to employees. He emphasized the severity of the financial situation and asked for ideas to improve performance and increase efficiency. Mixed groups of employees and managers were formed and spent the rest of the day talking about the plant. They compiled problems and presented solutions. Task forces were later created to analyze these solutions and implement promising ones. Within three months, several task forces had solved important problems, and the plant reached break-even performance. Day-to-day activities within the plant were still managed on a mechanistic basis. But the switch to an organic structure for idea generation proved to be very effective.

In larger organizations, the initiation and implementation of innovation is often divided between departments.[12] Staff departments such as research and development, engineering, operations research, and systems analysis are involved in the initiation of changes for adoption in other departments. Departments that initiate change are organically structured to facilitate generation of new ideas and techniques. Departments that use these innovations tend to be mechanistically structured, which is more suitable for implementation. Implementation often requires a single focus, formal authority, and employee compliance, which is characteristic of mechanistic organizations. Figure 7.4 indicates how one department is responsible for initiation and how other departments implement the innovation. Initiating departments often span the boundary to the environment. The dual tasks of initiation and implementation are achieved through division of labor. Horizontal linkage mechanisms can be used to achieve cooperation between the

Table 7.1. Structural Characteristics that Influence Initiation and Implementation of Change in the Ambidextrous Model.

Structural Characteristic	Influence on the Change Process	
	Initiation	Implementation
Formalization	Low	High
Centralization	Low	High
Professionalism	High	Low
Organic Structure	High	Low
Mechanistic Structure	Low	High

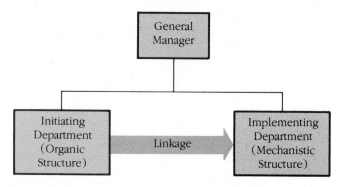

Figure 7.4. Division of Labor between Departments to Achieve Changes in Technology.

two units. The initiating department must establish a working relationship with using departments so that the idea solves a genuine problem in the user department. If the changes are not perceived as beneficial, the user department will resist change.

ADMINISTRATIVE CHANGES

The Dual-Core Model The procedures for administrative change differ from those for technology change.[13] Administrative change was addressed in the dual-core model of innovation.[14] Daft proposed that either bureaucratic or organic structures might be appropriate depending upon the need for administrative versus technological change. Many small and medium-sized organizations—schools, hospitals, city governments, welfare agencies, government bureaucracies, and many business firms—have dual cores, a technical core and an administrative core. Each core has its own inputs, outputs, participants, goals, problems, activities, and environmental domain. Innovation can take place in either core. The dual-cores are illustrated in figure 7.5.

The administrative core is above the technical core in the hierarchy. The domain of the administrative core includes the structure, control, and coordination of the organization itself, as well as environmental sectors that provide financial resources and legal constraints. The technical core is concerned with the transformation of raw materials into organizational products and services.[15]

An overall mechanistic structure is appropriate when the organization must make frequent changes in the administrative domain, which includes changes in goals, policies, strategies, control systems, and personnel. Administrative change is important in many government organizations that are bureaucratically structured. Low professionalism, high centralization, and high formalization facilitate the top-down implementation process that is used for administrative and structural changes. The very top levels of the organization, where ideas originate, is organic to facilitate the initiation of ideas. The middle and lower levels are mechanistic to facilitate the top-down implementation process.

An overall organic structure is appropriate when changes in organizational technology are important to the organization. Many of the technical departments will be organically structured to facilitate the inflow of new ideas for technological change. Lower-level personnel who are expert in the technological processes have the expertise and ability to identify problems and propose solutions, as in the Sunny Life Insurance case described earlier.

The appropriate organization structures for administrative versus technical change are summarized in table 7.2. Technical change is facilitated by a bottom-up process and an organic structure. Organizations that must frequently adopt administrative changes should use a top-down process and a mechanistic structure. In tightly structured mechanistic organizations, innovations are initiated at the top and implementation is downward.

The conclusion from the dual-core model is that a mechanistic structure is appropriate when organizations must adopt frequent administrative changes. An organic structure facilitates technological change, but not administrative change. The best structure for the organization depends upon its goals and environmental issues, and whether required changes are in the administrative or technical domain. The appropriate organizational form for administrative versus technical change is illustrated in the following example of a high school district.

Figure 7.5.   Administrative and Technical Activities in the Dual-Core Model.

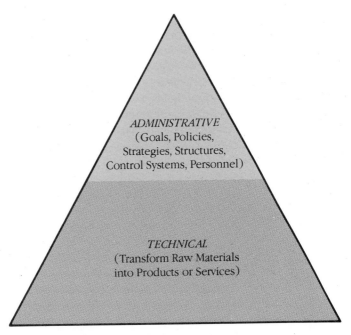

Table 7.2.   Dual-Core Model of Organization Change.

Organizational Characteristics	Type of Innovation	
	Technology	Administrative
Direction of Change	Bottom-Up	Top-Down
Structural Influence		
Formalization	Low	High
Centralization	Low	High
Professionalism	High	Low
Best Organizational Form for Change	Organic	Mechanistic

IN PRACTICE 7.4

Fairfield High School District

Fairfield High School is located in a medium-sized community in suburban Cook County, Illinois. This district was ranked as very innovative for educational (technological) innovations during the years 1959–64. During a later period of time, 1968–72, this district was one of the least innovative in the Cook County area. During the earlier period, the district scored high on many important structural characteristics for technological innovations, such as teacher professionalism, decentralization, and the absence of strict rules and regulations for teachers. The district was organically structured and adopted many changes in technology. The freedom of teachers to try new ideas encouraged a large number of proposals. Since teachers participated heavily in initiation, they understood the innovations and did not resist implementation. The administrators delegated the educational change process to the teachers.

About 1968, a new superintendent was hired to install a program, planning, and budgeting system (PPBS) in the district. This signaled a change in goals. The superintendent and school board wanted better control over expenditures, greater accountability, and greater value for dollars spent. The result of the new budgeting system was a very centralized decision-making process. Many rules and procedures were installed because all programs had to be cost analyzed, and program success was measured and reported back to the superintendent. All decisions were made by the superintendent in order to ensure compliance with the new procedures. Teachers no longer had professional autonomy to initiate innovations or to try new educational techniques on their own. Under the new superintendent, the basic structure of the organization changed from organic to mechanistic. The mechanistic system practically shut down the educational change process.

However, the district was very innovative in the administrative domain. It was the first in the county to implement PPBS and other administrative procedures. The mechanistic structure enabled the top-down initiation and implementation of administrative changes. Thus the same school district, under two different structural forms, was able to be innovative in different ways. The environment was also different. Technological innovation in the earlier period was a response to perceived community demand for the district to be educationally current and up-to-date. Administrative innovation in the later period was a response to perceived environmental demand for greater economy, reduced revenues, and the desire by community members for cost efficiency.[16]

This example illustrates many of the ideas expressed above. Administrative innovations followed a top-down process and were facilitated by a mechanistic structure. Technical innovations were bottom-up and were facilitated by an organic structure. The environment had substantial influence on the type and frequency of change. The appropriate structure for change depends on the type of change to be adopted.

NEW PRODUCTS

New products are different from changes in technology and administration because new products are used by customers outside the organization. Since new products are sold in the environment, uncertainty about the suitability and success of change is much higher. New product ideas are also less likely to be borrowed from outside the organization. Extensive creative and development work within the organization typically goes into new product development.

New Product Success Rate

The uncertainty associated with the development and sale of new products was illustrated in a survey by Edwin Mansfield from the University of Pennsylvania.[17] The survey examined nineteen chemical, drug, electronics, and petroleum laboratories to learn about success rates of technical projects. A sample of 200 projects was analyzed from these laboratories. The projects were followed from beginning to completion. To be successful, the project had to complete three stages of development—technical completion, commercialization, and market success. The findings about success rates for the three stages are given in table 7.3.

On the average, 57% of all projects undertaken in the R & D laboratories achieved technical objectives. All technical problems were solved and the projects had the opportunity of moving on to production. After technical completion, many projects still did not survive. Only 55% of the projects that came out of R & D went to full-scale production and marketing. The remaining projects were rejected because production cost estimates or test-market results were unfavorable. Of all projects that were started, only about one-third (31%) were fully marketed and commercialized.

Finally, of the new products that were commercialized, only 38% achieved an economic return. The other 62% did not earn sufficient returns to cover the cost of development and production. The products that achieved eco-

Table 7.3.   Probability of an R & D Project Success.

	Probability
Technical completion (technical objectives achieved)	.57
Commercialization (full-scale marketing)	
• Given technical completion	.55
• Given project is begun	.31
Market success (earns economic returns)	
• Given commercialization	.38
• Given project is begun	.12

Source: Adapted from Edwin Mansfield et al., *Research and Innovation in Modern Corporations* (New York: Norton, 1971), p. 57.

nomic success represented only 12% of all projects originally undertaken. The odds are only about one in eight that the development of a new product will return a profit to the company. New product development is thus very risky, and managers are interested in techniques that will improve the success rate.

Reasons for New Product Success

One of the laboratories surveyed in the Mansfield study had a market success rate of 29% of projects undertaken. This was more than twice the average for all laboratories. Further investigation found that this organization inserted marketing ideas much earlier into the product decision process. The majority of new products in other firms were initiated by people in research and development. The highly successful organization relied more heavily on new product ideas from the marketing staff. Marketing people provided information about customer complaints, suggestions by distributors or advertising agencies, competitive products, and many other potential sources of new product ideas.

The very significant discovery from the success of this laboratory is that new product innovation requires a coupling of technical and marketing expertise. Projects should not be undertaken solely because technical personnel are enthusiastic about the idea. Successful new products are tailored to the needs of customers. The needs of customers are analyzed by marketing personnel, who then provide suggestions for research projects.

An even more intensive study of new product success was project SAPPHO, undertaken by the Science Policy Research Unit at the University of Sussex.[18] Seventeen pairs of new product innovations were identified, with one success and one failure in each pair. Investigators ransacked the history of these projects, and the comparison between success and failure can be summarized as follows.

1. Successful innovators had a much better understanding of customer needs.
2. Successful innovators paid much more attention to marketing.
3. Successful innovators performed the development work more efficiently than failures, but not necessarily more quickly.

4. Successful innovators made more effective use of outside technology and outside advice, even though they performed more of the work in-house.
5. The responsible individuals in the successful attempts were usually more senior and had greater authority than their counterparts who failed.

This study shows a pattern very similar to the Mansfield study. New products were successful when they were designed to meet a well-understood user need, and when the company paid greater attention to marketing. New product failures did not incorporate customer needs early in the new product decision process. Other factors such as the use of up-to-date technology and having senior managers in charge of the project also made a positive difference.

Horizontal Linkage Model The appropriate organization design for achieving successful new product innovation involves three components: departmental specialization, boundary spanning, and horizontal linkages. These components are similar to the differentiation and integration ideas in chapter 2 and the linkage mechanisms in chapter 6. When organizations are able to achieve these three ingredients in their design and decision process, a high success rate of new product innovation will be attained.

1. Specialization means that research personnel and marketing personnel are highly competent at their own task. These two departments are differentiated from each other and have attitudes, goals, and structures appropriate for their specialized functions.
2. Boundary spanning means that each department involved with new products has excellent linkage with relevant sectors in the external environment. R & D personnel are linked to professional associations and colleagues in other R & D departments. They are aware of recent scientific developments. They can apply new developments to new product design. Marketing personnel are closely linked to customer needs. They listen to what customers have to say, and analyze competitor products and suggestions by distributors. Marketing personnel conduct periodic surveys to gather market-related information, and attend association meetings to learn about developments in the market. Boundary spanning by both the research and marketing departments is important if the organization is to launch new products successfully.
3. Horizontal linkages mean that technical and market information is shared. Research people inform marketing of new technical developments to learn whether the developments are applicable to customers. Marketing people provide customer complaints and information to R & D to use in the design of new products. If linkage between departments is good, the decision to develop a new product is a joint decision. Joint problem-solving will be used to resolve conflicts and problems during development and commercialization. Horizontal linkage during R & D and marketing is necessary if new products are to succeed. Figure 7.6 illustrates the horizontal linkage model.

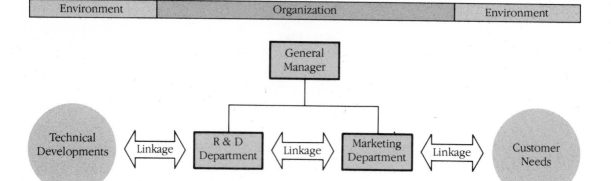

Figure 7.6. Horizontal Linkage Model for New Product Innovations.

IN PRACTICE 7.5
Rhody versus Crown

The importance of the horizontal linkage model was revealed in an analysis of two plastics manufacturing firms by Jay Lorsch and Paul Lawrence of Harvard.[19] The two companies were similar in size and structure, and both sold their products for industrial application. Both experienced demand for new products and for modifications of existing products. One company, Rhody, achieved an outstanding degree of successful new product innovation. Products developed in the previous five years accounted for 59% of Rhody's sales. The other company, Crown, was much less successful. New products accounted for only 20% of sales, or about one-third of Rhody's.

Discussion with executives in the two firms revealed striking differences in structure and decision-making. The departments at Rhody were more specialized and differentiated. They saw their tasks as unique and developed attitudes, values, and goals relevant to their department. An important part of specialization was to gather accurate information about activities in the environment. Each department performed boundary-spanning activities relevant to their function. Crown managers, on the other hand, reported less differentiation. Employees were assigned to departments, but had not fully acquired the goals, values, and attitudes needed for successful marketing or R & D performance. Managers at Crown were also less coupled to key elements in the external environment.

Each firm established a coordinating department to provide horizontal linkage between research and sales. At Rhody, the department orientation was toward overcoming differences between departments. Conflicts were raised and problems were thrashed out. The coordinating group was respected by all departments. It attempted to integrate each department's needs and goals into decisions that served the organization as a whole. At Crown, the integrating department was aligned with marketing and sales. The department was not respected by research or production, and hence was not effective in integrating diverse goals and decisions. Managers in the functional departments at Crown complained about the inadequacy of the coordinating group. Decisions tended to be made in the interest of individual departments rather than in the interest of the organization as a whole.

Rhody represents the ideal organization structure and decision process for new product innovation. Each department contained specialists who were oriented toward their own tasks. This orientation enabled high quality work and effective boundary spanning in each functional area. Differences between departments were integrated through the use of effective horizontal linkage devices. Specialists with diverse knowledge and information worked together to reach decisions that were best for the organization as a whole. The profitability of new products and an increasing market share testify to the success of Rhody's structural arrangement. Too often companies try to introduce new products without making use of horizontal linkages. As in the following case, the result is usually failure.

IN PRACTICE 7.6

National Service Co.

During the summer of 1974, an enterprising research engineer for National Service Co. obtained permission to study the problem of drive-wheel slippage on diesel locomotives. He was an expert on dampening devices and wanted to apply his ideas to the drivewheel slippage problem. The engineer learned that diesel locomotives occasionally suffered damage, especially from frequent starts on uphill grades. In steam locomotives, slippage caused no internal damage. But severe slippage could destroy a diesel locomotive. The engine would have to be completely rebuilt.

Over the next eighteen months, the engineer developed a "positive traction control" (PTC) device. He was able to use the extensive facilities in the R & D lab to refine the theory and test the PTC device. At the end of two years, the device was ready for application to diesel locomotives. It was designed to fasten near the drivewheels, where it sensed locomotive speed and dampened the surge of power to the drivewheel, thus preventing slippage. Drivewheels could turn at a maximum speed of three miles per hour faster than the motion of the train.

Initial tests were extraordinarily successful. The device was installed on several locomotives in regular use, and damage due to slippage was zero. The device cost only a few hundred dollars, but could save thousands. The engineer who designed the PTC was delighted. The Director of Research and Development sponsored a party celebrating technical completion of the project.

Three years later, the positive traction control device was still on the shelf. It never went into production. The engineer and others associated with the project were puzzled and discouraged by the lack of acceptance. They resented the marketing department that failed to develop a sufficient number of customers. They also resented the production managers who quoted an unrealistic high price for manufacturing the positive traction control device.

A later analysis of the events surrounding the PTC device indicated that the project was pushed exclusively by Research and Development personnel. The project was undertaken because of its technical merit and the engineer's interest in the project. Marketing was not involved in the decision. Top managers made no systematic effort to understand customer needs or to analyze whether there was a sufficient market for the device. As it turned out, many railroads were not experiencing locomotive damage. They were not willing to invest in a new piece of equipment. The demand was so small that only limited production was possible, which greatly increased the cost of production and hence the price. Moreover, General Motors, which produces most locomotives in the United States, developed a traction control device to include on locomotives as original equipment. They threatened to terminate the warranty on any locomotive that carried a PTC device manufactured by anyone but themselves.[20]

National Service Company made the decision to develop a positive traction control device with virtually no linkage to the external environment. Management did not survey customers to learn about their needs. Managers were not aware of the activities of other potential suppliers, such as General Motors. In addition to poor boundary spanning, collaboration within the organization was nonexistent. Research and Development had no linkage to Marketing. R & D undertook the project completely on its own. Research engineers did not want to consider marketing ideas. The engineers believed that marketing suggestions would simply slow down development of an excellent technical device. All in all, National Service Co. proceeded in exactly the wrong way to develop a successful new product.

PEOPLE CHANGES

The process of people change is often similar to technology and administrative change because the need for change occurs inside the organization. The target of change includes the values, attitudes, and skills of individual employees. Senior managers must sense the need for upgrading employee ability and provide a mechanism for initiating and implementing the appropriate change programs. These programs are provided internally through training departments or through the use of outside experts in organizational development.

Training Departments

Most large organizations establish training departments as the primary mechanism for implementing people change. Training departments use teaching techniques similar to those used in schools and universities. Formal classes may be held that include lectures, films, videotapes, and perhaps programmed instruction. Newer methods of training include case studies, role playing, and business games. Business games simulate the real world of the employee, and provide an opportunity to make decisions and practice skills in the classroom where mistakes are not costly to the organization.

When training departments cannot meet all training needs, organizations send employees to other organizations for a variety of seminars and courses. The American Management Association, consulting firms, universities, and junior colleges all offer specialized courses for management and technical employees. Management courses include topics such as supervisory skills, communication, motivation, leadership, bargaining, and time management. Many medium-sized companies realize the need to improve management skills, but do not have a sophisticated training department. Small and medium-sized firms rely heavily on off-the-job seminars and programs to meet their training needs.

Organizational Development Model

Organizational development (OD) has evolved as a separate field in the behavioral sciences that is devoted to organizational change. Some organizational development work pertains to the organization as a whole. These experts attempt to change people, structure, and technology simultaneously. However, a primary focus of organizational development is keyed to people change. Organizational development uses knowledge and techniques from the behavioral sciences to improve organizational and employee climate, values, health, functioning, and well-being.[21] The goal of organizational development is to improve organizational performance by creating a climate in which employees can be better performers. The needs of employees for growth and development are integrated with organizational goals.[22] Individual growth and interpersonal competence within the organization are important targets of OD. Examples of employee value changes that OD tries to bring about are given in table 7.4.

Organizational development is often undertaken in conjunction with outside experts. Many management professors and consulting firms provide organizational development services to organizations that have people-related problems. The first and most important step for these consultants is to determine whether a need truly exists within the organization. Without a perceived need and a willingness to accept change, implementation of new values and behavior patterns is nearly impossible. After the need is established, a variety of techniques is used to intervene in the organization to improve employee behavior and performance.

Sensitivity or Laboratory Training Often called T-groups or encounter groups, this procedure helps individuals increase understanding, insight, and awareness about their own behavior and its impact on others. Another objective is to increase understanding and sensitivity toward others. Partici-

Table 7.4. The Transition of Employee Values through Organizational Development.

Away from:	Toward:
1. A view of people as essentially bad	1. A view of people as essentially good
2. Resisting individual differences	2. Accepting and utilizing individual differences
3. Walling off personal feelings	3. Expressing feelings
4. Game-playing	4. Authentic behavior
5. Distrust	5. Trust
6. Avoiding risk-taking	6. Willing to risk
7. Emphasis on competition	7. Emphasis on collaboration

Source: Adapted and abridged from Robert Tannenbaum and Sheldon A. Davis, "Values, Man, and Organizations," *Industrial Management Review* (Winter, 1969): 67–86.

pants meet in unstructured group sessions to explore feelings, intentions, behaviors, emotions, effects they have on each other, and perceptions of each other. Most people find this a unique learning experience. A trainer skilled in sensitivity training is present in the group.[23]

Survey Feedback Organizational personnel are surveyed via questionnaires about their job satisfaction, attitudes, performance, leader behavior, and so on. A consultant then meets with the respective groups to discuss questionnaire results, to identify problem areas, and to discuss strategies for improvement.[24]

Intergroup Confrontation Meetings Members from separate departments are brought together in sessions designed to decrease intergroup conflict and to increase cooperation. Techniques are used to help members describe expectations for the other department, as well as their perception of the other department and its performance. (Conflict-reduction techniques are described in chapter 11.) These procedures help departmental employees understand each other and reduce intergroup conflict that limit organizational performance.[25]

Team-Building Team-development activities promote the idea that people who have working relationships can be trained to work as a team. Team-building improves employee performance both as team leaders and team members. Participants learn to build good relationships with other team members, to engage in joint problem-solving, and to reduce interpersonal friction. Improved communication, creativity, decision-making, and team performance typically result.[26] Team-building activities are useful for members of task forces, teams, and new product development groups.

Managerial Grid The managerial grid was developed by Blake and Mouton and consists of six training phases through which organization managers progress.[27] Early phases deal with the development of managerial skills and the use of these skills within the organization. Later phases deal with diagnosing and solving organizational-wide problems.

Relationship to Other Types of Changes

Team-building activities and intergroup confrontation meetings are often used to facilitate other types of innovation processes within an organization. The relationship between a staff department charged with initiating change and a user department in which change is implemented have to be positive in order for change to succeed. People change activities can break down barriers and improve the quality of collaboration so that the organization adapts more easily to changes in the external environment. Training sessions are especially effective when functional departments such as marketing and R & D are included. In the Crown Corporation described earlier, team-building activities would enable the representatives from Marketing and Research and Development to deal with one another more effectively. They could work together more closely, confront problems, and attempt to reach decisions that are good for the organization as a whole.

Team-building and confrontation meetings often take place away from the organization so managers can focus on themselves and the type of change needed. In the following case, top managers and an outside consultant diagnosed that the problems of customer complaints and poor performance were caused by people problems rather than by technology or administrative issues. Organizational development techniques were used to improve morale and working relationships. The behavior and attitudes of the president as well as those of several other key managers needed to be changed. The case was described by two OD experts, Wendell French and Cecil Bell.[28]

IN PRACTICE 7.7
Woodland Mills

Problems of lack of cooperation between subunits, increasing complaints from customers, sagging morale, and rapidly increasing costs induced the president of a medium-sized company to confer with a behavioral scientist consultant about ways to improve the situation. The two talked at length, and it became apparent to the consultant that the executive, while having some apprehensions, was generally agreeable to the desirability of examining the dynamics of the situation, including decision-making processes and his own behavior. He and the consultant agreed that certain organization development efforts might be worthwhile. It was decided that a three-day workshop away from the usual routine, with the executive and his entire work team, might be an appropriate way to start.

A few days before the off-site session, the consultant spent an hour interviewing each member of the team. In essence he asked them, "What things are getting in the way of this unit being as successful as you would like it to be?" The purpose of these interviews was to obtain the data around which the design of the workshop was to be built.

At the beginning of the workshop, the consultant first reported back to the group the general themes of the interviews, which he had grouped under these problem headings: "The Boss," "Meetings," "Administrative Services," "Customer Relations," "Relations Between Departments," and "Long-Range Goals." The group then prioritized these problems in terms of importance and immediacy and chose the problem areas to be worked on. With the consultant acting more as a coach than as a moderator, the group then examined the underlying dynamics of each problem area and examined optimal solutions to problems. The last morning was spent developing "next action steps" relative to a dozen or so items discussed under the above headings. One of the decisions was to spend a half day with the consultant three months in the future for the purpose of reviewing progress toward problem solutions. During a subsequent meeting between the company president and the consultant, the executive reported that the morale of the group was up substantially and customer complaints and costs were beginning to go down but that "we still have a long way to go, including making our staff meetings more effective." The two then agreed to have the consultant sit in on two or three staff meetings prior to the three-month review session.

The three-month review session with the consultant revealed that signficant progress had been made on some action steps but that improvement seemed to be bogged down, particularly in areas requiring delegation of certain functions by the president to his key subordinates. The matter was extensively worked on by the group, and the president began to see where and how he could "loosen the reins," thus freeing himself for more long-range planning and for more contacts with key customers.

STRATEGY FOR MANAGING CHANGE

The material so far in this chapter has described four types of change, and organization structure and processes that are associated with frequent adoption of each type. We also looked at six ingredients—need, idea, proposal, decision, implementation, resources—that have to be present for any change to succeed.

In this final section we focus on techniques for managing specific changes that a manager may want to implement. These are strategies and techniques that will improve the probability of initiating and implementing any type of change successfully. These ideas are summarized in table 7.5.

1. *Diagnose a True Need for Change.* A careful diagnosis of the existing situation is needed to determine the extent of the problem. If the people who are affected by the change do not perceive a genuine problem, the change process should stop right there. For new products, customers should feel a need. For other types of change, the need will be felt by

Table 7.5. Strategy for Managing Change.

1. Diagnose a true need for change.
2. Find an idea that fits the need.
3. Obtain top management support.
4. Design change for easy implementation.
5. Plan to overcome resistance to change.
6. Assign an idea champion.

people within the organization. A perceived performance gap is necessary to unfreeze users and make them willing to invest the time and energy to adopt new techniques and procedures.[29]

2. *Find an Idea That Fits the Need.* Finding the right idea often involves search procedures—talking with other managers, assigning a task force to investigate the problem, sending out a request to suppliers, or asking someone within the organization to create a solution. The creation of a solution requires organic conditions. People must have the freedom to think about and explore new options. A few organizations, such as General Motors, have created positions called corporate thinkers. These individuals have no deadlines and no day-to-day responsibilities. They think about social trends, economics, politics, television, and whatever else may be relevant to solving problems. The ultimate creative insight often provides a unique solution to a management problem.

3. *Obtain Top Management Support.* Successful change requires the support of top management. For a massive change, such as a structural reorganization, the president and vice presidents must give their blessing and support. For smaller changes, the support of influential managers in the relevant departments is required. The lack of top management support is one of the most frequent causes of implementation failure. If top management has other goals and priorities, the change may be swept aside. When managing a change project, top managers should be contacted. Top managers can add significantly to the change process if they understand the need for change and publicly state their support.[31]

4. *Design the Change for Easy Implementation.* Characteristics of the change itself can increase the likelihood of adoption and implementation. Implementation is easiest when the change is designed to provide high benefits in the form of profits or improved performance for the user. The prospects for success are also improved when the change can be broken into subparts and each part adopted sequentially. Users who see success at the first stage of implementation then throw full support behind the rest of the change program.[32]

5. *Overcoming Resistance to Change.* The most difficult part of any change is implementation. Many good ideas that are approved are never used because they are never implemented. This happened in the Valley Foods case at the beginning of this chapter. Top management did not anticipate or prepare for resistance to change by consumers, legislators, and em-

ployees. Consequently, the laser-scanning checkout system was never used.

No matter how impressive the performance characteristics of an innovation, its implementation will conflict with some interests and jeopardize some alliances in the organization. To increase the chance of successful implementation, management must acknowledge the conflict, threats, and potential losses perceived by employees.[33] Proposed changes often appear awkward and inefficient to people who are supposed to use them. They may be uncertain about the impact on their own job and careers. Change often generates uncertainty for the users, who may band together to resist implementation. Several strategies can be used by managers to overcome the resistance problem.

a. *Align the Change with Needs and Goals of Users.* The best strategy for overcoming resistance is to make sure that change meets a real need. Employees in R & D or other staff departments often come up with great ideas that solve nonexistent problems. This happens because initiators fail to consult with people who use the change. A major cause of resistance is that the change does not appear to be able to improve performance.[34]

Resistance can be frustrating for managers, but moderate resistance to change is good for the organization. If users believe that the change has no value, or if top management does not support it, the interest of the organization is probably not served by the change. Resistance to change provides a moderate barrier to avoid frivolous or fad changes, or change for the sake of change. The process of overcoming resistance to change normally requires that the change be good for the organization.

b. *Participation.* Early and extensive participation in the change should be part of any implementation strategy. Participation gives those involved a sense of control over the change activity. They understand it better, and they become committed to successful implementation. Participation should normally begin in the initiation stage so that ideas and proposals from users can be incorporated in the change design. The participation strategy was so successful at BF Goodrich's Oaks Pennsylvania Power Plant that managers repeated the strategy in four other plants. They successfully implemented a new maintenance management system in all plants in about two years by letting employees be heavily involved in the implementation process.[35]

c. *Open Communication.* Communication educates users about the need for change and informs them about the consequences of the proposed change. Full disclosure prevents false rumors, misunderstanding and resentment. Open communication often gives management an opportunity to explain what steps will be taken to ensure that the change will have no adverse consequences for employees.[36] A common mistake for managers is to assume that other people understand the change. Management should provide far more information than they think is necessary in order to be sure that users are properly informed.

6. *Assign an Idea Champion.* An effective strategy is to assign an individual or small committee to be responsible for all phases of initiation and implementation. The idea champion sees that all activities above are completed. Sometimes managers themselves have to be the idea champion. Other times champions will volunteer because they are enthusiastic and committed to the change. They will do all work necessary to see it implemented. An idea champion helps overcome resistance to change. The idea champion can communicate to people and explain how the change will help them perform their job. Training programs can be developed and users can be involved in the change process. An idea champion is absolutely essential for large changes, such as a new product, new organization structure, or major organizational development program.[37] Idea champions sometimes break the rules and push ahead even when there is user resistance. But the enthusiasm may pay off in successful implementation. A recent example of an idea champion occurred in the Papermate division of Gillette Company.

IN PRACTICE 7.8

Gillette Co.

Henry Peper is chief chemist at the Papermate division of the Gillette Company. Mr. Peper wanted to create an erasable-ink ballpoint pen. He was absolutely committed to the idea, even when marketing specialists balked. If customers wanted to erase what they wrote, they argued, they would use a pencil. Gillette gave Mr. Peper the opportunity to develop the idea anyway. He provided the time and resources to translate the concept into a new product.

The idea started by chance. One day on the job he used rubber cement to bind two pieces of paper together. He noticed that the excess could be picked up by rolling his hand over it. He wondered what would happen if he put pigment into the glue and put both into a ballpoint pen. He combined the elements and put them into a ballpoint cartridge. Nothing happened. The glue was too thick to come through the cartridge.

The next step was to add thinner. He also pressurized the cartridge to push the stuff out of the pen. It seemed to work. The pen would write and the ink was erasable. But it stayed erasable. Peper had to add something to allow the ink to dry.

The answer was a chemical called dioctyl phthalate. When added to the glue, it keeps the ink soft for a day or so before it dries into the paper.

Henry Peper is not the first idea champion to push through an idea against all odds and the advice of others. Edwin Land was told nobody would buy his instant camera. Millions did. Sometimes market surveys are not as accurate for predicting a need as the instincts of the inventor.

Gillette top management is quick to agree with Mr. Peper's inventiveness. Within months of the pen's introduction, it took 7% of the market for ballpoint pens. Its current sales are close to $50 million, which is about 25% of a $200-million-dollar market.[38]

Gillette broke the rules about including marketing in the decision to launch a new product. Once in a while it works, but it should not be done often. Mr. Peper championed the idea, and he did all the work. Gillette's investment was small. The reason for success was that Mr. Peper believed in the idea and plugged away until the erasable pen was developed and implemented. Most ideas need a champion or they never achieve fruition.

SUMMARY AND INTERPRETATION

Organizations face a dilemma. They prefer to accomplish their day-to-day activities in a predictable, routine manner. The fewer changes that are undertaken, the more predictable and efficient the organization can become. But the external environment is continuously changing. Innovation and change are required in order to adapt to the changes taking place in the environment. Change, not stability, is the natural order of things. Organizations need to achieve some degree of both stability and change, to facilitate both routinization and novelty. This is the dilemma they have to resolve.

The models and ideas described in this chapter can be thought of as solutions to this dilemma. Organizations handle the stability–change dilemma depending on the amount and type of innovation required. The organic organization is suitable when frequent technical innovations are required. The organic organization is oriented toward change rather than toward stability. It typically does not realize the efficiencies of routinized structure. Mechanistic organizations are oriented toward technological stability. Organizations thus resolve the stability–change dilemma by structuring in a mechanistic way whenever possible to obtain efficiency, and by structuring in an organic way when the organization needs new ideas and frequent changes. Some groups can be relieved of the day-to-day routine and be charged with developing and initiating new ideas. In this way, the organization can provide an inflow of new ideas for adaptation, yet increase efficiency through routinization and stability in other parts of the organization. The ambidextrous, dual-core and horizontal linkage models each describe how to design the overall organization to achieve specific types of change.

Another important idea from this chapter is the notion that bureaucracies can be innovative. Bureaucracies have been widely criticized for discouraging innovation and change. Bureaucracy has been accused of erring on the side of stability, and for being overburdened with rules and regulations that prevent change. The point from this chapter is that a bureaucratic structure is appropriate when the technical products or services are relatively stable and do not require frequent change. Bureaucracies are suited to change in the administrative domain. Government bureaucracies, for example, can adapt very quickly to new regulations or policies. The power balance favors administration, and the mechanistic structure provides a useful instrument for carrying out administrative changes in a top-down fashion.

This brings us to another dilemma: the underlying philosophy of organization theory versus the philosophy of organizational development. Organization theory takes an organizational point of view. It seeks to find the best organizational design contingent upon a variety of organizational factors. For many organizations, the best design may involve a mechanistic structure, routine work, and standardization. Organizational development, however, reflects a concern for humans within the organization. Organizational development changes are designed to make organizations more satisfying places to work. OD helps employees become more responsive and to acquire good interpersonal skills.

The underlying value of organizational development favors organic organizations. In the organization development view, workers should have freedom to participate in decisions, to do interesting work, and to initiate ideas for consideration. Both organizational development specialists and organization theorists are concerned with organizational effectiveness, but they seem to advocate different ways of achieving it. In organization theory, effectiveness is achieved by tailoring the organization to technological and environmental needs. In organizational development, the organization should be tailored to challenge the higher-level abilities and needs of organization participants.

The final point to consider is that of idea champion, because the role is new to the literature.[40] Idea champions are people within organizations who take it upon themselves to initiate a change and have it implemented. Idea champions often act on their own, in addition to the duties of their job. We know almost nothing about idea champions. They are scattered around the organization, and take it upon themselves to interpret needs and develop and propose solutions. Initiation activity takes a large amount of time, and faith. Idea champions push ahead even when others disbelieve and are critical of their ideas. Idea champions provide a tremendous service to the organization, because they provide the organization with an opportunity to change and improve. Without people willing to provide this energy, the change process would be thwarted.

DISCUSSION QUESTIONS

1. Name the four primary types of change. How do they differ from each other? Do they influence each other?
2. How is the organic model related to changes in technology? To administrative changes?
3. Describe the dual-core model. How does administrative change normally differ from technology change? Discuss.
4. When organizations free key employees from routine work in order to develop new ideas, how are they coping with the dilemma of needing both stability and change? Discuss.

5. Why do organizations experience resistance to change? What steps can managers take to overcome this resistance?
6. "Bureaucracies are not innovative." Discuss.
7. A noted organization theorist said, "Pressure for change originates in the environment: pressure for stability originates within the organization." Do you agree? Discuss.
8. Do the underlying values of organizational development and organization theory differ? Is there any way to accommodate both sets of values in organizational design?
9. What are the six elements required for successful change to be completed? Which element do you think managers are most likely to overlook when they are involved in a change project? Discuss.
10. "Resistance to change is good for the organization because it keeps frivolous and unimportant ideas from being adopted." Do you agree or disagree with this statement? Why?
11. Briefly describe the ambidextrous model. How do organizations meet the need for organic characteristics and mechanistic characteristics for certain changes?
12. What organizational traits have been found to be associated with successful new product introduction?
13. The manager of R & D for a drug company said that only 5% of their new projects ever achieve market success. He also said that the industry average is 10% and wondered how his organization might increase its success rate. If you were acting as a consultant, what advice would you give him concerning organization structure?

GUIDES TO ACTION

As an organization designer:

1. Facilitate frequent changes in internal technology by adopting an organic organizational structure. Give technical personnel freedom to analyze problems and develop solutions for technological problems, or create a separate organically structured department to conceive and propose new ideas.
2. Facilitate administrative change of policies, goals, performance evaluation systems, and organization structure by adopting a mechanistic structure. Use a mechanistic structure when the organization needs to adopt frequent administrative changes.
3. Establish a separate training department or work with organization development consultants when changes in the attitudes, values, or skills of people are required. Use organizational development consultants for large-scale people changes.

4. Encourage marketing and research departments to develop boundary spanning linkages to their environments when new products are needed. Use these linkages to provide information on new technical developments and changing customer needs. Incorporate horizontal linkages between research and marketing departments so that new-product decisions are made jointly.
5. Make sure that every change undertaken has a definite need, idea, proposal, decision, implementation strategy, and resources. Avoid failure by not proceeding until each element is present.
6. Use additional techniques to achieve successful implementation if necessary. Additional techniques include obtaining top management support, implementing the change in a series of steps, assigning an idea champion, and overcoming resistance to change by actively communicating with users and encouraging their participation.

Consider these Guides when analyzing the following cases and when answering the questions listed after each case.

CASES FOR ANALYSIS

I. DINETTES, INC.

Dinettes, Inc., feeds plant and office workers in over 400 businesses in the Southeastern United States. Forty retail cafeterias are also in operation. Dinettes' home office is in Atlanta, where economic growth has been rapid in recent years. Dinettes has not shared in that growth. From 1975 to 1979, the company lost $8 million. Management has been hit with a series of problems in the lunchrooms and cafeterias they run. Food prices skyrocketed, layoffs cut the number of customers, and the quality of meals dropped as lunchroom and cafeteria managers cut corners.

Dinettes' president, Ron Johnson, has been alarmed by the mounting losses. He analyzed the food operations and concluded that the root of the problem was in the administration of the food outlets. Cafeteria and lunchroom managers were cutting corners, and cooks were free to concoct any combination of sauces, gravies, and garnishings to go with suggested meals. The results often repelled customers.

In Johnson's opinion, a tighter administrative system was the order of the day. He proposed a new management by objectives system for lunchroom and cafeteria managers, with weekly reports to top management describing activities, costs, and income in each outlet. Meals were standardized. The Atlanta headquarters now ships recipe cards and premeasured packages of food. Cooks are forbidden to vary the recipes, and managers are forbidden to cut corners. Innovation in the preparation of foods is out. Rules and regulations are in. Standardization of food preparation and well-defined policies have brought food quality under control.

The new administrative system has other advantages. The jobs are routinized, so professional cooks are not needed. Anyone who can read the recipes can do the cooking. The new approach has brought additional traffic into the lunchrooms and cafeterias. The food is markedly better, which helped the company land twenty new accounts last month.

Costs have been cut too. By reducing the qualifications of cooks and reducing the number of menu changes, Dinettes is saving $1,500 per outlet.

"Tight management control is the wave of the future in cafeteria management," says Ron Johnson. "From now on, any changes will come from the top."[41]

Questions
1. What type of change—technology, administrative, people, product—was initiated by president Ron Johnson? What type of change will occur most often in the future?
2. Is Dinettes, Inc. more mechanistic after the change? Have formalization and professionalism changed? Was the change top-down or bottom-up? Will future changes be top-down or bottom-up?
3. Which model of innovation—organic, ambidextrous, dual-core—best describes the change that took place at Dinettes? Who was the idea champion?

2. DUN & BRADSTREET

Dun & Bradstreet Corp. has been a tightly run organization for 140 years. The strategy has been a winner, because D & B is now a $1.2-billion company. But the captain of the ship, Harrington Drake, is changing course. His goal is for D & B to be in a state of continuous transition to accommodate the changing environment of its clients. Achieving the new change orientation has required reshuffling within. Consider:

- Numerous managers are rotated among divisions. Rotation breaks emotional ties to a single product and gives executives broad exposure. Today nearly every divisional executive has worked in at least one other corporate area. People feel that they are going home to an old friend when they ask another department for help. Managers have a good working knowledge of other departments' capabilities, which facilitates cooperation and the exchange of ideas.
- Managers are being brought together more frequently for meetings. Meetings provide the interdepartmental cooperation that can lead to breakthroughs in technology and new products. In 1980, 140 senior managers were brought together in a single meeting to brainstorm about the company's new market thrust. Financial, data processing, and other functional specialists also pool ideas at their own interdisciplinary meetings.
- Managers are learning how to communicate. D & B has hired a staff of consultants to offer crash courses in information technology and the art of listening. Courses in technology enable managers to discuss the business of information technology. The art of listening removes interpersonal barriers to effective communication.
- The strategic planning staff pulls it all together. They facilitate cooperation across divisions. The planning staff is a diverse group that includes sales people, operating specialists, computer experts, and market researchers.

Several people are especially trained to debrief sales people on customer comments that might indicate a new product need.

Harrington Drake's reshuffling is paying off. At least 150 new ideas have been adopted in the last few years. Dun's "Financial Profile" provides detailed financial data on 800,000 companies. It cost D & B only $200,000 to develop, yet brought in $2 million in revenues in 1980 and about $5 million in 1981. The most exciting changes are the totally new products that arise when two diverse departments pool resources. One example is Keypoint, a service that provides on-line information on 500,000 Canadian businesses.

The future looks even brighter. Dun & Bradstreet managers do not miss the simpler and more stable life of the old days. They love the excitement of new developments.

Of course, new technology is not everything. Top management's primary concern is to not push change for the sake of change. Through speeches and memos they stress that no product, no matter how easily produced, is worth creating unless the need has been established. It is a dangerous and costly mistake to introduce new technology for any reason other than to meet a market need.[42]

Questions
1. The chief executive officer at Dun & Bradstreet wanted to facilitate change. Did D & B become more organic? What techniques did the chief executive use to create the correct orientation?
2. How was coordination achieved for new product innovations? Did Dun & Bradstreet use the horizontal linkage model? Explain.

NOTES

1. This case was inspired by "Giant Food, Inc.," distributed by the Intercollegiate Case Clearing House, Soldiers Field, Boston, MA 02163.
2. Alvin Toffler, *Future Shock* (New York: Random House, 1970), p. 11.
3. John L. Pierce and Andre L. Delbecq, "Organization Structure, Individual Attitudes and Innovation," *Academy of Management Review* 2 (1977): 27–37; Michael Aiken and Jerald Hage, "The Organic Organization and Innovation," *Sociology* 5 (1971) 63–82.
4. Richard L. Daft, "Bureaucratic versus Nonbureaucratic Structure in the Process of Innovation and Change," in Samuel B. Bacharach, ed., *Perspectives in Organizational Sociology: Theory and Research* (Greenwich, CT, JAI Press, 1982), pp. 129–166.
5. Lisa C. Anderson, Johnathan L: Dikes, and David W. Young, "Swearingen Aviation Corporation: A Case Study," unpublished manuscript, Texas A & M University, 1981.
6. Beth Falconer, Carol Stevens, Mark Richardson, and Brian Bartels, "GTE: A Case Analysis," unpublished manuscript, Texas A & M University, 1981.

7. Tom Burns and G. M. Stalker, *The Management of Innovation* (London: Tavistock Publications, 1961).

8. Aiken and Hage, "Organic Organization and Innovation"; Warren G. Bennis, *Changing Organizations* (New York: McGraw-Hill, 1966); Victor A. Thompson, "Bureaucracy and Innovation," *Administrative Science Quarterly* 10 (1965): 1–20.

9. This case is based on David G. Bowers and Stanley E. Seashore, "Predicting Organizational Effectiveness with a Four-Factor Theory of Leadership," *Administrative Science Quarterly* 11 (1966): 238–263.

10. James Q. Wilson, "Innovation in Organization: Notes Toward a Theory," in James D. Thompson, ed., *Approaches to Organizational Design* (Pittsburgh: University of Pittsburgh Press, 1966), pp. 193–218.

11. Robert B. Duncan, "The Ambidextrous Organization: Designing Dual Structures for Innovation," in Ralph H. Killman, Louis R. Pondy, and Dennis Slevin, eds., *The Management of Organization* (New York: North-Holland, 1976), vol. 1, pp. 167–188.

12. Judith R. Blau and William McKinley, "Ideas, Complexity, and Innovation," *Administrative Science Quarterly* 24 (1979): 200–219.

13. John R. Kimberly and Michael J. Evaniski, "Organizational Innovation: The Influence of Individual, Organizational and Contextual Factors on Hospital Adoption of Technological and Administrative Innovation," *Academy of Management Journal* 24 (1981): 689–713; Michael K. Moch and Edward V. Morse, "Size, Centralization and Organizational Adoption of Innovations," *American Sociological Review* 42 (1977): 716–725.

14. Richard L. Daft, "A Dual-Core Model of Organizational Innovation," *Academy of Management Journal* 21 (1978): 193–210.

15. Daft, "Bureaucratic versus Nonbureaucratic Structure."

16. Richard L. Daft and Selwyn Becker, *Innovation in Organizations: Innovation Adoption in School Organizations* (New York: Elsevier, 1978), pp. 124–126.

17. Edwin Mansfield, J. Rapoport, J. Schnee, S. Wagner, and M. Hamburger, *Research and Innovation in Modern Corporations* (New York: Norton, 1971).

18. Science Policy Research Unit, University of Sussex, *Success and Failure in Industrial Innovation* (London: Centre for the Study of Industrial Innovation, 1972).

19. Jay W. Lorsch and Paul R. Lawrence, "Organizing for Product Innovation," *Harvard Business Review* 43 (January–February, 1965): 109–122.

20. Richard L. Daft, *Research and Development in the Transportation Industry,* Technical Report 75-13 (Kingston, Ontario: Canadian Institute for Guided Ground Transport, 1975).

21. Richard Beckhard, *Organization Development: Strategies and Models* (Reading, MA: Addison-Wesley, 1969), p. 9.

22. W. Warner Burke and Warren H. Schmidt, "Management and Organizational Development," *Personnel Administration* 34 (1971): 44–56.

23. L. P. Bradford, J. R. Gibb, and K. D. Benne, *T-Group Theory and Laboratory Method* (New York: John Wiley & Sons, 1964), pp. 15–44.

24. David A. Nadler, *Feedback and Organization Development: Using Data-Based Methods* (Reading, MA: Addison-Wesley, 1977), pp. 5–8.

25. Richard Beckhard, *Organization Development: Strategy and Models* (Reading, MA: Addison-Wesley, 1969), pp. 33–35.

26. Wendell L. French and Cecil H. Bell, Jr., *Organization Development* (Englewood Cliffs, NJ: Prentice-Hall, 1978), pp. 117–129.

27. Robert R. Blake and Jane S. Mouton, *The Managerial Grid* (Houston: Gulf Publishing Co., 1964).

28. Wendell L. French and Cecil H. Bell, Jr., *Organization Development: Behavioral Science Interventions for Organization Improvement,* 2nd ed., © 1975, pp. 3–5. Reprinted by permission of Prentice-Hall, Inc., Englewood Cliffs, NJ.

29. Michael Aiken, Samuel B. Bacharach, and Lawrence J. French, "Organizational Structure, Work Process and Proposal-Making in Administrative Bureaucracies," *Academy of Management Journal* 23 (1980): 631–652; Gerald Zaltman, Robert Duncan, and Jonny Holbek, *Innovations and Organizations* (New York: John Wiley & Sons, 1973), pp. 55–58.

30. Judith R. Blau and William McKinley, "Ideas, Complexity, and Innovation," *Administrative Science Quarterly* 24 (1979): 200–219.

31. Daft and Becker, *Innovation and Organizations;* John P. Kotter and Leonard A. Schlesinger, "Choosing Strategies for Change," *Harvard Business Review* 57 (1979): 106–114; Beckhard, *Organization Development.*

32. Everett M. Rogers and Floyd Shoemaker, *Communication of Innovations: A Cross Cultural Approach,* 2nd ed. (New York: Free Press, 1971).

33. Mary Snepenger, "Implementing Change," unpublished manuscript, Texas A & M University, 1980.

34. *Ibid.*

35. Arthur E. Wallach, "System Changes Begin in the Training Department," *Personnel Journal* 58 (1979): 846–848, 872; Paul R. Lawrence, "How to Deal with Resistance to Change," *Harvard Business Review* 47 (January–February, 1969); 4–12, 166–176.

36. Kotter and Schlesinger, "Choosing Strategies for Change."

37. Richard L. Daft and Patricia J. Bradshaw, "The Process of Horizontal Differentiation: Two Models," *Administrative Science Quarterly* 25 (1980): 441–456; Alok K. Chakrabrati, "The Role of Champion in Product Innovation," *California Management Review* 17 (1974): 58–62.

38. Mitchell C. Lynch, "Mr. Peper Ignores Experts to Make an Indelible Mark on Penmanship," *Wall Street Journal,* September 29, 1980, p. 33; "Gillette to Market New Pen," *Wall Street Journal,* February 4, 1981, p. 17.

39. Paul R. Lawrence and Jay W. Lorsch, *Organization and Environment* (Homewood, IL: Irwin, 1969); Daft and Becker, *Innovations in Organizations;* Peter L. Szanton, "Urban Public Services: Ten Case Studies," in Richard R. Nelson and Douglas Yates, eds., *Innovation and Implementation in Public Organizations* (Lexington, MA: Lexington Books, 1978), pp. 117–142.

40. Daft and Bradshaw, "Process of Horizontal Differentiation"; Paul Jervis, "Innovation and Technology Transfer—The Roles and Characteristics of

Individuals," *IEEE Transactions on Engineering Management* 22 (1974): 19–26.

41. This case was inspired by "Canteen's Profitable New Menu," *Business Week,* August 15, 1977, p. 134.

42. This case is based on "How D & B Organizes for a New-Product Blitz," *Business Week,* November 16, 1981, pp. 87–90, and "Dun & Bradstreet Forms a New Business, Plans to Close Old One," *Wall Street Journal,* September 18, 1981, p. 38.

8

Information and Control

A LOOK INSIDE

S. I. NEWHOUSE AND SONS

In 1976, S. I. Newhouse and Sons was one of the largest publishing enterprises in the United States. The publishing empire included three types of business—newspapers (twenty-two, including the *Newark Star-Ledger* and the *Cleveland Dealer*); magazines (five, including *Vogue* and *House and Garden*); and broadcasting (four radio stations, six television stations, and twenty cable TV systems). The company is family-owned, yet *Business Week* estimated that the enterprise ranked number one in profits and number three in sales among companies in the communication media.[1] In 1981, profits were estimated at over $100 million.[2]

The senior Newhouse, called S. I., died in 1979. He started his empire at the age of seventeen, and stayed active until the end. S. I. adopted a rather unorthodox management style for the communication industry, which is carried on by his sons. He shunned elaborate management control systems, and cared little for elaborate planning and budgeting. He was not even sure how many people were on the payroll (approximately 15,000 in 1976). Relatives occupied a substantial number of management positions. One son was in charge of broadcasting, another was in charge of magazines. The two sons now jointly run the publishing empire. At one time, sixty-four relatives and in-laws were on the payroll, although a smaller number are now involved in management. A younger generation is coming along, who will be taught S. I. Newhouse's rule: "The ties that matter are the ties to each other."[3] All Newhouse descendents get together annually for a Thanksgiving feast.

The sons worked for their father for more than twenty-eight years, and have been carefully trained to take over the business. As one son explained, "We are essentially a nonbureaucratic, decentralized, highly autonomous organization, with each unit acting very much on its own initiative, but with personal or indirect contact with the various members of the family."[4] The Newhouses make frequent plant visits and then write memos to one another. Most reporting is informal. The family group also communicates frequently by telephone and in meetings. Major decisions are reached by consensus after substantial give and take. There is constant discussion between the various companies and the family group. Everyone knows what is going on all the time.

The newspaper and broadcast businesses operate under different environmental conditions. The newspaper industry is rapidly changing. Costs for newsprint, equipment, and labor have increased dramatically. Unions present many problems and often resist attempts to upgrade technologies. Most of the Newhouse newspapers have converted to cold-type composition, automated mail rooms, offset presses, and other new techniques. The success of each newspaper depends upon meeting area needs, which vary greatly by community. The family does not try to dictate editorial positions or management style for specific newspapers. Each paper is an autonomous business unit.

The broadcasting industry is more uniform and stable. Radio and television stations tend to use standard formats (e.g., network programming or top-forty music). Technological change is minimal. Broadcast media play a small role in local communities. Broadcast policies are less tailored to local conditions.

The newspaper part of the business is decentralized, and control is maintained through a single monthly report that is distributed to key family members. The report covers net profits, advertising lineage, circulation, and a few additional items such as labor costs.

In the broadcasting arm, the control system is centralized and bureaucratic. Budgets and statistical reports are compiled and reviewed frequently. The president of the broadcast division does not give individual stations much discretion. He keeps close tabs on day-to-day performance.

The Newhouse chain has enjoyed consistent growth and solid profits. Other newspaper chains have copied the Newhouse approach by reducing the level of administrative controls on local newspapers. The sons and other family members have now taken over complete operation of the Newhouse business. They have no plans to change the management control philosophy.[5]

The managers at S. I. Newhouse and Sons illustrate the use of information. They exchange memos, attend meetings, make telephone calls, and read a variety of reports. They spend a large amount of time processing information, and they use several channels, ranging from written documents to face-to-face meetings. Moreover, accurate information is not available on everything, such as number of employees. Managers often do not have accurate information to work with, and they get along without it.

The Newhouse case also suggests that the design and the use of information depends upon organization contingencies. The father disliked extensive formal planning and budgeting paperwork systems. Planning and budgeting information pertains to organizational control. A small amount of control information characterized the newspaper business, where the environment is changing, and uncertainty is great. Only a few key information cues are needed. The broadcasting business is quite different. The technology and environment are stable. Managers are concerned with frequent reports and check performance on a day-to-day basis.

Definition **Information** is that which alters understanding.[6] Information is not usually tangible or measurable. People represent what they know by pictures, symbols, verbal statements, and mental images. A change in the mental image is the result of information. A variety of cues, including verbal language, touch, personal observation, or computer printouts convey information if they add to or modify the receiver's understanding. Information provides insight and is perceived as useful by the receiver.

Data is the output of a communication channel. Data is tangible and can be counted. Data includes the number of words, telephone calls, letters, or pages of computer printout sent or received. Data does not become information unless people use it to improve their understanding.

The distinction between information and data is important. Managers want information, not data. Organizations try to provide information rather than data to employees. Most managers are overloaded with data in the form of reports, printouts, and procedures. Managers want information they can use to interpret the situation around them. They do not want endless reports that have little relevance to them.

This chapter deals extensively with two major purposes of information—information for task accomplishment and information for control. **Task information** conveys knowledge and techniques for accomplishing a task. Task information is used to perform work, solve problems, and make decisions. Task information at S. I. Newhouse was conveyed by memo and in frequent meetings among managers. **Control information** describes the performance of other people, departments, or the organization itself. Control information includes information about target setting, activity monitoring, and feedback. At S. I. Newhouse, control information was included in the monthly report from each newspaper, or in the more frequent reports from radio and TV stations.

Purpose of This Chapter Information is important in every organization because nearly every activity involves information-processing. Managers spend 80% of their time actively exchanging information.[7] Information helps hold the organization together. Employees and managers must interpret the external environment, coordinate activities, introduce innovations, resolve conflicts, and make decisions. The linkage mechanisms described in chapter 6 are designed to process information. Information moves up and down the hierarchy in the form of rules, policies, goals, and face-to-face discussions. Information moves horizontally in the form of memos, committees, task forces, and integrator roles. In order to perform their jobs, managers must attend meetings, send and receive reports, evaluate performance, read printouts, talk on the telephone, and disseminate instructions—each of which involves information-processing of some type.

The purpose of this chapter is to examine the nature and use of information in organizations. The next section looks at frameworks that describe information requirements for different tasks, and shows how to provide relevant information to people performing those tasks. Then the topic of control systems is explored. The design of control systems is contingent upon both the need for control information by upper management and the stability of technology and environment. The impact of control on employees is also discussed.

The last part of the chapter analyzes the role of computers in information-processing, and the impact of the revolution taking place in information technology. By the end of this chapter, students should understand organizational requirements for task and control information, and how to meet those requirements through the design of organization structure and information systems. Students will also be familiar with the impact of information technology on organization structure and manager behavior.

TASK INFORMATION

Information Amount

The first design consideration is the amount of information needed by employees to perform their tasks. **Information amount** is the volume of information about organizational activities that is gathered and interpreted by organization participants.[8] Amount of information is important because employees—especially managers—work under conditions of uncertainty. They do not have complete understanding of the external environment or of the problems occurring within the organization. When uncertainty is high, a greater amount of information has to be processed.[9] When uncertainty is high, the organization must encourage information-processing in the form of meetings, reports, procedures, etc., to meet the greater need for task information. More manager time and energy has to be devoted to problem interpretation and obtaining information to make decisions. When the organization does not experience uncertainty, the amount of information processed will be less.

Figure 8.1 indicates the organizational characteristics that increase uncertainty and hence the amount of information processed within the organization. The factors that influence the amount of uncertainty include task variety, organization size, environmental change, and interdependence between departments. Each of these characteristics adds to information-processing requirements in both vertical and horizontal directions.[10] When tasks are high variety, the amount of information processed to understand and solve frequent problems is greater. Organization size influences information because a larger number of people and departments has to be coordinated. Frequent changes in the environment induce uncertainty, which also requires more information. Changes occur when a client cancels an order, when another department changes its production schedule, when a supplier delays delivery by nine weeks, or when R & D cannot modify a product

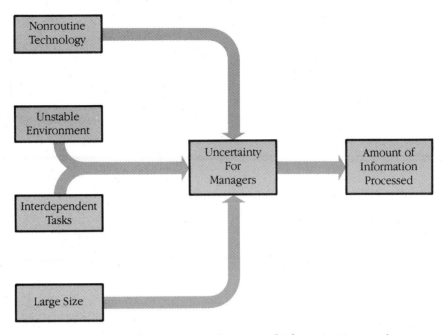

Figure 8.1. Sources of Uncertainty and Amount of Information Processed.
Adapted from Michael L. Tushman and David A. Nadler, "Information Processing as an
Integrating Concept in Organizational Design," *Academy of Management Review* 3
(1978): 613–624.

within cost estimates. These events create uncertainty for managers who
then have to process information. They must interpret what happened and
decide how to respond with a course of action.

Information   The other important information design variable is information richness.
Richness   **Richness** pertains to the information-carrying capacity of data.[11] Some data
cues are extremely informative for recipients while other cues provide little
understanding. Information richness is influenced by the medium through
which it is communicated. A scale of information media is presented in
figure 8.2. Face-to-face is the richest medium because it conveys several
information cues simultaneously, including the spoken message, body language, and facial expression. Face-to-face also provides immediate feedback
so that understanding can be checked and misinterpretations corrected. The
richness of face-to-face communication was illustrated in a study that found
93% of meaning conveyed was by tone of voice and facial expression.[12]

The telephone is somewhat less rich. Immediate feedback is possible, but
the visual cues are removed. Written communications are less rich still,
because feedback is slow and only the information that is written down is
transmitted. The least rich information is conveyed through numerical
reports. Numbers tend to be used to describe simple, quantifiable aspects
of organization.

Information richness is important because it relates to the analyzability of management problems, as illustrated in figure 8.3. When a manager's task or problem is unanalyzable, the factors surrounding it are unclear and poorly understood. In this situation, the manager has to acquire significant understanding in order to respond appropriately. Rich media, such as face-to-face, provide a variety of cues simultaneously that add greatly to the managers' understanding. If the manager relies on low rich media, such as a written report or a numerical document, the problem or solution will be oversimplified. The intangible, emotional, and difficult elements associated with unanalyzable problems can only be conveyed through rich media. On the other hand, when a problem is simple, a low rich medium is preferable. A written statement allows the verbal content to be transmitted uncluttered by other cues. In a face-to-face meeting, nonverbal cues may disagree with the simple message and cause confusion and misunderstanding in the receiver. The relationship in figure 8.3 suggests that unanalyzable and

Figure 8.2. Information Richness and Medium of Information Transfer.
Source: Adapted from Robert H. Lengel, "Managerial Information Processing and Communication-Media Source Selection Behavior," Unpublished Ph.D. Dissertation, Texas A & M University, 1982; and Winford E. Holland, Bette Ann Stead, and Robert C. Leibrock, "Information Channel/Source Selection as a Correlate of Technical Uncertainty in a Research and Development Organization," *IEEE Transactions on Engineering Management* 23 (1976): 163–167, © 1976 IEEE.

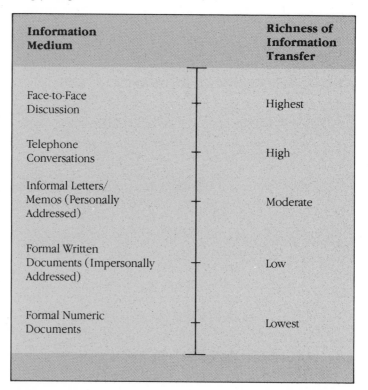

Figure 8.3. Unanalyzable Problems and Richness of Information Processed.

unclear problems require richer information. Analyzable, well-understood tasks can be interpreted and solved with less rich information.

FRAMEWORK FOR TASK-INFORMATION DESIGN

A framework for applying information concepts to organizations is given in figure 8.4. This framework is based upon Perrow's concept of technology, which was discussed in chapter 5. Technology represents the pattern of problems and tasks performed in different parts of the organization. Figure 8.4 identifies the two relationships that determine information requirements based upon the type of task performed.

1. When task variety is high, problems are frequent and unpredictable. Uncertainty is greater, so the amount of information processed will also be greater. Employees spend more time processing information, and they need access to larger data bases. When variety is low, the amount of information processed is less.[13] For example, the many problems associated with basic research require vastly greater amounts of information than do routine technical and drafting activities.[14]

2. When tasks are unanalyzable, employees need rich information.[15] Face-to-face discussions and telephone conversations transmit multiple information cues in a short time. Managers can move quickly to interpret the complexity of the problem and work toward a solution. When tasks are simple, managers will use less rich media. The underlying problem is clear, so only simple information is needed. Rich information would tend to overcomplicate the communication episode for an analyzable problem. For example, managers in finance departments rely heavily on written documents as a source of information, while general managers rely more heavily on human (face-to-face) sources.[16] Finance work tends to be more routine and better understood than general management, where many problems are unique and hard to analyze.

The implication of these relationships is reflected in the framework in figure 8.4. Organization structure and information support should be de-

Unanalyzable

Information Richness Increases

Analyzable

Craft Technology	**Nonroutine Technology**
Futures Buying  Small amount of rich information, personal observation, occasional face-to-face and group meetings, telephone.	_Strategy Formulation_  Large amount of rich information—frequent face-to-face and group meetings, unscheduled discussions, telephone.
Routine Technology	**Engineering Technology**
Bank Card Check Small amount of clear, often quantitative information—written reports, rules and procedures, schedules, some statistical data.	_Well-site Engineer_ 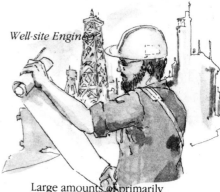 Large amounts of primarily quantitative information—large computer data bases, written and technical materials, frequent statistical reports.

Low   Information Amount Increases   High

Task Variety

Figure 8.4. Task Characteristics and Information-Processing Requirements. Source: Adapted from Richard L. Daft and Norman B. Macintosh, "A New Approach to Design and Use of Management Information," _California Management Review_ 21 (1978): 82–92. Copyright © 1978 by the Regents of the University of California. Reprinted by permission of the Regents.

signed to provide managers and employees with the appropriate amount and richness of information. Routine activities have few problems. When problems do arise they are fairly well understood. An available store of knowledge and procedures can be assembled to handle these problems. The amount of information can be small and directed toward a limited set of analyzable applications. The information available to the managers should be brief, clear, and point to an unambiguous action or decision. Economic order quantity (EOQ) reorder systems for inventory control is an example of information used for a routine task.

Engineering tasks have high task variety, which increases the demand for information. Many types of problems arise so it is not possible for the amount of information to be small. Engineering technologies are characterized by large bodies of established knowledge. Tasks are well understood. Consequently, information support should normally contain a large data base that reflects established knowledge. The huge store of engineering blueprints that support an engineering project is an example. So is the large data base made available to airline reservation agents. Airline travel schedules involve infinite combinations of routes (high variety), but the task is well understood. A large, low rich information base is appropriate.

Craft activities require a different form of information. Task variety is not high, but the few problems are unanalyzable. Problems are handled on the basis of experience and judgment. There are many intangibles, so managers need rich information. An example of the craft organization is a specialized psychiatric care unit. The success of the facility rests largely with the skills of individual psychiatrists. The process of therapeutic change is not well understood. Numeric information about costs and benefits cannot be directly related to this process. When psychiatrists have a problem, they discuss it face-to-face among themselves to reach a solution.

Nonroutine activities are characterized by high uncertainty. Many problems arise that are not analyzable. Large amounts of rich information have to be accessible or gathered. A great deal of effort is devoted to discussing and analyzing problems and to using information in the best way. Managers spend time in both scheduled and unscheduled meetings. A substantial amount of time must be allowed for information-processing. Employees in strategic planning units and basic research departments are normally involved in nonroutine tasks.

Design Implications   The design of the organization should provide information to managers based upon the pattern of tasks performed. The amount of information should be larger when tasks have many problems. Information media should provide richer information when tasks are poorly defined and unanalyzable. When the organization is designed to provide correct information to managers, decision processes work extremely well. Tasks will be accomplished. When information is poorly designed, problem-solving and decision processes will be ineffective, and managers may not understand why. The following two cases illustrate how an organization can be designed to provide the correct information for routine and engineering tasks.

IN PRACTICE 8.1

Bell Canada

The manager in charge of a district plant and facilities for a large public utility commented on the uselessness of a large operating report he received each month. He usually did not bother to open the report and simply threw it away when the next monthly report arrived. The report contained nearly forty pages of single-spaced numerical information. Other district managers also did not use the monthly operating report.[17]

The report was not used because the upkeep of plant and facilities was essentially a routine task. Few unanticipated problems arose, and maintenance activities (painting, repair) were analyzable. Hence, the large amount of data contained in the report was too much. The numerical information in the report was not rich, which was appropriate. Clearly defined information fit the clearly defined task. But too much data was provided because the task did not contain unexpected problems. Eventually the report was reduced to a more concise, one-page summary of monthly operations. The small amount of data was consistent with the requirements of the task.

IN PRACTICE 8.2

Co-op Sugar

A large sugar processor successfully evolved the chemical manufacturing process for transforming beets into sugar, so that consistent output was possible. Problems arose, however, in the variation from farmer to farmer in the sugar beets delivered to the plant. The manufacturing process had to fit the beets before maximum sugar output could be obtained.

Plant managers were not sure how to handle the sugar beet variation problem. They had meetings about it, but to no avail. A few general reports were issued, but they did not help either.

Sugar manufacturing is an engineering task. The transformation process is complex because of substantial variation in the sugar beets processed. The task is also well understood because research had revealed the step-by-step manufacturing sequence needed to obtain maximum sugar. After realizing the nature of the task, the company developed a large computer-based math model of the manufacturing process that covered the various types of sugar beets. From that time on, plant personel merely had to test the beets and check with the data base in the computer. The math model could calculate the appropriate manufacturing process for each batch of sugar beets. This large but low rich (numerical) information system was appropriate for the complicated yet analyzable task.[18]

Large amounts of data are appropriate when a task is well understood but has many problems. In the case of Bell Canada, a small amount of quantitative information was all that was needed. For Co-op Sugar, a larger amount of information was appropriate.

Quantitative information is not suitable for unanalyzable tasks, however. Providing large amounts of quantitative information to managers for poorly defined tasks creates a genuine problem. The reliance on quantitative information when richer information was needed almost caused the failure of a clothing manufacturer in England.

IN PRACTICE 8.3

Clothing Manufacturer

An information design problem occurred in one of two clothing plants, which are called Plant X and Plant Y. Each plant manufactured innerwear (underwear, socks) and outerwear (sweaters, jackets). The demand for innerwear was stable and well understood. Each plant independently developed a large information support system that used economic models based upon past sales, economic conditions, and related variables to predict the future demand for innerwear. The data base for this information system was large and precise. Managers at both plants used their information system to predict sales and thereby establish production targets and schedule plant operations.

The demand for outerwear, by contrast, was extremely unstable. Styles would change, total demand would change, and no one really understood why. Uncertainty for managers was high. The causes of demand changes were hard to analyze. Information system designers in Plant X tried to resolve this problem with the same type of information system used for innerwear. Extensive data were compiled about past and present economic conditions, sales records, competitors' sales, style changes, and so forth. Econometric models were used to predict outerwear styles, total demand, and to schedule production. The result was catastrophic. The manufactured clothing did not reflect consumer tastes and went unsold.

When problems are not well understood, it is better to trust rich information, which is what Plant Y did. Only a small amount of information was used in the decisions about outerwear styles. Key decision-makers made personal contact with a few store buyers. They visited stores to see what was selling. A few buyers discussed outerwear fashions in meetings. Based upon this face-to-face information and their own experience, buyers for Plant Y decided upon styles and production volume. Forecasting the demand for outerwear was essentially a craft decision. The estimates based upon rich information were much better than the forecasts based upon economic models. Plant Y prospered while Plant X nearly failed.[19]

The clothing plants illustrate how precise information fits a well-understood task (demand for innerwear), but richer information sources are more appropriate for tasks that are poorly understood and hard to analyze (demand for outerwear).

Managerial tasks differ by hierarchical level. The framework in figure 8.4 pertained to activities horizontally across organizations. Work activities and information requirements also differ vertically by managerial level. In terms of figure 8.4, top management work would tend to be unanalyzable and moderate to high in variety. This would mean a large amount of information, and most of it would be processed face-to-face or over the telephone. Top managers deal with poorly understood problems. They have to talk things out to define the scope of problems and explore various solutions.

Gorry and Morton proposed that information requirements could be defined for the lower, operational level of the organization and for senior management.[20] Senior management is concerned with a long-time horizon, for example, while lower-level personnel deal with day-to-day activities. Table 8.1 summarizes the proposed differences in information-processing by hierarchical level. Top management information is more likely to originate outside the organization, to be aggregated, to pertain to the future, and to be less accurate than information used by lower-level participants. Top managers value rich information over hard, formalized data.

Rich information provides greater insight into the ill-defined organizational processes with which they deal. One of the skills required as managers move up the hierarchical level is to learn to use the dramatically different sources and content of information compared to lower organization levels.

IN PRACTICE 8.4

Genesco, Inc.

Genesco, Inc. operates in the uncertain and fast-moving fields of retailing and apparel. Its product lines include Bonwit Teller retail stores and Jarman Shoes. Top management decision processes at Genesco were

Table 8.1. Information Characteristics by Organizational Level

Characteristics of Information	Organizational Level		
	Low	Medium	Top
Scope	Well-defined, narrow ⟶		Very broad
Aggregation	Detailed ⟶		Aggregate
Accuracy	High ⟶		Low
Frequency of Use	Very frequent ⟶		Infrequent
Source	Largely internal ⟶		External

Source: Adapted from G. Anthony Gorry and Michael S. Scott Morton, "A Framework for Management Information Systems," *Sloan Management Review* 13 (1971): 55–70, by permission of the publisher. Copyright © 1971 by the Sloan Management Review Association. All rights reserved.

uncertain. Frequent decisions had to be made to keep Genesco ahead of the competition in fashion, advertising campaigns, and store locations.

Franklin Jarman took over as chief executive of Genesco in 1973. He immediately acted on his belief in strong financial controls and precise analysis. He requested extensive reports and detailed analysis for every decision. Memoranda would accumulate in files several inches thick. On one occasion, Jarman demanded a seventy-five-page report for a $44,000 store investment. The report dealt with such minor details as whether the store should have a water cooler.

Within two years, Jarman's style resulted in personal isolation. He relied on paperwork and computer printouts for information. He cancelled management breakfast meetings that brought together top executives for discussion and planning. He refused to visit the company's plants and to discuss matters with executives face-to-face. Much of his time was spent checking reports and printouts for mistakes. He argued that managing a corporation should be like flying an airplane. Watch the dials to see if the plane deviates from its course, and then nudge it back with the controls.

What Jarman didn't realize is that detailed, precise information was not reflecting conditions in the environment, or in the stores and plants within the organization. His decision-making thus was inconsistent. Reports and data bases took a long time to develop, so decision-making was delayed. Indecision and missed opportunities caused trouble in a fast-moving field.

The paralysis caused by paperwork and indecision finally led to a palace revolt. Vice presidents working under Jarman teamed with board members to oust him as chief executive officer.[21]

A major problem at Genesco was that Jarman designed the organization to provide the wrong kind of information. In a top management position in a fast-moving industry, information should be broad, aggregated, general, and rich. Top managers must become quickly informed about complex and intangible issues. Formal reports and computer printouts oversimplify and fail to capture the unanalyzable aspects of problems. The information provided to Jarman would have been excellent for a low-level supervisor in a stable manufacturing or utility company. But for the top executive at Genesco, the information was dead wrong, and was largely responsible for Genesco's poor performance and Franklin Jarman's removal.

ORGANIZATIONAL CONTROL

The previous section described the use of information for task-accomplishment and problem-solving. The other major purpose of information is for organizational control. Control information includes downward communication about plans and targets, as well as upward communication about performance outcomes.

Organizational control is a cycle that includes the three stages of target setting, measuring and monitoring, and feedback.[22] The three stages of control are illustrated in figure 8.5. Target-setting involves planning and goal-setting for desired performance levels. Measuring and monitoring information indicates whether work activities are on target. Feedback information is designed to make corrections in either targets or work activities to bring them into alignment.

Control Cycle

The simple control cycle in figure 8.5 is based on the cybernetic model of control that was developed to describe machine systems. The thermostat, for example, has a machine-based control cycle in which a temperature standard is set, there is a temperature-monitoring device, and there is a mechanism for correcting the amount of heat or cooling in a home. An example of cybernetic control cycle is given in figure 8.6.

The control process for a thermostat in a home is clear-cut and easy to understand. The control cycle in organizations is much more complicated. As discussed in chapter 1, organizations are social systems, not machine systems. Machine concepts do not apply to organizations. One important difference in organizational control systems is that one or more stages may not be clear.[23] Targets may not be explicit or written down. Managers may carry general targets in their heads, and targets may change with changing conditions. Even when targets do exist, accurate performance data may not be available. This often happens in non-industrial settings where outputs or services are difficult to quantify and measure. Finally, feedback and correction of activities may be uncertain. Individuals don't always respond to or understand feedback in the way it is intended. In professional departments, employees may ignore directives and decide for themselves what to do. The three-stage cycle in figure 8.5 describes the control process, but in many organizations the cycle is implicit. Managers have a sense for what the organization is trying to accomplish. They judge progress toward those goals by a variety of indicators, many of which are subjective. The control cycle takes place, but not in the simple, clear fashion that characterizes a machine system.

Figure 8.5. The Organizational Control Cycle.

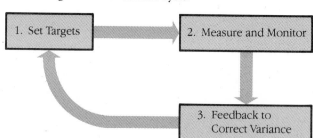

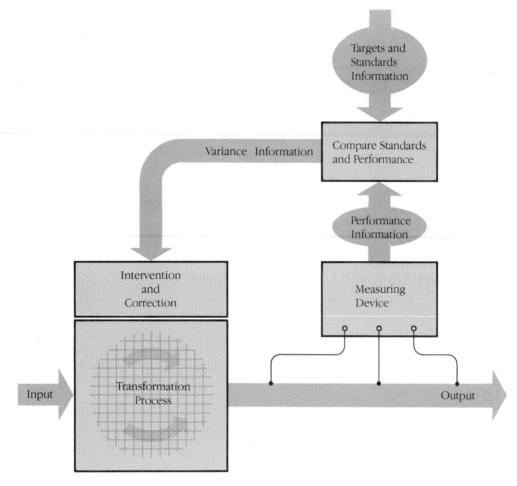

Figure 8.6. Cybernetic Control Cycle for Machine System.

Management Level and Control

Management control, whether explicit or implicit, differs by management level.[24] Top managers are concerned with a different set of control issues than first-line supervisors. Figure 8.7 indicates some differences in control systems by management level. The three management levels of institutional, managerial, and operational were described in chapter 1.

At the institutional level, managers are concerned with forecasting and target-setting for total organization performance, which includes targets for total sales and expected profits. Appropriate measures of performance are impersonal, and are aggregated to reflect performance of the organization as a whole. Managerial control pertains to specific departments. How does the marketing or engineering department perform? Targets are set and information is gathered to reflect departmental performance. Departmental control is similar to institutional control because information is general,

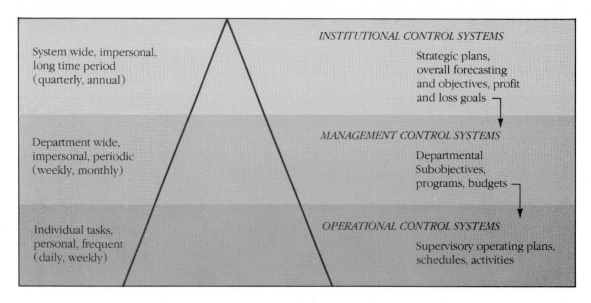

System wide, impersonal, long time period (quarterly, annual)	*INSTITUTIONAL CONTROL SYSTEMS* Strategic plans, overall forecasting and objectives, profit and loss goals
Department wide, impersonal, periodic (weekly, monthly)	*MANAGEMENT CONTROL SYSTEMS* Departmental Subobjectives, programs, budgets
Individual tasks, personal, frequent (daily, weekly)	*OPERATIONAL CONTROL SYSTEMS* Supervisory operating plans, schedules, activities

Figure 8.7.   Levels and Characteristics of Control Systems in Organizations.

periodic, and pertains to an entire unit as a whole. Operational control refers to the activities of individual employees. Operational control systems are very different from managerial and institutional systems. Operational control information is not aggregated, is very personal, and the control cycle is repeated on a frequent basis.

ORGANIZATIONAL CONTROL STRATEGIES

Managers at the top and middle levels of the organization can choose among three strategies for control. A framework for organizational control was proposed by William Ouchi of UCLA. Ouchi identified three control strategies that managers could adopt: market control, bureaucratic control, and clan control.[25] Each form of control uses different types of information. All three types may appear in an organization. The requirements for each control strategy are given in table 8.2.

Table 8.2.   Three Organizational Control Strategies.

Type	Requirements
Market	Prices, competition, exchange relationship
Bureaucracy	Rules, standards, hierarchy, legitimate authority
Clan	Tradition, shared values and beliefs, trust

Based upon William G. Ouchi, "A Conceptual Framework for the Design of Organizational Control Mechanisms," *Management Science* 25 (1979): 833–848.

Market Control

Price competition that is used to evaluate the output and productivity of an organization is called **market control.** The idea of market control originated in economics.[26] A dollar price is a very efficient form of control because managers can compare prices and profits to evaluate the efficiency of their corporation. Top managers nearly always use the price mechanism to evaluate corporate performance. Corporate sales and costs of resources are summarized in a profit and loss statement that can be compared to performance in previous years or to other corporations. The profit and loss statement provides information about how the organization is doing in a competitive environment.

Market control can be used to control major departments when they are profit centers. Profit centers are self-contained business divisions such as those described in chapter 6. Each division is responsible for all resource inputs needed to produce a product. Each division can be evaluated on the basis of profit or loss compared to other divisions. In the S. I. Newhouse and Sons case at the beginning of this chapter, market control was used in the newspaper business. Each newspaper was a profit center. Top managers only needed a few key profit figures to evaluate newspaper performance.

Market control is an efficient form of control because little surveillance is used. Relevant information can be summarized in numerical reports. Information on internal behavior is not needed.

Market control is not appropriate for many organizations. It can only be used when the output of the organization can be assigned a dollar price, and when there is competition. The market mechanism is not feasible in not-for-profit organizations. These organizations are not in competition with each other and they do not sell goods or services for a specific price.

Market control is also not efficient for the exchange of services among functional departments within a single organization. In a true market, prices are arrived at through a process of competitive bidding. Competitive bidding is an expensive and time-consuming process that is impossible to achieve for the thousands of day-to-day transactions between departments. The organization has no means of putting an accurate price on these services, or of comparing prices to competitive services in the marketplace.

IN PRACTICE 8.5

Bakersfield University

A prestigious private university in Bakersfield, California, organized its colleges into profit centers. The business college, engineering college, arts and science college, and graduate college all became profit centers. Each college received the tuition income from students and paid the cost for providing education to students. The university imposed tuition guidelines and academic standards, and then gave each college substantial freedom. The professional colleges, such as business and engineering, experienced a greater demand for services, and charged students a tuition premium. These colleges also paid more for resources because professors were in short supply and salaries were higher than in arts and science. Each college could not offer every course needed for a degree, so transfer payments were made between colleges for teaching courses to students enrolled in other colleges. An overhead payment was made to the university each semester for the use of centralized services such as the library, computer center, buildings, and utilities. Each college had to keep salaries and tuition rates at reasonable levels because other universities in the area competed for students.

After a trial period of two years, the profit center plan worked so well that top administrators decided to extend it to the centralized services provided by the university. They first examined the library, but decided that the cost of charging each college for every library transaction would be too expensive. This was not the case for computer services. Each user could be given a code that indicated the college to be billed, and all transactions could be automatically recorded by the computer. The university president decided to make the computer center a profit center. It was to become self-sufficient by selling its services to other colleges in the university.

Within about three years, the colleges were in an uproar. The computer center had steadily increased the price of computer services. The teaching and research budgets of the colleges were being drained. More and more money had to be allocated to cover the cost of computer services. The colleges joined forces and insisted that the computer center be brought back under the central administration. The colleges preferred to make a flat overhead payment to the university rather than pay cash to the computer center for each transaction.

A university committee met to analyze the computer situation and make a recommendation. They discovered that users of the computer center were being charged a price nearly three times the actual cost to the computer center. Computer center managers used the revenue to hire additional staff and to finance their own research. They were able to increase the price because no competitive computer services were available. Each college had to buy services from the computer center or use no service at all. The price thus did not reflect the true value of computer services.

The university committee recommended that the computer department once again be made a part of administration and that services be provided free of charge. The colleges were in unanimous agreement. They even agreed to increase the overhead payment to the university administration to cover computer costs.

The decision by administrators at Bakersfield University to use market control for a functional department did not work because competitive services were not available. Market control is effective only when the price is set in competition with other suppliers so that it represents the true value of services provided. Competitive services and fair-market prices cannot usually be determined for the exchange of information and services among functional departments within an organization.

Bureaucratic Control

Bureaucratic control is the use of rules, regulations, policies, hierarchy of authority, documentation, and other bureaucratic mechanisms to standardize behavior and assess performance. Bureaucratic control includes all the bureaucratic characteristics described in chapter 4 on bureaucracy. Within a large organization, thousands of transactions take place both vertically and horizontally. Rules and policies evolve through a process of trial and error to regulate this behavior. Bureaucratic control mechanisms are used when behavior and exchanges are too complex or ill-defined to be controlled with a price mechanism. An example of bureaucratic control occurred when Bakersfield University decided to make the computer center a part of administration. The provision of services to other departments was controlled by rules and policies rather than by price.

Bureaucratic control is used in almost every organization. Rules, regulations, and directives contain information about appropriate behavior. Bureaucratic mechanisms are especially visible in not-for-profit organizations. Prices and competitive markets do not exist, so bureaucratic control is the primary form of control. The lack of market mechanisms is one explanation why not-for-profit and government organizations are often so bureaucratic.

Bureaucratic Subsystems

A survey of twenty Canadian and American corporations found that managers use four subsystems for bureaucratic control.[27] The four subsystems are the operating budget, periodic statistical reports, performance evaluation system, and standard operating procedures. These four subsystems enable middle and upper management to control the organization and major departments.

The four bureaucratic subsystems are listed in table 8.3. The operating budget is used to set targets and record costs during the year. The budget is normally determined a year in advance, and actual expenditures are compared with estimates on a monthly basis. Periodic statistical reports are

Table 8.3. Bureaucratic Control Subsystems.

Subsystem	Content and Frequency
Budget	Financial, resource expenditures, monthly
Statistical Reports	Non-financial, outputs, weekly or monthly
Performance	Evaluation of department managers based on department goals and performance, annually
Standard Operating Procedure	Rules and regulations, policies that prescribe correct behavior, continuous

Based upon Norman B. Macintosh and Richard L. Daft, "Management Control Systems and Organizational Context," report to Society of Management Accountants and National Association of Accountants, Kingston, ONT., 1980 used to evaluate and monitor non-financial performance. These reports are tailored to the needs of specific departments and organizations. They are often used for the measuring and monitoring role in the control cycle because they give detailed information on performance activity.

Performance evaluation systems are mechanisms for evaluating managers and their departments. This report is often open-ended. Managers and superiors sit down and set goals for the next year for their department and then evaluate how well previous goals were met. Standard operating procedures are traditional rules and regulations. Managers use these to correct variances and bring activities back into line.

IN PRACTICE 8.6

Simpson Department Store

Simpson's is a department store chain in Canada. Like most retail organizations, each store is a profit center, and market control is used to evaluate store performance. Bureaucratic control is used to control functions within each store. One of the most important functions in a department store is the credit department. The credit department in one of the Simpson's highest volume stores uses four bureaucratic control subsystems.

The *budget* consists of five pages that report budgeted versus actual expense for each month and year-to-date. Expenses fall into three categories. The first category is personnel salaries, and includes the salary for each employee in the department. The second category is non-capital equipment, and includes expenditures for office machines and related equipment. The third category is day-to-day operating expenses, which includes all other expenditures, from the cost of entertaining clients to buying pencils and paperclips.

The credit department made extensive use of *statistical reports* for measuring and monitoring weekly and monthly activities. The statistical reporting subsystem included the following reports.

a. Comparative credit report—details of each charge account.
b. Effectiveness and efficiency report—income and payroll costs per credit account.
c. Credit sales ratio—percentage of credit sales to total store sales.
d. Delinquent accounts—analysis of delinquent accounts, including the ratio to active accounts.
e. Uncollectable accounts—analysis of uncollectable recoveries.
f. Growth report—details of credit account growth in the previous year.

The *performance evaluation* system at Simpson's was a simple two-page report that was filled out jointly by the credit department manager and the store manager. The credit department manager described the credit department performance targets for the coming year. Another meeting at the end of the year evaluated performance of the credit department. Results of this session determined pay increases, promotions, and bonuses for the credit department manager.

The *standard operating procedures* used within the credit department amounted to about 700 pages. They included step-by-step procedures for such things as disciplining employees, when to refund money to a customer, and job descriptions.[28]

The four bureaucratic subsystems, like the ones used at Simpson's, provide substantial control information to managers. The bureaucratic control process involves extensive paperwork, but enables managers to set targets, monitor performance, and make feedback adjustments. Bureaucratic control is used in most organizations.

Clan Control **Clan control** is the use of social characteristics such as values, commitment, traditions, and shared beliefs to control behavior. Organizations that use clan control require extensive trust among employees. Social control substitutes for market and bureaucratic control.[29] Clan control is important when ambiguity and uncertainty are high. High uncertainty means the organization cannot put a price on its services, and rules and regulations are not able to specify appropriate behavior. People may be hired because they are committed to the organization's purpose, such as in a religious organization. New employees may be subjected to a long period of socialization to gain acceptance by colleagues. The clan mechanism is used most often in small, informal organizations because personal involvement in the purpose and activities of the organization is possible. Clan control may also be used in smaller departments of a large organization where performance is difficult to measure in a systematic way.

An example of clan control was the S. I. Newhouse case at the beginning of the chapter. S. I. Newhouse and Sons hired family members in the upper echelons of the organization. Family members trusted each other, and shared common beliefs and traditions. With clan control, S. I. Newhouse and Sons did not need as many bureaucratic controls to regulate the behavior of its executives.

A subgroup of the organization that often uses clan control is the inner circle of top managers. Top managers work under extremely high uncertainty. They make decisions that affect the entire organization. To gain access to the inner circle, managers have to be trusted and socialized into the traditions, values, and climate of the top management team. People may even have to have a similar appearance in order to be accepted. A manufacturing firm called INDSCO was studied by Rosabeth Moss Kanter. She found that clan control was a primary control mechanism at the top. Middle-level managers were socialized into values and traditions. Anyone who did not appear to share the beliefs and values would never gain admittance to the top management inner circle.

INDSCO

Managers at INDSCO had to look the part. They were not exactly cut out of the same mold like paper dolls, but the similarities in appearance were striking . . . . The norms were unmistakable, after a visitor saw enough managers, invariably white and male, with a certain shiny, clean-cut look. The only beards, even after beards became merely daring rather than radical, were the result of vacation time experiments on camping trips, except (it was said) for a few in R & D . . . .[30]

Conformity pressures and the development of exclusive management circles closed to "outsiders" stem from the degree of uncertainty surrounding managerial positions. Bureaucracies are social inventions that supposedly reduce the uncertain to the predictable and routine. Yet much uncertainty remains—many situations in which individual people rather than impersonal procedures must be trusted . . . .[31]

The uncertainty up the ranks . . . puts trust and homogeneity at a premium. The personal loyalty normally demanded of subordinates by officials is most intense at the highest levels of organizations . . . . The lack of structure in top jobs makes it very important for decision-makers to work together closely in at least the harmony of shared understanding and a degree of mutual trust. Since for an organization to function at all requires that, to some extent, people will pull together around decisions, the solidarity that can be mustered through common membership in social networks, and the social control this provides, is a helpful supplement for decision-makers. Indeed, homogeneity of class and ethnic background and prior social experiences is one important "commitment mechanism" found to build a feeling of communion among members . . . . Situational pressures, then, place a great emphasis on personal relationships and social homogeneity as functional elements in the carrying out of managerial tasks.[32]

The disadvantage of clan control is its personal nature. It requires personal involvement of employees, which is only possible in small organizations, or within departments. Clan control may be used among a group of top managers or within a specific department, but it is difficult to extend clan control throughout a large organization. Bureaucratic mechanisms are more appropriate to provide systematic direction and standardization in a large corporation.

CONTINGENCY CONTROL MODEL

A contingency model that describes when organizations should use market, bureaucratic, and clan control is shown in figure 8.8. Each type of control may appear in the same organization, but one form of control will usually dominate at a given management level. Bureaucratic control mechanisms

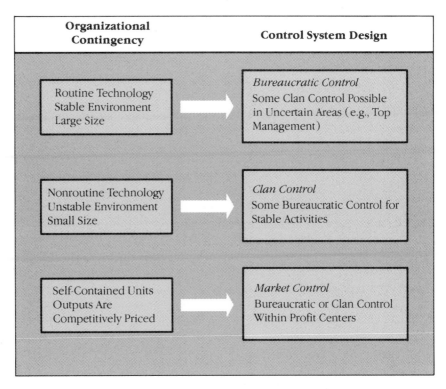

Organizational Contingency	Control System Design
Routine Technology Stable Environment Large Size	*Bureaucratic Control* Some Clan Control Possible in Uncertain Areas (e.g., Top Management)
Nonroutine Technology Unstable Environment Small Size	*Clan Control* Some Bureaucratic Control for Stable Activities
Self-Contained Units Outputs Are Competitively Priced	*Market Control* Bureaucratic or Clan Control Within Profit Centers

Figure 8.8. Contingency Model for Organizational Control Strategies.

are by far the most widely used control strategy. Some form of bureaucratic control is almost always necessary. Bureaucratic control is used extensively when organizations are large, and when the environment and technology are certain, stable, and routine. Clan control is used in the opposite circumstances. When organizations are small, and when the environment and technology are uncertain, unstable and nonroutine, then trust, tradition, and shared values are important. Bureaucratic control does not work well under unstable conditions because it is unable to measure and monitor the rapidly changing targets and outputs.

Market control has limited applications. Market mechanisms are used when costs and outputs can be priced, and when a market is available for price comparison. Market control is appropriate for self-contained divisions in a business corporation. Each division is a profit center. When applicable, market control is extremely efficient because performance information is summarized in a single profit and loss statement.

Control systems differ substantially from organization to organization. The use of these systems reflects the uncertainty of the technology and environment as well as the ability to price output. Bureaucratic control is extensive when technology and environment are routine and certain, and when the organization is large. Clan control is used when the organization is small and when activities are nonroutine and uncertain. Market control is best when outputs can be accurately priced and when competitive services are available.

IN PRACTICE 8.8

Metallic Finishes, Inc.

Metallic Finishes, Inc. is a producer of metals and chrome finishes and specialty metals. In 1982, the new executive vice president, Stuart Abelson, went on record saying that he was going to get the research and development department under control. Abelson came up through the manufacturing ranks, where extensive budgets and statistical reports were used. Almost every activity in manufacturing was counted and evaluated on a weekly or monthly basis. The research department, by contrast, seemed loosely controlled. Performance was satisfactory, but people had freedom to do as they pleased, such as to work whenever they wanted during the day or evening. Stuart Abelson was going to do something about it.

His first step was to install a detailed budget system. A budget was established for each research project rather than for the department as a whole. Even minor expenditures had to be budgeted. The research and development director was expected to keep each expense category on target. Statistical reports were implemented to keep track of all non-financial items, such as how employees spent their time and their productivity levels. Number of technical papers written, conferences attended, and use of equipment were all measured and monitored under the new control system. Abelson also wanted to install a market system, whereby users would be charged for R & D services. This system was not implemented. Most managers feared that if manufacturing had to pay for research services, R & D would go broke.

As the detail and intensity of the bureaucratic control system increased, satisfaction and productivity within research and development decreased. At least once a week the executive vice president and the R & D director battled over differences between actual expenditures and budget, or over the interpretation of activity reports. After about a year, the R & D director resigned, which was followed by the resignations of several key researchers.

The board of directors asked that a task force be created to examine problems in R & D. A management consultant was hired to assist the task force. They found that the control procedures were not appropriate in an R & D department characterized by ambiguity and uncertainty. Precise, detailed reports may work for a stable manufacturing department, but they do not capture the nature of R & D activities. Minor deviations from budget are the rule rather than the exception when uncertainty is high. A more generalized system was needed. A general control system used to plan future projects and to keep research output consistent with company goals would be more effective. The market control system that Abelson wanted to install was not appropriate either. Establishing a fair price for R & D services would be difficult. Competitive services are not available. Research and development exists because the goals of top management include innovation, not because R & D is able to sell its service to other departments. The task force recommended that the bureaucratic system be reduced and that clan control mechanisms be allowed to regulate employee behavior.

Stuart Abelson had not recognized or understood clan control. R & D employees were socialized into professional norms and practices. They shared common beliefs and values about work habits and departmental goals. Most researchers worked extra hours at night to finish projects. The absence of extensive bureaucratic control mechanisms did not mean that control was absent.

The lesson from Metallic Finishes, Inc. is that departments characterized by uncertainty should make greater use of clan control than departments characterized by routine work and a stable environment. Clan control takes advantage of participation, socialization, and shared norms and values. Clan control is an effective control mechanism when employees want to be a part of the organization and to contribute in any way possible. They do not need to be closely monitored, either by a supervisor or by a detailed bureaucratic system. On the other hand, when work is certain and unambiguous, bureaucratic control systems will be suitable. Bureaucratic reports will capture and report relevant activities. The following case illustrates the appropriate use of a bureaucratic control system.

IN PRACTICE 8.9

Canadian Finance Company

Canadian Finance Company has over 200 branch offices spread across Canada. Most branches were located in medium-sized cities and towns, and had from two to ten employees. The company needed good control for efficient cash management. Top management had to see that maximum available money was lent while bad loans were minimized. As the company grew larger, uniform procedures were established for use in the branch offices, but information about new loans and loan paybacks came into the home office every three weeks. Some reports were informal, and top management was unable to monitor branch activities.

Cash management is a fairly routine task. Over a period of about two years, the finance company installed an on-line computer system with terminals in each branch office. At the end of each day, someone in each branch office would insert information about the number of loans, payments, number of loans classified as a bad debt, repossessions, and so on. All activities from each branch were recorded in the system, including attendance, number of walk-in customers, and how employees spent their time. Each morning the control system produced for regional and top management a detailed listing of activities in each branch. Weekly and month-to-date performance was instantly calculated for each branch. The new control system was consistent with the routine and stable nature of loan office work. The new system, which complemented extensive rules and procedures, was effective for the finance company. Informal reports were no longer used. The control system was judged very satisfactory by middle management, and lower-level employees did not object to it.[33]

SUPERVISORY CONTROL STRATEGIES

Supervisory control pertains to the lower, operational level in organizations. Supervisory control systems focus on the performance of individual employees. The two types of supervisory strategies available to managers are output control and behavior control.[34]

Output control is based upon written records that measure employee outputs and productivity. Output control is very effective when the outputs of individual workers can be easily measured. Examples are piece-rate jobs where the number of units per hour can be easily calculated. Many sales jobs can be handled with output control because measurement of performance is reflected in the number of sales, the amount of sales, or in commissions earned. Output information is communicated through written records, a less rich media than personal observation.

The research productivity of university professors is normally evaluated by output control. The process of how to do creative research is not well understood, so procedures for researchers cannot be prescribed in advance. The test of good research is whether the output is accepted in journals and by colleagues. Research activity is normally measured by the number and quality of publications.

Behavior control is based upon personal observation of employees and the procedures they use. Behavioral control usually takes more time than output control because it requires personal surveillance.[35] Managers observe employees at work. Behavior control is used when outputs are not easily measured. High school and college teaching is often monitored and influenced through behavior control. The outputs of teaching are the amount of student learning and how long students retain what they have learned. These outputs are enormously difficult to measure. Consequently, teachers are usually evaluated on the process or behavior they use in teaching. A high school principal may personally observe teachers to learn whether they follow accepted practices. Student evaluations are often used at the college level to provide information about classroom behavior of teachers. Teaching and research activities are thus controlled in different ways. The form of supervisory control depends on whether employee output or behavior is measurable.

The choice of output control versus behavior control has implications for performance of employees. In many organizations, either approach can be used because both behavior and outputs can be evaluated. The choice of control emphasis should reflect the goals of the organization. A few department stores, for example, use strictly output measures, such as amount of sales by each salesperson.[36] Salespeople are free to use whatever procedures they find effective to increase sales. In other stores, especially expensive stores with a high-class clientele, output control does not achieve the goals desired by management. When employees are oriented exclusively toward sales, they often use hard-sell procedures that offend customers. Employees also fail to do other things consistent with the store's image, such as cleaning and dusting shelves. Many stores incorporate a balance of output and behavioral control to provide broader evaluation for employees.

THE CONTROL GRAPH

The control strategies identified in this chapter have implications for the distribution of control among employees. In some organizations, lower-level employees feel that they have substantial influence over what goes on. In other organizations, they feel as if they are completely controlled. The control group was formulated in the early 1960s as an approach to diagnose and measure the distribution of control in organizations.[37] Employees were surveyed to learn how much influence they had in day-to-day activities of the organization. Analysis of questionnaire responses determined how much control top managers, middle managers, and lower-level employees had in the organization. An example of the questions asked of employees is shown in figure 8.9.

Compilation of employee response yields a control graph such as the one in figure 8.10. The vertical axis in figure 8.10 represents the amount of control exercised by each level in the hierarchy. The typical organization

Figure 8.9.   Survey Question Used for Developing Graph Control.

In general, how much influence would you say each of the following persons or groups actually have on what happens in your plant?

	Almost no Influence	A Little Influence	Moderate Influence	Quite a Lot of Influence	A great Deal of Influence
Your Plant Manager	1	2	3	4	5
Supervisors in Your Plant	1	2	3	4	5
The Men in Your Plant	1	2	3	4	5

has a downward slope. Top management is perceived to have more control than lower-level employees. A truly democratic organization might have a flat slope or even an upward slope, which indicates that lower-level employees have extensive control. Organizations that have routine technologies and stable environments tend to have more extensive bureaucratic systems, and hence could be expected to have a steeper control curve. Clan control is often perceived as more democratic. The control curve might have a flatter slope because lower-level employees participate extensively in the control process.

The control graph provides a useful distinction between the distribution of control and the total amount of control in an organization. *The distribution of control is represented by the slope.* A steep downward slope indicates that most control is with top administrators, and a flat slope indicates equal distribution across levels of the hierarchy. *The total amount of control is represented by the height of the control curve,* as shown in figure 8.11. In some organizations the entire curve may be at a high level, which indicates that all employees in the organization believe they have influence over what happens. In organizations with a low curve, people feel they have little influence.

There have been numerous studies around the world using the control graph, and two consistent findings have emerged.[38] First, the slope of the control curve is not related to organizational effectiveness. The difference between hierarchical and democratic control does not influence organizational performance. Hierarchical and democratic slopes correspond to

Figure 8.10.   Control Graphs for Hierarchical and Democratic Organizations.

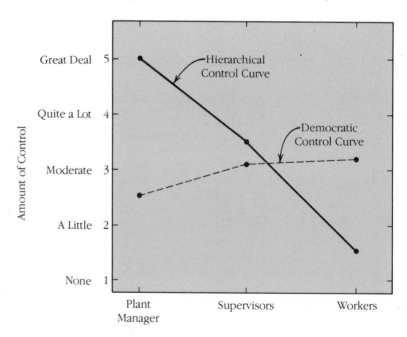

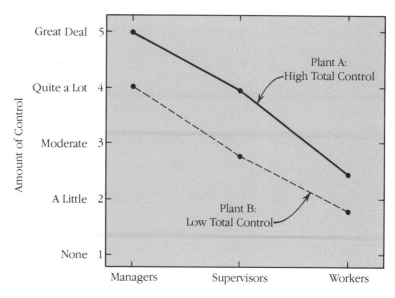

Figure 8.11. Difference in Total Control for Two Plants.

bureaucratic and clan control strategies. Either can be effective if it fits the organization's technology, size, and environment.

Second, organizational performance is influenced by the height of the control curve (total amount of control). Organizations with higher slopes tend to be scored as more effective. In figure 8.11, high performers have control graphs similar to the solid line and low performers have control graphs similar to the dotted line. The explanation is that employees at all levels are more involved in the organization. Employees have more influence over what happens. The total amount of control is not a fixed sum to be divided among lower- and upper-level employees. Even with bureaucratic control, the total amount of control can be increased by having people participate in target-setting or evaluation procedures. Top managers who encourage a sense of participation still have greater control than people below them in the hierarchy, but the organization is able to achieve higher performance.

COMPUTERS AND INFORMATION TECHNOLOGY

Organizations in recent years have undergone a revolution in the technology for processing both task and control related information. Computers provide a technology to rapidly process millions of pieces of data in a short time. Computers can handle the voluminous paperwork and manual activities required to provide information for task accomplishment and control described so far in this chapter.

Figure 8.12 shows the placement of a computer department in a large organization. The department often reports to an administrative or financial vice president, and is responsible for processing a variety of financial and operational information. The dotted lines in figure 8.12 show how information can be drawn from lower-level activities and provided to managers at upper levels. The computer is able to aggregate and summarize enormous amounts of data for managerial use. As computers are miniaturized and simplified, a single large computer may be replaced with several small computers located throughout the organization.

Computer Impact on Structure The introduction of a computer doesn't just add a computer department to the organization. It realigns power. It changes the need for certain types of jobs. Thomas Whisler, of the Graduate School of Business at the University of Chicago, studied the impact of computers on twenty-three insurance companies.[39] His study was especially informative because it provided information both before and after the computer was introduced. After computers became operational, organizations tended to change in the following directions.

1. *Reduced Number of Clerical Personnel.*[40] The impact on personnel was mostly at the clerical level. The computer replaced the need to hire clerical personnel because it absorbed the manual data-processing tasks performed by these personnel. A few personnel had to be hired to code data for the computer, but this was more than offset by savings in other clerical employees. There was also a small savings in supervisory personnel who directed clerical activities.
2. *Increased Power and Influence for Computer Specialists.*[41] Computer personnel have computer expertise. As more activities were taken over by the computer, computer personnel acquired greater control and authority over organizational activities. In some cases, production activities might even be rearranged to fit the requirements of the computer. Line managers become more dependent on staff specialists.
3. *A Tendency toward Differentiation into Functional Departments.* The computer is highly specialized, and can perform specialized tasks for individual departments. The functional form of structure (chapter 6) seemed to make more efficient use of the computer than self-contained units.[42]
4. *Greater Group Decision-Making.*[43] Several organizations saw the need to involve managers from different functions and subtasks in the decision-making process. A similar finding was that greater decentralization took place when computers were introduced.[44]
5. *Greater Proportion of Administrative and Professional Support Staff.*[45] Professional support staff, other than clerical, tended to increase with the introduction of a computer. Support staff were needed for computer programming and operations as well as to work with users around the organization.

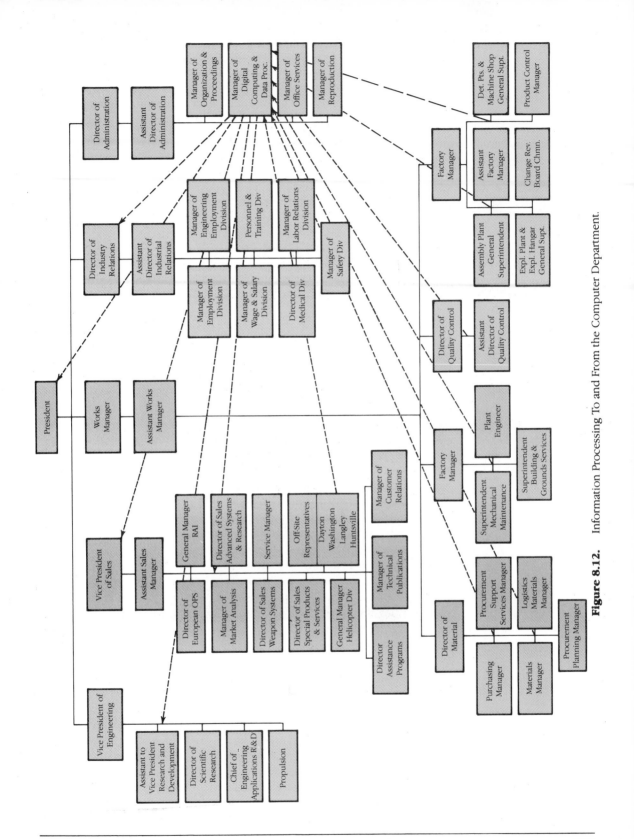

Figure 8.12. Information Processing To and From the Computer Department.

The introduction of a computer can have substantial impact upon the structure of an organization, which is not surprising if we think of organizations as information-processing systems. As the technology of information-processing continues to change, the design of the organization can also be expected to change to fit that technology. One corporation experiencing this change was Republican-Scobill.

IN PRACTICE 8.10

Republican-Scobill

Republican-Scobill manufactures lipstick, vanity, and aerosal containers for the cosmetics industry. Republican-Scobill had 2,400 employees in 1965 when they purchased their first IBM computer. Thirty months of hard work later, the computer had taken over many of R-S's clerical and financial recordkeeping.

In 1975, R-S purchased the largest, highest-power computer money could buy. Top management decided that every possible activity should be computerized. Three years after the introduction of the new computer, billings, customer orders, payroll, budgets, personnel records, inventory control, production schedules, sales records, salaries and bonuses, income and expenditures, shareholder records, and even policies and job descriptions were processed by the computer. Virtually every department in the organization was tied to the computer department.

In 1980, top management decided to adopt new forms of information-processing technology. Their first step was to create a separate department responsible for all typing and word processing. The newly centralized typing pool had recording equipment to handle dictation over the telephone. Sophisticated word processors were used to speed typing and make corrections. The centralized steno pool at headquarters was connected to other plants through electronic mail. The electronic hook-up handled memos and letters instantly.

In 1981, Republican-Scobill had grown to 5,100 employees at seven plant locations. The word-processing group was given departmental status under the Director of Computer Operations. In the fifteen years since the introduction of the first computer, the number of professional computer staff increased from three to thirty-three. These professionals were needed to write the programs, develop systems for computer application, and maintain computer files and hardware. Other managers at R-S were sometimes antagonistic toward the computer department. Their ability to achieve their goals and meet their own deadlines was no longer under their control. When the computer department experienced delays or shut-downs, everyone's work was held up. Top management initiated a series of weekly meetings between middle managers to work out problems between the computer department and users.

The introduction of the centralized word-processing system and steno pool also caused problems. Managers no longer had personal secretaries to do typing, although several executives admitted they liked the speed with which memos and letters could be processed between plants. During one weekly meeting, Mary Johnson, head of the word-processing group, commented that the number of secretaries at Republican-Scobill dropped by 18% after the introduction of the word-processing equipment. After a year, most managers were accustomed to the centralized steno pool and were satisfied with secretarial support. In March of 1982, the Director of Computer Operations was elevated to the rank of Vice President. His pay and stature were now similar to that of the Vice Presidents of Finance, Manufacturing, and Marketing.

Management Information Systems

A **management information system** is a computer-based data gathering and transmission system that provides management with information to make decisions. When management information systems (MISs) were first introduced, they were expected to have dramatic impact on the quality and speed of manager decision-making. The computer could gather the data, make sophisticated mathematical analyses of the data, and provide correct answers to managers. Computers could extend the minds of managers by processing vast amounts of information needed to solve complex problems.

The promise of MISs with its quantitative analysis to assist manager decision-making has not been realized.[46] Management information systems can convey excellent data, especially about such things as expenditures, billings, scrap rates, and human resources. But MISs have been widely criticized because they are often ignored within organizations. Many management information systems do not apply to or solve the problems with which managers deal.[47] The discussion earlier in this chapter about numerical information not being rich enough to solve unanalyzable problems points to one reason that MISs have not been successful. Computer specialists often do not understand the information needs of management, and hence try to provide quantitative data to solve every problem.

For example, the information system for a sales department will report quantified data on the number of completed sales transaction and perhaps the number of sales calls. These data can be processed through the computer, but are less important to sales management than understanding the reasons why specific sales were lost. This in-depth information cannot be processed through the computer, and needs to be obtained by talking directly to salespeople or customers. Moreover, face-to-face information sources provide additional cues such as facial expression, gesture, and tone of voice that may provide additional insight into a complicated problem. Information needs within organizations are much broader than what computers can supply.[48] The design of information systems should provide broad-based information for managers so that the richness of information suits the problem at hand.

Information Systems for the Future

Information technology has undergone dramatic changes since the advent of the computer. Computers have been miniaturized so that each department in the organization can have its own information-processing hardware. Even more exciting are new developments in the means for transmitting information. Executives at the Minneapolis Office of Control Data Corporation now hold televised conferences with executives in other parts of the country. They use an electronic blackboard so that information written down in Minneapolis automatically appears in the other locations. Atlantic Richfield is designing a complete teleconferencing network. This involves a satellite hookup and wall-size projection screens. Employees will be able to confer with each other visually, and will not have to fly to Los Angeles for their regular weekly meeting. Companies like Xerox use electronic mail to swap and file memos for executives. Secretaries can exchange memos in a minute or so. An exchange of memos previously would have involved typing letters and sending them coast to coast—a time lapse of several days.[49]

These developments are important because they may have great impact on the job of managers. The introduction of computers into organizations about twenty years ago helped solve the need for large amounts of data. But computers did not solve managerial needs for rich information. The importance of the current revolution in information technology is that new devices are beginning to process rich information. Word processors and electronic blackboards handle verbal languages, which are richer than simple numbers. Personal letters and reports can be written and communicated almost instantly. Telecommunication systems allow visual as well as audio contact among far-flung managers. These systems transmit face-to-face cues and provide instant feedback. Graphs and pictures can also be communicated, which are rich forms of information. All executives may eventually have their own mini-computer, television screen, and instant access to executives around the world. Information technology will play an expanded role in the management of organizations. The ability to use new forms of information technology may become a vital part of the effective manager's repertoire in the future.

SUMMARY AND INTERPRETATION

The ideas covered in this chapter are some of the newest in organization theory. In just the last few years, the field has begun to develop frameworks that explain information and control processes in organizations. One interesting discovery is that organizational requirements for information and control systems are very different from information and control systems designed for machines. Machine-based theories do not apply to human organizations.

The two important information dimensions covered are amount and richness. Determining how information requirements differ along these two dimensions, and how to design the organization's structure and information systems, are key problems for organizations to solve. Organizations also must solve the problem of directing and evaluating the performance of the overall organization, its departments, and individual employees. The concepts of market, bureaucratic, clan, output, and behavior control help explain how control is exercised in organizations.

The material in this chapter builds upon concepts described in earlier chapters. The discussion of information-processing relates to the chapter 6 discussion of organization structure and design. In chapter 6 we saw that organization structure serves to direct the flow of information. Vertical and horizontal linkage devices are used to ensure that information is passed where it is needed for problem-solving, decision-making, and coordination. Organization structure should facilitate and encourage both the amount and richness of information needed by managers to perform effectively.

The material on control systems corresponds to the material in chapter 4 on bureaucracy and in chapter 6 on structure. Chapter 4 described how bureaucracy is more extensive in large organizations, and in this chapter we saw that bureaucracy is a primary mechanism for controlling employees. By establishing a hierarchy of authority and by providing rules and procedures, budgets and statistical reports, the variation in behavior among employees is reduced. Outcomes are predictable. Clan control is used when organizations are small and less bureaucratic. Market control pertains to the material in chapter 6 on self-contained units. Self-contained units pay the cost of resources and sell outputs at competitive prices. This structural design is related to the choice of a market control strategy by top management.

Finally, the discussion of information and control corresponds to the material in chapter 2 on the environment and the material in chapter 5 on technology. The design of information and control systems reflects these two contingencies. An organization that has a nonroutine technology and unstable environment would require larger amounts of information and richer forms of information. Moreover, clan control would be more important. When technology is routine and the environment is stable, less information is required and control systems are more bureaucratic. The material in this chapter reinforces and elaborates earlier findings about technology, environment, bureaucracy, and the structural configuration of organizations.

DISCUSSION QUESTIONS

1. Define information. How does information differ from data?
2. Assume that students have two ways to inform professors about the quality of their teaching. The first way is for each student to rate the professor's teaching ability on a seven-point scale. The second way is for students to write a paragraph stating what they liked and disliked about the professor's teaching. Which of these techniques will provide the richest information to the professor? Is your answer consistent with the richness scale given in figure 8.2?
3. The manager of a computer processing department told his employees: "Top managers need the same data everyone else needs, only instead of all the details we'll aggregate it for the company as a whole." Agree or disagree with the manager's philosophy, and explain why.

4. Henry Mintzberg argued that managers need information support that is independent of computers. Explain why you agree or disagree with his point of view.

5. In writing about types of control, William Ouchi said "the Market is like the trout and the Clan like the salmon, each a beautiful highly specialized species which requires uncommon conditions for its survival. In comparison, the bureaucratic method of control is the catfish—clumsy, ugly, but able to live in the widest range of environments and, ultimately, the dominant species." Discuss what Ouchi meant with that analogy.

6. What type of controls do most professors use to control students—output, behavior, or both?

7. How do technology and environment influence the design of control systems?

8. Explain what it means when one organization has a control curve that is steeper than another organization.

9. What does it mean if one organization has a higher control curve (more area beneath it) than another organization?

10. What types of organizational and environmental conditions influence the amount of information-processing in organizations? The media used to process information?

11. Government organizations often seem more bureaucratic than for-profit organizations. Could this partly be the result of the type of control used in government organizations? Explain.

12. Discuss the following statements: "Things under tight control are better than things under loose control." "The more data managers have, the better decisions they make."

GUIDES TO ACTION

As an organization designer:

1. Provide information support to managers and employees that reflects the frequency and type of problems with which they deal. Design both the amount and richness of information to meet the problem-solving needs of managers.

2. Implement one of the three basic choices—bureaucratic, clan, market—as the primary means of organizational control. Use bureaucratic control when organizations are large, have a stable environment, and routine technology. Use clan control in small, uncertain departments. Use market control when outputs can be priced, and when competitive bidding is available.

3. Predict and plan for changes associated with the adaptation of information processing and computer technology. Prepare for a shift in power between those who manage the technology and those who do not. Hold frequent meetings to resolve disagreements between users and operators.

4. Diagnose the perceived distribution of control in the organization using the control graph. Increase the performance of employees by increasing total control. Encourage employees to participate in organizational planning and decision-making.

Consider these Guides when analyzing the following cases and when answering the questions listed after each case.

CASES FOR ANALYSIS

1. QUEEN'S CHILDREN'S PSYCHIATRIC CENTER[50]

With barbs, broadsides, and a parody of the bookkeeper mentality, a state hospital in Queens has answered an audit of its operations by State Comptroller Arthur Levitt by issuing a pseudo-scientific report entitled "Audit of an Audit."

Among the hundreds of tax-supported agencies that quake at the auditor's call, this was the first in memory that has dared to turn the tables on the Comptroller and audit the auditor.

Prepared by Dr. Gloria Faretra, the director of the [Queen's Children's] psychiatric center, and Dr. Abbas D. Nabas, the center's director of research, the hospital report, which accused the state's auditors of unbending bias, began with its conclusions:

"There is no more validity in employing an auditor to evaluate the treatment of programs of a hospital than there would be in employing a physician to audit the financial affairs of a bank."

Noting that there were no medical or clinical personnel on the team that audited the hospital's operations from May 12 to August 19, 1975, the report declared: "In the area of clinical evaluations and recommendations, the audit was found useless, time- and money-wasting, duplicative, unnecessary, and counter-therapeutic."

It said some recommendations in the areas of accounting, receipts, disbursements, payroll procedures, and voucher and inventory systems were of "some value," and either had been or were being implemented.

But the bulk of the auditors' work came in for some harsh criticism; "a startling measure of fancy," "impressions overruling arithmetic," "bias instead of objectivity," and "virtually an effort to practice medicine without a license," were some of the characterizations in an accompanying news release.

The report's litany of findings included the following:

- The longer hospital staff members worked with the auditors, the more they became convinced that the auditors were incompetent.
- "Auditors' 'biases' were unaffected by on-site information."
- While the auditors reported a "stable" census of about 300 children at the hospital from 1970 to 1975, the actual numbers dropped 45% during that period, from 480 to 275.

- The auditors compared the resident population of patients with the hospital's operating budget and concluded that the better (or longer or more detailed) the records kept on patients, "the shorter the patient's hospital stay," a leap of reasoning that prompted this response: "We have found neither professional opinion nor research results to validate this questionable comparison, but we are still searching."

The report's epilogue focused on paperwork, noting that a study two years ago had found that the professional staff at the hospital spent 40% to 50% of its time on it. The report said:

"Virtually every recommendation of the auditors, each suggested solution to a problem, each 'answer' to a question, calls directly or indirectly for still more forms, still more paperwork.

"It seems increasingly obvious that the conscious or unconscious goal of the auditor is the Perfect Form—something that can substitute for medical training, clinical field experience, and medical judgment, something that can be fed into a computer for an instant readout with all the answers."

Questions
1. To what extent are the complaints about the hospital audit a result of information media? Are standard forms and computer printouts appropriate for transmitting information about psychiatric care? Discuss.
2. The audit seemed to have value in the area of receipts, disbursements, payroll procedures, and voucher and inventory systems. Why would that be?
3. Why do auditors limit their data collection to paperwork types of information? How might organizations incorporate richer information in their audits? Discuss.

2. SUNFLOWER INCORPORATED[51]

Sunflower Incorporated is a large distribution company with over 5,000 employees and gross sales of over $400 million (1981). The company purchases and distributes salty snack foods and liquor to independent retail stores throughout the United States and Canada. Salty snack foods include corn chips, potato chips, cheese curls, tortilla chips, and peanuts. The U.S. and Canada are divided into twenty-two regions, each with its own central warehouse, salespeople, finance department, and purchasing department. The company distributes national as well as local brands, and packages some items under private labels. The head office encourages each region to be autonomous because of local tastes and practices. The northeast U.S., for example, consumes a greater percentage of Canadian whisky and American bourbon, while the West consumes more light liquors such as vodka, gin, and rum. Snack foods in the Southwest are often seasoned to reflect Mexican tastes.

Early in 1980, Sunflower began using a financial reporting system that compared sales, costs, and profits across regions. Management was surprised to learn that profits varied widely. By 1982, the differences were so great that management decided some standardization was necessary. They believed that highly profitable regions were sometimes using lower quality items, even seconds, to boost profit margins. This practice could hurt Sunflower's image. Other regions were facing intense price competition in order to hold market share. National distributors were pushing hard to increase their market share. Frito-lay, Bordens, Nabisco, Procter & Gamble (Pringles), and Standard Brands (Planter's peanuts) were pushing hard to increase market share by cutting prices and launching new products.

As these problems accumulated, Mr. Steelman, president of Sunflower, decided to create a new position to monitor pricing and purchasing practices. Mrs. Agnes Albanese was hired from the finance department of a competing organization. Her new title was Director of Pricing and Purchasing, and she reported to the Vice President of Finance, Mr. Mobley. Steelman and Mobley gave Albanese great latitude in organizing her job, and encouraged her to establish whatever rules and procedures were necessary. She was also encouraged to gather information from each region. Each region was notified of her appointment by an official memo sent to the regional managers. A copy of the memo was posted on each warehouse bulletin board. The announcement was also made in the company newspaper.

After three weeks on the job, Albanese decided that pricing and purchasing decisions should be standardized across regions. As a first step, she wanted the financial executive in each region to notify her of any change in local prices of more than 3%. She also decided that all new contracts for local purchases of more than $5,000 should be cleared through her office. (Approximately 60% of items distributed in the regions was purchased in large quantities and supplied from the home office. The other 40% was purchased and distributed within the region.) Albanese believed that the only way to standardize operations was for each region to notify the home office in advance of any change in prices or purchases. Albanese discussed the proposed policy with Mobley. He agreed, so they submitted a formal proposal to the president and board of directors, who approved the plan. Sunflower was moving into the peak holiday season, so Albanese wanted to implement the new procedures right away. She decided to send a telex to the financial and purchasing executives in each region notifying them of the new procedures. The change would be inserted in all policy and procedure manuals throughout Sunflower within four months.

Albanese showed a draft of the telex to Mobley and invited his comments. Mobley said the telex was an excellent idea but wondered if it was sufficient. The regions handle hundreds of items, and were used to decentralized decision-making. Mobley suggested that Albanese ought to visit the regions and discuss purchasing and pricing policies with the executives. Albanese refused, saying that the trips would be expensive and time-consuming. She had so many things to do at headquarters that a trip was impossible. Mobley also suggested waiting to implement the procedures until after the annual company meeting in three months. Albanese said this would take too long, because the procedures would not take effect until after the peak sales season. She believed the procedures were needed now. The telexes went out the next day.

During the next few days, replies came in from most of the regions. The executives were in agreement with the telex, and said they would be happy to cooperate.

Eight weeks later, Mrs. Albanese had not received notices from any regions about local price or purchase changes. Other executives who had visited regional warehouses indicated to her that the regions were busy as usual. Regional executives seemed to be following usual procedures for that time of year.

Questions

1. What type of control did the home office use to evaluate the performance of each region? What type of control did Mrs. Albanese try to use to change the behavior of regional purchasing and financial managers at Sunflower? What type of control were the executives used to? Discuss.

2. Mr. Mobley suggested that Albanese meet the executives personally, get to know them, and discuss the change in procedures directly with them. Would this approach represent a different form of control? Explain.

3. Mrs. Albanese had a choice of two information media—written and face-to-face. What information medium is most appropriate to resolve procedures in pricing and purchasing? Which medium is appropriate for announcing and providing authority to a new position? Why? Discuss.

NOTES

1. "S. I. Newhouse and Sons: America's Most Profitable Publisher," *Business Week,* January 26, 1976, pp. 56–64.
2. Daniel Machalaba, "Newhouse Chain Stays with Founder's Ways and with His Heirs," *Wall Street Journal,* February 12, 1982, pp. 1, 15.
3. *Ibid.*
4. "S. I. Newhouse and Sons," *Business Week.*
5. This case was based on "S. I. Newhouse and Sons," *Business Week,* and on Daniel Machalaba, "Newhouse Chain Stays with Founder's Ways and with His Heirs."
6. Richard L. Daft and Norman B. Macintosh, "A Tentative Exploration into the Amount and Equivocality of Information Processing in Organizational Work Units," *Administrative Science Quarterly* 26 (1981): 207–224.
7. Henry Mintzberg, *The Nature of Managerial Work* (New York: Harper & Row, 1972), p. 39.
8. Daft and Macintosh, "A Tentative Exploration," p. 210.
9. Jay R. Galbraith, *Organization Design* (Reading, MA: Addison-Wesley, 1977), pp. 35–36.
10. Michael L. Tushman and David A. Nadler, "Information Processing as an Integrating Concept in Organization Design," *Academy of Management Review* 3 (1978): 613–624; Samuel B. Bacharach and Michael Aiken, "Communication in Administrative Bureaucracies," *Academy of Management Journal* 20 (1977): 365–377.

11. Robert H. Lengel, "Managerial Information Processing and Communication-Media Source Selection Behavior," unpublished Ph.D. dissertation, Texas A & M University, 1982.
12. A. Meherabian, *Silent Messages* (Belmont, CA: Wadsworth, 1971), p. 44.
13. Daft and Macintosh, "A Tentative Exploration."
14. Michael L. Tushman, "Technical Communication in R & D Laboratories: The Impact of Project Work Characteristics," *Academy of Management Journal* 21 (1978): 624–645.
15. Daft and Macintosh, "A Tentative Exploration."
16. Warren J. Keegan, "Multi-National Scanning: A Study of Information Sources Utilized by Headquarters Executives in Multi-National Companies," *Administrative Science Quarterly* 19 (1974): 411–421.
17. Richard L. Daft and Norman B. Macintosh, "A New Approach to Design and Use of Management Information," *California Management Review* 21 (1978): 82–92.
18. *Ibid.*
19. Adapted from Richard L. Daft and Norman B. Macintosh, "A New Approach to Design and Use of Management Information," *California Management Review* 21 (1978), p. 89. Copyright © 1978 by the Regents of the University of California. Reprinted by permission of the Regents.
20. G. Anthony Gorry and Michael S. Scott Morton, "A Framework for Management Information Systems," *Sloan Management Review* 13 (1970): 55–70.
21. "What Undid Jarman: Paperwork Paralysis," *Business Week*, January 24, 1977, pp. 67–68; "Genesco Ousts Franklin Jarman as Top Officer," *Wall Street Journal*, January 4, 1977, p. 2.
22. William G. Ouchi, "The Relationship Between Organizational Structure and Organizational Control," *Administrative Science Quarterly* 22 (1977): 95–113; John Todd, "Management Control Systems: A Key Link Between Strategy, Structure, and Employee," *Organizational Dynamics* (Spring, 1977): 65–78.
23. Geert Hofstede, "The Poverty of Management Control Philosophy," *Academy of Management Review* 3 (1978): 450–461.
24. Anthony Hopwood, *Accounting and Human Behavior* (London: Haymarket Publishing, 1974).
25. William G. Ouchi, "Markets, Bureaucracies, and Clans," *Administrative Science Quarterly* 25 (1980): 129–141; and "A Conceptual Framework for the Design of Organizational Control Mechanisms," *Management Science* 25 (1979) 833–848.
26. Oliver A. Williamson, *Markets and Hierarchies: Analyses and Antitrust Implications* (New York: Free Press, 1975).
27. Norman B. Macintosh and Richard L. Daft, "Management Control Systems and Organizational Context," report to the Society of Management Accountants and National Assoication of Accountants, Kingston, Ont., 1980; Richard L. Daft, Norman B. Macintosh, and Becky Baysinger, "The Design of Management Control Systems," paper presented at the National Academy of Management Meetings, August, 1981, San Diego, California.

28. Macintosh and Daft, "Management Control Systems."

29. Ouchi, "Markets, Bureaucracies, and Clans."

30. From Rosabeth Moss Kanter, *Men and Women of the Corporation* (New York: Basic Books, 1977), p. 47. Copyright © 1977 by Rosabeth Moss Kanter. By permission of Basic Books, Inc., Publishers, New York.

31. *Ibid.* p. 48.

32. *Ibid* p. 53.

33. Macintosh and Daft, "Management Control Systems."

34. Ouchi, "Relationship Between Organizational Structure and Organizational Control"; William G. Ouchi and Mary Ann McGuire, "Organizational Control: Two Functions," Administrative Science Quarterly 20 (1975): 559–569.

35. Peter M. Blau and W. Richard Scott, *Formal Organization* (San Francisco: Chandler Publishing Company, 1962).

36. Ouchi and McGuire, "Organizational Control."

37. Arnold S. Tannenbaum, *Control and Organization* (New York: McGraw-Hill, 1968).

38. Arnold S. Tannenbaum and Robert S. Cooke, "Organizational Control: A Review of Studies Employing the Control Graph Method," in Cornelius J. Lamners and David J. Hickson, *Organizations Alike and Unlike* (Boston: Rutledge and Keegan Paul, 1980), pp. 183–210.

39. Thomas L. Whisler, *The Impact of Computers on Organizations* (New York: Praeger, 1973), p. 11.

40. *Ibid.*

41. Elmer H. Burack and Peter F. Sorensen, Jr., "Computer Technology and Organizational Design: Toward a Contingency Model," *Organization and Administrative Science* 8 (1977): 223–235.

42. B. C. Reimann, "Organization Structure and Technology in Manufacturing: System Versus Workflow Level Perspectives," *Academy of Management Journal* 23 (1980): 61–77. Whisler, *Impact of Computers on Organizations,* p. 11.

43. Whisler, *Ibid.,* p. 12.

44. Reimann, "Organization Structure and Technology,"

45. *Ibid.*

46. Harold J. Levitt, "Beyond the Analytic Manager: I," *California Management Review* 17 (1975): 5–12.

47. See Jackson Grayson, Jr., "Management Science and Business Practice," *Harvard Business Review* (July–August, 1973): 41–43; Richard L. Daft and John C. Wiginton, "Language and Organization," *Academy of Management Review* 4 (1979): 179–191.

48. Henry Mintzberg: "Impediments to the Use of Management Information," National Association of Accountants and the Society of Industrial Accountants, Canada, 1975; Daft and Macintosh, "A New Approach."

49. "Now the Office of Tomorrow," *Time,* November 17, 1980, p. 80.

50. Robert D. McFadden, "Audit of an Audit Spoofs Levitt's Staff as Liability," copyright © 1976 by the New York Times Company. Used by permission.

51. This case was inspired by "Frito-Lay May Find Itself in a Competition Crunch," *Business Week*, July 19, 1982, p. 186, and "Dashman Company," in Paul R. Lawrence and John A. Seiler, *Organizational Behavior and Administration: Cases, Concepts, and Research Findings* (Homewood, IL: Irwin and Dorsey, 1965), pp. 16–17.

PART V
Managing Dynamic Processes

9

Decision-Making Processes

Morgan Guaranty executives had been discussing the idea for several months. A majority of them were finally in agreement. A new "Morgan Guaranty Building" was needed. A lavish $250-million skyscraper would be comparable to their competitors' buildings, such as the Chase Manhattan Plaza and the Citicorp Center. It would also be a good investment, and would bring together most of the bank's New York employees who were scattered among half a dozen buildings. Morgan executives decided on it, and cast their eye on the Wall Street block next to their current building as a potential site.

Building a skyscraper in Manhattan requires an assemblage—the uncertain business of secretly buying individual properties located on the building site. Long-term leases also have to be purchased from tenants. Any seller who discovers the assemblage can hold out for a ransom price because the buyer has to obtain every parcel. Morgan's target block contained six highrises, of which the three largest were essential to the project. If any of the three was lost, the project was dead. The three critical properties were owned by some of the smartest and best-connected real-estate operators in Manhattan.

James Austrian was hired to direct the assemblage. He would try to grab the three buildings before the landlords realized what was happening. Then he would have to arrange to move out sixty tenants whose leases expired after the wrecking crews were to begin their work.

Economic conditions were in Austrian's favor. The real-estate market on Wall Street had been sluggish for several years, and the owners of the three key buildings wanted to sell. The first building was purchased in two weeks for $6.8 million. Negotiations with the second owner took less than two weeks, and were handled over the phone. The price was

$2.7 million. The deal for the third building was stickier, because it was owned by a limited partnership with 350 members. If the owners of the first two buildings were in the partnership, they would realize an assemblage was in progress. The cover would be blown. Austrian made a deal with the principal partner for $19 million. After "two months of sweat,"[1] the contract was ratified. Neither of the other owners were part of the partnership group.

While waiting for the third building to close, Austrian began the delicate task of persuading tenants in the first two buildings to leave. Within a few months, he had reached agreement or was near agreement with every tenant. Everything was moving nicely, certainly better than expected.

Except for one minor problem. The contract for the second building could not be legally closed because of $1.7 million owed in back taxes. The city of New York had filed a foreclosure proceeding against the building. Paying off back taxes was a routine matter, so the owner offered to settle up—after all, he was going to sell for $1 million more than the taxes owed. The city of New York refused. The Koch administration had adopted a tough new policy on delinquent landlords. The city became the new owner.

This was an uncertain stage. An assemblage normally should not be revealed. However, city administrators should be thrilled at the prospect of a new skyscraper that would pump over $13 million a year into the city's treasury. So Morgan executives and Austrian decided to come clean. They would inform the city of the assemblage, and buy the property outright. A veteran Morgan executive sat down with the deputy commissioner of general services. The commissioner said of course the city would sell the property to Morgan. The Morgan executive offered $2 million. If Morgan wanted the building, the commissioner said, the price was $17 million.

The city was trying to extract an assemblage ransom! The Morgan executive was furious. That price would destroy the assemblage budget. The price was six times the price of comparable property.

Morgan's vice chairman jumped into the negotiations. He pushed the decision up a notch or two in the city's hierarchy. The city stood firm. He called the city's price "highway robbery," and "a hold-up."

The assemblage is dead. The commissioner admitted that the building was worthless to the city, and that $17 million was too high, but said it was the negotiating price. If Morgan had wanted the building, why did they back out so quickly? One reason is that dissension within Morgan surfaced when the assemblage price increased. Several executives felt the price wasn't worth it. Morgan didn't need a new building that badly. The city believes someone will eventually build a skyscraper on that site. In the meantime, it will receive only about $1 million in property tax revenues instead of $13 million. As for Morgan Guaranty, they sold the other two buildings to a Canadian developer and made an unexpectedly handsome profit.[2]

Organization decision-making is the process of identifying and solving problems. The process contains two major stages. The problem identification stage is where information about environmental and organizational conditions is monitored to determine if performance is satisfactory and to diagnose the cause of shortcomings. The problem solution stage is where alternative courses of action are considered and one alternative is selected and implemented. Morgan Guaranty's decision to build a skyscraper came unravelled in the problem-solution stage. An unexpectedly high price by the city made the decision infeasible to implement. The barrier to implementation will cause Morgan to recycle to the problem-identification stage. The original problems were that Morgan's building was less than competitive and that the internal climate could be improved by bringing employees together. Executives will reevaluate whether the problems are serious enough to warrant another solution. In any case, it's back to the drawing board for Morgan Guaranty. A great amount of discussion and analysis will be undertaken to evaluate whether a problem truly exists and what the solution might be.

Morgan's skyscraper decision provided other insights into decision-making. First, decision-making in the corporate world can be a messy, uncertain process. Good information is scarce. Morgan executives could not be certain if a new building would improve business, or if poor employee working relationships were due to separate locations. And why propose the skyscraper for the next block over? Wouldn't another location be cheaper or more appealing? These issues were decided without complete information. Second, executives may not agree on the severity of the problem or with the proposed solution. The decision process often has to focus on reaching agreement among key people, which is called a coalition. Morgan had the coalition, which promptly fell apart when the building's price went up. Third, a big decision is not made all at once. Big problems are identified and solved through a series of small decisions, such as deciding that multiple locations are unproductive, that Morgan's image needs improving, that the next block is a good location, that the assemblage should be revealed to the city, and so on. Finally, corporate decisions don't always work out. Mistakes are made. The decision plan may fall apart. Working under uncertainty, the organization may cycle through the decision process several times, reassessing whether a problem truly exists, and trying new solutions.

Purpose of This Chapter

Decision-making processes represent the brain and nervous system of the organization. Decision-makers monitor the external environment, interpret internal information, detect shortcomings in expected behavior and performance, analyze potential alternatives, and implement new courses of action. Decisions are made about organization structure, innovation, goals, products, facilities, and technology. In this chapter, we explore models that describe how organizations can and should make decisions about these issues. Decision-making by individual managers and decision-making by the organization are interconnected, so both types of decisions are considered in this chapter. At any point, the organization may be identifying problems and implementing alternatives for literally hundreds of decisions. Organizations somehow "muddle through" these processes.[3] Our purpose here is to analyze these processes to learn what decision-making is actually like in organization settings.

In the next section, we examine how individual managers make decisions. Manager decision-making is important because individual decisions accumulate into decisions for the organization as a whole. Then we explore several models of organizational decision-making. These models include systems analysis, the Carnegie model, the incremental decision model, and the garbage can model. Each model is important because it is used in a different organizational situation. The final section in this chapter combines the models into a single framework that describes when and how they should be used.

MANAGER DECISION-MAKING

Rational Approach   The rational approach to individual decision-making has several versions, but each stresses the need for systematic analysis of the problem followed by choice and implementation in a logical step-by-step sequence. One rational approach consists of eight steps.[4]

1. *Monitor the Decision Environment.*   This means monitoring internal and external information that will indicate deviations from planned or acceptable behavior. Managers will review financial statements, performance evaluations, absentee reports, industry indices, competitors' activities, and so forth.
2. *Define the Problem.*   The manager responds to deviations by identifying essential details of the problem: where, when, who was involved, who was affected, and how are current activities influenced.
3. *Specify Decision Objectives.*   The manager determines what performance outcomes should be achieved by a decision.
4. *Diagnose the Problem.*   In this stage, the manager digs below the surface to analyze the cause of the problem. Additional data may be gathered to facilitate this diagnosis. Understanding the cause enables appropriate treatment.
5. *Develop Alternative Solutions.*   Alternative courses of action that may achieve decisional objectives are identified. The manager will rely on previous experience and seek ideas and suggestions from other people.
6. *Evaluate Alternatives.*   This may involve the use of statistical techniques or personal experience to assess the probability of success. The merits of each alternative are assessed as well as the probability that it will reach the desired objectives.
7. *Choose the Best Alternative.*   This is the core of the decision process. If the preceding steps have been performed well, selection will be easier.
8. *Implement the Chosen Alternative.*   The manager uses managerial, administrative, and persuasive abilities and gives directions to ensure that

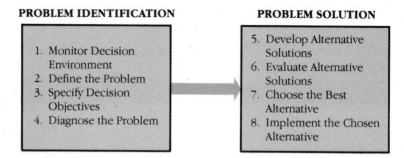

PROBLEM IDENTIFICATION	PROBLEM SOLUTION
1. Monitor Decision Environment 2. Define the Problem 3. Specify Decision Objectives 4. Diagnose the Problem	5. Develop Alternative Solutions 6. Evaluate Alternative Solutions 7. Choose the Best Alternative 8. Implement the Chosen Alternative

Figure 9.1.   Steps in the Rational Approach to Decision-Making.

the decision is carried out. Monitoring activity (step 1) begins as soon as the solution is implemented.

The first four steps in this sequence are problem identification and the next four are problem solution, as indicted in figure 9.1. All eight steps will normally appear in a manager's decision, although each step may not be a distinct element. Managers may know from experience exactly what to do in a situation, so one or more steps will be minimized. The following case illustrates how the rational approach is used to make a decision about a personnel problem.

IN PRACTICE 9.1

Alberta Manufacturing

1. *Monitor the Decision Environment.*   It is Monday morning, and Joe Defoe, one of Alberta's most skilled cutters, is absent again.
2. *Define the Decision Problem.*   This is the sixth consecutive Monday that Joe has been absent. Company policy forbids unexcused absenteeism and Joe has been warned about his excessive absenteeism on the last three occasions. A final warning is in order, but can be delayed if warranted.
3. *Specify Decision Objectives.*   Joe should attend work regularly and establish the production and quality levels of which he is capable. The time period for solving the problem is two weeks.
4. *Diagnose the Problem.*   Discreet discussions with Joe's co-workers and information gleaned from Joe indicate that Joe has a drinking problem. He apparently uses Mondays to dry out from weekend benders. Discussion with other company sources confirms that Joe is a problem drinker.
5. *Develop Alternative Solutions.*   (1) Fire Joe. (2) Issue a final warning without comment. (3) Issue a warning and accuse Joe of being an alcoholic to let him know you are aware of his problem. (4) Talk with Joe to see if he will discuss his drinking. If he admits that he has a

drinking problem, delay the final warning and suggest that the company will be reasonably flexible if he makes a serious attempt to seek professional aid. (5) If he does not admit he has a drinking problem, let him know that the next absence will cost him his job.

6. *Evaluate the Alternative.* The cost of training a replacement is the same for each alternative. Alternative 1 ignores cost and other criteria. Alternative 2 and 3 do not adhere to company policy, which advocates counseling, where appropriate, to assist employees in overcoming personal problems. Alternative 4 is designed for the benefit of both Joe and the company. It might save a good employee if Joe is willing to seek assistance. Alternative 5 is primarily for the benefit of the company. Final warning might provide some initiative for Joe to admit that he has a drinking problem. If so, dismissal might be avoided, but further absences will no longer be tolerated.

7. *Choose the Best Alternative.* Joe does not admit that he has a drinking problem. Choose Alternative 5.

8. *Implement the Best Alternative.* Write up the case, and issue the final warning.[5]

Decision Types   The complexity of the decision process depends upon whether the decision is programmed or nonprogrammed.[6] **Programmed decisions** are repetitive and well-defined, and procedures exist for resolving the problems. Programmed decisions are well-structured, because criteria of performance are normally clear, good information is available about current performance, alternatives are easily specified, and there is relative certainty that the chosen alternative will be successful. **Nonprogrammed decisions** are novel and poorly defined, and no procedure exists for solving them.[7] The organization has not seen the problem before, and may not know how to respond. Information about the extent of the problem is hard to obtain. Clear-cut criteria do not exist. Alternatives are fuzzy. Little certainty exists that a solution will solve the problem. Normally only one or two alternatives can be developed, so the solution will be custom-tailored to the problem.

Issuing the final warning to Joe Defoe was a programmable decision. The standard of expected behavior was clearly defined, information on the frequency and cause of Joe's absence was readily available, and acceptable alternatives and procedures were described. The rational procedure works best for programmable decisions. This procedure also works best when the decision-maker has sufficient time for an orderly, thoughtful process. Moreover, Alberta Manufacturing had mechanisms in place to implement the decision, once made. Circumstances in which goals are prescribed, information is available, implementation procedures are prescribed, and the manager has time to think things through are an ideal situation that is not typical of many decisions made in dynamic organizations. The decision to build a "Morgan Guaranty Building" described at the beginning of this chapter was a nonprogrammed decision. When decisions are nonprogrammed, ill-defined, and piling on top of one another, the individual manager may use intuition and experience rather than rational procedures.

Intuitive Approaches Medical scientists have known for some time that the brain has two hemispheres. Each hemisphere has distinct abilities for thinking, information-processing and decision-making. The left hemisphere functions in linear fashion.[8] It processes information in an orderly way, one bit after another, and is associated with logical, analytical thinking skills. The left brain works best with discrete symbols such as numbers. Analytical activities such as mathematics, statistics, and accounting are essentially left-hemisphere functions.

The right hemisphere is specialized for opposite processes. Information bits are processed simultaneously, rather than sequentially, and the brain looks for overall patterns and relationships among elements. The right brain handles fuzzy data and vague impressions rather than discrete elements, and seeks overall patterns rather than logical sequences.

Many organization decisions are made through intuitive processes, which is a right-hemisphere activity. Intuitive processes are used for nonprogrammed decisions. A study of manager problem-finding showed that thirty of thirty-three problems were ambiguous and ill-defined.[9] Bits and scraps of unrelated information from informal sources resulted in a pattern in the manager's mind. The manager could not "prove" a problem existed, but knew intuitively that a certain area needed attention. Examples of problems discovered through the informal, intuitive process are:

1. Reorganization to exploit opportunity for multidivisional projects.
2. Changing social attitudes toward company.
3. Need for department to develop new products.
4. Address long-term growth through reorganization.
5. Effect of changing technology on sales.
6. Creation and placement of new departments.[10]

Intuitive processes may also be used in the problem-solution stage. A survey found that executives frequently made decisions without explicit reference to the impact on profits or other measurable outcomes of the organization.[11] Many intangible factors, such as a person's credibility, concern for the support of other executives, fear of failure, and social attitudes, influence selection of the best alternative. These factors cannot be quantified in a systematic way, so intuition may guide the choice of a solution. Managers may make a decision based upon what they sense to be right rather than upon what they can document with hard data.

Intuition appears to originate in the "subconscious" part of a person's thinking process. Decisions are made with more than rational, discrete elements. The absence of conscious decision criteria should not be interpreted to mean that intuitive decisions are random or irrational. The manager's intuitive processes are built up through trial and error experience. Past experience with intangible elements is registered in the right hemisphere. In cases in which the manager's "gut feeling" or "hunch" disagrees with a decision made by analytical procedures, the intuitive decision is often correct. Some of the worst mistakes are made when managers ignore intuition in favor of hard data and so-called tangible evidence.[12]

Presidential Decision-Making

"The biggest poker pot I every raked in, I won with a pair of nines."
The company's president paused for effect before his waiting executive
group. "The point I'm trying to make is this: A sense of relative values
and timing—waiting it out and hanging in there when the big chips are
flying and the signals are confusing—is the key in our business, just as
it is in poker. Lately, we've had to call some stiff bets—extreme interest
rate fluctuations, an unprecedented sales drop, and a big inventory
buildup. Our stock hasn't come back like it should have, either.

"Well, what do we do?" he asked. "Do we fold and wait for the next
hand? Cut the dividend? Close down the new research center? Spin off
your business, Al?" (This with a glare at the manager of the troubled
WHIZ division, a high-technology growth business entered in the late
1960s that had consistently beaten its sales targets—and consistently lost
money.)

"That might look like plain common sense under the circumstances,"
the president continued. "But I think we'd be damn shortsighted to take
those kinds of steps. I'm convinced that we still hold winning cards.
Know what's going to happen when the economy finally absorbs this last
oil price increase completely, the Fed wakes up, and consumers start
feeling the tax cut? Well, I'll tell you. By the end of the year, inflation's
going to taper off to 5% or less, interest rates will settle back to normal,
and our customers will start spending again. Now when that happens,
do we want to be caught short of capacity.

"Of course we don't. If we're agreed on that, let's refigure the equity
issue we planned for the fourth quarter, take another cut at the capital
budget, tighten up where we can, and hold on to our cards for the next
round." And so, rejecting the alternative of major strategic or structural
change, the president and his executive group turned to a searching
discussion of cost-reduction possibilities.[13]

This president's metaphor is that business decision-making is like a poker
game. Hunch, feel, and intuitive processes are an important part of difficult
decisions.

Summary Individual managers use both rational and intuitive approaches
to make decisions. The rational and intuitive approaches complement one
another. Rational processes work best for analyzable, programmable problems. Intuitive processes are used for nonprogrammable decisions to incorporate non-quantifiable decision elements. Intuition is more than blind
faith. It works when managers have significant experience. Moreover, intuition will often be wrong. Managers often combine both processes for a
single decision. Analyzable elements of the decision will be quantified.
Intuition handles other, intangible elements. When the identification of a

problem or the implementation of a solution includes emotional, value, social, political, or other complex human elements, intuition and experience are an important part of the decision process.[14]

ORGANIZATIONAL DECISION-MAKING

Organizations are composed of managers who make decisions using both rational and intuitive processes. But a single manager making a decision is not representative of organizational decision processes. Many decisions involve multiple managers. Problem-identification and problem-solution involve many departments, multiple viewpoints, and even other organizations. These decisions are beyond the scope of an individual manager, because the decision is so complex and is relevant to many employees. Moreoever, large-scale organization decisions are often composed of sub-decisions made by individual managers. The overall decision may be less a conscious choice than a series of small, incremental decisions. The linking together of individual decisions into a significant organizational decision is a process that must be understood and controlled by the organization. Research into organizational decision-making has identified four models of organizational decision-making processes: the systems analysis model, the Carnegie model, the incremental decision process model, and the garbage can model.[15]

Systems Analysis Model

The systems analysis approach to organization-level decision-making is the analog to the rational approach by individual managers. Systems analysis came into being during World War II.[16] Mathematical and statistical techniques were applied to urgent, large-scale military problems that were beyond the ability of individual decision-makers. Consider the problem of a battleship trying to sink an enemy ship with its artillery. The enemy ship could be several miles away, and the calculation for aiming the ship's guns should consider distance, wind speed, shell size, the speed and direction of both ships, the pitch and roll of the firing ship, and curvature of the earth. Trial and error and intuition are not accurate, take far too long, and may never achieve success.

This is where systems analysis comes in. Analyses were able to identify the relevant variables involved in aiming the ship's guns, and could model them with the use of mathematical equations. Distance, speed, pitch, roll, shell size, and so on could be calculated and entered into the equations. The answer was immediate and the guns could begin firing. Factors such as pitch and roll were soon measured mechanically and fed directly into the targeting mechanism. Today, the human element is completely removed from the targeting process. Radar picks up the target and the entire sequence can proceed automatically.

Systems analysis yielded astonishing success for many military problems. This approach to decision-making diffused into corporations and business schools where techniques were studied and elaborated. Today, many corporations have departments assigned to systems analysis. The computer department develops information systems to provide data to managers on a continuous basis. These data pertain to problem-identification. Market research results, sales figures, market share calculations, and so forth signal potential deviations so that problems can be quickly identified. Operations research departments use sophisticated mathematical techniques to quantify relevant variables after a problem has been identified. Operations research personnel may work in conjunction with departments such as market research or engineering to gather information to feed into mathematical models. A quantitative representation of alternative solutions, and the probability of each one solving the problem, are developed using devices such as linear programming, bayesian statistics, PERT charts, and other analytical devices. These techniques have become established parts of the business college curriculum, and are typically taught in statistics and finance courses.

Systems analysis is an excellent device for organizational decision-making when problems are analyzable and when the number of variables is beyond the ability of individual decision-makers to handle. Mathematical models have been constructed that contain a thousand or more variables, each one relevant in some way to the ultimate outcome. Economic criteria can be inserted into these models so that cost-efficient methods as well as those most likely to achieve a given goal can be identified. Even relatively simple problems, such as moving a machine shop from one building to another, are appropriate for systems analysis. Each piece of machinery can be identified. Required moving time and human resources can be estimated. The appropriate moving sequence can be modeled on a flow chart that specifies all decision points for the most efficient and least expensive transfer to the new building.

IN PRACTICE 9.3

Commercial Airlines

The problem involved the training of stewardesses, of whom the company employed approximately one thousand. Most of these [women] left the airline before they had given two years of service, primarily to get married. Because of the high rate of attrition, the airline had a continuous need to recruit and train additional stewardesses.

The company had set up a stewardess training school. It was capable of conducting three classes of fifty [persons] each. Actual training took five and a half weeks. An additional half-week was required for outfitting; a week was required to get them to their bases after training. This made for a total of eight weeks "lead time."

The company wanted to know how often it should run a class and how large the classes should be. On examination it became apparent that this was a familiar problem in production and inventory control. The conversion of a young woman (the raw material) into a stewardess (the finished product) by training (the production process) has associated with it an inventory carrying cost (the salary paid to excess [women] whose available time for work is not completely used), shortage costs (those associated with emergency measures of cancellations of flights arising from shortage of stewardesses), and setup costs associated with preparing the school for a class. The problem, then, was one of determining the size and frequency of "production runs" so as to minimize the sum of these costs, that is, to find the economic "lot sizes."

The appropriate mathematical analysis was applied to this familiar problem and it was solved, yielding a set of tables that the school administrator could use to conduct his operation in an optimal way. The savings indicated were impressive.[17]

Systems analysis can accurately and quickly solve problems far too complicated for human processing. Systems analysis is at its best when applied to problems that can be structured in a logical way, but simply are too vast for the human mind to comprehend.

Systems analysis has also produced many failures.[18] When the technique is misapplied, the results can be a disaster. Part of the reason, as we discussed in the last chapter, is that quantitative data are not rich. The computer-based scanning systems of the organization provide abundant data, but only about tangible, measurable factors. Intangible, informal cues that indicate the existence of a problem have to be sensed on a more personal basis by managers.[19] The same is true in the decision-solution stage. The most sophisticated mathematical analyses are of no value if the important factors cannot be quantified and included in the model. Consumer "tastes," product "beauty," and the "warmth" or "feel" of an advertising campaign are qualitative dimensions. Numbers can be assigned to these dimensions but at the risk of oversimplification. When calculations are finished, the final answer may be wrong. In these situations, the important role of systems analysis is to act as a supplement to manager decision-making. Quantitative results can be given to relevant management groups for discussion and interpretation to use along with their informal opinions, judgments, and intuition. The final decision will include important qualitative factors as well as quantitative calculations.

The Carnegie Model

The Carnegie model of organizational decision-making is based upon the work of Richard Cyert, James March, and Herbert Simon, who were all located at Carnegie-Mellon University.[20] Until their work, research in economics assumed that business firms made decisions as a single entity, as if all relevant information was funneled to the top decision-maker for a choice. Research by the Carnegie group indicated that many managers are involved in organizational decisions. The final choice is based upon a political coalition among these managers. The coalition would include managers from line departments, staff specialists, and even external groups such as powerful customers, bankers, or union representatives.

Political coalitions are needed for two reasons. First, organizational goals are ambiguous, and operative goals of departments are inconsistent. When goals are ambiguous and inconsistent, problem-identification is difficult.

Managers disagree about problem priorities. They must bargain about problems and build a coalition around priorities. Coalition-building is thus very important for the problem-identification stage of decision-making.

The second reason for political coalitions is that individual managers are intendedly rational, but function with human cognitive limitations. Managers do not have the time, resources, or mental capacity to identify all dimensions and to process all information relevant to a decision. The world is far too complex to be known by a single person. Lack of understanding means that managers experience uncertainty. If customers decrease purchases, for example, managers cannot be certain of the cause or the best response. These limitations lead to coalition-building and political behavior. Managers talk to each other and exchange points of view to gather information and reduce uncertainty. People who have relevant information or a stake in the decision outcome are consulted. Joint decision-making will lead to an acceptable decision. A coalition is formed through the discussion and bargaining processes. The solution may be modified through discussion to meet the needs of managers whose support is needed to achieve implementation.

Bargaining and coalition-formation have several implications for organizational decision behavior. First, as discussed in chapter 2 on goals, decisions will be made to satisfice rather than to optimize problem solutions. An optimal solution cannot be identified, so the coalition will accept a solution that is perceived as satisfactory by coalition members. Second, managers will be concerned with immediate problems and short-run solutions. They engage in what Cyert and March called problemistic search.[21] **Problemistic search** means that managers look around in the immediate environment for a satisfactory solution to quickly resolve the problem. Managers don't expect a perfect solution when the situation is ill-defined and conflict-laden. This is in contrast to the systems analysis approach, which assumes that analysis can uncover every reasonable alternative. The Carnegie model says that search behavior is just sufficient to produce a satisfactory solution, and managers will normally adopt the first satisfactory solution that emerges. Third, discussion and bargaining are expecially important in the problem-identification stage of decision-making. Problems are identified through discussion and bargaining. Unless a coalition perceives a problem, the problem does not exist. The joint perception of whether performance is satisfactory is more important than any single manager's perception.

The Carnegie model thus points out that building a political coalition is a major part of organizational decision processes. Individuals are unable to be perfectly rational because of diverse goals and the complexity of organizational problems. This is especially true at upper management levels. Discussion and bargaining is a time-consuming process, so search procedures are usually simple, and the selected alternative satisfices rather than optimizes problem solution. When problems are programmed—they are clear and have been seen before—the organization will rely on previous procedures and routines. Rules and procedures resolve the need for renewed coalition-formation and political bargaining. Nonprogrammed decisions require substantial bargaining and conflict-resolution. The decision process described in the Carnegie model is summarized in figure 9.2.

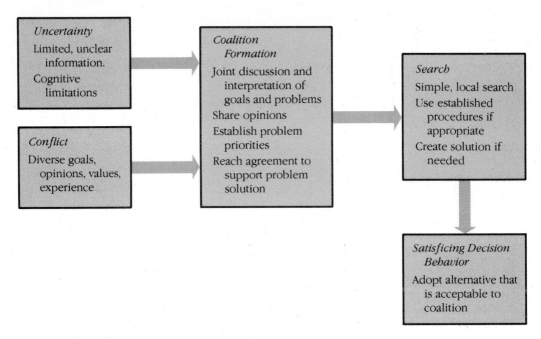

Figure 9.2. Choice Processes in the Carnegie Model.

Morgan Guaranty The decision by Morgan Guaranty executives to select a new building reflects the Carnegie model of decision-making. The identification of a problem and the desire to solve it by building a skyscraper were based upon a consensus of senior executives. Substantial bargaining and discussion took place in the months preceding the decision to act. Search was not extensive. The next block on Wall Street met their needs and was a satisfactory solution. After the cost of the solution skyrocketed because of the ransom price for the second building, the coalition began to fall apart. Some members no longer believed that the problem was urgent. Without a coalition to agree that a problem exists and to support a solution, a new decision will not be made. Morgan Guaranty still has not built a new Morgan Guaranty Building.

Incremental Decision Process Model

Henry Mintzberg and his associates at McGill University in Montreal approached organizational decision-making from a different perspective. They identified twenty-five decisions made in organizations, and traced the events associated with these decisions from beginning to end.[22] This research identified each step in the decision sequence. This approach to decision-making places less emphasis on the political and social factors described in the Carnegie model, but tells us more about the specific activities undertaken to reach an organizational solution.

Sample decisions in Mintzberg's research included the choice of which jet aircraft to acquire for a regional airline, development of a new supper club, development of a new container terminal in harbor, identifying a new market for a deodorant, selection of a new plant for a manufacturing firm, installing a controversial new medical treatment in a hospital, and the decision to fire a star announcer.[23] The scope and importance of these decisions are revealed in the length of time taken to complete them. Most of these decisions took over a year, and one-third of them took over two years. Moreover, most of these decisions were nonprogrammed and required custom-made solutions.

One of the important discoveries from this research is that major organization choices are usually a series of small choices that combine to produce the major decision. Most organizational decisions are a series of nibbles rather than a big bite. Organizations progress through several decision points and may hit barriers along the way. Mintzberg called these barriers "decision interrupts," and a small interrupt may mean that the organization has to cycle back through a previous decision and change direction. Decision loops or cycles are one way the organization learns which alternatives will work. The small decisions and trial and errors accumulate into a large organizational decision. A small interrupt may shift the whole decision sequence in a new direction, and the ultimate solution may be very different from what was initially anticipated.

The pattern of decision stages discovered by Mintzberg is shown in figure 9.3. Each box indicates a possible step in the decision sequence. The steps take place in three major decision phases: the identification phase, the development phase, and the selection phase.

Identification Phase The identification phase begins with *recognition*. Recognition means that one or more managers become aware of a problem and the need to make a decision. Recognition is usually stimulated by a problem or an opportunity. A problem exists when elements in the external environment change or when internal performance is perceived to be below standard. Recognition of the problem typically required several cues, and the cues often were equivocal. In the case of firing a radio announcer, a few good comments about the announcer would be intermingled with bad comments from listeners, other announcers, and advertisers. Managers must interpret these cues until a pattern emerges that indicates a problem has to be dealt with.

The second step is *diagnosis,* which is where more information is gathered if needed to define the problem situation. Diagnosis may be systematic and formal or immediate and informal depending upon the severity of the problem. Severe problems do not have time for extensive diagnosis, because the response must be immediate. Mild problems are usually diagnosed in a more systematic manner.

Development Phase The development phase is when the response is shaped to solve the problem arising in the identification phase. The development of a solution takes one of two directions. First, *search* procedures may be used to seek out standard solutions and alternatives within the organization's current repertoire. Organization participants may look into

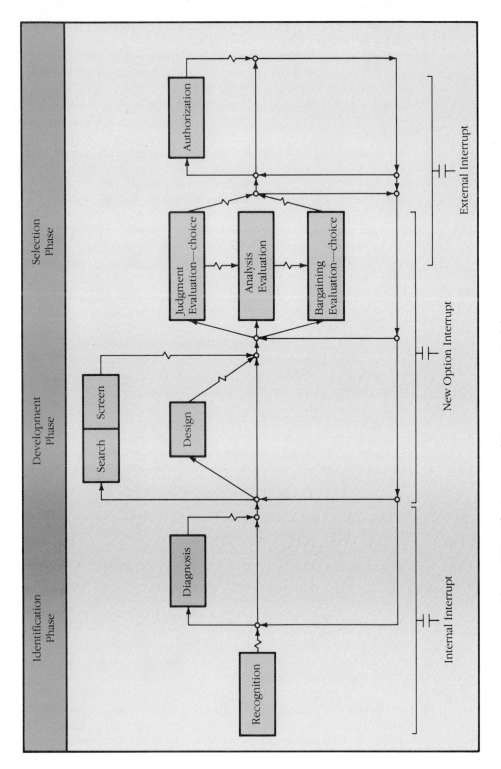

Figure 9.3. The Incremental Decision Process Model.
Source: Adapted and reprinted from "The Structure of Unstructured Decision Processes" by Henry Mintzberg, Duru Raisinghani, and André Théorêt published in *Administrative Science Quarterly* 21(2) (1976): 266 by permission of *The Administrative Science Quarterly.* Copyright © 1976 Cornell University.

their own memories, talk to other managers, or examine the formal procedures of the organization.

The second direction of search is to *design* a custom solution. This happens when the problem is novel so that previous experience has no value. Custom solutions require a complex, iterative procedure. Mintzberg found in these cases that key decision-makers have only a vague idea of the ideal solution. They work through a series of trials to test the feasibility of solutions and to learn more about them. Gradually, through a trial and error process, the custom-designed alternative will emerge. Development of the solution is a groping, incremental procedure, building a solution brick by brick.

Selection Phase   The *selection* phase is when the solution is chosen. However, the selection phase is not always a matter of a clear choice among alternatives. In the case of custom-made solutions, for example, selection is not so much a choice among alternatives as an evaluation of the single alternative that seems feasible.

Evaluation and choice may be accomplished in three ways. The *judgment* form of selection is used when the final choice falls upon a single decision-maker, and the choice involves judgment based upon experience rather than upon logical analysis. In *analysis,* alternatives are evaluated on a more systematic basis. Mintzberg found that the majority of decisions did not involve a distinct analysis and evaluation of alternatives. *Bargaining* occurs when selection involves a group of decision-makers. Each decision-maker may have a different stake in the outcome, so conflict emerges. Discussion and bargaining occur until a coalition is formed, as in the Carnegie model described earlier.

Authorization takes place when the decision is formally accepted by the organization. The decision may be passed up the hierarchy to the responsible hierarchical level. Authorization is often routine because the expertise and knowledge rest with the lower decision-makers who identified the problem and developed the solution. Top management does have the ability to commit or withhold resources, however, so they must approve it. A few decisions are rejected because of implications not anticipated by lower-level managers.

Dynamic Factors   The lower part of the chart in figure 9.3 shows lines running back toward the beginning of the decision process. These lines represent loops or cycles that take place in the decision process. Organizational decisions do not follow an orderly progression from recognition through authorization. Minor problems arise that force a loop back to an earlier stage. These are decision *interrupts.* If a custom-designed solution is not perceived as satisfactory, the organization may even have to go back to the very beginning and reconsider whether a problem truly exists, as happened in the Morgan Guaranty case at the beginning of this chapter. Feedback loops can be caused by problems of timing, politics, disagreement among managers, inability to identify an appropriate alternative or to implement the solution, turnover of managers, or the sudden appearance of a new alternative. For example, when an airline made the decision to acquire jet aircraft, the board authorized the decision. But shortly thereafter, a new chief executive was brought in and he cancelled the contract. He accepted the diagnosis of the problem, but insisted upon a new search for alternatives. New aircraft sources were considered. In the meantime, a foreign airline went out of business and two used aircraft became available at a bargain price. This presented an unexpected option, so the chief executive used his own judgment to authorize the purchase of the aircraft.[24]

Since most decisions take place over an extended period of time, circumstances change. Decision-making is a dynamic process that may require a number of cycles before a problem is solved. An example of the cycling that can take place is illustrated in the case below about a decision to build a new plant.

IN PRACTICE 9.4

Manufacturing Plant

A small manufacturing firm was faced with a series of pressures that indicated that its plant was obsolete. A proposal to sell the building was developed (design), and a real-estate agent then contacted (search), but no buyers were found. It was then realized that the city might expropriate the land (interrupt), and an agent was hired to negotiate a good price should that occur. Meanwhile, a neighboring firm moved out, and their adjoining parking lot was acquired to provide room for expansion or to increase the expropriation value of the property (evaluation-choice). At the same time, the firm employed architects to investigate two alternatives, but rejected both proposals as too expensive (evaluation-choice), and attention was then focused on moving. Three alternative sites were found (search), and employees were polled and road networks investigated (evaluation). One area proved to be the most desirable, and when an existing facility was found there at a good price (search), it was identified as a favorite candidate and purchased (evaluation-choice). The company planned the modification of the building (design), and commenced the alteration. Two months later, however, the provincial government expropriated at the same time both the old plant and the new and gave the firm a short time to vacate (interrupt). Now the firm faced a crisis. It did, however, have a considerable source of funds from the expropriation and could consider buying land and building a new plant. Only one area was investigated, and a suitable site was located (search). The firm obtained rezoning sanctions from the municipal government, a mortgage from the bank (design), and the assurance that this property would not be expropriated (authorization). The site was purchased (evaluation-choice), and the engineering department, in consultation with the architect, prepared building plans (design); the plans were quickly finalized (evaluation-choice).[25]

What started out as a basic sequential decision became a dynamic decision process. Several interrupts occurred so that several small decision cycles were completed before the plant was finally built. This single decision took over four years to complete.

Incremental Process versus Carnegie Model

At the beginning of this chapter, decision-making was defined as two stages—problem-identification and problem-solution. The incremental process model and the Carnegie model describe organizational responses to uncertainty in each stage of decision-making. The Carnegie description of political coalitions is most important when problem-identification is ambiguous and managers disagree. Discussion, negotiation, and coalition-building are necessary to reach agreement about problems and priorities. Once agreement is reached, the organization can move toward a solution.

The incremental process model describes the process organizations use to reach a solution when alternatives are not clear. After managers agree upon the problem, the step-by-step process is a way of trying various solutions to see what will work. When problem solution is unclear, various ideas may have to be tried to solve the problem.

The two models do not disagree with one another. They describe how organizations make decisions when either problem identification or solution is uncertain. The application of these two models to the stages in the decision process is illustrated in figure 9.4. When both parts of the decision process are highly uncertain simultaneously, the organization is in an extremely difficult position. Decision processes for organizations in that situation are described in the garbage can model.

The Garbage Can Model

The garbage can model is one of the most recent and interesting descriptions of organizational decision processes.[26] The garbage can model was developed to explain decision-making in organizations that have high uncertainty. Cohen, March, and Olsen, the originators of the model, called the extremely uncertain conditions an "organized anarchy."[27] Organized anarchies do not have the normal hierarchy of authority and bureaucratic decision rules. Instead, organized anarchies have three characteristics.

Figure 9.4. Organizational Decision Process When Either Problem Identification or Solution Is Uncertain.

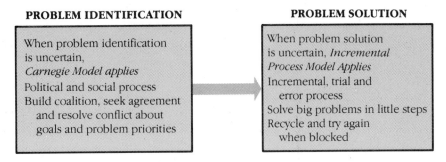

PROBLEM IDENTIFICATION

When problem identification is uncertain, *Carnegie Model applies*
Political and social process
Build coalition, seek agreement and resolve conflict about goals and problem priorities

PROBLEM SOLUTION

When problem solution is uncertain, *Incremental Process Model Applies*
Incremental, trial and error process
Solve big problems in little steps
Recycle and try again when blocked

1. *Problematic Preferences.* Problems, alternatives, solutions, and goals are ill-defined. Ambiguity characterizes each aspect of a decision process.
2. *Unclear, Poorly Understood Technology.* Cause and effect relationships are difficult to identify. The knowledge base that applies to decisions is not clear.
3. *Fluid Participation.* Organizational roles experience turnover of participants. In addition, the organization is energy-poor. Employees are busy and have only limited time to allocate to any one problem or decision. Participation in any given decision will be fluid and limited.

The organized anarchy describes organizations characterized by rapid change and a collegial, nonbureaucratic environment. One example is the university setting because traditional hierarchical decision-making procedures do not apply. No organization fits the organized anarchy circumstances all the time. Most organizations will occasionally find themselves in positions of making decisions under unclear, problematic circumstances. The garbage can model is useful for understanding some types of decisions in all organizations.

The unique and important characteristic of the garbage can model is that the decision process is not a sequential series of steps that begins with a problem and leads to a solution. Indeed, the problem-identification and problem-solution stages may not even be related to each other. Solutions often are not connected to problems. Problems may exist and never generate a solution. The reason problems and solutions are not connected is that decisions are the outcome of independent streams of events within the organization. The four streams relevant to organizational decision-making are as follows.

1. *Problems.* Problems are points of dissatisfaction with current activities and performance. Problems represent a gap between desired performance and current activities. Problems are perceived to require attention. However, problems are distinct from choices and solutions. The problem may lead to search or it may not. Problems may not be solved when solutions are adopted.
2. *Solutions.* "A solution is somebody's product."[28] Solutions represent a flow of ideas and alternatives through the organization. Ideas may be brought into the organization by new personnel, or be invented by existing personnel. Participants may be attracted to certain ideas and push them as logical choices. Attraction to an idea may cause an employee to look for a problem to which it can be attached. Solutions exist independently of problems.
3. *Participants.* Organization participants come and go throughout the organization. People are hired, reassigned, and fired. Participants vary widely in their ideas, perception of problems, experience, values, and training. The problems and solutions recognized by one participant will differ from those recognized by another participant. Time pressures lead participants to allocate different amounts of participation to a given problem or solution.

4. *Choice Opportunities.* Choice opportunities are those occasions when an organization makes a decision. An alternative is authorized and implemented. Choice opportunities occur when contracts are signed, when people are hired, or responsibilities allocated. Choice opportunities require a response from the formal organization. They may be precipitated by events such as an urgent problem, the proposal of an idea, or by a supplier who wants an answer on the purchase of new equipment.

The importance of the concept of independent streams is that organizational decision-making takes on a random quality. Problems, solutions, participants, and choices are flowing through the organization. In one sense, the organization is a large garbage can in which these streams are being stirred, as illustrated in figure 9.5. When a problem, solution, participant, and choice happen to connect at one point, the problem may be solved. But it also may not be solved. The solution may not fit because trial and error learning is required. An individual choice opportunity can be considered a small garbage can. Any problem and solution may be connected when a choice is made. But the problem does not always relate to the solution and the solution may not solve the problem. Organizational decisions simply are not the result of the logical step-by-step sequence of events that other descriptions of decision-making imply. Organization members are intendedly rational, but events are so ill-defined and complex that decisions, problems, and solutions are independent. Four consequences of the garbage can decision process for organizational decision-making are described below.

1. *Solutions Are Proposed Even When Problems Do Not Exist.* An employee may be sold on an idea and may try to sell it to the rest of the organization. An example was the adoption of computers by many organizations during the 1950s and 1960s. The computer was an exciting solution and was pushed both by computer manufacturers and systems analysts within organizations. The computer did not solve any problems in those initial applications. Indeed, some computers caused more problems than they solved.
2. *Choices Are Made Without Solving Problems.* A choice may be made with the intention of solving a problem, but under conditions of high uncertainty the choice may be incorrect. Moreover, many choices just happen. People decide to quit, the organization's budget is cut, or a new policy bulletin is issued. These choices may be oriented toward problems but do not necessarily solve them.
3. *Problems May Persist Without Being Solved.* Organization participants get used to certain problems and give up trying to solve them. Or participants may not know how to solve certain problems because the technology is unclear. Consequently, a problem often does not start the decision-making process. A university in Canada was placed on probation by the American Association of University Professors because a professor had been denied tenure without due process. The probation was not a severe hindrance because the university could still recruit new professors.

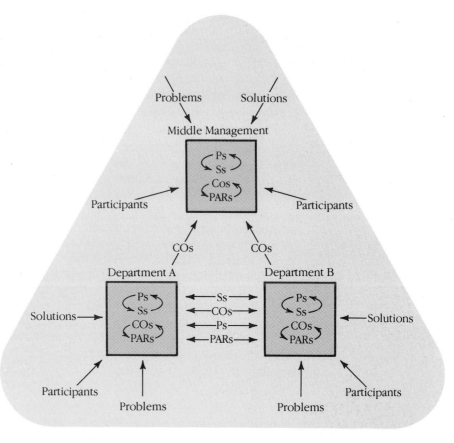

Figure 9.5. Illustration of Independent Streams of Events in the Garbage Can Model of Decision-Making. (P = problems; S = ideas for solutions; CO = choice opportunity; PAR = participants.)

Yet the probation was a nagging annoyance that the administrators wanted to remove. Fifteen years later, the nontenured professor died. The probation continues because the university did not acquiesce to the demands of the heirs or the Association to reevaluate the case. The university would like to solve the problem, but administrators are not sure how, and they do not have the resources to allocate to it. The probation problem persists without a solution.

4. *A Few Problems Are Solved.* The decision process does work in the aggregate. In computer simulation models of the garbage can model, important decisions were often resolved. Solutions do find appropriate problems and interested participants so that a choice is made. Of course, not all problems are resolved when choices are made, but the organization does move in the direction of problem reduction.

University Speech Program

The catalogue for 1970–1971 contains a section discussing the faculty and program for the Department of Speech and Drama. Twenty faculty members and 117 courses are listed. In 1971–1972, the catalogue was changed. There is now a Department of Drama with a faculty of fifteen members and 100 courses. There was no longer any mention of speech as a program or division . . . .

In 1956, a new dean was appointed to head the College of Liberal Arts. The dean came to the university with the expressed intention of making the university into one of the best in the country. Departments were encouraged to seek national reputations through new appointments. A series of events affecting the speech program followed the arrival of the new dean. Although he was not responsible for initiating all of them, there is no question that he contributed to the climate that produced them:

1. One of the full professors in rhetoric and public speaking retired in 1965 and was not replaced at that level.
2. In 1957, the faculty involved in speech correction, psychology, and audiology left the department to form a new section in the college of medicine at the university.
3. In 1958, the undergraduate major in speech was eliminated . . . .
4. Also in 1958, the most highly regarded young professor in the speech program was allowed to resign his assistant professorship to accept an appointment at a competing major university.

In a period when most programs at the university were expanding and improving, the speech program was contracting and allowing its best faculty to leave.

In December 1961, a new dean, with similar attitudes, became Dean of the College of Liberal Arts. Within the next two years, there was a new spurt of activity. By this time, the faculty in rhetoric and public speaking consisted of one full professor [Art Jensen], one assistant professor who had been there for several years, and three instructors or acting assistant professors who had only recently been appointed. . . .

A few weeks later, Professor Jensen died, leaving the program in rhetoric and public speaking without any tenured faculty members . . . . The associate dean was to say fifteen months later . . . that he had informed the faculty that "the situation obtaining in the speech program was unprecedented in university practice—namely, that work on the graduate level was being directed by a group of faculty members not one of whom had been carrying on an active program of research and publication such as is usually involved in graduate teaching and one of whom had not yet completed the work for his Ph.D. degree."

The speech professors involved interpreted the message of the meeting to be that the Ph.D. program in speech should be reorganized . . . .

At the same time, the deans were moving toward establishing a new Department of Communication Science as a modern, academically respectable form of "journalism" program . . . . In 1963, the new department was formally created and the second exodus of program and faculty occurred from the Department of Speech and Drama.

In [1968] two events occurred. The program in English for foreign students was transferred (along with the relevant faculty member) to the Department of Linguistics; and the senior assistant professor in speech was promoted to a tenure position as an Associate Professor of Speech and Education, in effect moving to the College of Education.

By this time, there was a new associate dean in the College of Liberal Arts. He was faced with the question of the renewal of contracts in speech for non-tenured faculty. On the basis of a brief review of other speech departments in the country and of the scholarly work of the faculty in this program, the associate dean recommended that the program in speech be discontinued. The recommendation came at the same time as pressures grew to find ways of saving money in the university budget and was accepted quickly by the dean and the provost of the university.[29]

The decision to eliminate the speech program illustrates many characteristics of the garbage can model. First, a number of participants came and went in the decision process. There was a turnover among deans and faculty members, and new participants brought new orientations and values to the decision. Second, the larger decision process was the result of streams of small events. Several small problems surfaced in the speech program. Several choices were made, such as increasing or decreasing the emphasis on the program, hiring and firing faculty, making transfers, and adding new administrators. These streams of events accumulated into the larger decision to eliminate the program. Third, many of the choices had little to do with problems. Letting a research-oriented faculty member leave, for example, was independent of the decision to drop the program, but was eventually connected with it. Fourth, the system had more than one solution. The faculty within the speech program pushed one set of ideas and the deans pushed another set. The proposed solutions represented outcomes each group wanted to achieve. Fifth, the ultimate decision to drop the program was made in response to a problem unrelated to the program itself, which was to save money for the university. Overall, the decision process had a random, chancy flavor characteristic of garbage can processes. But the apparent randomness did not necessarily work against the organization. An important problem was eventually resolved, although for reasons other than those in the immediate situation.

Garbage Can Strategies Garbage can decision processes occur in most organizations some of the time. They occur regularly in a few organizations that are dominated by problematic preferences, unclear technology, and fluid participation. In these settings, logical analysis and other traditional decision procedures are of little value. Cohen and March suggested strategic rules to follow that will accomplish choices in a garbage can setting.

Rule One: Spend Time. *Energy is a scarce resource in garbage can situations. People who spend time on a problem or situation find themselves in a strong position. By providing a scarce resource, they lay a claim for future consideration of problems they consider important. By spending time, they also become a major information source. Others turn to them for information and knowledge about the problem or solution. Finally, by being involved in something important to the organization, the individuals are likely to be present when something relevant is discussed.*

Rule Two: Persist. *Circumstances change rapidly in a garbage can decision situation. A different set of people and concerns will appear each time a problem is considered or a proposal discussed. Failure may occur today, but success may easily result at a future time. Always try again.*

Rule Three: Overload the System. *Overload means having a large number of projects for organizational action. The organization is energy poor so significant analysis, discussion, and negotiation will not occur on every issue. A person should not become committed to any single project. There are innumerable ways it can be defeated. But garbage can processes cannot cope with large numbers of projects. Any one project may be lost, but the organization will not stop everything. Some projects will get through.[30]*

CONTINGENCY DECISION-MAKING FRAMEWORK

This chapter has covered several models of organizational decision-making, including systems analysis, the Carnegie model, the incremental decision model, and the garbage can model. We have also discussed rational and intuitive decision processes used by individual managers. Each decision model is a relatively accurate description of the actual decision process, yet they differ from each other. Systems analysis, for example, reflects a different set of decision assumptions and procedures than does the garbage can model.

One very important reason for different models is that they appear in different organizational situations. The use of a model is contingent on the organization setting. Systems analysis is an appropriate decision process when the decision involves a large number of variables that can be measured and used in quantitative analysis. Garbage can procedures are appropriate when uncertainty is very high, so that problems, alternatives, and other relevant factors cannot be objectively identified.

Two characteristics of organizations that determine the use of decision models are (1) preferences about goals and (2) beliefs about cause-effect relationships.[31] Analyzing organizations along these two dimensions suggests which model will be used to make decisions.

Preferences about goals refers to the agreement among managers about which organizational goals to pursue. This variable ranges from complete agreement to complete disagreement. When managers agree, the goals of the organization are clear, and so are standards of performance. When they disagree, organization direction and performance expectations are in dispute. An example of goal disagreement occurred within the Penn Central railroad after it went bankrupt. Some managers wanted to adopt the goal of being a railroad organization, and to become efficient and profitable in that activity. Other managers wanted to diversify into other businesses. They believed Penn Central should not concentrate on railroad operations, and could make profits from other businesses. Eventually a strong coalition formed in favor of diversification, and that is the goal that was adopted. The disagreement among managers in Penn Central reflected a basic disagreement about the purpose and goals of the organization.

Agreement about goals is important for the problem-identification stage of decision-making. When goals are clear and agreed upon, they provide clear standards and expectations for performance. Problems can be identified. When goals are not agreed upon, problem-identification is uncertain, and more attention has to be focused on it.

Beliefs about cause-effect relationships reflect the knowledge and understanding about how to reach organizational goals. This variable can also range from complete agreement to complete disagreement among managers. An example of disagreement about cause-effect relationships is reflected in market strategies at 7-Up. The goal is clear and agreed upon—increase market share from 6% to 7% by 1982. But the cause-effect processes for achieving this increase in market share are not agreed upon. A few managers want to use discount pricing in supermarket outlets. Other managers believe they should increase the number of soda fountain outlets in restaurants and fast-food chains. A few other managers insist that the best approach is to increase advertising through radio and television. Managers can not agree on what would cause an increase in market share. To date, the advertising judgment has prevailed at 7-Up. It has not worked very well, which confirms the uncertainty about cause-effects processes.

Beliefs about cause-effect relationships are important to the problem-solution stage of decision-making. When cause-effect relationships are well understood, the appropriate alternatives can be identified and calculated with some degree of certainty. When cause and effect is poorly understood, rational alternatives are ill-defined and uncertain. Intuition and judgment become important decision criteria.

The contingency decision framework brings together the two organizational dimensions of preference about goals and beliefs about cause-effect relationships. Figure 9.6 shows how these two variables influence the decision situation. Agreement about goals and cause-effect relationships determines whether the problem identification and solution stages are uncertain. Low uncertainty stages mean that rational, analytical procedures can be used.

Figure 9.6. Contingency Decision Situations.

High uncertainty leads to greater use of judgment, bargaining, and other less systematic procedures.

Figure 9.7 describes the contingency decision framework. Each cell represents an organizational situation that is appropriate for certain decision-making approaches.

Cell 1 Rational decision procedures take place when goals are agreed upon and cause-effect relationships are well understood. Decisions are made in a computational manner. Alternatives can be identified and the best solution adopted through calculations. The rational models described earlier in this chapter, both for individual managers and for the organization, are appropriate when both goals and cause-effect relationships are well understood. The identification of problems is straightforward, and the calculation of the best solution is also straightforward. This type of decision process is used for programmed decisions. Performance standards are identified in advance. Expected behavior is known. When deviations occur, a logical process can be used to decide upon the solution. When an employee is absent from work for the fifth time, procedures can be identified for handling this problem and for bringing it to a speedy resolution. When a problem is large and involves many variables, systems analysis techniques are appropriate.

Cell 2 The important step here is to use bargaining and compromise to reach agreement about goals and problems. Diverse opinions about goals are present in this organization setting. One goal may be achieved at the expense of another goal. The priorities given to respective goals and the appropriate levels of performance are decided through extensive discussion and coalition-building.

Managers in this situation should use broad participation to reduce uncertainty in the decision process. Opinions should be surfaced and discussed until compromise is reached. The organization will not otherwise move forward as an integrated unit. In the case of Penn Central Railroad, the diversification strategy was eventually adopted, but only after extensive bargaining.

The Carnegie model reflects disagreement about organizational goals. When groups within the organization disagree, or when the organization is in conflict with relevant constituencies (government regulators, suppliers, union), bargaining and negotiation are required. The bargaining strategy is especially relevant to the problem-identification stage of the decision process. Cause-effect relationships are well understood, but problems are uncertain. Once the bargaining and negotiation is completed, the organization will have a sense of direction and standards against which to compare performance.

Cell 3 Judgment reflects the use of manager experience and intuition to choose among decision alternatives. In this situation, goals and standards of performance are well-defined, but alternative solutions are vague and uncertain. Cause-effect processes to solve the problem are ill-defined and poorly understood. When an individual manager faces this situation, intuition

Figure 9.7. Contingency Framework for Using Decision Models.

	Preferences about Goals	
	Agreement	Disagreement
Agreement	**Cell 1** Managers: Rational, Approach, Computation Organization: Systems Analysis	**Cell 2** Managers: Bargaining, Coalition formation Organization: Carnegie Model
Disagreement	**Cell 3** Managers: Judgment, Intuition Organization: Incremental Decision Model	**Cell 4** Managers: Inspiration, Imitation Organization: Garbage Can Model

Beliefs about Cause-Effect Relationships (vertical axis label, from Agreement at top to Disagreement at bottom)

will be the decision guideline. The manager will rely on past experience and judgement to make the decision. Rational, analytical approaches are not effective because the alternatives cannot be identified and calculated in a logical way. Hard facts and accurate information are not available.

The incremental decision process model reflects a judgment strategy on the part of the organization. Once the problem or crisis is identified, a sequence of small steps will eventually lead to a solution. Movement may be slow because of trial and error. As new problems or barriers arise, the organization may recycle back to an earlier point. Eventually, over a period of months or years, the organization will acquire sufficient experience to solve the problem in a satisfactory way.

Cell 4 Inspiration and imitation take place in the most uncertain of decision situations. Goals are not agreed upon, and cause-effect relationships are not clear. Inspiration refers to an innovative, creative solution that is not reached by logical means. A new idea from an unexpected source may be adopted. Sometimes the organization will imitate ideas adopted by other organizations simply because managers don't know what else to do.

For a manager experiencing this high level of uncertainty, intuition and creativity are important for both the problem-identification and problem-solution stages of decision-making. Indeed, the solution may precede the problem. In a university accounting department, faculty were completely dissatisfied with their current circumstances, but could not agree upon the direction the department should go. Some faculty members wanted a greater research orientation, others wanted greater orientation toward business firms and accounting applications. The disagreement about goals was compounded because neither group was sure about the best technique for achieving their goals. The ultimate solution was inspirational on the part of the dean. An accounting research center was established with funding from big-eight accounting firms. The funding was used to finance research activities for faculty interested in basic research, and to provide contact with business firms for other faculty. The solution helped provide a common goal and unified people within the department to work toward that goal.

When the entire organization is characterized by continuous high uncertainty with regard to goals and cause-effect relationships, the garbage can model applies. The rational decision sequence that starts with problem-identification and ends with a problem solution does not take place. Problems and solutions are encountered as independent streams. When problems, solutions, and participants make contact within the organization, decisions are made. Solutions will precede problems as often as problems precede solutions. In this type of organization, managers can encourage widespread discussion of problems and ideas to facilitate the opportunity for choices to be made. Choices will often not resolve problems, but choices must be made anyway. Eventually, through trial and error, the organization will solve some problems, perhaps by trying a variety of solutions. Substantial bargaining and political activity will also take place to decide upon goals and help identify relevant problems.

Adolph Coors Co.

In 1978, Adolph Coors Co. decided to enter the big time. An extensive marketing program was undertaken to thrust Coors into the national market and to stop competitors from encroaching on its territory.

By 1982, the plan clearly realized only limited success. Coors made some gains, such as with its new low-calorie beer. But overall the company was still having trouble hanging onto its territory and cracking new markets. In California, market share slipped by a third since 1976. In 1981, net income was down and so was total volume.

Industry observers say that Coors' goal of going national was associated with problems inside the company. Managers know what they want to achieve, but haven't yet learned to be a sophisticated competitor. The company's chairman suggested that Coors is on a learning curve to find out what works and what doesn't work.

The internal problems came to a head when two key marketing executives departed in 1981. The executives disagreed about marketing strategy. A few managers were pushing to go after new market segments. They wanted to spend money bolstering Coors' image in nontraditional areas. Senior management agreed with a partial effort in this direction, but decided the total marketing budget had to be cut back. Others criticized the decision to cut back, believing that Coors should be in hotter pursuit of the competition.

There are other disagreements as well. A few executives pushed to adopt a straightforward, national advertising campaign that would accompany price reduction. Another faction believed the company should direct its advertising toward developing a positive corporate image at the national level. A consultant claims that Coors is trying to sell a little bit of beer and a little bit of image, instead of putting forward a well-focused advertising program. Yet another idea proposed by an external consultant was that Coors should concentrate on entering the East coast market. He suggested building a plant there. Other advisors disagree, arguing that the East is a difficult market to crack. Coors should first square things away in its own backyard.

Why all the confusion and disagreement about how Coors should proceed? For years, Coors was a family-dominated corporation that didn't have to assert itself. Its original beer was so popular that people from other parts of the country would take trunkloads back home. Then Anheuser-Busch Co. and Miller Brewing Co. successfully penetrated Coors' following. Coors had to respond with bigger advertising budgets and a more aggressive marketing effort.

But the transition wasn't easy. The departure of the two marketing executives indicated the extensive disagreement about how to achieve Coors' national goals. Knowing what they want to achieve and doing it are two different things. Conflicts continued to persist, although not as severely. As one executive suggested, "We just see things a little differently."[32]

The executives at Adolph Coors Co. agree about goals, but disagree about cause-effect relationships (cell 3). Their goal is to move Coors into the national market and to increase market share, but the techniques for achieving that goal are not understood or agreed upon. Should advertising use a positive corporate image or a straightforward hard sell to accompany pricing promotion? These disagreements led to the departure of two executives. Coors' decisions reflect the incremental process model described by Mintzberg. Coors tries one strategy and then sees if it works. Coors can recycle and make new decisions as they understand the process better. The loss of key executives reduces the available experience, but Coors is rapidly gaining new experience about effective promotion strategy.

DECISION ERRORS

Organizational decisions, especially when made under conditions of uncertainty, produce many errors. The nature of organization decision-making does not enable managers to be certain about the correct alternative. This is especially true in situations characterized by little agreement about cause-effect relationships. Managers simply cannot determine or predict which alternative will correct the problem. In these cases, intuition, judgment, and trial and error are used to find solutions. But trial and error means that some trials will be in error. Solutions will be tried that do not work. Moreover, in situations characterized by disagreement over goals, political conflict and bargaining may result in the adoption of goals that are not compatible with the organization's skills or resources. In these cases, performance will be disappointing.

The point for managers is to move ahead with the decision process despite the uncertainty. Information about problems may be inadequate, and alternatives may seem ill-conceived. But managers must make decisions anyway. Managers must be willing to take risks. "Chaotic action is preferable to orderly inaction."[33] Action enables the organization to learn what works and to accumulate experience. When an alternative fails to improve performance, another alternative can be tried.

In many respects, decision-making in organizations is the opposite of decision-making in the college classroom. In most college courses, the problem is given and the appropriate alternatives and solutions can be identified. The classroom environment is a cell-1 situation. Problems are given, and students learn solution procedures. The students' responsibility is to find the right answer, and deviations from the correct answer are penalized. A correct answer is appropriate because both problems and cause-effect relationships are available to the students. That is not the case in most organizational settings, which are usually characterized by cells 2,

3, and 4. Only by making mistakes can managers and the organization acquire sufficient experience and knowledge to perform more effectively in the future. Robert Townsend, for example, gives the following advice:

Admit your mistakes openly, maybe even joyfully. Encourage your associates to do likewise by commiserating with them. Never castigate. Babies learn to walk by falling down. If you beat a baby every time he falls down, he'll never care much for walking.

My batting average on decisions at Avis was no better than .333. Two out of every three decisions I made were wrong. But my mistakes were discussed openly and most of them corrected with a little help from my friends.

Beware the boss who walks on water and never makes a mistake. Save yourself a lot of grief and seek employment elsewhere.[34]

Organizations stumble time and again. Notable mistakes include Braniff's disastrous and costly choice to invest $1 billion in new aircraft and to open new routes worldwide when air travel was declining; NBC's annual selection of promising TV series that immediately flop; Firestone's decision to manufacture the Firestone 500 radial tire without adequate technology and then to distort the facts when word of complaints and accidents began to surface; and Schlitz's decision to emphasize production efficiency over customer satisfaction and the change in beer ingredients that caused beer to turn flaky as it reached consumers. The possibility of failure must not stop organization decision processes. Based upon what we know about decision-making from this chapter, we can expect each of these corporations to form coalitions around key problems and follow a gradual, incremental process toward solutions. We can also expect an occasional new mistake.

SUMMARY AND INTERPRETATION

The single most important idea in this chapter is that most organizational decisions are not made in a logical, rational manner. Most decisions are not a series of steps that begins with problem-identification, then analysis of alternatives, and finally implementation of a certain solution. Decision processes are characterized by conflict, coalition-building, politics, trial and error, and mistakes. Intuition and hunch are often the criteria for choice. The decision process is disorderly, and may even seem random. In a few cases, the solution may actually drive the problem because someone likes an idea and tries to find a problem as an excuse to adopt it.

Another important idea is that individuals make decisions, but organizational decisions are not made by a single individual. Organizational decision-making is a social process. Only in rare circumstances do managers analyze problems and work through their solutions by themselves. Many problems are not clear, so widespread discussion and coalition-building take place. Once goals and priorities are set, alternatives to achieve those goals can be identified. A coalition also chooses the alternative in many cases. When managers do make an individual decision, it is often a small part of a larger decision process. Organizations solve big problems through a series of small steps. A single manager may initiate one step, but should be aware of the larger decision process in which it is embedded.

The greatest amount of conflict and coalition-building occurs when goals are not understood and agreed upon. Priorities must be established about which goals are most important and what problems should be solved first. If a manager attacks a problem other people do not agree with, the manager will lose support for the solution to be implemented. Thus, a substantial amount of time and activity should be spent in building a coalition in the problem-identification stage of decision-making. Once problems are identified and agreed upon, the organization can move toward solutions. Intuition and trial and error often characterize this part of the process. Under conditions of uncertainty the solution unfolds as a series of small steps that will gradually lead to an overall solution.

Finally, one of the most interesting descriptions of decision-making is the garbage can model. The garbage can model describes how decision processes can be random. It is not found in all organizations, but these processes do occur in most organizations some of the time. Decisions, problems, ideas, and people flow through organizations and mix together in various combinations. When a participant discovers an idea or makes a connection between a problem and a solution, the problem may be solved. But it may not, because neither the problem nor the solution was well understood. But through this process the organization gradually learns. Some problems may never be solved, but many will be, and the organization will move toward maintaining and improving its level of performance.

DISCUSSION QUESTIONS

1. A professional economist once told his class, "We assume that the firm's decisions are made by a single individual at the top of the organization. The organization is a single decision-making entity." Do you agree with the economist's view? Discuss.
2. The economist went on to say, "The individual decision-maker processes all relevant information and selects the economically rational alternative." Do you agree? Why or why not?
3. Briefly describe the eight steps in the rational approach to manager decision-making. Which steps are problem-finding and which are problem-solving?
4. When is intuition used in decision-making? Is intuition a valid decision technique? Is intuition likely to be used more often by decision-makers at the top or at the bottom of the organization?
5. For what types of organizational decisions would systems analysis be most appropriate?
6. The Carnegie model emphasizes the need for a political coalition in the decision-making process. When and why are coalitions necessary?

7. What are the three major phases in Mintzberg's incremental decision process model? Why might an organization recycle through one or more phases of the model?
8. An organization theorist once told his class, "Organizations never make big decisions. They make small decisions that eventually add up to a big decision." Explain the logic behind the organization theorist's statement."
9. What are the four streams of events in the garbage can model of decision-making? Why are they considered independent?
10. Explain the following statements in terms of garbage can decision processes: "Problems exist but may not be solved." "Solutions are proposed even when problems do not exist."
11. Why is persistence important to decision-making in an organized anarchy? Would persistence also be useful in other decision situations?
12. How does the amount of agreement among managers about goals influence the problem-identification process in organizations?
13. According to the contingency decision-making framework, what type of organizational situation is associated with the Carnegie model? The rational approach to decision-making?
14. Are there decision-making situations in which managers should always be expected to make the "correct" decision? Are there situations in which decision-makers should be expected to make mistakes?
15. Why are decision errors accepted in organizations but penalized in college courses that are designed to train managers?

GUIDES TO ACTION

As an organization manager:

1. Make decision processes fit the organizational situation.
2. Use a rational decision approach—computation, systems analysis—when the problem situation is well understood.
3. Use a coalition-building approach when organizational goals and problem priorities are in conflict. When managers disagree about priorities or the true nature of the problem, they should discuss and seek agreement about priorities. The Carnegie model emphasizes the need for building a coalition and maintaining agreement about goals and problem priorities.
4. Take risks and move the company ahead by increments when the problem is defined, but solutions are uncertain. Try solutions in a step-by-step manner to learn whether they work. Analytical procedures do not apply when possible solutions are unclear and uncertain.
5. Use garbage can procedures in a situation in which problems are not clear and underlying cause-effect relationships are not known. Move the organization toward better performance by flooding the organization with ideas, spending time working in important areas, and persisting with recommended solutions because the situation will change in the future.

Consider these Guides when analyzing the following cases and when answering the questions listed after each case.

CASES FOR ANALYSIS

1. FORT JACKSON HIGH SCHOOL DISTRICT

Part I July 17, 1969. Alan Ringlab, the new superintendent for the Fort Jackson School District, arrived in town to take over the new job as school superintendent. He was hired because he had impressive ideas for improving the school system. Parents and school board members had set a high priority on academic excellence.

Over the next few years, Mr. Ringlab set about achieving that goal. The school built a 2,000-seat auditorium and a 450-seat fine arts theater. The percentage of students going off to college increased to 85%. The football field was covered with astro-turf, and the school produced winning teams. The school district became a magnet for the community. Professional people and corporate executives wanted to move their families to Fort Jackson to take advantage of the school system. The district was free of racial and financial problems. Mr. Ringlab was the institutional leader, and the school board, parents, and teachers deferred to him.

Mr. Ringlab made occasional small mistakes when trying a new idea to improve academic excellence. They were corrected before any damage was done. The one lasting criticism was that the school's auditorium was too large for the school's needs. However, Mr. Ringlab is quick to point out that board members recommended an even larger auditorium, and he cut it back by 10%.

Mr. Ringlab's success was partly due to his previous experience as an educator. He had built up the academic reputations of two other school districts. Board members, teachers, and parents in Fort Jackson did not agree on, or understand, how to attain academic excellence. They were happy to turn the job over to him, and were pleased with the results.

Questions 1. In which quadrant of the contingency decision model (figure 9.7) was the Fort Jackson High School District when Mr. Ringlab arrived? Did the district experience uncertainty about goals for the school district, about how to achieve those goals, or both?
2. What organizational decision process was used at Fort Jackson? Did it fit the organizational situation? Discuss.

Part II June 22, 1982. Mr. Ringlab is preparing to leave Fort Jackson. He resigned under pressure from school board members, parents, and teachers.

The last straw was the teachers' strike last spring. The teachers were angry about the way the school was run and about budget cutbacks. They wanted salaries increased to keep ahead of inflation. Mr. Ringlab's labor relations skill was not sufficient to win over teachers who felt strongly about budget issues.

Parents were upset because the school district ran two consecutive deficits. Where was the money to come from? Other taxpayers complained about tax increases and were threatening a referendum to set a maximum limit on school taxes. They argued that the school received more and more money, and provided fewer educational services.

Selected parental groups were also becoming more assertive. They insisted on extensive special programs for underachievers, overachievers, and the handicapped. These demands came at a time when the cost of education was skyrocketing and revenues were not keeping pace.

The school board election in May demonstrated just how deeply the community was divided on the goals for the school system. Teachers, parental groups, and a taxpayer group all ran their own candidates. The three newly elected board members all disagreed with the direction Mr. Ringlab was taking the school. Mr. Ringlab knew that he had to either resign or be fired.

Board members and parents agree that Mr. Ringlab's strength was in building a first-rate academic school system. So long as there were plenty of resources to keep everyone happy, he did fine. But he was not skillful at getting to know teachers, parents, and taxpayers. The teachers would not rally behind him, and so they went on strike. The barriers existing between Mr. Ringlab and other groups are not insurmountable. Perhaps the new superintendent will do better.

The editor of the local newspaper said that the superintendent simply focused on the wrong problems. Mr. Ringlab continued working toward the goal of academic excellence when other groups no longer considered that so important. They wanted the budget under control, higher salaries, and special programs. He was unable to maintain his coalition, and could not build a new one. "You almost have to be a political broker in that situation," said a city council member. "Without a political coalition, you're out." [35]

Questions
1. In which quadrant of the contingency decision model (figure 9.7) was the Fort Jackson School District now? Did the district disagree about goals, about how to achieve those goals, or both? Discuss.
2. What decision process did Mr. Ringlab use? What model should he have used? Discuss.

2. EXXON CORPORATION

The toughest decisions in a corporation like Exxon concern future planning. What is going to happen between tomorrow and ten years from now? Many organizations try to develop a single scenario. Exxon, however, has moved to higher levels of planning sophistication. As a multinational corporation, events around the world can alter decision-making. Exxon forecasts include several game plans. They don't try to pin things down exactly, but project several courses of action depending upon critical events.

The stakes for decision-makers are high. In 1973, a $350 investment would produce a barrel of oil a day. The same amount of oil from the North Sea required an investment of $9,000. Today, the cost in some parts of the world is climbing toward $20,000. The executive decision-maker has to look years into the future, and consider the possibility of synthetic or other forms of fuel.

The shocker is that a large corporation like Exxon is not very good at projecting the future. They completely missed the oil boycott of 1973 and the high interest rates of 1974. The recession in 1981 and the accompanying high interest rates through 1982 also surprised planners.

To manage the enormous amounts of data, many corporations are using special computers. Computers monitor up to 140 inputs, which are used to project feasible courses of action. Executives then make decisions, such as whether to sell $100 million of long-term debt now or wait a year. A small mistake can cost millions of dollars.

Planners have become worried about the role of computers in decision-making. Computers tend to project from the past. Computer model builders are unable to spot unexpected events on the horizon. Econometric models have not been able to quantify key variables. Relationships among environmental elements change, and the computer is slow to detect the new relationships.

Exxon managers still use computer output. They feel that in an era of profound change, they need whatever information they can get. Computers provide a framework for analysis even if the answers are not always right. Computers do worst when projecting beyond the next twelve months.

The strategy at Exxon is to offset computer limitations with the skills of their planners. Theoretical types are intermingled with hard-nosed technicians. Planning has both an artistic component and a scientific component. The best planning decisions are a combination of both. Another strategy is to make planners out of doers. Line managers who have experience in the business are brought into the planning function. They can sense and interpret factors that computers miss.[36]

Questions
1. Why aren't computers relied on to a greater extent in corporate planning and decision-making?
2. Do you think it is effective for decision-makers to combine computer output with their own intuition and experience to reach a decision? Are these sources compatible? Explain.

NOTES

1. Shawn Tully, "The Block That Got Away," *Fortune,* July 13, 1981, p. 45.
2. This case was based on Tully, "The Block That Got Away," pp. 44–46; and Robert Guenther, "The Real Estate World's Version of Poker: Assembling Parcels for a Big-City Project," *Wall Street Journal,* May 18, 1982, p. 37.
3. Charles Lindblom, "The Science of 'Muddling Through'," *Public Administration Review* 19 (1954): 79–88.

4. Earnest R. Archer, "How to Make a Business Decision: An Analysis of Theory and Practice," *Management Review* 69 (February, 1980): 54–61.

5. Adapted from Earnest R. Archer, "How to Make a Business Decision: An Analysis of Theory and Practice," *Management Review,* February, 1980 (New York: AMACOM, a division of American Management Associations, 1980), pp. 59–61.

6. Herbert A. Simon, *The New Science of Management Decision* (Englewood Cliffs, NJ: Prentice-Hall, 1960), pp. 1–8.

7. *Ibid.*

8. Henry Mintzberg, "Planning on the Left Side and Managing on the Right," *Harvard Business Review* 54 (1976): 49–58.

9. Marjorie A. Lyles and Ian I. Mitroff, "Organizational Problem Formulation: An Empirical Study," *Administrative Science Quarterly* 25 (1980): 102–119.

10. *Ibid.*

11. Ross Stagner, "Corporate Decision Making: An Empirical Study," *Journal of Applied Psychology* 53 (1969): 1–13.

12. Thomas S. Isaack, "Intuition: An Ignored Dimension of Management," *Academy of Management Review* 3 (1978): 917–922.

13. From D. Bridgewater, D. Clifford, and T. Hardy, "The Competition Game Has Changed," *Business Horizons* 18 (1975): 5–20. Copyright © 1975 by the Foundation for the School of Business at Indiana University. Reprinted by permission.

14. Harold J. Leavitt, "Beyond the Analytic Manager," *California Management Review* 17 (1975): 5–12.

15. Charles J. McMillan, "Qualitative Models of Organizational Decision Making," *Journal of Management Studies* 5 (1980): 22–39; Paul C. Nutt, "Models for Decision Making in Organizations and Some Contextual Variables Which Stimulate Optimal Use," *Academy of Management Review* 1 (1976): 84–98.

16. Harold J. Leavitt, William R. Dill, and Henry B. Eyring, *The Organizational World* (New York: Harcourt Brace Jovanovich, 1973), ch. 6.

17. Russell L. Ackoff and Patrick Rivett, *A Manager's Guide to Operations Research* (New York: John Wiley, 1963), pp. 12–13. Reprinted by permission.

18. Leavitt, "Beyond the Analytic Manager." C. Jackson Grayson, Jr., "Management Science and Business Practice," *Harvard Business Review* 51 (July–August, 1973): 41–48.

19. Richard L. Daft and John C. Wiginton, "Language and Organization," *Academy of Management Review* 4 (1979): 179–191.

20. This discussion is based on Richard M. Cyert and James G. March, *A Behavioral Theory of the Firm* (Englewood Cliffs, NJ: Prentice-Hall, 1963), and James G. March and Herbert A. Simon, *Organizations* (New York: John Wiley, 1958).

21. Cyert and March, *Behavioral Theory of the Firm,* pp. 120–122.

22. This discussion is based on Henry Mintzberg, Duru Raisinghani, and André Théorêt, "The Structure of 'Unstructured' Decision Processes," *Administrative Science Quarterly* 21 (1976): 246–275.

23. *Ibid.*
24. *Ibid.,* p. 270.
25. *Ibid.,* p. 273.
26. Michael D. Cohen, James G. March, and Johan P. Olsen, "A Garbage Can Model of Organizational Choice," *Administrative Science Quarterly* 17 (March, 1972): 1–25; Michael D. Cohen and James G. March, *Leadership and Ambiguity: The American College President* (New York: McGraw-Hill, 1974).
27. Cohen, March, and Olsen, "Garbage Can Model."
28. *Ibid.,* p. 3.
29. James G. March and Pierre J. Romelaer, "Position and Presence in the Drift of Decisions," in James G. March and Johan P. Olsen, eds., *Ambiguity and Choice in Organizations* (Bergen: Universitepsfarbaget, 1976), pp. 254–258. Reprinted by permission.
30. Cohen and March, *Leadership and Ambiguity,* pp. 207–210.
31. Adapted from James D. Thompson, *Organizations in Action* (New York: McGraw-Hill, 1967), ch. 10, and McMillan, "Qualitative Models of Organizational Decision Making," p. 25.
32. This case is based on Lynda Schuster, "Internal Conflicts Inhibiting Coors Move to the Big Time," *Wall Street Journal,* July 10, 1981, pp. 23, 26, and "The Youth Movement in Coors Management," *Business Week,* May 24, 1982, p. 50.
33. Karl Weick, *The Social Psychology of Organizing,* 2nd ed. (Reading, MA: Addison-Wesley, 1979), p. 243.
34. Robert Townsend, *Up the Organization* (New York: Knopf, 1974), p. 115. Copyright © 1970 by Robert Townsend. Reprinted by permission of Alfred A. Knopf, Inc.
35. This case was inspired by Douglas R. Sease, "School Superintendent, Once Pillar of Society Now is Often a Target," *Wall Street Journal,* June 2, 1981, p. 1.
36. "Piercing Future Fog in the Executive Suite," *Business Week,* April 28, 1975, pp. 46–53; Grayson, "Management Science and Business Practice."

10

Power and Politics

McDONNELL DOUGLAS CORPORATION

At McDonnell Douglas Corp. there was never any doubt who was in charge. James S. McDonnell, chairman of the board, ran the company with an iron hand for more than forty years.

McDonnell Douglas is one of the few companies in which the founder was active so long and ran the huge corporation as if it were his personal property. Mr. Mac, as he was known, called the shots until he was eighty years old. Now he is dead.

What happens next? With a dominant figure to make all the decisions, other executives knew where they stood. Mr. Mac was so dominant that several strong-willed executives left because they had little impact. Now there is a power vacuum. Who will step in? What new order will emerge? Two of the contenders are Mr. Mac's sons—John F. McDonnell, executive vice president and a financial expert, and James S. McDonnell III, vice president for marketing. Sanford N. McDonnell, Mr. Mac's nephew, is currently president. Some people feel he will blossom into a strong, capable leader.

In addition to the loss of its chief executive, McDonnell Douglas has experienced other recent shocks. The emotional wounds of the American airlines DC-10 crash in Chicago persist. The company was picked apart by the press and humiliated when the FFA removed the DC-10's Certificate of Airworthiness for more than a month. Lawsuits and expensive repairs hang over McDonnell Douglas still.

So does the bribery scandal that began in 1973. McDonnell Douglas is accused of paying bribes to foreign airlines to purchase the DC-10. Four executives are currently under indictment for paying up to $1,000,000 in connection with the sale of DC-10 jets to Pakistan International

Airlines. Mr. Mac's son James is one of the indicted executives. This case is the first and only foreign payments case that could lead to criminal prosecution and jail terms for the individuals involved.

With Mr. Mac gone, many observers think a power struggle will develop. The board of directors is being recast to have an external majority. The additional members could provide the basis for a new coalition.

Marketing is not the strong suit of McDonnell Douglas, and son Jim is involved in the payoff scandal, which may weaken his chances. Stock ownership favors the sons. Mr. Mac and the two sons together owned 20% of the outstanding shares. Sandy, the nephew, owns less than one-third of one percent. But Sandy has the highest rank as president, and he has built up credibility after eight years in that position.

The major source of conflict could emerge over a new strategy. The DC-10 is petering out. McDonnell Douglas has to either come up with a new, fuel efficient mid-range aircraft or consider getting out of the business. A similar problem is the relationship between McDonnell and Douglas. The Douglas division is responsible for the DC-10, which has been a consistent money loser and a drain on the company's cash flow. The McDonnell side brings in three-fourths of the $4 billion revenues and provides the profit. McDonnell produces weapons for the defense department, such as the F-18, and has a reputation as an efficient, high-quality contractor.

If the power struggle occurs, it will be over the decision to build a new airliner. Each of the key executives may have a view that he wants to impose on the future of McDonnell Douglas. With so many uncertainties, someone will have to take charge. However, if the nephew and two sons are able to work as a team and make decisions jointly, the power struggle may be postponed indefinitely.

As of this writing, Sandy McDonnell, Mr. Mac's nephew, has been elected chairman and is chief executive officer. John McDonnell took Sandy's position as president. Jim McDonnell still holds his position as corporate vice president for marketing. The board of directors now has nonmanagement people in the majority. So far, no visible power struggle has appeared. The power vacuum has been filled by the top management team rather than by any individual.[1]

The McDonnell Douglas example illustrates the circumstances associated with power and political intrigue. The participants have high-level positions within the organization. They command extensive resources, and have the opportunity to build coalitions through a changing board of directors. Uncertainty is high. Mr. Mac's death left a power vacuum and the external environment is changing. The payoff scandal, the DC-10 crash, the need for more efficient aircraft, and the success of the McDonnell division compared to the Douglas division all create unpredictables for top management. The only missing ingredient is disagreement. If deeply held disagreements arise, the formal positions, experience, and resources will be thrown into the battle to determine the strategy and future of McDonnell Douglas.

Purpose of This Chapter
In the popular literature, power is often described as a personal characteristic. A frequent topic is how one person can influence or dominate another person.[2] Power in organizations, however, is often not the result of individual characteristics. Organizations are large, complex systems that contain hundreds, even thousands, of people. There is an extensive division of labor. Some tasks inevitably become more important regardless of who performs them. Some roles have access to greater resources, or their place in the organization is more central. Some people have high positions of great power compared to positions lower in the hierarchy. Horizontal differences across the organization are less visible, but nevertheless influence organizational goals and the allocation of resources. The important power processes in organizations reflect larger organizational relationships, both horizontal and vertical. Organizational power is invested in the position, not in the person. Control over vast resources and level in the hierarchy provide some roles with disproportionate power.

The purpose of this chapter is to explore these power issues. We examine sources of power in organizations, and the way power is used to attain organizational goals. Vertical and horizontal power sources are quite different, so we will treat them separately. We also look at politics. Politics is related to power because politics is the use of power and authority to achieve the ends of an individual or department. Political behavior occurs outside the formally prescribed rules and procedures of the organization.

POWER VERSUS AUTHORITY

Systematic studies of power in organizations indicate that power is not a well-understood concept.[3] Power is an intangible, illusive process in organizations. Respondents are often reluctant to discuss power. Many believe it detracts from organizational effectiveness. A few studies have been successful in learning about power processes, however, so a preliminary picture is emerging.

Power is a force that cannot be seen, but its effects can be felt. Power is often defined as the ability of one person (or department) to influence other persons (or departments) to carry out orders,[4] or to do something they would not otherwise have done.[5] Other definitions are less concerned with changing behavior, and emphasize the effect of power on goals or outcomes that powerholders desire.[6] The achievement of desired outcomes is the most important use of organizational power, so the following definition is used here: **power** is the ability of one person or department in an organization to influence other people to bring about desired outcomes. Power is used to influence others within the organization, but with the goal of attaining desired outcomes for powerholders.

Power exists only in a relationship between two or more people, and can be exercised in either vertical or horizontal directions. Power does not have to be exercised to be present. Only the potential needs to be present. The exercise of power depends upon the powerholder. If power truly exists, those being influenced will comply when asked. The following outcomes are indicators of power in an organization.

- Obtain a larger increase in budget than other departments.
- Get a hearing before top decision-makers.
- Obtain above-average salary increases for subordinates.
- Obtain production schedules that are favorable to your department.
- Get items on the agenda at policy meetings.
- Get a desirable position for a talented subordinate.[7]

Authority, by contrast, is much narrower in scope. Authority is also a force for achieving desired outcomes, but only as prescribed by the formal hierarchy and reporting relationships. Two properties that identify authority are:

1. *Authority Is Invested in Organizational Positions.* Incumbents have authority because of the positions they hold, not because of personal characteristics.
2. *Authority Is Voluntarily Accepted by Subordinates.* Subordinates comply because they perceive that incumbents have a legitimate right to exercise authority.[8]

Authority flows down the vertical hierarchy. The perceived legitimacy of authority and its acceptance are reflected in the following quotes from interviews with employees about authority.

"Authority to me is something you are bound to obey. It's something that I respect."
"The person with the rank has the final say. Whether you agree with him, you go along with him."[9]

Formal organization structure, including responsibility, centralization, and hierarchical level, influence the amount of authority held by various positions. Formal structure enables the exercise of authority along the vertical dimension of organizations.

VERTICAL POWER

Power Sources for Upper Management

The formal hierarchy of authority provides power and authority to top management. Tasks and responsibility are greatly subdivided at lower levels of the organization. Top management is responsible for a great number of people and many resources, and authority is equal to those responsibilities. The chain of command converges at the top of the organization, so authority is great for top offices. Surveys with the control graph in chapter 8 indicated that people at the top of the organization have greater influence than lower-level participants. The authority granted to top management to govern is reflected in the structure and design of the organization:

The design of an organization, its structure, is first and foremost the system of control and authority by which the organization is governed. In the organizational structure, decision discretion is allocated to various positions and the distribution of formal authority is established. Furthermore, by establishing the pattern of prescribed communication and reporting requirements, the structure provides some participants with more and better information and more central locations in the communication network . . . . Thus, organizational structures create formal power and authority by designating certain persons to do certain tasks and make certain decisions and create informal power through the effect on information and communication structures within the organization. Organizational structure is a picture of the governance of the organization and a determinant of who controls and decides organizational activities.[10]

A great deal of power is allocated to senior management from their position in the organizational structure. The power of top management comes from four sources—formal position, resources, control of decision premises, and experience.

Formal Position   Certain rights, responsibilities, and prerogatives accrue to top positions. Top managers have a great deal of responsibility, hence authority is also great. People throughout the organization accept the legitimate right of top managers to make decisions and direct activities. So long as the position and directives are perceived as legitimate, lower-level managers will obey. People in our society accept the right of top managers to direct the organization. Most of us believe, "Those in authority have the *right* to demand compliance; those subject to authority have the *duty* to obey."[11]

Resources   Organizations allocate huge amounts of resources. Buildings are constructed, salaries are paid, and equipment and supplies are purchased. Each year new resources are allocated in the form of budgets. These resources are allocated downward in organizations. Top managers have a substantial say about distribution to subordinates. Resources can be used to reward and punish, which are primary sources of power.[12] Resource allocation also creates a dependency relationship. Lower-level participants depend upon top managers for the financial and physical resources needed to perform well and to achieve their goals. Top management can exchange resources in the form of salaries, personnel, promotions, and physical facilities for compliance with the outcomes they desire.

Control of Decision Premises   Control of decision premises means that top managers place constraints on decisions made at lower levels. In one sense, top managers make big decisions while lower-level participants make smaller decisions. Top management, for example, decides which goal the organization will try to achieve, such as increased market share or profits. Lower-level participants may decide how the goal is to be reached. Top management can decide such things as the products to be manufactured, from whom supplies will be purchased, and the limits on signing authority for expenditures ("No more than $5,000 for department heads"). These decisions place limits on the decisions of lower-level managers and thereby influence their behavior.[13]

An additional source of power is the control of information. Information flows continuously into the organization and up and down the hierarchy. By carefully controlling this information, the manager has a major source of power. This power will influence choice processes at both upper and lower levels, and can be exchanged for compliance or can be released to define the decision premises for other people. Top managers control many kinds of information. In the following case, the senior manager controlled information given to the board of directors, and thereby influenced the decision outcome.

IN PRACTICE 10.1
Clark Ltd.

Clark Ltd., an English firm, decided to purchase and install a large computer system.[14] The board of directors had formal authority to decide from which company the computer would be purchased. The management services group was asked to recommend which of six computer manufacturers should receive the order. Jim Kenny was in charge of the management services group. Reporting to Kenny was Turner, who was in charge of programmers, and Reilly, who was responsible for systems analysts. Kenny, Reilly, and Turner each preferred a different computer manufacturer for legitimate reasons. As shown in figure 10.1, Reilly and Turner were subordinate to Kenny, which gave Kenny an advantage. He had access to the board of directors and controlled information to and from them. The views of Reilly and Turner had to be processed through Kenny to the board. Likewise, the board's views went through Kenny back to Reilly and Turner. The computer manufacturers did not have access to the board, so they also had to work through Kenny.

The decision process within the management services group developed into a competitive struggle for power between Kenny and his systems manager, Reilly, and between Reilly and the programming manager, Turner. By sitting at the junction of the communications channels for everyone involved, Kenny was able to exert biases in favor of his preference, and feed the board negative information about the preferences of his subordinates.

An analysis of board documents showed the extent of bias. Kenny discussed his preferred computer manufacturer more often than he did other manufacturers. His discussions of other manufacturers, when they occurred, tended to be negative. He influenced the board's selection of the computer to purchase by controlling information given to them.[15]

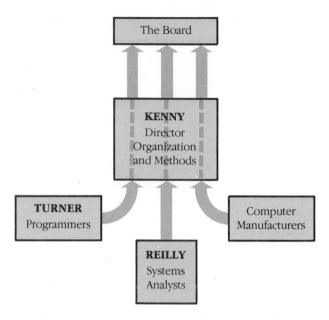

Figure 10.1. Information Flow for Computer Decision at Clark Ltd.
Source: Andrew M. Pettigrew, *The Politics of Organizational Decision-Making* (London: Tavistock, 1973), p. 235, with permission.

Experience Experience is often considered a characteristic of an individual rather than of the position. Top-level managers normally have substantial experience and ability. They have seen many situations in the past, and have developed a level of expertise for handling problems and situations that lower-level members lack. Top managers also view decisions from a larger perspective. Top-level problems are ambiguous and intangible, so good judgment is required. Indeed, when top managers are not performing at the ability level required of their positions, they are often moved off to the side, or even let go. Subordinates lack this judgment and expertise, which gives the manager power to provide direction and to make decisions to achieve desired outcomes.

Power Sources Along the Hierarchy The distribution of power down the hierarchy is influenced by organization design factors. Of course, top management will have more power than lower-level employees, but the amount of power provided to any given position or organizational group can be built into the organization's vertical design.

The design of positions along the hierarchy is important, because power enables employees to be productive. Managers need sufficient power and latitude to perform their jobs well. When positions are powerless, managers may seem ineffective, and may become petty, dictatorial, and rules-minded.[16] Several design factors are shown in table 10.1. Table 10.1 indicates how each design element contributes or takes away power from the position. Power is the result of both task activities and network interactions. When the position is nonroutine, it encourages discretion, flexibility, and creativity. When the job pertains to pressing organizational problems, power is more easily accumulated. Power is also increased when the position encourages contact with high-level people, brings visibility and recognition to employees, and facilitates peer networks both inside and outside the organization.

The variables in table 10.1 can be designed into specific roles or departments. For example, funds can be allocated to a department so members can attend professional meetings, thereby increasing visibility and stature. As participants accumulate power, they can accomplish more.

The logic of designing positions for more power assumes that the organization does not have a fixed amount of power to be distributed among high-level and low-level employees. The total amount of influence in an

Table 10.1. Ways in Which Vertical Design Contributes to Power.

Design Factor	Generates Power When Factor Is	Generates Powerlessness When Factor Is
Role activities:		
Rules inherent in the job	few	many
Precedents in the job	few	many
Established routines	few	many
Task variety	high	low
Rewards for reliability/predictability	few	many
Rewards for unusual performance/innovation	many	few
Flexibility around use of people	high	low
Approvals needed for nonroutine decisions	few	many
Relation of tasks to current problem areas	central	peripheral
Focus of tasks	outside work unit	inside work unit
Network Interactions:		
Physical location	central	distant
Publicity about job activities	high	low
Interpersonal contact in the job	high	low
Contact with senior officials	high	low
Participation in programs, conferences, meetings	high	low
Participation in problem-solving task forces	high	low
Advancement prospects of subordinates	high	low

Source: Adapted from Rosabeth Moss Kanter, "Power Failure in Management Circuits," *Harvard Business Review* 57 (July–August, 1979): 65–75. Reprinted by permission of the *Harvard Business Review*. Exhibit from "Power Failure in Management Circuits" by Rosabeth Moss Kanter (July/August 1979). Copyright © 1979 by the President and Fellows of Harvard College; all rights reserved.

organization can be increased, a situation similar to the control graph studies described in chapter 8. If the distribution of power is too heavily skewed toward the top so that others are powerless, the organization will be less effective.[17]

IN PRACTICE 10.2

Power Failures

Design factors can leave an entire level of the hierarchy, such as first line supervisors, in a position of powerlessness. Their jobs may be overwhelmed with rules and precedents, and they may have little opportunity to develop an interaction network in the organization. Minority group members often have little power because management is overprotective, and thereby precludes opportunities for initiative and exposure needed for power accumulation.[18] The same fate can befall staff specialists.

As advisers behind the scenes, staff people must sell their programs and bargain for resources, but unless they get themselves entrenched in organizational power networks, they have little in the way of favors to exchange. They are not seen as useful to the primary tasks of the organization. When staff jobs consist of easily routinized administrative functions which are out of the mainstream . . . and involve little innovative decision-making, [staff personnel may end up powerless].

Furthermore, in some organizations, unless they have had previous line experience, staff people tend to be limited in the number of jobs into which they can move. Specialists' ladders are often very short, and professionals are just as likely to get "stuck" in such jobs as people are in less prestigious clerical or factory positions.

Staff people, unlike those who are being groomed for important line positions, may be hired because of a special expertise or particular background. But management rarely pays any attention to developing them into more general organizational resources. Lacking growth prospects themselves and working alone or in very small teams, they are not in a position to develop others or pass on power to them. They miss out on an important way in which power can be accumulated.

Sometimes staff specialists, such as house counsel or organization development people, find their work being farmed out to consultants. Management considers them fine for the routine work, but the minute the activities involve risk or something problematic, they bring in outside experts. This treatment says something not only about their expertise but also about the status of their function. Since the company can always hire talent on a temporary basis, it is unclear whether management really needs to have or considers important its own staff for these functions.

Because staff professionals are often seen as aids to primary tasks, their effectiveness, and therefore their contribution to the organization, is often hard to measure. Thus, visibility and recognition, as well as risk-taking and relevance, may be denied to people in staff jobs.[19]

Without sufficient power, people cannot be productive. Power need not be taken for granted. Power can be built into positions and departments through the design of task activities and interaction opportunities.

Power Sources for Lower-Level Participants

Positions at the bottom of the organization have less power than positions at higher levels. Often, however, people at the bottom levels obtain power disproportionate to their positions. Secretaries, maintenance people, word processors, computer programmers, and others find themselves being consulted in decisions or having great latitude and discretion in the performance of their activities. The power of lower-level employees often surprises managers. The vice-president of a university may be more reluctant to discipline his secretary than to fire an academic department head. Why does this happen?

People at lower levels obtain power from several sources. Some of these sources are individual, as indicated in table 10.2. They reflect the personality and style of lower-level employees. Other power sources are position-based. One study found that unexpectedly high levels of power came from expertise, physical location, information, and personal effort and interest.[20] When lower-level participants become knowledgeable and expert about certain activities, they are in a position to influence decisions. Sometimes individuals take on difficult tasks and acquire specialized knowledge, and then become indispensable to managers above them. Power accumulation is also associated with the amount of effort and interest displayed. People who have initiative and who work beyond what is expected often find themselves with a great deal of influence. Physical location also helps because some locations are in the center of things. Central location lets the person be visible to key people and become part of interaction networks. Likewise, certain positions are in the flow of organizational information. One example is the secretary to a senior executive. The secretary has access to and can control information that other people want. The secretary will be able to influence those people.

Two additional sources of upward influence are persuasion and manipulation.[21] Persuasion is a direct appeal to upper management, while manipulation means arranging information to achieve the outcome desired by the employee. People who are highly motivated to attain power are also able to exert upward influence. Several of these power sources were used by Lyndon Johnson, when he was a university student, to build power and influence, as described in the following case.

Table 10.2.   Power Sources for Lower-Level Participants.

Personal Sources	Position Sources
Expertise	Physical location
Effort and interest	Information flow
Persuasion and manipulation	
Power motive	

Campus Politico[22]

From the beginning at San Marcos College (later Southwestern Texas State Teachers College), [Lyndon] Johnson set out to win the friendship and respect of those people who would assist his rise within the community which composed San Marcos. Most obvious was the president of the college, Cecil Evans, whose favor would have a multiplier effect with the faculty and student body. But Johnson was not alone in the desire to have a special relationship with Evans. "I knew," Johnson said later, "there was only one way to get to know Evans and that was to work for him directly." He became special assistant to the president's personal secretary.

As special assistant, Johnson's assigned job was simply to carry messages from the president to the department heads and occasionally to other faculty members. Johnson saw that the rather limited function of messenger had possibilities for expansion; for example, encouraging recipients of the messages to transmit their own communications through him. He occupied a desk in the president's outer office, where he took it upon himself to announce the arrival of visitors. These added services evolved from a helpful convenience into an aspect of the normal process of presidential business. The messenger had become an appointments secretary, and in time, faculty members came to think of Johnson as a funnel to the president. Using a technique which was later to serve him in achieving mastery over the Congress, Johnson turned a rather insubstantial service into a process through which power was exercised. By redefining the process, he had given power to himself.

Evans eventually broadened Johnson's responsibilities to include handling his political correspondence and preparing his reports for state agencies with jurisdiction over the college and its appropriations. The student was quick to explain that his father had been a member of the state legislature (from 1905 to 1909, and from 1918 to 1925), and Lyndon had often accompanied him to Austin where he had gained some familiarity with the workings of the legislature and the personalities of its leaders. This claim might have sounded almost ludicrous had it not come from someone who already must have seemed an inordinately political creature. Soon Johnson was accompanying Evans on his trips to the state capital in Austin, and, before long, Evans came to rely upon his young apprentice for political counsel. For Johnson was clearly at home in the state legislature, whether sitting in a committee room during hearings or standing on the floor talking with representatives. He could, in later reports to Evans, capture the mood of individual legislators and the legislative body with entertaining accuracy. The older man, on whose favor Johnson depended, now relied on him, or at least found him useful.

Consequences of Vertical Power

Behavioral versus Attitudinal Compliance Top managers have four major sources of power for influencing outcomes—from their formal position, resources, experience and expertise, and the ability to set decision premises. The type of power exerted will determine the type of compliance they receive from employees, as indicated in figure 10.2.[23] When managers rely upon resources such as rewards and sanctions to obtain compliance, employees usually conform in behavior only. They will do what is necessary, but they will not be committed to a course of action. Indeed, if employees are outside the direct eye of managers, they may not conform at all. Power sources such as expertise and legitimate authority are more likely to bring about attitudinal conformity. Employees believe in the ability and the right of the senior manager, and accept authority on a personal level. Consequently, employees are committed to a course of action, and will comply even when they are not watched. Decision premises may lead to either type of compliance, as indicated in figure 10.2. Setting decision premises represents a subtle form of power by providing goals and constraints for employees. Normally employees behave within these constraints, but attitudinal compliance may be only partial.

When managers wish to gain the commitment of employees, legitimate power and expertise are more potent power sources than rewards and sanctions. Rewards and sanctions are effective when only behavioral conformity is required.

Protection against Tyranny   One of the puzzlements in organizations is that the wide disparity in power between the top and bottom of the organization is seldom used to exploit employees. Indeed, upper-level managers are often frustrated because they try to move the organization in a new direction and employees are slow to respond. The wide differences in resources, prestige, expertise, and legitimacy should mean that top management can enforce its will upon the rest of the organization, even if the outcomes are illegal or immoral. This kind of power utilization is seldom seen in organizations, and the question is why?

Part of the answer is that lower-level employees have some power. The vertical dimension of organization is not a perfect hierarchical system.

Figure 10.2.   Vertical Power Source and Behavioral versus Attitudinal Compliance. Based upon Donald I. Warren, "Power Visibility and Conformity in Formal Organizations," *American Sociological Review* 33 (1968): 951–970.

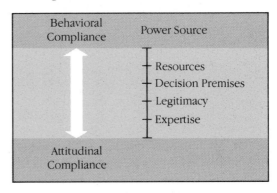

Lower-level participants acquire information and expertise, and they are able to persuade and manipulate, which is a source of power. There is enough latitude at all levels in the organization that absolute control is typically not possible.

The other reason is that the nature of organizations provides a built-in safeguard against top-management tyranny. Laboratory experiments have shown that power is greater over a single individual who is isolated from other people. Organizations, however, are composed of groups. Individuals are seldom isolated. In these experiments, power was applied to individuals alone and in the presence of a group.[24] Compliance dropped off dramatically when other people were present. Group members reinforced social norms so that illegal or immoral activities were blocked. Group members did not even have to talk to the person to whom power was applied. Simply having other people present who knew about the act was enough to prevent compliance. Employees provide support for each other and a defense against the undue use of power by people above them in the hierarchy.

Top managers do have a substantial amount of power, but the difference between the top and the bottom level is not so great that top managers can give orders without constraints. In only a few incidents, such as in the Watergate scandal during the Nixon administration, can the organization be taken in a direction that people do not want to go. In those situations, power was used on isolated people who did not have the social support of others, so compliance was easier to obtain.

HORIZONTAL POWER

All vice presidents are usually at the same level on the organization chart. Does this mean each department has the same amount of power? No. Each department makes a unique contribution to organizational success. Some contributions are of greater value than others. Some departments will have greater say and will achieve their desired outcomes, while others will not. For example, Charles Perrow surveyed managers in twelve industrial firms.[25] He bluntly asked, "Which department has the most power?" among four departments: Production, Sales and Marketing, Research and Development, and Finance and Accounting. The survey results are given in figure 10.3. In most firms, sales had the greatest power. In a few firms, production was also quite powerful. The average rank of department power was as follows: (1) sales, (2) production, (3) R & D, and (4) finance. Horizontal power differences were clearly perceived to exist in those firms.

Horizontal power is difficult to measure because power differences are not defined on the organization chart. Some initial answers that help us explain power differences such as those shown in figure 10.3 have been found. The theoretical concept that explains relative power is called strategic contingencies.[26] **Strategic contingencies** are those events and activities both inside and outside the organization that are essential for attaining organizational goals. Those departments that are involved with strategic contingencies

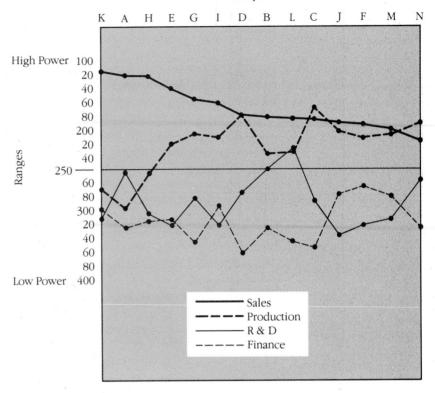

Figure 10.3. Ratings of Departmental Power in 12 Industrial Firms.
Source: Charles Perrow, "Departmental Power and Perspective in Industrial Firms," in Mayer N. Zald, ed., *Power in Organizations* (Nashville, TN: Vanderbilt University Press, 1970), p. 64, with permission.

for the organization will have greater power. Activities are important when they remove problems that have strategic value for the organization. If an organization faces an intense threat from lawsuits and regulations, the legal department will gain power and influence over organizational decisions because they cope with this threat.[27] If new products are the key strategic issue, the power of R & D can be expected to be high.

Strategic Contingencies   Jeffrey Pfeffer and Gerald Salancik, among others, have been instrumental in conducting research on the strategic contingencies theory.[28] Their findings indicate that a department rated as powerful may possess one or more of the following characteristics, which are illustrated in figure 10.4.

Dependency   Interdepartmental dependency is a key element underlying relative power. Power is derived from having something someone else wants. The power of department A over department B is greater when department B depends upon A.[29]

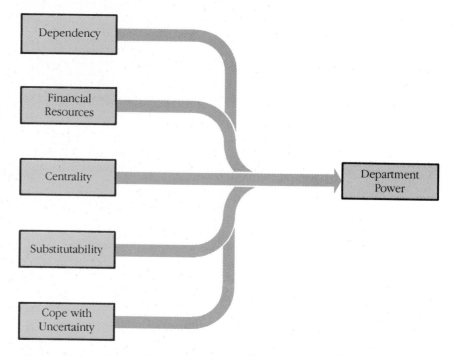

Figure 10.4. Strategic Contingencies that Influence Horizontal Power Relationships among Departments.

There are many interdependencies in organizations. In one sense, all organization units depend upon each other or they would not be part of the organization. But the strength of dependency between specific departments differs widely. Materials, information, and resources often flow in one direction, such as in the case of sequential task interdependence (chapter 4). The department receiving resources is in a lower power position than the department providing them. The number of dependencies is also important. When seven or eight departments must come for help or service to the engineering department, engineering is in a stronger power position than a department that is needed by only one other department. Likewise, a department that depends upon many other departments is in a very low power position.

IN PRACTICE 10.4

Cigarette Factory

Who would have more power in a cigarette factory, the maintenance department or the production department? The answer lies in the relative dependency between the two groups. These two departments were observed in a government-owned cigarette plant near Paris.[31] The production of cigarettes was a fairly routine process. The machinery was automated and individual production jobs were small in scope. The demand for cigarettes could be accurately predicted, so production was scheduled to maintain inventories at an adequate level. Supplies of tobacco and paper were also kept in inventory to ensure an uninterrupted production process. Production workers were not highly skilled, but they had job security since the manufacturing plant was government-owned. Production workers were paid on a piece-rate basis to encourage high production.

The maintenance department required highly skilled workers. They worked on the automated machinery, which was quite complex. Maintenance workers had many years of experience, which was needed to do their jobs well. Maintenance was a craft, because maintenance procedures and blueprints were not available. Vital knowledge was stored in the minds of maintenance personnel.

The dependency between the two groups was caused by unpredictable assembly-line breakdowns. Everything about the assembly process was routine and well-controlled except for machine failures. Managers could not remove the breakdown problem; consequently maintenance was the vital cog in the production process. Maintenance workers had the knowledge and ability to fix the machines, so production managers became dependent upon them. Maintenance was the only group that could solve the breakdown problem. There were no other groups either inside or outside the factory that could repair the machines on a continuous basis. Maintenance work required years of experience, so personnel could not be easily replaced.

Production's dependency on maintenance led to unusually high maintenance influence, even at top organization levels. Maintenance people began to dictate the production schedules. They had considerable say in plantwide operations as well. The reason for this influence is that maintenance managers had control over a strategic contingency—they had the knowledge and ability to prevent work stoppages. The organization depended upon them for this service, so they became extremely powerful. Maintenance had more power than production, which is normally a powerful group in an organization.

Financial Resources There is a new golden rule becoming popular, which goes something like: "He who has the gold makes the rules."[32] Control over financial resources is an important source of power. Money can be converted into other kinds of resources that are needed by other departments. Money generates dependency; departments that provide financial resources have something other departments want. Departments that generate income for the organization have greater power. The survey of industrial firms reported in figure 10.3 showed sales as the most powerful unit in those firms. Sales had high power because salespeople find customers and sell the product, thereby removing an important problem for the organization. Sales ensures the inflow of money. Financial resources also explain power relationships in other organizations, such as universities.

University of Illinois

You might expect that the budget allocation in a state university is a straightforward process. The need for financial resources can be determined by such things as the number of undergraduate students, the number of graduate students, and the number of faculty in each department. In some logical manner, central administration should be able to calculate the appropriate amount of resources to be allocated to each department. Resource allocation would reflect resource needs in a predictable way.

In fact, resource allocation in universities is not so clear-cut. Some departments have more power than others because of their resource contribution to the university. Departments that generate large amounts of outside funds in the form of research grants are more powerful. Research grants contain a sizeable overhead payment to university administration. The size of the graduate student body and the national prestige of the department also add to power. Graduate students and national prestige are nonfinancial resources that add to the reputation and effectiveness of the university. State universities have a relatively fixed resource inflow from state government. Beyond that, important resources come from research grants and quality of students and faculty. Overhead money from grants pays for a sizeable share of the universities' personnel and facilities. University departments that provide the most resources to the university have the most power.[33]

How do they use their power? Generally, to obtain even more resources from the rest of the university. Very powerful departments receive university resources, such as graduate-student fellowships, internal research support, and summer faculty salaries, far in excess of their needs based upon number of students and faculty.

Power accrues to those departments that bring in or provide resources that are highly valued by the organization. This power enables these departments to obtain more of the scarce resources allocated within the organization. "Power derived from acquiring resources is used to obtain more resources, which in turn can be employed to produce more power —the rich get richer."[34]

Centrality Centrality reflects the department's role in the primary activity of the organization.[35] One measure of centrality is the extent to which the work of the department affects the final output of the organization. The production department is more central and usually has more power than staff groups (assuming no other critical contingencies). Centrality is associated with power because it reflects the contribution made to the organization. In the departmental power relationships described in figure 10.3, finance tended to be low in power. Finance is also less central than other departments. It has the role of recording money and expenditures, but it is not responsible for obtaining critical resources or for producing the products of the organization. As a result, it is less powerful than marketing or production.

Substitutability Power is also determined by substitutability. A department will not increase in power if other readily available resources can perform the same function.[36] If personnel can be easily replaced, their power is less. If the organization has alternative sources of skill and information, the department's power will be less. This can happen when staff groups are assigned routine duties and management uses outside consultants when unexpected problems arise.[37] Availability of consultants as substitutes for staff people reduces the power of staff groups.

The impact of substitutability on power was traced for programmers in computer departments.[38] When computers were first introduced, programming was a rare and specialized occupation. People had to be highly qualified to enter the profession. Within organizations, programmers controlled the use of the computer because they alone possessed the knowledge to program it. Over a period of about ten years, computer programming became a more common activity. People could be substituted easily. The power of programming departments dropped:

> *Twenty years ago there were only a few dozen programmers in the world. They were all very competent professional mathematicians . . . . Today there are hundreds of thousands of them, but most of them are not even graduates. A few inspired mathematicians have invented some astonishing techniques which make it possible for ordinary men to communicate with computers and explore them. Today a schoolboy can use a computer to solve problems that would have baffled experienced mathematicians only fifteen years ago.*[39]

Coping with the Uncertainty The chapters on environment and decision-making described how elements in the environment can change swiftly; they can be unpredictable and complex. In the face of uncertainty, little accurate information is available to managers on appropriate courses of action. Departments that cope with uncertainty will increase their power.[40] The presence of uncertainty does not provide power, but reducing the uncertainty on behalf of other departments will. When market research personnel accurately predict changes in demand for new products, they will gain power and prestige because they have reduced a critical uncertainty. Forecasting is only one technique for coping with uncertainty. Sometimes uncertainty can be reduced by taking quick and appropriate action after the unpredictable event occurs. In In Practice 10.4, the maintenance personnel took action to reduce uncertainty in the cigarette manufacturing plant. They had the knowledge and expertise to respond to the uncertainty of machine breakdowns. By coping with this uncertainty, they made production dependent on them and greatly increased their power.

Departments can increase power if they cope with critical uncertainties. Three techniques for coping with an uncertainty are: (1) obtain prior information, (2) absorption, or (3) prevention.[41] Obtaining prior information means that the department can reduce the organization's uncertainty by forecasting the event. Absorption occurs when a department takes action after an event to reduce its negative consequences. Departments increase their power through prevention by predicting and forestalling negative events. In the following case, the industrial relations department increased its power by absorbing a critical uncertainty. They took action after the event to reduce uncertainty for the organization.

IN PRACTICE 10.6

Crystal Manufacturing

A new union is a crucial source of uncertainty for many manufacturing firms. The union can be a countervailing power to management in decisions concerning wages and working conditions. The workers in Crystal Manufacturing Company voted in 1980 to become part of the Glassmakers Craft Union. Management had been aware of union-organizing activities, but it had not taken the threat seriously. No one had acted to forecast or prevent the formation of a union in the company.

The presence of the union had serious consequences for Crystal. Glassmaking is a delicate and expensive manufacturing process. The float-glass process cannot be shut down even temporarily except at great expense. A strike or walkout would be a financial disaster. Top management decided that establishing a good working relationship with the union was critically important.

An industrial relations department was assigned to deal with the union. This department was responsible for coping with the uncertainties created by the new union. The industrial relations group quickly developed expertise in union relationships. They became the contact point for managers throughout the organization on industrial relations matters. Industrial relations members developed contacts throughout the organization and could bypass normal chains of command on issues they considered important. Industrial relations obtained nearly absolute knowledge and control over union relations.

In Crystal Manufacturing Company, the industrial relations unit was coping with the critical uncertainty by absorption. They took action to reduce the uncertainty after it appeared. This action gave them greatly increased power. Other units became dependent upon them for information and knowledge pertaining to union affairs. An example of their new-found power was displayed during the annual budget cycle. The industrial relations department obtained resources to add new personnel and office space, although the total company budget declined slightly. Less powerful departments lost out.

Politics, like power, is intangible and difficult to measure. Politics is hidden from view and is hard to observe in a systematic way. Managers are reluctant to discuss personal political behavior. One way to learn about politics is to survey managers anonymously about the political behavior of other people in their organization. Two recent surveys uncovered interesting reactions by managers toward political behavior.[42]

1. Most managers have a negative view toward politics, and believe that politics will more often hurt than help the organization achieve its goals.
2. Managers believe that political behavior is common to practically all organizations.
3. Most managers think that political behavior occurs more often at upper rather than lower levels in organizations.
4. Political behavior arises in certain types of decisions, such as structural change, but is absent from other types of decisions, such as handling employee grievances.

Based upon these surveys, politics seems more likely to occur at the top levels of the organization and around certain issues and decisions. In nearly all organizations, people do not approve of political behavior. In the remainder of this chapter we explore more fully the nature and role of political behavior, when it should be used, the type of issues and decisions most likely to be associated with politics, and some political tactics that may be effective.

Definition Politics is related to power. Power is the available force or potential for achieving desired outcomes. Politics is the actual behavior used to influence decisions in order to achieve those outcomes. Politics is the exercise of power and influence. Politics is associated with uncertainty and conflict because competing views may surface when only one can prevail. The formal definition of organizational politics used here is: **Organizational politics** involves those activities to acquire, develop, and use power and other resources to obtain one's preferred outcome when there is uncertainty or disagreement about choices.[43]

A department may have a given level of power, but politics is the activity through which power is exercised. Politics is neutral. This definition does not suggest that politics is harmful to the organization, only that politics exists where there is disagreement about choices. Managers, however, see politics as negative, and some writers have proposed definitions that adopt a negative view. One example is, "Organizational politics is the management of influence to obtain ends not sanctioned by the organization . . . ."[44] Another definition suggests that "Organizational politics denotes a subjective state in which organization members perceive themselves or others as intentionally seeking selfish ends in an organizational context . . . ."[45]

These two definitions miss the point. They state that politics is outside the acceptable behavior of the organization. This assumes that political behavior is used when the person or department wants something inappropriate, illegal, or unacceptable to the organization. Political behavior may be self-serving at times, but it can also be a very positive force. Politics is the use of power to get things accomplished, both good and bad. Politics emerges when there is uncertainty or conflict. Uncertainty and conflict are natural and inevitable, and politics is the mechanism for reaching agreement. Politics enables participants to arrive at a consensus and make decisions that otherwise might be stalemated or unsolvable. Politics is necessary. Powerful groups may prevail in political situations, but they are powerful because of their importance to the organization.

One reason for the negative view is that political behavior is compared to more rational procedures in organizations. Rational procedures are considered by many managers to be more objective and reliable, and to lead to better decisions than political behavior. Rational approaches are effective, but only in certain situations. Both rational and political processes are normally used in organizations.

Rational Choice versus Political Behavior

Rational Model The rational model of organization is summarized in table 10.3. Behavior in the rational organization is not random or accidental. Goals are clear and choices are made in a logical, computational way. When a decision is needed, the goal is defined, alternatives are identified, and the choice with the highest probability of achieving the desired outcome is selected. Alternatives are not selected on the basis of personal values or politics. The rational model of organization is also characterized by extensive, reliable information systems, central power, a norm of optimization, uniform values across groups, little conflict, and an efficiency orientation.[46]

The rational model in table 10.3 is an extreme case, and will not be found in most organizations. The rational model applies to organizations characterized by stable environments and well-understood technology. The rational model is a goal or an ideal.

Political Power Model The opposite view of choice processes within organizations is the political model in table 10.3. This model assumes that organizations are made up of separate coalitions that disagree about goals and that do not have good information about alternatives.[47] The political model defines the organization as made up of groups that have separate interests, goals, and values. Disagreement and conflict are normal, so power and influence are needed to reach decisions.

The political model in table 10.3 is also an extreme case. The political model is most common in organizations that face high levels of uncertainty and frequently changing conditions. To achieve goals, groups will engage in the push and pull of debate to decide goals and to reach decisions. Decisions are disorderly. Information is ambiguous and incomplete. Bargaining and conflict are the norm. Elements of the rational model will also appear in these organizations, but infrequently because of diverse goals, decentralization, and poor information.

Table 10.3.   Rational versus Political Models of Organization.

Organizational Characteristic	Rational Model	Political Model
Goals, preferences:	Consistent across participants	Inconsistent, pluralistic within the organization
Power and control:	Centralized	Decentralized; shifting coalitions and interest groups
Decision process:	Orderly, logical, rational	Disorderly, characterized by push and pull of interests
Rules and norms:	Norm of optimization	Free play of market forces; conflict is legitimate and expected
Information and computational requirements:	Extensive, systematic, accurate	Ambiguous, information used and withheld strategically
Beliefs about cause-effect relationships:	Known, at least to a probability estimate	Disagreements about causes and effects
Decisions:	Based on outcome maximizing choice	Result of bargaining and interplay among interests
Ideology:	Efficiency and effectiveness	Struggle, conflict, winners and losers

Source: Adapted from Jeffrey Pfeffer, *Power in Organizations* (Marshfield, MA: Pitman, 1981), p. 31.

Mixed Model   Neither the rational model nor the political model characterizes an organization fully, but each will be observed some of the time. Organizations fit on a continuum, as shown in figure 10.5. One model may dominate, depending on organizational environment and context. The important thing is that both models apply to organizational processes. Managers may strive to adopt rational processes, but it is an illusion to assume that an organization can be run without politics. The political model is an important mechanism for reaching decisions under conditions of uncertainty and disagreement. Many of management's efforts to make organizations efficient are designed to move from political to rational processes. But aspects of the political model will always remain in organizations, and will be the dominant model in organizations characterized by rapid change and high uncertainty. Power and political activity are needed to reach important decisions. The rational model is inadequate when there is uncertainty and conflict.

Domains of Political Activity   The definition of politics emphasizes the role of uncertainty and conflict. Uncertainty is a key variable because political behavior is a response to uncertainty. Politics is a mechanism for arriving at a consensus when rules and past experience are not available. Managers at the top of the organization

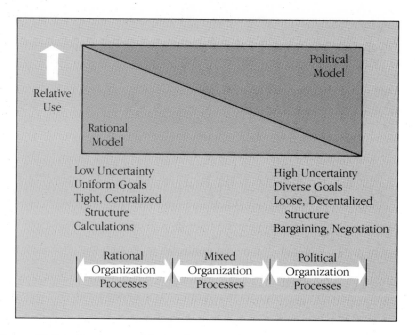

Figure 10.5. Continuum of Rational versus Political Processes in Organizations.

face greater uncertainty than those at lower levels, so more political activity will appear there. Certain decisions are associated with inherent disagreement. Resources, for example, are critical for the survival and effectiveness of departments, so resource allocation often becomes a political issue. "Rational" methods of allocation do not satisfy participants. Four areas in which politics play a substantial role in most organizations are structural change, interdepartment coordination, personnel changes, and resource allocation. These ideas are summarized in table 10.4.

Structural Change Structural reorganizations strike at the heart of power and authority relationships. Structural change reallocates legitimate authority on the organization chart. Reorganizations also change responsibilities and tasks, which affects the underlying power base from strategic contingencies. For these reasons, a major reorganization can lead to an explosion of political activity.[48] Managers want to learn the implications of reorganization for themselves, and will actively bargain and negotiate to maintain the responsibilities and power base they now have. Major reorganizations cause increases and decreases in power, hence a great deal of political activity is required to initiate and implement the change. Top management involvement and commitment is important for structural changes. Without their involvement, the imposition of a new structure would be very difficult because of resistance and political disagreements.

Table 10.4. Domains of High Political Activity in Organizations.

1. Structural change
2. Interdepartmental coordination
3. Personnel changes
4. Resource allocation

IN PRACTICE 10.7

Phillips Electrical, Ltd.

Phillips Electrical is a huge English electronics manufacturer. The director of the radio group, Don Keith, wanted to reorganize from a functional structure to a product structure. His group had 4,200 employees and manufactured four types of sophisticated radio equipment for airlines and air forces around the world. Coordination across the functions of procurement, finance, marketing, engineering, manufacturing, and quality control was poor. Keith was overloaded with decisions at the top of the hierarchy, and was frequently resolving disputes and facilitating coordination between departments. Keith knew the proposed reorganization would generate resistance because the functional managers (e.g., Manager of Engineering) would lose power and stature. The functions would become service groups to the major product lines rather than being the dominant managers in the organization.

Keith's first step was to persuade headquarters management that the reorganization was needed. Many of them believed that a functional structure was satisfactory. They did not understand the benefits of reorganization. A few headquarters managers said that a product structure overemphasized coordination and deemphasized the required competence in functional areas. Keith met with headquarters managers many times, often one at a time, and finally achieved the whole-hearted support of top management for the concept.

The next step was to sell it within his radio group. He knew that he could impose reorganization unilaterally without explanation, but the cost would be great. He would lose the cooperation of some managers, especially those in the functional areas that stand to lose stature. Keith introduced a series of meetings to explain the problems being faced by the organization and the potential benefits of reorganization. He spent a great deal of time teaching what product management was all about, especially to the functional managers. He also spent time talking to individual managers, thereby building a coalition in favor of the reorganization. Keith kept the allegiance of one key functional manager by agreeing to reassign him as a product manager to maintain his power base in the organization. For two other managers, Keith had to rely heavily on his formal authority to impose the new structure despite resistance.

The entire process of persuasion and reorganization took fourteen months. Once the organization structure was in place, eight additional months were required to change various systems, such as budgeting and accounting, to reflect the new lines of authority. Even after implementation, weekly meetings of functional and product managers were continued so that managers could see each other's problems and gain confidence in the new structure.

The effective use of politics by Don Keith early in the development of the product structure at Phillips made the ultimate outcome successful. Obtaining top management support and building a coalition in his radio group were critical to success. After the functional managers adapted to the changes, they became more cooperative and played an important support role to the product lines. Keith's use of politics was important, and the new structure enabled Phillips to attain a higher level of performance.

Interdepartmental Coordination[49]   Relationships between major organizational groups typically are not well-defined. When joint issues arise, managers have to meet and work out solutions on an ad hoc basis. These ongoing coordination activities are often political in nature. The ability of one group to achieve its goal often involves the cooperation of other departments. Interdepartmental coordination lacks rules and precedents to guide it. Uncertainty and conflict are common, especially when the issue is departmental territory and responsibility. Political processes help define respective authority and task boundaries. The following is an example of one such border clash.

IN PRACTICE 10.8

MIS Department

A management information systems (MIS) group was established to handle the company's data processing needs. The director of this group allocated resources on the basis of financial payoff. A marketing administration group found that although they had many worthy projects for the MIS group, their projects would not get done because of other, better justified, projects from other areas.

The marketing administration manager used his political power to rally marketing executives together. His strategy was to show the poor service of the MIS group and thus justify his solution, which was to use his own people for MIS work. He convinced his own management of the benefits of better service and got his own MIS group within marketing.

The MIS head then rallied the rest of the organization against the successful marketing administration group. Since the administration group was getting service that others weren't, the MIS head argued that this was done at the expense of the other department heads.

The result was that the marketing administration group's data processing expertise has been absorbed by MIS.[50]

In this case, MIS preserved its boundaries by using political influence. Rules and past experience did not prescribe how to handle the disagreement, which was unique, so political negotiation and influence resolved the problem.

Personnel Changes   Personnel changes involve promotions, transfers, hiring new executives, and career development.[51] These changes have great political significance at top organization levels where uncertainty is high, and trust and cooperation among executives is important. A manager with a new set of alliances or values can upset stable working relationships and previous agreements. Hiring decisions can generate uncertainty, discussion, and disagreement. Hiring and promotion can be used to strengthen internal alliances and coalitions by putting one's own people in prominent positions. Subordinates often feel obligated and will go along with their benefactor in critical decisions. This strategy was used by Fred Donner to consolidate the power of the finance group at General Motors:

> From him [Donner] developed what I call "promotion of the unobvious choice." This means promoting someone who was not regarded as a contender for the post. Doing so not only puts "your man" in position, but it earns for you his undying loyalty because he owes his corporate life to you . . . . A study of the past ten years of General Motors top executives and an examination of their business biographies make it obvious that some men with undistinguished business careers moved to the top and in many cases occupy positions of power within the corporation today. An understanding of their benefactors makes their ascension more explicable.[52]

Resource Allocation   Resource allocation decisions encompass the range of resources required for organizational performance, including salaries, operating budgets, number of employees, office facilities, equipment, use of the company airplane, and so forth. Resource allocation is something of a puzzle, because this is one type of decision that could be accomplished by the rational model. The value of resources is easy to compute, so if the criteria of allocation can be selected, the computations should be straightforward. Allocation of the travel budget could be based upon number of employees in a department, for example, and operating expenditures could be a function of previous operating needs. But this is rarely the case. Resources are so vital that disagreement exists, and political processes help resolve the dilemmas.[53] Even something so simple as the opening of a new building can cause problems in the allocation of offices. Some organizations resolve this by making offices identical for each rank. When offices vary in size and location, a great deal of discussion and bargaining may ensue as to who deserves which office. Power and influence determine the outcome.

Naive managers sometimes lose out in the resource allocation process because they see only the rational side of decison-making. The dean of an engineering department knew that the tuition received by the university was determined by the number of student credit hours. He calculated the number of students in his department and submitted it to the vice president for academic affairs, assuming that proportional resources would be given to each department. Little did he realize that allocations to departments are not calculated in a routine manner. There are many precedents, alliances, and special considerations to be made. The dean of engineering learned the realities too late, when his department's share was reduced in order to benefit the powerful arts and science department. In that university, the reputation of arts and science was responsible for student enrollment and the university's reputation. They dominated the resource allocation process. The dean of engineering, in order to counter that influence, must work to increase the stature of his own department and use political means to obtain what he sees as a fair share of resources. The following strategy, from another university, was more successful.

> *In a budget presentation of all departments in a local community college, one head made a very pious and long presentation outlining the very deep cuts to be made in his area. The rest were moved by his presentation and a portion of his funds were restored.*
>
> *Following the meeting, the head asked for feedback on his "performance" from a small group of his staff who were also at the meeting. All were unanimous in awarding full marks for presentation, piety, . . . and success of the game plan.*[54]

Summary   Political behavior typically does not emerge for routine, clear-cut decisions for which there are adequate rules, information, and precedents. Political behavior is a mechanism for reaching decisions and achieving outcomes when uncertainty and conflict are high. Decisions that are typically high in uncertainty and conflict are structural change, interdepartmental coordination, top level personnel changes, and resource allocation. Managers who ignore political processes in these decisions will have little influence over final outcomes.

POWER AND POLITICAL TACTICS

One of the themes in this chapter has been that power in organizations is not primarily a phenomenon of the individual. The greatest amount of power in organizations is related to the resources that departments command, the role departments play in the organization, and the environmental contingencies with which they cope. The vice president of marketing in an industrial organization may have substantial power because marketing removes a strategic contingency by generating income for the organization. Position and responsibility more than personality and style determine the marketing vice president's influence on outcomes in the organization.

Power is utilized through individuals, however. Individual managers decide upon the strategy to achieve their department's desired outcomes. Individual managers make decisions and adopt tactics that enable them to acquire and use power. The source of power comes from larger organization processes, but the use of power involves individual decisions and activities. Based upon the material covered in this chapter, this section briefly summarizes strategies that managers can use to increase the power of their departments and achieve desired outcomes. These tactics are summarized in table 10.5.

Tactics for Increasing Power

1. *Enter Areas of High Uncertainty.*[55] An important source of departmental power is to cope with critical uncertainties. If department managers can identify key uncertainties and take steps to remove those uncertainties, the department's power position will be enhanced. Key uncertainties depend upon the situation. Uncertainties could arise from stoppages on the assembly line, from the needed quality of a new product, or from the inability to predict the demand for new services. Once identified, the department can take action to cope with the uncertainty. By their very nature, uncertain tasks will not be solved immediately. Trial and error will be needed, which is to the advantage of the department. The trial and error provides experience and expertise that cannot easily be duplicated by other departments.

2. *Create Dependencies.* Dependencies are an important source of power.[56] When another department or the entire organization depends upon a department for information, materials, or knowledge, this department will hold power over them. This power can be increased by incurring obligations. Doing additional work that helps out other departments will obligate them to respond at a future date.[57] The power accumulated by creating a dependency can be used to resolve future disagreements in the department's favor.

3. *Provide Resources.* Resources are always important to organizational survival. Those departments that provide resources to the organization in the form of money, human resources, or facilities will be powerful. For example, university departments with the greatest power are those that obtain external research funds for contributions to university overhead.[58]

Table 10.5. Power and Political Tactics in Organizations.

Tactics for increasing power
1. Enter areas of high uncertainty
2. Create dependencies
3. Provide resources
4. Satisfy strategic contingencies

Political Tactics for Using Power
1. Build coalitions
2. Coopt key dissenters
3. Control decision premises
4. Enhance legitimacy and expertise
5. Make preferences explicit, but keep power implicit

Likewise, marketing departments are powerful in industrial firms.[59] As mentioned earlier, "He who has the gold, makes the rules."[60]

4. *Satisfy Strategic Contingencies.* The theory of strategic contingencies says that there are elements in the external environment and within the organization that are especially important for organizational success. A contingency could be a critical task, a task for which there are no substitutes, or a central task that is interdependent with many others in the organization.[61] An analysis of the organization and its external environment will reveal strategic contingencies. To the extent that those contingencies are not being satisfied and that there is room for a department to move into those critical areas, the department can increase its importance and power.

Summary The allocation of power in an organization is not random. Power is the result of organizational processes that can be understood and predicted. The ability to reduce uncertainty, increase dependency on one's own department, obtain resources, and cope with strategic contingencies will all enhance a department's power. Once power is available, the next challenge is to use it to attain helpful outcomes.

Political Tactics for Using Power The use of power in organizations requires both skill and willingness. Many decisions are made through political processes because rational decision processes do not fit. Uncertainty or disagreement is too high. Political behaviors that influence decision outcomes are as follows.

1. *Build Coalitions.* Coalition-building means taking the time to talk with other managers to persuade them to your point of view.[62] Most of the important decisions are made outside formal meetings. Managers discuss issues with each other and reach agreements on a one-to-one basis. Effective managers are those who huddle, meeting in groups of twos and threes to resolve key issues.[63] Other techniques are also effective, such as building alliances through the hiring, transfer, and promotion process. Placing people in key positions who are sympathetic to the outcomes of the department can help achieve departmental goals. The ability to build coalitions is a major requirement for achieving desired outcomes.

2. *Coopt Key Dissenters.* Cooptation is the act of bringing an outsider into one's group.[64] A dissenter can be asked to join the department for the accomplishment of a specific activity. This is often used at the board of directors level in firms. The company can coopt bankers, the media, the union, or other key people in the external environment by appointing them to board.[65] An example of cooptation in a university was the creation of a committee on the status of women. Several women professors who were critical of the tenure and promotion process were appointed to the committee. Cooptation brought them into the administrative function. Once a part of the administrative process, they discovered new information, could see the administrative point of view, and learned that administrators were not as evil as suspected. Cooptation effectively

reduced divisiveness so that the administration could then achieve its goals.[66]

3. *Control Decision Premises.* The control of decision premises means to constrain the boundaries of a decision. One technique is to choose or limit information provided to decision-makers. A common method is simply to put your department's best foot forward. Making a good impression often involves the rational side of the organization, such as selectively using objective criteria.[67] A variety of statistics can always be assembled to support the departmental point of view. A university department that is growing rapidly and has a large number of students can make claims on additional resources by emphasizing its growth and large size, and the need for a big increase in resources. Of course, objective criteria do not always work, but they are an important first step in making claims on organizational resources. Information can also influence outcomes by selective release. The manager of the computer department in In Practice 10.1 was able to influence the choice of which computer to purchase by limiting the information to decision-makers. With the limited information available, his preference was the obvious choice.

Decision premises can be further influenced by limiting the decision process. Decisions can be influenced by the items put on the agenda for an important meeting, or even by the sequence in which items are discussed.[68] Items discussed last, when time is short and people want to leave, will receive less attention than those discussed early. Calling attention to specific problems, and the suggestion of alternatives, also will affect outcomes. Pushing a specific problem to get it (rather than problems not relevant to your department) on the agenda is an example of agenda setting.

4. *Enhance Legitimacy and Expertise.* This is another technique that utilizes the rational side of the organization. Members can identify external consultants or other experts within the organization to support their cause.[69] They can also appeal to people in positions of legitimate authority to cooperate with the desired outcome.

5. *Make Preferences Explicit, But Keep Power Implicit.* If managers do not ask, they seldom receive. Political activity is only effective when goals and needs are made explicit so the organization can respond. Often there is organizational slack, and other managers are unsure about what the decision should be. An explicit, specific proposal will often receive favorable treatment, and will take priority over alternatives that are ambiguous and less well-defined. Effective political behavior requires sufficient forcefulness and risk-taking to at least try to achieve desired outcomes.

The use of power, however, should not be obvious.[70] If one formally draws upon his or her power base in a meeting by saying, "My department has more power, so the rest of you have to do it my way," the power will be diminished. Power works best when it is used quietly. To call attention to power is to lose it. Explicit claims for power are made by the powerless, not by the powerful.[71] People know who has power. There is substantial agreement on which departments are more powerful. Explicit claims to power are not necessary, and can even harm the department's cause.

When using any of the above tactics, managers should recall the survey described earlier that found that managers have a negative attitude toward self-serving political behavior. Many managers feel that political behavior hurts rather than helps the organization. If managers are perceived to be throwing their weight around, or are perceived to be after things that are self-serving rather than beneficial to the organization, they will lose respect. The power base will be eroded. The appropriate role of politics is to resolve conflicts and achieve ends that benefit the organization. Legitimate disagreements occur, but each point of view is believed correct by its proponents. Politics is a means to resolve disagreements. When political behaviors are perceived as illegitimate, as going too far, or as serving personal ends, they are dysfunctional. Political behavior is only appropriate and accepted when is is used to work toward outcomes that benefit the organization.

SUMMARY AND INTERPRETATION

This chapter presented two views of organization. One view, covered only briefly, is the rational model of organization. This view assumes that organizations have specific goals, and that environment and technical problems can be identified and logically solved. From this perspective, the management of organizations is basically an engineering problem. Decisions are the result of systematic selection of alternatives to achieve preferred levels of output or profit. The other view, discussed throughout most of the chapter, is based upon a political model of organization. The goals of an organization are not specific or agreed upon. Organizations are made up of departments that have different values and interests. Managers have different desires for organizational outcomes, and they come into conflict. Technical and environmental problems cannot be readily identified or solved. Decisions are made on the basis of power and political influence. Bargaining, negotiation, persuasion, and coalition-building decide outcomes.

The single most important idea from this chapter is the reality of power and political processes in organizations. Differences in departmental tasks and responsibilities inevitably lead to differences in power and influence. Power differences exist, and these power differences determine decision outcomes. Uncertainty about alternatives and disagreement about the correct choices lead to political behavior. Political behavior is inevitable. Understanding sources of power and how to use politics to achieve outcomes for the organization is a requirement for effective management.

Many managers prefer the rational model of decision-making. The rational model is clean and objective. The rational model should be used when decision factors are sharply specified so that the best outcome can be identified through a rational process. Rational processes are effective in situations of certainty, agreement, and good information. Political processes, however, should not be ignored. Political decision processes are used in situations of uncertainty, disagreement, and poor information. Decisions are reached through the clash of values and preferences, and by means of the influence of dominant departments.

Other important ideas in this chapter pertain to the analysis of power differences and political tactics. The research into power processes have uncovered characteristics that make some departments more powerful than others. Factors such as dependency, resources, and the removal of strategic contingencies determine the influence of departments. Political strategies such as coalition-building, cooptation of dissenters, and controlling decision premises help departments achieve the outcomes they desire. Organizations can be more effective when managers appreciate the realities of power and politics.

Finally, despite its widespread use in organizations, many people distrust political behavior. They fear that political behavior may be used for selfish ends that benefit the individual but not the organization. If politics is used for personal gain, other managers will become suspicious and withdraw their support. Politics is accepted when it is used to achieve the legitimate goal of the department or organization. Organizations can be more effective when managers appreciate the reality of power and engage in legitimate political behavior.

DISCUSSION QUESTIONS

1. One form of management tyranny occurs when male senior managers try to exploit sexual favors from female subordinates. These women experience extreme pressure because their jobs depend upon the recommendations of the manager, and they often need the job to support their family. Based upon the discussion in this chapter, what advice would you give to a woman to help her block the abuse of power by her manager?

2. Explain how control over decision premises gives power to a person.

3. In figure 10.3, Research and Development has greater power in firms A, B, L, and N than in the other firms. Discuss possible strategic contingencies that give R & D greater power in those four firms.

4. If you are a lower-level employee in an organization, how might you increase your power base.

5. Sometimes certain positions are practically powerless in an organization. Why should this be? How could those positions be redesigned to have greater power?

6. If a university department were suddenly to have its travel budget doubled so that members could present papers at other schools and attend professional meetings, would the power of the department be increased? Explain.

7. State University X receives 90% of its financial resources from the state, and is overcrowded with students. It is currently trying to pass regulations to limit student enrollment. Private University Y receives 90% of its income from student tuition, and has barely enough students to make ends meet. It is actively recruiting students for next year. Use the theory of strategic contingencies to analyze Universities X and Y. In which university will students have greater power? Discuss.

8. Define politics. How does politics differ from power?
9. If a position has power, does it also have authority? Does it need authority?
10. Why do you think most managers have a negative view of politics?
11. The engineering college at a major university brings in three times as many government research dollars as the rest of the university combined. To other departments, engineering appears wealthy, and has many professors on full-time research status. Yet, when internal research funds are allocated, engineering gets a larger share of the money, even though they already have external research funds. Explain why this happens.
12. Discuss the differences between the rational model and political model of organization decision-making. Would you expect both types of processes to appear in an organization?
13. Would the rational model, political model, or mixed model be used in the following decision situations: quality control-testing in the production department; resource allocation in the executive suite; deciding which division will be in charge of a recently built plant.

GUIDES TO ACTION

As an organization manager:

1. Do not leave lower organization levels powerless. If vertical power is too heavy in favor of top management, increase the power of lower levels by reducing rules, providing rewards for innovation, increasing visibility and outside contacts, and encouraging participation in important problem-solving task forces. Increase power of employees in order to increase performance.
2. Be aware of the less visible, but equally important, horizontal power relationship that comes from the ability of a department to deal with strategic contingencies that confront the organization. Increase the horizontal power of a department by increasing involvement in strategic contingencies.
3. Expect and allow for political behavior in organizations. Politics provides the discussion and clash of interests needed to crystallize points of view and to reach a decision. Build coalitions, coopt dissenters, control decision premises, enhance legitimacy, and make preferences explicit when outcomes are uncertain.
4. Use the rational model of organization when alternatives are clear, when goals are defined, and when managers can estimate the outcomes accurately. In these circumstances coalition-building, cooptation, or other political tactics are not needed and will not lead to effective decisions.

Consider these Guides when analyzing the following cases and when answering the questions listed after each case.

1. FEUDING STIFLES UMW REFORM[72]

Political feuding on the 24-man executive board of the United Mine Workers has turned into a desperate struggle for control of the union and has brought the administration of President Arnold Miller to a standstill. It has stymied organizing in the West—where the soft coal industry is growing fastest—and delayed programs to reduce wildcat strikes and improve safety in the mines.

The executive board is now split into irreconcilable factions, with Miller's enemies in control by a 2-to-1 margin. They have raised no issues of substance against Miller, although they disapprove of the liberal, innovative cast of his administration. Their immediate aim is to strip Miller of his administrative powers or to force him out as president. For coal-industry management, the UMW's internal struggle can only portend a weakening of control over a strike-prone work force.

Bitter Divisions   The conflict began when the Miners for Democracy ousted W. A. "Tony" Boyle, the former president, and his corrupt administration in 1972. The reformers had forced the union to grant rank-and-filers in the UMW's twenty-one districts the right to elect representatives to the policymaking board, which formerly had been largely an appointive body.

Predictably, the influx of rank-and-file miners—as well as many former Boyle staffers who retained political clout—resulted in what at first was a "healthy conflict" on the board. In recent months, however, old political loyalties have bred personal animosities. "The hatreds on the board are so intense," says a union insider, "that when Miller says something is black, his opponents say it's white."

The situation worsened last summer when Vice President Mike Trbovich, who had run on the reform ticket with Miller, and Secretary-Treasurer Harry Patrick swung over to the opposition. Virtually all administrative decisions made by Miller and Patrick, including the hiring and firing of staff personnel, down to clerks and secretaries, are subject to rejection by their enemies on the board. Miller's staff appointees are especially threatened. "We spend so much time protecting ourselves from political attack, we don't have any time to work for the members," says one.

The board has also attempted to impeach Miller by calling a special convention (although the UMW's constitution contains no such recall provision). It has tried to set up its own staff separate from the union's and to dictate when the board should meet.

Taking over the union is clearly the intention of opposition board leaders such as Lee Roy Patterson, representing UMW District 23 in western Kentucky. He is Miller's most vocal opponent, although the most articulate is Andrew Morris, of District 31 in northern West Virginia. Both were Boyle staffers.

Programs at Stake   Miller and Patrick contend that the political bickering has prevented the union from implementing vital programs in organizing, safety, and education.

"Ninety percent of the wildcat strikes could be stopped if our guys knew how to use the contract," Patrick says. "We need a rank-and-file education program, but the board's whole attitude makes us reluctant to propose it to them."

The anti-Miller forces have also tried to take control of organizing campaigns away from Miller's staff. As a result, the UMW's campaign to sign up miners on the big new stripping operations in the West—where output was expected to jump from 12% to 25% of total U.S. production by about 1980—is failing. The UMW has all but lost a crucial strike at the Gillette (Wyo.) mine of AMAX Inc., and if the Western mines remain outside the UMW, its national structure will be weakened.

Two months ago, Miller—who is a weak administrator and frequently loses control of meetings—began to crack down on the "dictators," as he calls them, who oppose him on the board. His toughest action was suspending District 23's Patterson for refusing to undertake a data-gathering mission to Alaska. In the UMW, board members have no administrative function but are required to travel on troubleshooting missions at the president's direction. Patterson balked on the grounds that Miller should have assigned someone to help him. Miller and an aide then made the trip.

At a board meeting two weeks ago, a "spirit-of-unity" compromise was proposed under which Miller agreed to reinstate Patterson if the board would reaffirm his power to suspend members for insubordination. Instead, Patterson demanded "vindication" and the board voted 15-1 to uphold his reason for rejecting Miller's order.

Management in the coal industry, which lost 15 million to 16 million tons of production because of wildcat strikes last year, views the split in the union with growing alarm. "The union is losing influence and is being held up to ridicule," says an industry man who feels that a strong union is necessary to keep discipline in the work force.

Coalfield Unrest

There is growing evidence that anger over the political bickering is welling up in the coalfields. Rank-and-file anger could force changes at a convention scheduled for late this year.

In the UMW's view, AFL-CIO President George Meany did not help matters recently when he said of the UMW: "I don't think they're any better off than they were three years ago." Meany's implication was that the coming of democracy has not changed the union. UMW officers considered this a gratuitous insult and asked Meany for an explanation. He has not replied.

Under Miller, the UMW has become stronger in some respects. But because Boyle stifled the rise of strong local leaders, there was virtually nobody with experience to step into top posts when democracy finally came. "We went from a dictatorship to a democracy overnight," says Patrick, "and it's been hard to handle. The tragedy is the rank-and-file isn't getting anything out of it."

Questions

1. For each organizational characteristic in table 10.3, decide whether the rational model or political model applies to the United Mine Workers. Overall, is this organization managed on a political or rational basis?

2. What are the sources of power for the UMW factions? Are the strategic contingencies for a union different from those for an industrial firm? Discuss.

3. Is political behavior appropriate for the UMW situation? Does it make the union more efficient?

2. DIAMY CORPORATION

Diamy Corporation is the second largest producer of household appliances in Canada. Three-quarters of Diamy's production is sold wholesale to retail chains who put their own brand on the product. Diamy also exports to the United States and Europe.

Len Schoenfeldt became transportation director seven years ago. He has spent his entire career with Diamy. In the early days, his job was to trace shipments and check freight rates in huge catalogs. Sometimes he did other transportation jobs, such as chauffuering VIPs or giving bus tours to groups of foreign visitors.

Times have changed in the transportation department. The director is a senior executive and his staff spends time negotiating with hundreds of carriers to reduce freight rates and improve service.

Freight rates have gradually increased to almost 10% of the wholesale price of appliances. Getting a good deal can make a real difference to Diamy's profit margin. Canada, like other countries, has also been hit with sharply higher fuel, labor, and raw material costs. Provincial regulations have been reduced in response to deregulation in the United States and to the federal government in Ottawa. Freight haulers used to set their rates by gentlemen's agreement, and they were all but identical. Now both truck and rail carriers are in head-to-head price competition to win the business of Diamy and other manufacturers.

The transportation department uses a computer to calculate the best freight rates. The cost of shipping a truckload of washing machines from Ottawa to Toronto could vary from $400 to $800. The computer keeps track of the dizzying array of changing freight rates and helps calculate the most economical mode of transportation.

Mr. Schoenfeldt recently met with Elizabeth Dee from InterCanada Lines, Inc. Ms. Dee explained that several trucks were returning from the Maritimes half empty. She proposed that if Diamy would rent space on the half-empty trailers, InterCanada would given them full truck load rates. This would save Diamy 10–15% on hauls from their plant in New Brunswick.

Mr. Schoenfeldt was noncommital, and offered to have his team look over the details and calculate competitive rates.

Mr. Schoenfeldt then casually mentioned that he hoped InterCanada would consider a proposal to be one of Diamy's major carriers. Diamy was considering giving increased business to carriers for discounts of up to 20%. He mentioned that InterCanada had not been enthusiastic when first approached by a Diamy representative. He also mentioned that Diamy did $150,000 business with InterCanada in the first eight months of 1982. Furthermore, he said, "Montreal Freight, a competitor of yours, has been signed on as one of our major carriers."

Elizabeth Dee wanted to know who at InterCanada sounded cool to the proposal. She would see what she could do. She promised to push for approval of Diamy's major carrier discount program.

Questions

1. Why has the stature and influence of the transportation department increased at Diamy over the last few years? Is transportation a strategic contingency? Would this happen in other companies for which transportation makes up a sizable percentage of sales cost?

2. Does Mr. Schoenfeldt use a rational or political model, or both? Does the decision model fit the type of decision? Does he seem willing to use his influence to achieve desired outcomes? Discuss.

3. Is Diamy a strategic contingency for other organizations? Would it be in Mr. Schoenfeldt's interest to use just a few trucking lines and have them dependent upon Diamy for the majority of their business? Discuss.

NOTES

1. William M. Carley and David P. Garino, "Big Changes Lie Ahead in Management, Board of McDonnell," *Wall Street Journal,* September 8, 1980, pp. 1, 18; Lee Smith, "They've Turned Off the Seat-Belt Sign at McDonnell Douglas," *Fortune,* December 17, 1979, pp. 60–64; "Where Mangement Style Sets the Strategy," *Business Week,* October 23, 1978, pp. 88–99; Dale Dobbins, Greg Owens, and Scott Wilder, "McDonnell Douglas Corporation," unpublished manuscript, Texas A & M University, 1981.

2. Examples are Michael Korda, *Power: How to Get It, How to Use It* (New York: Random House, 1975), and Robert J. Ringer, *Winning Through Intimidation* (Los Angeles: Los Angeles Book Publishing Co., 1973).

3. Jeffrey Pfeffer, *Power in Organizations* (Marshfield, MA: Pitman Publishing, 1981).

4. Robert A. Dahl, "The Concept of Power," *Behavioral Science* 2 (1957): 201–215.

5. Abraham Kaplan, "Power in Perspective," in Robert L. Kahn and Elise Boulding, eds., *Power and Conflict in Organizations* (London: Tavistock, 1964), pp. 11–32.

6. Gerald R. Salancik and Jeffrey Pfeffer, "The Bases and Use of Power in Organizational Decision-Making: The Case of the University," *Administrative Science Quarterly* 19 (1974): 453–473.

7. Rosabeth Moss Kanter, "Power Failure in Management Circuits," *Harvard Business Review* (July–August, 1979): 65–75.

8. A. J. Grimes, "Authority, Power, Influence and Social Control: A Theoretical Synthesis," *Academy of Management Review* 3 (1978): 724–735.

9. Robert L. Peabody, "Perceptions of Organizational Authority: A Comparative Analysis," *Administrative Science Quarterly* 6 (1962): 463–482.

10. Jeffrey Pfeffer, "The Micropolitics of Organizations," in Marshall W. Meyer et al., *Environments and Organizations* (San Francisco: Jossey-Bass, 1978), pp. 29–50.

11. Peabody, "Perceptions of Organizational Authority," p. 479.
12. John R. P. French, Jr., and Bertrand Raven, "The Basis of Social Power," in Dorwin Cartwright and Alvin Zander, eds., *Group Dynamics,* 3rd ed. (New York: Harper & Row, 1968), pp. 259–269.
13. Pfeffer, *Power in Organizations.*
14. Based on Andrew M. Pettigrew, The Politics of Organizational Decision-Making (London: Tavistock, 1973).
15. Andrew M. Pettigrew, "Information Control as a Power Resource," *Sociology* 6 (1972): 187–204.
16. Kanter, "Power Failure in Management Circuits."
17. *Ibid.*
18. *Ibid.*
19. *Ibid.,* p. 70. Reprinted by permission of the *Harvard Business Review.* Copyright © 1979 by the President and Fellows of Harvard College; all rights reserved.
20. David Mechanic, "Sources of Power in Lower Participants in Complex Organizations," *Administrative Science Quarterly* 7 (1962): 349–364.
21. Richard T. Mowday, "The Exercise of Upward Influence in Organizations," *Administrative Science Quarterly* 23 (1978): 137–156.
22. Doris Kearns, "Lyndon Johnson and the American Dream," *The Atlantic Monthly,* May 1976, p. 41. Specified material from *Lyndon Johnson* by Doris Kearns. Copyright © 1976 by Doris Kearns. Reprinted by permission of Harper & Row, Publishers, Inc.
23. Donald I. Warren, "Power, Visibility, and Conformity in Formal Organizations," *American Sociological Review* 33 (1968): 951–970.
24. Stanley Milgram, "Some Conditions of Obedience and Disobedience to Authority," *Human Relations* 18 (1965): 57–75.
25. Charles Perrow, "Departmental Power and Perspective in Industrial Firms," in Mayer N. Zald, ed., *Power in Organizations* (Nashville, TN: Vanderbilt University Press, 1970), pp. 59–89.
26. D. J. Hickson, C. R. Hinings, C. A. Lee, R. E. Schneck, and J. M. Pennings, "A Strategic Contingencies Theory of Intraorganizational Power," *Administrative Science Quarterly* 16 (1971): 216–229; Gerald R. Salancik and Jeffrey Pfeffer, "Who Gets Power—and How They Hold Onto It: A Strategic-Contingency Model of Power," *Organizational Dynamics* (Winter, 1977): 3–21.
27. Salancik and Pfeffer, "Who Gets Power."
28. *Ibid.;* Pfeffer, *Power in Organizations;* C. R. Hinings, D. J. Hickson, J. M. Pennings, and R. E. Schneck, "Structural Conditions of Intraorganizational Power," *Administrative Science Quarterly* 19 (1974): 22–44.
29. Richard M. Emerson, "Power-Dependence Relations," *American Sociological Review* 27 (1962): 31–41.
30. John P. Kotter, 'Power, Dependence, and Effective Management," *Harvard Business Review* 55 (July–August, 1977); 125–136.
31. Michel Crozier, *The Bureaucratic Phenomenon* (Chicago: University of Chicago Press, 1964).
32. Pfeffer, *Power in Organizations,* p. 101.

33. Jeffrey Pfeffer and Gerald Salancik, "Organizational Decision-Making as a Political Process: The Case of a University Budget," *Administrative Science Quarterly* (1974): 135–151.

34. Salancik and Pfeffer, "Basis and Use of Power in Organizational Decision-Making," p. 470.

35. Hickson et al., "Strategic Contingencies Theory."

36. *Ibid.*

37. Kanter, "Power Failure in Management Circuits."

38. Pettigrew, *Politics of Organizational Decision-Making.*

39. B. Bowden, "The Language of Computers," *American Scientist* 58 (1970): 43.

40. Hickson et al., "Strategic Contingencies Theory."

41. *Ibid.*

42. Jeffrey Gantz and Victor V. Murray, "The Experience of Workplace Politics," *Academy of Management Journal* 23 (1980): 237–251; Dan L. Madison, Robert W. Allen, Lyman W. Porter, Patricia A. Renwick, and Bronston T. Mayes, "Organizational Politics: An Exploration of Managers' Perception," *Human Relations* 33 (1980): 79–100.

43. Pfeffer, *Power in Organizations,* p. 70.

44. Bronston T. Mayes and Robert W. Allen, "Toward a Definition of Organizational Politics," *Academy of Management Review* 2 (1977): 675.

45. Gantz and Murray, "Experience of Workplace Politics," p. 428.

46. Pfeffer, *Power in Organizations.*

47. *Ibid.*

48. Madison et al., "Organizational Politics"; Jay R. Galbraith, *Organization Design* (Reading, MA: Addison-Wesley, 1977).

49. Gantz and Murray, "Experience of Workplace Politics," p. 248.

50. Victor Murray and Jeffrey Gandz, "Games Executives Play: Politics at Work," *Business Horizons* (December 1980): 14.

51. Gantz and Murray, "Experience of Workplace Politics"; Pfeffer, *Power in Organizations.*

52. J. Patrick Wright, *On a Clear Day You Can See General Motors: John D. DeLorean's Look Inside the Automotive Giant* (Grosse Point, MI: Wright Enterprises, 1979), p. 41.

53. Pfeffer, *Power in Organizations.*

54. Murray and Gantz, "Games Executives Play," p. 14.

55. Hickson et al., "A Strategic Contingencies Theory."

56. Pfeffer, *Power in Organizations.*

57. Kotter, "Power, Dependence, and Effective Management."

58. Pfeffer and Salancik, "Organizational Decision-Making as a Political Process"; Jeffrey Pfeffer and William L. Moore, "Power in University Budgeting: A Replication and Extension," *Administrative Science Quarterly* 25 (1980): 637–653.

59. Perrow, "Departmental Power and Perspectives."

60. Pfeffer, *Power in Organizations,* p. 101.

61. Hickson et al., "A Strategic Contingencies Theory."

62. Pfeffer, *Power in Organizations.*

63. V. Dallas Merrell, *Huddling: The Informal Way to Management Success* (New York: AMACON, 1979).
64. Pfeffer, *Power in Organizations.*
65. *Ibid.*
66. *Ibid.*
67. *Ibid.*
68. *Ibid.*
69. *Ibid.*
70. Kanter, "Power Failure in Management Circuits"; Pfeffer, *Power in Organizations.*
71. Kanter, "Power Failure in Management Circuits."
72. "Feuding Stifles UMW Reform," *Business Week,* February 16, 1976, p. 102. Reprinted from the February 16, 1976 issue of *Business Week* by special permission © 1976 by McGraw-Hill, Inc., New York, NY 10020. All rights reserved.

11

Intergroup Relations and Conflict

In early August, 1981, 12,000 of the United States' air traffic controllers joined together in a strike against the federal government. The controllers were supremely confident, dedicated to their cause, and certain they would win.

One month later, the controller's strike seemed to symbolize a suicide march rather than a courageous mission. The controllers' self-confidence was badly eroded. The reaction of the government had been seriously miscalculated. The Professional Air Traffic Controllers Organization (PATCO) was frantically seeking a salvage operation that would save the jobs of the controllers and the dignity of the union.

One year later the union was dead. Most of its members were fired from their government jobs. The union was found by the courts to have broken the law by striking against the government, and it was decertified.

What happened to bring about such a dramatic shift in the prospects of PATCO union members? Why couldn't the union and the federal government reach agreement? Why did PATCO leaders miscalculate so badly?

The most crucial error was overconfidence. Union members badly overestimated their importance to air travel and their worth to the government. Each member genuinely believed the government could not operate the nation's air transport system without the controllers. All they had to do was stick together and win. They also believed their enormous demands were justified. While controllers probably do endure more stress than ordinary government workers, they forgot they are more highly paid than other workers and also have job security. An average salary of $33,000 didn't seem that low to objective outsiders.

Several other problems also surfaced. One was internal cohesiveness. When the government issued its ultimatum with the backing of the full power of the presidency and the federal government, PATCO didn't flinch. Instead of compromising, PATCO members pulled together to stick it out. The emotional commitment to union solidarity became more important than the logical rationale for the strike.

Moreover, PATCO didn't listen. They refused to believe President Reagan, who insisted that federal strikes are illegal and would be broken regardless of cost. Drew Lewis, Secretary of Transportation, said that if a strike were called, the strikers would be dismissed, and there would be no amnesty. PATCO also failed to interpret the symbolic value of the President's position, and they underestimated his strength. The President had experienced successes in Congress and with foreign governments, and a firm stand here symbolized the decisive style of his presidency.

The negotiation process was mishandled. The two sides reached a crisis stage with no outlet. Demands were too extreme and notice was too short to allow a resolution. PATCO also didn't gain the support of other unions, such as the Airline Pilots Association or the Machinist's Union. They were overconfident to the point of believing they could shut down the airline system by themselves.

PATCO misperceived the larger external environment. They thought business would put pressure on the government to make a big settlement with the air traffic controllers. But business firms and the airlines supported the President, because of the importance of breaking a federal strike. Also, they went on strike in the fall, when air transportation is easy to manage. They should have waited until mid-winter when control problems are more severe.

The Professional Air Traffic Controllers Organization made several blunders and miscalculations, which had high human and financial cost. The union members are no longer air traffic controllers, and the union itself is dead at the tender age of thirteen.[1]

The clash between PATCO and the federal government is an example of intergroup conflict. Each side had different goals, and the achievement of those goals was blocked by the opposing group. In the heat of conflict, mistakes were made. Negotiations were not well-managed, and the judgment of PATCO officials was in serious error.

PATCO officials did not understand the nature of intergroup conflict. Overconfidence, solidarity, and failure to listen are normal for groups in conflict. These distortions must be recognized and discounted by managers involved in a negotiation process. Moreover, step-by-step negotiation strategies can reduce the intensity of the conflict and lead to a resolution that satisfies both sides. These techniques were not employed in the PATCO strike.

Purpose of This Chapter   The purpose of this chapter is to explore the nature of relationships among groups in organizations. The conflict between PATCO and the federal government is just one type of intergroup conflict. The very nature of organizations invites conflict, because organizations are composed of many groups. Groups are the building blocks of the total organization. Employees identify with the department or group to which they belong, which begins the phenomenon that leads to conflict between groups.

Organizational conflict comes in many forms. Conflict erupts among individuals when they simply don't like each other or have a personality conflict. Conflicts also arise between the individual and the organization. Some people just don't fit in, or disagree with the goals of the organization. The type of conflict we are concerned with in this chapter occurs between groups or departments. As we saw in the previous chapter, departments vie for the allocation of scarce resources and power. Conflict among groups is inevitable. Departments differ in goals, work activities, and prestige, and their members differ in age, education, and experience. The seeds of conflict are sown in these differences. Conflict has to be effectively managed for the organization to perform effectively and to achieve its overall goals.

In this next section, the nature of intergroup conflict is defined. Then the specific outcomes of conflict are identified. The poor judgment displayed by PATCO is not surprising to people familiar with the nature of intergroup relationships. Then the causes of horizontal conflict in organizations are analyzed, followed by a detailed discussion of techniques for preventing and reducing horizontal conflict. The final section of the chapter turns to vertical conflict, such as between management and unions, and considers techniques for controlling and resolving this conflict.

NATURE OF INTERGROUP CONFLICT

Intergroup conflict requires two ingredients. First, there has to be observable group differences of some form. Groups may be located in different parts of the building, members may have gone to different schools, belong to a different religion, vote for different political parties, or work in different departments. The ability to identify oneself as a part of one group and to observe differences in comparison with other groups is necessary.[2]

The second ingredient is frustration. Frustration means that two or more groups are potentially in competition, so that if one achieves its goal the other will not, and hence will be frustrated. Frustration does not have to be severe, and only needs to be anticipated to set off intergroup conflict. Simply perceiving that resources are scarce and other groups may try to increase their share can generate conflict. Intergroup conflict will appear when one group tries to advance its position in relation to other groups. We can define **intergroup conflict** as the behavior that occurs between organizational groups when participants identify with one group and perceive that other groups may block their group's achievement or expectations.[3]

Horizontal Conflict Most organizational conflict is horizontal. As shown in figure 11.1, horizontal conflict occurs between groups or departments, such as between line and staff.[4] Conflicting groups often have equal rank in the organizational hierarchy. Production may have a running dispute with quality control because quality requirements reduce production efficiency.

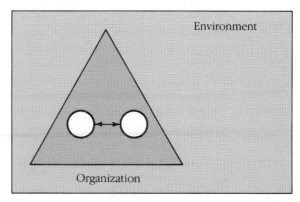

(a)   Horizontal Conflict

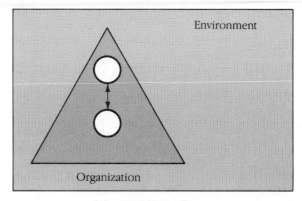

(b)   Vertical Conflict

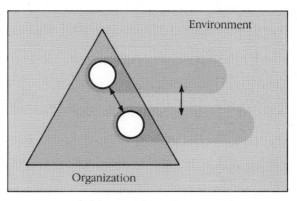

(c)   Social Conflict

Figure 11.1.   Types of Intergroup Conflict.
Source: "Managing Conflict Among Groups," by L. Dave Brown in *Organizational Psychology: A Book of Readings,* 3rd ed. edited by Kolb, Rubin, McIntyre, © 1979, p. 380. Adapted by permission of Prentice-Hall, Inc., Englewood Cliffs, NJ.

Purchasing may disagree with personnel about the qualifications or salaries of new purchasing agents. R & D and marketing may fight over radically different designs for a new product. Horizontal conflict is related to the process of differentiation described in chapter 2. Horizontal integration is needed to reduce conflict and achieve collaboration.

Vertical Conflict Conflict also arises between hierarchical levels.[5] Vertical conflict arises over issues of control, power, and wages and benefits. First-line supervisors and senior manufacturing management may misperceive each other's goals or control orientation. The most prevalent form of vertical conflict occurs between management and workers, and is often formalized by union-management relations. The PATCO strike was an example of vertical conflict.

Social Conflict A third type of conflict comes from the larger society. Group memberships and intergroup hostilities that exist outside the organization carry over into organizational relationships.[6] Religious, racial, or political differences may promote intraorganizational conflict. Mild intergroup conflict would result between graduates of rival universities, especially during the week before the big game. More severe conflict occurs if black managers and white managers identify with different organizational groups. Subtle prejudices and hostilities may carry over into promotions, raises, vacation schedules, or work assignments.

CONSEQUENCES OF
INTERGROUP CONFLICT FOR MEMBERS

Intergroup conflict has been studied in a variety of settings. Experimenters and consultants have been able to observe conflict and test methods for reducing or resolving conflict. This work has provided several insights into the behavioral dynamics that occur within and between groups. These insights are as follows.[7]

1. People identify with a group very quickly when members have a common goal or activity. Members think of their group as separate and distinct from other groups. They develop pride in group accomplishments, and they show signs of the "we feelings" that characterize an in-group. This in-group identification was very visible among members of PATCO.
2. The presence of another group invites comparison between "we" and "they." Members prefer the in-group over the out-group.
3. If a group perceives itself in conflict with another group, it will become more closely knit and cohesive. Members pull together to present a solid front to defeat the other group. A group in conflict tends to become more formal and accepting of autocratic leader behavior. This strong internal cohesiveness was also clearly visible among members of PATCO.

4. The cohesion and positive feelings among members within a group do not transfer to members of out-groups. Members tend to see other groups as the enemy rather than as a neutral object. PATCO perceived the federal government and the Department of Transportation as adversaries, and members displayed negative sentiments toward them.

5. Group members tend to experience a "superiority complex." They over-estimate their own strengths and achievements and underestimate the strength and achievements of other groups. This certainly took place in PATCO. Overconfidence in their abilities, strengths, and achievements was the biggest mistake PATCO made.

6. Communication between competing groups will decrease. If it does take place, it tends to be characterized by negative statements and hostility. Members of one group do not listen or give credibility to statements by the other group. PATCO, for example, did not fully assimilate the statements made by President Reagan and Secretary Drew Lewis.

7. If a superordinate goal is established, it will tend to reduce hostility between groups. A superordinate goal is a goal that has to be achieved in cooperation with another group.

8. When one group loses in a conflict, members lose cohesion. Group members also experience increased tension and conflict among themselves, and look for a scapegoat to blame for the group's failure.

9. Intergroup conflict and the associated changes in perception and hostility are not the result of neurotic tendencies on the part of group members. These processes are natural and occur when group members are normal, healthy, and well-adjusted.

These outcomes of intergroup conflict research were vividly displayed within PATCO. They also can be observed every day in other organizations. Members of one high school or college believe their school is superior to a rival school. People in one plant perceive themselves as superior and as making a greater contribution to the organization than people in other plants. Once these outcomes are understood, they can be accepted as a natural part of intergroup dynamics. Managers can concentrate on handling these processes in a logical way. Certain conditions lead to much more intense intergroup conflict than others. The next section examines the origins of intergroup conflict, and is followed by a description of techniques to reduce conflict when it becomes too great.

HORIZONTAL CONFLICT

Contextual Sources of Conflict

The potential for intergroup conflict exists in any situation in which separate groups are created, members have an opportunity to compare themselves to other groups, and the goals and values of respective groups appear mutually exclusive. Several of the topics covered in previous chapters explain why organizational groups are in conflict with one another. Let's review four of these.

Environmental Uncertainty and Complexity Departments are established to interact with major domains in the external environment. As uncertainty and complexity of the environment increases, greater differences in skills, attitudes, goals, and structure among departments are required. Each department is tailored to "fit" its task and environmental domain, and thus is differentiated from other organizational groups.

Size As organizations increase in size, subdivision into a larger number of departments takes place. Rules and regulations evolve to control behavior, but are not always effective. Relationships among departments are prone to conflict. The lengthening hierarchy also heightens status and prestige differences among departments.

Technology Technology determines task allocation among departments, as well as the interdependence among departments. Groups that have interdependent tasks interact more often and must share resources or exchange services. Interdependence creates more frequent contacts and situations that lead to conflict.

Strategic Choices The relationship among departments is also governed by the design choices of top management. Managers choose group incentives and reward systems, organizational goals, the physical location of groups, and the allocation of scarce personnel and financial resources. These managerial choices set the boundaries within which group relationships evolve.

Environment, size, technology, and strategic choices are elements of the organizational context that lead to more or less conflict between groups. These contextual dimensions determine the specific organizational characteristics that generate conflict, as illustrated in figure 11.2. The larger organizational context translates into seven attributes of interdepartmental relationships that influence the frequency, extent, and intensity of conflict between groups. These seven characteristics are: (1) operational goals, (2) personal backgrounds and traits of group members, (3) task interdependency, (4) resource allocation, (5) power, (6) uncertainty and ambiguity, and (7) incentives and reward systems.

Attributes of Intergroup Relationships

Goal Incompatibility Goal incompatibility is probably the greatest single cause of intergroup conflict in organizations.[8] The operational goals of each department reflect the specific objectives the department is trying to achieve. The achievement of one department's goal often interferes with another department's goal. University police, for example, have a goal of providing a safe and secure campus. They can achieve their goal by locking all buildings on evenings and weekends and not distributing keys. Without easy access to buildings, progress toward the science department's goals of research and development will proceed slowly. On the other hand, if scientists come and go at all hours and security is ignored, police goals for security will not be met. Goal incompatibility throws the departments directly into conflict with each other.

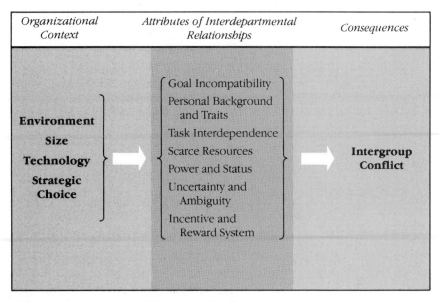

Organizational Context	Attributes of Interdepartmental Relationships	Consequences

Environment

Size

Technology

Strategic Choice

Goal Incompatibility

Personal Background and Traits

Task Interdependence

Scarce Resources

Power and Status

Uncertainty and Ambiguity

Incentive and Reward System

Intergroup Conflict

Figure 11.2. Sources of Intergroup Conflict.

Figure 11.3 provides examples of goal conflict between marketing and manufacturing departments. Marketing strives to increase the breadth of the product line to meet customer tastes for variety. A broad product line means short production runs so that manufacturing has to bear higher costs.[9] Other areas of goal conflict are quality, cost control, capacity planning, and new products. Goal incompatibility exists among many departments in most organizations.

Personal Background and Traits Specific organizational tasks require people with specific education, skills, attitudes, and time horizons. People may join a sales department partly because they have ability and aptitude consistent with sales work. After becoming a member of the sales department, they are influenced by prevailing norms and values characterizing that department. The underlying attitudes and traits of group personnel differ.[10] Consider an encounter between a sales manager and an R & D scientist about a new product.

The sales manager may be outgoing and concerned with maintaining a warm, friendly relationship with the scientist. He may be put off because the scientist seems withdrawn and disinclined to talk about anything other than the problems in which he is interested. He may also be annoyed that the scientist seems to have such freedom in choosing what he will work on. Furthermore, the scientist is probably often late for appointments, which, from the salesman's point of view, is no way to run a business. Our scientist, for his part, may feel uncomfortable because the salesman seems to be

Goal Area	Typical Marketing Comment	Typical Manufacturing Comment
1. Breadth of product line	"Our customers demand variety."	"The product line is too broad—all we get are short, uneconomical runs."
2. Capacity planning and long-range sales forecasting	"Why don't we have enough capacity?"	"Why didn't we have accurate sales forecasts?"
3. Production scheduling and short-range sales forecasts	"We need faster response. Our lead times are ridiculous."	"We need realistic customer commitments and sales forecasts that don't change like wind direction."
4. Delivery and physical distribution	"Why don't we ever have the right merchandise in inventory?"	"We can't keep everything in inventory."
5. Quality assurance	"Why can't we have reasonable quality at reasonable cost?"	"Why must we always offer options that are too hard to manufacture and that offer little customer utility?"
6. Cost control	"Our costs are so high that we are not competitive in the marketplace."	"We can't provide fast delivery, broad variety, rapid response to change, and high quality at low cost."
7. New product introduction	"New products are our life blood."	"Unnecessary design changes are prohibitively expensive."
8. Adjunct services such as spare parts inventory support, installation, and repair	"Field service costs are too high."	"Products are being used in ways for which they weren't designed."

Figure 11.3. Marketing/Manufacturing Areas of Potential Goal Conflict.
Source: Reprinted by permission of the *Harvard Business Review*. Exhibit from "Can Marketing and Manufacturing Coexist?" by Benson S. Shapiro (September/October 1977). Copyright © 1977 by the President and Fellows of Harvard College; all rights reserved.

pressing for immediate answers to technical questions that will take a long time to investigate. All the discomforts are concrete manifestations of the relatively wide differences between these two men in respect to their working and thinking styles . . . .[11]

Line versus Staff   Perhaps the greatest difference in personal style and background is between "line" and "staff." Employees that work in line management, especially near the shop floor, often have worked their way up from the bottom, are not college-educated, and have learned the manufacturing values of cost efficiency and short-run deadlines. Members of staff departments often are highly educated in a narrow specialty, are young, new to the organization, and are concerned with long-range projects. These projects require staff personnel to interact with people in line management, and this is where conflict emerges. In one study, a staff engineer proposed a plan for changing tool-room operations to line supervisors. The supervisors admitted privately that the plan had merit, but they rejected it anyway. As one of them said:

Jefferson's idea was pretty good. But his damned overbearing manner queered him with me. He came out here and tried to ram the scheme down our throats. He made me so damn mad I couldn't see. The thing about him and the whole white-collar bunch that burns me up is the way they expect you to jump when they come around. Jesus Christ! I been in this plant twenty-two years. I've worked in tool rooms, too. I've forgot more than most of these college punks'll ever know. I've worked with all kinds of schemes and all kinds of people. You see what I mean—I've been around, and I don't need a punk like Jefferson telling me where to head in. I wouldn't take that kind of stuff from my own kid—and he's an engineer too. No, his [Jefferson's] scheme may have some good points, but not good enough to have an ass like him lording it over you. He acted like we had to use his scheme. Damn that noise! Him and the whole white-collar bunch—I don't mean any offense to you—can go to hell. We've got too damn many bosses already.[12]

And the feelings of staff people show the same negative sentiment toward line managers.

We're always in hot water with those old guys on the line. You can't tell them a damned thing. They're bull-headed as hell! Most of the time we offer a suggestion its either laughed at or not considered at all. The same idea in the mouth of some old codger on the line'd get a round of applause. They treat us like kids.[13]

Task Interdependence   Task interdependence refers to the dependence of one unit on another for materials, resources, or information. As described in chapter 5 on technology, pooled interdependence occurs when departments have little interaction with each other. Sequential interdependence means that the output of one department goes to the next department, as on an assembly line. Reciprocal interdependence is the highest form, and means that departments mutually exchange materials and information.[14]

Generally, as interdependence increases, the potential for conflict increases.[15] In the case of pooled interdependence, units have little need to interact. Conflict is at a minimum. Sequential and reciprocal interdependence require employees to spend time coordinating and sharing information. They must interact frequently, and differences in goals or attitudes will surface. Conflict is especially likely to occur when agreement is not reached about the coordination of services to each other. Greater interdependence means that departments often exert pressure for a fast response, because departmental work activities have to wait on other departments.[16]

The following example of a purchasing department illustrates how the need to work together and depend upon each other provides the setting for intergroup conflict.

IN PRACTICE 11.1

Purchasing Department

The [Purchasing Department] had two primary functions: (1) to negotiate and place orders at the best possible terms—but only in accordance with specifications set by others—and (2) to expedite orders, that is, to check with suppliers to make sure that deliveries are made on time.

The purchasing agent would also like to suggest (1) alternative materials or parts to use, (2) changes in specifications or redesign of components which will save money or result in higher quality or quicker delivery, and (3) more economical lot sizes, and (4) to influence "make or buy" decisions. The agent calls these functions "value analysis."

Normally orders flow in one direction only, from engineering through scheduling to purchasing. But the agent is dissatisfied with being at the end of the line and seeks to reverse the flow. Value analysis permits him to initiate for others. Such behavior may, however, result in ill feeling on the part of other departments, particularly engineering and production scheduling.

Engineers write up the specifications for the products which the agents buy. If the specifications are too tight, or what is worse, if they call for one brand only, agents have little or no freedom to choose among suppliers. Yet engineers find it much easier to write down a well-known brand name than to draw up a lengthy functional specification which lists all the characteristics of the desired item . . . .

The size of the order and the date on which it is to be delivered are typically determined by production scheduling. The agent's chief complaint against scheduling is that delivery is often requested on excessively short notice—that schedulers engage in sloppy planning or "cry wolf" by claiming they need orders earlier than they really do—and thus force the agent to choose from a limited number of suppliers, to pay premium prices, and to ask favors of salesmen (thus creating obligations which the agent must later repay). Schedulers, on the other hand, claim that "short lead times" are not their fault, but the fault of the departments farther up the line, such as engineering (which delays its blueprints) or sales (which accepts rush orders).[17]

Engineering and production scheduling both depend upon purchasing to acquire products at favorable terms. Purchasing depends upon engineering for specification and production scheduling for delivery dates. These interdependencies, and the desire by purchasing agents to alter these interdependencies, cause frequent conflict.

Competition for Scarce Resources Another major source of conflict involves competition between groups for what members perceive as limited resources.[18] Organizations have only a limited amount of money, physical facilities, staff resources, and human resources to share among departments. In their desire to achieve goals, groups want to increase their resources. This throws them into conflict. Managers may develop strategies, such as inflating budget requirements or working behind the scenes, to obtain the desired level of resources. Resources also symbolize power and influence within the organization. The ability to obtain resources enhances prestige. Departments typically believe they have a legitimate claim on additional resources, but exercising that claim results in conflict.

Conflict over resources tends to be minimized in a growing organization. If the organization is prospering and new resources are flowing in, departments can increase resources without taking away from other groups. Conflict is minimized. In the case of organizational decline (chapter 4), the size of the resource pool is shrinking, and intergroup conflict is at its greatest intensity. The very survival of subgroups is at stake, and pressure to maintain resources will be great.

Power and Status As we saw in the previous chapter, power and status differences evolve even when departments are at the same level on the organization chart. Some departments provide a more valuable service, or reduce critical uncertainties for the organization. Power differences provide a basis for conflict, especially when actual working relationships do not correspond to perceived power.[19] In the following case, a department with less power tried to tell a more powerful department what to do.

IN PRACTICE 11.2

Production Engineering

The production engineering department took research designs and translated them into parts lists, production drawings, and fabrication and assembly specifications, and in addition processed engineering change orders (ECOs). Much of production's work—both its content and its timing—depended on production engineering's efforts, since product designs were constantly changing.

Production engineering was seen by production as telling production what to do and when to do it. On the other hand, production engineering was composed of people with skills no greater than—in fact, quite similar to—those possessed by production members. Production felt itself capable of performing not only production engineering's tasks but the more important tasks of job design and methods work that were within production's jurisdiction but outside production engineering's.

Production managers spent an inordinate amount of time checking for consistency among the various items produced by production engineering. When errors were discovered (as they seldom were), a cry of victory would ring out across the production office. A messenger would quickly be dispatched to carry the offending material back to production engineering, amply armed with a message elaborately outlining the stupidity that had produced such an error. The most common topic of production conversation centered about "those goddam ECOs," in spite of the fact that production originated as many ECOs (making changes for its own convenience) as did any other department.

In this case, energies were heavily focused on the impropriety of a low-prestige department like production engineering calling the tune for an equally prestigious or even superior department like production. Production devoted its energies to rebalancing trade between the two departments. In other words, production's prestige could be maintained only by calling more tunes that it danced. This rebalancing process had little to do with accomplishing any work. Yet it consumed vast amounts of production management time.[20]

Uncertainty and ambiguity Another important factor for predicting intergroup conflict is the uncertainty experienced by organizational departments. When activities are predictable, departments know where they stand. They can rely on rules or previous decisions to resolve disputes that arise. When factors in the environment are rapidly changing or when problems arise that are poorly understood, departments may have to renegotiate their respective tasks.[21] Managers have to sort out how new problems should be handled. The boundaries of a department's territory or jurisdiction become indistinct. Members may reach out to take on more responsibility only to find other groups feel invaded. Generally, as uncertainty about departmental relationships increases, conflict can be expected to increase. Uncertainty and change between departments at ENP Anchor Co. generated conflicts that lasted for a long time.

IN PRACTICE 11.3

ENP Anchor Co.

ENP started making anchors for sailboats in 1946, when Ed Pauley returned home from military service. The product line gradually expanded to include other fittings and pulleys used on both sail and power boats. The firm was relatively small, with about 500 employees, and operated in a stable industry. ENP had no salespeople of its own, relying for many years on field representatives to market its products.

Decisions about developing new products had always been in the hands of a small engineering group and the production department. In the fall of 1981, after a small decrease in sales of traditional product lines, Ed Pauley made the decision to broaden ENP's market and seek new uses for its technology. Two marketing executives were recruited and asked to establish a small marketing department. Marketing was given complete control over production development, previously handled by production and engineering managers. The marketing managers had worked in firms where they had controlled new product decisions. They felt their years of experience and educational background qualified them to handle product development activities.

Managers in both engineering and production felt that their control had been taken over unduly. These managers believed that their years of experience with ENP's anchors and fittings and procedures were important reasons why they should make new product decisions. Conflict between them and the new marketing managers became apparent in every meeting attended by both groups. Feelings ran high during discussion of new products. Ed Pauley was not sure how to handle this conflict, although he persisted in his decision that marketing should have new product responsibility. Eighteen months passed before the conflict subsided. Only one new product was implemented during that period.[22]

Incentive and Reward System   The incentive system governs the degree to which subgroups cooperate or conflict with one another.[23] An experiment with student groups illustrated how incentives influence conflict.[24] In one-half of the groups, called cooperative groups, each student's grade was the grade given for the group's project. All students in each group, regardless of individual contribution, received the same grade. In the remaining groups, called competitive groups, students were rewarded on the basis of their personal contribution to the group project. Each student was graded individually, and could receive a high or low grade regardless of the overall group score.

The outcome of these incentives on conflict was significant. When the incentive system rewarded members for accomplishing the group goal (cooperative groups), coordination among members was better, communication among members was better, productivity was greater, and the quality of the group product was better. When individuals were graded according to their personal contributions to the group (competitive groups), they communicated less with each other and were more frequently in conflict. Members tried to protect themselves and to succeed at the expense of others in the group. Quality of the group project and productivity were significantly lower.

Incentives and rewards have similar impact on conflict between organizational departments. When department managers are rewarded for achieving the goal of the organization, cooperation among departments is greater. Bechtel, for example, provides a bonus system to division managers based upon the achievement of Bechtel profit goals. Regardless of how well a manager's division does, the manager isn't rewarded unless the corporation performs well. This incentive system motivates division managers to co-operate with each other. If departments are rewarded only for departmental performance, managers are motivated to excel at the expense of the rest of the organization.

CONSEQUENCES OF CONFLICT FOR ORGANIZATIONS

In the previous section, we looked at several causes and examples of horizontal conflict. In this section, we want to consider whether conflict is healthy for organizations, that is, to what extent conflict should be reduced or suppressed. Then we explore several techniques for managing the level of horizontal conflict in organizations.

Two Views   ***Human Relations View***   Is conflict bad for the organization? Early writings on management said that it was. Members of the "human relations" school saw conflict as unhealthy, and said it should be eliminated from organizations.[25] Conflict was perceived as an unfortunate outcome that should be reduced as much as possible. An effective organization should be cooperative and peaceful.

Pluralistic View   More recent views argue that conflict is inevitable in organizations and, indeed, is beneficial. An organization without conflict is not sufficiently differentiated in goals, skills, and attitudes to be successful. Conflict is a sign of health and energy, and should be controlled only so that it does not get out of hand. This view has been called the pluralistic view of conflict.[26] Table 11.1 summarizes the two views.

Interdepartmental conflict can have both positive and negative outcomes. If an organization achieves the ideal of no conflict, the organization is probably in trouble. Conflict is a sign of an active, ongoing, forceful organization. Conflict becomes a problem when there is too much of it. Too much conflict leads to the waste of valuable human and material resources. Some of the benefits and wastes associated with conflict (summarized in table 11.2) are as follows.

Benefits   1. *Productive Task Focus.*   When a group is experiencing moderate levels of conflict, within-group differences are submerged, and members focus on the task at hand. The natural differences that evolve between groups, such as in dress, age, education, attitudes, and goals suit the task at hand. Engineering people can be successful at engineering tasks when they have a long-time horizon, are college educated, young, and project-oriented. Manufacturing personnel, on the other hand, can perform their task effectively when they have a short-time horizon, are oriented toward production goals, and are somewhat older and experienced. The charac-

Table 11.1. Underlying Assumptions about Conflict.

Human Relations Approach	Pluralistic Approach
1. Conflict, by and large, is "bad" and should be eliminated or resolved.	1. Conflict is good and should be encouraged; conflict must be regulated, however, so that it does not get out of hand.
2. Conflict is not inevitable.	2. Conflict is inevitable.
3. Conflict results from breakdowns in communication and lack of understanding, trust, and openness between groups.	3. Conflict results from a struggle for limited rewards, competition, and potential frustration of goals —conditions that are inherent in organizations.
4. People are essentially good; trust, cooperation, and goodness are givens in human nature.	4. People are not essentially bad, but are nevertheless driven by achievement, self-seeking, and competitive instincts.

Source: Adapted, with permission by the publisher, from Donald Nightingale, "Conflict and Conflict Resolution," in George Strauss, Raymond Miles, Charles Snow, and Arnold Tannenbaum (eds.), *Organizational Behavior: Research and Issues* (Belmont, Calif.: Wadsworth Publishing Company, 1976) p. 143. © 1976 by Industrial Relations Research Association.

teristics that lead to conflict are the same characteristics that enable departments to excel at their respective tasks.[27]

2. *Cohesion and Satisfaction.* "We-feelings" and in-group identification add to group cohesion. Members are attracted to the group, and obtain satisfaction from their membership. Members cooperate with each other and suspend the achievement of personal goals in order to achieve departmental goals. Group membership under conditions of mild intergroup conflict can be very satisfying to members.[28]

3. *Power and Feedback.* The occasional flare-up of intergroup conflict serves both to balance power relationships across departments and to provide feedback to managers about the department's standing in the organization. Employees often have distorted perceptions about their roles and importance. They may expect and demand undue amounts of organization resources. Conflict with other groups will blunt these ex-

Table 11.2. Benefits and Wastes from Interdepartmental Conflict.

Benefits	Wastes
1. Productive task focus	1. Diversion of energy
2. Cohesion and satisfaction	2. Altered judgment
3. Power equalization and feedback	3. Loser effects
4. Operational goals	4. Poor coordination

cesses.[29] Conflict calls attention to problems within the organization and balances disparities among groups. The feedback from conflict enables groups to correct their perceptions. Feedback acts as a regulatory mechanism. If a system is skewed out of balance toward certain groups, conflict will help correct the balance.

4. *Operational Goals.* The organization's ability to achieve overall goals is related to the energy directed toward operational goals at the departmental level. Moderate competition and conflict serve to stimulate participants to work hard.[30] Cohesion results in an enjoyable work atmosphere. The intensity of an athletic team achieving its goal is an example of the benefits of competition. Complacency can be as great a problem as too much conflict.[31] The organization can prosper and achieve its overall goals only when subgroups are actively doing their tasks well.

Wastes   When conflict is carried too far, several negative consequences for the organization may occur.

1. *Diversion of Energy.* One of the most serious consequences is the diversion of a department's time and effort toward winning the conflict rather than toward achieving organizational goals.[32] When the most important outcome becomes defeating other departments, no holds barred, resources are wasted. In extreme cases, sabotage, secrecy, and even illegal activities occur.

2. *Altered Judgment.* One of the findings from intergroup research is that judgment and perceptions become less accurate when conflict becomes more intense. The overconfidence and unrealistic expectations of PATCO members is an example. Groups may mistakenly blame opponents within the organization rather than acknowledge their own shortcomings. People involved in conflict also have a poor understanding of ideas offered by competitors.[33]

3. *Loser Effects.* Another unfortunate aspect of intense organizational conflict is that someone normally loses. The losing department undergoes substantial change. Losers tend to deny or distort the reality of losing. They often seek scapegoats, perhaps even members or leaders in their own department. Dissension replaces cohesion. Losers generally tend toward low cooperation and low concern for the needs and interests of other group members.[34]

4. *Poor Coordination.* The final problem with conflict is the emphasis given to achieving departmental goals. Departmental goals serve to organize employees, but these goals should not become an all-consuming priority. Departmental goals must be integrated to achieve the goals of the organization. Under intense conflict, integration does not happen. Collaboration across groups decreases. Groups have less contact, and they are not sympathetic to other points of view. Under intense conflict, departmental goals and defeating the enemy take priority. There is no room for compromise. This rigid point of view is not in the interest of the organization.[35]

STRATEGIC CONFLICT

The benefits and wastes of conflict are related to amount of conflict. With too little conflict, the benefits of stimulation, cohesion, and task focus are lost. With too much conflict, the organization suffers negative outcomes. Managers should try to maintain a balance between too much and too little conflict.

Strategic conflict is an intermediate level of intergroup conflict.[36] Strategic conflict recognizes that conflict can be both beneficial and harmful. Managers strive for the benefits, while avoiding harmful effects. Strategic conflict recognizes that organizational conflict is inevitable, even necessary. Managers should actively manage conflict toward an appropriate level rather than ignore or suppress it.

A continuum of conflict in organizations and the outcomes at each level are shown in figure 11.4. The zones of too much or too little conflict should be avoided. The ideal conflict strategy is to maintain the organization in the intermediate zone. In the level of strategic conflict, group members identify with their group, are cohesive, and strive toward group goals. They also will compromise their goals for organizational benefit, and cooperate with other groups. Strategic conflict means that moderate conflict should be encouraged, but conflict should not get out of control.

TECHNIQUES FOR MANAGING
CONFLICT BETWEEN GROUPS

The ideal situation for most organizations is to have moderate inter-unit competition and conflict. In many organizations, the problem is intense conflict rather than complacency. Conflict often gets out of hand. The

Figure 11.4.   Levels of Interdepartmental Conflict and Organization Outcomes.

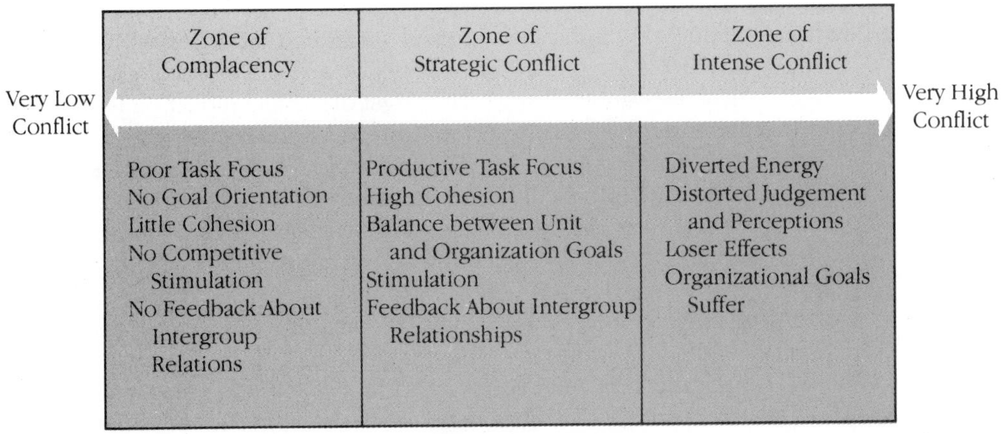

Zone of Complacency	Zone of Strategic Conflict	Zone of Intense Conflict
Poor Task Focus No Goal Orientation Little Cohesion No Competitive Stimulation No Feedback About Intergroup Relations	Productive Task Focus High Cohesion Balance between Unit and Organization Goals Stimulation Feedback About Intergroup Relationships	Diverted Energy Distorted Judgement and Perceptions Loser Effects Organizational Goals Suffer

Very Low Conflict ←——————————————————————→ Very High Conflict purchasing department simply will not cooperate with the engineering department; the finance clerks won't talk to the accounting clerks. In these situations, departments adopt the goal of fighting each other. Most of the techniques developed for managing conflict between groups are designed to reduce conflict. In this section, we briefly cover ways to prevent and reduce conflict as needed.

Preventing Conflict

Techniques for preventing conflict are used to keep conflict from increasing. Managers are often satisfied with the level of conflict, but wish to prevent it from getting out of control. Preventing conflict is often easier than undoing conflicts that have reached an intense level.

1. *Emphasize Total Organizational Goals and Effectiveness.* When members are hired, organizational accomplishments should be emphasized so that department outcomes are not the only goals. Stressing total organizational performance helps employees see the big picture and their role in it, which leads to greater cooperation and collaboration.[37]
2. *Provide Stable, Well-Structured Tasks.* When activities are well-understood and clearly defined, conflict is less likely to erupt. Employees know the limits of their authority and their place in the organization. Conflict is most likely to occur when activities and responsibilities are not well-defined and groups have to negotiate their respective positions.[38]
3. *Communication among Groups.* Stimulating group contact prevents the development of misperceptions about the abilities, skills, and traits of other departments. Senior managers can see that relevant organizational information about departments is passed horizontally across the organization.[39]
4. *Avoid Win-Lose Situations.* Do not put groups in the position of intense competition for scarce organizational resources or rewards. Win-lose conflicts force one group to be the ultimate loser in the competition. Emphasize pooling resources to achieve maximum organizational effectiveness. Rewards can be given for each group's contribution to overall effectiveness.[40]

Reducing Conflict

Reducing conflict is a greater challenge than preventing conflict. When conflict is too great, participants may actively dislike each other, and simply may not want to change. The target of conflict reduction techniques is either the *behavior* or the *attitude* of group members.[41] By changing behavior, open conflict is reduced or eliminated. Department members will still dislike people in the other departments. A change in behavior makes the conflict less visible, or keeps the groups separated. A change in attitudes is deeper and takes longer. Attitude change is difficult and requires a reduction in the negative perceptions and feelings of department members. Attitude change improves the quality of the ongoing relationship between groups.

The techniques available for reducing conflict are arranged along a scale in figure 11.5. Techniques near the top of the scale, such as physically separating groups, will change behavior but not attitudes.[42] The techniques near the bottom of the scale, such as rotating group members or intergroup training, are designed to bring about attitude change. In practice, the reduction of conflict, especially if attitudes need changing, is more difficult and time-consuming than preventing intense conflict.

Physical Separation Physical separation is sometimes the fastest and easiest method of reducing conflict. Groups are simply not allowed to interact with each other. Separation is useful when groups are not working on a joint task, and when a temporary solution to the conflict is needed. Separation provides time to seek a more permanent solution. Separation does not encourage members of the conflicting groups to change their attitudes toward one another.[43]

Bureaucratic Method The bureaucratic method means that top management invokes rules, regulations, and authority to resolve the conflict issue or to suppress the conflict. The disadvantage is that it does not change attitudes and may only treat the immediate problem. The bureaucratic method is effective in the short run when members cannot be separated.[44]

Limited Interaction Interaction between conflicting departments should be limited to issues with common goals. Common goals occur when the groups must work together to achieve them. They force the group to cooperate, at least for the achievement of that goal. This technique is most effective when decision-making rules and boundaries of interaction are well-defined. This technique may make a small impact on attitude change long enough to achieve the joint goal.[45]

Figure 11.5.   Strategies for Reducing Conflict Between Groups.
Source: Adapted from Eric H. Neilsen, "Understanding and Managing Conflict," in Jay W. Lorsch and Paul R. Lawrence, eds., *Managing Group and Intergroup Relations* (Homewood, IL: Irwin and Dorsey, 1972), pp. 329–343.

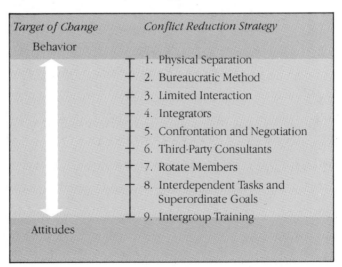

Integrators Integrators were described in chapter 6 as people who are assigned the role of spanning the boundary between departments. Integrators must have legitimacy and expertise in the eyes of both groups, otherwise they will not be trusted. The integrator works full-time to achieve cooperation and collaboration by meeting with members of the respective departments and exchanging information. The integrator has to understand each group's problems and be able to move both groups toward a solution that is mutually acceptable. The integrator may work continuously to keep conflicts between key departments at modest levels.[46]

Confrontation and Negotiation This technique brings key members of respective groups together to confront the conflict and work it out themselves. This technique involves some risk. There is no guarantee that the discussions will focus on the conflict or that emotions will not get out of hand. However, if members are able to resolve the conflict on the basis of face-to-face discussions, they will find new respect for each other and future collaboration becomes easier. The beginnings of relatively permanent attitude change are possible through direct negotiation.

Confrontation is successful when managers engage in a "win-win" strategy. Win-win means that both departments strive to resolve the conflict in a way that will benefit each other.[47] If the negotiations deteriorate into a strictly win-lose strategy (each group wants to defeat the other), the confrontation will be ineffective. Prior to confrontation, top management can urge group members to work toward mutually acceptable outcomes. The differences between win-win and win-lose strategies of negotiation are shown in table 11.3. With a win-win strategy—which includes defining the problem as mutual, communicating openly, and avoiding threats—attitudes can often be changed for the better.

Table 11.3. Negotiating Strategies.

Win-Win Strategy	Win-Lose Strategy
1. Define the conflict as a mutual problem.	1. Define the conflict as a win-lose situation.
2. Pursue joint outcomes.	2. Pursue own group's outcomes.
3. Find creative agreements that satisfy both groups.	3. Force the other group into submission.
4. Use open, honest, and accurate communication of group's needs, goals, and proposals.	4. Use deceitful, inaccurate, and misleading communication of group's needs, goals, and proposals.
5. Avoid threats (to reduce the other's defensiveness).	5. Use threats (to force submission).
6. Communicate flexibility of position.	6. Communicate high commitment (rigidity) regarding one's position.

Source: Adapted from David W. Johnson and Frank P. Johnson, *Joining Together: Group Theory and Group Skills* (Englewood Cliffs, NJ: Prentice-Hall, 1975), pp. 182–183.

Third-Party Consultants A third-party consultant is brought in from outside the organization and meets with representatives of both departments. These consultants should be experts on human behavior, and their advice and actions must be valued by both groups. Third-party consultants can make great progress toward changing attitudes and reducing conflict. Typical activities of third-party consultants are as follows.

- Reestablish broken communication lines between groups.
- Act as interpreter so that messages between groups are correctly understood and are not distorted by preconceived biases.
- Challenge and bring out into the open the stereotyping done by one group of the other. Exposing stereotypes often leads to their dissolution.
- Bring into awareness the positive acts and intentions of the other group. This forces a cognitive reassessment of their stance toward the other group.
- The specific source of conflict must be defined and focused on and the surrounding emotions removed. Extraneous issues have to be ignored while the group is brought back into concentration on the key cause of conflict.[48]

Member Rotation Individuals from a department can be asked to work in another department temporarily. Rotation might last for three months to a year. The advantage is that these individuals become totally submerged in the values, attitudes, problems, and goals of the other department. In addition, the individuals can explain the problems and goals of their original departments to their new colleagues. This enables a frank, accurate exchange of views and information. Rotations works slowly to reduce conflict, and requires a long period of time, but it is very effective for changing the underlying attitudes and perceptions that promote conflict.[49] The following case illustrates the successful use of member rotation in one company.

IN PRACTICE 11.4

Canadian-Atlantic

Canadian-Atlantic, a transportation conglomerate headquartered in Vancouver, British Columbia, experienced intense conflict between research managers and operating managers at the home office. Research managers were responsible for developing operational innovations, such as for loading railroad cars, to increasing operational efficiency. Operations managers were responsible for scheduling and running trains.

Operations management had absolutely no use for research personnel. They claimed that research personnel took far too long to do projects. One manager said, "A 50% solution when we need it is much better than a 100% solution 10 years from now when the crisis is over." Operating managers were also offended by the complicated terminology and jargon used by research personnel. Research personnel had developed several useful innovations, such as automated loading platforms and training simulators, but resistance to the innovations was great. Research personnel wanted to cooperate with operations managers, but they could not go along with certain requests. Researchers refused to release half-completed innovations, or to water down their ideas for less well-educated personnel in operations. One manager commented that the extent of communication between research and operations "was just about zero, and both groups are beginning to like it that way."

The vice president of research and development was worried. He believed that intergroup hostility was dramatically reducing the effectiveness of R & D. Morale in R & D was low and operations managers had little interest in new developments. The vice president persuaded the president to try rotating managers between operations and research. Initially, one manager from each department was exchanged. Later, two and three were exchanged simultaneously. Each rotation lasted about six months. After two and one-half years, the relationship between the departments was vastly improved. Key individuals now understood both points of view and could work to integrate the differences that existed. One operations manager enjoyed the work in research so much that he asked to stay on. The operations vice president tried to hire two of the R & D managers to work permanently in his division.

Interdependent Tasks and Superordinate Goals Another strategy is for top management to establish superordinate goals that require interdependence and cooperation between departments.[50] These goals and interdependent tasks, in order to be effective, must be major and must consume a substantial amount of each group's time and energy. One powerful goal is company survival. If the organization is about to fail and jobs will be lost, groups forget their differences and try to save the organization. The goal of survival has dramatically improved relationships in meat packing plants and auto supply firms that have been about to go out of business.

Intergroup Training The strongest intervention is intergroup training. This technique has been developed by psychologists such as Blake, Mouton, and Walton.[51] When other techniques fail to reduce conflict to an appropriate level, or when other techniques do not fit the organization in question, extensive group training may be required. This training requires the attendance of department members at an outside workshop away from day-to-day work problems. The training workshop lasts for several days, and various activities take place. This technique is expensive, but has great impact on attitude change. Groups learn about themselves and about each other.

IN PRACTICE 11.5

Intergroup Training Process

An intergroup training process developed by one specialist has been successful with several corporations.

1. The competing groups are both brought into a training setting and the common goals are stated to be an exploration of mutual perceptions and mutual relations.
2. The two groups are then separated and each group is invited to discuss and make a list of its perceptions of itself and the other group.
3. In the presence of both groups, representatives publicly share the perceptions of self and other that the groups have generated, while the groups are obligated to remain silent. The objective is simply to report to the other group as accurately as possible the images that each group has developed in private.
4. Before any exchange takes place, the groups return to private sessions to digest and analyze what they have heard; there is great likelihood that the representatives' reports have revealed discrepancies to each group between its self-image and the image that the other group holds of it. The private session is partly devoted to an analysis of the reasons for these discrepancies, which forces each group to review its actual behavior toward the other group and the possible consequences of that behavior, regardless of its intentions.
5. In public session, again working through representatives, each group shares with the other what discrepancies it has uncovered and the possible reasons for them, focusing on actual, observable behavior.
6. Following this mutual exposure, a more open exploration is permitted between the two groups on the now-shared goal of identifying further reasons for perceptual distortions.
7. A joint exploration is then conducted of how to manage future relations in such a way as to minimize a recurrence of the conflict.[52]

After this training experience, department employees understand each other much better. The improved attitudes lead to better working relationships on the job.

VERTICAL CONFLICT

Management versus Workers

The discussion so far in this chapter has dealt with horizontal conflict between departments. The other major form of conflict is between vertical groups. Some of the same concepts apply to vertical conflict, but the groups and issues tend to be different.

Vertical conflict can take various forms. Student groups may find themselves in conflict with faculty or administration about the teaching versus research goals of the university. Individual employees may have conflicts with their bosses. One visible and sometimes troublesome area of conflict within organizations is between management and workers, who are often represented by a union. All too often we see union or management representatives on television explaining why the other side is wrong and why a strike or lockout is necessary. These conflicts often occur in major industries such as transportation and steel, and in specialized areas such as sports or air traffic controllers.

Status and power differences are greater for vertical conflict than for horizontal conflict. Part of the reason for vertical conflict is to equalize these differences. Unions try to give workers more power over wages or working conditions. Moreover, the ground rules for conflict between workers and management are formalized by laws and regulations. Formal negotiation procedures are available in which appointed representatives work to resolve differences. The conflict between union and management is similar in some ways to the conflict that occurs between lateral groups, but it can be expected to be more severe. In this section, we explore some of the reasons for union-management conflicts, and techniques for its reduction.

ORIGIN OF
UNION-MANAGEMENT CONFLICT

Vertical conflict exists with or without a union, but conflict is more visible when workers join a union. The union formalizes vertical differences, and provides a mechanism for resolving these differences. Workers form into unions for a variety of reasons:

1. *Psychological Distance.* Workers do not feel involved in the organization. They perceive that their needs are not being met. A union is a way of giving voice to these needs. The union provides workers with a clearly defined group identity. Once the union is formed, members identify with the union, not the company, and try to achieve gains through the union. This usually throws union and management into a win-lose conflict situation.

2. *Power and Status.* Workers are at the bottom of the hierarchy, and often feel powerless and alienated. They have little say in decisions that directly affect their lives, such as wages and benefits. Standing together in a union gives them strength that equalizes their power with management's. This power is restricted to areas directly affecting workers, but it is still much greater than workers have alone.[53]

3. *Ideology.* Values of management and workers differ along a number of dimensions. These differences represent basic beliefs about the purpose and goals of organizations and unions.[54] The major ideological differences are listed in table 11.4. Unions believe that managerial control has clearly defined limits, that employees should be loyal to the union first and the company second, and that the union should extract greater and greater benefits for union members from management. Management, on the other hand, believes that they have the right to manage the organization, that employees should be loyal to the organization, and that the primary purpose of the organization is to provide products and services for a profit.

4. *Scarce Resources.* One important issue between unions and management is financial resources. Salary, fringe benefits, and working conditions are dominant bargaining issues. Workers look to the union to obtain

Table 11.4. Ideological Characteristics of Union and Management that Lead to Conflict.

Unions	Management
1. Limits to managerial control	1. Right to manage organization
2. Loyalty of members to union	2. Loyalty of employees to organization
3. More, more, more wages and benefits	3. Profits
4. Right to participate in determining own destiny	4. Labor as a factor of production

Based on John T. Dunlop, *Industrial Relations Systems* (New York: Henry Holt Co., 1958), pp. 16–18.

financial benefits. Unions will strike if necessary to get what they want, just as PATCO did.

5. *Contextual Factors.* Other factors sometimes influence unionization or the amount of conflict that occurs between union and management. These include the technology of the organization, which can vary from white-collar jobs in banks to assembly-line work. Other settlements in the same industry may determine worker expectations. State and local laws and public opinion are also important. Unions are less powerful in states with right-to-work laws. The personalities of the representatives may influence the goals and conflicts between workers and management.

Experiment in Union-Management Conflict

One of the most interesting studies to explore the underlying dynamics in union-management relationships was conducted by Blake and Mouton.[55] The study involved only managers, but they were placed in competing roles similar to those experienced in union-management conflict.

The managers from a large company were brought together in a laboratory training session. They were divided into groups of from nine to twelve persons. Participants worked intensively with their own groups and developed a strong in-group identification. They worked as a group throughout the training period of from ten days to two weeks.

Each group was placed in conflict with another group. The groups were given a problem that would measure problem-solving effectiveness. The problem was presented so that both groups realized that one group would be a winner and one group a loser. This forced the groups into an intensive win-lose situation. Each group was given thirteen hours (overnight) to develop a solution.

Under this form of conflict, several behaviors were observed.

1. *Increased Group Cohesion.* Differences in senior, middle, and lower managers disappeared as group members closed ranks and concentrated on winning.
2. *Distorted Perceptions.* Each group developed a superiority complex. Virtually all groups saw themselves as "above average."

3. *Distorted Judgment.* After all solutions were presented, each group evaluated its own solution as best. Members were not fairminded or rational in making judgements. They believed in their own group's solutions and downgraded solutions of other groups.

4. *Unequal Knowledge.* Experimenters worked with each group to ensure a full understanding of their own and their competitor's solutions. When group members indicated full understanding of the other group's solution, an examination was given. All those surveyed had much greater knowledge of their own group's solution, despite the systematic effort made to ensure complete understanding of both solutions.

To simulate the negotiation strategies of unions and management, each group was asked to elect a representative who would meet with a representative from the competing group. The two representatives were asked to select one solution as the winner. An interesting thing happened.

5. *Representatives Stayed Loyal to Their Own Group's Solution.* The two representatives were asked to analyze and discuss each solution and to agree on a winner. After thirty-three such incidences, only two representatives agreed that the other group's solution was superior. Thirty-one representatives remained loyal to their own group, regardless of solution quality. Representatives supported their group's proposal, and never did agree on a winner.[56]

These findings are striking because they emphasize just how difficult it can be for elected representatives to reach a solution. The first priority for representatives is loyalty to their group. Conflict between management and unions is often intense because of differences in attitudes, values, and power. The resolution mechanism is to use negotiators, yet negotiators are committed to their group's proposal, regardless of the quality of competing proposals. In an intensive, win-lose situation, the fair resolution of conflict through the use of negotiators may seem impossible.

RESOLUTION OF UNION-MANAGEMENT CONFLICT

Collective Bargaining

Collective bargaining is the negotiation of an agreement between management and workers. The bargaining process is usually accomplished through a union, and it follows a prescribed format. **Collective bargaining** involves at least two parties that have a defined interest. The collective bargaining activity usually begins with the presentation of demands or proposals by one party that are evaluated by the other parties. This is followed by counterproposals and concessions.

The approach taken in collective bargaining is determined by the compatibility of the goals of the respective parties. Three types of bargaining approaches are common:[57]

1. *Distributive bargaining.* Distributive bargaining refers to the attainment of one party's goals when they are in basic conflict with those of the other party. This is bargaining in the traditional sense. Conflicts can relate to any issue, but they are typically economic. This type of bargaining usually takes place in a "fixed-sum" situation in which one person's gain is the other person's loss. Both parties perceive a win-lose situation. This was the situation in the negotiations leading to the PATCO strike.

2. *Integrative Bargaining.* Integrative bargaining refers to the attainment of objectives that are not in conflict with those of the other party. The two parties define a common concern or problem. Integrative bargaining exists when the problem is such that solutions can be developed that benefit both parties rather than benefit one party to the exclusion of the other. Integrative bargaining characterized the UAW negotiations with Ford and General Motors in 1982. Each side was willing to help the other attain common objectives, such as lowering the price of cars to increase both sales and jobs.

3. *Attitudinal Structuring.* Distributive and integrative bargaining pertain to economic issues. An additional function of negotiation is to influence attitudes such as friendliness, trust, and respect. Attitudinal structuring occurs when negotiators take advantage of the interactions to develop a more positive attitude between parties. One recent example of attitudinal structuring occurred in the steel industry.

IN PRACTICE 11.6

Steel-Mill Negotiations

Union-management relationships in the steel industry were for many years governed by a distributive bargaining approach. The United Steel Workers and steel industry management are now in the forefront of industries that are trying to achieve both integrative bargaining and attitudinal structuring. The approach is based upon what is called "labor-management participation teams" in several plants.

The participation-team concept, first provided for in the 1980 contract, was devised as a means of improving steel's sluggish productivity growth rate, as well as a means of enhancing the quality of work for steelworkers. Consisting of ten to fifteen rank-and-file workers and supervisors, the teams are being formed at the department level within plants to solve problems that are not addressed in the traditional union-management procedures. The teams will give workers a chance to contribute ideas to deal with problems such as production bottlenecks, safety and health issues, the efficient use of tools, absenteeism, incentive pay, product quality, and other matters.[58]

The participation team reflects the belief that both industry and workers can benefit. They have a cooperative attitude. The company gets increased productivity, and workers receive a better quality of work life. This approach reflects integrative bargaining and a concern for attitudinal structuring.

Collaborative Win-Win Approach   One approach that has successfully reduced union-management conflict is for management and union leaders to adopt a win-win attitude in negotiations.[59] The win-win approach was summarized in table 11.3. A win-win approach occurs if union officials and management have had training in conflict-reduction and are aware that the traditional attempts to win their goals at the expense of the other party will not be effective. The application of these ideas to remove the win-lose dynamics was used in an organization in which the history of the union-management relationship was characterized by tension and strife.[60] The consultants began their implementation by first working with managers in training sessions to help them avoid the pitfalls that arise when each group has a strongly preferred solution to a given problem. The results of the collaborative process are described in the following case.

IN PRACTICE 11.7

Union-Management Collaboration

One of the applications of the collaborative approach involved a sixteen-man bargaining unit in the petroleum industry. Eight men were from management and eight from the union. The union approached the bargaining table with sixty demands. Management's initial reaction was a negative and rejecting attitude toward the union's demands. However, since they had been trained to avoid the problems of intergroup conflict, management examined their attitudes before intergroup antagonism arose. The union's demands were grouped into topic areas that then became targets for exploratory discussions.

The basic strategy involved establishing a number of subgroups, each consisting of two union and two management representatives, to accept a single responsibility. It was their obligation to investigate and to establish the *facts* behind each of the identified problem areas. The subgroups were *not* to work on solutions.

In due course, the joint subgroups reported the facts to the total union and management bargaining team. At this point, a fascinating result was observed. In many cases, the facts developed and agreed on in the subgroups were conspicuously different than the "facts" that either management or the union had thought to lie behind the problem before the subgroup investigations took place.

Given a mutually acceptable statement of facts within each problem area, the situation was ripe to search for solutions that would meet the common needs of both union and management as well as the needs unique to each. The procedure adopted for taking the step toward finding acceptable solutions in each problem area involved breaking the total group of sixteen into two subgroups of eight, with each composed of four from management and four from the union.

In the final stage, the two eight-person subgroups reunited into a total bargaining group of sixteen to compare the quality of the solutions by one group with the solutions by the other. They were able to evaluate and, when necessary, to further modify the most highly agreed-upon suggested solutions as the basis for formalized agreements. This sequential procedure for problem-solving between groups has proved outstandingly successful as a basis for statesmanlike union-management problem-solving.[61]

Cross-Cultural Approaches A variety of new ideas has been advanced in the last few years for overcoming barriers between workers and management. The goal of these approaches is fewer crippling strikes and greater harmony. These ideas range from the participation-team concepts used in the steel industry to actually appointing union representatives to task forces or to membership on corporate boards. Douglas Frazer, President of the UAW, for example, was appointed to Chrysler Corporation's board of directors in 1980.

European managers tend to be ahead of the United States in drawing workers into the process of running the company. This is partly the result of socialist governments that provide a different legal climate within which workers and management bargain. These approaches usually encourage greater worker influence in management decisions than would normally be expected in the United States and Canada. They may, however, indicate the wave of the future.

West Germany New forms of employee involvement in top management decision-making were legislated in 1975. The process is called co-determination. Union and employee representatives participate in all fundamental top management decisions. Union representatives are primarily involved in decisions affecting employment levels and job security.[62]

Sweden Since 1971, management in every Swedish factory has to consult employees on important operational decisions. Organizations have adopted several devices for gathering employee views, including questionnaire surveys and electing worker representatives.[63]

Yugoslavia Yugoslav enterprises are theoretically owned by society as a whole, which includes the employees. Responsibility for a firm rests with a committee of employees. All workers must have an opportunity for direct or indirect participation. Participation takes the form of worker meetings and the election of representatives. The workers' council, an elected group, is responsible for the firm, and it selects the top managers. Managers report to the workers' council. Managers serve for a limited term, but may be reappointed after each term of office.[64]

SUMMARY AND INTERPRETATION

This chapter contains several important ideas. Probably the most important idea is that intergroup conflict is a natural and useful outcome of organizing. At a personal level, most of us dislike conflict. Whatever the reason for interpersonal conflict—personality clash, basic value differences—we tend to avoid conflict scenes because they are uncomfortable. But the dislike for conflict should not be applied to intergroup relations in organizations. Differences in goals, backgrounds, tasks, and so on are necessary for departmental excellence. Unfortunately, these differences throw groups into conflict. Intergroup conflict is healthy and should be directed toward successful outcomes for everyone. Conflict should not be suppressed or avoided. Understanding the appropriate role of organizational conflict and the importance of achieving strategic levels of conflict is probably the single most important lesson from this chapter.

Conflict between groups represents a dilemma for the organization. Intergroup conflict has very clear advantages *within* each group. The increased focus on achieving group goals, increased cohesion, satisfaction, and stimulation represent the type of group atmosphere organizations strive for. Intergroup conflict is a powerful device for achieving a positive group atmosphere within departments. The atmosphere within departments does not translate into relationships *between* departments. The improved identification with one's own group leads to disregard and dislike for external groups. Members begin to see other departments as inferior, as the enemy, and cooperation may decrease as the within-group atmosphere improves. In order to achieve high-quality collaboration between departments, some of the in-group identification has to be given up. The dilemma for managers is to obtain the advantages of in-group feelings without the disadvantages of intense intergroup conflict. This is accomplished in the zone of strategic conflict. A strategic level of conflict allows organizations to balance the within-group and between-group forces at a satisfactory level.

Intergroup conflict has been a concern of researchers and managers for a long time. The material in this chapter presents two trends in organizational research. The first trend began with the belief that conflict is bad for the organization, and led to the belief that it is good. Early theorists thought organizations should be warm, conflict-free places to work. Our understanding of conflict in organizations has now evolved to where we understand that conflict is healthy, and in correct amounts can have great benefits for an organization's productivity.

The other trend has been the focus of research on intergroup conflict, begun over twenty years ago. The pioneering work in boys' camps and with managers in the laboratory provided rich insights into the causes of conflict. That early research was so well done and so informative that there has been little to add in the years since. Recent research has focused on techniques for managing conflict. At this point in the development of organization theory, we now have an understanding of the causes of conflict, and a large repertoire of techniques for managing conflict when it occurs.

Much of the work in organization theory has been concerned with horizontal rather than vertical conflict. Horizontal conflict is the day-to-day preoccupation of most managers. Horizontal relations among departments are less predictable than vertical relations, and there are fewer rules and regulations to prescribe conflict resolution. A large part of managerial activity includes handling horizontal conflicts on a day-to-day basis. The dominance of horizontal conflict in organizational theory reflects its frequency in organizations. Vertical conflict is reflected in union-management relationships and is equally important. But it follows formal procedures and has been delegated to specialists, such as industrial relations personnel and attorneys.

Finally, the material in this chapter corresponds to material in earlier chapters. The causes of intergroup conflict lie in the basic underlying structure of organizations, which was covered in the chapters on environment, size, and technology. To the extent that students understand these basic organizational processes, it is possible to predict factors that increase or decrease conflict in organizations. The material on conflict resolution also corresponds to the material on organizational development in chapter 7 on change. Many techniques for handling conflict evolved from organizational development work, for example, third-party negotiation and intensive intergroup training. Research in one area of organization theory (organizational change) has provided assistance in developing solutions in another area (intergroup conflict).

DISCUSSION QUESTIONS

1. What is vertical as opposed to horizontal conflict? What issues or topics would tend to characterize one type of conflict as opposed to the other?
2. Define intergroup conflict? Does this definition apply to social conflict as well as to vertical and horizontal conflict?
3. Briefly describe how differences in personal background lead to conflict between groups. How does task interdependence lead to conflict between groups?
4. What is meant by strategic conflict?
5. Discuss the benefits and wastes of interdepartmental conflict. At what level of conflict do these benefits and wastes appear?
6. Intergroup training is located at a higher level on the scale of conflict-resolution techniques than is member rotation. What does this mean in terms of the amount of impact the two techniques have on attitude change? Can you think of situations in which rotation might have greater impact on attitude change than would intergroup training?
7. What techniques can be used to overcome conflict between workers and management? Describe.
8. What is meant by the organizational dilemma involving within-group and between-group relations? Discuss.

GUIDES TO ACTION

As a manager:

1. Do not eliminate or suppress conflict. Recognize that some interdepartmental conflict is natural and even necessary. Obtain the benefits of conflict without the waste by maintaining conflict at a strategic level.

2. Associate the organizational design characteristics of goal incompatibility, difference in personal traits, task interdependence, resource scarcity, power and status differences, and competitive reward systems with greater conflict between groups. Expect to devote more time and energy in resolving these conflicts.

3. Reduce conflict by diagnosing underlying causes, and then changing them. This approach may not be successful because some causes, such as environmental uncertainty or task interdependence, cannot be adjusted on a short-run basis.

4. Do not allow intense conflict to persist. Intense conflict is harmful to the organization because departments direct their resources toward sabotaging or defeating other groups rather than working with other departments to achieve unit goals. Intervene forcefully with conflict-resolution techniques.

5. Use the techniques of physical separation, bureaucratic regulation, limited interaction, integrators, confrontation, third-party consultants, member rotation, superordinate goals, and intensive intergroup training to reduce conflict between groups when it is too high. Select the techniques that fit the organization and the conflict.

6. Avoid placing groups in direct win-lose situations when managing either horizontal or vertical conflict. Direct the conflict toward enabling both groups to be partial winners. When negotiating, do not place representatives in the dilemma of choosing between loyalty to their group or loyalty to the best interest of the company as a whole. Representatives will usually be loyal to their group, even if their proposals are not the best solutions for the entire company.

Consider these Guides when analyzing the following case and when answering the questions listed after the case.

CASE FOR ANALYSIS

VALENA SCIENTIFIC CORPORATION

Part I   Valena Scientific Corporation is one of the largest manufacturers of health-care products in the world. The health-care market includes hospitals, clinical laboratories, universities, and industry. Clinical laboratories represent 52% of VSC's sales. The laboratories are located in hospitals and diagnostic centers where blood tests and urine analyses are performed for physicians. Equipment sold to laboratories can range from a five-cent test tube to a blood analyzer that performs eighteen blood tests simultaneously for $195,000.

During the 1970s, many large energy and industrial corporations began to move into the clinical market. Eli Lilly, Dow Chemical, Revlon, and E. I. DuPont shifted more research dollars to medical products. Fifty percent of the nation's health-care bill goes into testing, and the medical profession is demanding more accurate tests as well as tests for a variety of new diseases.

By 1980, the industry experienced a new twist: genetic engineering. New companies such as Genentech Corp. and Cetus Scientific Laboratories were created as venture capital companies and were staffed with a handful of university microbiologists. These companies were designed to exploit the commercial potential for gene splicing.

Senior executives at VSC saw the trend developing, and late in 1979 decided to create the Biotech Research Department. Skilled microbiologists were scarce, so the department was created with only nine scientists, who had experience in the fields of biology and engineering. Twenty technicians, who helped with research at the scientists' direction, were also assigned. The department was divided into three groups—gene splicing, recombination, and fermentation. The organization chart for the Biotech Research Department, is shown in figure 11.6. It is the smallest of three research departments at VSC. An important characteristic of the new department was that the employees from each group were expected to work closely together. The most competent personnel had been selected to serve as part of the new department. They would be doing leading edge research compared to other departments at VSC. Each group was located on a separate floor in the research building, although they would be located together after a new research wing was constructed sometime in the future.

For the first eighteen months of operation, the work in the Biotech Department was moderately routine. The biotech department concentrated

Figure 11.6. Organization Chart of VSC's Biotech Research Department.

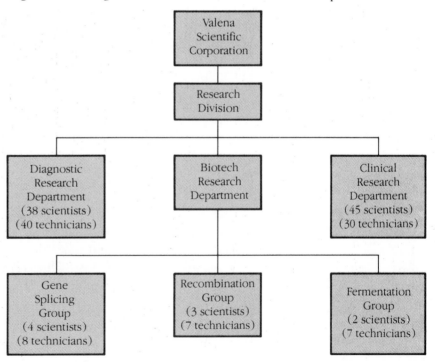

on applying principles established elsewhere. One example was the production of human insulin by gene splicing. The basic research was performed by a scientist at Harvard. The work required by private companies was to produce insulin in large amounts. Other work included the refinement of blood tests, such as for the identification of hereditary diseases (e.g., sickle-cell anemia). The initial projects all followed a similar pattern. The work was started in the gene-splicing group, followed by work in recombination, and then to fermentation. Fermentation is used to breed the bacteria created by the other two groups in sufficient numbers to enable mass production.

The senior scientist in each group was appointed group leader and the three leaders reported to the director of the biotech department, who did not have a scientific background. The structure within each group was very informal and collegial.

Questions
1. Would the scientists and technicians be enthusiastic or unenthusiastic about becoming part of the new department? Would they identify more strongly with the department as a whole or with their subgroup? Explain.
2. Would conflict among group leaders be high or low during the initial eighteen months? Explain.
3. Would social relationships among technical personnel tend to be department-wide or limited to subgroups? Explain.

Part II
The scientists and technicians were enthusiastic about the new department. They felt proud to be selected and quickly identified with the new department. They were happy with the division of labor, but lunch and coffee gatherings included members from all three groups. Group leader meetings were cooperative, quickly resolved any coordination problems, and were conflict free.

During the summer of 1982, the Biotech Department received a special project. Hoffman-LaRoche was developing leukocyte interferon to use as a treatment against cancer. The company was unable to clone the bacteria in its own lab and hired other companies to do the job. VSC contracted with Hoffman-LaRoche to develop a technique for interferon production. The company had only six months to come up with a production technology. Because of the intense time pressure, the research could not be done in the sequence of gene splicing, recombination, and fermentation. Each group remained in its own geographic confines, and began immediately to test ideas relevant to its own work. Each group also examined the current research literature and contacted university colleagues in their own areas of specialization. The groups were aware that if findings from another group were strong enough to dictate the entire production sequence, the work undertaken by their own group would be lost.

Questions
1. Would department employees be enthusiastic or unenthusiastic as the interferon project developed? Would they identify more strongly with the department as a whole or with their own subgroup? Explain.

2. Would conflict among group leaders be high or low during this period? Explain.
3. Would social relationships tend to be department-wide or subgroup-oriented? Explain.

Part III   In September 1982, the group leaders met for the first time to explore the technical progress and discoveries made by each group. The goal of this meeting was to exchange information and to establish parameters for each group's subsequent research activities. It quickly became apparent that each group had taken a different research direction and had discovered concepts that the group considered paramount. The position of any one group required considerable extra work by the other two groups. The group leaders argued vehemently for their positions, and the meeting was concluded without compromise of original positions.

During the following six weeks, each worked desperately to complete its research before complementary segments were completed in the other groups. Haste was necessary because the late groups would have to reformulate their research based on what was found by the group that finished first. Future meetings among group leaders were conflict-laden and did not resolve the issues. No research approach was proven to be superior for cloning and manufacturing interferon. All three avenues looked promising, but mutually exclusive. A number of personal frictions developed between the groups. Enthusiasm for the project was initially high, but gradually dropped off as conflict increased. Social activities were limited to members in each subgroup and were dominated by talk of research and the need to beat the other groups.

On November 15, a Stanford professor with extensive research experience in recombinant DNA technology was hired. His first assignment was to be project leader for the interferon project. His title was Chief Biologist, and all scientists, engineers, and technicians working on the project were to report to him. The group leaders in each area discussed their work with him. After one week, the chief biologist selected the basic approach that would be taken in future research. The new approach was a technique developed at Stanford, and in many ways was similar to the line taken in the fermentation group. Technical objections from the other groups were dismissed. The new approach was to be followed by everyone. Each group was assigned a set of research instructions within the overall research plan. Firm deadlines were established based upon group interdependence. Weekly progress reports were required from each group leader.

Questions   1. Would members of the three groups be enthusiastic or unenthusiastic after these developments? Would the scientists and technicians identify with the overall department or with their respective subgroups? Explain.
2. Would conflict among group leaders be high or low as work progressed on the project?
3. Would social relationships tend to be department-wide or subgroup-oriented? Explain.

For several weeks after the chief biologist decided the direction of the interferon project, the group leaders from gene splicing and recombination disagreed with him. Considerable time was spent trying to find a weakness in the new plan and to prove that their previous research was superior. Few problems in the new plan could be found. The chief biologist defended his position and demanded that deadlines be met.

Schedules were met, and the three groups simultaneously developed the approach in their respective areas. Communication with the chief biologist became more frequent. Communication between groups became common. Problems discovered by one group were communicated to other groups so that effort was not expended needlessly. Group leaders coordinated many problems among themselves.

Cohesion within each group became less pronounced. Lunch and coffee groups comprising several members of each group began to appear. Group leaders had daily discussions and cooperated on research requirements. Enthusiasm for the department and for the interferon project was expressed by department members.[65]

Questions

1. What intraorganizational changes in Valena Scientific Corporation led to heightened intergroup conflict? Explain. Why couldn't the group leaders resolve the conflict by themselves?
2. What factors account for the reduction of conflict after the chief biologist took over?
3. Should intergroup conflict be completely removed from the biotech department? Will departments like this produce better if strategic levels of conflict are present? Discuss.

NOTES

1. Harry Bernstein, "Union Misjudged Government," *Houston Chronicle,* September 4, 1981, copyright © Los Angeles Times-Washington Post News Service; Paul Galloway, "Negotiating Consultant Says Air Controllers Can't Win Strike," *Houston Chronicle,* August 25, 1981, copyright © Chicago Sun-Times.
2. Muzafer Sherif, "Experiments in Group Conflict," *Scientific American* 195 (1956): 54–58; Edgar H. Schein, *Organizational Psychology,* 3rd ed. (Englewood Cliffs, NJ: Prentice-Hall, 1980).
3. Kenneth Thomas, "Conflict and Conflict Management," in M. D. Dunnette, ed., *Handbook of Industrial and Organizational Psychology* (Chicago: Rand McNally, 1976); Joseph A. Litterer, "Conflict in Organizations: A Re-Examination," *Academy of Management Journal* 9 (1966): 178–186; Stuart M. Schmidt and Thomas A. Kochan, "Conflict: Toward Conceptual Clarity," *Administrative Science Quarterly* 13 (1972): 359–370.
4. L. David Brown, "Managing Conflict Among Groups," in David A. Kolb, Irwin M. Rubin, and James M. McIntrye, eds., *Organizational Psychology:*

A Book of Readings (Englewood Cliffs, NJ: Prentice-Hall, 1979), pp. 377–389.

5. *Ibid.*
6. *Ibid.*
7. These conclusions are summarized from Sherif, "Experiments in Group Conflict"; M. Sherif, O. J. Harvey, B. J. White, W. R. Hood, and C. W. Sherif, *Intergroup Conflict and Cooperation* (Norman, OK: University of Oklahoma Books Exchange, 1961); M. Sherif and C. W. Sherif, *Social Psychology* (New York: Harper & Row, 1969); and Schein, *Organizational Psychology.*
8. Thomas A. Kochan, George P. Huber, and L. L. Cummings, "Determinants of Intraorganizational Conflict in Collective Bargaining in the Public Sector," *Administrative Science Quarterly* 20 (1975): 10–23.
9. Benson P. Shapiro, "Can Marketing and Manufacturing Coexist?" *Harvard Business Review* 55 (September–October, 1977): 104–114.
10. Eric H. Neilsen, "Understanding and Managing Intergroup Conflict," in Jay W. Lorsch and Paul R. Lawrence, *Managing Group and Intergroup Relations* (Homewood, IL: Irwin and Dorsey Press, 1972), pp. 329–343; Richard E. Walton and John M. Dutton, "The Management of Interdepartmental Conflict: A Model and Review," *Administrative Science Quarterly* 14 (1969): 73–84.
11. Jay W. Lorsch, "Introduction to the Structural Design of Organizations," in Gene W. Dalton, Paul R. Lawrence, and Jay W. Lorsch, eds., *Organization Structure and Design* (Homewood, IL: Irwin and Dorsey, 1970), p. 5.
12. Melville Dalton, *Men Who Manage* (New York: John Wiley, 1959), p. 75.
13. *Ibid.*
14. James D. Thompson, *Organizations in Action* (New York: McGraw-Hill, 1967), pp. 54–56.
15. Walton and Dutton, "Management of Interdepartmental Conflict."
16. Joseph McCann and Jay R. Galbraith, "Interdepartmental Relationships," in Paul C. Nystrom and William H. Starbuck, eds., *Handbook of Organizational Design,* vol. 2 (New York: Oxford University Press, 1981), pp. 60–84.
17. George Strauss, "Tactics of Lateral Relationship: The Purchasing Agent," *Administrative Science Quarterly* 7 (1962): 161–186. Quoted by permission.
18. Neilsen, "Understanding and Managing Intergroup Conflict"; Louis R. Pondy, "Organizational Conflict: Concepts and Models," *Administrative Science Quarterly* 12 (1968): 296–320.
19. John A. Seiler, "Diagnosing Interdepartmental Conflict," *Harvard Business Review* 41 (September–October, 1963): 121–132.
20. *Ibid.,* pp. 126–127.
21. Walton and Dutton, "Management of Interdepartmental Conflict"; Pondy, "Organizational Conflicts"; Kochan, Huber, and Cummings, "Determinants of Intraorganizational Conflict"; Kenneth W. Thomas and Louis R. Pondy, "Toward an 'Intent' Model of Conflict Management Among Principal Parties," *Human Relations* 30 (1977): 1089–1102.

22. Neilsen, "Understanding and Managing Intragroup Conflict," pp. 331–332.
23. Walton and Dutton, "Management of Interdepartmental Conflict."
24. Morton Deutsch, "The Effects of Cooperation and Competition Upon Group Process," in Dorwin Cartwright and Alvin Zander, *Group Dynamics* (New York: Harper & Row, 1968), pp. 461–482.
25. Donald Nightingale, "Conflict and Conflict Resolution," in George Strauss, Raymond E. Miles, Charles C. Snow, and Arnold S. Tannenbaum, *Organizational Behavior: Research and Issues* (Belmont: CA: Wadsworth, 1976), pp. 141–164.
26. *Ibid.*
27. Paul R. Lawrence and Jay W. Lorsch, *Organization and Environment* (Homewood, IL: Irwin, 1969); Pondy, "Organizational Conflict"; Thomas and Pondy, "Toward an 'Intent' Model of Conflict Management."
28. Robert R. Blake and Jane S. Mouton, "Reactions to Intergroup Competition Under Win-Lose Conditions," *Management Science* 7 (1961): 420–435; Sherif et al., *Intergroup Conflict and Cooperation.*
29. Thomas and Pondy, "Toward an 'Intent' Model of Conflict Management"; Joe Kelly, "Make Conflict Work For You," *Harvard Business Review* 48 (July–August, 1970): 103–113.
30. Kelly, *ibid.*
31. Stephen P. Robbins, *Managing Organizational Conflict: A Nontraditional Approach* (Englewood Cliffs: NJ: Prentice-Hall, 1974).
32. Seiler, "Diagnosing Interdepartmental Conflicts."
33. Blake and Mouton, "Reactions to Intragroup Competition."
34. Schein, *Organizational Psychology;* Blake and Mouton, "Reactions to Intergroup Competition," pp. 174–175.
35. Pondy, "Organizational Conflict."
36. This discussion is drawn from J. Victor Baldridge, *Power and Conflict in the University* (New York: John Wiley, 1971) and Mary Zey-Ferrell, *Dimensions of Organizations* (Santa Monica, CA: Goodyear, 1979).
37. Harold J. Leavitt, William R. Dill, and Henry B. Eyring, *The Organizational World* (New York: Harcourt Brace, 1973).
38. Pondy, "Organizational Conflict."
39. Schein, *Organizational Psychology,* p. 179.
40. Robert R. Blake, Herbert A. Shepard, and Jane S. Mouton, *Managing Intergroup Conflict in Industry* (Houston: Gulf Publishing Company, 1964).
41. Neilsen, "Understanding and Managing Intergroup Conflict."
42. *Ibid.*
43. *Ibid.*
44. Pondy, "Organizational Conflict."
45. Neilsen, "Understanding and Managing Intergroup Conflict."
46. *Ibid.;* Paul R. Lawrence and Jay W. Lorsch, "New Management Job: The Integrator," *Harvard Business Review* 45 (November–December, 1967): 142–151.
47. Blake, Shepard, and Mouton, *Managing Intergroup Conflict in Industry.*
48. Thomas, "Conflict and Conflict Management."
49. Neilsen, "Understanding and Managing Intergroup Conflict."

50. *Ibid.;* Sherif et al., *Intergroup Conflict and Cooperation."*

51. Schein, *Organizational Psychology;* Blake, Shepard, and Mouton, *Managing Intergroup Conflict in Industry;* Richard E. Walton, *Interpersonal Peacemaking: Confrontation and Third-Party Consultations* (Reading, MA: Addison-Wesley, 1969).

52. Edgar H. Schein, *Organizational Psychology,* 3rd ed., © 1980, pp. 177–178. Reprinted by permission of Prentice-Hall, Inc., Englewood Cliffs, NJ.

53. Leon C. Megginson, *Personal and Human Resources Administration* (Homewood, IL: Irwin, 1977), pp. 519–520.

54. John T. Dunlop, *Industrial Relations Systems* (New York: Henry Holt Co., 1958).

55. Blake and Mouton, "Reactions to Intergroup Competition."

56. *Ibid.*

57. These bargaining approaches were developed by Richard Walton and Richard McKersie, *A Behavioral Theory of Labor Negotiations: An Analysis of the Social Interaction System* (New York: McGraw-Hill, 1965), ch. 1.

58. "A Try at Steel Mill Harmony," *Business Week,* June 29, 1981, pp. 132–133.

59. Blake and Mouton, "Reactions to Intergroup Competition."

60. *Ibid.*

61. *Ibid.,* pp. 433–434. Reprinted by permission of Robert R. Blake and Jane S. Mouton, "Reactions to Intergroup Competition Under Win-Lose Conditions," *Management Science* 7, no. 4, (July 1961). Copyright © 1961 The Institute of Management Sciences.

62. George S. McIsaac, "Thinking Ahead," *Harvard Business Review* 55 (September–October, 1977): 34.

63. *Ibid.*

64. A. Tannenbaum, B. Kavcic, M. Rosner, M. Vianello, and C. Wieser, *Hierarchy in Organizations* (San Francisco: Jossey-Bass, 1974), pp. 27–32.

65. This case is based on "Genetic Engineering's Manpower Problem," *Dun's Business Month,* January, 1982, pp. 92–95; "Reid Scientific" case, distributed by the Intercollegiate Case Clearing House, Soldiers Field, Boston, MA 02163; and "Daniels Computer Company," in Robert E. Coffey, Anthoney G. Athos, and Peter A. Reynolds, *Behavior in Organizations: A Multidimensional View,* 2nd ed. (Englewood Cliffs, NJ: Prentice-Hall, 1975), pp. 416–420.

PART VI
Integrating the Total System

12

The Top Management Domain

HARTMAN LUGGAGE COMPANY

The last time I was in Chicago, I was making a speech before the Executives Club. I don't know if you're familiar with that organization, but it's impressive for a couple of reasons. First, they have over 3,000 paid-up members. Second, they get anywhere from five hundred to one thousand of the members to come to a luncheon every Friday. The week before my speech, they'd had Senator Charles Percy. The week after me, they had Nelson Rockefeller. I felt good about the company I was in until I was introduced with the polite explanation to the audience by the club's president that a "change of pace" was desirable.

Anyway, the point of my telling you about this organization is that before each luncheon, they ask the speaker to meet with a half dozen high school kids whom they've invited as guests. When I met with them, they took one look at me, looked at each other, and almost in one voice wanted to know what kind of education you needed to be in management. Was there a major course of study, a *degree* in management that they could pursue in college?

Naturally, I refused to answer a stupid question like that.

But if you know kids, you know they don't let go, especially if they smell a phony. They'd been told I had been president of the Plaza Hotel and had had no previous hotel experience, and no hotel schooling, and they seemed skeptical about what the BS degree I'd gotten in college really stood for.

"Mr. Lavenson," one particularly obnoxious little smart alec asked me, "If you had no experience running a hotel and you started at the top, how did you know what to do? Just what did you do?"

"I ran the place, that's what! Next question?" I snapped back and figured I'd won. I hadn't.

"Come now, Mr. Lavenson, these students won't accept that answer." It was their teacher who interrupted this time, a guy with a beard and a pipe and very high forehead. I hated him on sight. "What about an MA degree? Wouldn't you say that a master's degree in business from a school like Harvard or The Wharton School would qualify a man or woman for management?"

I didn't have an MBA degree and it was painfully obvious this teacher did. If I let him win that point, I knew I was lost, so I resorted to a trick I'd learned through years of experience: I lied.

"Not an MBA degree," I said very calmly. "It takes an MBWA degree to qualify as a manager." With that one, I'd stopped the beard and pipe dead in his tracks. But he recovered and just before someone came in and announced lunch was starting, he growled a last question. "Just exactly what *is* an MBWA degree?"

I gave him my most generous smile, and gave him a pearl of wisdom in one sentence that I'm going to stretch out into a full speech today. You see, I'd never really thought about it before and my glib answer to that poor teacher and group of kids was the lucky, accidental, off-the-cuff, wise-guy response of a cornered rat. On my way home from Chicago, I thought a lot more about the questions the kids were asking and my answer. The longer I thought about it, the more I realized that MBWA *is* the qualification for management, and it's one I'd unwittingly been using in every job I've been in. And when I'd started each of the management jobs I've had over the past 20 years—in advertising, in toy products, in luggage, in publishing, in food processing, in sunglasses, T-shirts, dresses, and, yes, if you'll excuse the expression, in women's pants, there's one thing you can say about me without fear of contradiction from anyone with whom I ever worked. I didn't know from beans about any of these businesses. I don't really mean I didn't know *anything*. Naturally, since I was over 30, I did know a thing or two about ladies' pants. But what I didn't know about any of the businesses when I started in them was how to *run* them. And I certainly didn't have any of the technical experience necessary to mold a doll, sew leather into a suitcase that would come out the other end of the production line as Hartman luggage, or dig clams out of the Atlantic Ocean, clean them, and vacuum pack them into cans labeled Doxsee. And what I knew about ladies' sportswear was confined to whistling—mostly at my wife's bills from Saks Fifth Avenue and Bergdorf Goodman . . . .

Oh my, that's right! I still haven't told you what MBWA stands for, have I? MBWA stands for *Management By Walking Around*. Just walking around with your eyes and ears open, asking questions like crazy, and trying to understand what the [people] working for you are doing. A good place to start is to see if *they* understand what they're doing . . . .

One day about ten years ago, I suddenly found myself chairman of the Hartman Luggage Company. Like you, I'd known the name for years and before I'd seen the figures, I would have guessed that Hartman was at least a ten- or twenty-million-dollar company. I was shocked to learn that its sales volume was under two million, so I started by walking around the territory with a couple of salesmen to see why they weren't selling more. They all told me the same thing—Hartman was a prestige name without a truly prestige product, a real top-of-the-line, expensive piece of luggage which by its very price had the snob appeal to get it into stores like Saks Fifth Avenue and Neiman Marcus. I brought that story back to the president, who pooh-poohed the idea but reached into a secret compartment in his office safe and produced the loveliest, richest looking attache case made of belted leather and brass trim that I'd every dreamed of. "Why isn't that in the line?" I wanted to know.

"Too expensive. It would never sell. We'd have to retail this thing for close to two hundred bucks."

I walked around again, taking the sample attache case with me and asking the salesmen if this was the kind of thing they had in mind. "Yeah, man!" was their reaction.

"How much should it sell for?" I wanted to know from the guys who had to sell it. The consensus was three hundred bucks. That MBWA attache case went into the Hartman line along with overnighters and two-suiters all made of belted leather with price tags that would shock the Shah of Iran. Today, Hartman is stocked by Saks and Neiman Marcus and doing one helluva lot more than two million dollars in sales.

Probably the most important principle of MBWA is really a philosophy —a philosophy that says that the boss's job is to make sure of three things: first, that his staff understands what they are doing; second, that his staff has the tools *they* think they need to do the job; and last, that the boss lets the staff know he has an *appreciation* of what the employee is doing.

You hear a lot of management types talk sanctimoniously about their "open door" policy. Their door is "always open to the staff," they tell you. In my book, the best reason for a boss's open door is so he can go out the door and walk around . . . .[1]

James Lavenson has definite ideas about how to manage an organization. His experience suggests that skillful top management involves several activities. The manager must spend time taking the pulse of the organization— talking to people, asking questions, and developing an accurate mental picture of the organization. The top manager also works to build bridges between departments to make sure they work well together. Lavenson got sales and product design together at Hartman Luggage. The top manager also has to make strategic decisions. Lavenson decided to launch a new line of luggage to tap a new market. This kind of decision is made under great uncertainty because market response is hard to predict. Top managers also set goals and have a vision for organizational performance. In the above case, Lavenson had a goal of increased sales and market share for Hartman. Finally, Lavenson's speech provides a clue to management succession. Turnover in the chief executive's position was a good thing for Hartman Luggage. Replacing the previous manager led to a new line of briefcases that greatly increased Hartman's sales and profits.

Purpose of This Chapter

In this chapter, we explore the domain of top management. This book has been about organizations, and top managers are responsible for the entire organization system. The chief executive is involved in the areas already covered in this book, such as organization structure, interacting with the environment, overseeing information and control systems, mediating group relations, innovations, and politics.

The purpose of this chapter is to bring together new findings about the top management domain that go beyond the material covered in previous chapters. The next section describes the responsibilities and activities of top managers, which provide a flavor of the day-to-day work of chief executives. Then we examine the types of choices top managers make, with special emphasis on organizational strategy. The discussion of strategy provides an introduction to policy and strategy issues. The symbolic role of top managers and their impact on organization culture is also discussed. The final section of the chapter explores the issue of managerial succession. Here we answer the questions: Why does turnover occur, and does the top executive make any difference to organizational effectiveness? By the end of this chapter, students should understand the role of top management and how top managers steer the organization through an uncertain environment.

TOP MANAGEMENT RESPONSIBILITIES AND ACTIVITIES

One of the frustrations of management scientists has been the inability to develop a concise description of the chief executive's job; it is so complex and contains so many elements that complete documentation is nearly impossible. Some insight into the top manager's job has been obtained by following managers around and observing everything they do.[2] Information has also been obtained by analyzing speeches made by leading executives.[3] Another technique is to gather chief executives in a seminar and ask them to talk about their jobs.[4] These sources of information indicate that the top executive domain can be narrowed down to a set of areas both external and internal to the organization.

External Environment

Chief executives work directly with elements in the external environment. Uncertainty in the external environment is felt more directly by the chief executive than by anyone else in the organization. One of the critical roles of the top manager is to help the organization reach out and manage the external environment, and at the same time make internal adjustments to cope with changing external conditions. The external conditions that concern top executives are:

1. *Government.* Tax regulations and depreciation allowances have direct economic impact on corporations. Government regulations are excessive in the minds of most administrators.[5] Rules concerning safety, employee

discrimination, mergers, exports, and the natural environment require the organization to hire employees and generate paperwork. A number of executives claim that government regulations cost corporations more than $100 billion a year. Top management is also responsible for influencing government policy through lobbying, campaign contributions, and voter appeals.

2. *Economic Conditions.* Top executives continuously try to interpret economic conditions.[6] Inflation, unemployment, the value of the dollar overseas, and productivity all influence the demand for products, the availability of labor, and corporate economic well-being. Economic stability and prosperity enable the corporation to plan for capital investments and orderly growth.

3. *Industry and Market.* Decisions made by competitors and customers have major impact on chief executives.[7] Top managers try to anticipate the strategies and new products adopted by competitors, as well as the needs of customers in the marketplace.

4. *Public Opinion.* Most chief executives believe that their job is to represent the organization to the public.[8] Public opinion overestimates corporate profits and underestimates the social contributions made by business and its employees. Top executives take advantage of speech-making opportunities and advertising campaigns to influence these opinions.

5. *Social Responsibility.* Most top managers agree that free enterprise is not completely "free." The profit motive, if pursued without restraint, can lead to the exploitation of people and the environment. Many chief executives are concerned with the organization's contribution to the larger society.[9] They are personally involved in decisions to correct problems their organization may have caused. Chief executives are also responsible for decisions to use their businesses to solve social problems or to make donations to universities, the arts, or other not-for-profit institutions.

Internal Organization   The internal domain of the chief executive includes:

1. *Organization Design and Structure.* The chief executive is responsible for the arrangement of positions, responsibility, and authority to achieve the organization's goals. For example, how much authority should be centralized with the chief executive or delegated down the hierarchy? Should a functional form or a divisional form of structure be adopted? These decisions ultimately rest with the chief executive, who is responsible for the entire corporate entity.[10]

2. *Relationships among Divisions and Departments.* Another responsibility is to cope with internal conflict.[11] Regardless of the chosen organization structure, departments and divisions will come into competition and conflict with each other. The chief executive monitors and arbitrates these conflicts. Resources must be allocated and priorities set, even when all parties are not in agreement.

3. *Internal Goals and Values.* Another domain of the chief executive is to define the goals and set the values of the organization.[12] What does the

organization stand for? What is it trying to achieve? What are its values? Organizations develop unique internal cultures, and the chief executive has greater impact than anyone on internal climate and values.

4. *Strategy Formulation.* Top managers are responsible for the organization's strategy-making machinery.[13] Strategy includes the techniques and decisions for achieving organizational goals. Strategy formulation is the integration of environmental conditions and internal organization characteristics.[14] The chief executive achieves this integration by setting the course of the organization through the pitfalls and unexpected changes in public opinion, economic conditions, and competition. Strategy involves an assessment of company strengths and history, and decisions about which products to produce, which technology to invest in, and whether to acquire new companies. Strategy involves the surveillance and interpretation of problems and opportunities in the external environment, and the selection of means to solve the problems and take advantage of opportunities.

Top Manager Activities

The domain of top managers includes events in the external environment, processes within the overall organization, and the organization's strategy. What day-to-day activities do top managers perform in these domains? Henry Mintzberg of McGill University systematically observed five top managers at work. Mintzberg identified three characteristics of top managerial activities:

1. *The Manager Sits between the Organization and a Network of Contacts.*[15] The manager is the center of a large information system, as illustrated in figure 12.1. The manager is surrounded by a "diverse and complex web of contacts."[16] These contacts include associates, suppliers, staff experts, top managers of other organizations, trade organizations, government officials, clients, independent people, and boards of directors. Eighty percent of the manager's time is spent on direct interaction, and a substantial portion of the remaining time is spent processing information in the form of paperwork. Top managers process enormous amounts of information both to and from others.

2. *Managerial Activity Is Characterized by Variety, Fragmentation, and Brevity.*[17] The manager's involvements are so widespread and voluminous that there is little time for continuous thought and reflection. The average amount of time spent on any one activity is less than nine minutes. Top managers must shift gears quickly. There is no continuous pattern in the manager's work. Significant crises are interspersed with trivial events in no particular sequence. One morning's work for the president of a large organization included the following activities.

As he enters his office at 8:23, the manager's secretary motions for him to pick up the telephone. "Jerry, there was a bad fire in the plant last night, about $30,000 damage. We should be back in operation by Wednesday. Thought you should know."

At 8:45, a Mr. Jamison is ushered into the manager's office. They discuss Mr. Jamison's retirement plans and his cottage in New Hampshire. Then the

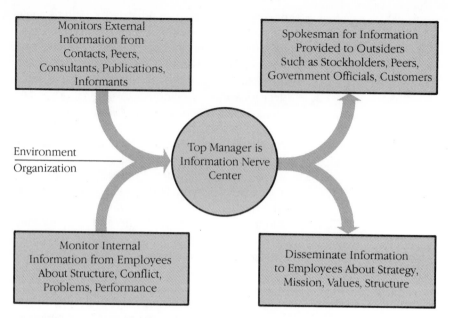

Figure 12.1. The Top Manager as Information-Processing System.
Source: Adapted from Henry Mintzberg, *The Nature of Managerial Work* (New York: Harper & Row: 1973), pp. 65–77.

manager presents a plaque to him commemorating his thirty-two years with the organization.

Mail processing follows: An innocent-looking letter, signed by a Detroit lawyer, reads: "A group of us in Detroit has decided not to buy any of your products because you used that anti-flag, anti-American pinko, Bill Lindell, upon your Thursday night TV show." The manager dictates a restrained reply.

The 10:00 meeting is scheduled by a professional staffer. He claims that his superior, a high-ranking vice president of the organization, mistreats his staff, and that if the man is not fired, they will all walk out. As soon as the meeting ends, the manager rearranges his schedule to investigate the claim and to react to this crisis.[18]

3. *The Manager Performs a Great Quantity of Work at an Unrelenting Pace.*[19] The work of top managers is fast-paced and requires great energy. The people observed by Mintzberg processed thirty-six pieces of mail each day, attended eight meetings, and took one tour. After their daily schedule is set, unexpected disturbances appear. New meetings are required. During time away from the office, chief executives catch up on work-related reading and detail work. Sloan Wilson, who wrote *The Man in the Grey Flannel Suit,* made the following observation about top managers.

Top Managers

When I was a young man newly out of World War II, Roy E. Larsen, the president of Time, Inc., hired me as a minor assistant to help him get together a do-good committee of big shots to do something nice for public education.

I was dutifully interested in public education, but I was much more interested in the big shots, which included the presidents of several vast corporations, famous journalists and educators, James B. Conant, the president of Harvard, pollster George Gallup, and Walter Lippman.

When this committee met, I was able to study closely some of the most successful men in the world and I worked over a period of four years with some of them, including Roy Larsen himself, Dr. Conant, and Neil McElroy, the president of Procter and Gamble (later to serve as secretary of defense).

How in the world did these people get so famous, so rich, so successful? Could I see in them any common denominators of success?

These questions, I confess, fascinated me more than the problems of the public schools, which we were supposed to study. The truth was that these very successful men did not look any different from the people next door, if one happened to live in a fairly prosperous neighborhood.

They were obviously intelligent, but no more so, so far as I could make out, than the average run of graduate students. How did they get so good at what they did?

It was not pull or influence that got them their impressive jobs—most of these people were self-made. Larsen, Gallup, and McElroy had impressive charm, but so did plenty of second-rate salesmen I knew, and some of the big shots were simply glum.

So what was the secret? As I attempted to work around the clock on the many projects they undertook in addition to their real jobs, one simple answer came to me: raw energy. Super-abundant, inexhaustible energy—that was the one thing all these very successful men had.

They were people who enthusiastically could undertake the fifth rewriting of a speech on education at three in the morning when they were up against a deadline, fly across the continent to deliver it and fly back again, working out of a briefcase on a plane all the time. And when they got to their offices, they were fresh and eager to see what their engagement calendar had to offer for the day and evening ahead. I never understood how they did it, and I was never able to keep up with them.[20]

Top Manager Roles The day-to-day observations of chief executives enabled Mintzberg to identify ten manager roles. The ten roles provide a framework for understanding the activities performed by chief executives. The ten roles are listed in table 12.1 along with a brief description of the role and an example of role activity.[21] Interpersonal roles describe interactions with others. These interactions occur as figurehead of the organization, as leader of subordinates, and with others of equal stature both inside and outside the organization. Information roles describe the activities of monitoring and disseminating information both inside and outside the organization. Decisional roles describe the types of decisions made by chief executives, such as taking a risk with a new strategy or improvement project, handling crises, allocating resources, and negotiating with external groups.

The ten roles describe the activities undertaken by chief executives to meet the demands of domains described in the previous section. The figurehead role is used to define the mission and values of the organization for employees. The spokesperson role is used to influence public opinion about the organization. The monitor and dissemination roles cut across several domains—economic conditions, the industry, government, organization structure—about which information is monitored and passed along to people who can act on it. The entrepreneur and disturbance handler roles are part of the strategy domain. Acquiring a new business or launching a new product are strategic decisions that are the responsibility of the chief executive because they are in the strategy domain.

IN PRACTICE 12.2

Robert Townsend

One of the important functions of a leader is to make the organization concentrate on its objectives. In the case of Avis, it took us six months to define one objective—which turned out to be: "We want to become the fastest-growing company with the highest profit margins in the business of renting and leasing vehicles without drivers."

That objective was simple enough so that we didn't have to write it down. We could put it in every speech and talk about it wherever we went. And it had some social significance, because up to that time Hertz had a crushingly large share of the market and was thinking and acting like General Motors.

It also included a definition of our business: "renting and leasing vehicles without drivers." This let us put the blinders on ourselves and stop considering the acquisition of related businesses like motels, hotels, airlines, and travel agencies. It also showed us that we had to get rid of some limousine and sightseeing companies that we already owned.

Once these objectives are agreed on, the leader must be merciless on himself and on his people. If an idea that pops into his head or out of their mouths is outside the objectives of the company, he kills it without a trial.[22]

Robert Townsend of Avis used the figurehead role to define the mission of Avis for employees and for people in the environment. He also used his position to hold the company on course toward that goal.

Table 12.1.   Ten Roles of Top Managers.

Role	Description	Identifiable Activities of Chief Executives
Interpersonal		
Figurehead	Symbolic head; obliged to perform a number of routine duties of a legal or social nature	Ceremony, status requests, solicitations
Leader	Responsible for the motivation and activation of subordinates; responsible for staffing, training, and associated duties	Virtually all managerial activities involving subordinates
Liaison	Maintains self-developed network of outside contacts and informers who provide favors and information	Acknowledgments of mail; external board work; other activities involving outsiders
Informational		
Monitor	Seeks and receives wide variety of special information (much of it current) to develop thorough understanding of organization and environment; emerges as nerve center of internal and external information of the organization	Handling all mail and contacts categorized as concerned primarily with receiving information (e.g., periodical news, observational tours)
Disseminator	Transmits information received from outsiders or from other subordinates to members of the organization; some information factual, some involving interpretation and integration of diverse value positions of organizational influencers	Forwarding mail into organization for informational purposes, verbal contacts involving information flow to subordinates (e.g., review sessions, instant communication flows)
Spokesman	Transmits information to outsiders on organization's plans, policies, actions, results, etc.; serves as expert on organization's industry	Board meetings; handling mail and contacts involving transmission of information to outsiders
Decisional		
Entrepreneur	Searches organization and its environment and initiates "improvement projects" to bring about change; supervises design of certain projects as well	Strategy and review sessions involving initiation or design of improvement projects
Disturbance Handler	Responsible for corrective action when organization faces important, unexpected disturbances	Strategy and review sessions involving disturbances and crises
Resource Allocator	Responsible for the allocation of organizational resources of all kinds—in effect the making or approval of all significant organizational decisions	Scheduling; requests for authorization; any activity involving budgeting and the programming of subordinates' work
Negotiator	Responsible for representing the organization at major negotiations	Negotiation

Source: From *The Nature of Managerial Work* by Henry Mintzberg: After Table 2 "Summary of Ten Roles" (pp. 92–93). Reprinted by permission of Harper & Row, Publishers, Inc.

Interpretation and Choice

During the early chapters of this book, we explored how the organization's environment, size, and technology influenced structure. When the organization is able to develop structural arrangements consistent with these requirements, it will be more effective.

Top manager choices are important because they intervene between these variables.[23] Top managers are not passive elements who respond predictably to requirements of size, technology, or environment. Managers are in the middle of this process, and they impose their own values and goals upon decisions.[24] Just as important, the demands associated with environment are not clear. Interpretation is difficult, so the appropriate structural response is not obvious. There are a range of alternatives associated with any single environmental problem, and the impact of management is to choose one alternative. Factors such as size and technology, which seem fixed in many organizations, are an outcome of top manager choices, as indicated in figure 12.2.

In figure 12.2, the top management group interprets environmental characteristics, and then responds with basic choices about the appropriate size and growth of the organization, the technology that should be used, the products to be produced, the best organization structure to meet these needs, and the deployment and utilization of human resources. The concept of top management choice is important because it means that the response of the organization is not perfectly predictable. Knowing size, technology, or environment does not allow one to predict the exact dimensions of organization structure. Indeed, almost every characteristic of the organization is a result of choices made by top executives.

Top management is located at the interface between the environment and the organization. The external environment is characterized by complexity and uncertainty. From this complexity and uncertainty top management must interpret, assess, and evaluate, and then make decisions about future strategies and courses of action. By making choices about the appropriate size, technology, structure, and strategy, they provide guidelines and directions within which the rest of the organization can function. Top management thereby absorbs and reduces uncertainty and provides a stable decision environment for lower-level managers and personnel. This type of assess-

Figure 12.2. The Relation of Management Choice to Environment, Size, Technology, Structure, and Products.

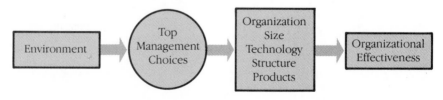

ment and decision-making takes place in group meetings, retreats, and day-to-day discussions, as illustrated in the following example from General Mills.

IN PRACTICE 12.3
General Mills

Shortly after becoming CEO [Chief Executive Officer] of General Mills, Mr. James McFarland decided that his job was "to take a very good company and move it to greatness," but that it was up to his management group, not himself alone, to decide what a great company was and how to get there. Consequently he took some thirty-five of the company's topmost managers away for a three-day management retreat. On the first day, after agreeing to broad financial goals, the group broke up into units of six to eight people. Each unit was to answer the question, "what is a great company?" from the viewpoints of stockholders, employees, suppliers, the public, and society. Each unit reported back at the end of the day, and the whole group tried to reach a consensus through discussion.

On the second day the groups, in the same format, assessed the company's strengths and weaknesses relative to the defined posture of "greatness." The third day focused on how to overcome the company's weaknesses and move it toward a great company. This broad consensus led, over the next several years, to the surveys of fields for acquisition, the building of management's initial "comfort levels" with certain fields, and the acquisition-divestiture strategy that characterized the McFarland era at General Mills.[25]

Enactment   Top management plays another interpretation and choice role also. The external environment must be enacted by the organization. **Enactment** is the process of defining which environmental elements are important enough to be attended to by the organization.[26] Since the environment is theoretically infinite, those subsets of the environment that are of primary importance have to be identified. Enactment is the process of defining the external environment into a manageable subset of elements that top managers can cope with effectively. The enacted environment is the limited set of external organizations and factors that the organization deals with on a continuous basis. Other elements in the environment may exist, and may even influence the organization. But if these elements are not enacted, management will not pay attention or respond to them.

The interesting aspect of enactment is that the environment is not assumed to be fixed.[27] Top management describes what the environment is. They choose and define the environment, as shown in figure 12.3. Top managers actually select the environmental elements that are imposed upon the organization. The process of top management decision-making thus includes those decisions that define the environment as well as those decisions about how the organization will respond to the environment.

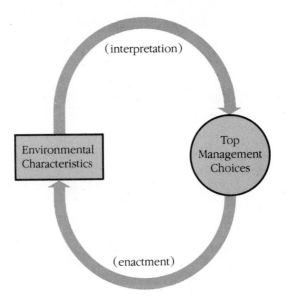

(interpretation)

Environmental
Characteristics

Top
Management
Choices

(enactment)

Figure 12.3. Management Choices Enact as Well as Interpret External Environment.

The enactment process often has a fuzzy beginning, and leads to the identification of a new environmental domain with which the organization must cope, as illustrated in the following case.

IN PRACTICE 12.4

Consumer Products Company

The president of a large consumer products company was troubled by what seemed to be increasing government regulation. Managers from several functions within the organization commented on increasing paperwork and time being consumed in government-related activities. Government also influenced the company indirectly through its impact on customers. Gradually, from talking to his managers, he began to build up an image of how important government regulation was for the company. He began to define the government as a critical environmental contingency for his organization. He asked for advice of people within the company about how to deal with government regulation, and at the same time he identified the government as an important element to other managers. "I have started conversations with anyone inside or outside the company who can help . . . . I collect articles and talk to people about how things get done in Washington in this particular [industry]. I collect data from any reasonable source. I begin wide-ranging discussions with people inside and outside the corporation. From these a pattern eventually emerges. It is like fitting together a jigsaw puzzle. At first a vague outline of an approach appears like the sail of a ship.

Then suddenly the rest of the puzzle becomes quite clear. You wonder why you didn't see it all along. And once it's crystallized, it's not difficult to explain to others."[28]

In this company, government activities in Washington became part of the enacted environment. The manager defined this external element and then communicated his perception to others in the organization. In the future, the organization will concentrate specifically on the governmental domain.

ORGANIZATIONAL STRATEGIES

The process of interpreting and enacting the environment provides the basis for strategy formulation. Strategy formulation and implementation is probably the single most important responsibility of top managers. A **corporation's strategy** is the current set of plans, decisions, and objectives that have been adopted to achieve the organization's goals. Recall from chapter 3 that goals are the desired future state of the organization. Strategy pertains to the short-term objectives and decisions used to achieve those goals. Top managers formulate strategy based upon their interpretation of opportunities in the environment and the strengths and weaknesses in the organization. Organizations facing similar environments often adopt different strategies because of different enactment processes.

One classic example of differing strategies is illustrated by Sears Roebuck and Montgomery Ward in the retailing industry. Immediately after World War II, both companies were similar in size and reputation. The top management at Sears perceived the business environment at the end of the war as having two characteristics—economic prosperity and population migration to the suburbs. Prosperity meant that immediate expansion was necessary to cash in on the spending habits of American families. The move toward the suburbs meant that the location of stores should shift from urban to suburban locations. In response to these perceived environmental conditions, Sears launched a strategy of expansion into suburban areas. They borrowed heavily and built large stores in major shopping centers throughout the country.

Montgomery Ward also interpreted the environment. Sewell Avery, the chief executive, saw a different trend. He believed that the war would precipitate a severe depression. Costs would be depressed, so affluent companies could invest money and make purchases at bargain rates. The strategy adopted by Wards was to not build new stores. They adopted a strategy of retrenchment and cost-cutting to save cash for expenditures during the coming business downturn. The strategy adopted by Avery and Montgomery Wards was the opposite of Sears', and much less effective. They misdiagnosed the external environment. The strategy of retrenchment meant they would always be smaller than Sears. After realizing the inappropriateness of Ward's strategy, the Board of Directors voted to have Avery removed as Chief Executive. He did not go willingly, and had to be physically carried out of his office. Meanwhile, Sears grew by leaps and bounds. Wards was never again a well-matched competitor. By 1973, when Sears moved into their new office building—the tallest in the world—Sears had grown to almost four times the size of Wards, with sales of $12.3 billion compared to $3.2 billion for Wards.[29]

Corporate versus Business Strategy

Corporate strategy is developed at the top level in large corporations and is concerned with the combination of business units and product lines that make a coherent business portfolio.[30] Decisions at this level pertain to the acquisition of new businesses, divestments, joint ventures, and reorganizations. Strategies determine how much to grow by acquisition, and which type of businesses complement current lines. Corporate strategy also includes statements about the corporation's creed, values, and responsibility to society.

Business strategy is concerned with a single business or product line.[31] The question addressed by business strategy is: How do we compete? Strategic decisions at the business level pertain to marketing and advertising strategies, investments in new production facilities, product changes, and R & D planning. The difference between corporate and business strategy is illustrated in figure 12.4.

Figure 12.4.   Hierarchy of Corporation and Business Level Strategies.
Source: From *Strategies for Diversification and Change,* Milton Leontiades, Exhibit 5-4 and 5-5. Copyright © 1980 by Milton Leontiades. Reprinted by permission of the publisher, Little, Brown and Company.

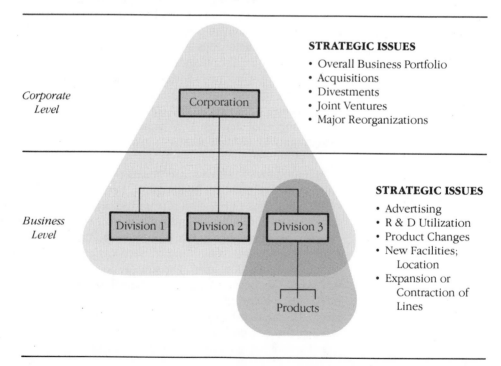

In large, diversified corporations, corporate and business strategies are easily distinguished. Corporate strategies originate with the chief executive at the corporate level, and business strategies are developed within each business unit or product line. When the corporation has only a few products that are very similar, corporate and business strategy are the same. R. R. Donnelley and Sons Co., for example, is in the business of printing catalogues, magazines, books, and directories. These products are all included within the printing business. Corporate and business strategy are the same in a single-line business.

Corporate-Level Strategy

At the corporate level one successful strategy is to acquire businesses that complement each other to achieve market and profit goals. Each business represents a different investment in the corporation portfolio.

The Boston Consulting Group developed a framework to analyze corporate businesses and product lines. The two dimensions in the strategies framework are overall *market growth* and *share of the market* held by the product line. Market growth refers to the product stage in the life cycle.[32] Some products are in a stage of ascendancy and rapid growth, which typically occurs early in the product's life. After products have been widely consumed, growth levels off. The product becomes mature, so that increases in sales only come from increased market share rather than from total market growth. Market share is the percentage of the market held by the business. Regardless of market size, those products that have a low percentage are considered low market share products. Attaining a high market share requires greater investment, but provides the opportunity for greater cash flow if it can be held.

The dimensions of market growth and market share combine to form four cells in figure 12.5. Each cell describes a business in a different stage of development, each stage having unique implications for corporate cash flow and profits.

1. The star has both high market share and a rapidly growing market. The star has additional growth potential. The star provides increasing sales for the corporation, and the profits are plowed back into the business in the form of investment for future growth. The star is highly visible and attractive, and will generate profits and a positive cash flow as the product matures.
2. The cash cow is a mature business. This business has a large market share but the market is no longer growing. Investment in advertising and plant expansion is no longer required, so the corporation receives a huge positive inflow of cash. The corporation can milk the cash cow to invest in new product lines that have the potential to become stars.
3. The new venture is a new business with high market growth potential. In the initial stages, market share is low. When market share increases rapidly, the business is a prize heifer and will become a star. When market share stays low, it is a problem child. Under ideal conditions, the prize heifer becomes a star, and eventually a cash cow. Under poor conditions, a problem child becomes a dog.

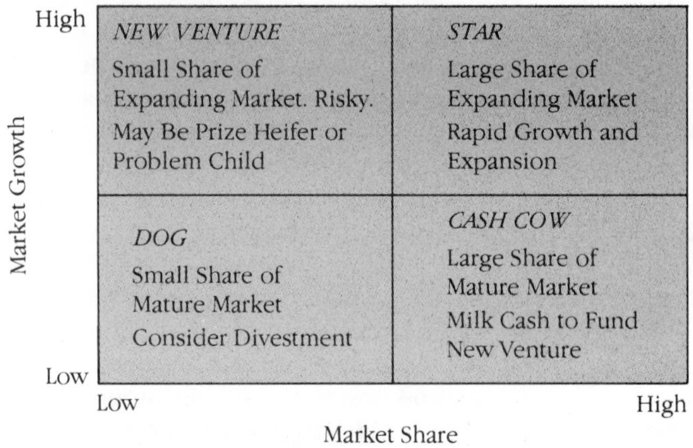

	Low	High
High	*NEW VENTURE* Small Share of Expanding Market. Risky. May Be Prize Heifer or Problem Child	*STAR* Large Share of Expanding Market Rapid Growth and Expansion
Low	*DOG* Small Share of Mature Market Consider Divestment	*CASH COW* Large Share of Mature Market Milk Cash to Fund New Venture

Market Growth (vertical axis) — Market Share (horizontal axis)

Figure 12.5. Framework for Corporate Portfolio of Integrated Businesses.

4. The dog is a poor performer. The market is stagnant and mature, and the dog has only a small share of the limited market. The dog typically adds little profit to the corporation and is often identified for sale to other corporations.

Corporate strategy seeks to maintain a balanced portfolio of business and product lines. Cash cows are needed to provide the cash for new ventures. Stars are needed to provide rapid growth. Prize heifers are needed to become stars of the future. Dogs are not needed and are only kept if they break even. If they provide a small positive cash flow, they may be kept. If dogs are a money loser, they will be divested or abandoned. Corporations that achieve a balance across the cash cows, stars, and new ventures can be enormously successful, as at Chesebrough-Ponds.

IN PRACTICE 12.5

Chesebrough-Ponds

Ralph Ward took over as chief executive officer of Chesebrough-Ponds in 1968. Corporate strategy was his responsibility. Ralph Ward is a thoughtful, careful decision-maker, but he is also willing to take risks. The transformation he brought about in Chesebrough-Ponds is considered by some to be little short of a miracle.

When Ward took the helm in 1968, Chesebrough-Ponds consisted of two cash cows. Ponds Cold Cream and Vaseline Petroleum Jelly were profitable products that provided a steady inflow of cash. In 1969, Ward purchased Ragu Spaghetti Sauce. This seemed like an unusual business for a health-care products company. Ragu was a regional brand, but it was the market leader in the regions where it was sold. Ward immediately opened up the national market with extensive advertising and dealer promotion. By 1972, Ragu had over 60% of the national market. In three years, Ragu sales increased from $25 million to $350 million a year.

In 1973, Health-Tex, a manufacturer of children's clothing, was acquired. This also seemed like an unusual business for Chesebrough-Ponds, but it was the next star in the corporate portfolio. Health-Tex was a successful regional manufacturer that had great potential on the national level, which Ward exploited over the next few years. Shortly thereafter, he purchased G. H. Bass shoe manufacturing company. Once again, a regional manufacturer made a big kick on the national level. In three years, revenues soared and profits rose over 50%. An additional bonus was that Weejuns Loafer and Sunjuns Sandals were included in the preppy craze that boosted sales beyond expectations.

Other new products followed. Chesebrough-Ponds launched Rave home permanent to take on Toni in what had been a sleepy market for several years. Then came Prince Matchabelli men's fragrance, Chimere perfume for women, and hospital-care products such as Filac electronic thermometers. Vaseline Intensive Care lotion and Pond's Cream and Cocoa Butter lotion were introduced to complement the old cold cream and petroleum jelly products.

Chesebrough-Ponds has been transformed from a mature business into a highly diversified corporation in which no business has more than 14% of sales. The corporation has grown rapidly, and has been consistently profitable. What is most astonishing is that they have market leaders in five different product lines.

Ward's corporate strategy has been extraordinarily successful. He has used cash from traditional products to invest in new ventures in growth markets. Many of these new ventures matured to become stars in their markets. They provided corporate growth and cash inflow as they matured and maintained a dominant position. These new cash flows enabled further investments in new businesses. Chesebrough-Ponds is considered one of the best managed companies in the country.[33]

Business-Level Strategies

Within a given business or product line, what strategy should be adopted? Business strategy depends on demand for the product from the environment, internal structure, and resource allocation. Depending on how the external environment is interpreted, strategy may range from rapid expansion to retrenchment.

A typology of business strategies was proposed by Ray Miles and Charles Snow.[34] They proposed that individual businesses can be classified as defenders, analyzers, or prospectors, depending on how managers interpret the external environment and the product's stage in its life cycle. Table 12.2 summarizes the three strategies.

The *defender* is characterized by stability and retrenchment. Top management perceives that environmental demand is not growing. The product market is mature and stable. The primary strategy is to protect the market share the product now has. Managers strive for efficient internal production and tight control of the organization. This type of business would be organized along the lines of a classic bureaucracy.

The *prospector* is at the other extreme. Managers anticipate a dynamic, growing demand from the environment. The market is young and increasing in size. The strategy is to seek new market opportunities. Internal structure will be diverse in order to scan the environment and provide latitude for new ventures. Internal structure will be flexible and loosely controlled to encourage growth and change. The primary structural concern is to facilitate operations and coordinate activities so that growth is achieved.

The *analyzer* adopts an intermediate strategy. The environment is perceived as experiencing moderate change. The strategy of top management is to maintain the stable business while also innovating moderately. Top management wants to protect what they have and also to devote attention to locating new opportunities. Internal production is oriented toward efficiency of current methods, but with some flexibility for new product variations. The structure will provide tight control over existing activities but looser control for growing lines and new activities.

The key element in choosing either the defender, analyzer, or prospector strategy is interpretation of the external environment. Interpretation is a function of the priorities and perceptions of management. The top managers determine whether the organization will retrench and defend what they have, or expand into new market opportunities. The importance of manager interpretation is illustrated in the strategies of Goodyear and Firestone.

Table 12.2. Three Business Level Strategies.

| Characteristic | Strategic Types | | |
	Defender	Analyzer	Prospector
Environment	Stable	Moderately changing	Dynamic, growing
Strategy	Seal off share of market. Protect turf. Advertise to hold customers.	Maintain market but innovate at edges. Locate opportunities for expansion while protecting current position.	Find and exploit new market opportunities. Scan environment, take risks.
Internal orientation and structure	Efficient production. Retrench. Tight control. Centralized, mechanistic.	Efficient production, yet flexibility for new lines. Tight control over current activities, looser for new lines.	Flexible production. Innovation and coordination. Expansion. Decentralized, organic.

Adapted from Raymond E. Miles, Charles C. Snow, Alan D. Meyer, Henry J. Coleman, Jr., "Organizational Strategy, Structure, and Process," *Academy of Management Review* 3 (1978): 546–562, with permission.

Goodyear versus Firestone

The two giants of the tire industry are debating a multi-million dollar question: Will the American motorist continue to drive less as the price of gasoline increases?

Probably not, says Goodyear Tire & Rubber Co., the nation's leading tire maker.

Yes, on the average, quite a bit less, replies Firestone Tire & Rubber Co., the nation's number-two tire producer.

Goodyear is the industry's optimist, Firestone the pessimist. The conflicting forecasts have led to sharply different business strategies. Upbeat Goodyear invested several hundred million dollars in new tire plants. Firestone has closed five domestic plants, will close two more, and plans no new factories.[35]

For tire makers, what matters is the number of tires that drivers have to replace. Replacement makes up about 70% of total tire sales. Goodyear predicts that American motorists will buy 138 million replacement tires in 1985. Firestone thinks the figure will be only 105 million or 14 million fewer than 1980's replacement sales.

On what evidence are these forecasts based? Goodyear and Firestone both scan the environment and have evaluated their own previous experience. Goodyear points to the years from 1970 to 1980 when gasoline increased from $.36 to $1.26 a gallon. U.S. auto mileage increased about 30% in the same period. Goodyear also thinks that the increasingly fuel-efficient car will increase driving. Goodyear knows that motorists in Europe drive more, even though European gas prices are more than double those in the U.S. Two-income families and the extra commuting required plus the trend toward suburban living will require more driving.

Firestone agrees that the number of cars on the road will increase by 1985, but believes that each car will be driven much less. Greater mileage will come at the expense of car size. Small cars won't be used for vacation travel. Firestone believes people will fly rather than drive. Firestone can point to a 7% drop in mileage per car from 1978 to 1980. Firestone also thinks that nonessential driving will be cut back. Carpools to and from work and public transportation will handle any trend toward commuting and suburban living.

Part of Firestone's pessimism may spill over from its other businesses. Nearly broke in 1979, and under fire for unethical handling of defective Firestone 500 tires, Firestone has been cutting back in several areas. Firestone plants have outdated technologies, and the plants need to be gotten off the books. New chief executive officer John J. Navin is retrenching in several areas. Several plants and subsidiaries around the world have been closed or sold. He claims they were only "dogs, begging to be shot."[36]

Firestone and Goodyear are in the same industry and environment, but their interpretation and strategies are poles apart. Firestone sees the need for a defender strategy. They are retrenching, and are protecting current market share while pushing for production efficiencies. Goodyear sees a rosier future. They have adopted a prospector strategy. Goodyear executives expect a growing demand for tires, and they are preparing to meet that demand.

ORGANIZATIONAL CULTURE AND SYMBOLS

The external environment and organization strategy as described above are the responsibility of top management. Another area of responsibility is the internal culture of the organization, which is influenced by symbolic management.

Culture   **Culture** consists of the behavioral patterns, concepts, values, ceremonies, and rituals that take place in the organization. Culture should be congruent with strategy and the external environment. An organization in a state of retrenchment will have a different internal culture than one in a state of expansion. The chief executive can influence internal culture to be consistent with corporate strategy. Cultural values provide employees with a sense of what they ought to be doing, and how they should behave to be consistent with organization goals. Culture represents the feeling, emotional, intangible part of the organization. Each organization has a distinct culture. Two such cultures exist within J. C. Penney and PepsiCo.

IN PRACTICE 12.7

J. C. Penney and PepsiCo

J. C. Penney Co. cares about its employees and customers. J. C. Penney is a great place to work, and its customers will always receive satisfaction. These are the dominant values in Penney's corporate culture. Management actions have reinforced these values since founder James Cash Penney laid down the seven guiding principles, called "the Penney idea." These principles have brought forth tremendous loyalty from staff and customers. One store manager was reprimanded by the President for making too much profit, which was unfair to customers. Customers can return merchandise with no questions asked. Everyone is treated as an individual. Employees are encouraged to participate in the decision-making process. Layoffs are avoided at all costs. Unsuccessful employees are transferred to new jobs instead of being fired. Long-term employee loyalty is especially valued.

PepsiCo. has a completely different value system. Pepsi is in hot competition with Coke for a larger share of the soft drink market. Pepsi's values reflect the desire to overtake Coke. Managers engage in fierce competition against each other to acquire market share, to squeeze more profits out of their business, and to work harder. Employees who do not succeed are terminated. They must win to get ahead. A career can be made or broken on one-tenth of a point of market share. Everyone knows the corporate culture and thrives on the creative tension thus generated. The internal structure is lean and adaptable. The company picnic is characterized by intensely competitive team sports. Managers change jobs frequently and are motivated to excel. The culture is characterized by a go-go atmosphere and success at all costs.

One tangible indicator of the difference in culture between J. C. Penney and PepsiCo. is the length of employee tenure. Penney's executives have been with the company thirty-three years on average, while Pepsi's executives have averaged only ten years.[37]

Symbolic Management

Top executives do not drive trucks or run machines. They deal in symbols.[38] Managers consciously or unconsciously signal values and goals to organization participants. Top executives are watched by employees just as professors are watched by students. Students look for signs about which topics are important for the exam, what the professor likes, and how to get a good grade. In the world of business and government, symbols reach large numbers of people. After President Reagan fired the air traffic controllers, he could not change his mind. The firing symbolized to leaders around the world that the President of the United States was firm and decisive. To renegotiate with the controllers, even if justified on humanitarian grounds, would have signaled indecisiveness by the President. The symbolic value of his action was important and outweighed the rightness or wrongness of the firing itself.

The underlying value system of the organization cannot be managed in the traditional way. Symbols represent a mechanism for managing organizational climate and values that are hard to measure or shape by conventional means.[39] Symbols provide information about what counts in the organization, and where people fit into the organization. Issuing a written rule or policy, for example, will have almost no impact on the value system. The following examples illustrate the use of symbols by managers to influence internal culture.

- In a major midwestern firm, old employees tell how every Christmas the chairman of the board, a grandson of the founder, used to come down from his office on the top floor to walk through every department, shaking hands with each employee. This was the only time he would be seen by many, and the appearance served as a symbol of concern for his "family."
- In a Boston investment firm, during an interdepartmental power struggle, one director's employees took him to dinner and gave him a silver disk inscribed with their signatures and a pledge. Only those present know what was inscribed on the disk but departmental cohesion and effort were greater following this event.
- In a major bank, election as an officer is seen as the key event in a successful career. A series of acts that accompany every promotion to

bank officer includes the official method of notification, the new officer being taken to the officers' dining room for the first time, and the new officer buying drinks on Friday after his notification.[40]

Symbols are one technique for managing culture and underlying values. A **symbol** means that one thing represents another thing. In the examples above, a silver disk represented commitment and support for a director. Shaking hands represented family concern. The ritual associated with promotion to bank officer symbolized entry into the new group and oneness with it.

Symbols are powerful tools. Executives can use symbols to manage images relevant to organizational values. Symbols are signs and signals that can be communicated to large numbers of employees. The types of symbols that managers manipulate fall into three categories—language and logos, ritual and ceremony, and physical space.

Language and Logos Chief executives use a variety of public statements, metaphors, and physical symbols to influence organizational climate and direction. The impact of the chief executive is often to put the values of the company into words that can be disseminated widely. T. J. Watson, Jr., son of the founder of International Business Machines, used the metaphor "wild ducks" to describe the type of employees needed by IBM. The metaphor originated from a story about ducks flying south for the winter that found food set out on a lake. Some ducks continued to fly south while others stopped to eat and stayed for the winter. After a time, the ducks that stayed had difficulty flying at all. The moral was, "you can make wild ducks tame, but you can never make tame ducks wild again."[41] "Wild ducks" symbolized the freedom and opportunity that must be available to keep from taming creative employees at IBM.

Logos represent company symbols created specifically for employees and customers. Most companies have a logo of some sort, such as the Pillsbury Doughboy or Betty Crocker. Eastern Airlines made paperweights that included metal from each aircraft it had flown during its history. This paperweight was distributed to key employees and was never again to be duplicated. It took on almost spiritual value among the employees who received it.[42] Employees would not trade or sell them. Employees identified with the symbol and felt they were an integral part of the company.

Ritual and Ceremony Ritual and ceremony represent a wide range of behaviors that chief executives use to indicate what is important.[43] The concern for minorities can be symbolized by appointing a member of a minority group to the board of directors. Most presidents of the United States appoint women and other minorities to the Cabinet and other government positions. Universities have elaborate ceremonies when a new president is installed. The pomp and circumstance indicate the academic importance of presidential succession.

Simple day-to-day activities of chief executives have symbolic value for employees. When the chief executive "appears" at a planning meeting, the value and importance of planning is emphasized. The location of meetings, such as holding them in regional offices, symbolizes that the regions are important to headquarters. Even the ordering of items on an agenda communicates signals to subordinates. Other rituals such as retirement or award dinners indicate which behavior is valued and important to the chief executive. Watson at IBM installed elaborate rituals to instill the appropriate company spirit. The Hundred Percent Club rewarded sales representatives who had succeeded in fulfilling 100% of their quota. Special conventions were held and awards were passed out to Hundred Percent Club members. Attaining 100% of quota became a dominant value in the IBM culture.[44]

Physical Space Another symbol is the physical environment of the corporation. The chief executive can give attention to the physical environment within the organization. Physical facilities can symbolize a sparse, lean, hardworking climate. Or they can symbolize opulence and luxury. The signal sent to employees and customers should not be left to chance. One brokerage firm made little investment for furnishings for its regional offices. The offices were overcrowded and tacky-looking. Business was poor. A consultant pointed out how a competing brokerage firm attended to physical surroundings. The feel and image created by the office environment was the first impression made on customers.

Physical space also sends signals within the organization. Office size or floor level (penthouse to basement) sends signals about power and influence within the organization. Since these symbols are observed by participants, top executives make decisions to be sure the correct signals are sent.

IN PRACTICE 12.8

The U.S. Post Office

One important use of symbols is to guide a major reorganization. Those symbols that characterize the previous structure and value system must be destroyed, and new symbols brought forth to represent new structure and values. Nicole Woolsey Biggart studied the 1971 reorganization of the U.S. Postal Service (USPS), and observed the extraordinary role of symbol destruction and creation. The Post Office change was so vast, involving 700,000 workers, and was so revolutionary that extraordinary measures were required.

Politicians and employees could not imagine replacing the political patronage system with a corporate structure. And employees were not anxious to go along with the new system. In order to change the cultural ideology, several symbolic actions were taken.

The 200-year-old name of the organization was changed. Only federal agencies are called "departments," so the name change to United States Postal Service symbolized its new role as an independent agency.

An industrial design firm was hired to develop new symbols. These symbols included a new logo, a new type-face for all publications, stationery, and contracts, and new postal colors. Olive-green trucks and mailboxes were replaced by patriotic red, white, and blue colors. A new sign system was used for post offices, and lobbies were repainted.

A birthday party theme was chosen to symbolize the birth of USPS. A stamp was issued, and ceremonies were held. Public tours were given through facilities at post offices around the country.

The cultural value of "service-at-all-costs" was replaced with a value of business-like, efficient service. The service-at-all-costs ideology was enormously expensive and inefficient. The old cultural value was attacked along several fronts. Internal publications emphasized efficiency standards. Articles such as "What Makes Fort Worth Number One" appeared in the house organ, *Postal Life*. Internal newsletters carried the same theme. Over 2,000 senior employees were encouraged to retire so they could be replaced by employees who held the new ideology. By replacing older managers, a signal was sent to remaining employees that the USPS does not operate under the same values as the POD. Large numbers of MBAs were hired for middle management positions, an unheard-of procedure in earlier years.

Through all these techniques, the formal structure, cultural values, and leadership were changed. New work methods, technological improvements, and work values were instilled. Top management in the post office used symbolic management to change culture as well as structure. By using the power of symbols to communicate new values and goals, top management successfully achieved change that was enormous in scope.[45]

MANAGEMENT SUCCESSION

Several components of the top manager's role have been discussed so far in this chapter. Top managers interpret and enact the external environment. They make choices about organization structure, technology, size, and products. Managers develop strategy for achieving organizational goals, and are responsible for the cultural system within the organization.

The final section explores the process of executive turnover, and the extent to which it can help or hurt the corporation. The type of questions to be addressed here are: Should organizations develop succession procedures to replace top managers on a regular basis? Does the chief executive make that much difference to corporate performance?

Succession and Adaptation

The flow of managers through the management hierarchy is a form of organizational adaptation. In organizations characterized by turbulent environments, rapid change, and uncertainty, the turnover of organizational leaders is greater.[46] Organizations in a turbulent environment are more difficult to manage, so new energy and vitality is needed on a frequent basis.

Top manager turnover also allows the organization to cope with specific contingencies. The selection of the new chief executive may reflect the need for a specific skill or specialization.[47] If the dominant issue confronting the organization is financing mergers, choosing a finance person as chief executive gives priority to financial activities. In a hospital, the background of the chief administrator often indicates that one medical specialty or environmental domain is important. A background in business, for example, is helpful if the hospital must raise funds from private corporations.[48] The selection of the top manager enables the organization to adapt to specific environmental needs.

Large organizations tend to experience greater rates of succession than small organizations.[49] Large corporations have specific turnover policies. Managers are promoted into the chief executive slot at the age of fifty-five or sixty, so they will not occupy the position for more than ten years. Turnover every few years can have a dramatic effect on the organization. If a corporation chief executive and the top management team serve continuously for long periods of time, say twenty years or more, organizational stagnation is inevitable. New executives are not coming in to provide fresh energy, new goals, or expertise on changing environmental problems.

A recent example of how management succession is used for adaptation is Coca-Cola Co. In recent years, Coca-Cola became a tradition-bound, stagnating corporation. Most of its business was international, but Coke was not adapting to the turbulent international environment. Coca-Cola was also losing ground to PepsiCo in the U.S. market. That has all changed with the appointment of top executives who provide new blood and an international perspective. The new chief executive of Coca-Cola was born in Havana, Cuba. The chief financial officer is Egyptian. The president of Coke USA is an Argentine. The marketing vice president is a Mexican. Two other members of the top team are U.S. born. Wall Street analysts are optimistic that these changes in top administrators will revitalize Coke in both U.S. and foreign markets.[50]

IN PRACTICE 12.9

Exxon

Perhaps the company most totally committed to succession planning as a way of corporate life is Exxon. From the moment a young engineer, chemist, or MBA joins the company, his or her performance is not only evaluated but continually compared with that of other employees doing similar work. Such comparative ranking, from the top to the bottom of the pyramid, is probably the most distinctive element of Exxon's master plan for finding and training executives of outstanding promise.

Every one of Exxon's scores of operating units has its own compensation and executive development committee, which keeps individual files on all employees in the unit. Each employee's job performance is evaluated on a score of 1.0 (outstanding) to 4.0 (inadequate); so is his or her promotability, including a timetable for promotion. The unit is also required to maintain a list of replacements for every job, ranked in order of preference.

In filling Exxon's top job, the ultimate decision is of course made by the board, which includes a majority of eleven outside directors, who may or may not accept the recommendation of the outgoing chairman. But over the years, observes T. H. Tiedemann, Jr., manager of compensation, organization, and executive development, those board members will have been exposed many times to all the people at the level from which a new CEO is most likely to be chosen.

As a matter of corporate policy, Exxon consistently fills management positions from inside. "We go outside only in unusual circumstances—for instance, when we need some highly specialized expertise," Tiedemann says. "And we don't have to use a computer to find the best candidate for any given job in a hurry, because our system brings all the potential candidates to light."[51]

Succession and Performance

Ritual Scapegoating Does managerial succession influence organizational performance? One type of organization that can help answer this question is athletic teams. The coach is the top manager of the team, and coaches are regularly replaced in both college and professional sports. Several studies have analyzed coaching changes to see whether an improvement in performance occurs. The general finding is that manager turnover does not lead to improved performance.[52] Teams that are extremely bad tend to get better, whether or not the coach is replaced.

An interesting finding from these studies is that performance leads to turnover.[53] Teams with poor records experienced greater succession. The relationship between turnover and performance is the opposite of what we might expect. Rather than a new manager leading to a better record, the poor record leads to the firing of the old manager. The new manager does not make the team better, but firing the previous manager serves as a symbol for what the team is trying to achieve. Thus the term "ritual scapegoating" is a signal to fans and others associated with the team that efforts are being made to improve the team's performance record.[54] The firing of the manager is more of a ceremonial symbol than a strategy for improvement.

Corporate Performance A corporation is much larger and more diverse than an athletic team. Can the chief executive make a difference in a corporate setting? Top managers in large corporations function under many constraints. Corporations have a huge number of employees, many of whom are unionized. Demand for a company's output is influenced by the nature of the industry and economic conditions, which are outside anyone's control. In the steel industry in recent years, for example:

> . . . there have been Presidential pressures against price increases, a long strike against the industry's largest single customer, a steel hauler's strike and sharply increasing costs of input materials. Contract negotiations with the United Steel Workers affect wages and, therefore, production costs. Further, because steelmaking technology has changed radically, the earlier conventional economics of the process have become obsolete . . . . In addition, pressures from important customers like the auto and appliance

industries have affected the industry's concern with product quality. Also the
industry is under growing competitive pressures from both the use of
substitute metals and foreign steelmakers. Finally, options are also restricted
by new regulations governing pollution control.[55]

Clearly, chief executives work within many restrictions. But can they influence the corporation to perform well, even within these constraints? An important study of chief executives surveyed 167 corporations over a twenty-year period.[56] Each time a chief executive was replaced, the changes in sales, net earnings, and profits were recorded for the next three years. Analysis of these data indicated that sales and net earning levels were the direct result of general economic conditions and industry circumstances. When conditions were good and the industry was successful, all corporations had high sales and net earnings regardless of chief executive succession.

However, leader succession was associated with profits. Top managers seemed to influence the factors that translated into profits. Chief executives influenced profits by changing the goals of the organization, by selling off unprofitable subsidiaries, or by adopting new strategies.

Chief executives had more impact in some industries than in others. Profit margins were most responsive to top executive actions in industries in which advertising was important and consumers formed a sizable percentage of the market. These industries deal in areas of consumer taste, and success is a function of consumer manipulation. Hence, management decisions about advertising strategies and consumer interests had more immediate impact on profit margins than in industries not oriented toward consumer tastes.

Another survey of 193 manufacturing companies indicated similar findings.[57] Measures of chief executive turnover and financial strategies were associated with corporate profitability and improved stock prices. Stock prices represent the perception of company performance by investors. Strategic choices made by top management can have a positive influence on corporate performance.

Corporate performance is thus the result of several factors. General economic conditions affect changes in sales and net earnings. Net profit is heavily influenced by the chief executive because net profit is an outcome of strategic choices. The chief executive can use strategic choices and symbolic action to alter the direction and the performance of the corporation. The chief executive does make a difference.

IN PRACTICE 12.10

Arkla Utility Co.

Arkla has been a household word in Arkansas for twenty-five years. Now the word is spreading to Wall Street, where the stock price has doubled in the last year to $40 a share. The price-earnings ratio recently was 12 to 1, one of the highest in the industry. In just three years Standard & Poor's and Moody's have upgraded the company's bond rating four times; both now give it a double-A. Security analysts expect earnings to increase by at least 20% annually for the next five years. Net income was $73 million last year on sales of $975 million.

Arkla is in an extraordinarily powerful position. With the help of an aggressive gas exploration and acquisition team, the company has cornered supplies to last fourteen years at the present rate of sale, versus an industry average of nine years. Having contracted for a lot of this gas when it was cheap, Arkla pays less than competitors. Although it supplies five states, most of its customers are in Arkansas, and it's just now gearing up to penetrate the huge Louisiana industrial market. Many customers there will be petrochemical plants that use gas not only for fuel but also as a raw material.

Arkla is firmly in the grip of a brash young chairman, president, and chief executive, Sheffield Nelson, 40, who has proved to be a tangible asset in his own right. "Nelson has performed a staggering feat by turning Arkla from a humdrum utility into the best-positioned company in the industry," says Richard Lilly, an analyst who specializes in up-and-coming southern companies for Raymond James & Associates of St. Petersburg, Florida. Nelson has managed the company well and bargained the Arkansas Public Service Commission into some remarkably liberal rates. And he did this while waging a protracted struggle with his own mentor: Arkla's former boss and a big stockholder, William R. "Witt" Stephens, 74, patriarch of one of the South's wealthiest families.

By the early 1970s, Arkla executives now say, the company was turning into "junk." Talent was leaving, and half the company's cars were so old and ill-maintained that they had to be jump-started every morning. Stephens was earning, by choice, only $100,000 when he retired in January, 1973. He had refused increases offered by the board, saying he didn't need the money and the government would only tax it away. Unfortunately, he was paying comparably low wages to employees who didn't own investment banks to supplement their paychecks. At the end of Stephens' tenure, some full-time Arkla employees qualified for and collected food stamps.

Nelson's flair for sales and public relations has been vital in Arkla's success. Like Stephens, Nelson projects a down-home image; he listens to country music and serves black-eyed peas and cornbread at board meetings. ("They don't eat that kind of cookin' anywhere else," he says.)

Nelson nurtures his and Arkla's image by raising funds and speaking for such causes as the United Way and a home for battered women. Four years ago, Arkla cut its lines of credit to New York banks and replaced them with a web of credit lines to 350 local banks in the five states where Arkla has operations. Three Arkla board members are active in politics: a woman who sits on the Little Rock city council, a state senator, and the former chairman of the state Democratic party.

Nelson's popularity seems to have helped him with the regulators. In 1975, he persuaded the Arkansas Public Service Commission to allow the company to charge large industrial customers prices based on the replacement cost of gas. Most state commissions apply a rate formula

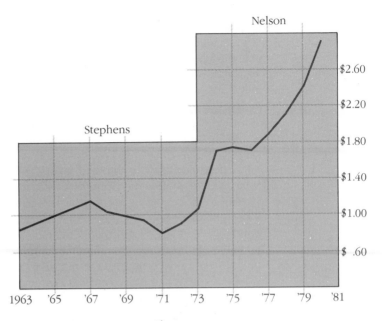

Figure 12.6. Arkla's Earnings per Share.
Source: Peter Nulty, "Little Rock's Hot-Cookin' Gas Company," *Fortune,* October 5, 1981, pp. 148–153, with permission. Copyright © Time, Inc. All rights reserved.

based on the average cost, which is almost always lower than replacement cost. Arkansas laws also permit Nelson to bill customers for anticipated rate increases before they're approved. This permits Arkla to move rates up gradually, avoiding sudden jumps that attract attention, and brings in cash without the usual delay. Nelson avoids the appearance of greed; he'll take a good rate without dickering for extra pennies. Says Mac Norton, head of the Arkansas utility commission, "Nelson knows if the hog gets too fat, it'll be slaughtered." [58]

Nelson's success with Arkla illustrates many of the themes in this chapter. He works at a fast pace and is involved in many activities. Nelson manages key elements in the external environment, such as the public service commission and area banks. He is socially responsible and nurtures Arkla's public image. He established an improved corporate culture. He adopted a strategy of supplying gas to petrochemical plants in Louisiana, and it paid off. Management turnover, with Nelson succeeding Stephens, led to dramatically increased profits and stock prices (figure 12.6), thanks to a new internal culture and an effective corporate strategy.

SUMMARY AND INTERPRETATION

The purpose of this chapter has been to look at processes and techniques associated with the management of large organizations. Top management choices illustrate the importance of top management. These choices influence all the characteristics of organizations, including structure and design, technology, size, and strategy. These characteristics are shaped to fit the external environment. Even the environmental elements the organization responds to is a function of top manager choice. Both the enactment of the external environment and the design of internal characteristics evolve from the chief executive.

Within this array of decisions, the single most important decision for corporate performance is strategy. At the corporate level, top managers seek a balanced portfolio. Each business under the corporate umbrella can provide a different benefit. Some may be risky new ventures, but with the possibility of becoming a fast-growing star of the future. Other businesses represent stable sources of cash that can be used to finance other activities. Some new ventures will not work out, and will have to be dropped from the portfolio. At the level of individual businesses or product lines, strategic decisions are concerned with advertising campaigns, product changes, and whether to retrench or expand. Success at both the business and corporate level is closely related to the selection of correct strategies that integrate the needs of the external environment with the abilities of the organization.

Research into top management activities indicates just how complex and multi-dimensional the job is. Top managers deal with great uncertainty, especially when environmental conditions are changing. Decisions pertain to policy matters, strategy, the government, competitors, future planning, jurisdictional disputes among executives, and the organization's general relationship with the external environment. Many of these problems have few precedents, and for nearly all problems the solution is not obvious or clear-cut. Managers rely heavily on accumulated experience and judgment in order to cope with the randomness and variety in the job. The ability to process large amounts of information to and from a large number of actors appears to be one important management skill. Another requirement is high energy. There are so many activities and demands facing top managers that the ability to work long hours at a fast pace is essential.

Within the complexity and variety of the manager's job, a few patterns have emerged. The most important are the ten roles identified by Mintzberg. Top managers interact with other people as figurehead, leader, and liaison person. They also act as information processor and monitor, disseminator, and spokesperson. They make decisions that pertain to the roles of entrepreneur, distrubance handler, resource allocator, and negotiator. These ten roles provide the best look at top manager behavior available in the literature.

Finally, recent research has discovered the impact of top managers on the corporate culture and the importance of succession procedures for organizational health. Top managers make a difference. Top managers stand for and symbolize cultural values and images they consider important. Symbols reinforce management strategy. Top manager turnover provides new energy and perspectives for organizational leadership. Succession also provides new skills to cope with changing environmental conditions, and may even symbolize a new organizational direction. Enforced succession on a periodic basis is an important mechanism that enables the organization to adapt to the environment.

DISCUSSION QUESTIONS

1. Briefly describe the internal and external domains of top managers. Why are these the responsibility of top management rather than of specialists lower in the organizational hierarchy?
2. Define strategy. How does it link the internal and external domains of top managers.
3. What does it mean to say that managerial activity is "characterized by variety, fragmentation, and brevity"?
4. Describe and give examples of the figurehead, monitor, and disturbance handler roles. Which domains among external environment, internal organization, and strategy would these roles apply to?
5. Strategic choice means that the top managers interpret the environment and make decisions about size and technology. How does that differ from the concept of "enactment"?
6. Pitney-Bowes Corporation recently decided to change strategy in the copier business. They closed down their research and development facility. They will rely on Japanese suppliers for their new technological developments. Would their strategic decision be considered a corporate or business level strategy? Discuss.
7. What is the difference between a prize heifer and a problem child?
8. What role do cash cows play in the corporate portfolio?
9. How does internal organization structure and emphasis differ between organizations adopting prospector versus defender strategies?
10. What is organizational culture? Describe the symbolic tools managers can use to influence internal culture.
11. Top management succession is one technique organizations use to adapt to the external environment. Describe how this happens and give an example.
12. What is ritual scapegoating? Do corporations ever do this?
13. A consultant said, "The individual who occupies the chief executive position can have substantial impact on profits, but not on sales." Explain why you agree or disagree with that statement.

GUIDES TO ACTION

As an organization top manager:

1. Pay attention to the environment. Interpret the external environment and enact measures that will allow the organization to be successful over the long run.

2. Monitor external information and disseminate it to subordinates. Act as a spokesperson for the organization by communicating information to constituents in the external environment.

3. Make choices about technology, size, and structure based on your interpretation of the external environment. Take advantage of environmental opportunities and problems to further the interests of the organization. Define and act upon those elements considered important enough for organizational attention.

4. Take control of the organization's strategy-making machinery. Achieve organizational goals through strategy involving plans, decisions, and technique. Decide such things as which products to produce, growth rate, advertising budget, and acquisition or divestment of product lines. Affect corporate profits and stock prices through the selection of corporate strategies.

5. Act as a symbol for the internal culture and values that are important to the organization. Influence the value system of the organization through the use of metaphors, logos, and ceremonies. Communicate important values and organizational direction to employees.

6. Encourage periodic top management succession. Use built-in succession procedures to ensure a continuous flow of fresh energy and ideas into the upper ranks. Adapt to specific environmental conditions by bringing needed skills and experience into the chief executive positions through this periodic succession.

Consider these Guides when analyzing the following cases and when answering the questions listed after each case.

CASES FOR ANALYSIS

1. PILLSBURY COMPANY

Pillsbury Co. bought Green Giant Co. in 1979. This acquisition was heralded as the biggest and best of several acquisitions in recent years. A little over a year later, Pillsbury executives met for a strategic planning session. What were they to do about Green Giant's miserable profits? The Pillsbury Doughboy was getting a case of indigestion.

Pillsbury's mainstay grocery business—including flour, cake mixes, cookies, biscuits, and rolls—has been a steady money maker. But markets haven't grown much as shoppers turn to convenience foods. Green Giant was an opportunity to get into the frozen food growth business with its frozen vegetables and frozen entree lines. Green Giant also has a major line of canned vegetables.

Green Giant's frozen entrees have been a flop. The products are medium quality at high prices. One example is Toast Toppers—single portions served over toast. They aren't very good and the line is being dropped. Green Giant's well-established line of frozen vegetables remains profitable, but sales have been sluggish.

An unexpected problem occurred with the inefficient canned vegetable operation. It has been cut back. Green Giant's policy was to can everything that it could buy, whether it made money or not. During bumper crop years, its plants would can an enormous volume of vegetables, which resulted in no profits because of low retail prices. Pillsbury closed four of Green Giant's thirteen canning plants at a loss of almost $7 million.

Pillsbury hasn't given up on the frozen entree line. Back in the test kitchen, several new frozen entrees are being developed, including pea pods, pepper steak, and beef and noodles. These will be launched in the next year or two.

Aside from Green Giant, Pillsbury's restaurant line, which provided growth in the 1970s, is stagnating. The Steak & Ale chain has halted expansion. The chain grew to 195 units in 1980, but last year Pillsbury sold eleven and opened only four. In 1982, Pillsbury plans to sell twelve or thirteen more restaurants. Pillsbury is being more selective with its Steak & Ale restaurants to keep up with the competition.

The Poppin Fresh Pies chain is at sixty-nine restaurants and holding. Pillsbury had high hopes for the chain, but it has made no money. No new restaurants are planned.

Burger King is continuing to grow, but at a slower rate than in the past. It opened 311 restaurants in 1979, and 344 in 1980. This dropped to about 275 in both 1981 and 1982. Pillsbury once hoped to build 400 units a year, but they couldn't sustain it. High interest rates made financing difficult for franchises.

Pillsbury's greatest hope in the restaurant business is a new concept called Bennigan's. Bennigan's stood at 50 restaurants in 1981 and plans are to increase it to at least 300 and perhaps 500 units by the end of the decade. Bennigan's restaurants are very popular and Pillsbury plans to exploit its growth potential.

Growth has slowed on several Pillsbury fronts, but Pillsbury executives are optimistic. They'll cut back where they have to, and look into new businesses, perhaps outside the food industry, to generate growth in the future.[59]

Questions
1. Do the product lines at Pillsbury fit into the Boston Consulting Group's framework for corporate planning? Which of Pillsbury's lines would be considered new ventures, dogs, stars, and cash cows? Explain.
2. Which product lines would you say are using the prospector strategy? The defender strategy? Analyzer strategy?

2. JOHN MUIR & CO.

Raymond L. Dirks, a very well-known man not only in financial circles but in the best restaurants and hotels, gets a kick out of the fact that for years American Express wouldn't give him a credit card because of his debts. He had made it a habit every since to carry a thick roll of $100 bills in his pocket, as if to demonstrate his indifference to the finicky standards of credit-card companies.

Mr. Dirks's bundle of carry-around cash is considerably skinnier these days than it used to be. On August 17, his securities firm, John Muir & Co., voluntarily filed for bankruptcy in New York federal court . . . .

One thing is certain: Although Muir is gone, it won't soon be forgotten on Wall Street. The firm's crowded, chaotic boardrooms were staffed with some of the sharpest big-volume stock salesmen in the business—and some of the rankest beginners. And then there was "Dirks's Dozen," a group of handsome young women who had been coached into becoming some of the firm's biggest producers. At Muir offices, complete informality was the order of the day. Nobody cared whether you wore a coat or a tie. And on birthdays, it wasn't unknown for striptease dancers to come in to pep up the celebrations.

"I guess they wouldn't do such things at Morgan Stanley," Mr. Dirks concedes, mentioning one of Wall Street's more prosperous—and more straitlaced—concerns. He says that Muir's swinging style was all part of a plan and that he was deliberately trying to foster "a free-form atmosphere . . . ."

On a few really big days, Mr. Dirks, a short, plump Kewpie doll of a man in his late forties, would leap atop a desk in Muir's crowded main boardroom and exhort the sales staff like a cheerleader. "Get it while you can," he would shout. Many of the salesmen, meanwhile, were making $10 and $20 bets among themselves about which of Muir's many low-priced speculative issues would appear on the daily over-the-counter 10-most-active list . . . .

Although Mr. Dirks asserts, "We ran a low-overhead operation," others who worked there say that money was spent lavishly on parties and other forms of entertainment to promote the firm's underwritings. "The standard drill was a cocktail party at Windows on the World (a restaurant atop New York's World Trade Center) followed by dinner there or at some other swank restaurant," a former salesman says.

The affairs were supposed to introduce Muir's underwriting clients to Wall Street's money managers, but sometimes not enough money managers showed up. "At some of the parties, 80% or 90% of the people were Muir employees, passing themselves off as money managers," the former salesman says. "I got a call from my boss late one afternoon. He told me: 'Bring your wife, bring somebody, bring anybody! We gotta fill up this place.'"

Inevitably, the unstructured atmosphere bred some bizarre abuses of good business practices. A former employee recalls that two salesmen took their girl friends to Europe on a Concorde jet and wrote it off as a business trip. And there were "near fist fights" over who would get to use Muir's rented Cadillac limousine on many nights . . . .

However, Mr. Monberg, Muir's former sales manager, [said] "Philosophically he was correct. He provided an unstructured environment where creative people could flourish. Working for a major firm today is like working for the Post Office."[60]

Questions
1. Did Mr. Dirks's personal style and behavior influence the internal climate and cultural values at John Muir & Co? Discuss.
2. Was the internal culture congruent with the goals and strategy Mr. Dirks adopted for his company? Was it congruent with the type of business he was in? Discuss.

NOTES

1. James H. Lavenson, "How to Earn an MBWA Degree," *Vital Speeches of the Day* 42 (April 15, 1976): 410–412.
2. Henry Mintzberg, *The Nature of Managerial Work* (New York: Harper & Row, 1973).
3. Robert J. Myers and Martha Stout Kessler, "Business Speaks: A Study of the Themes in Speeches by America's Corporate Leaders," *The Journal of Business Communication* 17 (1980): 5–17; Thomas Christ, "A Thematic Analysis of the American Business Creed," *Social Forces* 49 (1970): 239–245.
4. A Brearley, "The Changing Role of the Chief Executive," *Journal of General Management* 3 (1976): 62–71.
5. Myers and Kessler, "Business Speaks."
6. *Ibid.*
7. *Ibid.*
8. Maynard S. Seider, "American Big Business Ideology: A Content Analysis of Executive Speeches," *American Sociological Review* 39 (1974): 802–815.
9. *Ibid.*
10. A. van Cauwenbergh and N. van Robaeyf, "The Functioning of Management at the Corporate Level," *Journal of General Management* 5 (1980): 19–29.
11. Phillip Selznick, *Leadership in Administration* (New York: Harper & Row, 1957).
12. *Ibid.*
13. Mintzberg, *Nature of Managerial Work,* p. 95.
14. Henry Mintzberg, "Patterns in Strategy Formation," *Management Science* 24 (1978): 934–938.
15. Henry Mintzberg, "Managerial Work: Analysis from Observation," *Management Science* 18 (1971): B97–B110.
16. *Ibid.,* B100.
17. *Ibid.*
18. *Ibid.,* B97. Reprinted by permission of Henry Mintzberg, "Managerial Work: Analysis from Observation," *Management Science,* Volume 18, Number 2, October 1971, copyright 1971 The Institute of Management Sciences.
19. *Ibid.*
20. Sloan Wilson, "What Do Successful Men Have in Common? Raw Energy," *Houston Chronicle,* March 30, 1980. Copyright 1980 Independent News Alliance. Reprinted by permission.
21. Mintzberg, *Nature of Managerial Work,* pp. 55–57.
22. Robert Townsend, *Up the Organization* (New York: Alfred A. Knopf, 1974), pp. 129–130.
23. John R. Montanari, "Operationalizing Strategic Choice," in John H. Jackson and Cyril P. Morgan, *Organization Theory: A Macro-Perspective for Management* (Englewood Cliffs, NJ: Prentice-Hall, 1978), pp. 286–298.

24. John Child, "Organization Structure, Environment and Performance: The Role of Strategic Choice," *Sociology* 6 (1972): 1–22; H. Randolph Bobbitt and Jeffrey D. Ford, "Decision-Maker Choice as a Determinant of Organizational Structure," *Academy of Management Review* 5 (1980): 13–23.

25. James Brian Quinn, "Strategic Change: 'Logical Incrementalism,'" *Sloan Management Review* 20 (1978): 7–19.

26. Karl E. Weick, *The Social Psychology of Organizing* (Reading, MA: Addison-Wesley, 1979), pp. 130–131.

27. *Ibid.,* p. 130.

28. Adapted from Quinn, "Strategic Change," p. 14.

29. Milton Leontiades, *Strategies for Diversification and Change* (Boston: Little Brown, 1980), p. 63.

30. *Ibid.,* pp. 102–105.

31. *Ibid.*

32. William L. Shanklin and John K. Ryans, Jr., "Is the International Cash Cow Really a Prize Heifer?" *Business Horizon* 24 (1981): 10–16.

33. Howard Rudnitsky with Jay Gissen, "Chesebrough-Pond's: The Unsung Miracle," *Forbes,* September 28, 1981, pp. 105–109; "A Shoe-In?," *Forbes,* November 13, 1978, p. 218.

34. Raymond E. Miles and Charles C. Snow, *Organizational Strategy, Structure, and Process* (New York: McGraw-Hill, 1978).

35. Ralph E. Winter, "Goodyear, Firestone Split on Future Demand for Tires," *Wall Street Journal,* February 23, 1981, p. 21.

36. Subratan Chakravaty, "Firestone: 'It Worked,'" *Forbes,* August 17, 1981, pp. 56–58.

37. "Corporate Culture," *Business Week,* October 27, 1980, pp. 148–160.

38. Thomas J. Peters, "Symbols, Patterns, and Settings: An Optimistic Case for Getting Things Done," *Organizational Dynamics* (1978): 2–23.

39. Jeffrey Pfeffer, "Management as Symbolic Action: The Creation and Maintenance of Organizational Paradigms," in L. L. Cummings and Barry M. Staw, eds., *Research in Organizational Behavior,* vol. 3 (Greenwich, CT: JAI Press, 1981), pp. 1–52.

40. Thomas C. Dandridge, "Symbols at Work," working paper, School of Business, State University of New York at Albany, 1978, p. 1.

41. Richard Ott, "Are Wild Ducks Really Wild: Symbolism and Behavior in the Corporate Environment," paper presented at the Northeastern Anthropological Association, March, 1979.

42. Personal communication from Thomas Dandridge.

43. Thomas C. Dandridge, Ian I. Mitroff, and William S. Joyce, "Organizational Symbolism: A Topic to Expand Organizational Analysis," *Academy of Management Review* 5 (1980): 77–82.

44. Ott, "Are Ducks Really Wild."

45. Nicole Woolsey Biggart, "The Creative-Destructive Process of Organizational Change: The Case of the Post Office," *Administrative Science Quarterly* 22 (1977): 410–426.

46. Gerald R. Salancik, Barry M. Staw, and Louis R. Pondy, "Administrative Turnover as a Response to Unmanaged Organizational Interdependence," *Academy of Management Journal* 23 (1980): 422–437; Jeffrey Pfeffer

and William L. Moore, "Average Tenure of Academic Department Heads: The Effects of Paradigm, Size, and Departmental Philosophy," *Administrative Science Quarterly* 25 (1980): 387–406.

47. Jeffrey Pfeffer and Gerald R. Salancik, "Organizational Context and the Characteristics and Tenure of Hospital Administrators," *Academy of Management Journal* 20 (1977): 74–88.

48. *Ibid.*

49. Oscar Grusky, "Corporate Size, Bureaucratization, and Managerial Succession," *American Journal of Sociology* 69 (1961): 261–269.

50. John Huey, "New Top Executives Shake up Old Order at Soft-Drink Giant," *Wall Street Journal*, November 6, 1981, pp. 1, 17.

51. "Management Succession: A Hard Game to Play," *Dun's Review,* April, 1981, pp. 54–55. Reprinted with the special permission of *Dun's Review,* April 1981, copyright © 1981, Dun & Bradstreet Publications Corporation.

52. Michael Patrick Allen, Sharon K. Panian, and Roy E. Lotz, "Managerial Succession and Organizational Performance: A Recalcitrant Problem Revisited," *Administrative Science Quarterly* 24 (1979): 167–180.

53. Oscar Grusky, "Managerial Succession and Organizational Effectiveness," *American Journal of Sociology* 69 (1963): 21–31.

54. M. Craig Brown, "Administrative Succession and Organizational Performance: The Succession Effect," *Administrative Science Quarterly* 27 (1982): 1–16; William Gamson and Norman Scotch, "Scapegoating in Baseball," *American Journal of Sociology* 70 (1964): 69–72.

55. Stanley Lieberson and James F. O'Connor, "Leadership and Organizational Performance: A Study of Large Corporations," *American Sociological Review* 37 (1972): 119.

56. *Ibid.*

57. Nan Weiner and Thomas A. Mahoney, "A Model of Corporate Performance as a Function of Environmental, Organizational, and Leadership Influences," *Academy of Management Journal* 24 (1981): 453–470.

58. Peter Nulty, "Little Rock's Hot-Cookin' Gas Company," *Fortune,* October 5, 1981, pp. 148–153, with permission. Copyright © Time, Inc. All rights reserved.

59. Lawrence Ingrassia and Meg Cox, "Sluggish Green Giant Slows Pillsbury's Pace From the Frantic '70s," *Wall Street Journal,* November 4, 1981, pp. 1, 14; "Green Giant Merger into Pillsbury Voted," *New York Times,* January 31, 1979, p. D4.

60. Richard E. Rustin, "How Ray Dirks Led His Firm to Prosperity Before the Roof Fell in," *Wall Street Journal,* November 6, 1981, pp. 1, 16.

13

Organization Theory:
An Overview and Assessment

ABC Television Network

"When the ABC Television Network soared to the top of the prime-time ratings in the fall of 1976, broadcasters and Wall Street alike were skeptical. After all, the network had spent nearly a quarter of a century running a poor third behind CBS and NBC, and there was little reason to believe that ABC's remarkable string of hit programs was anything more than a temporary run of luck.

"But those doubts soon faded. ABC not only increased its lead in prime-time but shocked the competition by taking over leadership of the lucrative daytime viewing hours and registering impressive gains both in the early morning time period long thought to be virtually owned by NBC's Today Show and the news area long dominated by CBS."[1]

ABC appeared to come out of nowhere in the 1970's. For years it had been a weak third network, but in 1980 it was in first place in ratings and profits.[2] ABC's remarkable success was no accident. It resulted from good strategic planning, a willingness to take risks, and the right organization structure.

In the early 1950's, NBC and CBS jumped out ahead of ABC because of popular personalities from radio programs. ABC also lacked member stations. In 1955 it could reach only about 25 percent of the TV audience compared to 85 percent for the other networks. Using strong programming in urban areas, ABC made sufficient profits to increase the number of affiliates and to innovate.

In the 1950's two new shows, "Cheyenne" and "77 Sunset Strip," were introduced. They were the first regularly scheduled adult western and private-eye series. Both were enormously successful. A string of innovations followed. Turning their attention to sports, ABC purchased rights to broadcast NFL games on Monday nights. They outbid other networks for the 1976 Olympics and established popular weekend sports shows. ABC introduced the mini-series concept with shows like "Roots." "Good Morning America" was launched to compete with NBC's "Today" show, and new soap operas began taking over the lead in daytime programming.[2]

Since 1970, the number of ABC affiliates has increased significantly. Many stations call ABC and ask to join the team.

By any standard, ABC has enjoyed tremendous success. It was picked as one of the best managed companies by *Dun's Review*.[3] For five years, ABC had an annual compounded earnings growth rate of nearly 28%. Revenues in 1981 were over $2 billion and profits were over $45 million.[4]

Leonard H. Goldenson, ABC's chairman, has directed ABC for over twenty years. He developed the strategic plan of making profits in one area and then moving on to a new target. The strategy has achieved success in evening programming, daytime programming, and sports. The last frontier is news programming, which is next on Goldenson's list. A multimillion-dollar news center was recently built. Organization structure has helped Goldenson achieve his strategy. ABC has decentralized management groups. This design encourages innovation and entrepreneurship. The overall structure is sufficiently tight that each division can be evaluated, but managers remain free to take risks. ABC also has in-depth management talent and experience that keeps it from being dependent upon any one person, and enables it to meet the challenge of changing conditions.

Purpose of This Chapter

In the first chapter of this book, the fall of the Joseph Schlitz Brewing Company was analyzed. ABC, by contrast, has experienced a string of successes, and continues to rise even higher. ABC and Schlitz represent two organizational stories, one successful and one not so successful.

The purpose of this chapter is to compare the management of successful and unsuccessful organizations to materials taught in organization theory. Research in organization theory typically is not undertaken to solve specific management problems. Most organizational research is reported in academic journals. Research findings sometimes seem sterile and unrelated to organization problems. Throughout this book we have used examples of organizations to illustrate and apply organization theory concepts. The next part of this chapter takes those applications one step further by comparing the overall set of concepts in organization theory to the views of management consultants. Management consultants have developed their own frameworks for explaining organizational success and failure. Consultants' perspectives on organizations are important in their own right, and they also provide a basis for evaluating the applicability for organization theory.

Another purpose of this chapter is to analyze the development of organization theory and consider where it is headed in the future. New topics on the horizon, such as theory Z and the population ecology model, are discussed. These topics will be of increasing concern to both managers and organization theorists of the future.

DOES ORGANIZATION THEORY RELATE
TO REAL MANAGEMENT ISSUES?

The goal of any scientific discipline is to acquire knowledge about the physical or social world. At the very forefront of knowledge, discoveries and techniques are complex and difficult to understand. But if a scientific discipline achieves its goal of new knowledge, elements of those discoveries should help laypeople understand the world around them. The question of whether organization theory relates to management issues has been partially answered throughout this book. Specific case examples and illustrations have suggested that organization theory is applicable to management in ongoing organizations.

A different approach to assessing organization theory concepts is to examine the viewpoint of consultants who work with organizations, but who are not organization theorists. These people are problem-solvers. Comparing their views of key management issues to the topics in this book provides additional insight into which topics are relevant to the management of organizations. To accomplish this comparison, reasons for corporate success and failure reported in the business literature by consultants were compiled.[5] These management issues were used to explain both corporate success and failure, and are summarized in table 13.1. They are based on work with private corporations, but most of these ideas and insights are applicable to organizations of all kinds.

The management issues in table 13.1 represent valuable findings about organizations. The consultants have wide experience with successful and unsuccessful organizations. They have provided valuable insight into organization performance. The lessons they have learned are important for current and future managers. Their analyses were based on giant corporations like Hewlitt-Packard, McDonald's, Dana Corporation, and Texas Instruments as well as small and medium-sized corporations around the U.S.

Reasons for Corporate Success or Failure Fifteen characteristics were identified from studies by management consultants as relevant to management excellence or management problems. Eight characteristics led to corporate success (S); seven led to severe problems which often resulted in failure (F). These characteristics are classified into four categories: environment, management, structure, and other.

Environment Environmental characteristics identified by consultants pertain to the quality of relationships with other organizations, and sensitivity to external changes.

1. *Closeness to the Customer (S).* Successful companies are customer driven. In terms of the chapter on innovation, new product ideas arise from customer needs, not from engineering desires. In terms of the chapter on environment, managers are boundary spanners and must pay attention to key environmental sectors, the most important of which is the customer. Customers are the most important element in business decision-making.

If anything, successful companies thrive on sales and service overkill. Top managers interact directly with customers whenever necessary. When management is out of touch with customer needs, the organization will eventually find itself in difficulty.

2. *Changes in Technology (F)*. Production and product changes by other companies lead to trouble when one's own products become obsolete or less competitive. Adapting to these changes was the topic of the chapter on innovation and change. Organizations must develop mechanisms to encourage change, such as staying in touch with customer needs and technical developments, or establishing a separate department to create and implement new developments.

3. *Company Hostage to Others (F)*.   4. *Depending on a Single Customer (F)*. These issues pertain to dependence on the environment. The first relates to the supply domain and the second to the market domain. As described in the chapter on environment, organizations can reduce their dependence by seeking relationships with multiple organizations. If large loans are owed to a single banker, the banker may force the organization into actions that promote short-term payback rather than long-term growth and development. A single customer may drive down prices or prove unreliable and turn elsewhere. Failure to manage the environmental relationship has led to catastrophe for many firms.

Management   Management characteristics that distinguish successful from unsuccessful companies relate to decisiveness, expertise, and the goals and business values that management stands for.

1. *Bias toward Action (S)*.   In the language of the chapters on innovation and decision-making, successful companies are oriented toward implementation. They don't talk problems to death, or spend all their time

Table 13.1.   Reasons for Corporate Success or Failure. (S = Associated with Corporate Success; F = Associated with Corporate Failure.)

Environment	*Management*
1. Closeness to customer (S)	1. Bias toward action (S)
2. Changes in technology (F)	2. Management short of courage (F)
3. Company hostage to others (F)	3. Company outgrows managerial expertise (F)
4. Depending on single customer (F)	4. Stress on a key business value (S)
Structure	5. Stick to what company knows best (S)
1. Simple form and lean staff (S)	*Other*
2. Autonomy to increase entrepreneurship (S)	1. Internal conflict (F)
3. Inadequate control systems (F)	2. Productivity improvement via consensus (S)
4. Simultaneous loose-tight controls (S)	

Sources: John Banaszewski, "Thirteen Ways to Get a Company in Trouble" *Inc.*, September 1981, pp. 97–100; Thomas J. Peters, "Putting Excellence into Management," *Business Week*, July 21, 1980, pp. 196–205.

creating exotic solutions. These companies "do it, fix it, try it."[6] These companies are also goal-directed, and managers strive toward a limited set of well-defined goals. Effectiveness is measured in results, which are in the output domain described in the chapter on goals and effectiveness. Managers learn what works by doing it.

2. *Management Short of Courage (F).* In a similar vien, when change is needed, such as new people, new structure, new products, or new markets, management must make decisions and push ahead. This issue pertains to several chapters, especially those on decision-making. If managers wait until they are sure of the answer, they will get nowhere. They must make decisions to move the company ahead, even without perfect information.

3. *Company Outgrows Managerial Expertise (F).* This issue was described in the chapter on size and growth, and occurs in small and medium-sized companies. If the company experiences growth and success, but the owner still wants to make every decision, the company is in trouble. New management structures must be designed to allow the company to grow beyond the ability of the founding entrepreneur.

4. *Stress on a Key Business Variable (S).* In successful companies, chief executive officers push a dominant value with a single-minded focus. This value shapes the culture for the company, as described in the chapter on top management. At Dana, the value is cost reduction and productivity improvement. At Texas Instruments, innovation is the theme. At McDonald's, the values of quality, cleanliness, and value are stressed in all training programs. These values reflect the dominant competitive issue for each organization. Lower-level managers in these corporations do not suffer from mixed signals or doubts about what the company is trying to accomplish.

5. *Sticking to What Company Knows Best (S).* Most companies diversify in order to manage environmental uncertainty, but when they do, the best companies stay in their area of expertise. They define their internal strengths, whether it be marketing, innovation, or manufacturing efficiency, and build on them. This is part of the strategy-making process and is the responsibility of upper management, as discussed in the chapter on top management. It is also a way of managing the external environment.

Structure   Structural characteristics apply to the allocation of personnel across departments, the use of self-contained units, and the design of internal information and control systems to complement overall structure.

1. *Simple Form and Lean Staff (S).* Successful organizations adopt bureaucratic structural characteristics to meet their needs, but they don't overdo it. McDonald's has extensive bureaucracy at the store level, where procedures keep the work simple and ensure reliably good food. Upper levels are less bureaucratic and are not bloated with staff personnel. Very large corporations are divided into divisionalized structures by product or by territory. Each self-contained division can act like a small or medium-sized corporation.

2. *Autonomy to Encourage Entrepreneurship (S)*. Successful organizations are designed to encourage innovation and change. The product form of structure gives each unit a specific product focus so innovation and creativity will be rewarded. As discussed in the chapter on innovation, idea champions are encouraged, and risk-taking is rewarded when innovations succeed. The self-contained unit structure encourages the lateral coordination required to accommodate customer needs in the innovation process.

3. *Inadequate Control Systems (F)*. When management does not have adequate control systems to direct behavior, set targets, or detect trouble spots, problems fester too long. This tends to occur in smaller organizations. As discussed in chapter 8, information and control systems should be designed to reflect key variables, such as product quality, customer satisfaction, or rate of innovation. Managers should supplement these control systems with their own personal information sources and evaluations to stay on top of system performance.

4. *Simultaneous Loose-Tight Control (S)*. Successful large companies use tight controls in some areas and loose control in others. Market control is used to evaluate the performance of divisions as described in chapter 8. Division managers have specific growth and profit goals to achieve, and accurate information on performance is available. Within these controls, however, managers have flexibility. They are free to innovate, take risks, and adopt whatever procedures are needed to achieve desired outcomes and high levels of effectiveness.

Other Two other characteristics also distinguish successful from unsuccessful corporations—the ability to cope with internal conflict and to move the company ahead by consensus.

1. *Internal Conflicts (F)*. As described in the chapters on power and politics and intergroup conflict, too much conflict can hurt the organization. When groups' goals are to obtain political advantage, corporate performance suffers. Mechanisms must be built into the organization to allow decisions to be made in the company's benefit and to reduce conflict to a strategically suitable level.

2. *Productivity Improvement via Consensus (S)*. Productivity can be improved by motivating and stimulating employees throughout the organization. Some organizations use shop floor teams and cross-functional groups to provide input to the goal-setting and decision-making process. The improvement of productivity through human motivation was covered briefly in the discussion of organizational development in the chapter on change.

Summary Consultants deal with issues very similar to the topics discussed in this book. The most relevant organization theory topics seem to be innovation and change, the environment, top management domain, decision-making, information and control systems, and goals and effectiveness. Beyond those topics, a connection between consultant viewpoint and organization theory can be found for practically every concept in this book, with only one exception. According to consultants, one reason for excellence in corporations is productivity through human resources, an issue that has not been stressed in organization theory. This topic has normally been in the domain of organization behavior, and is now emerging as a topic relevant to organization theory. One of the newest approaches in this area, Theory Z, is described later in this chapter.

Comparing consultants' views to organization theory also shows that each group divides the field of organization and management into different categories. For example, the consultant point of "bias toward action" cuts across the topics of goal setting, decision-making, innovation, and information-processing. The chapter on environment describes several issues that consultants deal with, including contact with customers, technological change, depending on a single customer, company held hostage, and location disadvantage. Thus organization theorists and consultants provide different categories for understanding organizations, but the content of these viewpoints is very similar.

TWENTY YEARS OF PROGRESS

Organization theory is a new field of study. It is not a mature discipline, with a large, well-defined body of knowledge. Organization theory is still in the formative stages, and is just now being recognized as a separate discipline in universities, where separate courses are being established. Because of its newness, the last twenty years have seen remarkable progress. Several significant developments on the topics of organization technology and structure were published in the 1960s. Since then a vast amount of new research has been reported. Not all organization theory topics have been studied equally or have developed at the same pace. In some areas, organization theory can be quite specific about how an organization should be designed. In other areas, knowledge and frameworks are scarce. Many contingencies have not yet been discovered.

The topics that are part of organization theory are reflected in the chapter titles in this book. These topics are also consistent with a survey of organization theorists that asked their opinions about the field's boundaries.[7] Each topic can be classified according to whether the level of development is high, moderate, or low compared with other topics within the discipline. This classification indicates where significant progress has been made in the last twenty years and, conversely, where we can expect the most rapid development in the future. The classification of organization theory topics by level of development is given in table 13.2.

High Development   Three topics that have a high level of development in organization theory concern organization structure and design. Research into (1) size and bureaucracy, (2) technology and structure, and (3) functional versus product structural processes has been reported since the 1960s. A substantial amount of information has accumulated. Relationships among variables such as bureaucracy, size, formalization, complexity, administrative ratio, and clerical ratio are well understood. Organization theorists can say with some certainty when a bureaucratic structure is appropriate or is not appropriate. We know that small-batch technology should be associated with a quite different organization structure than assembly-line technology. At the department level, nonroutine departments require a different structure than routine departments. Similarly, organization theorists can suggest when a product form of structure is preferable to a functional structure for an organization.

Recall from chapter 1 that organizations are social systems, and are not characterized by the same level of precision and prediction that occurs in the physical and biological sciences. The amount of bureaucracy or extent of functional structure cannot be calculated with mathematical precision. Even in this well-developed area of organization theory precise formulas do not exist. But definite patterns do exist, and organization theorists can say with some certainty that large deviations from these patterns will lead to serious problems.

Moderate Development Several of the topics in organization theory have experienced moderate development. These include (1) the environment, (2) goals and effectiveness, (3) innovation and change, (4) decision-making, and (5) intergroup relationships. These topics are moderately developed because a few models have been developed for analyzing organizations. For instance, organizations can be analyzed by the amount of change and complexity in the external environment. Techniques for managing the environment have also been reported. Another example is the dual-core and ambidextrous models that apply to innovation and change. Organizational decision-making can be understood with reference to the rational model, the Carnegie model, and the garbage can model.

These topics are considered only moderately developed because while there are specific frameworks in each area, many unexplored contingencies still exist. Moreover, the application of these models requires substantial training and experience within the specific organization. The models are not sufficiently developed or comprehensive to fit every organizational setting.

Table 13.2. Areas of High, Moderate, and Low Development in Organization Theory.

High	Moderate	Low
1. Bureaucracy and size	1. Environment	1. Power and politics
2. Technology and structure	2. Goals and effectiveness	2. Information and control
3. Functional versus product structure	3. Innovation and change	3. Top management domain
	4. Decision-making	
	5. Intergroup relations	

Also, there has not been a large amount of research which has confirmed or replicated patterns and relationships. As that kind of research is reported, the body of knowledge will become more well-developed and the models will become more precise. Models in these areas are relatively conceptual and abstract, and do not translate into managerial applications as easily as findings from the highly developed topics.

Low Development   Three topic areas are classified as low development: (1) information and control, (2) power and politics, and (3) top management domain. These areas are considered low in development because the body of knowledge is new and relatively small. Ten years ago, chapters on these topics could not have been written. Sufficient research did not exist. Even five years ago, the amount of research was small. The work in information-processing, for example, has been dominated by research on communication and data. Chapter 8 defined data as the outcome of a communication channel. But information is the interpretation of meaning, which has been studied only recently in the form of information amount and richness. Likewise, only in the last few years have theories of control moved beyond the simple feedback mechanisms used in machine systems. Machine concepts do not apply to organizational control, so new theories concerned with market control, clan control, and bureaucratic control have been reported. Power and politics has been an especially difficult area of study because managers are reluctant to report their perceptions of power and politics. The top management domain is also difficult because strategy formulation, symbolism, and culture are difficult to define, and top managers are extremely busy and reluctant to be interviewed.

Future Research   One explanation why topics have developed at different rates is the difficulty of research for organization theorists.[8] The greatest development in research methods over the past twenty years has been the use of questionnaires and statistical analysis. These techniques are very effective for measuring well-defined characteristics of organizations. With a questionnaire, the researcher can ask about the organization's size, formalization, structure, technology, and administrative ratio, and these data can be analyzed with statistics.

But the topics in the moderate and low developed categories are more complicated. They pertain to internal behavioral processes that are more elusive and ambiguous. Organization scholars are now beginning to attack these more complex topics, and they are doing so with new methodologies. Richer forms of research, such as intensive case analyses, observation, and open-ended interviews are able to reveal insights about complex organizational processes. These richer methodologies are able to provide more exhaustive descriptions of organization.[9] The new methodologies are less precise, but they can capture and communicate ideas and emotions that cannot be quantified. They are able to capture some of the complexity and variety inherent in complex social systems.

Organization theory is rich and exciting. It seems to be changing almost daily. Future research can be expected to reveal new knowledge about information processes, power, and top management domain. In information-processing, future studies will explore the use of organizational languages and jargon for interpreting activities. Power and politics will be more closely linked to the process of decision-making as well as to goals, innovation, and conflict. Top management strategic choices, which decide the direction of the organization, are extremely important. The field has not yet defined the general pattern of strategic decision-making or the options normally available to top management. Additional developments can also be expected in the areas of organization environment, innovation and change, and other areas in the moderately developed topics. Models that describe new variables and that give more elaborate frameworks for manager application will be forthcoming. Research is accumulating at a rapid rate in these topic areas.

ORGANIZATION THEORY OF THE FUTURE

A few new developments are emerging in organization theory that have not yet accumulated much research data and were not included earlier in this book. Three areas that have great promise and will be prominent in text-books of the future are Theory Z, Mintzberg's typology of organizations, and the population ecology model. Theory Z is important because it provides a framework for managing human resources in organizations. Mintzberg's typology of organizations is significant because it pulls together several organization theory concepts to describe five basic types of organizations. The population ecology model provides a new framework for understanding organizational relationships with the environment and the process of adaptation and change.

Human Resource Management: Theory Z

Since World War II, Japan has undergone what many observers would call an industrial miracle. Japan has adopted Western technologies and has equalled or exceeded American corporate performance in domains considered to be exclusively American, such as autos and electronics. This extraordinary performance has received a great deal of attention. Organization scholars are studying and writing about Japanese methods. The Japanese have also purchased selected American and Canadian companies, and have applied their management techniques in these firms. These companies have provided additional sites for studying Japanese management techniques.[10]

A major ingredient of Japanese management is that managers seem to make better use of human resources. Moving American corporations toward a Japanese style of management means increasing the responsibility and influence of rank-and-file employees. Japanese managers assume employees want to work together and will share a common purpose. Unlike traditional American organizations, Japanese organizations do not separate the work of producing the goods and the work of management and planning. Everyone is involved in planning, decision-making, and other management activities.

Ideas about participative leadership style and worker motivation have appeared in the Western literature for a long time. But the new trend is different. Japanese-style management concerns the organization as a whole and the organization's culture, which are topics in the organization theory domain. This change is more than a leader simply including subordinates in a decision. The new approach attempts to change basic assumptions that have characterized American corporations for years and that have excluded workers from extensive participation in the management process.

The most significant work in the area of Japanese management is Theory Z by William Ouchi.[11] Ouchi and Alfred Jaeger studied Japanese and American firms and discovered that management style reflects the larger culture. Ouchi and Jaeger identified seven dimensions along which Japanese and American firms differ. These seven characteristics provide the basis for characterizing type A (American) and type J (Japanese) organizations.[12]

Length of employment refers to the average tenure of employees. Long tenure means that employees will be familiar with organizational workings and co-workers. Anticipation of a long career with a single organization encourages an employee to become integrated into the organization. The modes of *decision-making* and *responsibility* refer to whether the organization culture values individual action or a collective approach to decision-making and responsibility. *Speed of evaluation and promotion* refers to the frequency of employee review. When evaluations and promotions are slow, employees have an opportunity to become fully integrated into the organizational culture. They also adopt a longer term perspective. *Control* refers to whether employees are controlled with explicit standards, rules, and measurement, or whether less explicit social values and norms are used to control behavior. *Career path* pertains to whether employees are highly specialized within a single functional area or whether they are exposed to several functions. Lateral transfers enable employees to become more committed and involved in the entire organization. Finally, *concern* refers to how the organization views the employee. Segmented concern means the employee is valued only during time involved on the job. Holistic concern is oriented toward the total personal life circumstance of the employee.

The differences between traditional American and Japanese firms on these seven dimensions are summarized in table 13.3. The American organization values individual mobility, personal independence and self reliance, rapid promotion, explicit forms of control, and is concerned with only the

Table 13.3. Characteristics of Type A and Type Z Organizations.

Type A (American)	Type J (Japanese)
Short-term employment	Lifetime employment
Individual decision-making	Consensual decision-making
Individual responsibility	Collective responsibility
Rapid evaluation and promotion	Slow evaluation and promotion
Explicit, formalized control	Implicit, informal control
Specialized career path	Nonspecialized career path
Segmented concern	Holistic concern

Source: William G. Ouchi and Alfred M. Jaeger, "Type Z Organizations: Stability in the Midst of Mobility," *Academy of Management Review* 3 (1978): 308, with permission.

work behavior of employees. This type of organization is oriented toward the short-run and toward getting measurable benefits from the employee in exchange for quick promotion opportunities.

Japanese organizations reflect a culture in which individual mobility is low. Employees are expected to be with a firm for a lifetime, and social norms rather than rules and regulations control behavior. Employee involvement and commitment to the organization enable a consensual decision-making process to emerge. Employees will be with the organization for an extensive period. They are able to invest time working in diverse functions learning the organization. The Japanese firm is concerned with the total needs of employees since they are to be with the organization for a lifetime.

Managers in type J organizations have a longer time perspective than do managers in type A firms. Coordination problems are less in type J firms because employees are familiar with each other and with the entire organization, and they try to accommodate each other in decision-making. Credit is given to the collective so that rapid evaluation and promotion of individuals is inappropriate.

It would not be logical to transplant the Japanese system intact into American culture. It wouldn't fit. But the type Z organization proposed by Ouchi and Jaeger integrates key Japanese ideas with management style from American firms.[13] The type Z characteristics are listed in table 13.4. The type Z organization combines the best characteristics of traditional Japanese and American management to meet current needs of American organizations.

The type Z organization retains the American cultural value of individualism, but combines it with a collective approach to decision-making. Employment is for a longer term, which slows down the evaluation and promotion process and enables employees to become integrated into the organization. Explicit, formal control procedures are retained, but are combined with implicit, social control. Career paths in the type Z organization are moderately specialized. Paths may include only a few diverse activities but are no longer limited to a single specialized function. Slow evaluation and stability of membership is associated with greater concern for employees, including their families. The combination of these processes embodies the type Z philosophy.

Table 13.4.   Characteristics of Type Z Organizations.

Type Z (Modified American)

Long-term employment
Consensual decision-making
Individual responsibility
Slow evaluation and promotion
Implicit, informal control with explicit, formalized measures
Moderately specialized career path
Holistic concern, including family

Source: William G. Ouchi and Alfred M. Jaeger, "Type Z Organization: Stability in the Midst of Mobility," *Academy of Management Review* 3 (1978): 311, with permission.

When firms successfully achieve the theory Z management structure, distinct characteristics emerge. Employees experience a sense of equality and involvement, as if they were members of the enterprise. Employees have greater understanding of each other's point of view, so shared norms and values begin to emerge. Extensive amounts of time are spent identifying problems. In a type Z firm, seventy or eighty people may be included in an initial discussion because they eventually may be affected by the decisions. But while problems are discussed at length, implementation is a snap. Traditional American firms have great difficulty with implementation, which is overcome by theory Z management processes.[14] The sense of collective responsibility also increases productivity. For example, workers on a type A assembly line have clearly prescribed individual jobs, and they follow specified instructions. When an incomplete component comes down the line, no one reports it, because it is not their responsibility. Employees act individually and will do only the required task. In a type Z firm, each worker is part of the organization and is collectively responsible with other employees. An incomplete component will be called to the attention of others by the first person to spot it, so that it will not proceed any further down the assembly process.

IN PRACTICE 13.1

Westinghouse

Westinghouse Electric corporation decided to experiment with theory Z management. The guinea pig was the company's construction group, which was an example of traditional American-style management. It had an established chain of command and a large number of tradition-minded engineers. Westinghouse's goal in this experiment was to overturn traditional boss-employee relationships to enhance performance. In a period of difficult economic conditions, top management felt they must make better use of human resources. Bosses will no longer be expected to issue orders. Instead, they will seek consensus. Rather than chew out workers, they will ask for suggestions. New committees and councils will be involved in both major and minor decisions.

The Westinghouse Construction Group will not suspend performance measurement. They will measure productivity improvement, and are going to test whether theory Z management allows them to increase productivity faster than the 2–3% increases of the last three years. Visits to Japanese plants deeply impressed Westinghouse managers with the potential to improve productivity. "When you visit Japanese factories and see everyone, but everyone, working like tigers to make that product more reliable at a lower cost, it's awesome . . . . They even come back early from their breaks."[15]

Implementation of theory Z has not been easy. Top management first expected it to be implemented at lower levels so they could see how it would work. Consultants insisted that this approach wouldn't do. Either top executives made their own decisions by consensus and moved the process downward, or theory Z would never work on the shop floor.

Once top management agreed to be involved, the construction group was blitzed with training programs. Managers at all levels in the construction group were exposed to theory Z ideas and began to practice the techniques in five-day seminars. Once lower-level managers realized that top management was serious, the rumor mill helped diffuse the program. People at all levels began to look forward to attending the training programs and trying the new techniques.

Committees and decision groups have been set up at all management levels. At the top, general managers meet to discuss common interests monthly. Councils under them meet with counterparts with common problems from other units. Sixty quality circles were formed at lower levels, which brought together workers and supervisors to discuss production problems. Other areas were affected as well. A new cafeteria was designed to replace the vending machine area by a committee of workers and managers. Even a problem of restroom vandalism was tackled by a committee. New business systems, such as inventory and manufacturing controls, are being established through group processes. The most difficult decision of all—the allocation of budget resources— has also been handled by the committee. Instead of fighting with each other for limited resources, once all problems were laid on the table the group moved quickly to a consensus. Some divisions gave up expected budget increases to help divisions that had more severe needs. The open decision process led to a much better allocation of resources than the group president could have accomplished alone.

At this point, the results look promising for Westinghouse. Full results won't be realized for up to ten years. Changing management culture is a slow process. Productivity in the construction group was up 8% last year, more than any previous increase.[16] At Westinghouse, the proverbial belief that the camel was the result of a group decision to create a horse is rapidly being replaced by the belief that group decision-making can be effective after all.[17]

Theory Z management builds upon several topics covered earlier in this book. The chapters on power and control both reported research showing how greater influence by lower-level participants was associated with better organizational performance. The material on organizational development in the innovation and change chapter stressed techniques for upgrading the skill and participation of employees. The chapter on top management described how organizations have distinct cultures. Top managers can influence culture, but a strong commitment is required. Theory Z uses these ideas because greater participation and influence at lower levels become part of the organization's culture. Theory Z is not temporary, but a new value system. Structural and management characteristics, such as promotion and succession, control systems, appraisal systems, and concern for the individual must also be changed throughout the organization. When these ideas are combined into type Z management, increased productivity and effectiveness is a genuine possibility.

Organizational Typologies

One fundamental element in the development of a scientific discipline is a scheme to order, classify, or group objects under investigation. A comprehensive typology is important to science because knowing an object's category provides significant information about many of the object's characteristics.[18] Most classifications in this book have included only one or two dimensions. Organization environments, for example, can be classified by the rate of change or by complexity. This type of classification helps us understand organizations, but it does not provide a compehensive set of categories into which groups of organizations can be placed.

A few attempts to develop organization typologies have been reported in the literature on organizational theory. In chapter 1, organizational subsystems were categorized by production, boundary spanning, maintenance, adaptation, or managerial functions in the organization. The same classification has been used to classify organizations according to their contribution to the larger society.[19] Schools are maintenance organizations because they supply trained people to maintain society. Business firms are production organizations. Government organizations provide the managerial function for society. Universities and research centers are responsible for adaptation. Boundary-spanning is handled by the foreign services and multinational corporations. Thus the function an organization performs for the larger society is one basis for categorizing organizations.

Another typology classified organizations by who benefits from the organization's existence. Blau and Scott proposed four organizational types: (1) Mutual-benefit organizations are those in which the prime beneficiary is the membership, such as in a union. (2) Business concerns are organizations in which the owners are beneficiaries. (3) Service organizations are those in which the client group is the prime beneficiary. (4) Commonwealth organizations benefit the public at large.[20]

Several other typologies have been proposed, but most have problems.[21] The typologies are very limited. They consider only one or two dimensions of organizations so that enormous differences emerge within a single category. The category of business firms, for example, is so vast that many firms will not be similar at all. Knowing a category does not enable an observer to predict structure, design, or management techniques. For the most part, the development of typologies has not been a very fruitful area in organization theory.

Despite the problems, typologies are of great importance. If accurate typologies could be developed, they would be very useful because organizations could be classified into homogeneous subgroups. Then dimensions such as structure, technology, power, control systems, innovation, and strategy could be prescribed with considerable accuracy. The development of an accurate typology is an important goal for the field.

Henry Mintzberg recently proposed a five-category typology that incorporates many of the variables described in this book, such as environment, power, structure, formalization, configuration, technology, and size.[22] Mintzberg's analysis of organizations suggests that these variables hang together in identifiable clusters. This development is important because it combines several key organization theory variables and suggests that relatively uniform groupings of organizations may be possible.

The five organization types proposed by Mintzberg are simple structure, machine bureaucracy, professional bureaucracy, divisionalized form, and adhocracy.[23] These organization types summarize many of the organizational characteristics described throughout this book. Each type is listed across the top of tables 13.5a and 13.5b along with a description of organizational characteristics typically associated with each type.

Simple Structure   The simple organization is typically a new, small entrepreneurial company. The organization consists of a top manager and workers in the technical core. Only a few support staff are required. There is little specialization or formalization. Coordination and control is from the top, where power and influence are located. Employees have little discretion, although work procedures are typically informal. This organization is suited to a dynamic environment. It can maneuver quickly and thereby competes successfully with larger, less adaptable organizations. Adaptability is required to establish its market. The organization is not powerful and is vulnerable to sudden changes. Unless adaptable, it will fail.

Machine Bureaucracy   Machine bureaucracy describes the bureaucratic organizations discussed in chapter 4. This organization is very large, and the technology is routine, often oriented to mass production. Extensive specialization and formalization are present, and key decisions are made at the top. The environment is simple and stable because this organization is not adaptable. The machine bureaucracy is distinguished by large support staffs. Technical support staffs, including engineers, marketing researchers, financial analysts, and systems analysts, are used to scrutinize, routinize, and formalize work in other parts of the organization. The technical support staff is the dominant group in the organization. Machine bureaucracies are often criticized for lack of control by lower employees, lack of innovation, and an alienated work force, but they are suited to large size and a stable environment.

Professional Bureaucracy   The distinguishing feature of professional bureaucracy is that the production core is composed of professionals, as in hospitals, universities, and consulting firms. While the organization is bureaucratized, people within the production core have autonomy. Long training and experience replace the need for extensive internal control structures. These organizations often provide services rather than tangible products, and they exist in complex environments. Most of the power rests with the professionals in the production core. Technical support groups are small or nonexistent.

Divisionalized Form   Divisionalized organizations are extremely large, and are subdivided into product or market groups. The key part of the organization is middle management, which runs the division. There are few

Table 13.5a.   Dimensions of Five Organizational Types.

	Simple Structure	Machine Bureaucracy	Professional Bureaucracy	Divisional-ized Form	Adhocracy
Key part of organization:	Top management	Technical support staff	Production core	Middle management	Support staff and technical core
Contingency factors:					
Age and size	Typically young and small	Typically old and large	Varies	Typically old and very large	Typically young
Technology	Simple	Machines but not automated, not very sophisticated	Not machine or sophisticated	Divisible, other-wise like machine bureaucracy	Very sophisti-cated, often automated
Environment	Simple and dynamic; some-times hostile	Simple and stable	Complex and stable	Relatively simple and stable; diversified markets	Complex and dynamic

liaison devices for coordination between divisions, and there is emphasis on performance control using profit and loss statements. The divisionalized form can be quite formalized within divisions because technologies are often routine. The environment for any division will tend to be simple and stable, although the total organization will serve diverse markets. Many large corporations, such as General Motors, Procter & Gamble, Ford, and Westing-house are divisionalized organizations. Centralization exists within divisions, and a headquarters staff may retain some functions, such as planning and research.

Adhocracy   Adhocracy develops to survive in complex, dynamic environ-ments. The technology is normally sophisticated, as in the aerospace and electronic industries. Adhocracies are typically young or middle-aged and quite large, but need to be adaptable. A matrix form of structure typically emerges with extensive horizontal information-processing and mutual adjust-ment. Both support staff and the production core are important because both have authority over key production elements. The organization has an elaborate division of labor, but is not formalized. Employee professionalism is high. There is selective decentralization to individuals who have the expertise to handle problems, so people at any level may be involved in decision-making. The adhocracy is almost the opposite of the machine bureaucracy in terms of structure, power relationships, and environment.

Table 13.5b.   Dimensions of Five Organizational Types.

	Simple Structure	Machine Bureaucracy	Professional Bureaucracy	Divisionalized Form	Adhocracy
Design elements:					
Specialization of jobs	Little specialization	Much horiz. and vert. spec.	Much horiz. spec.	Some horiz. and vert. spec.	Much horiz. spec.
Professionalism	Little	Little	Extensive	Some	Much
Formalization, bureaucratic/ organic	Little formalization, organic	Much formalization, bureaucratic	Little formalization, bureaucratic	Formalization within divisions, bureaucratic	Little formalization, organic
Structure	Functional	Functional	Functional or product	Product	Functional and product (matrix)
Key coordinating mechanism	Direct supervision	Standardization of work	Standardization of skills	Sophistication of outputs	Mutual adjustment
Decentralization	Centralization	Limited decent.	Decent.	Limited decent.	Selective decent.
Technical core	Informal work with little discretion	Routine, formalized work with little discretion	Skilled, standardized work with individual autonomy	Tendency to formalize	Merged with administration to do project work
Technical support staff	None	Many to formalize work	Few	Many at HQ for performance control	Small and blurred within project work
Clerical support staff	Small	Often elaborated to reduce uncertainty	Elaborated to support professionals	Split between HQ and divisions	Many but blurred within middle in project work
Flow of authority	Significant from top	Significant throughout	Insignificant (except in support staff)	Significant throughout	Insignificant
Flow of informal communication	Significant	Discouraged	Significant in administration	Some between HQ and divisions	Significant throughout
Power	Chief executive	Professional staff and external control	Professional operators	Division Managers	Expert control
Flow of decision-making	Top down	Top down	Bottom up	Differentiated between HQ and divisions	Mixed, all levels

Adapted from Henry Mintzberg, *The Structuring of Organizations: A Synthesis of the Research,* © 1979, pp. 466–467. Adapted by permission of Prentice-Hall, Inc., Englewood Cliffs, NJ.

Human Resources Administration

In late 1971, New York City's welfare operation was totally out of control and heading for sure fiscal disaster. In October there were 1,255,000 individuals receiving a total of about $1.3 billion in welfare assistance and another $1.2 billion in medical assistance; six out of every seven applicants were accepted. Quality control studies revealed that one-third of all recipients were receiving the wrong amount of money and 15% were probably ineligible for any assistance. Approximately $150 million in taxpayer funds was being misappropriated through fraud, error, and mismanagement. Welfare rolls were climbing at the disastrous rate of 10,000 persons a month; costs were increasing at the rate of $120 million per year.

Field operations were in a state of absolute and perpetual chaos. Welfare centers closed their doors routinely at 10:00 or 11:00 o'clock in the morning, unable to handle the crush of desperate recipients. Acts of violence against welfare workers were commonplace, and police measures to protect them proved inadequate. Each of the city's forty-four welfare centers had a unique layout with a different client flow; each seemed equally senseless. Over 165,000 critical transactions were backlogged, including $27 million in cases that were supposed to have been closed. Employee productivity was below 40%.

The application procedures and processing system could best be described as irrational, negligent, and chaotic. A person merely had to sign a name to an application form to receive welfare, then be recertified annually by signing a statement that nothing had changed. Over $8 million was lost in duplicate check frauds—when recipients cashed their checks, fraudulently claimed to have lost them, and then received replacements in addition.

Management was virtually nonexistent. Over one-third of the employees exceeded their allotted lateness limit, at a cost of $1.3 million a year to the city. The average employee took eleven and one-half of his twelve days of sick leave, with disproportionate concentrations around holidays and weekends. Absenteeism cost the city another $7.5 million per year. Although misconduct was prevalent, the agency terminated only nineteen employees for flagrant abuses.

On staff, there were no industrial engineers, less than twenty professional systems analysts, and few professional managers. In short, the system was out of control and the existing organization lacked the capability to bring it back in check.

In late 1971, faced with the appropriate political and fiscal climate and a consultant's in-depth report on welfare operations, Mayor Lindsay resolved to overhaul the welfare system and bring the caseload under control. To accomplish this, the mayor brought in a new management team, authorized the expenditure of $10 million a year for professional staff and computer support, and gave the effort full political backing . . . .

The project management group was the pivotal unit in the overhaul strategy . . . .

At the end of the first year, the project management staff had successfully identified and documented the system's problems, publicized "horror stories," and made appropriate recommendations. Many new systems had been implemented, special operations like "photo ID" had been completed, a comprehensive overhaul plan had been scheduled, and certain line managers had been "spun off" to run new programs.

At the end of eighteen months, the following major results had been obtained:

- The $5.5 million duplicate-check problem was solved by referring over 1,900 cases to the District Attorney for prosecution and by recouping funds from the fraudulent individuals.
- Backlogs in the processing of cases were reduced from 165,000 to 50,000; employee productivity increased by 16%. At welfare centers, the lines of waiting clients disappeared and directors regained control of their centers.

The bottom-line result of the overhaul has been a dramatic reversal in welfare expenditures. Whereas in 1971 the welfare rolls were growing at the rate of 10,000 persons a month, in 1972 this growth was arrested; the rolls remained fixed at 1,275,000 persons. In November of that year, the rolls began to decline steadily at an average rate of about 9,000 persons per month. This trend should continue through the end of 1973. The bottom line of the overall effort is a $230 million annual cost turn-around for the City of New York.[24]

The initial design of the Human Resources Administration was all wrong. In terms of Mintzberg's typology, it was run as a professional bureaucracy when it should have been designed as a machine bureaucracy. Consider the key elements: processing welfare applicants was a routine technology, the professional level of production employees was low, the organization needed mass production techniques to handle thousands of people, technical specialists were needed to develop and implement efficient management systems, and field units needed to be formalized and standardized to achieve HRA goals. These elements all point to a machine bureaucracy. Once the technical support staff were in place and received power to do their job, the organization became much more effective. The correct organizational design made a real difference.

Mintzberg's typology is a useful way to categorize organizations along several dimensions found to be important in previous chapters. These dimensions evolve in clusters so that environment, technology, structure, support staff, and employee professionalism fit together in logical patterns. Mintzberg's categories represent a significant development toward a useful typology. Additional research can be expected to refine and elaborate organizational categories, which will provide important information to managers about how their organizations should be designed.

Population Ecology   The third area in which increased research activity can be expected in the future is the environment. The environment is already a moderately developed topic of study, but it is so rich and important that extensive new work will be undertaken. Future research will seek to identify new dimensions of organizational environment, how they influence the organization, how organizations sense and interpret external elements, and how organizations reach out and manage those elements.

There is another pressure that also makes the study of organizational environments especially valuable. The organizational world is becoming more crowded.[25] As the human population increases, so does the organizational population. Thousands of new organizations are started annually. The mortality rate is high, but a number of organizations do survive. The total environment becomes more crowded. Organizations are bunched together, which requires closer cooperation. Organizations are no longer free to act on their own, but must share scarce resources and work under constraints. Interorganizational cooperation is necessary for organizations to survive. The process of environmental crowding makes the environment for any single organization more complex and less stable.

An important focus of future research will be on the set of organizations that comprise the environment, and how the set of organizations adapt and interrelate to each other. A new model that explores this aspect of organization and environment is called the population ecology model.[26] The population ecology model is drawn from theories of natural selection in biology. Theories of biological evolution try to explain why certain forms of life appear and survive while others perish. Those that survive are typically best fitted to immediate environmental circumstances.

The population ecology model is concerned with organizational forms. **Organizational form** is the configuration of technology, products, goals, and personnel that are selected or rejected by the environment. Each new organization tries to find a niche—a combination of environmental resources and needs—sufficient to support it. The niche is typically small in the early stages of an organization, but may increase in size over time if the organization is successful.

In the population ecology model, luck, chance, and randomness play an important part in survival. New products and ideas are continuously being proposed by entrepreneurs and by large organizations. When these ideas are pushed into the external environment, success or failure is often a matter of chance—whether external circumstances happen to support it. An idea that failed in the 1960s can be a smashing success in the 1980s because the environment is different. The population ecology model assumes continuous change, both in the environment and in the development of new organizations and products trying to find a niche in that environment. The process of change in the population ecology model has three stages: variation, selection, and retention. These stages are summarized in figure 13.1.

Variation   Variation is similar to mutation in biology. New organizational forms continuously appear. They are initiated by entrepreneurs, established with venture capital by large corporations, or set up by a government seeking to provide new services. Some forms may be deliberately conceived to cope with a perceived change in the external environment. Others may be pushed as an idea that has great potential. At any point, there are a great number of variations in new organizational forms appearing in the population of organizations. These variations add to the scope and complexity of organizational forms in the environment.

Selection   Some variations will suit the external environment better than others. Those that find a niche and are accepted by the larger environment will survive. Others will fail to meet the needs of the environment and will perish. When there is insufficient demand for the product or insufficient resources made available to the organization, it will be selected out. Most organization variations fail. Only a few are selected and have a chance to survive over the long term.

Retention   Retention is the institutionalization of selected organizational forms. If the organization's form and output are valued by society, it will become a dominant part of the environment. Many forms of organizations are currently institutionalized, such as government, schools, churches, and the makers of television sets and automobiles. They are relatively permanent features in the population of organizations. But they are not permanent in the long run. The environment is always changing, and if the dominant organizational forms do not develop variations with which to adapt to external change, they will gradually diminish and perhaps perish.

From the population ecology perspective, the environment is the important determinant of organizational success or failure. The organization must read and interpret environmental needs correctly, or it will be selected out. Those organizational forms that happen to meet the needs of the environment will survive. For the hundreds of organizational forms initiated each year, chance largely determines which survive and which perish. A small percentage of the new variations will succeed, and a large percentage will fail.

An example of environmental change and organizational variation was the emergence of motels. During the 1950s, motor hotels appeared along highways to meet the needs of the traveling public. This variation in organizational form met an environmental need and quickly found its niche. The

Figure 13.1.   Elements in the Population Ecology Model of Organizations.

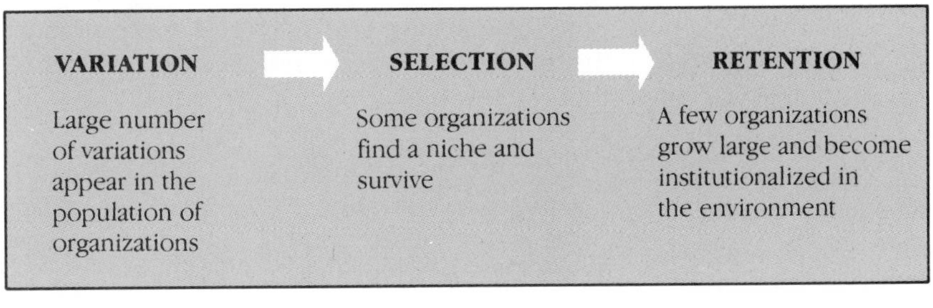

VARIATION		SELECTION		RETENTION
Large number of variations appear in the population of organizations	⇒	Some organizations find a niche and survive	⇒	A few organizations grow large and become institutionalized in the environment

best ones were filled quickly, so people had to stop early to find quarters for the night. But the environment changed. Super highways were built that crisscrossed the country. Organizational forms were also changing. The most important variation came from a group in Memphis, Tennessee, that developed a motel chain with standardized quality and a system of advance reservations. These motels were built along the new freeway systems and away from the old two-lane highways. Soon Holiday Inns stretched from coast to coast, and small independent hotels could only attract the overflow. Other variations of motel chains emerged and became the dominant organizational form. The small independent motels have been largely selected out because they were unable to adapt to the changing external environment.

The process of variation, selection, and retention leads both to the creation of new organizational forms and to changes in current organizational forms. Variations of existing ideas may emerge within an organization and lead to new products and internal changes that meet environmental needs. The population ecology model explains why change takes place both within and between organizations, and why new organizational forms continuously appear.

IN PRACTICE 13.3

Timex Corporation

During World War II, Timex effectively manufactured clock-timers for artillery shells. But in 1945, the environment changed. The war was over, and there was little demand for these timing mechanisms. Timex's niche was disappearing. Top management decided to adapt the organization to the manufacture of wristwatches. Top management identified a new niche in which Timex could become established. The goal was to produce a highly accurate watch at low cost. Manufacturing technology instead of craft technology would be used to produce the watches. Manufacturing efficiencies could be realized by using a pen-level movement instead of a jeweled movement.

The manufacturing process was successful, but marketing presented a new set of barriers. Jewelry stores would not handle Timex watches because they were outside the traditional price range. Timex watches would undercut current lines of watches that provided larger profits. The answer was to develop a new distribution system through drug stores and supermarkets. The development of this niche required several years of teaching and selling to these organizations. After eight years, the entire distribution system was in place. Timex watches were distributed through about 250,000 stores.[27]

The new watch manufacturing process and distribution system were organizational mutations, which were eventually selected by the environment. A need existed in the external environment that was coupled with Timex's ability to manufacture watches at low cost. Timex took the chance, and the variation succeeded. Low-cost watches are institutionalized today. Traditional manufacturers who produced costly handcrafted watches have added low-cost watches to their lines. Timex became the dominant organization in the environment to which other organizations had to adapt. The environment for watch manufacturers continues to change with new shifts away from mechanical watches. Electronic and digital watches are the new variations in this environment, and these variations now threaten manufacturers of low-cost mechanical watches.

SUMMARY AND INTERPRETATION

The purpose of this chapter was to compare organization theory to real world views of organizations, and to assess both the past and future of organization theory. One of the most important conclusions is that organization theory does relate to the world of organization and management. Although research is normally undertaken from an academic perspective, the results have implications for understanding and managing organizations. The key issues identified by consultants overlap all the key topics described in this book. Consultants use their own categories for defining important issues, but the content is very similar to that of organization theory.

Another important point is that areas within the field of organization theory are in different stages of development. The highly developed topics, such as technology, structure, and bureaucracy, have the greatest applicability to organizations. These topics have larger bodies of knowledge based upon research findings, so definite frameworks are available for application to organizations. The less developed areas, such as power and politics or top management domain, will receive greater research attention in the future. Less developed topics tend to be more complex and ambiguous than other topics in the field. These areas have the greatest potential for new knowledge.

The future of organization theory is exciting. There are three areas in which new research is already being reported. The first is in the area of productivity through human resources. Achieving increased productivity through motivation and participation of all employees as a dominant cultural value is just beginning. Theory Z, which integrates management concepts from Japan and America, is an initial step in this field.

The second area is organization typologies. Mintzberg proposed five types of organizations that summarize several of the variables covered in this book. While this typology does not include every kind of organization, it provides a very useful framework for combining characteristics such as environment, technology, bureaucratic characteristics, and power. Additional work on typologies has great potential for providing new knowledge as well as specific guides to managers.

The third area of new research is the population ecology view of the environment. Population ecology examines the whole population of organizations, and how it changes. New organizational forms continuously emerge, and the environment is always changing. Those new organizational forms that fit the environment are selected in. Others fail. Those that are retained in the environment may grow and become institutionalized as dominant forms in the future. Over time, however, even institutionalized organizations must adapt. Change, although gradual, is always present. Without variation in the organization's form and products, the organization will eventually find itself out of step with environmental needs.

DISCUSSION QUESTIONS

1. Issues considered by consultants to be important to organizational success or failure are: closeness to customer, management short of courage, and autonomy to increase entrepreneurship. Which topics covered in this organization theory book are similar to these issues?
2. An entire chapter of this book was devoted to the environment and to innovation and change. Which management issues identified by consultants are similar to the material in these chapters? Explain.
3. Which topics in organizational theory are classified as low in development? What does low development mean? How do topics in this category differ from those in the high development category?
4. Are research methods related to the extent of development of organization theory topics? Explain.
5. Briefly describe the seven characteristics of theory Z. How does a type Z firm differ from a traditional type A firm?
6. What is a machine bureaucracy? A divisionalized form? How do professionalism, power, technical support staff, and formalization differ between these two types of organizations?
7. What is the key part of an organization in a "simple structure"? In an "adhocracy"? What do you think explains why a different part of the organization is more important in each organization type?
8. What role does chance play in the population ecology model?
9. Briefly define variation, selection, and retention as used in the population ecology model. How do these processes apply to the evolution of the population of organizations?
10. Population ecology has been called a highly theoretical model. What significance does it have for managers?

GUIDES TO ACTION

As an organization designer:

1. Make your organization successful by emphasizing closeness to the customer, changes in technology, simple form, and lean staff. Structure to encourage entrepreneurship, simultaneous loose-tight controls, bias toward action, stress on a key business value, and productivity improvement by consensus.

2. Identify and avoid problems that can keep an organization from achieving corporate excellence. Avoid being held hostage to other companies, depending on a single customer, having inadequate control systems, having management that is short of courage, outgrowing manager expertise, and having internal conflicts.

3. Use organization theory to provide explicit tools and concepts that can assist and guide managers and future managers. Environment, innovation and change, top management domain, decision-making, information and control systems, organization structure and design, and goals and effectiveness are all things that need to be considered when supplying guidance for managers.

4. Use Theory Z as one way to increase productivity through employee participation by creating an internal culture with more stability and involvement of employees.

5. Identify an organization type by using Mintzberg's typology, and then use the typology to implement appropriate structure and power relationships.

6. Encourage variation within an organization so that new products and new organizational forms will fit the needs of the continuously changing environment. Without variation, the organization will not survive over a long period of time.

Consider these Guides when analyzing the following case and when answering the questions listed after the case.

CASE FOR ANALYSIS

GULF OIL CORPORATION

Gulf Oil recently found itself with a new president and a new organization structure. Gulf has slipped in recent years, and is no longer considered one of the "seven sisters," the major international oil companies. The previous president resigned because of political scandals and an apparent lack of corporate direction. The new president and organization structure were implemented to correct these problems.

The corporate reorganization was started by the former chief executive. Gulf set up seven independent strategy centers. Each center is a distinct company with profit and loss responsibility. The seven centers are Refining and Marketing, Energy and Minerals, Science and Technology, Real Estate, Trading and Transportation, Chemicals, and Canada. The reorganization also added a large corps of corporate planners at headquarters.

Establishing a new direction and making the new corporate organization work have been the responsibility of the new chief executive, Jerry McAfee. Gulf will no longer consider acquisitions outside the energy field, such as CNA Financial and Ringling Bros., which it previously tried to acquire. Instead, Gulf will invest in petroleum exploration and coal and uranium operations. McAfee insists that Gulf will stick with the things they know best. "We see a sense of direction and purpose emerging. There is no longer any uncertainty about our strategy or our goals."[28]

During initial reorganization and changeover of chief executives, middle managers were uncertain about where they stood. Although they had authority to make decisions, many of them were reluctant to push ahead. The headquarters planning group seemed to have the power. McAfee quickly pushed operating responsibilities back to the managers of the strategy centers. The headquarters group has been reduced in number and is strictly advisory.

Each strategy center is evaluated on a strict profit and loss control system. This system led to initial competition among operating units because each unit tried to look good at others' expense. Transfer payments were boosted to make one's own performance look good. Strategic center activities are now better coordinated, and profit centers are only rewarded when total corporate profits are good.

The reorganization is still being fine-tuned. The Refining and Marketing group has undergone severe cost-cutting. The president of that group reduced the payroll by 1200 in order to break even on the bottom line. McAfee is still not satisfied, so more cuts are expected. Several of the headquarters staff were also cut, and the European operation is next up for surgery.

McAfee's personal style is quite different from his top-down approach to cost-cutting and decision-making. He is affable and likes to rub shoulders with rank-and-file employees. He appears on closed-circuit television periodically to address employees.[29]

Questions
1. Does Gulf Oil Corporation reflect any of the traits identified as characteristic of successful or unsuccessful corporations? Would you consider Gulf successful or unsuccessful at this time?
2. In which of the five organizational types proposed by Mintzberg would you place Gulf? Are characteristics such as headquarters support staff, middle manager power, environment, and other dimensions similar to what Mintzberg suggested? Does Gulf differ on any characteristics?
3. Does McAfee's approach to decision-making, responsibility, and performance evaluation reflect organizational type A or Z? Discuss. Would you expect consensus decision-making to be effective for decisions about corporate reorganizations or cutbacks?

NOTES

1. "ABC: How to Become Number One," *Dun's Review,* December, 1979, p. 46.
2. *Ibid.;* Steven Flax, "Stay Tuned to Tomorrow," *Forbes,* July 19, 1982, pp. 66–72.
3. "ABC: How to Become Number One," pp. 46–47.
4. "Form 10-K," American Broadcasting Companies, Inc., Securities and Exchange Commission, for the fiscal year ending January 2, 1982, p. 47.

5. The following discussion is based upon Thomas J. Peters, "Putting Excellence into Management," *Business Week,* July 21, 1980, pp. 196–205, and John Banaszewski, "Thirteen Ways to Get a Company in Trouble," *Inc.,* September, 1981, pp. 97–100. Thanks to Don Parks for suggesting this analysis.

6. Peters, "Putting Excellence into Management," p. 196.

7. Allen C. Bluedorn, "The Teaching of Organization Theory: A Report on a Survey of the Management/Organization Theory Division of the Academy of Management," paper presented at the National Academy of Management Meetings, San Diego, CA, August, 1981.

8. Richard L. Daft, "The Evolution of Organization Analysis in *ASQ:* 1959–1979," *Administrative Science Quarterly* 25 (1980): 623–636.

9. *Ibid.*

10. R. T. Johnson and W. G. Ouchi, "Made in America (Under Japanese Management)," *Harvard Business Review* 52 (September-October, 1974): 61–69.

11. William G. Ouchi, *Theory Z: How American Business Can Meet the Japanese Challenge* (Reading, MA: Addison-Wesley, 1981).

12. William G. Ouchi and Alfred M. Jaeger, "Type Z Organizations: Stability in the Midst of Mobility," *Academy of Management Review* 3 (1978): 305–314.

13. *Ibid.*

14. *Ibid.*

15. Jeremy Main, "Westinghouse's Cultural Revolution," *Fortune,* June 15, 1981, p. 76.

16. *Ibid.*

17. This discussion was drawn from Main, "Westinghouse's Cultural Revolution," pp. 74–93, and Bruce A. Jacobs, "Does Westinghouse have the Productivity Answer," *Industry Week* 208 (1981): 95–98.

18. Bill McKelvey, "Guidelines for the Empirical Classification of Organizations," *Administrative Science Quarterly* 20 (1975): 509–525.

19. This classification was proposed by D. Katz and R. L. Kahn, *The Social Psychology of Organizations* (New York: John Wiley, 1966), and T. Parsons, *Structure and Process in Modern Societies* (New York: Free Press, 1960).

20. P. M. Blau and W. R. Scott, *Formal Organizations* (San Francisco: Chandler, 1962).

21. William B. Carper and William E. Snizek, "The Nature and Types of Organizational Taxonomies: An Overview," *Academy of Management Review* 5 (1980): 65–75.

22. Henry Mintzberg, *The Structuring of Organizations* (Englewood Cliffs, NJ: Prentice-Hall, 1979), pp. 215–297.

23. *Ibid.;* Henry Mintzberg, "Organization Design: Fashion or Fit?" *Harvard Business Review* 59 (January-February, 1981): 103–116.

24. Adapted from Kenneth L. Harris, "Organizing to Overhaul a Mess." Copyright © 1975 by the Regents of the University of California. Reprinted from *California Management Review,* vol. XVII, no. 3, pp. 40–49 by permission of the Regents.

25. Harold J. Leavitt, William R. Dill, and Henry D. Eyring, *The Organizational World* (New York: Harcourt Brace Jovanovich, 1973), pp. 303–314.
26. The discussion of the population ecology model is based upon Howard E. Aldrich, *Organizations and Environments* (Englewood Cliffs, NJ: Prentice-Hall, 1979).
27. Charles E. Summer, *Strategic Behavior in Business and Government* (Boston: Little-Brown, 1980).
28. "Gulf Oil Gets Back to What it Knows Best," *Business Week,* January 31, 1977, pp. 78–80.
29. *Ibid.;* and Bryan E. Calame, "At Gulf Oil Nowadays, A 'Questionable' Deal is One to be Shunned," *Wall Street Journal,* January 25, 1977, pp. 1, 37.

Name Index

Burns, Tom, 61–62, 269
Bushnell, Robert A., 143

C

Calame, Bryan E., 526
Cameron, Kim S., 93, 104
Carley, William M., 381
Carper, William B., 514
Cartwright, Dorwin, 384, 433
Chakrabrati, Alok K., 287
Chakravaty, Subratan, 481
Chandler, Alfred D., Jr., 69
Child, John, 130, 136, 141–142, 180, 202, 248, 472
Christ, Thomas, 465
Clark, John P., 94, 96, 108
Clifford, D., 349
Coffey, Robert E., 452
Cohen, Michael D., 359–360, 365
Cohen, Todd A., 153
Coleman, Henry J., Jr., 480
Conlon, Edward J., 102, 104
Connolly, Terry, 102, 104
Connor, Patrick E., 177
Cook, James, 46
Cooke, Robert S., 324
Cooper, William C., 176
Coulter, Phillip B., 101
Cox, Meg, 495
Crozier, Michel, 394
Culver, Melinda, 145
Cummings, Larry L., 150, 426, 432, 483
Cunningham, J. Barton, 98–99
Cyert, Richard M., 27, 89, 92, 352–353

D

Daft, Richard L., 12–13, 93, 128–132, 174, 176–177, 262, 272, 275, 280, 285, 287–289, 299–300, 303–304, 306–307, 315, 317, 322, 329, 352, 508
Dahl, Robert, 382
Dalton, Gene W., 59, 192, 213–214, 429
Dalton, Melville, 429
Dandridge, Thomas C., 484
Davis, Stanley M., 237, 239–241, 244
Davis, Sheldon A., 282
DeLong, David, 140
Delbecq, Andre L., 178, 184–185, 262
Deutsch, Morton, 433
Deutsch, Stuart Jay, 102, 104
Dewar, Robert, 129
Dikes, Johnathan L., 265

Dill, William R., 350, 438, 520
Dobbins, Dale, 381
Doehring, J., 229
Doreian, Patrick, 129
Downey, H. Kirk, 49
Duncan, Robert B., 49, 51, 61, 227, 230, 242, 271, 285
Dunlop, John T., 444–445
Dunnette, M. D., 422, 441
Dutton, John M., 427, 430, 432–433

E

Elgin, Dwayne, 143
Emerson, Richard M., 393
Emery, Fred E., 52
England, George W., 94
Etzioni, Amitai, 81, 89, 92
Evan, William M., 70, 100
Evaniski, Michael J., 272
Eyring, Henry B., 350, 438, 520

F

Falconer, Beth, 269
Famularo, Joseph J., 218
Fayol, Henry, 27, 226
Ferry, Diane L., 177
Flabe, C. M., 180
Flack, Kevin, 104
Flax, Steven, 500
Fogerty, John E., 248
Ford, Jeffrey D., 130, 149, 181, 472
Fox, Bertrand, 22
Frazer, Douglas, 449
Freeman, John, 97
French, John R. P., Jr., 384
French, Lawrence J., 285
French, Wendell L., 282–283
Friedlander, Frank, 103

G

Galbraith, Jay R., 208, 213, 222, 245, 300, 402, 430
Galloway, Paul, 421
Gamson, William, 488
Gantz, Jeffrey, 399, 404–406
Garino, David P., 50, 80–81, 381
Getschow, George, 153
Gibb, J. R., 282
Gissen, Jay, 479
Glisson, Charles, 177
Goode, Kathy, 127

Goodman, Paul S., 96–97
Gorry, G. Anthony, 308
Gracey, J. F., 192
Graves, Robert, 35
Grayson, C. Jackson, Jr., 329, 352, 377
Greiner, Larry E., 136–137, 141
Grimes, A. J., 177, 383
Grubert, Jim, 3, 5
Grusky, Oscar, 487–488
Guenther, Robert, 343
Guest, Robert, 24
Gulick, Luther, 226

H

Haas, Eugene, 129
Hahn, Betty, 127
Hage, Jerald, 70, 129, 177, 262, 269
Halbrooks, John, 111
Hall, Richard H., 94, 96, 108, 128–129, 146
Hamburger, M., 275–276
Hannan, Michael T., 97
Hardy, T., 349
Harrigan, Kathryn Rudie, 147
Harris, Kenneth L., 519
Harvey, Edward, 161, 166
Harvey, O. J., 424, 435, 442
Hawley, A., 130
Hellriegel, Don, 49, 244
Henderson, A. M., 124–125
Herden, Richard P., 105
Herker, Diane, 57–58
Hickson, David J., 14, 20, 161, 169–171, 173, 324, 392–393, 396–398, 407–408
Hinings, C. R., 14, 20, 392–393, 396–398, 407–408
Hirsch, Paul M., 70, 97
Hofstede, Geert, 310
Hogue, Ken, 71
Holbek, Jonny, 61, 285
Holdaway, E. A., 130
Holland, Winford E., 302
Holusha, John, 4
Hood, W. R., 424, 435, 442
Hopwood, Anthony, 311
Hrebiniak, Lawrence G., 177
Huber, George P., 426, 432
Huey, John, 487
Hummon, Norman P., 129

I

Indik, B. P., 130

Ingrassia, Lawrence, 495
Isaack, Thomas S., 348

J

Jackson, Brooks, 148
Jackson, John H., 472
Jacobs, Bruce A., 513
Jaeger, Alfred M., 510–512
James, T. F., 130
Jenkins, Jeff, 236
Jervis, Paul, 289
Johnson, David W., 440
Johnson, Frank P., 440
Johnson, Norman J., 129
Johnson, R. T., 509
Jones, Barry, 236
Joyce, William S., 484
Jurkouich, Ray, 49–50

K

Kahn, Robert L., 10, 382, 514
Kanter, Rosabeth Moss, 318, 383, 386–388, 397, 409
Kaplan, Abraham, 382
Kasarda, John D., 130
Katz, Daniel, 10, 514
Kearns, Doris, 390
Keegan, Warren J., 303
Keely, Michael, 102
Kelly, Joe, 436
Kessler, Martha Stout, 465–466
Khandwalla, Pradip, 161, 180
Kilmann, Ralph H., 105, 271
Kimberly, John R., 128, 146, 272
Kline, S. M., 177
Kochan, Thomas A., 422, 426, 432
Koenig, Richard, 184–185
Kolb, David A., 422–424
Korda, Michael, 382
Kotter, John P., 55, 65–66, 285–286, 394, 407

L

Lamners, Cornelius J., 324
Lavenson, James H., 464
Lawrence, Paul R., 22, 59–61, 192, 213–214, 217, 237, 239–241, 244, 278, 286, 288, 334, 427, 429, 431–433, 435, 439, 440
Leavitt, Harold J., 329, 350, 352, 438, 520
Lee, C. A., 392, 396–398, 407–408
Leibrock, Robert C., 302

Paulson, Steven, 70
Peabody, Robert L., 383–384
Pennings, Johannes M., 96–97, 392–393, 396–398, 407–408,
Perrow, Charles, 25, 83–88, 91, 94, 123–124, 142, 159, 161, 173–174, 178, 181, 392–393, 408
Peters, Thomas J., 483, 502–504
Pettigrew, Andrew M., 385–386, 397
Peywell, Harry E., 239
Pfeffer, Jeffrey, 43, 55, 65, 67, 70, 177, 181, 382, 384–385, 392–393, 395–396, 399–401, 405, 407–409, 483, 486–487
Pheysey, Diana, 161, 169–170, 173
Pickle, Hal, 103
Picou, J. Steven, 71
Pierce, John L., 262
Pondy, Louis R., 13, 271, 431–432, 435–436, 438–439, 486
Porter, Lyman W., 399, 402
Price, James L., 94
Price, Jorjanna, 229
Pugh, D. S., 14–15, 19–20, 161, 169–171, 173

Q

Quinn, James Brian, 473, 475

R

Raisinghani, Duru, 354–356, 358
Randolph, W. Allen, 177
Rapoport, J., 275–276
Raven, Bertrand, 384
Reimann, Bernard C., 128, 180–181, 326
Renwick, Patricia A., 399, 402
Reynolds, Peter A., 452
Richardson, Mark, 269
Ricklefs, Roger, 149
Rigsby, S. Renee, 71
Ringer, Robert J., 382
Rivett, Patrick, 352
Robbins, Stephen P., 436
Rogers, David C., 98
Rogers, Everett M., 285
Romans, John R., 192
Romelaer, Pierre J., 364
Rosenheim, Daniel, 221
Rosner, M., 449
Rosseau, Denise M., 159, 181
Rubin, Irwin M., 422–424
Rudnitsky, Howard, 479
Rumelt, Richard, 226

Rushing, William A., 128, 161
Rustin, Richard E., 496
Ryans, John K., Jr., 477

S

Salancik, Gerald R., 43, 55, 70, 382, 392–393, 396, 407, 486–487
Schein, Edgar H., 422, 424, 436, 438, 443
Schlesinger, Leonard A., 285–286
Schmidt, Stuart M., 422
Schmidt, W. H., 141
Schmidt, Warren H., 281
Schneck, R. E., 392–393, 396–398, 407–408
Schnee, J., 275–276
Schoenherr, Richard A., 130, 177
Schulz, Mark, 3, 5
Schuster, Lynda, 371
Scotch, Norman, 488
Scott, B. R., 141
Scott, W. Richard, 322, 514
Sease, Douglas R., 376
Seashore, Stanley E., 98, 270
Seibert, Cindy, 127
Seider, Maynard S., 466
Seiler, John A., 334, 431–432, 436
Selznick, Phillip, 466
Shanklin, William L., 477
Shapiro, Benson S., 427, 428
Shepard, Herberta, 438, 440, 442
Sherif, C. W., 424, 435, 442
Sherif, Muzafer, 422, 424, 435, 442
Shoemaker, Floyd, 285
Sills, David L., 90
Simmons, Doug, 104
Simon, Herbert A., 83, 89, 91, 143, 347, 352
Slevin, Dennis, 271
Slocum, John W., Jr., 49, 130, 244
Smith, Lee, 381
Snepenger, Mary, 286
Snizek, William E., 514
Snow, Charles, 434–435, 479–480
Sorensen, Peter F., Jr., 326
Stagner, Ross, 348
Stalker, G. M., 61–62, 269
Starbuck, William H., 135–136, 430
Starrels, John M., 248
Staw, Barry M., 13, 483, 486
Stead, Bette Ann, 302
Steers, Richard M., 92, 95
Stevens, Carol, 269
Strauss, George, 431, 434–435

Street, David, 181
Stuart, Alexander, 153
Summer, Charles E., 522
Szanton, Peter L., 288

T

Tannenbaum, Arnold S., 323–324, 434–435, 449
Tannenbaum, Robert, 282
Teuter, Klaus, 129
Théorêt, André, 354–356, 358
Thomas, Kenneth, 422, 432, 435–436, 441
Thompson, James D., 8, 56, 63, 70, 84, 89, 106–108,
    111, 161, 168, 182, 184, 270, 365, 430
Thompson, Victor A., 142, 269
Thorton, Horace, 192
Todd, John, 310
Toffler, Alvin, 262
Townsend, Robert, 372, 470
Tracy, P. K., 180
Trist, Eric L., 52
Tully, Shawn, 343
Tung, Rosalie L., 50, 63
Turner, C., 14, 20, 169, 171
Tushman, Michael L., 177–178, 300–301, 303

U

Urwick, Lyndall F., 226
Uttal, Bro, 46

V

Vaill, Peter D., 33
Van Cauwenbergh, A., 384
Van de Ven, Andrew H., 70, 177–178, 184–185
Van Robaeyf, N., 384
Vaugh, John, 145
Veiga, John F., 76, 112, 180, 186–187, 257
Vianello, M., 449
Vinter, Robert, 181

W

Wagner, S., 275–276
Wallach, Arthur E., 286
Walton, Richard E., 427, 430, 432–433, 442, 446–447
Warren, Donald, 391
Weber, Max, 124–125
Weick, Karl E., 93, 371, 473
Weiner, Nan, 489
Whetten, David A., 69–70, 93, 146–149
Whisler, Thomas L., 326
White, B., J., 424, 435, 442
Wieser, C., 449
Wiginton, John C., 13, 329, 352
Wilder, Scott, 381
Williamson, Oliver A., 313
Wilson, James Q., 270
Wilson, Sloan, 469
Windhager, Ann, 229
Winter, Ralph E., 481
Withey, Michael, 176
Woodward, Joan, 161–165
Wright, J. Patrick, 405

Y

Yanouzas, John N., 76, 112, 180, 186–187, 257
Yates, Douglas, 288
Young, David W., 265
Yuchtman, Ephraim, 98

Z

Zald, Mayer, N., 392
Zaltman, Gerald, 61, 285
Zander, Alvin, 384, 433
Zey-Ferrell, Mary, 437
Ziegler, P. Thomas, 192
Zwerman, William L., 165

Subject Index

ESB Ray-O-Vac, 200–201, 231
Executive recruitment, 66
Exxon Corporation, 376–377, 487–488

F

Fairfield High School District, 274–275
Feuding Stifles UMW Reform, 413–415
Fire departments, 101
Firestone Tire and Rubber Company, 481–482
Ford, 41
Formalization
    definition, 15
    and other bureaucratic characteristics, 132–134
    and size, 128
Fort Jackson High School District, 375–376
Framework for book, 27–31
Functional structure,
    definition, 226
    compared to other structures, 244–246
    strengths and weaknesses, 227

G

Garbage can model of decision making, 359–365, 368–369
General Foods, 54
General Mills, 220, 473
General Motors, 41
General Telephone and Electric Corporation, 267–269
Genesco, Incorporated, 308–309
Gillette Company, 287–288
Goal approach to effectiveness, 94–97
Goal preferences and decision making, 366–369
Goals
    changes, 89
    coalition, 91
    conflicting, 88–90
    defined, 81
    differences among departments, 60
    and effectiveness, 94–97
    horizontal linkage, 212–213
    intergroup conflict, 426–428
    multiple, 88–90
    preference ordering, 89
    purpose, 82–84
    satisficing, 89
    sequential attention, 89
    top manager, 91
    types, 84–88
Goodyear Tire and Rubber Company, 481–482

Government,
    environment, 47
    interorganization relationships, 69
Greeting Card Company, 191
Growth,
    and bureaucracy, 135–141
    crises, 136–138
    reasons for, 135–136
    stages of, 136–138
    and structural characteristics, 140–141
Gulf Oil Corporation, 525–526
Gypsum Plant, 122–123

H

Hartman Luggage Company, 462–464
Hierarchy of authority
    definition, 15
    and information processing, 308
    and power, 383–392
Hierarchical level. *See* Management level
Horizontal linkage. *See* Linkage
Houston Oil and Minerals Corporation, 151–153
Human relations view of conflict, 434–435
Human resources, 45
Human Resources Administration, 518–519

I

In Broken Images, 35
INDSCO, 318
Information, 299–303
    amount, 300–301
    defined, 299
    richness, 301–303
    versus data, 299
Information processing, 298–309
    computer impact on structure, 326–329
    design implications, 303–307
    for control, 309–325
    for tasks, 299–309
    and hierarchical level, 308–309
    implications for management, 332–333
    management information systems, 329–330
Information systems, 209, 329–330
    computer based, 329–330
    vertical linkage, 209
Innovation. *See* Change
Institutional level of management, 28–29
Integration. *See also* Linkage
    definition, 60
    and differentiation, 60–61

New products, 266, 275–280
    horizontal linkage model, 277–280
    management of, 284–287
    reasons for success, 275–277

O

Ohio State University, 58
Olson's Locker Plant, 192–196
Operational level of management, 28–29
Organic structure,
    defined, 61
    and environment uncertainty, 61–62
    and technology, 176
    and technological change, 269–271
    versus mechanistic, 61
Organization
    definition, 8
    dimensions of, 14–19
    contextual dimensions, 17
    structural dimensions, 15–17
    subsystems, 10
    as a system, 8–10
    typologies, 514–519
Organization development, 281–283
Organization set, 69–70
Organization structure. See Structure, organization
Organization theory
    amount of development, 506–508
    application to real world, 25–27, 502–505
    contingency theory, 20
    definition, 20
    future research, 508–509
    levels of analysis, 22
    and organizational behavior, 24
    twenty years of progress, 506–508
Organizational development, 281–283
Organized anarchy, 359–360
Output control, 322
Output standards, 106, 366

P

The Paradoxical Twins: Acme and Omega
    Electronics, 112–116
People change, 266, 280–284
    laboratory training, 281
    managerial grid, 282
    organizational development, 281–283
    survey feedback, 282
    team-building, 282

PepsiCo, 482–483
Performance evaluation system
    and control, 315–316
    and intergroup conflict, 433
Performance, reasons for, 502–505
Phillips Electrical, Ltd., 403–404
Pillsbury Company, 494–495
Placid, clustered environment, 52–54
Placid, randomized environment, 52–54
Plankton High School District, 84–85
Political activity, 67
Political model of organization, 400–401
Politics, 399, 400–410. See also Power
    and coordination, 404
    defined, 399
    domains of activity, 401–406
    manager attitudes toward, 398
    and personnel changes, 405
    and resource allocation, 405–406
    and structural change, 402
    tactics for using, 408–410
    versus rational choice, 400–401
Population ecology model, 520–523
Post Office, 485–486
Power, 395–410. See also Politics
    consequences of, 309–392
    definition, 382
    horizontal, 392–398
    and intergroup conflict, 431
    lower participants, 389–392
    protection against, 391–392
    strategic contingencies, 393–398
    tactics, 407–410
    and task design, 386–388
    uncertainty, 397–398
    upper management, 383–386
    vertical, 383–392
Presidential decision making, 349
Problem identification, 344–346, 355, 359, 360–361.
    See also Decision making
Problem solving, 344–346, 357, 359, 360–361. See
    also Decision making
Proctor and Gamble, 54
Product structure
    defined, 230
    compared to matrix structure, 244–246
    strengths and weaknesses, 230
Production Engineering, 431–433
Products, new. See New products
Professional Air Traffic Controllers Association
    (PATCO), 420–421

Professional bureaucracy, 515–517
Professionalism
   and bureaucracy, 145–146
   and technology, 177
Public relations, 66
Purchasing Department, 430–431
Putnam Plastics, 185–186

Q

Queen's Children's Psychiatric Center, 333–334

R

Ralston Purina Company, 80–81
Rational approach
   to decision making, 345–347, 366–368
   versus political approach, 400–401
   versus social approach, 27–28
Rational-legal authority, 125
Rational model of organization, 400–401
Raw materials, 44
Regulation, 67
Republican-Scobill, 329–330
Requisite variety, 55
Resistence to change, 285
Resource dependence, 55
Resource exchange, 69
Resources and conflict, 431
Responsibility chart, 206
Retrenchment. *See* Decline
Rhody Company, 278
Richness of information, 301–307
Ritual scapegoating, 488
Rodney Hunt Company, 217
Rules,
   and control, 315–316
   and formalization, 15, 128
   and vertical linkage, 208

S

Satisficing, 89
Scullin Steel Company, 50
Sears, Roebuck and Company, 133–134
Self contained units, 222–224
Simpson Department Store, 316–317
S. I. Newhouse and Sons, 297–298
Size, organizational
   administrative ratio, 130, 133
   bureaucratic dimensions, 127–131

clerical ratio, 130–131, 133
complexity, 129, 133
decentralization, 129, 133
definition, 17
formalization, 128, 133
intergroup conflict, 426
Parkinson's Law, 130
professional support staff, 130–131, 133
structural characteristics, 132–133
Small-batch technology, 162–164
Social approach to organization, 27–28
Specialization, 15
Standard Oil, 67–69
Standardization, 15
Strategic choice, 472–474
   and intergroup conflict, 426
Strategic contingencies, 393–398
Strategy, 485–482
   analyzer, 480
   business level, 476, 479–482
   cash cow, 477–478
   corporate level, 476–479
   defender, 479–480
   definition, 475
   dog, 478
   new venture, 477–478
   portfolio, 477–478
   prospector, 480
   star, 477–478
   top management, 467
Structural deficiency, 248–250
Structural change. *See* Administrative change
Structural dimensions of organization, 15–18
Structure, organization
   adhocracy, 516–517
   boundary spanning, 56–57
   buffers, 56
   and corporate success, 504–505
   definition, 202
   departmentation (grouping), 204
   and differentiation, 59–60
   dimensions, 15–18
   divisionalized form, 515–517
   and environment, 55–65
   functional form, 227–229
   geographical, 232
   grouping (departmentation), 204
   and horizontal linkages, 212–221
   hybrid, 233–237
   and integration, 59–60
   matrix, 237–248

and politics, 399
and power, 397–398
and structural linkage, 208, 212–213
United Mine Workers, 413–415
United Parcel Service, 126–127
Upper management. *See* Top management
U. S. Postal Service, 485–486

V

Valena Scientific Corporation, 452–456

Valley Foods, 260–261
Variety, 173
    and information amount, 303–304
Vertical linkage. *See* Linkage

W

Westinghouse, 512–513
Woodland Mills, 283–284
Workflow integration, 170
Workflow rigidity, 169

†